GETTING INTO PRINT

GETTING INTO PRINT

The Decision-Making Process in Scholarly Publishing

WALTER W. POWELL

The University of Chicago Press
Chicago and London

WALTER W. POWELL is associate professor
of behavioral and policy sciences in
the Sloan School of Management at
the Massachusetts Institute of Technology.
He is also associate professor of
organization and management and sociology
at Yale University.

The University of Chicago Press, Chicago 60637
The University of Chicago Press, Ltd., London

94 93 92 91 90 89 88 87 86 85   54321

Library of Congress Cataloging in Publication Data

Powell, Walter W.
 Getting into print.

 Bibliography: p.
 Includes index.
 1. Scholarly Publishing—United States—Decision-
making. 2. Book industries and trade—United States—
Decision-making. 3. Editing—Decision-making.
4. Authors and publishers—United States. 5. Organization theory. I. Title.
Z479.P68 1985   070:5′0973   84-23962
ISBN 0-226-67704-4

To Marianne

CONTENTS

LIST OF TABLES

PREFACE

This is a study of how editors in scholarly publishing houses decide which books to publish. Answering this question required many hours of interviews and fieldwork inside publishing houses, but the study also took me outside the formal boundaries of the firms and into contact with authors, reviewers, advisers, brokers, and patrons. In tracing how choices were reached on particular manuscripts, I came to see the ways in which publishing departs from many of the assumptions commonly found in the literature on organizations. Markets and hierarchies, the twin concepts on which so much contemporary theory and research on organizations are based, presuppose that organizations are independent entities, separate from society, driven by economic and administrative logics. Contact with suppliers, consumers, or other organizations is guided by contract and principles of economic exchange. Yet in book publishing, and, I suspect, in many other organized economic endeavors, it is hard to tell where society ends and economic organization begins. Decisions are embedded in an environmental context that can transform the choice process in a number of surprising ways. The rational elements in formal decision processes often turn out to be more symbolic than real, while chance, or serendipitous contact, appears to be strongly tied to one's location in the social structure. Editorial decisions are a form of mating—a matching of editors looking for manuscripts to make

up their lists with authors searching for a publisher to dissemi-
nate their ideas and to enhance their career prospects. Both
parties to this mating process are frequently guided by a sense
of appropriateness, and long-term relationships are sealed by
an implicit norm of reciprocity. Years of contact with editors
and the social worlds they inhabit have made these observations commonplace to me, and it is only in the context of
reading otherwise superb work in organization theory that I
am reminded of the disjunction between the world I have
observed and the world our theories purport to describe.
While the primary purpose of this book is to explicate the
decision-making process in scholarly publishing, I hope that
the observations and explanations I offer will raise questions
about current theories and stimulate the development of
models of organizations that do a better job of capturing the
richness of organizational choice processes and their intimate
linkage to a broader social context.

This book has had a long gestation period. It began in 1975
as a pilot study of two organizations. That research grew into
a large-scale study of the book industry, undertaken by Lewis
Coser, Charles Kadushin, and me. In an earlier form, the
book was my doctoral dissertation, but the manuscript that
the University of Chicago Press accepted five years ago bears
little resemblance to this final version. The first half of the
earlier manuscript became the basis for three chapters in
Books: The Culture and Commerce of Publishing, the larger
industry study to which this volume, an expansion of the
second half of my dissertation, is a companion. My work on
Books required setting aside the revisions for this book, and a
new job, teaching, other writing, and another research project—this one on public television—also intruded. But the
study of Apple Press and Plum Press did not sit idly gathering
dust. I kept in contact with my respondents, even following
them as they moved to other houses. My understanding of the
industry was enhanced by my participation in various publishing conferences and annual meetings. Most important,
the passage of time allowed me to gain distance from the case

studies and to see beyond them to more general social processes.

Along the way I have incurred a great many debts. Like most people, I get by with a little help from my friends, and I have been blessed with many supportive colleagues at both Stony Brook and Yale. The members of my dissertation committee at Stony Brook—Lewis Coser, Charles Perrow, and Mark Granovetter—were both exemplary teachers and good friends. I learned from and shared many good times with the members of our research team—Lewis Coser, Charles Kadushin, Michelle Caplette, Laurie Michael Roth, and Frank Sirianni. Richard Peterson and Barry Schwartz provided insightful comments on the dissertation, which greatly improved it, and I benefited immensely from the careful reading of the revised manuscript by Becky Friedkin and Connie Gersick. For me, the best thing about Yale has been my friendship and collaboration with Paul DiMaggio. Not only is Paul all that one could ask for in a friend; he is a marvelous and speedy editor as well. I also had the good fortune that Chick Perrow "followed" me to New Haven. He has provided the kind of advice and criticism, on this book and on much else in my life, that comes only when the best of friends also happens to be an excellent scholar. Finally, for the past eight years, Dan Deutsch has been a dear friend and probing critic of everything I have written.

My research was supported by NIMH grant MH-26746, and release time for writing was made possible in part by a grant from the Yale Program on Non-Profit Organizations. The Yale School of Organization and Management has provided excellent support facilities. Very special thanks are due to Linda Vessicchio, Dolly Bonisch, and Linda Knudsen for their expert typing of the manuscript.

Finally, my greatest debt is to the many people whom I cannot thank publicly: the employees and executives of Apple Press and Plum Press and the many other members of the book community who gave so generously of their time. Without them, this book would never have been possible. Their openness and accessibility were extraordinary, and I am extremely grateful for their help.

I would like to thank the publishers of the following articles of mine for permission to draw on these papers for use in this book: "Publishers' Decision Making: What Criteria Do They Use in Deciding Which Books to Publish?" *Social Research* 45:227–52 (used in chapter 5), and "Political and Organizational Influences on Public Television Programming," pp. 413–38 in E. Wartella and D. C. Whitney, eds., *Mass Communication Review Yearbook*, vol. 4 (Beverly Hills: Sage, 1983) (used in chapter 6).

INTRODUCTION

Publishers are the key intermediary between writer and reader. This book describes two successful scholarly publishing houses that perform this linkage, thereby providing the institutional and organizational framework for the production and dissemination of academic research. The book thus offers a map and an interpretation of a sector of the book industry that is central to the intellectual advancement of our society.

Books compete with newspapers, radio, and television for the shaping of public discourse. In part because of their comparative cheapness and convenience, books enjoy some advantages that newer forms of communication lack. Books are more respected than the more ephemeral media, and they still carry a measure of dignity. Books have more permanence; the reusage rate for books is vastly higher than for the other mass media. The tactile pleasures and physical attractiveness of books are unmatched by other means of transmitting the written word. Books are also an individual medium: the reader proceeds at his or her own speed. While the growth of the modern electronic mass media has stripped publishing houses of some of their formerly uncontested influence in the cultural arena, publishing nevertheless remains a vital force in the world of ideas.

Publishers, like classical entrepreneurs, link creators of products with interested consumers. Publishers decide which

kinds of books will be offered to the public and how vigorously they will be marketed. In doing this, they shape the
creation and dispersion of ideas, scientific knowledge, and
popular culture. But, despite the publishers' central role, we
have only recently begun to learn why some book manuscripts get published and others do not.[1] This is not to say that
little has been written about the book trade. There are many
histories of individual companies,[2] treatments of key periods
in the industry's history,[3] memoirs and biographies of editors
and publishers,[4] informative journalistic accounts,[5] and treatises on the nature of the book business.[6] There are many fine
studies of the development of reading publics and of the social
context in which literature is produced.[7] There are, however,
few systematic analyses of the decision-making process in
book publishing.[8] Compared to the attention paid to other
media, such as newspapers or television, the book industry
has gone unnoticed by those who could provide rigorous
analysis.

Book publishing is a commercial enterprise, and product
design, sales strategy, pricing, and order fulfillment are just as
important in it as in any other business. Yet, as we shall see,
book publishing is a fascinating and complex industry, with
traditions that often frustrate the standard business practices
associated with other, more bureaucratized industries. As
Charles Horton Cooley (1929:188) observed many years ago:

> Commercial institutions . . . have in general obvious func-
> tions, but an adequate characterization of a successful institu-
> tion of trade would have to include all those subtle traits of
> organization and spirit which explain how and why this institu-
> tion is viable while others, if they are viable, are so in a
> different way. I have had to do, for instance, with several
> publishing concerns, and am of the opinion that their distinc-
> tive behaviors would make an instructive study.

As an industry, book publishing is beset with a number of
competing demands and internal contradictions. It is both a
labor-intensive craft and a business that realizes economies of
scale from high-volume production. Highly dependent on the

success of a large number of new "products" issued annually, some firms are nevertheless sustained by the steady earnings of their backlists. In recent years the industry has experienced both an exceptionally high birthrate of new firms and a pronounced tendency toward mergers. The labor force is generally overeducated yet is frequently ill prepared for careers in publishing. There is widespread use of subcontractors for nearly every function save the initial decision to publish. The most persistent and unresolved problem has been distribution—how to get books into the hands of interested consumers (see Shatzkin 1982; Powell 1983). College and university libraries, themselves major consumers of scholarly books, offer books as public goods, obviating the need for scholars to purchase them.

A thorough study of the sociology of scholarly publishing must address a wide variety of concerns. The decision to publish a book involves such factors as the credentials of authors ("He's from Stanford," "Her previous book won the C. Wright Mills Award," or "He's an unknown"); the social networks in which authors and editors are enmeshed ("This editor, who is a good friend of mine, is coming for a visit. Would you like to join us for dinner and tell him about the book you are working on?"); the process through which decisions are made (which is sometimes a slow, cumbersome affair, bogged by delays; sometimes a lengthy period of solicitation of an author by an editor; sometimes fast—a snap decision resulting from a chance encounter on an airplane); the occupational characteristics of editors ("I'm not a professional, I'm more like a skilled craftsman" or "An editor is like a cabdriver: he knows the feel of the road, where the ruts and bounces are"); and the mechanisms through which employees are socialized ("After you are here for a while, you acquire a kind of cognitive map—you learn what goes over and what doesn't").

The relationship between scholarly publishing and social science research is an intricate one. One task of this book is to analyze the way in which the success of two scholarly publishing houses is inextricably tied to the organization of the

American academy. The forces of supply and demand and the pressures of environmental selection do influence the growth and development of scholarly publishing, but these pressures are strongly attenuated by the network ties and the cultural and historical elements that form the nexus of social relations between editors and academics. Of course, any recurrent economic transaction becomes overlaid with social content (see Macaulay 1963; Williamson 1975:106–8; Granovetter 1983a:31–38 and 1983b:33–35); however, in book publishing preexisting social relations often form the basis of economic exchange.

For the community of American scholars, books are very important commodities. They are written, read, debated, and reviewed. Reputations are tied to the success or failure of one's latest book. Promotion, tenure, and even one's first job are tied to the quality of one's writing. Publishing is the primary measure of academic achievement. A few scholars and unattached intellectuals command so significant an audience that their writings are also a source of considerable income. So, for the academic community, books serve a highly utilitarian purpose, and it is scholarly publishing houses that are the gatekeepers to this important medium of communication.[9]

The primary focus of this book is the local political economy—the set of relations both within the two houses that I studied and between them and a variety of external advisers and service-providers. The immediate ties to the task environment form a critical part of this local political economy. A publishing house lies at the center of a large and complicated web whose strands reach out in a variety of directions: to authors and the social worlds they inhabit; to libraries; to the reading public; to employment agencies and to unions; to banks or parent corporations, which extend credit or lend money; to the federal government, which sets policies dealing with copyright legislation, the tax treatment of books held in inventory, postal rates, and import regulations; and to the scientific communities in foreign lands.[10]

The case studies on which this book is based describe the boundary-spanning roles played by editors and explain the influence exerted by such key outsiders as senior academic advisers and series editors. I present a detailed ethnographic account of how the structure of social relations, both inside and outside the firm, influences the crucial decisions about what should be published. In general, I am concerned with three main questions. (1) How do editors decide which few manuscripts to sponsor, out of the hundreds that flood their desks? The view of the decision-making process presented here suggests that choices are seldom strategic, nor are they guided by stable preferences. Choices more commonly represent the fulfillment of duties and obligations. Preferences and meaning develop in the course of making decisions, through a combination of socialization and experience. (2) What is the nature of the editorial task? In short, how do editors ply their trade? Here I analyze the different strategies employed by editors to acquire manuscripts and show how the search process fits into a network of social relations among editors and authors. I illustrate the way in which the structure and operation of the two publishing houses I studied create standard operating assumptions that guide editorial activities. (3) What are the specific ways in which scholarly houses are embedded in a larger social context? To answer this, I describe the relationships between the two scholarly houses and their respective parent corporations, discuss the role of the two houses within the scholarly sector of the book industry, and illustrate how most of the activities that publishing houses must engage in—the acquisition and evaluation of manuscripts, the promotion and sale of books—require making contact with outsiders. The formal organization of the two houses—and of the publishing industry in general—is not well suited to meeting these demands; recurrent informal connections are one way of filling in the gaps in the formal structure.

In chapter 1, I provide an overview of the publishing industry. Several trends—in particular, increased concentration and commercialization—have of late been attracting a considerable degree of attention. It is my view that culture is more resilient and resourceful than we generally take it to be. Periodic crises in the publishing industry have come and gone, and the feared collapses have not occurred. The history of the industry can be characterized as a long series of conflict-laden episodes, none of which has proved terminal, however threatening each seemed at the time. In taking this long view, I do not intend to understate the risky, unsupportive financial environment in which some sectors of the book industry currently operate. Yet, however much we may deplore the blockbuster complex in trade publishing or the production of "managed" textbooks, it is not only the economic structure of publishing that has changed in recent years. As Elisabeth Sifton (1982) suggests, it is not rapacious, profit-minded corporations that threaten quality work so much as the sad but simple fact that, for the first time since the early eighteenth century, readership is declining.[11] A complete assessment of the health of scholarly publishing must ask whether scholars read outside the narrow confines of their disciplinary subfields. Do they buy books within their fields, or do they rely on libraries to purchase them? How valid are the charges made by some scientific publishers that books are no longer bought but instead are photocopied?

The most significant feature of book publishing as an industry is its internal diversity and segregation into a number of distinct, separate worlds, marked by important cultural and organizational differences. Across industry sectors we find significant variation in recruitment patterns, career security, interfirm mobility, and promotion prospects.[12] Each sector of the book industry operates within a distinctive institutional environment, with dissimilar amounts of risk and uncertainty. The various types of publishing houses are staffed by people from different social backgrounds, and the status and influence of the occupants of similar positions contrast significantly across industry sectors. Such sectoral differences influence the quality of an employee's life: the nature of interdepartmental conflicts, patterns of friendship, and leisure-time activities all vary according to the branch of publishing in which a person works.[13]

In chapter 2 I introduce the two companies that I studied. One of them, Apple Press, is a small scholarly house that publishes fewer than a hundred books a year, almost exclusively in the social sciences. The other, Plum Press, is a large monograph house that publishes over four hundred books a year, of which fewer than a hundred are in the social and behavioral sciences. Apple has approximately thirty employees; Plum, more than four hundred. Both companies are on a sound financial footing. In the years just preceding my fieldwork the smaller one cleared a double-digit profit margin, while the larger one had a somewhat smaller profit margin on annual sales in excess of forty million dollars. At both Apple and Plum the organization of work shapes the editorial process in important ways. As I argued in an earlier book, "What directly affects an editor's daily routine is not corporate ownership or being one division of a large multidivisional publishing house . . . ; on a day-to-day basis, editorial behavior is most strongly influenced by the editorial policies of the house and the relationship among departments and personnel *within* the publishing house or division" (Coser, Kadushin, and Powell 1982:185). We shall see that, although both Apple and Plum direct their books toward an audience of academics and professional practitioners, there are sharp differences between them with respect to organizational structure and editorial policy and practice.

In chapter 2 I also look at an intriguing dimension of publishing: the time cycle. Publishers engage in a delicate balancing act involving previously published books that continue to generate revenue, the search for new acquisitions, and books that are presently being released. The various departments of a publishing house operate within very different time frames, and the disparity between their perspectives is, in addition to being an indicator of an employee's discretionary power, a frequent source of conflict and disagreement. Cyert and March (1963) observed that finance departments estimate resource requirements on the low side, whereas comparable estimates by sales departments are high. This is not at all surprising, given that it is the task of finance to conserve resources and of sales to stimulate growth; yet it serves to emphasize that organizations have multiple goals and perspectives and that these often conflict.

Organization theorists are familiar with numerous studies that point to the tensions that arise between administrators and professionals, between the demands of the organization as a whole and the personal concerns of career-minded individuals. Nowhere is this tension more evident than among book editors. For no one person oversees or controls the whole publishing process, and at no one time do all or even most of the personnel work on the same set of manuscripts; yet it is the editor who decides which book others in the house will have to produce and sell, and this clearly is the most important decision to be made in a publishing house.

Editors, as we shall see in chapter 3, are situated in structurally ambivalent positions: loyalty to their authors and their craft often outweighs their allegiance to the firm that employs them. All but one of the editors at Apple and Plum had worked for three or more different companies. The high turnover commonly reported in publishing partially reflects the extent to which craft loyalties outweigh corporate ones. Theodore Caplow (1954) and Rosabeth Kanter (1968) have noted that many organizations attempt to instill commitment in their members by inducing newcomers to renounce previous associations. Editors, however, are frequently hired precisely because of their extensive contacts. When editors change houses, some of their authors move with them. Indeed, the number of authors that follow an editor from one publishing house to another is a good measure of that editor's prestige and influence. In chapter 3 I look at the craft of editing and examine the daily tasks performed by editors, paying particular attention to the different search methods used by editors, the problems involved in rejecting authors, the services that editors provide for authors, and the extent to which editor's jobs spill over into their private lives. A great part of an editor's skill lies in his or her ability to judge which topics will attract a sufficiently broad audience. At both Apple and Plum the editors were continually looking for books with the backlist in mind, for an ideal book is one that will sell steadily for many years.

The editors I observed rebelled at any overt attempts by their bosses to tell them how to do their work. They claimed that editing demands special sensibilities and that they knew their subject matter better than anyone else. Their descriptions were very much akin to Mary Quant's characterization of fashion designers: "Good designers . . . know that to have any influence they must keep in step with public needs, public opinion . . . and with an intangible 'something in the air'" (Quant 1965:74).

In chapter 4 I discuss a variety of situations that illustrate the degree of discretion that editors are allowed. Most editors have a considerable amount of freedom in conducting their daily affairs. Indeed, they all made a point of telling me this and offered data in support of this view. For example, one editor had had only one book proposal turned down in four years, and another estimated that 95 percent of his projects were approved without question. What are the reasons for this apparent autonomy, and how real is it? The second part of chapter 4 provides an answer and offers an alternative account of editorial discretion. Despite considerable evidence of editorial freedom and autonomy, it often seemed to matter very little which particular editor happened to make a decision. I argue that editorial choice is strongly shaped by the force of moral and organizational obligations. As Howard Becker (1974:770) shows, "People who cooperate to produce a work of art do not decide things afresh. Instead, they rely on earlier agreements that have become customary." These agreements become conventions and suggest a shared understanding that allows for easy and efficient coordination of activity. The routinization of the decision process at Apple and Plum allows for the appearance of autonomy while simultaneously enforcing limits beyond which decisions rarely stray. I describe the methods publishers use both to socialize editors into organizational roles and to shape the premises of editorial decision-making. Once editors accept their employer's premises, they can then be permitted considerable latitude. Of course, conventions are seldom rigid and unyielding; much may be left unsettled and subject to interpretation and negotiation. I conclude the chapter with a discussion of how the tastes of individual editors blend with the overall "character" of their respective houses.

In chapter 5 I examine the criteria that influence an editor's decision to accept or reject a manuscript. A crucial reality of editorial work is that the demand for editorial time far exceeds its supply. At both publishing houses, systems of preemptive priorities allow some clients to jump ahead of earlier arrivals in the queues awaiting editorial attention. The conventions vary with the context of production. There are significant differences for authors with regard to waiting and access, and this variation in queuing at the two houses helps amplify some of the differences between them. As we shall see, authors located in different positions in the respective queues meet with different rates of acceptance and rejection.

Queuing rules operate as filtering systems; however, even in the most preferential queues, only a minority of the authors receive contracts for their manuscripts. A variety of other factors—the house's history and tradition, finances, and scheduling considerations—influence the decision-making process. An author's academic status is reputed to determine his or her chance of being published, yet, as we shall see, the actual influence of an author's academic position is modified by his or her position in social networks.

Many of the chapters provide examples of how authors are cared for by editors, how authors may suffer from delays they experience during the review process, and how they may be mishandled during the production process. Publishing houses and their employees treat as routine what authors regard as their crowning achievements. There is obviously considerable opportunity for disparities of opinion to emerge. Meyer Schapiro (1964), in describing the system through which an artist agrees to exhibit and sell exclusively with a particular dealer, notes that the contractual relation is beset with many strains and difficulties. There are clearly many parallels between the author-publisher relationship and that of artist and dealer. It is worth quoting Schapiro at length:

> The dealer may be dissatisfied with the artist, either because he has produced too little altogether or falls below the expected level of quality. The artist may not approve the looks or location of the gallery, the method of publicity, the clientele, the dealer's personality and calculations; he may feel less favored by the dealer than other artists in the same gallery who are more successful in attracting purchasers; he may suffer because the works of the others cast a shadow on his own, because they are better or worse, or in a style with which he feels no sympathy. There are then many tensions within this freely chosen relationship of artist and dealer. In general, an artist desires a dealer who admires his work wholeheartedly and will continue to show it even though there are few sales; who gives no sign of disapproval when the artist changes his style and passes through a period of searching or experimentation, without fully realized results; whose publicity is dignified, original, or personal in a way that appeals to the imagination and taste of the artist; and who respects the personality of the artist. There have been dealers for whom the art business was a genuine personal expression, a means of participating in the deeply interesting, often exciting world of original artists with whom they have formed lasting friendships. [Schapiro 1964:368]

The comments of authors illustrate the separation process that occurs as an author gains distance from his or her work with the passage of time. As one author whom I interviewed stated, "When it comes to my scholarly work, I consider it tinkering with my soul. I went through a period where I would have liked to shoot my editors and copyeditors. But, in retrospect, I now think the job they did was quite good . . . I'd readily publish with them again."

In the sixth and final chapter I place the analysis of the choice processes at Plum and Apple in the context of recent debates within organization theory. Most formal theories of organization-environment relations ignore both the role of organization qua organization (see Zucker 1983) and the manner in which organizations represent clusters of patterned relations embedded in more inclusive social arrangements (see Granovetter 1983a). Prevailing conceptions of organizations view firms as being at the mercy either of the internal necessities of production or of external market forces over which they have little control. I argue that the comparative case studies I present here suggest the need for a rethinking of the relationship between organizations and their environments. I draw upon my research on another industry, public television, and contrast the fragmented environment of public TV with the tightly coupled world of scholarly publishing. I show that environments are enormously invasive and that firms are capable of altering and managing them. I close by examining how the decision process at Apple and Plum in particular, and in scholarly publishing in general, influences the academic development of the social sciences.

When Lewis Coser, Charles Kadushin, and I began our study of the book-publishing industry, we were motivated above all by our common love for books, our interest in the institutions responsible for producing and disseminating ideas, and our conviction that much of the fate of our culture and our educational system hinges on the health of the publishing industry. I have painted scholarly publishing with all its warts precisely because I care about books so deeply. Even if, on the basis of our research, my colleagues and I can give only two cheers for the publishing industry as it is presently constituted, we can give three wholehearted cheers for the future of ideas, writing, and the book in America.

Research Chronology

In order to judge the reliability of many of the observations in this book, the reader needs to know something about my research methods and the arrangements I made with the two publishing firms. Case studies have many virtues and many liabilities. They avoid some of the simplistic causal assumptions found in some quantitative work. Thick description is necessary if we are to capture the range of events and practices that go on within organizations. But a publishing house does not sit still while we study it. Indeed, any organization that did not change while being studied would be a peculiar one. And a case study can give too much credence to the interpretation favored by its author. Selective emphasis of material and decisions about what to include and exclude are, however, problems shared by both qualitative and quantitative research. I have attempted to avoid overemphasizing my own views by systematically describing the two publishing houses and the events that I observed within them. The reader can thus use the ethnography to develop his or her own explanation. In some cases, I suggest competing analyses for interpretation of the field data and argue why I think a particular interpretation is the correct one. Of course, it is almost always possible to find a plausible explanation for a set of observations; the reader will have to judge how systematic and consistent the views offered in this book are.

When I began my research in May, 1975, my central concern was to locate publishing houses that would give me more or less free rein to study them. I drew up a list of prominent scholarly or monograph houses in the New York City metropolitan area, developed a prospectus that outlined the aims of my work, and began contacting the firms. The first two companies declined; although they expressed interest in the research, they maintained that their staffs were overworked and could not spare the time I would require of them.

Apple Press

I used a well-known academic as an intermediary to introduce me to the editor-in-chief of the third house I approached. For purposes of confidentiality, this very successful and well-regarded scholarly publishing house will be referred to as Apple Press. The editor-in-chief consented to my studying the house. I was introduced to the company's employees as a graduate student in sociology who was interested in understanding how the publishing business operated. Being re-

garded as a novice was extremely useful in establishing rapport with people. I was not viewed as a threat by anyone; in
fact, I was treated very much like someone who had just
started to work for the company. I began visiting Apple Press
in late May of 1975 and spent at least one day a week there
during the months of June, July, September, October, and
November. These visits were generally arranged in advance. I
would telephone either the editor-in-chief, a department
head, or one of the editors and arrange to spend the day with
the person I had contacted.

During this initial period, I listened to people describe
their work and explain the details of the specific projects with
which they were involved. A typical day would find me sitting
in someone's office, reading mansucripts that had been submitted, going through editors' correspondence with authors,
and looking at sales records. During this time the person
would carry on with his or her business more or less as usual,
with the exception that about fifteen minutes out of every
hour would be spent in answering my questions.

By December, 1975, my visits became less frequent, and
they were not arranged in advance. The nature of my interaction with Apple Press changed considerably. Several factors
influenced this. First, I had formulated hypotheses I wished to
test, and I had specific requests for information that I wished
to collect. My questions were no longer general inquiries but
detailed, specific probes, aimed either at explicating processes that were unclear to me or at filling in gaps in my
knowledge. Second, in the fall of 1975 I assumed a position as
field director of a major study of "publishers as gatekeepers
of ideas," funded by a grant from the National Institute of
Mental Health to Lewis Coser and Charles Kadushin. In that
capacity I was responsible for overseeing the interviewing of
over a hundred people in editorial positions in a variety of
houses throughout the United States. With the added resources provided by the grant, in terms of both personnel and
finances, I was quickly becoming more knowledgeable about
all aspects of the book business.

I was no longer regarded as a novice at Apple Press; in fact, my opinions and advice were sometimes solicited. I was recognized and greeted by maintenance staff and employees of the parent company located in the same building. Whether they thought I was a meddlesome author or an employee I do not know. With the added responsibilities of the grant, I had less time for fieldwork. Instead of spending the day from 9:00 A.M. to 5:00 P.M., observing the goings-on, I would see people for lunch or for short, focused interviews. This continued until July, 1976, when I finally concluded my work at Apple Press. In retrospect, I realize that the patience of these people and their willingness to spend countless hours with me were truly remarkable. I hope the final product of my work will in some small way compensate for their generosity.

Plum Press

My next attempt to gain access to a publishing house was made within the context of our larger study of the publishing industry. I was rebuffed by an independent house that I sought to use as a comparison to Apple Press, since Apple was a division of a large corporation. Then one of the senior investigators of our research team received the approval of the chief executive officer of a very large publishing corporation to study all of the company's operations. I was assigned to the task of studying a monograph house that was one of its major subsidiaries. I lost the chance to draw a comparison between independent and corporately owned firms, but I gained the opportunity to study a very large, commercially successful, and academically reputable monograph house.

Again for the sake of confidentiality, I will refer to this house, pseudonymously, as Plum Press. My field relations and experiences at Plum were substantially different from those at Apple. In a real sense, my presence was imposed on the company. The nature of my first meeting with the editor-in-chief and the psychology editor was indicative of this: they took me to lunch at a posh restaurant. (On my first day at

Apple Press the editor-in-chief and I had had sandwiches at a nearby fast-food stand.) In short, I was treated as a professional social scientist involved in organization research, not as a young graduate student. This created some problems in building rapport, but, in general, these difficulties were overcome. For example, my first introduction to production and manufacturing personnel occurred at a transmittal meeting, where the social science editor presented me as having "the imprimatur of Mr. ———— [the president of the parent company] and God." One young union organizer was taken aback by this and asked what, if any, association I had with a recent management consulting team that had been at the house. He asked if I had spoken with any of the participants in the union drive. I mentioned that I had talked to the union's leaders at the union office and that I knew of the organizing drive that was presently under way at Plum Press. I later met with several union organizers off the job site and gained their confidence and trust.

Establishing rapport with the social and behavorial science editors at Plum Press was not difficult, since we had a number of interests in common. Regrettably, I never established good relations with the company's editor-in-chief, who found my presence intrusive and bothersome.

My field experiences at Plum Press were both more focused and more concentrated than at Apple. By this time I had accumulated a great deal of general knowledge about the publishing industry, so that my concern now, in addition to collecting specific data, was to learn what, if any, characteristics were unique to Plum Press. My observations were not stretched out over a period of months. Instead, I visited the company two to three times a week from mid-September, 1976, through mid-December of that year, for a total of about thirty observations.

Other Sources of Information

In addition to my fieldwork at Apple and Plum, I visited a large university press, where I interviewed several editors and the director. I also attended a variety of industry meetings and workshops, such as the annual meetings of the American Booksellers Association, the Society for Scholarly Publishing, and the Association of American University Presses, and I closely followed events in various trade publications, among them *Publishers Weekly, Scholarly Publishing*, the *Author's Guild Bulletin*, and the *BP Report on the Business of Book Publishing*. I also read numerous reports issued by the Association of American Publishers, the Association of American University Presses, Knowledge Industry Publications, and the Book Industry Study Group. Finally, my associates and I formally interviewed approximately one hundred thirty people in editorial positions and informally interviewed roughly four hundred other publishing personnel. I also supervised participant-observation studies of eight other publishing houses.

A word of explanation about the sources of information cited in this study is necessary. In the course of our research, my colleagues and I promised confidentiality to all the people with whom we talked. Since people were rarely aware of the ultimate use that I would make of the information they gave me, it is important that their confidence not be violated. Occasionally, I have altered minor details of incidents in order to protect respondents' identities. All data collected at Apple Press and Plum Press (as well as additional material collected in the course of the general research project on publishing) are reported anonymously. When individuals or corporations are identified by name in the text, it is because this information was obtained from publicly available sources.

1

THE ORGANIZATION OF AMERICAN BOOK PUBLISHING

Publishing has acquired something of a mythic heritage as a genteel profession that attracts people because it is a lively and urbane occupation concerned with ideas, contemporary affairs, and literature. The traditional prerequisites for being a successful publisher are a certain flair—a certain taste and sense of discrimination. How close this myth is to reality would be difficult to ascertain, but, suffice it to say, it has had considerable staying power. As recently as 1976 the Association of American Publishers sponsored a seminar called "The Money Side of Publishing," and one of the speakers, Erwin Glikes, criticized the seminar for perpetuating the pervasive myth that the industry has two sides, the "sunny side of editors, writers, and other gentle folk sitting at sidewalk cafes, sipping aperitifs, talking about Art," and the shady side, where the sun does not shine, where "sharp-eyed accountants and heavy-jowled financial types pause every now and then to shake their fists at the children of the sun across the street, who sit there, oblivious to the bottom line, whiling away their hours and the profits in blissful ignorance."[1] Much of the current outcry over commercialism in publishing is a reflection of the belief held by some parties that book publishers should be concerned with more than just making money. These tensions between the demands of commerce and the obligations of culture have persisted throughout the history of the book trade.

Such debates go back over a century and a half because book publishing is one of the oldest industries in the United States. There are few other American businesses in which it is possible to trace a direct family lineage from the original founders to the executives of contemporary firms. Nor are there many industries where so substantial a number of the leading companies have maintained their dominant position since the turn of the century. Moreover, some of the practices and policies associated with the book trade's cottage-industry era persist in modern-day publishing. Nevertheless, there have been a number of profound changes, particularly during the past three decades. In the 1950s, William Jovanovich regarded his occupation as "a halfway house between art and business."[2] By the late 1970s, Michael Korda, editor-in-chief at Simon and Schuster, quipped to an interviewer, "We sell books, other people sell shoes. What's the difference? Publishing isn't the highest art."[3]

In this chapter I briefly review the principal changes that have shaped the social and economic organization of the book industry in recent years and assess the consequences of these changes. In particular, I review the emergence of various market segments within the industry, the rapid growth of the past few decades, and the bifurcation of the industry into large vertically integrated publishing and entertainment firms and smaller specialist houses that cater to well-defined audiences. I conclude with a comparative analysis of the three branches of the industry—general "trade" books, college textbooks, and scholarly monographs—that are most significant for the production and dissemination of social science knowledge. Although editors in almost all branches of the book industry share a common task—the location of manuscripts with sales potential—the means for accomplishing this task vary, depending on the sector of publishing in which the editor works.

Differentiation: A Highly Segmented Industry

A great many different types of books—textbooks, encyclopedias, reference books, Bibles, mass-market paperbacks, serious fiction, and research monographs, to mention only a few—are produced by the publishing industry. Each type of publishing commonly requires special skills and knowledge. As we shall see, the problems that people must solve in their work roles differ significantly across the different branches of the industry. Given the varying requirements for successfully publishing a particular type of book, it is not surprising that publishing houses tend to specialize in one type of book or that, in the larger firms, such as McGraw-Hill or Harcourt Brace Jovanovich, there are separate divisions or departments, each concentrating on a particular type of book.

In terms of its social organization, the book-publishing industry is a universe of loosely connected firms, linked sometimes by ownership but more often by nothing more than the common enterprise of producing books. This universe of firms is subdivided into a number of smaller, distinct, and tightly knit social systems. This process of differentiation, or the creation of various subsectors within the industry, dates back to the nineteenth century. John Tebbel (1974:119) reports that, "by 1860, book production had assumed the general proportions it has today—that is, textbooks were the largest part, 30 to 40 percent of the whole." Book publishers have long known that publishing "trade books"—books of wide general appeal—"has ordinarily been too shaky a business to stand firmly by itself" (Miller 1949:19).

By the early part of the century, many of the larger publishers of general literature had expanded the scope of their operations to include the more reliable and predictable areas of publication, such as medicine and law and, especially, school and college textbooks. Macmillan was the first house to establish a college textbook division, which it did in 1906 (see Madison 1966). By 1913, George P. Brett, president of Macmillan, observed that few large publishers were confining their publications to books in general literature (Brett 1913:455). The strategy of diversifying into new areas was a means of reducing the risks typically associated with trade publishing.

Not only publishing houses but a wide variety of American industries began to diversify during the early years of this century. As the historian Alfred Chandler (1977:473) has shown, the strategy of diversification evolved from the concept of the "full line," the adding of new product lines which permitted companies to make more effective use of their expertise and to exploit the by-products of their existing product lines. Initially, many of these moves were ad hoc responses of middle managers to fairly obvious opportunities. By the 1920s, however, in much of American industry, diversification became an explicit strategy of growth. By diversifying, businesses hoped to achieve several aims: to decrease risks by spreading resources across several domains of activity; to achieve economies of scale in those activities that were common to all lines of the business; and to smooth over rough periods and allow for the maintenance and development of product lines during periods of adversity.

Book publishing lagged behind these general business developments, pursuing its own independent path. Some publishers diversified into new lines of publishing, but the industry did not grow. In fact, in the period 1911–45 it had a negative compounded annual growth rate of − 0.8 percent (Noble 1982:100). After a remarkable year in 1910, when 13,470 books were published, an increase in the number of new books and new editions released annually did not occur again until almost five decades had passed. Although these years were not propitious for growth, they were years of significant literary and intellectual accomplishment. Books of genuine merit commonly made the best-seller lists. This was also the heyday of valuable and productive editor-author relations, typified by the legendary Maxwell Perkins of Scribner's and his close association with, among others, Thomas Wolfe and Ernest Hemingway (see Wheelock 1950).

Although the book industry began to develop distinct submarkets early in the twentieth century, it was not until midcentury that it began to grow. And grow it did, turning out 14,876 titles in 1959, more than 30,000 by 1966, and reaching a peak of 48,793 in 1981.[4] The number of publishing companies jumped from 804 in 1954 to 1,650 in 1977.[5] I turn now to a discussion of this growth and the changes that have accompanied it, but we should not lose sight of the fact that the industry's recent growth has also accelerated the move toward differentiation. Thus any effort to chart overall industry trends is risky, because book publishing today is not so much a single industry as an assemblage of subsectors, and few trends or changes are uniform in their consequences across industry sectors.

Expansion and Modernization

The speedy growth of book publishing since 1960 is the result of the confluence of a number of factors. In the midst of the baby boom and post-Sputnik funding, higher education burgeoned. As the globe shrank and literacy rates increased, there was a worldwide information explosion. The popular entertainment industry, with its insatiable appetite for new products, also grew at a rapid clip. Publishing-industry analyst John Dessauer recalls that the sixties were

> times when books seemed to sell despite the inadequacies of their publishers, when even inferior materials were readily absorbed by a well-funded, gluttonous market. So many factors worked together to benefit the various segments of the industry that almost everyone enjoyed a slice of the pie. Research projects supported by government and foundation grants encouraged acquisition of professional books; generous federal and state budgets, bringing unaccustomed affluence to colleges, universities, and their faculties, augmented sales of scholarly materials; newly founded colleges were stocking libraries; parents eager to strengthen their children's educational resources avidly bought encyclopedias for the home; general and specialized book clubs were flourishing. [Dessauer 1974:8]

The expansion of the book industry attracted many outside interests. Companies such as Time, CBS, ITT, Xerox, and others in the information or entertainment fields were eager to join in the book trade's growth or to finance it. Publishing houses themselves raised new sources of capital by public stock issues or by merger, the latter route becoming very common. This outside capital further fueled the industry's swift rise. The book industry became rife with mergers and acquisitions, and during two peak periods, 1965–69 and 1974–80, the merger rate in publishing was four to five times higher than in most American industries. Outside ownership also brought modern management practices that fundamentally altered the craftlike nature of book publishing. These changes, as I discuss in more detail below, have been a mixed blessing.

The debate over the consequences of the book industry's growing absorption by the entertainment industry, through the acquisition of publishing houses by film companies and television networks, has been loud and long. Some have termed these developments a "sinister process," while others have welcomed them.[6] Statistics on the publishing industry are sparse, and one can easily marshal data to support a wide variety of competing arguments. Heather Kirkwood, the attorney who coordinated the Federal Trade Commission's investigation of media concentration, has remarked:

> I have been frequently startled by the amount and intensity of disagreement which revolves around the media. Yet I have found that little of this controversy involves disagreement on facts. Instead, people disagree on how the facts should be categorized, judged, analyzed, or valued. Hardcover trade book publishing provides a good illustration of this type of controversy . . . ; frequently one side will point to a particular set of figures as proof positive that the industry is, indeed, concentrated. The next day, a different group will point to the exact same figures as proof positive that the industry is unconcentrated.[7]

A plausible case can be made that industry concentration has been enhanced by the formation of large vertically integrated publishing/entertainment companies. Huge multimedia giants, such as MCA, Gulf and Western, Times Mirror, and Time, Inc., own various combinations of magazines, television stations, film companies, cable television, and other entertainment activities. The ten largest mass-market paperback lines, all owned by large corporate entities, accounted for 83.3 percent of mass-market paperback sales in 1980.[8] The eleven leading hardcover trade publishers were responsible for 71 percent of the sales of hardcover titles in 1980.[9] Six of these houses are owned by larger corporations; the others are themselves large diversified publishing companies. These figures suggest that certain subsectors of the industry are controlled by a small number of firms, many of them in cross-ownership of other mass media. But other statistics paint a very different picture. Measures of overall industry concentration show scant change. The four largest firms accounted for 18 percent of the industry's sales in 1947, and in 1977 the four-firm concentration index was 17 percent. The U.S. Bureau of the Census considers the publishing industry to be "one of the least concentrated sectors among all U.S. manufacturing activities."[10] A recent Congressional Research Service report notes that the number of publishing establishments increased by 45.2 percent over the 1972–77 period and concludes that the industry is highly competitive and open to new entrants (Gilroy 1980).

I find that neither set of statistics—those that stress the industry's competitive health as against those that indicate a trend toward concentration and a narrowing of editorial choices—fully captures the complex reality of contemporary book publishing. The interviews and field observations that my colleagues and I obtained in our general study of book publishing provide a different perspective. I argue that changes in ownership have had a subtle but nonetheless significant impact on the manner in which many publishers conduct their business. I will also suggest—and this may initially strike the reader as counterintuitive—that the heightened quest for large audiences, common in many corporately owned houses, has provided new opportunities for specialist firms. The basic economic structure of the book industry is fragmented, and only in a few submarkets do any significant financial gains accrue from large size.

Changes in the Labor Process

Arthur Stinchcombe's (1959) classic paper on bureaucratic and craft modes of production beautifully delineates the difference between work systems that are bureaucratic and hierarchical and those that are autonomous and personal. In bureaucratic mass-production systems, both the product and the work process are planned in advance by persons who are not members of the work crew. The engineering of work processes and the evaluation of work by economic and technical standards takes place in specialized staff departments. Such systems are hierarchical in nature, and communication generally is in a vertical direction. In contrast, Stinchcombe observed that the construction industry consists of a loose coalition of small organizational units, each having considerable autonomy. In construction, the task calls for many intermittent and highly skilled operations that follow a sequence. The skills are such that control by direct surveillance or by rules will not render the desired outcomes; considerable reliance must be placed on workers making their own judgments. Management confines itself largely to inspecting outcomes. In a craft system of production, such as construction, the work process is governed by workers in accordance with the empirical lore of their occupation. Planning and execution are decentralized at the work level, where entrepreneurs, foremen, and craftsmen carry the burden of technical and economic decision-making. Such systems are not bureaucratically organized except for their administrative components, which generally are considerably smaller in size than their counterparts in bureaucratic organizations. Stinchcombe finds a strong association of craft systems with a minimization of fixed overhead costs. This is necessary because of variations in work volume and product mix.

Occupations that involve the production of cultural goods exhibit many of the characteristics associated with craft systems of production. Because of their uncertainty about the necessary ingredients for a successful book or phonograph record, executives are forced to trust the professional judgments of their employees, relying on their track records as indicators of their abilities (Peterson and Berger 1971). Paul Doebler, a publishing-industry analyst, has described these arrangements in the following way:

Unlike many other industries, where costs can be managed more tightly from higher echelons, book publishing costs depend heavily on the actions of those working at the lower and middle levels of the organization. It is impossible to centralize all the myriad decisions to be made on the thousands of books published each year, and these cost-determining decisions are spread throughout the company in publishing. So, in a very real sense, people at most levels of publishing have direct impact on how well the organization uses its resources to attain its goals, whether to earn a profit or to produce fine books or both. [Doebler 1976:33]

For years, the view that publishing is a craft was the orthodox one. The following comments, made by two highly regarded senior editors, both with distinguished careers in trade publishing, aptly summarize this perspective. One of them had this to say:

Publishing is a very chaotic industry . . . ; it begins with the fact that you exert very little control over the person who creates the product. Nor does anyone actually know what the public wants or what it will buy. I think it would be impossible to try and create a list of books, each of which would have high-volume sales. I don't think it can be done, not intentionally anyway. Over and over, publishers are surprised by their lists. Some books sell better than expected, others do much worse. What I try to do is to publish books I think are important, or informative, or needed by someone out there. I think about the "market," but, in my mind, what is crucial ultimately is how I feel about the book.

The other said:

I firmly believe that publishing cannot be made rational or efficient because it is like a factory that turns out sixty, eighty, a hundred or more custom-produced objects . . . each of which has to be sold to a different market, talked about in a different way. Each book is a separate product, with an essentially autonomous fate.

Not only has the nature of the labor process in publishing long resembled a craft occupation, but the industry as a whole has been able to maintain low operating costs by arranging for services on an as-needed basis. Overhead costs are minimized by contracting with authors on a royalty basis, and editors' salaries may sometimes be tied to the sales of the books they sign. Even the largest houses routinely call upon free-lancers, either individuals or agencies, for such services as copyediting, design and artwork, indexing, promotion, and publicity for individual books; smaller houses rely on free-lancers to an even greater extent. The overwhelming majority of publishing houses contract with independent firms for the printing, binding, and manufacturing of books. Additionally, many publishing houses market a substantial number of their books indirectly, through independent distributors or wholesalers, who sell to libraries and bookstores. This is true even for large houses who have their own sales staffs. Most of the small and some of the medium-sized houses have no in-house sales force; instead, they contract with either commission salespersons or larger publishing houses, or they form a consortium with other small publishers to handle the sales, distribution, and warehousing of their books.

Yet, in the past decade or so, many of these features have disappeared from the publishing scene, usurped by new arrangements and practices. The conversion of a craft occupation into a corporate enterprise has been initiated in part by new owners and managers, who have sought to rationalize book publishing and bring its idiosyncratic and often determinedly old-fashioned habits into line with modern management techniques. Much more attention is now paid to orchestrating a book's release and reception. Both trade and textbook publishers have embraced the idea that books should be carefully packaged. Houses now have large and sophisticated marketing and publicity departments, whose advice is frequently sought, and in some instances is required, before any publishing decisions are made. The result is that more attention is paid to actually selling a book; this is in marked and rather welcome contrast to the previous notion that a book sold itself by favorable word-of-mouth. The down side, of course, is that not all books are deemed worthy of such favorable treatment.[11] At some publishing houses, it does not seem worthwhile to crank up the marketing machinery for a book of quality and merit but of only modest commercial potential. (Such books, I should note, are not going unpublished. As I discuss in more detail later, they are increasingly likely to be published by small specialized firms, or under a special imprint by a larger house, or by a nonprofit university press.)[12]

Other changes in the work process are the natural by-product of the close alliance of publishing with television and film.[13] The huge sums paid for the subsidiary rights to hardcover books have kept many trade houses afloat;[14] at the same time, these developments signal a displacement of editorial prerogatives. Editors in trade and textbook houses can no longer simply sign a book and then tell their house to sell it. Instead, other departments must be consulted before decisions are reached. The task of negotiating a trade-book contract has become quite complex, involving complicated subsidiary-rights agreements. Negotiations require hard bargaining, legal expertise, and shrewd manipulation. For assistance, authors have turned to agents and lawyers to help them stay abreast or ahead of the publishing community. The links between authors and agents are but one part of a more general reduction in contact between authors and major publishing houses.

Perhaps the most fundamental shift has been in the role of the editor, especially in large trade and textbook houses. Publishing-industry historian John Tebbel observes (1981:732) that the widely used term "acquisitions editor" is an indicator that today's editors seldom edit. He notes that, in the 1940s, "acquisition editors were confined to textbook publishing, and the so-called line editors of the 1970s had not been invented." Editors used to be generalists who did everything. Now the time of an acquisitions editor is considered too valuable to be spent on working with an author. In the past, editors read manuscripts, worked with authors, assisted them, and edited their manuscripts to whatever extent was required. Today's editors spend much more time talking,

arranging deals, and consulting with lawyers, corporate managers, and marketing and subsidiary-rights directors. This not
only signals a power shift within publishing houses—one in
which editors are on the decline and others are in ascendance;
it has also led to a restructuring of the relationship between
authors and editors.

One editor described the changes in his work at a large
trade house by noting, "I'm spending a lot more time planning the lives of my books. Much less time is spent with
authors and much more time with other departments—
marketing and subsidiary rights, especially." Another trade
editor, commenting on the hurly-burly pace of his job and the
need to move quickly, remarks that, "with multiple submissions, editor and author never get together to judge the
chemistry between them, and we find ourselves up against
fifteen other houses, having to make fast decisions." Moreover, both authors and editors seem to move from one house
to another more frequently than they used to. A *New York
Times* story on publishing's declining sense of community
summed up the state of affairs by noting that loyalty is now
spelled "M–O–N–E–Y."[15] Of course, few complaints are being
voiced by the authors who are reaping the benefits of the new
era of large contracts or by the employees, who have found
that the highest salary levels are paid by houses owned by
large corporations or conglomerates.[16]

Transformation or Transition?

How fundamental or permanent are the changes I have just
described? One indicator of whether new forms of ownership
and work organization will endure is the strength of their
financial performance. Clearly, when measured by increases
either in sales receipts or in the number of new titles and
editions, the book industry's gains have been remarkable.
But have the new methods and practices resulted in higher
profits? The data needed to fully answer this and related
questions are not available;[17] however, the calculations of
J. Kendrick Noble, analyst of media stocks and vice-president

of Paine Webber Mitchell Hutchins, Inc., offer us some insights. It is important to note that, prior to the industry's recent transformation, hardcover trade publishing was a marginally profitable activity, while textbook publishing was fairly stable and prosperous. Have the new practices altered these traditional standards of performance? Moreover, are the greatest financial gains realized by the largest firms within specific industry sectors? And, finally, is it the more concentrated sectors of publishing that earn the more robust profits?

Tables 1 and 2, below, provide tentative answers to these questions. They report 1980 profit margins for different sectors of the book industry, as well as a trendline, based on normalized estimates of operating margins for the period 1971–80. Noble (1982:113–16) cautions that these data, which are derived from voluntary reports by member firms of the Association of American Publishers, have several limitations. The number of companies reporting varies annually, and it is reasonable to assume that the larger publishers are more likely to report. It is best to regard the data as reflecting the performance of members of the AAP and not as necessarily representative of the entire industry.

Table 1
Estimated Operating Margins of Publishing Firms, by Sector

Sector	Operating Margin 1980 (%)	Rank	Trendline, 1971–80 (%)	Rank
College textbooks	20.4	1	16.3	3
Trade books (total)	8.2	10	0.9	9
Adult hardbound trade (subcategory of above)	5.6	11	4.2	7
Mass-market paperbacks	1.4	14	− 5.6	11
Professional books (total)	12.4	7	10.6	5
Technical and scientific books (subcategory of above)	9.4	9	18.6	1

NOTE: Operating margins are pretax.
SOURCE: Excerpted from Noble 1982: 113. The full table includes data for fourteen industry sectors.

Table 2
Estimated Operating Margins for Different-sized Publishers, 1980

Sector	Smallest Third (%)	Middle-sized Third (%)	Largest Third (%)
Trade books (total)	8.8	8.8	8.7
Trendline, 1971–80	1.6	9.8	8.5
Professional books (total)	12.8	11.3	13.0
Trendline, 1971–80	9.6	10.2	12.0
College textbooks	9.4	14.2	25.4
Trendline, 1971–80	1.9	17.1	25.4

SOURCE: Adapted from Noble 1982:114.

In 1980 and for the period 1971–80, college textbook publishers performed very well. They were the industry leaders in 1980 and were among the top performers in the previous decade. Textbook publishing's economic status clearly did not suffer from any changes in work arrangements or increases in concentration; in fact, this sector's financial performance was quite likely improved as a result of these developments. Trade publishing presents a different story. Financially, it remains a fairly marginal activity. Of course, it is possible to argue that, had there been no changes in operating practices, trade publishers might have fared even worse than they did; but that is hardly a strong justification for significant changes in the organization of work. It is also worth speculating that, while trade publishing is not particularly lucrative in and of itself, firms that own trade publishing houses in tandem with film companies or television studios realize some economies of scope. That is to say, they benefit from common ownership of several media, and they gain added understanding of their markets as well as greater access to potential "products" from such arrangements. The data do not permit us to assess whether this is true, but this would be one reason for remaining in this line of activity. Note that mass-market paperback publishing, one of the most concentrated sectors of publishing, is also one of the least rewarding financially. Finally, professional books, the unglamorous and seldom-recognized sector that we will shortly be examining, performed extremely well in the decade 1971–80.

The data in table 1 do not provide strong support for the notion that changes in the organization of work have dramatically improved performance. Textbooks continue to be rewarding, while trade books are not. Nor do the data offer a clear picture of the advantages of market concentration. The college textbook market is fairly concentrated, with a small number of firms controlling the lion's share of industry receipts. On the other hand, mass-market paperback publishing is even more concentrated, and the performance of these dominant firms is hardly auspicious.

When we turn our attention to differences in the size of houses within specific industry sectors, we find somewhat more stable results. The larger companies in each sector tend to show the highest profit margins. The advantages of bigness seem particularly strong in the college textbook market, somewhat less powerful in trade publishing, and even more modest in professional books. Nevertheless, the message of table 2 is fairly clear: greater financial gain is associated with larger size. We should, however, be somewhat cautious about the actual importance of size. The proposition that large size generates high profits raises tricky problems of causality. Both size and profitability may be the result of growth, of expertise, or of historical trends. The strongest association between size and high profit margins is found in college textbook publishing, a sector of the industry which has long been regarded as highly predictable and profitable. Textbook publishing is one of the few areas of the industry where there are any significant economies of scale. Large textbook publishers, unlike large houses in other sectors of the industry, appear to be able to maintain high profits without facing significant challenges from new entrants, whom we would normally expect to be attracted to this rewarding line of activity.

If the available data on financial performance do not provide an unequivocal rationale for the recent alteration in the traditional practices of book publishers, are there other reasons why we might expect the developments of the past decade to be more or less irrevocable? For example, to what extent are there sunk costs, either psychological or economic, attached to existing modes of operation? The general portrait of the rise of modern business enterprise sketched by such scholars as Max Weber, Alfred Chandler, and Oliver Williamson suggests an evolutionary progression. Weber averred that rationalization was the dominant trend in modern industrial societies. Bureaucracy, as an organizational form, has rendered calculable and predictable what was once governed by intuition, personal appeal, or passion. Once established, bureaucracy is very resilient in responding to challenge. Chandler (1977) and Williamson (1980) see the growth of modern corporate organization as the triumph of a superior form of administration, one that is able to outperform competing modes. Hence, once an economic activity moves from a decentralized, craft form of organization to a more centralized corporate form, it is unlikely to return to its earlier craft status. Though they differ in some important respects, the implication to be drawn from Weber, Chandler, and Williamson is that a return to a craftlike form of organization would be an unexpected regression. These broad portraits of social change are meant to capture general trends and are not necessarily applicable to specific industries, particularly one as idiosyncratic as publishing, but they do suggest that, in the absence of strong contrary factors, we should expect the recent changes in publishing to constitute a fundamental transformation in both the means and the relations of production. Thus we now turn to the key question: Are there any factors that would render the recent changes in book publishing more transitory than transformative?

Mergers by themselves do not necessarily make companies any less efficient or their activities any less valuable. But as the concerns of book publishers shift in a way that leads them to spend more time on business issues and less time on cultural matters, it is natural to worry that the social consequences of these developments may not be altogether beneficent. The production of books is a special enterprise. What may be logical from the point of view of efficient management may not be beneficial when examined with respect to such different criteria as enhancing cultural diversity, promoting civil liberties, or advancing scientific knowledge.

There is little evidence, however, that books of merit are going unpublished. Even the Authors Guild, the most vehement critic of recent changes in book publishing, observes that "it is not that fewer books are being published than formerly, or even, at least not provably, that books of exceptional merit are going unpublished."[18] The Authors Guild points instead to a kind of degradation of the publishing process. But books of quality continue to be published, occasionally with considerable success, both critical and financial. *The Name of the Rose*, a demanding first novel by Umberto Eco, a professor of semiotics at the University of Bologna, spent many weeks in 1983 and 1984 atop both the hardcover and paperback best-seller lists. Successes such as this are, however, uncommon; more typically, books that are challenging and rewarding are published with limited fanfare. The works of a great number of talented novelists, historians, social scientists, and foreign writers are currently in print. One may have to look carefully for these books and pay dearly, because their prices are generally very high even when they are published in a quality-paperback format. And, outside of a few large cities, such books may require special ordering. Yet they are available.

One reason for this relatively promising state of affairs is the growing specialization of the book industry, brought about, in part, by the proliferation of small publishing concerns. The rate of merger and acquisition in publishing is high in comparison to other industries, but it is only a fraction of the rate of formation of new publishing companies. As a result, the industry's overall concentration rate does not increase. Noble (1982) shows that the average new book is selling fewer copies and that the average firm has fewer employees than before; hence the book industry's productivity is being achieved in terms of more titles per employee. In short, the industry is becoming more specialized.

These new houses are not replacements for the medium-sized firms that have been gobbled up in the recent mergers. The publications of small firms do not receive the attention in national review media that books published by larger houses do. Small firms also lack the distribution capability of larger publishers.[19] What is significant about the small publishers is that they are demonstrating that a specialist strategy—that is, catering only to particular segments of the reading public—is quite viable in book publishing. A small but highly specialized publisher can make as much profit with small print runs of expensive titles as the very large publisher of titles can with big print runs and low prices.

Glenn Carroll (forthcoming) has pointed out that many industries are characterized by the simultaneous success of apparently opposing strategies. In such industries as brewing, newspapers, music recording, and book publishing, generalist firms and specialist firms not only coexist but are fundamentally interrelated. The success of the generalists creates the conditions for the success of the specialists. Carroll (1984) describes this phenomenon as "resource-partitioning," a process which results in an environment that is split into general and specialized markets. In the newspaper industry, for example, general-audience newspapers strive to reach the widest possible audience; in so doing, they are vulnerable to the competition of specialized newspapers, who appeal, for example, to ethnic or suburban readers or to those interested in business news (Carroll, forthcoming). More generally, "by attempting to secure large market shares through universalistic appeals to all potential customers, generalists avoid making extended particularistic appeals to special groups of customers" (Carroll 1984:131–32). The net result is that, by pursuing large audiences, generalists neglect many specialized pockets of consumers.

Resource-partitioning seems to be an apt characterization of the current state of the book trade. As large trade and also college textbook publishers increased their expectations about the number of copies that a book must sell in order to be considered successful, they became less willing to take on eminently worthwhile books that had modest sales potential. This change in the marketing strategies of many large publishers has created new opportunities for small trade houses, scholarly houses, and university presses, all of whom are moving into the territory the large trade houses have vacated in their quest for blockbusters. Other small publishers have found specialized niches and have concentrated on how-to books or books of regional interest. There are also small publishers driven by social, religious, or political causes. Still other small houses, such as David Godine, are concentrating on books noted for their exceptional design. And there are small firms that are surviving by reissuing titles that the large companies have allowed to go out of print.

Perhaps the key difference is that, unlike general-interest publishers, small specialty houses operate with the knowledge that the readers of their books are, to a large extent, the same kind of people as those who write them or else are professionally like them. This makes information-gathering much simpler. It is easier to stay in close contact with authors who are more likely to know one another. Decisions can be made faster. The marketing advantages of specialization are even more pronounced. Direct-mail advertising can be highly targeted and cost-effective. Special markets have more predictable sales. The same benefits of specialization also extend to finding skilled copyeditors, compositors, and other production personnel. The growth of special-interest publishers is only one factor, albeit a significant one, in the dramatic increase in the total sales of books, from approximately half a billion dollars' worth in 1952 to more than eight billion in 1983.

Part of the success of the small, more specialized houses is due to the declining quality of author-publisher relations in the larger houses, along with the exceptionally high rejection rate for manuscripts that is characteristic of almost any publishing house of significant size. Small firms and large firms not only aim at different audiences; they also differ with respect to their internal structure and operating policies. While the books published by the small, specialized houses generally receive less national exposure and attention, the titles are kept in print longer than the typical book published by a large house. Employees are likely to feel a stronger sense of identification with a small press, even though their pay is usually less than they would receive at a large firm. The administration of a small house tends to be fairly simple, in contrast to the intricate organizational structures, involving complex decision rules and costly monitoring practices, that are standard at many large houses.[20]

Of course, not all small houses are specialists, and not all of the large publishers are generalists. Although organizational size and strategy are correlated, the association is not terribly strong because other factors affect this relationship. Despite the many problems faced by small houses in their struggle for survival, particularly with regard to access to bookstores in general and to chain bookstores in particular, some do succeed. A crucial issue is how they react to success. Do they continue their specialty operations or attempt to standardize their products and enlarge their resource base? Or do they become acquisition targets for larger houses, who can provide much-needed financing for the smaller firm? Some may even go out of existence if the person who founded them dies.

Moreover, I have treated large publishing houses as if they are uniform in their policies when, in fact, they are not. The relationship between one division or subsidiary of a large firm to the corporate office is rarely the same across companies. Ownership strategies and practices vary considerably. Some parent companies follow a hands-off policy with their divisions and subsidiaries, while others become involved in the minute details of daily business. Many large houses and conglomerates encourage internal competition among their various divisions and subsidiaries.[21] And, as the specialist strategy has demonstrated its viability, large firms themselves are embracing it, whether through diversification into specialized lines of publishing, the establishment of personal-imprint lines within trade publishing houses, and the spinning-off of small subsidiaries, or directly, via the acquisition of successful small publishing houses.

This diversity of practices reflects the basic fragmentation of the book business. In order to retain authors as well as valuable personnel, large houses have moved to set up small "boutique" or personal-imprint lines within their larger operations. In this manner, editors enjoy some freedom from corporate constraints and responsibilities and are freer to stay in close contact with their authors. The diversification into new areas of publishing is a recognition that some of the less glamorous areas of book publishing are the most remunerative. But, most broadly, these developments illustrate that even large publishers have found it difficult to transform some of the basic structural features of the book business. It is a type of work in which there are some important diseconomies of scale (Porter 1980:197–98). There is a constant need for new products. These products have a creative content that cannot be supplied by the publishing house itself but must be competed for in the marketplace. While the competition for authors is sometimes determined on financial grounds, it also frequently rests on personal service and matters of image and reputation. Outside of the textbook and mass-market paperback fields, there are neither barriers to entering the publishing business nor economies of scale to be reaped from high-volume production. And there are "peculiar" barriers to exit, such as a strong emotional desire to be associated with books, that keep people and firms in the business for reasons other than financial reward. In sum, these enduring features of the book trade have led to a fairly diverse, highly segmented industry, populated by corporate giants, semiautonomous firms backed by corporate owners, and small "Mom and Pop" houses, all competing in many different areas of book publishing.

Major Sectors of the Industry

Although I maintain that it is the branch of publishing—not ownership or size—that has the greatest influence on the way people carry out their jobs, it is by no means easy to come up with a widely shared set of definitions that nicely discriminate

among the various sectors of the industry. The fact that
people distinguish between types of books, not only locating
them individually but also categorically, is nothing new. Jane
Austen, in *Northanger Abbey*, made the point for her own
generation in this ironic passage:

> "I am no novel reader—I seldom look into novels—Do not
> imagine that I often read novels—It is really very well for a
> novel." Such is the common cant. "And what are you reading,
> Miss———?" "Oh! It is only a novel!" replies the young lady,
> while she lays down her book with affected indifference, or
> momentary shame. "It is only *Cecilia*, or *Camilla*, or *Belinda*"
> . . . Now, had the same young lady been engaged with a
> volume of the *Spectator*, instead of such a work, how proudly
> would she have produced the book, and told its name . . .
> [Quoted in Lane 1980:13]

The definitional problem is further confounded by the fact
that few publishing houses catalogue their books in the same
way. The primary consideration may well be the overall con-
stitution of a house's list, and this will therefore influence how
individual books are to be typed. For example, a publisher
whose list is largely trade-oriented may designate as academic
a book that a scholarly house would regard as "general." Nor
would it be correct to claim that publishers never handle
books that lie outside their normal range; for a variety of
reasons, many publishers do books that seem out of character
for their particular house. But these exceptions only serve to
emphasize the extent to which publishers' lists do have an
identity, which can be described in terms of the types of books
they have previously published.

A number of different methods are currently used for
categorizing books. There is the Dewey system, which clas-
sifies books according to twenty-three subject categories.
This method is not particularly helpful for our purposes here,
because it does not allow us to distinguish among publishing
houses. (It also appears to have its share of problems with
subject matter; to take an example from my local library,
Union Democracy, a classic study of the politics of the typog-
rapher's union, is classified as a book about printing.) Nor are

the thirteen categories established by the Association of American Publishers (AAP) all that useful from a sociological standpoint. (We will, however, have to rely on the AAP statistics, because other figures are virtually nonexistent.) The problem with the AAP categories is that they fail to employ a consistent set of criteria for discriminating among houses. Some categories are based on type of publisher (textbook); others signify the manner in which books are distributed (mass-market paperbacks, mail order, book clubs); still others rely on a book's content (religious); and one describes ownership (university press).

Another manner of classifying books is by their channel of distribution. There are five major means of distribution: general retail stores, college stores, libraries and institutions, schools, and export.[22] While the great majority of texts are sold in college stores, and most trade books are handled by retail outlets, neither professional books nor university-press titles have a primary distribution outlet. For example, in 1981 professional publishers used a variety of channels, with direct sales to consumers, sales to libraries and institutions, and export sales the three primary means of distribution. University presses relied on sales to libraries and institutions, to college stores, and to general retailers, in that order of importance (Dessauer 1983:101–4).

I choose instead a simple typology that distinguishes among three sectors of the book industry—publishers of trade books, including adult hardcover and trade paperbacks, as well as mass-market paperbacks; publishers of college textbooks; and scholarly publishing, including specialized commercial monograph publishers, nonprofit university presses, and for-profit generalists who publish primarily for an academic audience. The usefulness of this scheme is that the interviews and fieldwork that my colleagues and I conducted revealed significant differences in the organization of work across these three sectors; hence it is a sociologically interesting way of dividing up the industry.

The three sectors differ in the following important ways: the audiences they seek to reach and the methods they employ to reach them; in the standards and criteria they use for accepting manuscripts; in the differential chances for unpublished authors to be discovered; in the size of their print runs and in their time schedules; and in their definitions of what is successful, as well as in their strategies for attaining success. Scholarly editors seek the approval of the oligarchs of academic networks or "invisible colleges."[23] Trade editors try to create the illusion of success by generating media publicity, talk-show spots for authors, and high-priced subsidiary-rights auctions. Textbook editors rely on research that purports to tell them what professors who teach introductory college courses are looking for. While Harvard University Press would be pleased with a book that sold 5,000 copies in a three-year period and garnered a Bancroft Prize as the best book in the field of history, Prentice-Hall or Simon and Schuster might be very disappointed by a book that sold "only" 20,000 copies during its first six months of shelf life. It is a business in which one publisher's peacock is another's turkey.

Perhaps most important, the three sectors show very significant differences in profitability. One review of the performance of the industry in 1981 concludes, "As usual, text and professional books were among the profit leaders" (Dessauer 1983:100). Table 3 shows estimated book-industry sales according to the AAP classification. If we combine the categories that I have marked 1, we approximate what I call the trade sector. College texts are marked 2, and the categories labeled 3 roughly correspond to my definition of the scholarly sector. These are general approximations, but they will prove useful in the context of a discussion of profitability and market shares. Professional books and college texts have both been consistently strong performers over the past decade (see, for example, Most 1977 and Quirk 1977). The 1981 pretax operating margins of around 13 percent for professional books and an even stronger 22 percent for college texts typify the year-in, year-out solidity of these two sectors. In contrast, adult hardcover trade, trade paperbacks, and mass-market paperbacks all had lower than 10 percent operating margins in 1981, which, though weak, represented a marginal improvement over 1980 (Dessauer 1983:100). If we use the data in table 3 for 1982 book sales, we find that trade books accounted for 22.8 percent of total industry sales, professional books for 15.7 percent, and college texts for 14.6 percent. The three sectors combined account for more than half of all book sales. I turn now to a brief overview of the major features that distinguish these three branches of book publishing.

The nature of college textbook publishing has undergone tremendous change since the 1950s and 1960s. Back then, all manner of books—research monographs, basic texts, paperback anthologies, and books designed for advance upper-level courses—were published by textbook companies. In the interim, textbook publishing has witnessed a growing concentration of ownership and a reduced willingness to take risks.[24] Since the 1970s, the large textbook houses have concentrated on producing books for the largest undergraduate courses. They no longer produce for the smaller upper-level and graduate courses, and they publish no research monographs at all. These large textbook publishers may employ more than a hundred college travelers, who visit the campuses, urging adoption of the latest texts. Orders are placed with college bookstores, who obtain the books from the publisher at a discount of 20–25 percent.

In contrast to the large houses, the small college publishers, frequently located in publishing's hinterland, outside the New York metropolitan area, survive by locating the specialized niches that the large firms disdain. They concentrate on producing one "quality" introductory text, on doing books for smaller advanced courses, or on publishing texts with a particular point of view, such as a Marxist political sociology text. Medium-sized text houses face the greatest threat to their survival, because they are too large to rely on specialized texts, yet they lack the sales force and other economies of scale necessary to take on the dominant giants, such as Prentice-Hall or McGraw-Hill.

The days when a college text editor would "eyeball" the

Table 3
Estimated Book Publishing Industry Sales
(In Millions of Dollars)

	1972 $	1977 $	1977 Pct Chg From 72	1982 $	1982 Pct Chg From 77	1982 Pct Chg From 72	1983 $ (Preliminary Est.)	1983 Pct Chg From 82
Trade (Total)	444.8	887.2	99.5	1344.4	52.8	204.7	1595.2	17.7
(1) Adult Hardbound	251.5	501.3	99.3	671.6	34.0	167.0	807.6	20.3
(1) Adult Paperbound*	82.4	223.7	171.5	452.0	102.1	448.6	531.6	17.6
Children's Hardbound	106.5	136.1	27.8	180.3	32.5	69.3	190.3	5.5
Children's Paperbound	4.4	26.1	493.2	51.5	97.3	1071.3	65.7	27.6
Religious (Total)	117.5	250.6	113.3	390.0	55.6	231.9	454.9	16.6
Bibles, Testaments, Hymnals & Prayerbooks	61.6	116.3	88.8	163.7	40.8	165.8	182.0	11.2
Other Religious	55.9	134.3	140.2	226.2	68.4	304.7	272.9	20.6
(3) Professional (Total)	381.0	698.2	83.2	1230.5	76.2	223.0	1373.0	11.6
Technical & Scientific	131.8	249.3	89.2	431.4	73.0	227.3	491.0	13.8
Business & Other Professional	192.2	286.3	49.0	530.6	85.3	176.1	561.2	5.8
Medical	57.0	162.6	185.3	268.5	65.1	371.0	320.8	19.5
Book Clubs	240.5	406.7	69.1	590.0	45.1	145.3	654.4	10.9
Mail Order Publications	198.9	396.4	99.3	604.6	52.5	204.0	554.5	-8.3

(1) Mass Market Paperbacks								
Racksize	250.0	487.7	95.1	665.5†	36.5	166.2	706.1	6.1
(3) University Presses	41.4	56.1	35.5	122.9†	119.1	196.9	129.9	5.7
Elementary & Secondary								
Text	297.6	755.9	51.9	1051.5	39.1	111.3	1149.7	9.3
(2) College Text	375.3	649.7	73.1	1142.4	75.8	204.4	1228.6	7.5
Standardized Tests	26.5	44.6	68.3	69.7	56.3	163.2	79.7	14.3
Subscription Reference	278.9	294.4	5.6	396.6	34.7	42.2	443.0	11.7
AV & Other Media (Total)	116.2	151.3	30.2	148.0	−2.2	27.4	143.0	−3.4
Elhi	101.2	131.4	29.8	130.1	−1.0	28.6	124.3	−4.5
College	9.2	11.6	26.1	7.9	−31.9	−14.1	7.6	−3.8
Other	5.8	8.3	43.1	10.0	20.5	72.2	11.1	11.1
Other Sales	49.2	63.4	28.9	77.1	21.6	56.8	80.0	3.8
TOTAL	3017.8	5142.2	70.4	7844.3	52.5	159.9	8592.0	9.5

SOURCE: *Publishers Weekly*, June 22, 1984, p. 34.
*Includes Non-racksize sales by Mass Market Publishers of $113.5 million in 1982 and $139.9 million in 1983.
†Previously reported 1982 figures revised to conform to information available at a later date.

market to see what was needed, find a professor to write a book on the subject, wait for it to be written, and then hope the book would sell have largely passed from the scene. One reason for this is that the process took too long. Sometimes as many as three or four years would be spent in writing the text. Nowadays college publishers are anxious to produce books that are lively and topical. They are also asserting much greater control over both the writing and the content. Textbooks no longer just get written; they are now carefully designed packages, heavily illustrated and accompanied by manuals, test banks, and other paraphernalia. In other words, college texts are now produced with the very active participation of the publishing house, much as elementary and high-school texts have always been prepared. Utilizing market-research data, editors develop a plan for a text and then carefully oversee the writing, testing, design, and manufacture to make sure that the plan is followed. The editor-author relationship is essentially a buyer-seller relationship in which the editor contracts for certain specified services from the author. There are tight deadlines and strict controls. The aim is to produce a small number of products that have been carefully researched and tested in advance of publication.

College text publishing is strongly sex-typed: nearly 75 percent of the college text editors whom we interviewed were men who had begun their careers in sales or marketing (see Coser, Kadushin, and Powell 1982: chap. 4). Thus, editorial decisions—which ultimately determine what college students will read—are influenced by historical patterns of career mobility, the market demands of a highly concentrated sector of the book industry, and a set of internal social relations in which an emphasis on sales predominates. Introductory texts are expensive to produce; a quarter of a million dollars or more is often spent before the first copy is adopted for classroom use. This large expenditure puts heavy pressure on editors to ensure that their decisions will pay off. As a result, the majority of college editors handle less than a dozen books each year—much less than the yearly workload of scholarly editors. Much of their time is spent in meetings—much more than is the norm for editors in scholarly or trade houses. Every step of the production process is closely coordinated by editors and key members of other departments.

Competition among text houses is fierce. Unlike scholarly or trade publishers, text houses are in direct competition with one another for customers—the professors who decide which text to adopt. One indication of the competitive nature of text publishing is the reluctance of text editors to assist their counterparts at other houses; they are the least likely of all editors to refer manuscripts to editors at competing houses. The decision process in text publishing is highly formalized; text houses are among the most bureaucratic of publishing firms. In Perrow's (1967) terms, the task of the text publisher is routine. There is little variation in the production process even though the subject matter of the books may differ greatly. With such high stakes involved, most houses opt for a fairly conservative strategy, and there is a good deal of imitation of competitors' products.

Text editors feel that their skills are interchangeable from discipline to discipline (one text editor claimed that he could "easily be as efficient in electrical engineering or physics as in psychology"), but scholarly editors take a different perspective on their work. Although few scholarly editors profess to be experts in their respective fields, they do believe that a certain amount of knowledge of a subject—whether acquired through education or experience—is necessary. "You *have* to understand the differences among subfields within a discipline," an editor at Plum Press asserted. More generally, our interviews revealed a difference in intellectual disposition between scholarly and text editors. The latter believe that they possess a general skill, while the former have more passion for a particular set of interests. Scholarly editors read much more widely and well; they were more likely to read such periodicals as *Science*, for example, and more than a third of the scholarly editors we interviewed regularly read three or more "highbrow, intellectual" magazines.[25] In contrast, college editors were light readers; they seldom read publications such as the *New York Review of Books*, the

American Scholar, the *Atlantic*, or the *New Yorker*. Most scholarly editors attended top undergraduate colleges and universities, and more than a third had one or more advanced degrees. Of all the editors we interviewed, it was the scholarly editors who were the most likely to have done some writing themselves, while the text editors were the least likely to have done so.

Many scholarly editors underwent some anticipatory socialization before entering a career in publishing. Almost half intended to pursue a career in book publishing. In contrast, text editors typically entered publishing by accident. Scholarly editors honed their network-building skills early: many used personal contacts to land their first job. As a group, scholarly editors are, by publishing standards, the most diverse; for example, the largest percentages of females and Jews are found in the ranks of scholarly editors. This diversity also holds up in terms of career mobility. Scholarly editors started in a much wider range of positions than did editors in either textbook (where sales is the entry point) or trade publishing (where editorial secretary or assistant is the first step on the ladder).

Academics and other professionals constitute the primary audience of scholarly publishers. Within this terrain, however, there is room for a considerable variety of publishing houses. There are a small number of for-profit scholarly houses, as well as the elite, nonprofit university presses, who try to reach what is, by scholarly standards, a fairly wide audience. These houses publish books aimed at a broad spectrum of academics from several disciplines rather than a narrow subfield of specialists. Ideally, their books either deal with important public issues or make a serious contribution to scholarship and thus continue to sell for many years. In addition, there are also a great many professional monograph houses who publish for very specialized audiences. Whether the audience is broad and interdisciplinary or narrow and specific, the comments of the editor-in-chief at a large monograph house aptly summarize the intended model: "The best scholarly books are those that professors have to buy for their personal libraries—the ones they have to read in order to keep up with their field."

The economics of scholarly publishing is the major factor that distinguishes it from trade publishing. While there are trade publishers, such as W. W. Norton or Pantheon, whose lists bear some resemblance to those of scholarly presses, the manner in which their books are costed out and distributed is fundamentally different. Trade books are sold at a trade discount (40–45 percent) in general bookstores. Their print runs are typically much larger than those of a scholarly book. Scholarly publishers survive by conservatively estimating a book's sales potential and then budgeting the book in such a way that a small profit can be made on a limited number of sales. The amount of money involved in terms of advances, production costs, and advertising budgets is relatively small. It is not unusual for a small scholarly book to cost less than $15,000 to produce.

Professional monograph houses represent the most specialized branch of the scholarly publishing field. The essence of monograph publishing is the delivery of timely research to small groups of consumers in need of the information. The editor-in-chief of a large monograph house described his firm's activities in the following way: "The way we look at it is that we don't publish books; we produce research tools—the latest in scientific advances. Scientists need our books the same way they need a new piece of hardware. We are at the cutting edge of science."

As scientific fields have become more specialized, and as new areas of professional activity have opened up, the number of monograph houses has grown dramatically. Among the many monograph houses or companies with monograph divisions are Wiley Interscience, Greenwood Press, Lexington Books, Jossey-Bass, Praeger Special Studies, Routledge and Kegan Paul, Ballinger, Academic Press, JAI Press, McGraw-Hill, Plenum Publishing, Transaction Books, Sage, and Westview Press.

The very specialized content and audience are the key factors, and they are unique to monograph publishing. Because the audiences for them are small, monographs are extremely high-priced. Authors receive low royalty rates, and advances are rare. The assumption is that an author's main interest is in rapid dissemination of his or her ideas to relevant colleagues. It is not unusual for a monograph to be published in less than six months. Little editing is done, and artwork and design are minimal. It is a steady and profitable, if unspectacular, business in which cash-flow problems are minimized by low overhead costs and by the short publishing schedules, which result in money returning much sooner than in other types of publishing.

The ninety-odd university presses can be arrayed along a continuum from general scholarly publisher to specialized monograph publisher. The larger and more prosperous ones, such as Oxford, Cambridge, and the university presses at Chicago, Harvard, California, and Yale, are very similar to commercial scholarly publishers and, in fact, frequently compete with them for authors. The smaller university presses have lists that are more like those of the commercial monograph publishers. One important exception is the fact that many university presses publish books in the humanities and even fiction, both of which are regarded as unprofitable by commercial scholarly houses.[26]

University presses, however, operate under different economic circumstances and, as a result, decision-making in university presses is less oriented toward the profit motive. As a part of nonprofit educational institutions, these presses are tax-exempt. Their overhead costs are lower because they are typically located in university towns rather than metropolitan centers, and their parent universities may assume various expenses for them. Many presses have endowments or other forms of subsidy. As a general rule, it would be fair to say that most university presses would be satisfied to break even. But university presses face other, more stringent constraints than do commercial houses. Manuscripts undergo much more critical scrutiny at university presses. Any manuscript that is seriously considered for publication must be favorably reviewed by two experts in the field and must later pass muster with a governing board composed of members of the senior faculty. As a result, the decision process is often lengthy, and university presses may lose authors to commercial scholarly or trade publishers. As one university press editor-in-chief remarked ruefully, "We publish an author's dissertation and then they take their next book to commercial publishers in Manhattan."

If, in trade publishing, the importance of editors is being challenged internally by subsidiary-rights personnel and externally by agents, and if, in text publishing, an editor's duties are segmented and often subservient to the marketing and sales departments, in scholarly publishing the role of editor remains the most powerful position. Scholarly editors often oversee the publication of twenty-five or more books each year. That may sound like a lot, but we will soon see that the academic community greatly assists these editors in carrying out their duties.

While scholarly publishers generally operate in a context of low risk, the high-stakes world of hardcover trade books and mass-market paperbacks is characterized by considerable risk and great uncertainty. On the other hand, the readers of scholarly books are a demanding lot, and a publisher's prestige can suffer if books of little substance are issued. In particular, the elite university presses and top scholarly houses are quite concerned with maintaining prestigious reputations. (For large monograph publishers, who issue hundreds of very specialized research treatises, reputation is not so overriding a concern.) Trade publishers compete for a broad mass audience and often publish outright junk with little negative consequence. Authors, agents, librarians, and others in the book-buying trade may be put off by a list of dubious quality, but the general book-buying public is not considered to be sensitive to a trade publisher's reputation. Each trade book is regarded as an individual commodity in its own right.

Trade editors lack both the market-research data that college editors utilize and the tightly connected academic circles that scholarly editors depend on. Text and scholarly editors readily turn to outside experts for advice; in contrast, trade editors rely on other members of their house for guidance. The world of academic and professional authors is well organized; there are even regular gatherings, such as conferences and annual meetings, where text editors and scholarly editors come in contact with authors and with one another. A consensus on what is new and valuable is developed through these institutionalized contacts. For trade editors, the outside world is much more anonymous; they lack easy access to authors, and they also tend to be somewhat isolated from editors in other houses.[27]

Trade books, whether published in hard covers or in rack-sized mass-market paperback format, are regarded as "perishable" commodities.[28] A scholarly book is sold over a fairly long time period and may wait a year or more for recognition, but a trade title has but a few months in which to make an impact or else be forgotten. If they are published with little fanfare, trade books will die a quiet death upon publication. Mass-market paperbacks expire in a most unceremonious fashion: their covers are ripped off and returned to the publisher for reimbursement by the bookstore. Hardcovers that do not "move" are consigned to be "remaindered"—that is, sold at sharply reduced prices in discount bookstores. But when success strikes, trade publishing comes alive with a kind of intoxication. Subsidiary rights are auctioned off to the highest bidder, with book clubs, movie studios, and others all clamoring for a piece of the action. Authors jet around the country on whirlwind tours, promoting their books on television and radio talk shows. Books are reviewed in newspaper and magazine columns, and large sums may be spent on publicity and advertising.

Trade publishing is a high-stakes world, with little room for the cautious. The president of a major trade house sadly notes that "only one out of every seven or eight titles pays for itself."[29] Because of the risks involved, most trade houses rely on established writers, well-known public figures, and those temporarily in the limelight as sources for new books. Trade editors typically receive a good portion of their books from agents, who have already carefully sifted through the ranks of potential authors. Few of the major trade publishers will take a chance on a manuscript from someone whose name is not known. Previously published authors or celebrities are much more likely to receive attention from reviewers and book-buyers.

Although it may not be as lucrative as text or scholarly publishing, trade publishing plays an enormously important role in shaping our popular culture. The debate over whether the high-powered world of entertainment has eclipsed the less exciting but more consequential world of serious literature cannot be resolved here; we can, however, note that the two currently coexist, with the lists of various trade publishers tilting more strongly toward entertainment or toward literature, depending on the predilections of their editors and owners.

* * *

The revenues of book publishers pale in comparison with those of other mass media. The policies of the book industry are discussed infrequently in the halls of Congress. We seldom read about book publishers in the business press, nor should we expect to, since, as a whole, the industry employs only about 66,000 people. But we should not allow its comparatively small size to obscure the book industry's importance. Moreover, in contrast to other media industries, where decisions are dictated by the imperatives of mass production, the book industry does a better job of serving the diverse interests of small groups of consumers with special tastes. We move now from a discussion of the general landscape of the industry to specific portraits of two scholarly publishers. In doing so, we move from an assessment of the direction the industry is taking to the question of how a very small number of individuals make choices of considerable consequence for the academic community.

2

THE SETTING

Apple Press occupied a portion of one floor of a multistory building located in one of Manhattan's main business districts. The other floors of the building were inhabited by the various divisions, and also several of the subsidiaries, of the parent corporation. There were many other publishing houses in the neighborhood and also an abundance of restaurants, shops, and department stores. Editors could choose among a wide variety of restaurants, their selection often guided by the status of their lunch date.

The offices at Apple were cramped, with books and manuscripts stacked everywhere. Employees frequently inquired if and when they could get more space. The editors, department heads, and production editors all had small personal offices. The two top executives—the president and the vice-president, who was also the editor-in-chief—had somewhat larger, but by no means spacious, offices, which doubled as reception areas for guests and visitors. The remaining staff had desks in a small open area. The personal occupancy of the offices and desks was marked by posters, plants, and family pictures.

Besides offices, the building contained a newsstand, a company cafeteria for employees, and a posh corporate dining room for executives, which was rarely used by the editors of Apple Press. Each floor had a bulletin board for posting job openings within the corporation, company news, and special-interest stories, such as the one that announced the winners of the college-scholarship competition among the children of company employees. There was a monthly company newsletter, which sought to boost the company's internal image. This reflected a recent effort by the parent company to repair the damage that had stemmed from serious labor-relations problems a few years earlier. While some Apple Press employees welcomed the corporation's increased concern, others viewed it with suspicion. Contact between Apple and members of the parent company was both formal and infrequent.

The working conditions at Apple were "hygienic," or, as one employee described it, "nothing to get excited about . . . I mean, we don't have a great view or fancy chairs or anything, but it's all right." The offices were close and compact. All employees were on a first-name basis. Contact among the employees was both frequent and informal. If the head of production had a question for an editor, he would walk into the editor's office to get an answer. When a member of the manufacturing department wanted the editor-in-chief's approval of a book's jacket design, it was easy to obtain. There was a great deal of socializing both on and off the job. Employee birthday parties were common, and if the press gave a party for an author when a professional convention was in town, the entire staff was invited. Apple Press had something of the image of a happy team, working together in pursuit of a common goal. This was clearly the picture that Apple's executives drew for me. As we shall see, it was not entirely accurate. I should note, however, that, despite constant questioning on my part, few employees voiced wholesale dissatisfaction. Most of their complaints were more on the order of frustrated suggestions as to how things could be done more efficiently.

At Plum Press, the atmosphere and setting were markedly different from this. Plum occupied most of the floors of a multistory building that was located in a part of Manhattan where there were few other publishing houses and a limited number of restaurants and shops. The editorial offices were on one floor; production and manufacturing, accounting, sales and promotion, customer services, and the journals department were on other floors. Two floors were occupied by subsidiaries of Plum Press. Most of the contact between personnel on different floors was formally arranged. Employees comported themselves in a quiet and reserved manner. On-the-job socializing was limited to pleasant exchanges. Editors and executives were often referred to as Mister or Doctor by rank-and-file employees. The formality of social relations was of course due in part to the large size of Plum Press, which precluded face-to-face working relationships for most people.

The offices at Plum were not well furnished. The building was old and undergoing renovation. On very cold days the heating system warmed the building to the point that fans or air conditioners had to be turned on for relief. Top executives, editors, and managerial personnel had private offices that could best be described as adequate. Other employees worked at desks that were crowded together and separated only by short glass partitions. There were few signs of personal occupancy of offices or desks. Reception areas were sparsely furnished. Bulletin boards on the editorial floor listed the weekly travel schedules of the editors; on the other floors there was only information about fire regulations and company rules. There was little, if any, company "news" or publicity.

A Short History of the Two Firms

Apple Press was founded after the Second World War with an initial investment of less than two thousand dollars. In its early years, reprints of classical European works in the social sciences were its staple publications. One employee who worked with the company during the 1950s reports that Apple in those days was "chronically undercapitalized; we operated on a shoestring." Another remarked, "We were always stalling off creditors." The company had only five full-time employees during the mid-1950s, so it relied heavily on the services of free-lancers and a number of academics who served as advisers and uncommissioned scouts. The company's founder was a "master at exploiting personal ties," according to one former editor. He got authors to forgo royalties until their books had recouped their production costs. He found scholars who were willing to translate foreign classics for very small fees. During most of the 1950s Apple Press published fewer than thirty titles a year.

In the late 1950s and early 1960s the publishing industry was rife with mergers and public stock issues. College enrollments were expanding rapidly, and publishers wanted a piece of the burgeoning educational market. Apple Press was constantly short of money, a chronic problem for many fast-growing but small companies. To remedy this, the president of Apple agreed to an acquisition offer from a larger publishing company. At the time of the merger, the firm had annual sales of somewhat less than a million dollars.

Initially, Apple Press was "lost" within the larger parent corporation. The founder of Apple moved on to "bigger and better things with the parent company." During the 1960s there were frequent corporate reorganizations, and Apple Press eventually wound up as a division within another publishing division of the parent corporation. The parent firm itself then became, through the merger process, a large diversified, multinational educational corporation. Apple Press was encouraged by the parent company to become more textbook-oriented and to publish in a wider range of fields. The press experienced some initial but short-lived success with college textbooks. The transition to more texts and fewer scholarly books was reflected in the smaller number of titles published by the press in the late 1960s.

An editor who was with the company in the 1960s and is now editorial director of another house had this to say:

I believe that ———— [the parent corporation] thought they had purchased a potential textbook house. But clearly Apple Press lacked that capability. We were encouraged to go after college adoptions, and we didn't even have a sales force! We relied on theirs [the parent corporation's], but they were busy selling their own books. The press wasn't successful in changing its list. There were rapid changes in leadership. The house's economic performance was poor. There was no direction to their program. Their relations with authors deteriorated, and they lost many of the good ones. The publication program suffered [and, with it,] their reputation, performance, and profits. It was not until the current management redefined itself that they came near to making the kind of impact they made in the 1950s.

The parent company grew dissatisfied with Apple Press and installed a new administration in the early 1970s. The new president and the editor-in-chief were promoted from within the parent company. In the editor-in-chief's words, "We were hired to do a full-scale first-aid operation." Major changes soon took place. The new editor-in-chief described them as follows:

> Only six of our present employees worked for the press under the previous administration. We've tried to disassociate ourselves from that period. I guess it started going downhill about eight or ten years ago. [This conversation took place in late 1975.] The press published a freshman English textbook with spectacular success—it sold something like 40,000 copies. That won everyone over—texts became the order of the day. They quit selling scholarly books that sold only 2,800 copies. They didn't work with their superb backlist authors. They did not develop good relations with authors. They started publishing readers and texts—both of which can require big investments. Then, if they don't click, you lose big! Plus, they were not contributing to their backlist or promoting it. Their sales sagged. They lost their contacts and the authors who used to publish with them . . . Shortly after we took over, we had to destroy thousands of copies of textbooks the press had done in the sixties. It was a difficult decision, but there was no way these texts were ever going to sell, and warehousing costs aren't cheap!

The new president of Apple Press took a somewhat more sanguine view of the past:

> You must realize that it was a minority opinion, both within the parent corporation and among authors, that Apple Press

was seriously deteriorating. You might say that it was also the more perceptive opinion, but there were plenty of people who would have been delighted to have their books published by Apple. You should remember that the press published some of the leading social scientists in the world during the sixties. Many of these books did a lot for the house's reputation and also sold extremely well. But clearly a lot of errors were made. It was essential for me to reestablish a certain sense of trust in the press, both within the parent corporation and among authors.

One of the current employees who had worked with the press in the 1960s recalled that "the delays were just incredible. It often took two years to put a book between covers. There were no schedules. No one talked to each other. Authors were furious at us. Now we are a professional publishing house."

The two new top executives hired their own staff, reestablished contacts with authors who had left the press, instituted more efficient production schedules, and exploited the press's fine backlist, which had gone relatively ignored. Both of them told me it was impossible for them to come into Apple Press with any preset philosophy about what types of books they wanted to publish because, for the first year at least, they were saddled with publishing books that had been signed by their predecessors. In fact, manuscripts of books that had been contracted for in the late 1960s sometimes arrived at the press as late as 1976 and 1977.

By 1974, in the opinion of Apple's executives as well as in the minds of the top people in the parent corporation, the press had made a successful turnaround. This was a very good year financially for the press. Most of the books published had been signed during the reign of the current administration. Publications in the humanities had been cut back, and very few texts were published. Once again the house was publishing "respectable works of scholarship in the social sciences." In contrast, the parent corporation of Apple Press fell on hard times in the mid-1970s, partially as a consequence of their aggressive and rapid growth during the prosperous sixties. As firings and layoffs became part of "a general strategy of corporate belt-tightening," the corporation received a considerable amount of bad publicity as a result of charges of "unfair labor practices." Apple Press had only an indirect involvement in this tumult. Moreover, the success of Apple Press was a small beacon of light in the generally gloomy corporate picture; as a result, it was permitted to operate increasingly under its own direction.

In the years since my fieldwork at Apple, the press has gradually moved from publishing basic social science research into more applied areas. It has expanded its list into economics, law, management, and policy analysis and has trimmed the number of monographs in anthropology, history, political science, and sociology. There is greater concern that a new title in, say, the sociology of deviance also appeals to potential readers in the fields of criminal justice, law, and police administration. The number of titles published has remained fairly constant, ranging between sixty and eighty annually. The most pronounced change has been the editorial turnover. Only one acquisitions editor remains from the period when I did fieldwork. The president has moved on to an important position at a larger publishing house, and the editor-in-chief also has changed jobs. The reputation of Apple Press in the scholarly community remains strong, despite the changes in the nature of its list and its staff.

Plum Press was founded by an émigré during the Second World War. Few commercial publishers at that time were specializing in professional monographs in the hard sciences. The founder was the company's president for over two decades. His second-in-command—the vice-president and editorial director—assumed the presidency in the '60s, upon the founder's death.[1] There has been stability at the top executive levels throughout the press's existence. Plum Press remained relatively small during the 1950s; not until 1960 did it begin to publish more than a hundred books a year. A London branch was established in the mid-1950s, and it has developed a separate editorial program. A reprint program and a small monograph house were also set up as Plum Press subsidiaries.

The company went through a period of accelerated growth in the 1960s, publishing more than two hundred books in 1963 and topping three hundred by 1968. It also started a number of journals, opened a west-coast office, and established branches in Europe and Canada. A specialized textbook program was begun, but its record has been spotty. Textbook sales have never exceeded 10 percent of the company's total sales. The text department has had a number of different directors, in sharp contrast to the relative absence of executive turnover in other departments.

The press began publishing in the fields of chemistry, physics, and the earth sciences, later branching into the biological sciences, mathematics, medicine, and engineering. A publishing program in the behavioral sciences, defined by the press as psychology and as the speech and hearing sciences, was begun in the mid-1960s, but the emphasis has always been on the "hard" sciences. It was firmly believed that other disciplines, such as the social sciences and the humanities, were not sufficiently empirical and could not support the publication of expensive monographs.

The press went through a series of significant changes in the late 1960s. First, it went public in order to raise capital for expansion. Second, the founder of Plum Press died. The editorial director assumed the presidency, and other executives moved up a level in the hierarchy. Most of the top executives whom I met in the course of my fieldwork moved into middle-management positions at Plum during the late sixties. The new president's family became the company's major shareholder. Third, a few years after the founder's death, a merger agreement was reached between a large publishing corporation and the new president's family, in which the family's majority holdings were exchanged for stock in the larger publishing company. Plum Press and its subsidiaries became part of a conglomerate that had, like Apple Press's parent corporation, embarked on a campaign of mergers and acquisitions throughout the sixties. One key difference is that Plum Press's parent corporation continued its active expansion into the 1970s.

By the early 1970s, Plum Press was issuing more than four hundred books a year. This growth was partly attributable to a decision to initiate a publishing program in the social sciences. At the outset, a separate imprint for the social sciences was established, because there were fears that the social sciences were not "scientifically respectable." The press did not want to damage its reputation in the "hard" sciences through association with the "softer" sciences. The social science editor recalls that, "after a few years, in which I demonstrated that an estimable list could be developed in the fields of anthropology, archeology, demography, linguistics, and sociology, the separate imprint was dropped."

A major falling-out occurred between Plum Press's president and the parent corporation's top executives in the mid-1970s. As a result of the exchange of stock at the time of the merger, the president of Plum Press and his family had become large shareholders in the parent corporation. Whether the president of Plum Press was regarded by the parent firm as a potential threat or as too independent is not clear, but relations were not good. The president of Plum Press soon left the press, sold his stock in the parent firm, and formed a small publishing company of his own. His second-in-command assumed the position of editorial director.

The parent corporation was then restructured into a multidivisional firm. Plum Press, which had not been very visible within either the parent corporation or the industry, now became the major component of one of the divisions; in fact, it was one of the largest subsidiaries of its parent corporation. Plum's parent, like the parent of Apple Press, is a large diversified multinational educational and communications conglomerate, and Plum Press itself is an international publishing company, with branch offices in numerous foreign countries and, in some disciplines, very sizable foreign sales. In addition, much of its printing, mainly in the fields of mathematics, chemistry, and physics, is done by specialized printers in foreign countries.

Since the period when I did my fieldwork, Plum Press has continued to grow and to expand its publishing programs.

There has also been some editorial turnover, but the personnel changes have not, it appears, led to any changes in editorial policy or corporate strategy; however, Plum's position
within the hierarchy of its parent firm has changed somewhat
of late. The parent firm has continued to expand into the
areas of educational and entertainment services while selling
off or reducing many of its traditional publishing operations.
Plum Press is now the major publishing arm of the corporation. While the parent firm's involvement in trade and textbook publishing has been reduced, its commitment to Plum
Press has strengthened. A good example of this support has
been the elevation of several Plum Press executives to high-
level staff or advisory positions within the parent company.

Domain

James Thompson has argued (1967) that every organization
must establish a "domain": the claims that it stakes out for
itself in terms of goods or services produced, client population, geographical location, and services rendered. Organizational domain is a primary concern of the top administrative
levels of responsibility and control in an organization. For-
profit organizations have considerable freedom in choosing
their domain. It is important to understand, however, that the
selection of a domain is also the selection of an environment
in which to operate. The domain determines the points at
which an organization is dependent on its environment. A
domain can be viable only if an organizations's claims to it are
recognized by the essential forces in the environment that
provide the organization with its necessary resources. Thus
the environment poses both constraints and opportunities for
organizations that seek to exchange their goods and services
for resources. (We shall see that this process of exchange in
publishing houses is characterized by strong norms of reciprocity.) The choice of domain is both fundamental and
strategic. Thompson (1967) and also Hannan and Freeman
(1977) have maintained that no two domains are identical and
that two organizations cannot occupy the same domain. A

good portion of the success that both Apple Press and Plum Press have achieved can be credited to their ability to stake out domains in a way that was recognized and accepted by key external actors. In short, they have achieved what Thompson (1967) refers to as "domain consensus"—a set of expectations, both for the members of the respective houses and for outsiders with whom they must interact, about what the houses will and will not do.

Plum Press is, according to the vice-president for sales, a "well-established scientific publishing company that does four to five hundred books a year in over three-hundred subfields." He went on to say, "We also do over a hundred journals. With the exception of business, law, the humanities, and history, we cover almost every scientific discipline." Plum Press titles are almost always done in hardcover and are sold to individuals through direct mailings and at conventions. Library sales are also a substantial part of total sales. "It would be odd if you saw one of our books in a regular bookstore. You'll find them in a few college bookstores but never in your local shopping-mall bookstore," remarked another member of the sales department.

"Normal science" was clearly the dominant model at Plum Press. One editor described the press as "a very conservative house":

> We'd never do anything earth-shaking. We tend to stay away from controversy or anything topical. The emphasis is on signing books that deal with significant empirical research. That way, scientists who are working in the area will have to buy our books. We want our books to be an essential part of the research process. We like books with numbers in them because we think people will be attracted to them, not just for the book's arguments or thesis, but because they contain useful data sets.

The economics of the publishing program were deceptively simple. A senior editor summed it up well:

> It is a low-investment, low-return operation. All sales are projected for a five-year period; that means that, at a mini-

mum, the book will not go out of print for five years. We rarely give advances. A book is expected to sell at least 600 to 800 copies, and that covers the cost of investment; if it sells another 600, then we have covered the cost of our overhead. Above that, it's gravy. So you can see that, if a book sells 1,500 or 1,800 copies in its first year, that's fantastic.

The director of sales elaborated on Plum Press's marketing strategy, noting that

It's fairly unusual for one of our books to sell more than 4,000 copies. Oh, sure, some of the books signed by [the social sciences editor] have sold more. But his books are different. We have trouble promoting books to a larger audience. We don't do enough to enjoy any economies of scale, and ads for one or two books in the major media are too expensive. We just aren't equipped to promote them. We have several books that have received a great deal of attention and are selling well. We're trying to promote them accordingly . . . but, by the time all is said and done, they probably will turn out to be less profitable than a steady monograph, where we printed 1,800 copies, advertised them through the mail and in professional journals, and sold most of them over a several-year period. That's the name of our game.

The great majority of Plum Press's publications were monographs and treatises dealing with a particular subfield or topic and published as part of a series. The strategy of concentrating on well-defined topics was one means of attracting attention to, and facilitating the advertising of, their new books. Given the large number of scientific monographs on the market, a series of books has definite advantages over individual books. If a publisher has a particularly strong series in, say, anthropology, it is likely to attract new authors who wish to be associated with the series. Series are particularly economical to market and promote. It is anticipated that libraries and institutions will want to have a complete series and so will purchase new additions to it as a matter of routine. If the series prospers, it will grow in reputation and attract both authors and purchasers.[2]

Plum Press has been particularly adept at recruiting well-known academics to serve as series editors. These editors receive a small royalty, usually of 2 or 3 percent, on books published as a part of their series. Then, for books that they locate that do not appear in their own series, they may receive a finder's fee of several hundred dollars. Series editors are efficient and inexpensive talent scouts. They are the functional equivalent of quick and accessible market research. Monetary gain is not what motivates someone to take on the task of editing a series. For all the time and effort involved, the pay is quite low. More likely, the power and influence to shape the development of a field of research is a key incentive for many academics. Yet we should not underplay the fact that the position is also an obligation that is owed to the profession that has accorded one a position of prominence. Moreover, being a series editor gives one access to new work that may not become available to others for several years; it also affords one the opportunity to offer one's students and colleagues a publication outlet.[3]

Multiauthored serial publications are equally attractive to monograph publishers like Plum Press. Among the various types of multiauthored volumes regularly published by Plum are Proceedings, Recent Advances, Current Topics, and Annual Reviews. The audiences for these publications are quite small, but they are well defined and easily reached.[4] Prices for these volumes are extremely high. Print runs can be accurately predicted because the market is ascertainable—a limited but definite number of scientists, libraries, and institutions will purchase each volume in these series. Despite all these advantages, there are certain problems connected with serial publications. The new growth area one decides to exploit may fail to develop rapidly, or other publishers may overcrowd the market in this area. Editors also have to be concerned with ensuring a continuous flow of books of consistently high quality; several poorly done volumes can give an entire series a bad name and do irreparable damage.

Plum Press is not highly visible either within the book industry or to the reading public at large. In part this is because its books are rarely reviewed outside the professional journals. The company's executives tend to regard their house as unique and so do not compare themselves to other publishing houses. While few of the general developments within the publishing industry are of concern to Plum Press, events in the scientific world, or developments that affect the academic community, such as government spending for basic research, are of considerable importance and are closely watched by company executives.

The strength of the list at Apple Press was in the social sciences, particularly in international affairs, criminology, sociology, and political science. During my fieldwork, Apple Press was rapidly expanding into new areas, such as history, law, and psychology. The house was strongly committed to its backlist, and in fact most of its annual sales came from books that were more than a year old. The editor-in-chief echoed this commitment in his description of an "ideal" Apple Press book:

> The perfect Apple Press book is well reviewed in the major journals, cited for many years . . . it's a book of lasting value . . . it does not have to sell spectacularly, but [it should sell] steadily over the years. As a result, we stay away from fads, and we don't try to keep up with intellectual fashions. If good stuff is being done by important people, then we will either hear about it or they'll come to us. We may not always live up to this image, but that's our goal.

Like Plum Press, Apple Press was not very active in book-industry affairs. The president commented, "I'm certainly not very flamboyant personally, and the house reflects this somewhat. We don't belong to the AAP [Association of American Publishers], and none of us is part of any cocktail set. We don't have much pizzazz, I guess you could say." Apple Press editors and executives did stay informed about what was happening in other scholarly publishing houses, and contact with editors and personnel at competing houses was frequent. The primary focus of attention, however, was the academic social science community. Extreme importance was

given to maintaining good relations with house authors and to
fostering a positive image of the house. As an example of the
concern about image, the top executives felt that it was "very
tacky to remainder books. Authors wouldn't care for that."
The press routinely called on its authors for advice, and the
more prestigious senior authors were heavily relied on. As
the president of the company remarked,

> It has been my viewpoint for a long time that there are people
> out there in academia and the foundations who will act as
> scouts for us and that, if you treat them right, you will build up
> a loyal relationship. There are probably forty to fifty people
> we rely on. [I act surprised at this large figure.] You just can't
> survive on only six or seven scouts. We won't publish every-
> thing they refer to us, and sometimes they tell us we made a
> mistake when we turn down one of their referrals. But they
> know it will get a fair shake—that the project will receive
> serious attention.

Apple Press's strategy of using a large number of "scouts"
on an informal basis was a sound one from both a business and
a sociological point of view. As Emerson (1962), Blau (1964),
and Pfeffer and Salancik (1978) have demonstrated, if a
much-needed resource can be obtained from a variety of
sources, the power of any single source is reduced. Moreover,
the referral of manuscripts by scouts is a flexible and manage-
able way for editors to cope with the great mass of projects that cross their desks. The scouts used by Apple Press
were commonly senior academics who acted as patrons and
brought younger academics to the attention of the house.[5]
The role that such patrons play in scholarly publishing is in
certain respects equivalent to the role of literary agents in
trade publishing. Like agents, they help to screen potential
manuscripts. These informal ties are bound by a norm of
reciprocity but have the appearance of serendipity. Unlike
agents, the scouts do not receive financial remuneration or
any fixed reward. They may receive a polite note from an
editor, a free book or two, or a dinner invitation. Bourdieu
(1977) has pointed out that it is of the essence that reciprocal
relationships not be openly acknowledged as formal ex-

changes. Calling attention to the exchange nature of reciprocity offends participants. In contrast to formal exchanges, in which there is a quid pro quo, reciprocal ties are highly implicit, returns are uncertain and long-range, and compensation may occur at a much later date. It is precisely these characteristics that make reciprocal relations more trustworthy than formal exchanges. And, as Kenneth Arrow (1974:23) has noted, trust is "extremely efficient; it saves a lot of trouble to have a fair degree of reliance on other people's word." In sharp contrast was the disdain with which literary agents were generally regarded by most scholarly editors. Apple Press understood altruistic ties very well and used them frequently. It had a large circle of scouts whom it could count on for referrals and for advice. As we shall see later, these scouts were amply rewarded, in a noneconomic sense, for their assistance.[6]

Apple Press published a wide range of social science titles in both hardbound and paperback editions. The bulk of its list consisted of scholarly professional books whose average print runs ranged between 2,500 and 6,000 copies. These books were the press's "bread and butter." The president underscored this publishing philosophy when he stated:

> As you know, we estimate things conservatively; our print runs are small. You call it the "cover your ass" principle. Well, it is. But I try to encourage my editors to translate unit sales into income and return on investment. Many publishers talk only about unit sales, especially in trade publishing but in our business too. But often big sales don't mean big profits. You have to consider all the angles, the costs and discounts involved . . . Looking at it from this perspective, you can see how a small book can make a good contribution. The important point is that the book doesn't have to be a big seller for us to do it and consider it a success.

The press also published a small number of reference books and an occasional specialized multivolume encyclopedia. Each season they did a few upper-level, advanced textbooks as well as several books targeted for a general trade audience. The print runs for the few trade books were considerably larger, as many as 15,000 copies for a biography of a major politician or a book on the history of an important institution. There were even instances when a successful hardcover book was released in a mass-market paperback format with an initial printing of 25,000 copies. The press was also developing an agency account, whereby a bookseller commits himself to stocking some minimum number of copies of Apple Press titles in a given subject area and in return receives an intermediate discount (generally 33.33 percent as opposed to the more common "short" discount of 20 percent for professional books). The press's parent corporation handled the sales of the texts and trade books; the press itself was responsible for direct mail and library sales. When Apple Press (or, very rarely, Plum) published a book with potential broad appeal, the parent company's trade sales force was responsible for placing the book in the bookstores. As can be expected, such arrangements did not always work well. A trade sales force is usually not well prepared to handle academic or professional books. The sales force's performance is usually evaluated on the basis of how successful they are in selling the parent company's list, so there is little incentive to work hard at promoting Apple Press books. Bookstores are seldom enthusiastic about ordering one or two copies of an academic title. Nevertheless, through a variety of means, some Apple Press books received limited distribution and were available in more discriminating bookstores, particularly in university towns.

Apple Press sold its books in a wide variety of ways. The editor-in-chief estimated that the sales breakdown in 1976 of the various channels of distribution was as follows:

Library and institutional sales	25 percent
College adoptions	25
Direct mail	20
General bookstores	20
International sales	10

Many academics are accustomed to ordering scholarly books directly from a publisher. Scholarly houses also advertise widely in journals like the *New York Review* or the *American Scholar*, and if readers cannot obtain an advertised book in their local bookstore, they can write the publisher directly. A house like Apple Press may sell several thousand copies of a book individually, filling one order at a time.[7] Both Apple and Plum did a considerable amount of their promotion and sales through direct mailings to academics and other professionals. Plum Press maintained up-to-date mailing lists of academics and professionals, while Apple Press more commonly leased appropriate mailing lists from professional societies, scholarly journals, or list brokers. The mailing lists allow houses to pinpoint the professionals who are likely to be interested in their recent publications. Even if the recipients of a catalog or mailing do not purchase a book, they may recommend purchases to their university libraries. Direct mailings permit flexibility in the design and format of advertising copy, and it is easy to chart and analyze their effectiveness. Publishers can build a data base from mail-order responses that will help them determine print runs and audience size for comparable books in the future.

The more specialized a book's topic, the more the publisher will rely on direct mailings rather than other sales methods. When it comes to specialized monographs that are not addressed to a whole academic discipline, say, economics, but to a narrower field within a discipline, such as industrial organization, total sales will be comparatively modest, but knowledge of who will buy the book is quite high. The publisher, or the academic editor of a specialized series, knows with some accuracy who will be inclined to acquire a particular book. This is why Plum Press monographs, though usually priced very high, have a relatively certain market and so can be profitable even with very modest print runs.[8]

Another important outlet for Apple and Plum was library sales. Editors at both houses mentioned that if they chose the right books, they could count on anywhere from one to two thousand sales to libraries. For some books, this alone would put them into the black. Here again, a publishing house's reputation is important. With declining library budgets, li-

braries have become more selective and will rely on publishers with a reputation for, and tradition of, publishing good
scholarship.[9]

During my fieldwork at Apple Press in 1975 and 1976 and
in subsequent interviews in 1977 and 1978, I observed that
Apple editors were signing more books with trade or agency
potential. The current sales mix would probably include a
larger percentage of trade books. Even with the somewhat
increased emphasis on "bigger" books at Apple Press, the
publishing philosophy did not change. Almost all of its books
were written by academics or professionals. Advances were
seldom extravagant. The average advance in 1975 was approximately $1,300, which masks a range that includes many
authors who received no advance at all and a handful who
were given several thousand dollars.[10] The press took a conservative approach to academic books that might possibly
appeal to a wider audience. They usually waited until the
publication date drew near; then any of a number of factors,
such as a rave prepublication review in *Publishers Weekly*,
enthusiastic comments from reviewers, heightened interest in
the book's subject, or an excited response from the parent
company's sales force, would increase confidence in a book,
and the size of the printing would accordingly be increased.
The important point, however, is that Apple Press was very
careful in these matters. Its prices for trade books were comparatively high, and the books were budgeted to earn back
their initial investment on a limited number of sales.

The Structure of the Two Houses

Apple Press is a small house and is organized quite simply.
There are two chief executives: the president, who is also an
officer of the parent corporation, and a vice-president, who is
the editor-in-chief and also an executive of the parent firm.
There are four departments: editorial, production, manufacturing, and marketing. All other functions are performed
either by the parent company or by free-lancers. The formal
chain of command is simple: each employee reports to his or

her department head, who then reports to the editor-in-chief, who is responsible to the president. In daily practice, since it is a small company, there is constant interaction among almost all staff members.

The editor-in-chief functioned as the company's chief troubleshooter. His days were characterized by constant interruptions, telephone calls, visitors, and employees dashing in and out of his office for advice. He worked on many projects simultaneously, juggling problems and projects back and forth, jumping from issue to issue, depending on the needs of the day. His office door was almost always open. Because of the many intrusions on his time, his attention span was short, and many tasks were glossed over. If he had something very important to attend to, such as a monthly report for the president or an important manuscript he wished to read or edit closely, he took it home with him. Like most managers, he thrived on oral communication (see Mintzberg 1973).

The editor-in-chief usually had several major appointments a day. Often they were of a ceremonial nature, such as taking an important author or a visiting foreign publisher to lunch or meeting with an important member of the parent corporation. During such occasions there were rarely pressing items that demanded discussion; the meetings served as an opportunity to exchange pleasantries and information and to do some public relations work for the press. Most of the editor-in-chief's daily work contacts were unplanned.

When key employees were absent or there was an important position that was temporarily vacant, the editor-in-chief would often fill in. He functioned as the sociology editor for a nine-month period and, for a shorter period, helped out with marketing and promotion. The latter task was shared with the president until the help of a free-lance person was secured. Eventually, a full-time department head was hired. The editor-in-chief still found time to acquire manuscripts, and he was personally responsible for dealing with some of the press's most prestigious authors. The time span of matters under his attention varied from the short run of daily and mundane affairs to long-range projections, often several years into the future. At one moment he would be concerned with prodding employees, approving the jacket copy for a new book, or sending out an advance copy of a book in the hope of obtaining an important person's favorable reaction. At the next moment he would be working out future scheduling problems, analyzing the backlist, or planning a new reference series that might reach fruition in five years.

In contrast to the editor-in-chief's harried pace, the president of the press maintained a low profile. A large portion of his time was spent in interaction with the parent corporation. He wanted "the corporate shadow to end in his office and not affect the rest of the press." His primary duties were fiscal management, planning, and the preparation of detailed monthly summaries for the parent company that reported Apple Press's progress in title acquisitions and sales. The weekly meeting of the four department heads was run by the president. He wanted lines of communication within his company to be direct and open; however, he was acutely aware that satisfied employees were a small factor in the parent company's evaluation of how well he was performing; it was interested strictly in the bottom line, in seeing that Apple did as well or better than had been predicted at the year's outset. Occasionally the president signed a few titles—in his words, "for the sake of my own sanity."

Both of the top executives worked long hours and were very devoted to the press. Both maintained that "companies are reflections of the people who run them." They prided themselves on their style of collegial leadership. They wanted their employees to identify with the company and to be committed to their work, yet they also believed in hiring bright young people, knowing full well that they would not remain with the company for very long. The parent company's personnel office had a different approach, preferring to hire prospective employees who professed a long-term commitment. They were therefore reluctant to hire college-educated people for low-level positions. The attitude of Apple Press was, "Why shouldn't you hire educated persons if they want a job? Hell, nobody that's any good should want to stay in a lousy job very long anyway."

For most of my fieldwork period, the editorial department consisted of two senior editors and an assistant. Their principal responsibility was manuscript acquisition. Editorial turnover is commonplace in book publishing and is a key source of author dissatisfaction (see Coser, Kadushin, and Powell 1982: chapters 4 and 9).[11] Within commercial scholarly houses and university presses, career patterns are even more varied than in trade or textbook publishing, where career ladders are fairly standard and recognizable. The editors whom I interviewed, not only at Apple Press and Plum Press but at other scholarly houses as well, began their publishing careers in a variety of different positions. A fair percentage were once editorial assistants or secretaries, a few began as salespeople or in promotion departments, and a surprising number were hired as editors from the beginning and did not have to work their way up. Almost all of the latter were people with academic backgrounds; frequently they were advanced graduate students who, for one reason or another, never completed their dissertations. Knowledge of a particular discipline, however, does not seem to be a particularly valued asset in scholarly publishing. Only a few editors actually did advanced studies in the field in which they became editors. The psychology editor at Plum Press had an advanced degree in biology. He explained that he was better off working in a field in which he was not an expert because he could be more "objective."

A key feature of editorial work is its forward-looking character. An editor's primary interest lies in finding manuscripts that will constitute future lists. Few of their concerns lie in the present, except for worrying over the whereabouts of an author's long-overdue manuscript or the status of a reviewer's promised critique. Editors are structurally conditioned not to pay much attention to books that are currently being released (for a more detailed discussion, see Coser, Kadushin, and Powell 1982:244–59). For most editors, this is a taken-for-granted aspect of their work, and few reflect on the unusual temporal nature of their activities. One exception, however, was a woman I interviewed at a competing house. She was an author and had previously worked as a magazine editor. When she became a senior editor at a scholarly house, she brought with her a very different personal time frame. Her reactions to the reviews of her first crop of books are most suggestive.

> This is a very anxious period for me. I discovered that I respond to the reviews of the books that I published—that I care about—very badly. Not as much as if they were my own books, but almost. The big difference is that, as an editor, you are already busy doing other things. As an author you are not as busy, so reviews can really get to you. What keeps you from worrying too much around here is that you learn that it is all in a day's work. By the time you face the prospect of success and failure of a particular project, you're already very much involved in another. You're too busy doing other things. And then, of course, if you see someone with long experience who laughs about the failures that he's had, then you learn to take it all in stride. They're part of the whole scene. But it horrified me at first.

The production department at Apple Press was responsible for overseeing the editing of manuscripts for style, consistency, spelling, and punctuation. It consisted of a department head, three to five production editors, and a department secretary. As a rule, the production editor did not work on more than eight books at the same time. The manuscripts were farmed out to free-lancers for the actual copyediting, which was then checked by the production editors. In a year's time, a production editor would see between twelve and fifteen manuscripts "put between covers." The time frame of these editors was very limited, since they were always focusing on manuscripts that would by published in the upcoming months.

The manufacturing department at Apple was similarly organized, with a department chief, three manufacturing editors, two clerks, and a secretary. This department spent the bulk of the press's money. Manufacturing was responsible for creating books as physical entities, which involved making

cost estimates, scheduling, planning an overall uniform design, selecting suppliers, purchasing paper and cover materials, and supervising the typesetting, printing, and binding.
All of the artwork and design were done by free-lancers. The
head of the department also kept track of the inventory of the
backlist.

The press's smallest, and most overworked, department
was marketing, staffed by the marketing director, two copy-
writers, and a secretary. They were responsible for advertising, publicity, and promotion for all of the press's titles
except the textbooks and trade books, which the parent company handled. Other marketing functions, such as the sale of
translation rights and book-club rights, were also performed
by the parent company. During my stay at the press, the
marketing director was never satisfied with the efforts of the
parent company, and she increasingly took on the tasks herself. This built to a point where she was working seventy
hours a week, and she eventually resigned. It was six months
before a full-time replacement was hired.

This department was the press's weakest link. In contrast
to Plum Press, Apple Press did not have an easily identifiable
style of promoting its books. Each year a new format was
adopted. Various experiments were tried with journal ads,
but no consistent promotional strategy was evident. Marketing experts in scholarly houses are split in their evaluation of
the utility of journal ads. Most believe that, at the very least,
they have "institutional" value, in that they promote the
publishing house's reputation and show that the house supports its authors. In addition, readers of scholarly journals
may also be potential authors, so that advertising current
books may help to insure a future supply of publishable
manuscripts. Whether the ads also sell books is a matter of
some dispute.

Both Apple Press and Plum Press knew that successful
promotion of a scholarly book depends on utilizing the author's network and the "invisible college"—a fact that many
authors do not fully appreciate.[12] Publishers provide authors
with a questionnaire, asking them, in effect, to describe the

key nodes of their academic network and the key access points to the "invisible college" to which they belong; they are also asked to list the names of professional journals in which it would be appropriate to advertise. The author naturally knows much more about these matters than the publisher does. More frequently than not, however, the author naively thinks that book promotion is solely the publisher's responsibility. The publisher may know the principles of promotion, but the author knows who the audience is.

While Plum Press used its proven mailing lists for book promotion, Apple Press exerted more effort at obtaining good prepublication blurbs from noted persons in an author's academic discipline or in an important policy-related position. Blurbs are used by all types of publishers, but they are especially useful for the scholarly market, since the network of potential readers and opinion leaders is so clearly delineated. Apple Press was most successful in getting favorable quotes to grace the covers and ads for new releases. They were less successful in bringing new books to the attention of the "intelligentsia press"—such journals of opinion as the *New York Review of Books*, the *New Republic*, and *Commentary*. When its books were reviewed in these "elite" magazines, Apple Press seldom knew about it in advance and would have to scurry about trying to place copies in bookstores. To this observer, the most surprising market strategy was an omission: Apple Press had no catalogue of its backlist titles, nor did it distribute seasonal catalogues, describing its new titles. Nor were there separate catalogues for the various social science disciplines. In effect, the press's impressive backlist sold itself. To some extent, it can be viewed as a testament to the quality of the press's publications that, with the exception of ads in professional journals and some promotional work on a title-by-title basis, little was done to sell them. The press was a very profitable operation, so additional marketing efforts were perhaps viewed as unnecessary.

Plum Press had twelve times more employees than Apple Press and published approximately six times more books. Doing fieldwork in a large organization presents many more difficulties. One is not afforded the luxury of sitting in one particular office where, in the course of the day, the majority of the company's employees would come and go. Large corporations appear more reserved and formal because face-to-face interaction is limited and the pace of activity seems much slower. Top executives are surrounded by assistants and secretaries, who shield them from intrusions. As a result of their relative isolation, the actions of individuals seem to have less consequence. One editor at Plum Press noted, "It's very easy to become detached from the actual process of publishing books. All the work is done by people on other floors; you have to go out of your way to see what's going on. And that means extra work, which you seldom have time for."

Hence Plum Press seemed like a large machine with replaceable parts. No employee or executive appeared to be indispensable. This was in sharp contrast to Apple Press, where the absence of a few key employees or executives threw the firm into turmoil. Georg Simmel (1950) was one of the first social scientists to eloquently analyze "the bearing which the mere number of associated individuals has upon the forms of social life." In small groups, the views and needs of individuals are a more immediate consideration. In large groups, individuals are submerged in the mass and count for less. Studies that have assessed the effects of individual administrators in large organizations have found that they account for, at best, 10 percent of the variance in organizational performance (Lieberson and O'Connor 1972; Salancik and Pfeffer 1977). Moreover, Pfeffer (1977) has shown that personalities and personal characteristics are more apparent, and that factors of personal style have a greater effect on career progress, in smaller organizations. The differences in size and strategy at Apple and Plum created different organizational climates, which greatly influenced the nature of intraorganizational relations and conflicts. The latter are discussed in more detail in the next section.

Besides its much larger size, Plum Press differed from Apple Press in the manner in which it was organized. Unlike Apple, it was not broken down into specific departments, each with a department head of equal importance; instead, it was run by ten executives, two of whom were on the premises on only a part-time basis. The company's president was also an executive of the parent corporation and president of the London branch of Plum Press. His time was thus divided among three commitments. There were three senior vice-presidents. One was the editorial director, another was the chief financial officer, and the third was head of the sales department. This third man was also an executive of the parent corporation and spent time there as well. The sales department was run on a day-to-day basis by one of the six company vice-presidents. Two of the other vice-presidents were senior editors, who, along with the editorial director, constituted the editorial committee, which met weekly. Another vice-president was the company treasurer, and the head of the textbook division was also a vice-president. The only woman in the executive group was in charge of the journals. The company's various floors were overseen by floor managers.

One of Plum's senior vice-presidents described departmental responsibilities in the following way:

> It's the duty of the editorial department to acquire, sign, and contract for manuscripts, to oversee the reviews and refereeing process, to recheck final manuscripts and ready them for production. The function of production is to take a finished manuscript and produce it. We do very little artwork and our designs are standardized. Some free-lancers are used for copyediting. The sales department handles the promotion, marketing, distribution, direct-mail advertising, and library sales.

The company's concentration and strength lay in two areas: editorial and sales. In the New York office there were twenty-five people involved in editorial acquisitions. This group included twelve Plum Press editors, each in charge of monograph publications in a particular set of disciplines; six editors in the textbook department; and four in one of the company's small subsidiaries. Each editor reported to one of the two editorial vice-presidents, who in turn reported to the editor-in-chief. Plum Press also had a field office on the west coast, where three additional editors were located.

The sales department was extremely large, with over seventy-five employees in its various branches. It was one of the company's best assets. Every book that was published was featured at least once in a direct mailing and a journal ad, and, if a book belonged to a series, it was likely to be promoted many times a year. The sales department kept hundreds of mailing lists on computer file, which greatly facilitated promotion. The importance of international sales has already been mentioned; one consequence of the overseas sales was that few translation rights were sold. Book-club sales were not common; the largest order on record was for 2,000 copies.[13]

Interdepartmental Relations and Conflicts

As I have argued elsewhere (Coser, Kadushin, and Powell 1982:198–99), conflict is endemic to the publishing process. It is not at all surprising that different departments within an organization develop different outlooks on the organization's activities. Certain departments have tasks that require them to focus inward while others face outward. Differing perceptions of similar situations easily occur. As Dearborn and Simon (1958) noted, executives perceive situations in terms of the specific activities and goals of their own departments rather than from a company-wide viewpoint.

Furthermore, employees will attempt to use an organization to achieve their own ends and maximize their own careers. People also identify with their jobs and derive status from their positions. Within an organization, status is commonly associated with discretion in the use of time and freedom from routine. Publishing houses generally are two-tiered systems, with executives and editors enjoying the lofty positions and the rest of the employees consigned to the routine, more mundane, chores. Ever since the work of March and Simon (1958) and Cyert and March (1963), organization re-

searchers have viewed organizations as political arenas, characterized by subgroup struggles and attempts at maximizing
subunit interests. Organizations are commonly rife with internal disagreements over the distribution of power and discretion. One of the paradoxes of organizational life is that
while the division of labor into specialized departments encourages the development of expertise and the coordination
of activities within a department, such an arrangement can
also create coordination problems and conflicts among departments. Different departments, particularly in large organizations, can become so isolated from one another that they
develop their own goals and perspectives. An editorial department wants all books promoted heavily, while the
marketing department wants to get the maximum use of its
small advertising budget by promoting only the few titles that
have potentially broad appeal. In publishing we find that
authors are often caught in the crossfire of battles between
different departments.[14] Such disputes are not uncommon in
cultural industries.

Intraorganizational conflicts in publishing are further complicated by the particular character of publishing's labor force
and the unusual temporal phasing of the publishing process.
Publishing has long had a strong, somewhat romanticized,
attraction for many young people, fresh out of college, who
have dabbled in writing or worked for campus publications.
Publishing also is an appealing occupation for frustrated
teachers, librarians, journalists, and writers who are thinking
of changing to a second career. It is an occupation that is
tempting to people who believe they have creative talents.
This attraction results in a perennial supply of new recruits for
most publishing houses. Unfortunately, most of these people
aspire to editorial positions. Starting positions, however, are
usually at lower levels, often in noneditorial departments. At
both Apple and Plum a significant proportion of the rank-
and-file employees were highly educated. Yet they were saddled with low-paying and not very glamorous positions, with
few prospects for advancement. This situation is not unique
to publishing; Hagstrom (1976:94) notes that young persons

employed at substandard wages are important in almost all types of cultural endeavors. Epstein (1977:435) finds that one of the marks of a "romance" industry is that it can get away with paying small salaries at its lower echelons because so many are lined up outside, waiting to get in.[15]

The temporal phasing of work has significant consequences for intraorganizational conflicts. The pace at which work proceeds depends on one's position. While editors are concerned with the lists that will be published two and three years down the road, the rest of the house is struggling to produce next season's list. Publishing is arranged in interlocking lines of work, so that the output of editors—that is, manuscripts—constitutes the input of the production, manufacturing, and marketing personnel. In effect, the rest of the company is preoccupied with books that have left the purview of editors. There are even formal occasions—called "launch meetings" at Apple Press, "transmittal meetings" at Plum Press—where editors turn manuscripts over to the other departments. As the editor's concerns must turn to other matters, the launch or transmittal meeting is the first step in an editor's gradual relinquishing of control over a manuscript. From this point on, the manuscript becomes increasingly remote from an editor's interest. Yet it is the editor who is generally the author's sole contact with the publishing house.

It is at this point that conflicts and disagreements most often develop. Authors feel they are at the mercy of members of the publishing house whom they have never met. The employees of the house will have a much closer relationship with the free-lancers to whom they regularly farm out work and with whom working relations are established. Authors are frequently wary of the way their books will be copyedited, designed, and promoted, but at this stage they have very little voice in these matters and can only react to more or less finished work. Authors can, of course, complain; but to whom and with what effect? Their editors are now in pursuit of other authors. Moreover, at least at Apple and Plum, authors who become extremely bothersome can be threatened with cancellation of their contract.

At both Apple and Plum, books were normally produced in a period of seven to nine months. A large number of "raw materials" were always being transformed at the same time. Every employee had a sizable workload and a schedule to meet. To work in the face of a deadline is to work under pressure, and this affects the way employees evaluate their work. Given this pressure, we should not be surprised that the service-providers occasionally expressed irritation at clients—in this case authors, who were a source at once of livelihood and burdensome demands.

Other factors also create conflict. At Apple Press, the top executives encouraged the active participation of all members of the company. They frequently said, "Everyone around here contributes." One of the biggest problems of the previous administration at Apple was an erratic and slow production schedule. The new administration wanted books published promptly and on schedule, a sensible philosophy, since, the quicker you publish a book, the sooner the money that you've invested begins returning.[16] In order to produce books efficiently, the press allowed the noneditorial departments a sense of responsibility and autonomy. These departments were also staffed by young well-educated persons. Once they were encouraged to play an active role, it is not surprising that they sometimes attempted to alter an author's work to bring it more into line with their image of the type of books their press should be publishing.

The head of the production department at Apple remarked, "I like to challenge the author. When a manuscript needs a lot of work, I let it be known. A lot of manuscripts we get are very uneven." Authors frequently did not welcome these changes. In some instances serious disputes arose, and the acquiring editor or the editor-in-chief had to intervene. This was usually done on the author's behalf, and the editor would inform the employee, "If we hadn't liked this manuscript in the first place, we wouldn't have signed it. So cool it!" This fostered disagreements and led employees to question whether their contributions were really valued. Some of the turnover in the production and manufacturing departments was attributable to disagreements of this type.

The situation differed at Plum Press, for a number of reasons. First, although the rank-and-file at Plum were also young and well educated, they did not receive any signals that could be read as encouragement to devote themselves to a manuscript. The suggestions for improvement that were made by employees were seldom received with enthusiasm. Hard work on a manuscript was not rewarded. Second, over four hundred books were produced yearly. This meant that the manuscript that an author regarded as a unique accomplishment was, to Plum employees, a routine product in need of prompt processing. Third, working conditions were not good; lunch breaks were only forty-five minutes long, and supervision was tight. One response of employees was to initiate a union-organizing drive. In the opinion of several key organizers, this drive improved morale, but it also met with difficulty precisely because turnover was so high. One organizer remarked in the autumn that over 30 percent of the employees who had signed union cards during the previous summer had since left the firm. Fourth, the type of books being produced also had an effect on employee involvement. At Plum Press the products were highly technical treatises that were usually of little immediate interest to those working on them. At Apple Press, more of the books appealed to the employees who worked on them; the staff enjoyed reading some of the titles and occasionally took copies home. This increased attachment, however, could result in greater disappointment when an employee's efforts to "improve" the books were rebuffed. I once asked a production editor if employees ever took Plum Press books home as personal copies. He responded, "Who would want to? Besides, no one can ever read them. They are really very difficult books." Disputes at Plum were, as a rule, less often between departments than was the case at Apple. Instead, conflict more typically pitted the rank-and-file against top management. Editors who were members of top management were identified as hostile to the rank-and-file, while other editors were seen as bystanders to the conflict.

In sum, we see that a number of features of book publishing—a talented, young, and underpaid labor force; problems in keeping to tight schedules; and a craft legacy that frowns on one department's offering too much advice or commentary on the activities of another—all contribute to organizational conflicts. The very common organizational problem of attributing credit and responsibility for successes and failures often boils down in publishing to disputes between the editorial and sales departments, and the perennial question of which books should receive the most promotion is an ongoing debate that involves, the editors, the sales and promotion departments, and the top executives.

Summary

How do we account for the differences between Apple Press and Plum Press? Apple is more informally organized, the work process is less standardized, and a lively atmosphere pervades the house. In contrast, Plum is more bureaucratic and routine, and, for most employees, it is rather dull. At Apple there are disagreements among the staff and between departments over the handling of particular books. At Plum there is little comparable debate over publishing matters; conflict there is more like the traditional production politics that characterize labor-management relations in other industries. Questions about the amount of time that employees had for lunch or for breaks and conflicts over the prohibition of fraternizing on the job or the quality of work conditions were continually arising at Plum but seldom at Apple.

Both houses were owned by a parent publishing corporation. In neither case did the policies of the parent firm influence decisions made by the subsidiary. Both parent companies were pleased with the financial performance of their respective subsidiaries and generally left them alone. One obvious difference is the disparity in size between Apple and Plum. Work is much more likely to be formally organized in large organizations than in smaller ones. However, Plum differs from other large scholarly publishers in that the work process is not finely distributed among numerous departments. There were only a few departments at Plum, and they were quite large. The two houses were roughly comparable in age, but Apple had installed a new management team, while Plum had had considerable continuity of leadership.

Perhaps the most significant difference between the two firms is in the relationship between the type of books they publish and the degree of uncertainty they feel about selling their books to the scholarly market. I argue that while both houses had considerable ability to influence and manipulate their operating environments, the technology adopted at Plum Press was so effective that it permitted the routinization of the work process. By "technology" I refer to the strategies and techniques utilized to get work done. At Plum Press there was very little uncertainty about its publication strategy. There was a clear notion of what a scientific monograph was. Ideally, it was a book for which there was a limited but known demand—a book that could be sold easily. There was little variance from the practice of publishing this kind of book. Indeed, when the social science editor occasionally had a "surprise" on his hands—a book that was reviewed in the popular media and had the potential for sales outside a particular discipline—the sales director was not thrilled, because such a book would disrupt well-established routines.

Apple Press showed mastery in exploiting external contacts with senior-scholar brokers and journal editors. While Apple did publish some scholarly monographs, similar to those published by Plum, it also published a mixture of textbooks, some trade books, and professional books aimed at a wider audience. Plum was highly effective in selling its monographs by direct mail, targeting them to carefully chosen lists of people with similar professional interests. Apple used a variety of promotional and distribution mechanisms: direct mail, ads in the *New York Times Book Review*, and general bookstore sales. In short, while Apple's list was more interesting than Plum's, it was the diversity of its list that created uncertainty and led to internal policy debates. The comparison of the organization of work at Apple and Plum suggests a general logic that informs the production of cultural goods: as a firm's work process becomes more rationalized, its output becomes more homogeneous and its capacity for innovation diminishes.

I should note that, personally, I would much prefer to work at Apple Press. There is more opportunity for having a voice in decisions, and the list is more varied and interesting. At Plum there is little voice but ample opportunity for exit. The publications are highly specialized and routinely handled. However, as an author, and depending on the type of book in question, I might take a different view of the two houses. Apple Press did fairly well in terms of author-publisher relations. Most authors were happy with the services they received, but there were "horror stories": cases where an enterprising staff member decided that the author's manuscript needed improving and the author was not happy with the wholesale revisions. Author-publisher relations at Plum Press, on the other hand, were extremely good, partly due to Plum's adroit use of its series editors, who served as vital links between the house and the scholarly community. Given the limited advertising done by Plum Press, I was particularly struck by the fact that over 70 percent of its authors responded to a questionnaire I sent them by stating that they were extremely satisfied with the advertising, promotion, and distribution their books received. Slightly less than half of the Apple Press authors expressed similar satisfaction.

The initial acceptance of a book and, many months later, its publication occasion great expectations in an author. The book is a product of years of research and writing. The author naturally hopes that his or her efforts will be repaid, if not in money, in attention and prestige. It is precisely such expectations that explain why the majority of authors are displeased with their publishers (see Coser, Kadushin, and Powell 1982: chap. 9). That Plum Press is an exception to this unhappy rule is due to its unusual approach to its authors. Plum Press editors were direct and open: they told their authors what kind of services they would receive; explained that every book is featured in a direct-mail ad and in an ad in a major journal; solicited the author's advice about the appropriate audience for the book and asked for useful mailing lists; and followed up on the author's suggestions.[17] They were honest about the very limited sales prospects, were open to ideas, and were responsive to the author's concerns. Plum compensated for the lack of widespread exposure for its books by bringing new titles to the attention of the author's invisible college. By contrast, Apple's efforts to reach a broad audience occasionally resulted in a failure to bring the book to the attention of an author's professional colleagues, thus creating author dissatisfaction.

3

THE NATURE OF
EDITORIAL WORK

Editors are the essential players in the publishing process.[1]
They are responsible for acquiring the manuscripts that the
rest of the publishing house will turn into books. They start
the wheels turning. In essence, it is their job that is unique.
The director of a leading university press reinforced this view
when he said:

> Let me tell you something, and don't you repeat it to anyone
> else around here. Editors are irreplaceable! I think very
> highly of the staff I have assembled. They are very good; but if
> any one of them left, I could find someone else to do their job.
> That's not true with my editors. If one of them left, it would be
> a disaster. Editors are very special people.

The majority of the people employed by a publishing house
are administrative and clerical workers whose skills are easily
transferable to any of a number of commercial or public
organizations. Those with more specialized talents could find
work in other media organizations or advertising agencies.
Then there are executive positions, such as president or director, that pay much better and carry more power than editorial
jobs. Such positions, however, require that considerable time
be spent on administrative matters and managerial duties.
They afford little time for locating new authors and working
with them. In fact, executive positions, such as editorial director, require that the executive be the manager of an editorial

staff. Chester Kerr, former director of Yale University Press, described a meeting with another press director in the following manner:

> "The list," said Arthur Rosenthal, "the list is everything. So if you don't have any smart editors, you don't have any list." He had just become director of Harvard University Press, after a brilliant performance as founder and head man of Basic Books, and I was having lunch with him in Cambridge to see how things were going. He had walked into a bad financial picture, not to mention a somewhat disoriented organization, and I had supposed the marketing and business sides would receive his first attentions. But here he was firing and hiring editors, just as though new feats of list-building could be performed overnight. [Kerr, 1974:211]

An editor at a scholarly or monograph house performs a set of varied tasks.[2] Perhaps the key to scholarly editing is staying informed about developments that are taking place in various academic fields. Knowing who the leading scholars are, who the up-and-coming people are, and what fields are growth areas is an editor's primary responsibility. The extent of an editor's knowledge is a key measure of his or her skills, and many editors jealously guard their talents. A senior editor at Apple Press was very clear about this, as his comments to me attest:

> The president will send me suggestions from time to time . . . ideas from the newspaper or somewhere. But they are just suggestions. If I deem them useful, I'll follow up on them . . . We don't have any editorial meetings. Why should we? I don't see how someone can tell me what's best to sign. It's *my* area; I *know* it. Who else around here knows anything about cognitive psychology or what new developments are taking place in administrative science? The normal course is for me to develop things on my own. When I give the editor-in-chief the rough draft of the "proposal to publish" form, it is usually the first thing he knows about the project.

Another important task for editors is to establish good relations with authors, because this enables an editor to use

them as sources of information about what is going on in their
specialty, as reviewers of manuscripts, or as sources of news
about college enrollment trends. Editors must also stay informed about new lines of research in the various disciplines
they cover. It is their job to evaluate these developments and
determine whether work in a new area is related to subjects
they are already publishing or, if not, whether it is worth
expanding into. Usually it is younger scholars, often without
commitments to a particular publishing house, who are doing
research in these new areas. Hence they represent "a new
field to mine." Editors realize that if all their time is spent on
authors whom they have already published, their lists can
become stale and inbred. Depending on their position in the
market vis-à-vis their competitors, editors will spend more or
less time scouting new fields. Apple Press devoted some
attention to this but not nearly as much as Plum Press, whose
social science authors were generally much younger than
those published by Apple.[3]

The primary means for editors to keep *au courant* of the
professional disciplines in which they work is through building and maintaining a wide and active personal network or, as
one Apple Press editor dubbed it, a "stable" of advisers
whom she could readily call on for good advice—for "objective comments about the merits and marketability of a particular project." Advisers can also be counted upon to refer
promising manuscripts. Boundary-spanning activities are not
unique to scholarly publishing, but in many important respects they are more crucial for scholarly editors than for their
editorial counterparts in trade houses, who can rely on literary agents for referrals, or those in textbook houses, who rely
on the lure of cash rather than reciprocity to attract authors.

Active "networking" outside the confines of the publishing
house is rewarding in a variety of ways. Advisers and friends
in academia are accessible sources of advice and information
about who is doing what, who recently received a large research grant, and what new journal articles are worth reading. A good network is also invaluable when it comes to

traveling. Despite the avalanche of unsolicited materials received by both Apple and Plum, all the editors agreed that "getting out and knocking on doors" was both the best way to find good books and the most rewarding. Senior editors at both houses favored an active style and enjoyed traveling to college campuses, to think tanks, to public policy institutes in Washington, and to the meetings of scholarly associations. Editors with a wide network are also more productive travelers. Friends in various universities can be dinner companions or provide a place to stay, both of which are preferable to spending a lonely night in a motel. Such contacts also enable an editor to be in the right place at the right time: an invitation to a small departmental party can be the occasion for a serendipitous find. Discovering a promising manuscript at a dinner party may seem accidental, but it is the result of maintaining a good network. Obviously, networks are not only good for business leads, they are also personally rewarding for an editor who combines scouting trips with a number of enjoyable social occasions. The comments of a senior editor, who had recently joined the staff of a major university press after a distinguished career in trade publishing, underscore the importance of traveling. He had just returned from a trip to a number of midwest campuses.

Can you imagine: here it was, the dead of winter, snowing like mad, and I'm knocking on people's doors. Suffice it to say, most people were very flattered that I paid them a call. Not many editors make the rounds out there, certainly not in January. Publishing is a crazy business. We receive so many unsolicited manuscripts . . . and there is always work to be done, paper to push, manuscripts to read, forms to fill out . . . It's like anything else, I guess; if you let yourself, you can become nailed to your desk. You have to force yourself to get away. It is imperative that an editor be well informed. To do this you have to get out and knock on doors. I wrote the "big names" in advance and set up lunches and dinners. You can learn something, however, from all sorts of people. You can't ignore librarians, junior faculty, or graduate students if you

> want to keep up with a discipline's fads and fashions . . . to
> learn what's going on . . . where a field is growing. You don't
> always learn these things from senior faculty. Traveling is an
> essential part of an editor's work.

Networks are formed by traveling, by "hanging out"
wherever scholars gather, and by maintaining a large volume
of correspondence. There can, however, be costs in having an
extensive personal network. Every social relationship is constrained and shaped by its own history. Strong tensions can
develop when editors feel more strongly committed to their
authors and network members than to the firm for which they
currently work. From an organizational point of view, editors
are persons trapped in the middle. They are the author's only
friend and voice within the publishing house. At the same
time that they must represent the house in negotiations with
authors, they are the firm's liaison with an author. Such
competing demands of craft and commerce frequently create
problems for editors in determining where their loyalties lie.[4]
These competing demands can be particularly problematic
when an editor moves to another publishing house. In such
cases, authors often feel that the editor has abandoned them.

Editors also have many in-house responsibilities. They
must act as an information resource for their books, advising
the sales department on promotional plans or writing or
overseeing the preparation of jacket copy. They also oversee
the production process for the books they have acquired.
They see that schedules are kept to, possibly recommend a
free-lance copyeditor whom they know and trust, and act as
intermediaries when authors are dissatisfied with the services
rendered by other departments. In short, editors must be
managers and promoters of their books within the house. As
one editor put it, "You have to sell your colleagues—convince them that a book deserves care."

With all these responsibilities, plus the work involved in
guiding and helping authors in the preparation of their books,
it is no surprise that none of the editors find the job boring.
Quite to the contrary, they worry that their work load pre-
vents them from becoming sufficiently knowledgeable to

make good decisions. Although they may be well informed about several fields, editors are essentially amateurs in a world of professionals. No doubt some scholars view editors as dilettantes. The editor-in-chief at Apple Press recalled a comment someone made many years ago that "a bookman's knowledge is as wide as the Amazon and about an inch deep." Another editor at Apple mentioned that "an editor could talk about any subject in the world for two minutes." One editor said, "It is the nature of an editor's job to get interested in an area, locate promising manuscripts by authors with some claim to fame in that field, build up a list in that subject, drop it, and get started on something else." Editorial work involves close association with an author for a relatively brief period of time. Then the editor must move on to other authors and other topics. Moreover, editors work with authors in different fields; however, it is fair to say that at any one time there are only a few topics with which an editor is deeply involved.

Some comments made by the president of Apple Press touch on the manner in which editors move from one subject to another:

> What my editors talk about is what they are doing at the moment. Talk to ———— and he will mention social work or criminal justice; six months from now it may be research in the area of stratification, while six months ago it was the sociology of education. At the moment, ———— is into organizational studies and administrative science. A month ago she was working with a number of psychologists. That's the nature of an editor's job. You get into topics, follow your leads, develop contacts, accomplish something, then move on to another topic. If your work bears fruit, you'll return to that subject in the future.

In this chapter I explore two main questions: How do editors, despite their limited knowledge of the fields in which they work, make reasonable decisions about which books to publish? and How do they balance the problems created by competing loyalties and conflicting values? In focusing on editorial decision-making, I analyze both the formal decision process within the house and the more informal choices that are made by editors as they acquire and evaluate manuscripts and work with authors and reviewers.

The Formal Process of Contracting for a Book

The key question to ask in any study of organizational gatekeepers is How do decision-makers narrow down a large number of competing items and decide which few to devote some attention to in order to select an even smaller number for eventual sponsorship? To answer this question, I initially studied the formal decision-making process within each of the two publishing houses. I quickly learned that the formal process of obtaining approval to publish a book involved little actual decision-making. The important decisions about what to publish are made by editors well in advance of the formal process of securing a contract.[5]

At Apple Press, the standard procedure for obtaining a contract was for an editor to solicit one or two outside reviews of a promising manuscript. Once these had been obtained, and if they were generally favorable, the editor would notify the author that Apple wanted to publish his or her book. A proposal-to-publish form was then filled out (a rough version is usually drafted prior to sending a manuscript out for review). This is a standard form that editors in every house must submit for each book they wish to publish. The form contains information about an author's professional background; a description of the manuscript and the reasons for publishing it (this usually contains several quotes from the reviewers' reports); contractual information, such as royalty terms; preliminary information about the manuscript's length and estimated production costs; a sales estimate; and a timetable for recouping the costs of publication. The editor sends this form to the editor-in-chief, who, on occasion, will return it with questions. It is then referred to the president of the company; after he signs it, the form is forwarded to the contract officer of the parent corporation, who draws up a contract. The entire process usually takes from four to six weeks.

During my fieldwork at Apple Press, I came across only two instances in which a proposal advanced by either of the two senior editors was turned down. In about 10 percent of the cases, the editor-in-chief would return a proposal to the originating editor with comments such as "Tell me less about the book and more about its marketablility or sales potential." After a proposal had passed the editor-in-chief's scrutiny, it was uncommon for further discussion to occur. Once in a while, the president of Apple would raise questions about a book's sales prospects. If a proposal met with approval at Apple, it was extremely rare for an officer of the parent company to question it; if he did raise questions, they usually had to do with the suggested list price, not the feasibility of the project.[6] With a book that the editor-in-chief wished to publish, the decision-making process was even more routine. In the case of the beginning assistant editor, the process differed somewhat: she would discuss projects in detail with the editor-in-chief before drawing up a proposal-to-publish form.

One of the senior editors at Apple Press described the procedure in the following manner: "If I like a manuscript, I propose it to the editor-in-chief; if he concurs, it goes on to the president. Then we wait for the parent company to draw up a contract. If the editor-in-chief doesn't like my proposal, I may or may not choose to argue with him; if I do, he lets me have my way."

At Plum Press, the formal process was somewhat different; nevertheless, the outcome was the same. The social science editor could recall only one proposal of his that had been rejected over a four-year period. This was a translation of a Polish monograph; the reason for the rejection was that it was deemed to involve too much work. The behavioral science editor could not remember any of his proposals being turned down. The procedure at Plum Press was for an editor to complete a proposal-to-publish form after having obtained a favorable review by a scholar in the relevant discipline. The proposal form was more detailed than the one used at Apple Press, but the forms were seldom completely filled out. Once the review was in, the editor would contact the author and convey an interest in publishing his or her book. If the author agreed to certain deadline stipulations, the editor would tell the author that he would submit the book to Plum's editorial committee and that a contract should be in the mail very soon.

The editor would then send the proposal-to-publish form to the appropriate editorial vice-president and to the sales department, where the editor's estimates were checked to see if they were "in the ballpark," to use the words of the sales vice-president. Only once did I observe that a question was raised by the sales department, and this was due to the fact that a secretary had inadvertently typed 15,000 instead of 1,500 for a book's projected sales. After the proper signatures were obtained, the proposal was routed to the editorial committee for consideration at its weekly meeting. The committee could be called to meet more frequently in special cases— for instance, if other publishing houses were interested in a manuscript and a quick decision was needed. The editor-in-chief commented, "We probably approve 99.8 percent of the proposals that our editors submit." The entire process could be executed expeditiously within a week, or it could take as long as a month. Once the editorial committee's approval was secured, a contract was drawn up. The parent corporation of Plum Press had no involvement in this process or any knowledge of what books Plum Press was publishing.

In many respects, the formal decision-making process was ceremonial (see Meyer and Rowan 1977). At neither house was it likely that questions would be raised about a proposal, and it was even more unusual for a proposal to be turned down. At Plum Press, the process was both routine and prompt. At Apple Press, although the steps were routine, they were seldom prompt. This was because the last step involved sending the proposal "upstairs" for approval. The parent corporation was responsible for issuing all contracts. The contract officer dealt with proposals from each division of the parent company, and, as a result, there was a great deal of paperwork involved. A lengthy delay for a contract was not uncommon. This could create problems if Apple Press was competing with another house for an author or if the author did not have full confidence in the editor and began to worry about the cause of the delay. Eventually an executive at the parent company recognized the need for Apple to issue contracts more expeditiously. A new policy was established which required obtaining corporate approval only for projects that involved a sizable outlay of funds; otherwise, the president of Apple Press could grant final approval.

The Process of Deciding What to Decide Upon

Clearly, the process of winnowing out manuscripts occurred prior to the formal decision-making stage. Bachrach and Baratz (1962; 1963), in their critique of methods of community-power research, argue that an important "face of power"—the power tactics that prevent a decision from being made at all—is often ignored. This is the power of nondecision, the forces that influence whether an issue ever becomes part of the agenda. Many issues die before they ever gain access to the decision-making arena. Researchers who accept that nondecisions are an important part of decision-making must therefore be concerned with the process by which social actors determine what to decide upon.

At Apple Press, I studied these issues in two ways. First, I examined all the manuscripts, proposals, and prospectuses that had been submitted to the press for evaluation. I sought to learn which projects attracted the attention of editors and what features distinguished these few from the many others that received scant attention. Second, I repeatedly asked the editors to explain how they ascertained whether a manuscript had commercial potential. During this period most of my time was spent in the editors' offices reading manuscripts and going through correspondence.

The editors were not particularly helpful in accounting for how they determined whether a manuscript had commercial possibilities. Editors repeatedly claimed that the ingredients for a successful scholarly book are not well known in advance. "You have to take your chances . . . go with your sense of

smell, and learn how to hedge your bets. And, as you know,"
they would continue, "these books aren't terribly expensive;
so if you make a few mistakes, it doesn't matter that much,
just as long as you don't make a habit of it."

While sitting in the offices at Apple Press, I observed what
were, to me, anomalous situations. In one instance, a manuscript came in over the transom, and, to judge from its tat-
tered condition and the marks on it, it had already been
rejected by several other publishing houses. The psychology
editor at Apple Press, once he finally got around to reading it,
liked the manuscript a great deal. He decided it would best be
divided into two books, and he thought up snappy titles to
replace the drab ones selected by the author. The editor sent
the manuscript to a prominent sociologist to review, who
concurred with the editor that the material was very worthy of
publication. The editor decided to start off by publishing only
the first part of the manuscript; then, if it was a failure, he
could refrain from publishing the second part. The book did
very well and caught Apple Press completely off guard. It was
surprised by a review in the daily *New York Times*, a review
column that is normally reserved for trade books. The book
went on to win a Pulitzer Prize and sell over 100,000 copies in
a mass-market paperback edition. The editor was unable to
articulate what it was that initially attracted him to this manuscript.

There were other things that puzzled me initially. One was
the rejection of a book even though it was well regarded.
Another was the signing of books that were noncommercial,
that is, books that would not sell well or, for that matter,
break even. The editor-in-chief would never openly acknowl-
edge that these things occurred. He said, "We publish only
the best material, and the brightest scholars, in the social
sciences. Sometimes we may err, but our goal is to produce
good scholarship and make a profit. I firmly believe that good
books sell well. . . . Nobody published Max Weber because
they thought they were doing a service for humanity; they did
it to make money!"

The other editors resisted such generalities and pointed to a number of compelling reasons for rejecting what appeared to be "good" books and for signing "marginal" ones. For example, an editor might turn down a promising manuscript because it was outside the competence or interests of the house. This is not unusual; authors do detailed research on their subject matter but seldom do any at all on which publishing house is appropriate for their work.[7] For example, neither Apple Press nor Plum Press was interested in introductory textbooks or anthologies, yet hardly a day passed when proposals for these types of books were not received. Neither house published books in the humanities or did popular trade books, but proposals for such books arrived frequently.

I discuss in more detail in chapter 4 the way in which a house's tradition and backlist influence choices; for now it should be noted that the size and strength of a house's list strongly affect consideration of a manuscript, regardless of its merits. For example, an editor may have on his or her desk five excellent manuscripts dealing with deviance, but, if you publish only fifteen or so sociology books in a year, you are severely restricting your coverage of the whole field if you publish all five. In the interests of balance, it is more sensible to publish a "so-so" book on the topic of ethnic relations.

Editors may also reject promising manuscripts because they cover the same ground as another book that was recently published or soon will be. For example, I found that one editor was reluctant to sign a book on the history of the black family until Herbert Gutman's research on the topic had been published and reviewed. The editor was worried that other projects would pale in comparison with Gutman's work, and he also wanted to see the reviews of Gutman's book so that he might better gauge the market for this topic.

Manuscripts are also turned down because they will demand too much of an editor's time and energy. An important consideration for an editor is whether he or she has sufficient time to devote to a manuscript and wants to spend it on that particular manuscript. If an editor is expected to sign between twenty-five and thirty-five books a year, there is no way that every book can be a major book, for that involves a great deal of effort.[8] Editors occasionally turn down big books by well-known academics because they think these will involve more work than they can handle. Manuscripts of considerable appeal by cantankerous authors may be rejected because the editor would prefer not to relive previous unpleasant experiences. Projects may also be declined because they require too large a financial commitment. Such an investment could create cash-flow problems, and the editor may decide that it is preferable to do several less expensive books instead. There are also cases when an author's status has risen to the point where the house can no longer afford him or her. The author's name now commands an advance or royalty terms that are outside the house's normal range, and it is unwilling to spend that much money.

Not surprisingly, editors reject material that they do not understand. As one Apple editor noted, "Unfortunately, I tend to turn down things that are too difficult for me, such as a highly theoretical manuscript as opposed to something about voting behavior, political machines, or an interesting political biography." To some extent this practice reflects good business sense, for dense, complex books are not as likely to sell as well as intriguing case studies or engaging political analyses, but at Apple Press there was some reluctance to tackle highly abstract theoretical material simply because the editors did not feel competent to evaluate it. At Plum, demanding manuscripts could be referred to the series editors for review.

As for commercial considerations, cases in which editors signed books that were not expected to make money were not uncommon. Not making money and losing money are, however, separate issues. An editor at a commercial house very rarely publishes a book that he or she *expects* will lose money, and, on the rare occasion that he or she decides to publish such a book, the losses can be minimized by keeping the print run small and the production costs low. Of course, there are decisions where an editor's judgment, experience, or intuition is incorrect. Or an editor may rely on the advice of a noted scholar and the advice turns out to be commercially unsound. Publishers can also "miss" with books; that is, a popular topic may be played out by the time they publish a book about it. In trade publishing, timeliness is a major concern. It is less of an issue in scholarly publishing, although one means of reducing uncertainty is to "run with the crowd" and publish topics that other houses have found to be successful. As one university press director remarked:

> Some publishers will be smart enough to publish books that help set the agenda of our nation's culture, that capture our intellectual pulse. Other publishers will merely imitate that success until it is a tired old story. Look at the lists of houses— you name the fad, and every company has as least one book on it. The successful publisher—and whether it is the result of acumen or luck is difficult to say—is the publisher who got there first.

Of particular interest are the books that were deemed worthy of publication even though their commercial prospects were not bullish. It is important not to view publication of this kind as wholly charitable; rather, the publisher is concerned with, in the words of Pierre Bourdieu (1977:177– 83), "symbolic capital" as opposed to economic capital. For example, I once mentioned to the social science editor at Plum Press that a particular author had taken a very novel approach to his subject. The editor responded enthusiastically, "You just have to publish books like that one. I doubt that we've made a penny on it, but I wouldn't hesitate to do it again. I personally enjoyed reading it; it's an important book. Besides, books like this don't cost that much, and they are worth doing."

The publication of books that maximize symbolic capital can also be viewed as a public relations strategy, designed to maintain the loyalty of house authors and attract others. The editor-in-chief at Apple Press spent a considerable amount of time "wooing several distinguished scholars back into the fold." These academics had published with Apple in the 1950s; they grew dissatisfied with the editorial staff in the 1960s and moved to other houses. The editor-in-chief made it one of his top priorities to regain these authors. He felt that their return would help signal Apple's resurgence in the 1970s. The press published books of essays, with limited commercial prospects, by these eminent scholars and vigorously pursued younger academics who were collaborators with the well-known scholars. In one case a younger colleague was offered a lucrative contract for his most recent book. This person promptly canceled his contract with another publishing house that he felt had not been particularly hospitable. A senior editor at Apple noted that this book should be well received, but then he remarked, "You can't live on prestige alone, and, given the financial terms, we haven't a prayer of making any money on it." This was an atypical example, and it involved the editor-in-chief; it would have been unlikely that any of the other editors could have done something quite like this. The example does illustrate, however, the way in which decisions can be based on non-financial criteria. In a similar vein, the editor-in-chief at a publishing house that was one of Apple Press's chief competitors described the publication of two books by a leading young British social scientist in the following manner: "We considered these books to be our research and development costs. We don't expect either of them to make any profit, but they are important books, and we anticipate that his third book will be a significant success."

A publisher with a well-known author under contract may also want to keep as much of that author's *oeuvre* in print as possible. This is one means of keeping authors happy and preventing them from moving to another house. If the author is highly regarded, it certainly pays, in the long run, to allow his or her less successful books to remain in print. There is always the possibility that, if the author's latest work is acclaimed, the earlier work will also attract attention.

Decisions about books that will add to symbolic capital can be vexing, and the evaluation process is complicated by the fact that editors usually must evaluate projects on the basis of a short synopsis and perhaps one or two sample chapters. Very few authors submit completed manuscripts. Several factors explain this. In the opinion of a senior editor at Apple Press, "Most of those who send in the entire manuscript are young people who don't know any better. They finish their work, which is probably their dissertation, and then look for a publisher." At the other end of the prestige pendulum are prominent scholars who are confident that any number of publishing houses would jump at the opportunity to publish their work. As one editor remarked, "Well-known, esteemed academics do not always want an editor telling them they have to change certain things. So they submit completed manuscripts and expect the publisher to either take on the project or pass on it." "It permits them to call their own shots," is the way another editor at Apple Press explained a prestigious author's submission of a completed manuscript. However, the great majority of authors submit only a prospectus and a sample chapter; they do not wish to invest a great deal of time and energy in preparing a manuscript unless they can first secure the interest of an editor and, ideally, a contract and a small advance to defray the costs involved in writing the book.

The need to make a quick decision on the basis of a small amount of material means that an editor must be a fast learner, one who can quickly acquire sufficient knowledge of a topic in order to discuss an author's proposal intelligently. This also means that editors must become proficient at finding experts who can evaluate projects. (The use and cultivation of outside readers is discussed more fully later in this chapter.) Knowing who will be able to ascertain the merits and value of a proposed manuscript is a special talent in itself. The editors must evaluate outside readers, not on the basis of their professional expertise, since that is assumed, but rather on their competence to assess an author's arguments without a great deal of bias. Editors become judges of others' judgments.

In theory, giving an author a contract on the basis of a proposal, which can be a very slim example of their skills, seems somewhat risky. In practice, however, all publishers' contracts state that the final manuscript must be "acceptable" to the publisher in form and content. This provision gives the publisher an out, permitting cancellation of the contract if he is dissatisfied with what the author delivers. Coser (1979) analyzes the asymmetrical nature of this relationship, which permits publishers to say no after they have initially said yes.[9] From a publisher's perspective, the house must retain the right to reject a manuscript that turns out not to be up to reasonable standards. The investment in reputation as well as money is too large a risk. However, a standard contract does bind an author to a publisher without imposing a parallel claim on the publishing house. One good reason for an author to ask for an advance is that the money helps cement the publisher's commitment. Of course, authors can and do break publishing contracts.

The Acquisition of Manuscripts

Although a voluminous amount of unsolicited material was received by editors at both Plum and Apple, their work involved much more than reacting to what arrived in the mail. An editor cannot decide that he or she does not want to publish any books in a particular season just because the manuscripts that have been sent in are not good enough. Sitting back at one's desk and waiting for materials to arrive is a poor way to do one's job. To begin with, some houses are more respected than others and receive much more promising material. Even editors with a list of renowned authors cannot afford to rest on their laurels. If they do, someone else will surely try to lure their authors way from them. A good scholarly editor must actively search for manuscripts.

One of the more remarkable features of the editorial search process is the extreme variation in the amount of time that this effort involves. I watched editors at both houses reject projects in less than fifteen seconds. On other occasions an editor would agonize over a manuscript for as much as six months, then set it aside, then agonize some more before finally deciding against publication. For some projects that were eventually accepted, the process lasted months and involved obtaining several readings from well-known academics, who frequently had contradictory opinions. Other projects were handled more routinely, with the editor reading the material, becoming excited about it, doing a very rough cost analysis on a pocket calculator, deciding the book wouldn't have to be priced at $35, and then sending the project out for evaluation by a person, knowledgeable in the field, whom the editor could count on to provide a favorable review. Normally the reader would reply within four to six weeks, and, if the response was favorable, the editor would propose a contract. Finally, some deals are concluded over a lunch or on the telephone; in these the project seems so obviously a winner and the author's track record is so successful that any subsequent consideration by the house is merely *pro forma*—the book is going to be signed.

It is common knowledge that unsolicited manuscripts have very slim chances of being published. (The acceptance rates at Apple and Plum are presented in chapter 5. For the acceptance rate for unsolicited materials in other branches of book publishing, see Coser, Kadushin, and Powell 1982:129–32.) Authors who send materials in "over the transom" had somewhat better odds of being published at Plum than at Apple. Yet, even at Apple, there were a few occasions when an editor responded favorably to a well-written cover letter and read the enclosed unsolicited manuscript. One such letter went as follows:

Dear ———:
I know that many new Ph.D.'s clutter up your desk with badly written typescripts on obscure subjects, and I've heard it is hard to break into a large and prestigious house such as ———. But I thought I'd give it a go anyhow. The few people who *have* read the book have either described it as "fascinating" or said that it may change the course of the sociology of religion for the next ten years. I myself am so familiar with the work that I no longer feel competent to judge either its intellectual worth or its readability.

So, enclosed in this envelope you will find the introductory
pages and the first chapter of my dissertation, along with the
Abstract prepared for the oral defense, which, although very
stilted in style, gives more information about the basic argument of the work than does the first chapter. If you shudder at
the thought of even having to look at the first chapter of a
dissertation, let me just say that my dissertation adviser has
already made me revise it five times, and it seems pretty
presentable to me for right now.

My main reason for going to a house such as ———— is that
I'm convinced that [my book] can appeal not only to an
academic market but to the wider one of religionists as well.
There are maybe twenty-five million people going to church
these days, and some of them I feel sure will be curious about a
book which says it knows why they do that. If you do like the
first chapter, and feel the book might appeal to a wide audience, I am ready to put considerable energy into the extensive
revisions I know will be necessary. With good feedback and
being sure of publication, I know I can smooth out the rough
places.

Sincerely yours,

————

Instances in which editors played such a reactive role were
unusual; much of their time is spent gathering information
and building intelligence networks. Each of the editors had
his or her own way of doing this. The editor at Apple Press
who handled the disciplines of sociology, anthropology, and
social work actively socialized with scholars in these fields,
and her circle of close friends consisted not only of academics
but of editors in other scholarly houses. "I call them all the
time, I lunch with them," she said; "it's terribly useful to talk
frequently with your competitors." She attended parties regularly and liked to go to small conventions or lectures, where
she was often the only editor in attendance. In developing a
social-work list, her initial step was to make personal calls on
the authors of the leading social-work titles that Apple had
published prior to her joining the firm. She spoke with them
at considerable length and persuaded one to edit a series for

her. Her next step was to have lunch with the editor of a major social-work journal. She soon became close friends with both the author and the journal editor.

The Apple editor responsible for the fields of psychology, economics, and law pursued a different strategy. He would telephone people he did not know and say, "I'm looking for a book about [some particular topic], and I've heard you are the person to write it." He constantly fired off letters to prospective authors, frequently writing professors who had recently received research grants or awards. Two of his more successful books resulted from his dogged determination during a trip to Harvard. It was late one afternoon and snowing heavily. The editor-in-chief, who was traveling with him, wanted to call it a day, but the editor wanted to drop in, unannounced, on someone his sources had recommended that he talk to. He located this young scholar and found that he was at work on two books. Both were later published by Apple to much critical acclaim.

This editor spent a good deal of time corresponding with the contributors to the various reference books or anthologies that Apple Press had published. In the following entry in my field notes, I recorded his description of this process:

> This book [of ours] is a presidential commission report that has around sixty contributors. I sent a list of the contributors to a top scholar who knows the areas of law and psychiatry. He will evaluate the list for me and choose the top people. So when I send each author a copy of the book, I'll include a special letter to these people and ask if they have anything in the works. I've been doing the same thing for the Encyclopedia we're publishing, as well as that Handbook we did. Not only did I write to all the contributors, but I went through the bibliography. There were some very productive people, like ———, who was referenced over a dozen times. You know people like this have ideas for books.

The editor-in-chief at Apple Press pursued overseas contacts by staying in touch with editors at scholarly houses in Great Britain. Whenever he was abroad or British editors were in New York, he would dine with them. He would often purchase the American rights to British books and, on occasion, sell the British rights to his books.

The editor-in-chief was also a strong believer in staying in close personal contact with his authors. He commonly used them as a sounding board for his ideas. The following letter is a good example.

Dear ———:

I thought of you on your vacation up there and tried to figure out a way to disturb you. Here it is!

Please look over all the introductory material and as much of the manuscript as you wish in order to make a decision. Is this really a first-class piece of work which political scientists would buy in cloth and/or adopt in paper? Is this original and well written, and does he know what he is talking about?

If you really get into this, find it very interesting, and wish to read the whole thing, just let me know how much we owe you.

I received an excellent response to my letter regarding ———, and I will be ready to move into the next phase soon. I appreciate your kind offer of help and I will embark on this important project feeling much better because of it.

Where does your next book stand? I desperately need an excuse to get away. Isn't there some pressing business we must discuss?

Under separate cover I am sending you a very interesting book. After you have had a chance to look it over, I would like to know what you would think of a similar book on political scientists.

Best wishes,

———

At Plum Press, all of the editors stayed in close contact with their series editors. Each of them maintained a busy travel schedule.[10] The behavioral sciences editor kept an index file that listed all of his authors by geographical area so that, when he traveled to a certain city, he could get in touch with them. He also went to numerous professional conventions and, unlike many scholarly editors, attended most of the sessions;

he would then contact the speakers whose work he found promising. The social sciences editor at Plum felt that "the key to this business is to surround yourself with the right people, develop your own sense of taste, and let the opportunities present themselves." He also kept on the lookout for translation possibilities and the opportunity to reprint government reports. But most of all he liked to travel, more so than any other editor I spoke with. He described his job in this manner:

> I have about ten series editors, and I try to stay in constant touch with them. I want to hear what they are doing, as well as keep them informed about what's going on at my end. I visit my series editors personally at least once a year and preferably more. I love to travel. I probably travel a week out of every month. I spend between $7,000 and $9,000 a year on travel expenses. Some of it has to do with the fact that we are neophytes in the social sciences. But it is also a matter of personal taste. I like for a publishing relationship to be a personal one.

Analysis of Search Behavior

The relationship between an editor's preconceptions about what he or she is looking for and the eventual outcome of a particular search procedure is loosely coupled. The term "loose coupling" is used to describe the disconnectedness of behavior and its consequences (see Weick 1976). Organization theorists have come to question the assumption that individual and organizational decision-making is necessarily purposive and goal-directed. Initial work in this direction began with March and Simon's (1958) ideas on the cognitive limits on rationality and Charles Lindblom's (1959) notion of the science of muddling through, wherein organizations muddle through because of the proliferation of preference orderings and the complexity of cause-effect relations. Weick's (1969) discussion of rationality as "post hoc dissonance reduction" conveys a marked skepticism about calculated, instrumental behavior. To these theorists, organizations have

many competing distractions, and they labor under such formidable constraints as bounded rationality (March and
Simon 1958), uncertain or contested goals (Perrow 1961), and
unclear technologies (Cohen and March 1974).

The efforts by Apple Press editors to procure manuscripts
vividly illustrate loose coupling. A few examples will suffice.
In the process of looking for someone to write a book on
medical experimentation on dependent populations, an editor found a book on the shady and fraudulent practices that
retail stores engage in to exploit consumers. On another
occasion, when the same editor asked a noted academic to
review a manuscript that his house was considering, he
learned that the reviewer was finishing his own *magnum opus*
and was planning to look for a publisher in a few weeks; he
did not need to look further. Another editor, who attended a
conference called "Sociologists for Women in Society" in the
hope of finding several books in women's studies, met several
women who were currently engaged in research projects that
she felt were worthy of publication, though none of the projects dealt with women per se. Finally, while the editor-in-
chief was scanning the ads of competing houses in scholarly
journals and trade publications, he decided he wanted a book
on a new "hot" topic; without making any effort in this
direction, he received, three days later, a manuscript that
filled this newly found need. In short, the choices made at
Apple frequently depended on the order in which alternatives
presented themselves.

Other examples were perhaps not as serendipitous, though
they resulted from unexpected or unplanned personal contacts. It often happened that editors working at other houses
referred projects to Apple that they felt were not right for
them. These referrals were welcomed, but it is important to
realize that the editor usually had no prior knowledge that the
project was on its way and rarely had any preexisting desire
for a manuscript on that specific subject.

What I am arguing is that some decisions were made by
doing very little or by following a course of action that at its

outset was aimed in a different direction. Decisions at Apple Press are not analyzable as a discrete choice among various alternatives. Faced with five good manuscripts, an editor may decide to publish one, two, three, four, five, or none, depending on their subject matter, the authors' academic status, the house's financial situation, and the editor's current work load. The steps in a decision sequence are rarely clear in the beginning and are sometimes difficult to reconstruct in retrospect. The particular problem an editor is working on changes as new information and gossip reveal new problems. External events constrain possible alternatives and shape outcomes, yet often go unanalyzed within the organization. The fate of a manuscript at Apple Press depended on the support and interest that it generated within the house, the extent to which it avoided bottlenecks, where personnel or operating capital were tied down on other projects, and on how well the manuscript fit with the track record of the respective editor and the house's overall list.

Thus the decision to publish a book at Apple took place within a complex swirl of simultaneous occurrences that involved other individuals besides the author and editor, other firms than Apple, other projects besides the book in question, and other developments that were as yet unresolved. This results in part from the fact that the acquisition of "raw materials" took place on a highly personal, idiosyncratic basis, as in the following example. The editor-in-chief of Apple Press frequently voiced his "folk wisdom" that "people in the best schools write the best books." "If I received," he once said, "a manuscript on sociological theory from someone at East Delta State University, I would not consider it for a minute. If the manuscript is any good, why isn't the author at Berkeley or somewhere?" Nevertheless, what was preached was not always practiced. A number of Apple Press authors are from colleges and universities that have little claim to elite status. When I asked the editor-in-chief why he had published two books by a previously unknown academic from a small school, he responded, "I met him at a convention and we had a few drinks; he was a friendly and interesting guy. I had his work reviewed, and people liked it. Besides, I wanted to publish a couple of short ethnographies anyway."

Time and again, editors at Apple Press would comment, "I was dubious about that one when I received it; I never expected it to turn out so well," or "I had never heard of the author, and I knew little about the topic, so I didn't think we would want to publish it," or "It's pleasant surprises that arrive like this that make life enjoyable." My point is not that things always occur by accident but that precisely how a manuscript will be obtained cannot be planned or calculated. Editors do know, however, what are useful methods for acquiring manuscripts. Closeness and familiarity with academics on the part of editors is expected to be productive. This is why publishing houses allow editors generous expense accounts for travel and meals. We should also recognize that, at the same time that editors are looking for manuscripts, authors are looking for someone to publish their work.

In some important respects, the process of acquiring manuscripts at Apple Press resembled what James March and his colleagues (Cohen, March, and Olsen 1972; Cohen and March 1974; March and Olsen 1975, 1976) have termed the "garbage-can model of choice." Tossed into a garbage can is a loosely coupled mix of (1) problems or issues looking for solutions; (2) solutions looking for problems to resolve; (3) participants with different amounts of time and energy; and (4) choice situations waiting to be actualized. The term "loosely coupled" is meant to underscore the independence of these various streams and the lack of temporal ordering; that is, solutions may precede problems, and both solutions and problems can await appropriate choice opportunities.

In garbage-can situations the social structure of the organization influences each stream's arrival and departure times, the allocation of participants' attention to the choice opportunity, and the set of possible links among the various streams. In publishing, the cast of participants changes over time as both editors and authors come and go. Timing is a crucial element. Opportunities are the result of a particular blend of situations, problems, and participant availability. The dynamics of acquiring manuscripts include chance elements that appear to have been rationally calculated only after a manuscript has been secured; rationales are then constructed to explain events. Beliefs or preferences may appear to be the results of behavior at least as much as they are determinants of it (see March 1978); motives and intentions are then discovered after the fact. March and Olsen (1976:15) argue that we must recognize the "possibility that there may be attitudes and beliefs without behavioral implications, that there may even be behavior without any basis in individual preferences, and that there may be an interplay between behavior and the definition of self-interest."

I am not arguing that decision-making at Apple Press was irrational or totally dictated by chance. In fact, it is important to recognize that Weick (1976) is probably correct in arguing that, because loose coupling lowers the probability that an organization will have to respond to each little change in its environment, a loosely coupled organization probably devises more novel solutions than a tightly coupled organization would devise. Moreover, there were editorial decisions that were clearly intelligent, calculated moves, such as publishing the latest work of a well-known scholar whose previous books had sold well, or buying the American rights for a book originally published in England to considerable acclaim and purchasing the rights for a price that means you have to sell only a thousand copies to recoup your investment. As one editor quipped, "With a deal like that, you can't miss!"

There were, however, many situations in which the participants were faced with too many things to attend to, and decisions seem to have been made by flight or oversight. Here is one illustration:

> I asked an editor about the status of a particular project that had arrived in the house several months before. He responded, "Oh, I had forgotten all about it." He hunted around the cluttered office, found it, and glanced at it for a few minutes. He then said, "You've helped me to make up my mind for me. I'll reject it."

Situations such as these were not uncommon. Fortunately, the projects were not always rejected. Sometimes the editor would say that he would send the lost project out for review as soon as he had had time to think about who would be appropriate. Then the project would be placed on top of another pile of papers, and, if it wasn't attended to that day, it would once again be buried in the stacks of undecided projects.

The key element at Apple was not the informality or haphazardness of the decision-making process but the fact that an editor usually did not know when—or whether—his or her search activities would pay off. Quite often the process of acquisition did not appear to be strongly related to making a decision. Feldman and March (1981:177–78) assert that the main point of a decision process may not be an outcome; the central purpose may be the process itself. In such a view, decision-making is an arena for exercising social values, for displaying authority, and for expressing and discovering self-interest. Choice processes of this type are probably most common in organizations where goals are either unclear or inoperative, technologies are imperfectly understood, history is difficult to interpret, boundaries are not fixed, and participation is fluid. The last factor is particularly important because most theories of decision-making do not recognize that attention varies, decision-makers have competing distractions, and participants wander in and out of the choice process. March and his coauthors argue that decision-making is rarely a discrete event; it is far more likely to be a stream of activities with multiple inputs. Nor does all the ambiguity come from the external environment, for these authors also see the decision-making process as a receptacle into which many kinds of personal and organizational problems are dumped: group relations, departmental conflicts, and career frustrations are all played out in the process of making decisions.

Garbage-can decision processes no doubt occur in most organizations under certain kinds of circumstances. More generally, organizations that cope with diverse points of view about appropriate technologies, rapid technological innovation, divergent consumer demands, multiple or mixed goals, and a disparate and/or irregular labor supply seem particularly ripe for garbage-can situations. Thus garbage-can theory is likely to be applicable to organizations other than the "exotic" ones, such as universities, free schools, and voluntary associations, that have been studied thus far. One could argue that the more contact points, at both the input and output boundaries, an organization has, the more divergent is the information it receives. As a result, competing views develop about what would be an appropriate course of action, and internal consensus declines. Such a condition characterizes not only much government policymaking (Pressman and Wildavsky 1973; March and Olsen 1983) but policymaking by business firms that operate in uncertain international markets or in intensively competitive and innovative fields.

Garbage-can choice processes are also likely to be common in service organizations that employ a professional labor force. This is due, in part, to the fact that professionals differ among themselves about what the organization should be doing. Indeed, organizations can become an arena for the clash of different reference groups and ideologies. In publishing, for example, to assert that acquiring and signing books is a talent not subject to quantification or empirical analysis is, in part, a form of mystification that serves the self-interest of editors. Such an assertion by editors can be viewed as an ideological justification of their craft, a means for fending off the demands of accountants, corporate executives, and sales directors. The claim that the craft of editing is a special skill is part of the culture of publishing professionalism. It is a part of the struggle of the members of an occupation to define the conditions and methods of their work or, in Larson's words (1977:49–52), to control "the production of producers" and to establish a cognitive base and legitimation for their occupational autonomy (Collins 1979). As Larson shows, the professional project is rarely achieved with complete success. Nevertheless, the ambiguity and variability that typify such organizations as publishing houses, advertising agencies, universities, law firms, research institutes, and other culture-producing industries indicate that the resident professionals are attempting to define their work in a manner that does not lend itself to routinization and formal standards.

The terms "organized anarchy" and "garbage can" suggest a choice process that is quite different from what a rational model of choice would imply. The difference, however, should not be exaggerated. I would argue, and I suspect March would agree, that there are regular patterns in the apparent disorderly process of decision-making. All organizations have rules of evidence, that is, standard operating assumptions about what information is relevant to a particular decision and how past history should be interpreted in the light of current choices. For example, the history and traditions of a publishing house have a major impact on the amount and quality of attention that a particular author receives. Organizations also have decision structures that determine who is permitted to participate in a decision. Such subtle forms of control are discussed in the next chapter.

The search behavior of editors at Plum Press contrasted sharply with the more free-wheeling style of Apple Press editors. The editorial staff at Plum relied heavily on their various series editors for advice and used the suggestions of their other academic advisers as a means of reducing uncertainty and problems of information overload. Some of the uncertainty faced by editors has to do with not knowing which new areas of scholarly research are likely to be "growth industries" and which scholars can be counted on to provide high-quality, marketable books. To cope with these concerns, Plum editors routinely used series editors as "trail scouts." For instance, the social science editor met with one of his series editors and went over the list of faculty members at every major sociology department in the country. The series editor checked off the names of the people he knew personally. The social science editor then sent each of them a letter, informing them about Plum's series and inquiring about their research in progress. This process was repeated with series editors in other fields. Another Plum Press editor made it a regular practice to dine with his series editors. He always asked his academic advisers to invite their colleagues to join them. The editor used these occasions to learn about recent academic developments.

At Apple Press the editor was assumed to be the resident expert in a given field. It was very rare for anyone else to ask to see what an author had submitted; other members of the house relied on the editor's evaluation. At Plum Press, editors were not considered experts; instead, the series editors served this function. The primary responsibility of editors was to locate hard-working series editors who had extensive academic contacts and exercised good judgment. The selection of appropriate series editors was extremely important. An inappropriate choice—that is, someone who would use the position to repay debts to colleagues, or to reward students, or to push his or her own particular view to the exclusion of other approaches—not only would be a financial loss but could seriously harm the house's reputation. And, in time, the series editor's reputation would suffer as well. The prestige system of science serves to attenuate self-aggrandizing behavior on the part of series editors.

Pfeffer and Salancik (1978:145–47) have demonstrated that, when situations of exchange are uncertain, organizations may attempt to establish linkages with key elements in their environment and use such linkages to acquire needed resources. Linkages can expedite the search for information; they are a means of social coordination that reduces uncertainty and increases predictability. The establishment of links to the academic community in the form of series editors also provided Plum Press with a forum for communicating its intentions and for generating exposure. Moreover, prestigious series editors were a sign of support; their reputations enhanced the legitimacy of the press's publishing program.

In several relevant ways, the search for scholarly books by Plum editors resembled shopping in a Moroccan bazaar, where information also is scarce, maldistributed, inefficiently communicated, and intensely valued. As Clifford Geertz (1978) has shown, the village bazaar is marked by uncertainty about the quality and reliability of goods; he describes (1978:30–31) "clientelization" as a means of coping with the uncertainty that pervades the Moroccan bazaar in Sefrou. This is the "tendency for repetitive purchasers of particular goods and services to establish continuing relationships with particular purveyors of them, rather than search widely through the market at each occasion of need." Clientelization partitions the bazaar crowd into those who are genuine candidates for attention and those who are merely theoretically such. It is a means of personalizing the exchange relationship in order to limit the search process. This mechanism narrows the relevant field and permits in-depth, intensive search rather than broad, but superficial, extensive search. Geertz (1978:32) shows that:

> Search is primarily intensive because the sort of information needed most cannot be acquired by asking a handful of index questions of a large number of people but only by asking a large number of diagnostic questions of a handful of people. It is this kind of questioning, exploring nuances rather than canvassing populations, that bazaar bargaining represents.

Search behavior at Plum Press resembled the strategy of clientelization in that, instead of casting their nets widely, Plum editors utilized a few series editors to guide them in their efforts to locate new authors. There was a strong preference for a few repeated dealings; thus the search process employed by Plum Press editors was purposive and highly targeted. The uncertainty of the search was reduced through the assistance of the series editors. It is worth noting the parallels between the Plum strategy and that of a business firm facing an uncertain market for its products. One response to such a state of affairs is for the sales department to sign long-term purchase agreements with various customers. By doing so, the sales force eliminates some of the uncertainty faced by the firm, but it also sharply reduces the organization's dependence on the sales department. In the same manner, the use of series editors greatly lessened the problems of information overload and information impactedness commonly faced by editors. Yet this practice also reduced the editors' power within the house and rendered them less irreplaceable. Indeed, as long as a series editor's loyalty was to the house and not to an individual editor, an editor at Plum could be replaced and the new editor would not have to build a new network of advisers. The differences in the hiring process at the two houses aptly demonstrate this. At Apple Press, editorial positions remained vacant for long periods of time—in some cases for as much as six to nine months. Job candidates were asked to provide letters of reference from authors with whom they had worked. In contrast, editorial vacancies at Plum were quickly filled, and outside candidates were evaluated on the basis of the sales records of the titles they had published at other houses.

Evaluating Manuscripts and the Use of Outside Reviewers

Once a manuscript is under consideration, an editor must evaluate it. (The speed, or lack of it, with which a manuscript is reviewed is discussed in chapter 5.) Editors have a list of questions that they ask of each manuscript under serious review. They want to know what groups of scholars will be attracted to a book. They must judge whether a book has adoption possibilities for graduate or upper-level undergraduate courses and whether it has book club or foreign sales potential. An editor must also determine how well written a book is and how much work will be involved in publishing it. An editor has to decide whether to spend his or her time on a particular book. Finally, and most important, the editor must determine whether the manuscript makes a substantial intellectual contribution; for assistance in deciding whether the scholarship is respectable, editors frequently turn to outsiders.

To help them solve some of these questions, or if these questions have been answered affirmatively, editors will "cost out" a manuscript—that is, estimate, at least roughly, the costs of producing and manufacturing the book. To do this, the editor must decide on the number of copies to print.

In making this decision, the editors at Apple Press "take the most pessimistic view possible and try to make it work." At Plum Press the strategy is similar, except that the social science editor often feels that his books have greater sales potential than the other books the house publishes. This generally has been true, and his outlook is usually more optimistic than that of his more conservative colleagues. At this point, all of the figuring is very speculative; the editor is concerned, in a general way, with whether the project is "doable."

If these preliminary computations (they will be revised at a later stage) demonstrate that a project is worth undertaking, the editor must then decide whether the book should be sent to someone who can provide an authoritative judgment on its merits. Editors cannot send every manuscript out for review, nor need they. Unlike university-press editors, commercial scholarly editors are not required to obtain outside assessments in order to sign a book. If a book is by a well-known author, an Apple Press editor may not bother with obtaining a review. Or the editor might seek an independent judgment, after the book has been contracted for, as a service to the author to aid him or her in the revision process. At Plum Press, if a manuscript was strongly supported by a series editor, no further review was considered necessary. However, if an editor had questions about the material, the market, or comparable books on the same topic, an outside review could help answer these concerns. In addition, if a Plum editor felt particularly enthusiastic about a project, he or she might obtain an outside review in order to bolster the case for publication.

One simple reason why every manuscript under serious consideration cannot be sent out for review is the cost, in both time and money, that is involved. Equally important is that, in sending a manuscript out for review, an editor is making demands on the reviewer's time. The honorarium that is paid for evaluating a manuscript is rather small compensation. Scholars review manuscripts out of loyalty to a house and because they are interested in reading new material. If an editor sends a reviewer several poor manuscripts, the reviewer's enthusiasm will naturally wane, and he or she will begin to question the editor's ability. No editor wants a reviewer to think, "Why is this stupid person sending me this junk?" Any manuscript that passes in-house screening should be presumed to include new work that will need to be read by others in the field when it is eventually published.

Harman and Schoeffel (1975:333) state, "The care of readers [i.e., manuscript reviewers] is . . . central to the work of an editorial department—locating them, ensuring that their time is not wasted on evident dross, persuading them to tackle yet one more manuscript, and shielding them from direct confrontation with the author." Editors select reviewers in several ways. Here is one editor's strategy:

> Ask the author if he can recommend anyone, or if there's somebody he does *not* want it sent to, because there may be cases where he attacked somebody in the book, or something like that, or he knows somebody is down on him—it's only fair to do that, sometimes. Often I will say, "Can you name two or three people—people you do not personally know—as reviewers for the manuscript?"

Editors may also select reviewers from an author's bibliography. But the largest source of potential reviewers are the authors who have already been published by the house. Becoming an author is often the start of a long-term relationship with a publisher. If a book is a commercial or critical success, an editor will then freely call on the author for advice and for assistance in evaluating manuscripts. The relationship between a scholarly press and its authors can be close and long-lasting. It is of paramount importance that editors sustain these relationships. At Apple Press, the editors frequently called on their authors for assistance in reviewing manuscripts. Following are three examples of cover letters that accompanied manuscripts sent out for review by Apple Press.

Dear Professor ———:

Under separate cover, I have sent you the complete manuscript of ———. I very much appreciate your agreeing to read it for me in view of the incredible demands on your time now.

You need not read it all, because the book is not yet under contract and I want only your general impressions of his work at this stage. I fully believe it will be an important book, and, as I said, my major question is, how important. What are the chief books already published on this subject, and how do they compare?

I am enclosing with this letter the table of contents and the 56-page introduction to the author's first book, ———, on which the manuscript in question builds. It may be of help.

I'll send you $—— for your brief overview, as we agreed. I fully appreciate your time problems. Whatever you can do will be most welcome.

Sincerely,

———

Dear ———:

Although, as you will see from the enclosed, I received this letter and proposal some months ago, I have spoken to the author several times since, most recently in ———.

May I please have your comments on the need for such a book, its potential market, and his ability to do it properly? Is this a work that will be used widely? To what audience will it appeal? Is the material suitably organized?

I am really quite hesitant to send you too much material, knowing how busy you are, but you and I have discussed projects like this in the past, and I do not feel it would take up too much of your time.

Regards,

———

Dear ———:

Please excuse my inordinate delay in getting you a contract. Suffice it to say that we will be very proud to publish another book by you and that I will put a contract in your hands as soon as I dig out far enough to do the detestable paperwork. Let me add to my excuse by telling you that I just returned from a

combination business trip–vacation to England. It was, needless to say, an unforgettable trip. However, I know that you
are a patient man, and I promise to get you a contract soon.

I will now add insult to injury by asking you to do me a
favor. I enclose the uncorrected proof of ————. You will see
that it is from ———— in England, and they want to know if we
are interested.

We recently published ————, and it is selling exceptionally well. Is this the same kind of book? In a word, do you
recommend we publish it in the U.S.? Why, or why not? Is it a
respectable work of scholarship? Is the research sound?
Could the manuscript be cut without loss of effectiveness?

Upon receipt of your review, I will send you an honorarium. Thanking you in advance, I very much appreciate your
help.

Best wishes,

The responses of reviewers play an important role determining the fate of a manuscript. Unless the editor feels
strongly about a manuscript, one negative review may kill its
chances. Yet there are also times when an editor overlooks
unfavorable reports. Responding to a negative review, the
editor-in-chief at Apple Press quipped, "I wasted $—— on
that." In other cases, when a manuscript was already under
contract, a sharply critical review served only to dampen an
editor's enthusiasm. As a rule, if the editor did not have a very
strong opinion about a manuscript, the reviewer's comments
weighed heavily; if the editor was favorably inclined, he or
she would be likely to select a reviewer who would be interested in the work.

Reviewers' reports varied considerably, in both length and
substance. This was due partly to the style of an individual
reviewer, but it was also a consequence of the editor's having
provided an indication of whether he or she wanted the
manuscript "sniffed" or thoroughly read. The comments re-
produced below are typical reviewer responses.

Dear ———:

This is written confirmation of my earlier oral report to you concluding that the manuscript, ———, should not be accepted for publication. I think the book is at most superficial, and frequently downright misleading. This is due to the authors' abortive attempt at viewing both criminal and civil law simultaneously. The result is enormous distortion. Even had they succeeded in eliminating the distortion, I see very little need for such a work. There are a host of books which cover this area that are better written and more soundly conceived than this one.

Please let me know if you desire further details.

Sincerely,

———

Dear ———:

The manuscript is an impressive piece of work. He manages to present in this rather smallish book the essentials of the notion of verstehen (understanding) as it developed from its origins in German classical philosophy to such luminaries as Rickert, Dilthey, Simmel, Weber, to more recent discussions in the Frankfurt School (Habermas), in phenomenology and ethnomethodology and in British linguistic philosophy (Wittgenstein and his successors). It is a very remarkable job of critical discussion and tight logical argumentation. In fact, this is probably the best thing on the topic that exists in English.

However, this was written with a British audience in mind. British social scientists are much more sophisticated when it comes to philosophical or epistemological issues than their American counterparts, who are often totally innocent of any philosophical knowledge. This would raise issues as to how widely a book of this kind would be used here. A counterargument is, on the other hand, that with the rise of ethnomethodology, phenomenology, and Frankfurt-style Marxism there has emerged a younger group of social scientists who are interested in these questions. (And you know that the ethnomethodological studies you have published have done pretty well, even when couched in esoteric language.

Summa summarum: I think that you should probably take this little book. Not only has it considerable intrinsic merit, but the overall series of which it is a part looks promising enough to warrant an initial outlay on the first of the series, so as to have an option on later volumes.

One last thought: You probably won't sell much of that book in the Middle West, but it might do quite well in quality schools on both coasts, and it might also do well in smaller places, where one now can find instructors of phenomenological or Marxist persuasion. There will also be some interest in certain departments of philosophy.

Cordially,

In a few cases, the comments of reviewers were extensive. The following summary concluded a detailed eight-page review of a work of diplomatic history:

> The reader believes the work to be unusually attractive, both as scholarship and as literature. I recommend publication enthusiastically and without reservation. No major revision is required. The authors do not hesitate to come to clear and authoritative conclusions when evidence permits. In situations when evidence is not complete and where previous authors have indulged in speculation the authors review those speculations. They provide both judicious and bold statements. Readers will like the book; it seems destined to enjoy a market well beyond most efforts of comparable scholarly quality.

At Plum Press, the editors utilized their authors considerably less than was the case at Apple Press. As I have noted, they relied much more heavily on the opinions of their series editors. The following entry from my field notes captures the workings of this relationship:

> Upon returning from lunch, an editor discovered that a manuscript had arrived in the mail, referred by one of the series editors. The accompanying letter from the series editor stated that "this book will grace our list." The series editor instructed the editor "not to send it out for review, as it has already been favorably commented upon by a noted demographer." The editor at Plum Press stated that this manuscript represented several years of work on the part of the series

editor——making suggestions, reviewing drafts, editing, etc.
I asked the editor if he would get another outside review. "In
cases like this, where the manuscript is right up my editor's
alley, generally not, especially since he has worked so hard on
it. If it was outside of his immediate area of expertise, I might
get it reviewed and then tell him about it afterwards."

The series editors at Plum Press functioned as minipub-
lishers—scouting for manuscripts, evaluating them, making
suggestions, and even editing in some cases. Thus, when the
series editors referred material to the house editor, the
chances of its being published were quite good but certainly
not automatic. As one Plum Press editor commented,

> No, we don't publish just anything that a series editor recom-
> mends. For sure, everything they submit gets serious atten-
> tion. Anyway, you don't want to upset them. But you have to
> bullshit them from time to time. You don't want to say that
> you don't like the manuscript, so you blame its rejection on
> your supervisor or the editorial committee.

Saying No Gracefully

Declining to publish an author's manuscript is a part of every
editor's job. Many of the rejections are handled mechanically. The editor writes "reject" on a sheet of paper and
attaches it to the letter or manuscript and turns it over to his
or her secretary, who then sends out a fairly standard rejection letter. Two of the most common lines in rejection letters
are "publishing is not an exact science" and "given the nature
of our publishing program." A typical letter of this sort often
goes as follows:

> Dear Dr. ———:
>   I regret to tell you that we have decided against publication
> of your book on ———. This decision in no way reflects on the
> quality of your work but has to do with the nature of our
> publishing program and our appraisal of the needs of the
> market.
>   Publishers differ, of course, in their programs and evalua-

tions, and we hope that you are successful in finding a suitable publisher for your book. Thank you for giving us the opportunity to consider it.

Sincerely,

Some rejection letters, on the other hand, are handled quite thoughtfully and with great tact. The sociology editor at Apple Press exhibited much concern over rejection letters, as her comments to me attest:

> I feel I owe it to authors who have submitted reasonably good ideas to make a serious effort. If we decide not to publish, I always try to write a helpful rejection letter. When I think it's appropriate, I'll provide the names of friends in other houses who might react more favorably. If I do not know anyone right off, I may still suggest other houses that might be interested. Taking the time to write a well-thought-out rejection letter can mean that the author will think of you for their next manuscript.

The following letter is an example of this editor's consideration for an author she is currently declining to publish:

> Dear ———:
> You write awfully well, and you've done a remarkably good job of integrating work by several authors so that the book reads as an integrated whole—but I'm afraid I don't think it's for us. Our list as a whole is small, as you know; my personal list is overwhelmingly large, as you also know; and the reason for the rejection boils down to a matter of triage. I don't think the manuscript holds sufficient commerical promise to vanquish some among the flood of others awaiting a yea or nay. I certainly think it's publishable and interesting, but not a big potential money-maker. Maybe try ——— at ———? If he doesn't bite, you could send it to ——— and tell them I suggested it.
> I'm sorry, but please don't rule us out for your next product.

Best,

The psychology editor at Apple Press remarked that you never know what can happen as a result of a poorly conceived, perfunctory rejection letter. "They may tell their colleagues you treated them cavalierly." The unanticipated consequences of tactfully declining an author's work were demonstrated when this editor received a job offer from another publishing house as a result of his having treated an author in a straightforward manner. As he commented to me:

> Remember last fall, when I was talking with you about ———? Well, I had his manuscript reviewed; the reviews were so-so at best. The thing needed a *lot* of work, but I assumed we would sign him because he is a big name. Then we would try to improve the manuscript after the contract was signed. I submitted the proposal and told him that things looked good. Much to my surprise, the editor-in-chief kicked the proposal back to me; he wasn't enthusiastic about signing the book unless we could get a promising review. So I had to get back to the author and break the news. I figured I had made an enemy for life. I called him, and yes, he was upset. But he mentioned that ——— had offered him a contract. I doubted that he wanted to revise the manuscript for us, so I suggested he sign with them; I made a number of recommendations to him, and I figured that was that. Now it turns out that it was ——— [the author] who had recommended me to the executives at ——— [the other publishing house]. An unusual way to get put up for a job, isn't it?

An inappropriate or thoughtless rejection letter can, by the same token, have dire consequences. As the psychology editor noted, "Academics have well-organized grapevines; word gets around the academic community very quickly."

The social science editor at Plum Press spoke of the inherent difficulties in rejecting manuscripts from certain people. As he explained:

> This is the outline of a book that was referred to me by ——— [one of the editor's favorite authors, whose latest book is a critical success]. This is the second project that he has referred to me that I will can. I just can't see where the audience is for this book. It's a real problem, though; I'd love for him to refer

something to me that I could accept. In this case I'll write a nice personal rejection letter to the author of the manuscript and send the recommender a copy of it too.

The decision to reject books by important people or by "friends and supporters" of the house is often a very trying experience. These are what editors call "political problems." In certain cases it is simply unwise to disappoint an important scholar because of the danger that he or she will move to another house. For example, a distinguished author or the editor of a series published by the house may wish to publish a collection of his or her own papers or may highly recommend another person's manuscript. The editor must weigh the risks involved in turning down either the scholar or his protégé. The risks may not be worth taking. Editors who work for university presses encounter similar problems. Sometimes they receive manuscripts that have been recommended by a member of their board of directors or publications commit- tee. When this occurs, they are quite naturally concerned with the possible consequences of rejecting these manu- scripts. As August Frugé (1976:5), former director of the University of California Press, recalls, "We once rejected, and with no repercussions, a manuscript by the then president of the university. We also passed up two manuscripts by the dean of a school in Los Angeles, but it is not so clear about the repercussions; our offices were in his building, and we had to move not long thereafter."

I do not wish to contend that well-known authors who have prior associations with a house have *carte blanche*. Their manuscripts may on occasion be rejected, but this is done with great discretion. A "regular" author may submit a proj- ect that the editor is not favorably predisposed toward; however, the editor does not want to personally say no. In such cases the editor will go through the review process and then point to a reviewer's lack of enthusiasm or raise a ques- tion about the potential market. These are acceptable reasons for rejecting the project. Or, at a university press, the editor may take the project before the publications committee, knowing full well that the committee rarely approves anything that has received a negative review. The editor is then able to tell the author that it was the committee that turned the project down.

In the final analysis, the rejection of a manuscript—whether it presents a "political problem" or not—can be a troubling decision for an editor. Every editor with whom I have spoken can recount an extraordinary "one that got away" story. They each can remember at least one manuscript that they rejected, secure in their opinion that it lacked commercial appeal or intellectual promise, only to have another house publish it with great success. Editors also recalled turning authors down, firm in the belief that their work had little potential; they would later watch with dismay as another firm published the author's *next* book to critical acclaim.

The Publishing of Journals

The editors at Plum Press spent between 10 and 20 percent of their time either working on the various journals that the press published or evaluating proposals for new journals. Deciding whether to start a journal or, alternately, assuming the responsibility from a professional society for publishing its journal, is handled in the same manner as a proposal for a new book, but the stakes are higher. As the social science editor remarked: "Publishing a journal is a most serious responsibility. A bad book is one thing, but a bad journal can be a major embarrassment."

The social science editor at Plum would ask the following questions about a journal proposal: What are the competing journals? Can this journal attract material away from them? Is there a community of scholars large enough to support it? Who is the journal editor going to be, and what are his credentials? If a journal proposal was of interest to the editor, he would get reviews of the person who had proposed the journal. The editor would also ask the house's authors in the relevant discipline about their impression of the need for a new journal. The editor would also try to speak with the editors of existing journals in the area to learn whether any other publishers were planning a similar journal. The sales department would assist in the whole evaluation process.

In some cases successful journals will spin off a monograph series. There was one case where a journal editor had received a number of articles that were too long for his journal. He mentioned this to the editor at Plum, and they agreed to develop a monograph series. The journal editor then contacted the authors of the lengthy articles and attempted to persuade them to expand their articles into books. The social science editor noted that "journals generally play an important role in aiding the acquisition of manuscripts."

The editors at Plum Press assist in the selection of a journal's editorial board and, on occasion, provide ideas if an issue of the journal is to focus on a special topic. Once the journal is on its feet, the editor of the journal is usually left to his own devices. There is an annual financial evaluation. However, two editors and the editor-in-chief each remarked, "Plum would never discontinue a journal. If things were terribly bad, we might merge two journals if that would help." The behavioral sciences editor said, "It would look very bad if we stopped publishing a journal, even if it was unprofitable. Even though we can't count its profitability in pennies, journals bring in and maintain a clientele. They are often very prestigious."

The vice-president of the sales department pointed out that, although the academic editors run the journals on their own, his department helps them as much as it can. He commented:

> Developing journals is like developing books, but it is much more difficult. These days you have to be very careful. In 1976 we will not begin any new journals, nor do we have any plans for 1977 at this time. In 1975 we started two, and they first appeared in print in 1976. Both look to be coming along well, but it takes two to three years to tell. Some of our journals aren't all that great, but by no means would we ever quit doing one. That could be a fatal mistake.

Journal publishing was another strategy used by Plum Press to cover a particular discipline effectively and fully exploit all the available opportunities. The sales department's vice-president describes the "dynamics of our publishing program" in this manner:

> You approach a scientific area this way: you try to set up a primary journal first, then begin publishing advances, reviews, serial, or continuation lines. Then you bring out a multivolume state of the art. After all this, a monograph series can be spun off. Then you tie it in with a reprint line, particularly if the reprints in this area date back before 1900 and are in the public domain. At the end of each year, our journal subscriptions bring in hundreds of thousands of dollars of income, on which we don't have to deliver any goods immediately. The orders for the serial publications build up in advance. We have large standing orders for many of our books. We try to send out promotion mailings prior to publication, and then we get a number of advance orders. We can use our journals to advertise our books. It's a very effective program; it's really the classical European approach to scientific publishing.

Apple Press publishes no journals. It has, however, recently had success with handbooks, annual reviews, and encyclopedias. The Apple management wants to publish more of these, for not only are they profitable in themselves, but reference works of this type are useful for establishing contacts with, and acquiring manuscripts from, the various contributors.

Relations with Authors

The editors at Apple Press were very supportive of their authors. As one of them remarked, "Authors like to know they are appreciated; they have to be stroked and curried." This particular editor would explain a contract in detail to each author, warning about clauses that were strongly to the publisher's advantage. These clauses were rarely removed from the contract, but the authors were at least informed, and this might prevent disagreements at a later date. Another editor noted that "in our kind of publishing we don't compete on the basis of money. We can't give authors big advances or outlandish royalty rates and still publish profitable books. Instead, we go all out in trying to assist our authors every step of the way." In marked contrast to trade and textbook publishing, negotiating a contract for a scholarly book is generally a simple matter. In part this is because advances are low and royalty rates are standard at almost every scholarly house. An added factor is the absence of costly competition among houses for an author. Scholarly houses certainly compete with each other, but rarely does this competition lead to lucrative contracts for authors. Instead, the competition revolves around editorial services and the comparative prestige of the houses. Scholarly houses are all competing for roughly the same market, and authors are aware of this and usually do not expect that their books will make them rich.

Many authors relished the attention they received from the editors at Apple Press. Yet there were a few who felt that such attention was unnecessary; they were, in fact, suspicious of the press's solicitousness, particularly after their book had been published and they were unhappy with the marketing campaign. One author commented that what he liked most about Apple Press was the "cheerfulness and enthusiasm for his work" but that he "distrusted it."

The editor-in-chief went to great lengths to keep distinguished Apple Press authors content. He would send birthday and seasonal greeting cards. For "one of the deans of American history," he went to an out-of-print bookstore and purchased several books, which he sent to the historian with a note saying, "Please accept these with my gratitude for your having published with us . . . ; if you already have copies, you can donate them to your university's library." Whenever an Apple Press author visited New York, the editors would try to take him or her out to lunch. Authors who lived in the New York metropolitan area were fortunate to receive such treat-

ment frequently. When one long-time author was hospital-
ized, the editor-in-chief took the time to send a card and a
lovely plant, as well as the following letter:

> Dear ——:
>
> I was very sorry to hear that you are not feeling well. After
> a long and very pleasant meeting with your colleagues yester-
> day, however, I was glad to find that you are in the hands of
> such talented doctors.
>
> Please let me know if there is anything I can do for you or if
> there are any errands you would like taken care of. You know
> that I will be delighted to help in any way possible.
>
> Get well soon! I won't know what to sign up until you get
> well and back to work. Please don't hesitate to call me if I can
> do anything. I really mean it.
>
> Best wishes,
>
> ——

Efforts such as these reflect genuine concern. Such policies
at Apple Press stemmed from its high regard for its successful
authors. Problems sometimes developed when authors came
to expect exceptional treatment as a matter of routine and the
editors were too busy working on acquiring books to attend to
already published authors. While editors were genuinely interested in their authors, they naturally expected the authors
to reciprocate. In return for the services that were provided to
particular authors, the editors felt that they could call on
these people for advice, to "pick their brains," or for assistance in promoting a particular book. One example of this
type of request goes as follows:

> Dear Professor ——:
>
> In January, 197—, we will publish ——, by ——. The
> reviewers who have already read this material in an earlier
> form report that it is a magnificent piece of work on an
> important subject and that it should take its place as one of the
> two or three most important books in legal philosophy in the
> twentieth century.
>
> It is very well written, and it examines the literature in

depth in at least five languages without ever bogging down in too much detail.

I enclose a copy of the uncorrected bound proof of this work. I would very much appreciate it if you would look through this work and, assuming that you like it, send me your reaction, from which I may glean a prepublication "quotable quote." I would then, of course, send you a copy of the bound book upon publication in January.

Thank you very much for your help; I hope to hear from you.

Yours truly,

———

It is common in all branches of publishing for editors or promotion personnel to write to well-known people and ask them to read a manuscript and provide a "quotable quote." Our research has shown that the success rate for such queries is normally rather low unless the person being asked is a close friend or admirer of the author. At Apple Press, however, the rate of response to requests for quotable "blurbs" is very high, and this is in part attributable to the "stroking and currying" of successful authors.

One of the most upsetting things for an author is to have his or her meaning changed by editing. The author often feels that no one has the right to tamper with his or her thoughts. Many authors fail to see that an editor is trying to understand and clarify what they have written. Few authors stop to consider that, if a reasonably intelligent editor finds a certain idea ambiguous, other readers will probably be puzzled by it also. An editor must feel confident that he or she can work with an author and produce a publishable manuscript. This process can take months, sometimes years. Editors must be sympathetic; yet they have to be capable of saying that they dislike something. The timing of suggestions can also be important. As a senior editor at another scholarly house observed, "Occasionally there may be a really important book being written by someone who hasn't got hold of it, and you need to keep intervening . . . and then there are people who simply sit down and write a book, and the manuscript requires only a few internal changes." It is important for editors to be able to "read" their authors and judge how they react to criticism. Some writers look to the rewriting, polishing, editing, or changing stage as a major step in the development of their work. Other authors are literally uneditable; they may react vehemently to even the slightest suggestion of alterations. Once their thoughts are down on paper, their book becomes so real for them that they cannot conceive of it any other way.

The editors at Apple Press often found themselves caught in the middle of disagreements between authors and the production department. Such cases were often no-win situations for editors, although they usually intervened on behalf of their authors at the expense of making the production staff angry. This created extra work for the editors. Going out on a limb for an author or spending a great deal of time working on a manuscript was not considered an important part of an editor's job. As one editor noted, "Editors win points, raises, promotions, etc., on how many books they sign and how many they get out. If you don't feel obliged to work on manuscripts yourself, then it's no problem. If you do, it's another matter, and it means you lug your work with you everywhere—to home, on vacation, on trips, etc."

One editor faced serious problems as a result of the attention she lavished on manuscripts. It took her longer to process paperwork, and this created a bottleneck. She found herself retyping material that had been copyedited and then editing it herself so that the author would not be upset by the original poor copyediting. Her relations with the production department deteriorated. Eventually the president approved of her extra efforts when he spoke with several authors who were extremely enthusiastic about her work. But another problem arose: word spread about this editor's skills. Her fine editorial hand was a major plus in acquiring manuscripts. In addition, the editor-in-chief would turn over to her the manuscripts that he considered very important but in need of polishing. It soon became a vicious cycle. As she confessed to me:

I'm having real trouble with my work load. I've been signing lots of books; then I have to find time to give each of them my personal touch, which is one reason authors are attracted to me and I sign so many books. Now if I don't provide them with excellent comments, they get upset. I'm going to have to ask if I can work at home one or two days a week.

A senior editor who worked for a scholarly house that was one of Apple Press's major competitors also felt the conflict between the demands of signing manuscripts and her personal feelings that doing line-by-line editing was something her authors valued:

If I think a really big difference could be made, then I'll copyedit the manuscript myself. Sometimes the author requests this of you. I feel that I would prefer to do the copyediting myself, because I am infinitely better at it than anyone we would hire. We still use a lot of free-lance copyeditors. Frequently, then, when my manuscripts come back from having been farmed out, I go over them to remove what I consider asinine . . . so that the author shouldn't be driven to a frenzy. It is a painful process to get a manuscript back with all these pink flags all over it, and marked up, even if it is done well. It is always painful, even if you are edited by the very best. Because it hurts your vanity and makes you anxious. . . . But to be copyedited by an incompetent is the most anxiety- and rage-producing experience. But there isn't time to copyedit as many books as I would like. The trick, of course, is to get good writers. Then you can say to the copyeditor, "This person knows more about writing than you. Leave them alone. Just make sure that there are no spelling errors and that all the numbers are spelled out or written out, or whatever."

On occasion there were manuscripts that needed work, and the editors at Apple approved of the extensive revisions made by the copyeditors. In one special case the editor-in-chief had hired a free-lance person to add more "punch" to what he regarded as a "dry" treatment of a subject that potentially had a wide audience. The editor-in-chief knew that he had a lot of tough negotiating to do with the author over these additions, as the tone of his letter indicates:

Dear ———:

Before you scream, I implore you read through the entire manuscript. I believe that our helper, whose name is ———, has done exactly what I asked her to do, which was to write a new introduction, to plug in material on prisoner labor, food, behavior modification, the use of prisoners in experimentation, punitive transfer, and other points, as well as adding some punch to the manuscript throughout.

I believe that you will find that she has done what I asked and more. I don't expect that you will accept 100% of what she has done, but I frankly would be disappointed if you rejected more than 10%. I went through the entire manuscript, and you will see my notes throughout. Often I kicked myself for not seeing and recommending what she did.

Call me as soon as you have looked over this, and we will talk about it.

Best wishes,

———

Finally, there were those unusual cases in which the editors at Apple Press did not intervene on an author's behalf when disputes arose over copyediting. In one instance the author wanted to rewrite his manuscript while it was in the galley stage. He was told that if he did so his contract would be canceled. Another author wrote the press, saying, "Please restore the pre-penciled purity of the text." He had erased the 700 pages of copyediting that had been done on his manuscript. His contract was promptly canceled.

There were two other problem areas in author-publisher relations at Apple Press. One concerned the marketing department. As I have noted, this was Apple's weakest link, and the authors I interviewed consistently gave low marks to its sales and marketing efforts. The psychology editor took it upon himself to try to remedy this situation. He would send complimentary copies of recent books to noted academics, and he contacted the editors of various journals and magazines and alerted them to a new book that he was enthusiastic about. When he traveled to college campuses, he would stop in and chat with the manager of the campus bookstore. In short, he did everything he possibly could to increase his books' exposure. Not surprisingly, the sales staff did not always applaud his efforts. Moreover, as word spread through academic networks about the editor's promotional efforts, authors would contact him, rather than the marketing department, to suggest additional ideas for promoting their books.

Another perennial problem is the "stepchild" book: manuscripts signed by predecessors and passed on to the next person hired. Editors felt some responsibility toward these books, but they were seldom enthusiastic about them. This was particularly true when completed manuscripts suddenly arrived unannounced. If the author first contacted the new editor and a relationship was initiated, there was usually more enthusiasm on the editor's part.

At Plum Press, none of the acquiring editors did any line-by-line editing. It was generally felt by editors not only at Plum but at competing houses that editors simply cannot meticulously edit detailed, specialized monographs. On the rare occasion when a book was thought to have some appeal to a broader audience, the sponsoring editor would spend some time going over it. However, few books of this sort were published by Plum Press, and it was even more unusual for the book to be regarded in this manner prior to publication. More often than not, the fact that a book appealed to a larger audience came as a surprise, and it was not until a book received reviews in such magazines as the *New Republic* that the people at Plum Press realized what they had on their hands.

A constant problem for editors at Plum Press was delay in the publication of multiauthored books that reported on the latest advances in a field. Prompt publication is essential for such books. However, the job of selecting authors and persuading them to get their chapters in on time was the responsibility of the volume editor. A Plum Press editor could intervene but had to do so cautiously, so as not to affront the editor of the volume. Considerable delays, which created many difficulties, were not uncommon. Too long a delay in publication could mean that the reports on the "latest" advances or developments in the fields would be embarrassingly out of date. Often there were awkward situations when punctual contributors were being penalized by those who were less prompt. Delays were frustrating for Plum, since they upset all the planning and budgeting for printing, advertising, and promotion.

The following letter to overdue authors illustrates the problems inherent in multiauthored works. In this case there was a real danger that the annual review for the following year would be in print before the work in question was published. This would not only be most embarrassing but could seriously hurt sales as well.

Dear ———:

In my capacity as sponsoring editor of ———, I met this week with the volume editor, Dr. ———. As you know, all chapter authors agreed to submit their final manuscripts to the volume editor by September of last year. In truth, only some of the chapters were submitted at that time. However, the overwhelming majority of the chapters are now in the editor's hands, and I am sorry to have to write you as one of the very few overdue authors.

From the publisher's point of view, there is very little we can do in terms of production work until we have a complete manuscript. We are, of course, disappointed, for had we received the manuscript on schedule, the book would now be nearing publication.

More important, however, is the situation regarding your colleagues in the field, whose chapters have been in the hands of the editor for some time. They feel rather put upon, since their work is now lying dormant and going out of date as time passes.

Dr. ——— has informed me that he will be required to present a report on the volume's progress to the membership of the association at the business meeting, during the annual convention. He wants to be able to report that all chapters are in his hands at that time.

As you know, other volumes, designed along similar lines, are planned for the future. In fact, the next one is now being organized. I would hope that we will not see this book preceded by the aforementioned work!

Dr. ———, your coauthors, and I expect that you will respond to this letter by the 30th of May, hopefully enclosing your chapter. At the very least, we ask for a realistic indication of a final submission date. Considering the amount of time we have lost, I feel that June 15th is not an unrealistic target for receipt of a final manuscript.

We look forward to hearing from you, and to a rapid solution to this problem.

Sincerely yours,

———

The Plum editors did not exert as much effort in "stroking and currying" authors as the Apple editors did. Nor were they as concerned with whether an author remained loyal and published all of his or her future work with Plum. Both the nature of the publishing program at Plum and the sheer size of its operations meant that author-publisher relations were less personal. Although individual authors were seldom personally catered to at Plum, the press was exceedingly diligent at maintaining good working relationships with their series and journal editors. Plum authors did, however, receive some special attention. At most publishing houses, many steps in the publishing process are delegated to free-lance outsiders; such services as copyediting, artwork and design, and even promotional work are entrusted to them. As we have seen from Apple Press examples, this can lead to problems for authors. At Plum Press, very little use was made of outsiders. In-house staff handled most of the steps in the production process. In particular, Plum was very capable of doing first-rate work with highly technical, heavily statistical manuscripts. Moreover, every book was promoted and marketed in the same fashion. There were no favorites or multitiered lists, which are common at other houses. Every book was promoted through journal ads and direct mailings; hence, although authors were treated with more distance and less affection, the product of their work was produced by Plum Press with considerable professionalism.

Summary

The editors at both Plum Press and Apple Press enjoyed considerable latitude in executing their work. This was particularly evident in the acquisition of manuscripts, but the editors also had a great deal of discretionary power in other parts of their jobs as well. They also had a substantial amount of influence over the activities of other departments. There is a considerable literature demonstrating that the higher one's rank in a hierarchy, the greater one's time advantages (Coser 1961; Merton 1957; Mintzberg 1973). Publishing represents a partial exception to this observation. While editors are not at the very top of publishing hierarchies, in their role as boundary-spanners they have considerable freedom of movement, lowered observability, and greater choice in the use of their time. In this regard, time can be viewed as a resource for social control (Schwartz 1975; Zerubavel 1979). Editors work on their "own" time, devoting their attention to the pursuit of their own interests. Other members of the publishing house do not have this freedom; they work according to the directives and desires of others. Moreover, their work pace is largely determined by the acquisition efforts of editors. Of course, editors usually devote a greater amount of their time on behalf of the firm, but they have considerable leeway about when and where to do so. As Merton (1957:76–77) has argued, lowered observability and greater choice in the use of time can be viewed as evidence of trust that the individual will live up to organizational values or goals without overt supervision.

Editors exhibited not only considerable freedom of movement within houses but a good deal of mobility across houses. David Jacobs' perceptive analysis (1981) of the relationship between individual performance and organizational success helps us to understand the underlying basis of this mobility; it also suggests that editorial freedom may depend on an editor's track record. Jacobs argues that there are three types of relationships between individual performance and organizational success: (1) an exemplary individual performance in some positions adds a significant increment to an organization's total performance; (2) an exemplary individual performance has little effect on the total performance of the organization; (3) an exemplary individual performance adds little to overall performance, but the occasional mistake will reduce the total performance of the organization by a significant amount. Editorial positions fit category one, for successful books can make a significant contribution to a firm's annual performance. In addition, editorial failures are not all that costly. Jacobs (1981:693) goes on to show that when poor performance is not very damaging and stellar performance has a big impact, firms will engage in a continuous search for new talent, and "lateral movements between such organizations should be common."

In the following chapter I examine in some detail the rationales offered by editors to account for their autonomy; I then go on to suggest some reasons why editorial discretion may be more apparent than real. In the present chapter I have illustrated how editorial duties are embedded in a network of personal relations that extend across houses and backward in time. In the next one I examine how these boundary-spanning ties influence the allocation of power within firms. I also introduce what I take to be an equally crucial observation: just as individual networks are embedded in personal career histories, so the structure of authority within organizations is embedded in social relations that extend backward in time, well beyond the individual tenures of particular editors, and outward in scope, in a manner that is far more dense than the associational contacts of any one editor.

4

DISCRETIONARY POWER AND UNOBTRUSIVE CONTROLS

At both Plum Press and Apple Press the senior editors worked under their own direction, with apparent immunity from supervision by others. If they needed to go on the road for a few days or spend the afternoon with an author, they did so, letting their secretary or the editor-in-chief—depending on how long they would be out of the office—know their intended whereabouts. Members of other departments had little voice in editorial decisions. Such freedom is largely limited to scholarly publishing. Trade-book editors are far more likely to discuss projects with members of other departments—most commonly, subsidiary-rights directors and the promotion and marketing staff. Whether such discussion takes place informally, in the hallways, or requires a formal presentation by an editor to an editorial board, composed of executives, differs from house to house. Trade houses vary as to who attends editorial meetings and whether an actual vote is taken. Moreover, editors may have enough influence to prevail in spite of general skepticism on the part of the others in attendance. Editors in textbook houses are even more likely than trade editors to be required to obtain formal approval for their projects from top executives in other departments. In addition, textbook editors spend a great deal of time in meetings, coordinating the production of their books with the staff members of other departments. Finally, in both trade and text houses the approval rate for projects proposed by editors is considerably lower than the 99 percent enjoyed by editors at Apple and Plum.

In this chapter I analyze, and provide illustrations of, the discretionary power that is apparently enjoyed by the editors at Apple and Plum. There are several strong theoretical traditions that help to account for editorial autonomy. Nevertheless, it is important to realize, as Weick (1969:40) does, that the basic raw materials with which many organizations operate are ambiguous, uncertain, and equivocal bits of information. A focus on individual choices is much more likely to capture this uncertainty, for it is only when we look at a population of choices made over time that we recognize that most organizational activities are directed at establishing a tolerable level of certainty. The answer obtained thus depends on the question that is posed; the focus—on individual decisions or on a population of decisions—will shape the reality that is observed. The format of this chapter reflects my learning curve about editorial choices. At first I was struck by the amount of apparent freedom that editors had. I was also impressed by the strong craft elements that typify editorial work. It was only after many months of fieldwork that I began to ask, Where do decision rules and performance programs come from? The answer to that question is that editorial work is subject to a number of powerful, if unobtrusive, controls.

The Case for Editorial Autonomy

The editors at Apple and Plum made frequent reference to the autonomous nature of their work, claiming that they knew their fields best and that it would be both impractical and unprofitable for their supervisors to dictate how they should go about doing their jobs. The editors were subject to little, if any, formal evaluation, and no attempts were made to hold them accountable for each book they signed. Editors at both houses felt that they worked best without guidance. As one Apple Press editor put it:

I work under my own direction. Sure I have disagreements with the editor-in-chief, but rarely is it over whether to do a book or not; instead, it's a question about pricing or sales potential. We don't have editorial meetings here. The editors are left on their own. No one here knows my fields better than I do. It stands to reason, then, that I should be the one to decide which books to publish.

Another Apple editor strongly concurred that editors are best left to their own devices and that good editors must be permitted flexibility:

As you know, I feel that the individual editor has much more personal clout than is generally believed, even by most editors. There are editors who are in high favor (usually this depends on their track record, but it sometimes applies to new employees who come from the right backgrounds, have the right connections, or for other reasons are able to impress people); they have very little trouble getting approval of anything they submit, whereas editors lower in the pecking order may be required to submit more documentation, pare down their royalty proposals, etc., in order to get the go-ahead.

There's also an element of personal salesmanship involved. In almost every house that I've worked for, the top brass never sees the manuscript or proposal on which the editor's initial decision is based but instead depends on the editor's highly selective presentation of the gist of the book and often on a highly selective assortment of reviews. Sometimes an editor gets a proposal or a manuscript that is not really up to snuff but feels pretty certain that the author can pull off a good book, with lots of help, and in essence the editor writes a proposal describing the book he or she would *like* to have. I'm well aware that this is a kind of cheating. I feel guilty, and anxious, about it, but I've done it.

The editor-in-chief at Apple felt that his senior editors "didn't need telling how to do their jobs." Moreover, he certainly expected to be the judge of what he himself should be doing. As for the young assistant editor, he said: "This is her first editorial job, so naturally she needs help. But if she'd go out there and start lining up authors on her own, I'd be overjoyed."

Members of the noneditorial staff of Apple Press commented about how "editors run the show" and that the other departments had little influence over what books were signed. The head of the production department grumbled, "The usual hardcover print run is around 2,500 copies. Even when they do a hot item, then it's only 10,000. I don't know why they do such small stuff. But I don't have any say. It's all up to the editors. Me, I just work here." And the marketing director at Apple Press remarked, "An editor is interested in how a book sells over the long haul. They may also be satisfied if a book wins a prize or gets good reviews even if it doesn't sell well. I don't have that luxury. I'm evaluated on a more short term basis—the amount of annual sales." On another occasion when I spoke with the marketing director about how she determined which books have good sales potential, she responded:

> Presumably they wouldn't have been signed up if they wouldn't sell, although sometimes I look at a book and I'm not at all sure why it was signed. But, once I have them, it's my job to sell them. I certainly have no voice in whether or not they are signed . . . I see the proposal, which has the suggested price of a book, but I have no say as to what the books will cost. If books aren't selling well, it isn't up to me to suggest that they shouldn't have been published or that they be revised or updated. That's up to the editors.

The president of Apple Press, echoing these comments of the marketing director, noted that:

> A formal profit-and-loss statement is not prepared for each book. The editors do have access to all the pertinent records, but I guess they are too busy to keep tabs on the past. Editors will tell you it's their job to sign books, not sell them. They are oriented toward the future, and sales records serve only to tie them to the past.

At Plum Press, too, the editors had a great deal of discretion in the execution of their duties. Not only did they make

the decisions as to which books to sign, with very little input
from other members of the house, but most of the services
performed by other departments required the final approval
of the sponsoring editor. The editor-in-chief described the
responsibilities of Plum editors the following way:

> The sponsoring editor has the broadest, most general respon-
> sibility for each book, from the time it is signed to the time it is
> declared out of print. To a very unusual degree, our editors
> work with other departments. Almost everything done by
> other departments, from ad copy to the jacket design, *has* to
> be approved by the book's sponsoring editor.

The social sciences editor at Plum alluded to the free rein
his job afforded him in the following comment: "As for the
company's editorial committee—I know what they get their
jollies on. I've had only one contract rejected since I have
been here, and it was a translation. Often I commit the
company to a contract before the editorial committee has
approved the idea." The behavioral sciences editor maintained, "There's no quota or understanding as to the minimum or maximum number of titles an editor must sign. I
honestly couldn't tell you how many books I signed last year.
Nobody tells us, 'Thou must produce.' I work on my own,
doing what I think is necessary."

I asked the director of the sales department what input his
department contributed to the editorial process, and he replied:

> Very, very little . . . and what little there is really comes after
> a book is signed. Oh, sure, we're asked to check every pro-
> posal; but we don't give comments unless we think a particular
> project is very badly conceived . . . like, if it's an immunology
> book projected for 3,000 sales, and the professional associa-
> tion has only 700 members . . . then we would wonder where
> the audience is coming from. But it remains entirely up to
> editorial to decide what is or is not signed. We can't even give
> any specific figures about promotion costs until we see the
> actual book, and by then the contract has long been signed.

Having observed that sales had no influence on the decision to publish, I still assumed that editors would, at the very

least, receive feedback from sales regarding the performance of books that had already been published. The vice-president of sales pointed out that this was rarely the case:

> Well, there are weekly and monthly stock-status reports, but very few editors pay any attention to them. Most [editors] are uninterested in checking the sales records, probably because they are sure of what they publish. The only exception is ——— [the social sciences editor], and that's because (1) his publishing program is the youngest and (2) his books have the greatest potential to take off and reach larger markets. I'm well aware that, in trade and text houses, sales departments have much more influence. Here the power lies in editorial . . . I used to be an editorial vice-president before I moved up here . . . it's an unusual career pattern, I know . . . but, given my background, I approve of our setup.

I followed up on the comments by members of the sales staff in a later conversation with the social sciences editor:

> Q: The head of sales tells me that you keep a closer eye on the sales of your books than the other editors. He claims that you check on your books while none of the other editors do. He seemed to appreciate your concern. Could you tell me why you are more interested?
>
> A: Sure. It's because my publishing program is new. I'm trying to get an idea how it's doing. Also, I anticipate more sales of my books than do others, and I push for lower prices; that means I'm cutting it closer, and the books have to sell more to make it.
>
> Q: What happens when they don't?
>
> A: Nothing. Oh, on occasion the editor-in-chief might stop by and say, "That book was a bomb. Well, how come?" I'll say, "I'll look into it," and that's that. He usually forgets to check back. Or I might say, "I blew that one. It doesn't look as if that subfield is a growth area."
>
> Q: So you don't lose any sleep over it?
>
> A: Oh, no; it's part of the job.

In discussions with editors at both houses I suggested that, despite their seeming autonomy within the firm, they ulti-mately were forced to rely on outside reviewers for the final judgment of a manuscript. Every editor disagreed, many pointing out that not all books receive an outside review. Moreover, one editor compared the use of reviewers' reports to the way film companies make use of negative reviews by well-known film critics. "Few reviews are ever totally negative, so it's always possible to excerpt a few favorable lines if you really want to do the book."

The psychology editor at Plum Press noted that, if a manuscript comes in under contract (that is, it has already been signed on the basis of a proposal or a sample chapter), he never seeks an outside review. As he said, "We already own the book, so why spend money on a review?" At Apple Press, on the other hand, the editor-in-chief frequently sent manuscripts out for review even if they were already under contract. "It doesn't have anything to do with the decision to publish," he said; "we've already bought the manuscript. But I want to find out what we've got on our hands. The reviewer can tell us that and maybe provide suggestions for improvement." Another editor said, "I use outside reviewers for questionable books; for manuscripts that I lack the qualifications to evaluate properly; for books that I like, but I'm unsure of the market; and when I want to build support for signing a book that I really like and I don't want my proposal questioned."

Control over Uncertain Aspects of the Work Process

One explanation of why editors have so much discretion would stress that their power is a structural phenomenon. Because their role spans organizational boundaries and attempts to deal with an uncertain environment, editors are in a strategic position. A report to the Board of Governors of Yale University Press by the university's Ad Hoc Committee on What to Publish begins with this statement: "One of the greatest joys and griefs associated with publishing springs from an inability to predict with precision the success or failure of a book" (Kerr 1974:212). In short, editors work in a situation where the origin of conventions about what is or is not commercially feasible remains something of a mystery.

Given the uncertainty about the acquisition of manuscripts, editors are permitted considerable leeway. Their work requires flexibility.

What do we mean by uncertainty? Decision theorists such as Knight (1921) and Luce and Raiffa (1957) have defined as uncertain those situations where the probable outcome of events is unknown. Lawrence and Lorsch (1967:27) argue that uncertainty consists of three components: (1) a lack of clarity of information, (2) a long time period before definitive feedback can be obtained, and (3) ambiguity concerning casual relationships. More generally, uncertainty can result when (1) the flow of resources to an organization is unpredictable, (2) the technology utilized to transform the resources is complex or nonroutine, and (3) the organizational field in which a firm competes is dynamic, diverse, or hostile.

External environments that change in ways that are difficult to analyze or predict create problems for organizations for which there are no easy and ready solutions (Thompson 1967). Perrow (1967) has illustrated the various ways in which a complex and changing environment poses special problems for organizational personnel: the exceptions to organizational routine are many; established procedures for problem-solving cannot be developed; and "no formal search is undertaken, but instead one draws upon the residue of unanalyzed experience or intuition, or relies upon chance and guesswork." The greater the variability of the "raw materials" that arrive as inputs from the environment, the greater is the need for adaptiveness and worker autonomy. Thus, an appropriate organizational design depends on matching internal structure to the requirements of an organization's environment.

Editors maintain that their jobs cannot be standardized because each case with which they deal is unique. Many researchers, in particular Hage and Aiken (1967) and Pugh and his associates (1968), have shown that, in organizations where work is repetitive, work roles can be formalized. Rules, procedures, instructions, and communications are specified, and employees are clear as to what is expected of them. In highly formalized situations, work behavior is very

routine, and there are few options as to how a job can be
carried out. On the other hand, where work is nonroutine and
variable, organizational roles are not formalized, and employees are permitted considerable autonomy in dealing with
the problems they encounter.

The literature is replete with studies that illustrate the
thesis that organizations operating in uncertain environments
are more successful if they adopt flexible and adaptive internal structures rather than more formal, bureaucratic arrangements (see, e.g., Burns and Stalker 1961; Lawrence and
Lorsch 1967; Duncan 1972; Lorsch and Morse 1974). Thompson and Tuden (1959) contend that universalistic standards
are likely to be used in circumstances where there is agreement on the connection between actions and results. However, in the face of uncertainty, it becomes far more likely
that particularistic criteria will be used, simply because no
criteria are universally accepted. This permits the employee
to determine which criteria he or she deems relevant. Peterson and Berger (1971) argue in similar vein when they show
that in cultural organizations, where there is widespread uncertainty over the precise ingredients of a successful product,
administrators must rely on the experienced judgments of
their employees. Close supervision in the product sector is
impeded by ignorance of the relations between cause and
effect.

Thompson (1967) has maintained that organizations seek
to cope with uncertainty by allowing the segment of the
organization that directly interacts with the turbulent elements of the environment to be loosely organized, so that it
can adapt to the continuous changes in the market. The other
parts of the organization, which make up the technical core,
are thus segregated, or "buffered," from the environment
and can be organized in a more routine, hierarchical manner.
From Thompson's perspective, editorial autonomy is an
efficient structural arrangement. The assumption is made that
editors have been hired because they are fluent and skilled in
their tasks. They know their work and how to go about it.

Hickson and his associates, in their study of intergroup

power within organizations (1971), maintain that the distribution of power within organizations is related to (1) a subunit's ability to cope with situational uncertainties and (2) the extent to which those who perform these activities are replaceable. Salancik and Pfeffer (1974) found that departmental power at the University of Illinois was best predicted by the amount of outside grant and contract money a department brought in; the power of a department was a function of the amount of important resources it controlled. More generally, Pfeffer and Salancik (1978) argue that the differential ability of different sections of an organization to deal with environmental contingencies determines the internal arrangement of power within an organization.

From a resource-dependence perspective, the autonomy of editors is derived from their control over the most uncertain aspect of the publishing process: the acquisition of commercially and critically successful "products." Power in organizations is related to the ability to solve critical uncertainties (Crozier 1964; Hickson et al. 1971; Pfeffer and Salancik 1978). Thus it is no surprise that other departments in scholarly and monograph houses are in a dependent position vis-à-vis editors, for it is the editors who have the skills that are necessary to procure the products the others in the house need in order to perform their jobs.

Craft and Occupational Control

The concept of occupational control refers to "the collective capability of members of an occupation to preserve unique authority in the definition, conduct, and evaluation of their work" (Child and Fulk 1982:155). My conversations with the editors at Apple and Plum, quoted at the beginning of this chapter, show that they had this capability. Child and Fulk (1982) go on to argue that occupational control includes the capacity to "determine the conditions of entry to and exit from the practice" of an occupation. Such control is exercised by only a handful of professions, such as medicine and law, that are able to restrict access to the profession's knowledge base. Both law and medicine provide services based on the authority of expertise—on keeping their professional knowledge at arm's length from their clients. This practice differs both from "people-working" professionals, who share their knowledge with clients, and from other professionals, such as accountants, whose work activities are directed toward serving the goals of the administration of the organization that employs them.

Editors generally do not possess a monopoly of access to the knowledge that is needed to perform their tasks. In publishing, the management of the firm controls the process of hiring and firing. Career and income progression for editors requires meeting the general goals established by management. An important distinction that is relevant to the question of occupational versus organizational control is made by Jamous and Peloille (1970). They describe two types of occupational knowledge and draw a distinction between "technicality" and "indetermination." Technicality refers to a rationalized, systematized, and hence transferable body of occupational knowledge; indetermination refers to the tacit, esoteric elements of occupational knowledge that defy rules and rationalization and are possessed by individual practitioners. It is over this special, personal, and indeterminate knowledge about writers and networks that editors attempt to maintain exclusive control.

There is much disagreement over who or what is "professional."[1] The established professions, such as law, medicine, engineering, architecture, and accounting, are undergoing a process of routinization of their professional knowledge and are increasingly subject to outside definition (Oppenheimer 1973). Computer technology serves to hasten the codification of professional knowledge and has the potential for permitting outsiders to carry out some of the tasks formerly reserved for members of the profession (Haug 1977). In addition, Scott (1965) has shown that many professionals work in "heteronomous organizations"—organizations over which they do not exercise strategic control and within which they are constrained by an administrative framework. At the same time, many occupations are lobbying for professional status. Despite the diminution of the term "professional" through the decline in the power of the traditional professions and through the success of practitioners of what were once regarded as nonprofessional work activities in having their professional aspirations legitimated by the state (DiMaggio and Powell 1983), editors cannot, by most standards, be considered professionals. Even in comparison to practitioners in the somewhat related fields of journalism and library science, editors receive far less systematic training and preparation for their eventual work.[2]

The Association of American Publishers (AAP), concerned over the lack of available training for careers in publishing, has organized a committee to develop educational standards and criteria for such careers and to establish reasonably uniform descriptions of the various jobs in the industry.[3] In the committee's report, issued in 1977, the president of the AAP, Townsend Hoopes, is quoted as saying, "If we are honest, we will admit that publishing is only beginning to address the question of whether it constitutes a body of attitudes and practices sufficiently tangible and delimited to be defined in a coherent curriculum" (AAP Education for Publishing Committee 1977:6).

I asked the two senior editors at Apple Press whether they regarded themselves as professionals. Their comments are illuminating. One of them said:

> No, I guess I am a practitioner of a certain skill. My job doesn't require an advanced degree. Certain things I do are the same every day. My job is to sign up books and turn them over to production. That's my job description. I don't do original research—nothing far-reaching, anyway. I am supposed to estimate trends. I read scholarly journals, but I read them first for publishing ideas and second for my own knowledge.
>
> I'm more of a custodian. There are ideas that deserve to be made public, and I help to do that. My primary self-interest, of course, is to publish good books. I don't see myself as a censor. I am a selector . . . I look at numerous ideas that

> people offer and choose certain ones because I think they are important and will sell. I'm not interested in influencing our foreign or domestic policy. I have no illusions about leaving a legacy. Even books that are important contributions won't change the world.

The other editor said:

> I'm very evasive about that term . . . anyway I'm not [a professional]. I'm a skilled worker, plying my trade. Education is irrelevant to a career in publishing. What is essential is social and professional contacts, experience, and gut smarts. The ability to work with people and having worked in the same area for a number of years also help. You have got to know whom to ask for help. You must understand what the author is trying to say and help him or her to say it better. The mistake many young people in publishing make is to try to change what the author is saying.

Many editors pride themselves on their sense of "smell"— their flair for finding just the right book. They contend that the traits of a good editor—judgment, expertise, intuition, and character—cannot be taught. Editors argued that success is a combination of luck, hard work, and timing. It was most difficult to get editors to be precise about how they reach decisions. One editor said, "You have to be a reader of the culture. If it's something you like and you think it is a good book, you supply the reason to publish it. If it's something you don't necessarily like and you reject it, then you are reading the culture."

Editing can best be viewed as a skilled craft. Becker (1978:864–65) states that a "craft consists of a body of knowledge and skill which can be used to produce useful objects, or . . . from a slightly different point of view, it consists of the ability to perform in a useful way." Editorial skills are developed through a process of technical socialization, characterized by an apprenticeship system. Editors learn on the job, beginning as either editorial assistants, promotional assistants, sales representatives, or secretaries. Learning to be an editor is a gradual process. As one first-rate editor commented, "You can learn all the technical stuff in six months; the rest takes a lifetime." Editors move through a series of positions, from assistant to associate to senior editor. If they attain senior-editor status, they are at the top of the editorial job ladder and their income is maximized. The only career alternatives for senior editors are in administration, as editors-in-chief or editorial directors, or in top management, where the acquisition of manuscripts is no longer the primary part of the job.[4]

Both Stinchcombe (1959) and Hall (1975:188–201) have shown that skilled craftsmen and professionals exhibit a number of similar characteristics. They are alike in that both have a strong sense of autonomy. They differ in that professionals lay claim to possession of a body of theoretical knowledge, while the skilled craft workers claim mastery of techniques, practical knowledge, and creative intuition. Due to their lack of powerful professional associations, the crafts have much less status than the professions. Although both exert some occupational control over recruitment, the professions are much more powerful in this regard.

Craft occupations are characterized by occupational communities with extensive social interaction and informal ties. Indeed, for many editors, editing is much more than a job; it is a way of life. Most editors' jobs spill over into their private lives. Their circle of personal friends often consists of other publishing people and authors. As one scholarly editor commented, "Many of my authors and reviewers can also be considered personal friends, with easy and informal access to me and I to them." I often observed editors doing special favors for their authors and friends (e.g., editing an encyclopedia article for a friend, informally acting as an agent for an author's manuscript, advising authors about points in their contracts, and editing a friend's manuscript that was being published by another house).

There are strong informal ties and interaction between people in different scholarly houses. Socializing and collegiality are important; a good reputation enhances one's chances for occupational mobility. Publishing is characterized by an

extremely high rate of turnover. Lateral movement from
house to house is frequent, and manuscripts are often referred through networks that link houses through previous
employment ties.[5] The standard editorial career ladder permits only limited mobility; this, along with the craft features
discussed above, encourages turnover. Turnover and promotion chances are inextricably linked: turnover is more likely
when upward mobility and the challenges associated with it
are not available. If a senior editor does not wish to move into
a managerial position, taking a job in another house is the
only option open. As the psychology editor at Apple Press
reflected, when offered a job by a competing house, "Actually I wouldn't want to advance; I couldn't stand being in a
management position. Keeping track of how many paper
clips are used is not for me. But another house would mean
new faces, new vistas." Another aspect of editorial work that
encourages turnover is that many scholarly editors find it
challenging to start a publishing program from the ground
floor or to revitalize a list that has seen better days. But once a
list is established and the normal routine of exploiting existing
contacts sets in, much of the excitement vanishes, and an
editor may decide it is time to move on.[6] And even though
editors may have substantial discretion in terms of how they
acquire manuscripts, every editor I've spoken with knows
that the selection of repeated "failures" is grounds for dis-
missal. There are no tenured appointments in publishing.[7]

In scholarly and monograph publishing, editors are solitary
workers. That is to say, while an editor may have personal ties
to other editors at their press, their in-house colleagues work
in different disciplines. It is rare for a house to employ two
editors to work in the same area. This kind of specialization is
also the rule in textbook publishing, but it is not found in
trade houses, where editors handle books on a wide variety of
subjects. At scholarly, monograph, and textbook houses, as
well as university presses, editors find that it is editors in
competing houses, working in the same field, who share their
interests, problems, and concerns. As the editors at both
Apple and Plum pointed out, they are more likely to know

and be interested in what an editor with the same specialty in a competing house is involved in than in what their own editorial colleagues are up to. An editor's reference group is thus scattered across many publishing houses rather than within his or her own house. Like university faculty members who work in different departments and have little contact with each other, editors in nontrade publishing houses work in different disciplines and engage in little in-house collaboration. An editor's key ties are extraorganizational: they are to authors, to reviewers, to free-lancers they regularly work with, and to editors in other houses who work in similar fields.

Informal interaction between editors in different houses is further promoted by the fact that, although most individuals in publishing have at least a college degree and many scholarly editors have advanced degrees, they are paid comparatively low salaries. Starting annual salaries in publishing are often under $10,000. Senior editors in scholarly and monograph houses, with many years of experience, seldom earn more than $30,000 a year.[8] In 1975, *Publishers Weekly* reported the results of a nineteen-industry survey which showed that executives at publishing houses received the lowest salaries of all the industries in the sample. Positive evaluation of one's work by others in the industry helps to compensate somewhat for the lack of financial remuneration.

The changes described in chapter 1 have left their mark on trade and textbook publishing (see also Powell 1982b), but changes in corporate ownership and editorial policies have not had a comparable effect on scholarly publishing. The scholarly sector has had to cope with inflation, declining library budgets, and many of the same general problems currently facing higher education, but pressures from top management to change the decision process at scholarly houses are not common. In this sector of the industry, editors still appear to have more discretion than their counterparts elsewhere. Because scholarly publishing is highly specialized and lacks mass appeal, a scholarly house does not need an expensive publicity, marketing, or subsidiary-rights staff. Much of the information that is systematically collected by these departments in trade and text houses is informally gathered by scholarly editors. As one editor explained, "One of the reasons scholarly editors tend to get mystical when asked how they make their decisions is that they don't really think about, much less quantify, what goes into seat-of-the-pants judgment." Another scholarly editor noted that "the craft of editing is a combination of many things—experience, including many discussions with colleagues in other houses and academics in your network, awareness of the histories of other books, and gut feelings. We don't have time to be systematic about these things, but they figure into any decision."

Watson (1980:147) has argued that "the history of Western occupations has been very much one of the rise and fall of the degree of occupational self-control maintained by various groups." Scholarly editors are clearly aware of the discretion they possess, and they are naturally reluctant to lose it. They are quick to resist any effort to impose on them an administrative framework for the conduct and evaluation of their duties. It is to an editor's personal and occupational self-interest to assert that choosing books is a talent not subject to market analysis. The comments of editors that the skills required to be a good editor cannot be taught reflect an effort to maintain possession of the knowledge required to do their jobs. Control over such knowledge can provide scholarly editors with an enduring basis for the maintenance of their discretionary power.

The Power of Informal Controls

As I spent more time at Apple and Plum, I came to question the amount of discretion that editors actually exercised. A number of factors were responsible for this skepticism.[9] First, the editors had a strong sense of priorities. They knew which authors should receive prompt service and which ones could be put off without penalty. Second, editors never proposed publishing certain kinds of atypical books, such as a 2,000-page manuscript, a novel written by a social scientist, or a

book replete with photographs. There clearly were boundaries around what was permissible. Third, I found it hard to
reconcile high editorial turnover with the view that editors
were the dominant group within the firm. Bluedorn
(1982:108–9) points out that, in organizations where turnover
is variable among units, the departments with less turnover
should reap some advantages, in terms of influence, from
their greater insight into the operation of the firm. I began to
wonder how editors could understand and manipulate the
internal decision process within publishing houses if they
frequently moved from house to house. Finally, I personally
became very adept at predicting which manuscripts would be
accepted and which ones would be rejected. The choice process was no longer mysterious to me. I had learned that
editorial decision-making is guided by a number of informal
control processes. In one sense, a statement that decisions are
guided by conventions or informal premises is almost a
sociological truism. The key question is where such conventions come from; as the philosopher Croce (1968:31) puts it,
"But if there are to be conventions, something must exist
which is no convention but is itself the author of convention."
In the remainder of this chapter I analyze the genesis, persistence, and operation of unobtrusive control processes.

Direct bureaucratic controls are commonly used at the
lower levels of an organization, but such obtrusive controls do
not work well with a highly educated or professionally trained
staff. (Indeed, recent work suggests that bureaucratic controls are counterproductive *whenever* they are used [Hack-
man and Oldham 1980].) Professionals and other highly
skilled workers object to rules and tight control. Moreover,
organizations stifle innovation when they attempt to direct all
aspects of work behavior (Kanter 1983). Formal controls also
require constant surveillance and monitoring, and neither is
feasible in organizations where tasks are nonroutine. Even
professional employees, however, do not like complete freedom of choice. An endless range of choices can lead to chaos
and confusion. An effective way for an organization to exercise control is to channel and shape behavior unobtrusively.

A number of organization theorists suggest that the predominant form of control in many modern organizations has shifted from formal, obtrusive supervision to a process that relies on the internalization of organizational values and preferences (Edwards 1979; Perrow 1976; Ouchi 1980; Williamson 1975). This change is a profound one, yet there is little consensus on what has caused it. Williamson (1975) argues that the creation of internal labor markets and reward systems is more efficient than contracting through market mechanisms. Ouchi (1980) contends that goal congruence, achieved through socialization, affords efficiency advantages because of the reduced need for supervision. For theorists in the transaction cost tradition, the problem is to discover how work can best be organized under conditions of idiosyncratic or firm-specific knowledge. Edwards (1979) and Perrow (1976) see this change less benignly; they suggest that a different problem is being solved: unobtrusive controls represent a sophisticated means of maintaining control over the labor force. Such a shift makes the exercise of arbitrary power less necessary; unobtrusive controls are viewed as more legitimate and tolerable.

When behavioral boundaries are well defined, employees can be permitted a good deal of latitude. They will voluntarily restrict their range of alternative behaviors, relieving superiors of the need to process routine information and make minor decisions. Decision-making authority can be delegated to the persons most immediately involved, who thereby learn from the experience and develop special skills. Because such delegation requires a particular model of authority, organizations rely on inconspicuous controls and effective socialization so that employees will perform in a manner that is not injurious to the organization.

According to Herbert Simon (1957), the superior can structure the perceptions of subordinates so that the latter see things in the manner the superior wants them to be seen. Such a model fits well with recent ethnographic research that shows that managers give few direct orders; instead, they set priorities and channel behavior (Mintzberg 1973; Peters 1978).

Simon has argued that the decision-making process can be deliberately modified. He states (1957:79): "Individual choice takes place in an environment of 'givens'—premises that are accepted by the subject as bases for his choice; and behavior is adaptive only within the limits set by these 'givens.'" He then goes on to show that, once attention and behavior are initiated in a particular direction, they tend to continue in the same direction for a considerable period of time because psychological "sunk costs" limit the range of future options. Williamson (1975:121) also notes the tendency for organizational activities to persist, regardless of their utility. These sunk costs "insulate existing projects from displacement by alternatives which, were the program not already in place, might otherwise be preferred."

Crucial to Simon's model of authority is the distinction between the premises that underlie decisions and the decisions themselves. Simon argues that, in all choice situations, attention is paid to only a fraction of the possible stimuli, meanings, and responses. Individuals are capable of coping with uncertainty only because they have acquired premises that interpret the meanings of various stimuli and the possible responses to them. When premises are controlled and shaped by others, the range of behavior is more predictable. Premises provide order in uncertain situations and allow employees to feel independent. Perrow (1976) has argued that, as long as an organization can control the premises that are used to make choices among alternatives, it can leave the actual choices up to subordinates. In other words, when policy is centralized, its execution can be decentralized. Mechanic (1962) recognized this when he stated that "an effective organization can control its participants in such a way as to make it hardly perceivable that it exercises the control that it does." One of the principal means of establishing organizational premises is through socialization.

Most adult socialization entails little attempt to change closely held values or to influence basic motivations. Instead, it involves the learning of new role expectations and performances as newcomers try to meet the demands of significant others. Indeed, it can be argued that most occupants of middle- and upper-class work roles have sufficiently internalized, both cognitively and effectively, the norms of appropriate behavior so that they are likely to perform competently, or at least try to do so, when placed in appropriate work settings. One reason for this is, as Inkeles (1969:629) has observed, that each organization is a "consumer" of the products of prior socialization by other organizations. Perrow (1974) recognizes this when he argues that professionals are the ultimate eunuchs: because of their extensive socialization, they can be turned loose in an organization and relied on to properly discipline themselves.[10]

Socialization theory argues that "scripts" are laid down for an individual by the groups to which he or she belongs. Both the person's social self and the behavior of others will influence how he or she will act out the script, but the script determines most of the appropriate behavior. This argument holds up well for occupations in which there is formal schooling or training, extensive anticipatory socialization, or processes of mortification or conversion.[11] In publishing, the "scripts" provided for new employees are largely blank. They are filled in on the job, through trial and error and through assimilation. Much of what is learned is not explicitly taught but is derived, rather, from casual and unscheduled contacts. New employees must learn to "sink or swim" on their own. This type of socialization is informal and often unexamined. Yet it must be recognized that it can be costly: failures in apprenticeships or new senior appointments are extremely expensive to the organization.

Organizational socialization refers to the manner in which the experiences of people learning the ropes in a new position are structured for them by other members of the organization (Van Maanen 1978). Socialization strategies may be intentional or unconscious. As Van Maanen (1978) has shown, different forms of organizational socialization produce remarkably divergent results. Socialization processes are most overt when employees first join an organization or when they are promoted or demoted; however, the process of socialization goes on continuously.

How are editors socialized into the mores of a publishing house? The following entries from my field notes illustrate one unobtrusive, yet effective, method. One day, not long after she had been hired, I found the sociology editor going through a stack of a dozen or so previously published books. I asked her what she was doing. She responded,

> These are books that the president asked me to look at. He's exceptionally clever, always looking for old areas that can continue to be mined. This is exceptionally rare in publishing; most houses couldn't care less about books they published ten years ago. He wants me to look these books over to see if any of them could be revised or brought out in a new edition or if the author has continued this line of research. It's a good idea for using old information in new ways. There are two or three here that look promising. I'll contact some friends and ask them to look them over and tell me if they think a revision is in order and what new material should be added.

I later spoke with the president of Apple Press and mentioned that one of his editors felt he was very adept at exploiting the past. I asked if he did this frequently. Did he regularly pore over sales data from previous years or study the performance of particular titles? He responded:

> Oh, no, that isn't an important part of my job at all. You see, [the sociology editor] is new here and unfamiliar with our backlist. This was just a way to help her become acquainted . . . to let her learn on her own the type of books we do around here. It shows her the importance we attach to our backlist. For us, many of our bestsellers are backlist titles. We publish with a conscious notion that every book should become part of a backlist. I just thought that would be a good way for her to become comfortable with our image of the type of books we do.

The result of the editor's research was that two books were brought out in new editions, and one author was encouraged to update and expand an earlier volume.

A similar example can be gleaned from an interview with a woman who had recently been hired as a senior editor at a scholarly house that was one of Apple Press's principal competitors. I inquired how she had learned to make an assessment of what the audience was for a particular book. She responded:

> Mostly by seeing what the books that were being published did. And when I got here, I had no authors of my own and no books that I had commissioned. And so, as frequently happens—certainly in a small house like this—I became a house editor. I was given manuscripts to handle that had already been signed. So that, very quickly, I had books that were my books—book that I was looking after—and I got a lot of experience seeing what happened to them—or didn't happen to them. Also, it was mostly from sitting in on meetings and listening to the conversation . . . Let's see, if you have to actually describe the learning process, it's very hard to do . . . Now, you know, we are a very big backlist house. So we often have reprint meetings. Sometimes the meetings are once a week, sometimes every two weeks. All the editors are there . . . and the business manager and her assistant. She says, "We are getting low on inventory on this book and that book." And of course the essence of good backlist publishing is to have just the right amount . . . never to run out but never to be overstocked. That's why we do this frequently; it's a sort of fine tuning process. So, by sitting in on those meetings, by hearing about whether we should reprint and how many, what the book did last year, what we expect it to do now . . . all this dealing with the old books gave me a much better sense of how to go about my work.[12]

These examples illustrate how simple reinforcement and reassurance can lead to patterns of recurrent behavior on the part of editors. An editor who learns which of his or her behaviors is rewarded in certain situations will repeat those behaviors in situations that are perceived to be similar. Cognitive social learning theory (Mischel 1973; Bandura 1977) suggests that an individual learns behavior-outcome expectancies, or contingency rules, that lead him or her to generate the response pattern perceived as most likely to obtain the outcome that is subjectively most valuable for a particular situation. Behavior is a function of previous organizational experience: choices that were approved or rewarded tend to be repeated, while efforts that did not bear fruit are replaced in favor of more approved behavior.

Previous educational and occupational experiences are also important elements in the socialization process. Many occupational career ladders are so closely guarded, both at the entry level and throughout the career progression, that individuals who make it to the top are virtually indistinguishable. For example, March and March (1977) found that individuals who attained the position of school superintendent in Wisconsin were so alike in background and orientation as to make further career advancement random and unpredictable. They attributed this randomness to the existence of a filtering process, common to all Wisconsin school systems, that ensured a high degree of similarity among acting superintendents. Barnard (1938) and Kanter (1977) both describe the same kind of filtering of aspirants to top management positions in American corporations; Kelsell (1955) notes the homogeneity of entrants into the higher civil service in Great Britain; and Hirsch and Whisler (1982) contend that there is very little variation among the directors of the boards of the Fortune 500 companies. DiMaggio and Powell (1983) argue that to the extent that key staff members of an organization are drawn from the same universities and filtered by a common set of attributes, they will tend to view problems in a similar fashion, see the same policies, procedures, and structures as normatively sanctioned and legitimated, and approach problems and decisions in much the same way. Filtering may even be more personal and subtle. Driscoll (1980) maintains that almost all new hires in business are made by informal means—word of mouth, personal contacts, and special school-employer relationships built up over time (see also Granovetter 1974; Lin et al. 1981).

Organizational vocabularies are another means of premise-setting. Organizational "lexicons" (Cicourel 1970) are important in directing attention to types of behavior and attitudes that are regarded as appropriate. C. Wright Mills (1963:433) recognized that "a vocabulary is not merely a string of words; immanent within it are social textures—institutional and political coordinates. Back of a vocabulary lie sets of collective action." Perrow (1976:14) suggests that there are even more subtle symbols: "a superior may simply give signals, such as frowns, impatience, blue-pencilling memos or highlighting words and repeating them, to show what distinctions are no longer important and which are." In this manner, employees learn that certain things are simply not done, while other behavior is considered normal and is taken for granted. Individuals in an organization are also socialized into common expectations about their personal behavior, appropriate style of dress, and standard methods of speaking, joking, or addressing others (Ouchi 1980). Peters (1978) has suggested that there are numerous "mundane tools" that managers use to influence their organizations. He views managers as transmitters of signals, and he notes that signals take on meaning as they are reiterated. Frequent and consistent positive reinforcement is a primary shaper of expectations. Employees are also attentive to what kinds of questions managers ask of them. Through various mechanisms—agenda management, the interpretation of an organization's history, modeling behavior—managers provide a sense of direction that permits latitude for employee discretion.[13] Pfeffer (1981) argues that the most important managerial function is to interpret organizational action for participants so that they will develop a shared system of meaning.

I observed the hiring and socialization of a new editor at Apple Press. In her first weeks on the job, she was terribly conscious that the customs there were very different from ones she had known at the press where she had formerly been employed. She worried that she would not be permitted to work closely with authors. None of the other editors did careful line-by-line editing. She found the company to be bureaucratic and its people blunt and gruff. She felt that there were forms to fill out for everything. She said she just knew "that the red tape would be incredible." She complained that editors had to do all the computing of the costs of their books. Within a short while, however, she fitted in very nicely. She learned that, although other editors did not edit manuscripts, they labored long and hard to satisfy the whims of their authors. She found that her colleagues' bluntness was their style of humor and openness. The forms and computations that she had feared turned out to be routine and easy to do with a pocket calculator.

Caplow (1964:171–72) has observed that "even a small organization has an intricate complex of ideals and ideologies, of norms and standards, of beliefs and prejudices, and of expectations and myths." The force of tradition and the constraints imposed by social structure do not control so much as they enforce limits. They restrict the range of options and lead to a commitment to doing things in a certain way. Naturally, organizations differ in the amount of their commitment to the past. Some become superstitious, believing that what worked for them before will be successful in the future. Most constraints on organizational behavior are the result of prior decision-making or the resolution of conflicts between competing groups.

Just as organizations may take on a life of their own, so do the lists of publishing houses. Books can endure longer than those who wrote or published them. When editors are in the process of signing books, the list that is already in print will impose its own logic on them, in both obvious and imperceptible ways. Editors-in-chief from all sectors of publishing have told me they believe that editors are attracted to a particular house more because of their affinity for a house's image, style, or list than because of the salary and other emoluments they are offered.

As Tuchman and Fortin (1980) note, both literary critics and historians of the publishing industry suggest that publishing houses have personalities. Editors maintain that their lists have a certain character or identity, that they are able to describe the quintessential type of book for their house. The house's identity, or tradition, finds expression in its backlist,

which constitutes those wise choices of previous years that
continue to sell well today. I argue that in houses such as
Apple Press and Plum Press, where the sales from the backlist
constitute at least 60 percent, and in some years a much
higher percentage, of total sales, there is an ever-present
consideration of how well the material currently under review
"fits" with the previous books done by the house.[14]

The social sciences editor at Plum Press mentioned that,
after you have worked there long enough, "you tend to
acquire a kind of cognitive map—you know what goes and
what doesn't." An Apple Press editor remarked that "each
house has its own image that no one can quite specifically
define. It may take several weeks or many months to learn it,
but, once you do, you've got it, and you know what will float
and what won't."

A crucial premise-setting characteristic at both Apple and
Plum was complementarity. Certain subjects, regardless of
how well they are treated, are considered outside the competence of the house and are seldom considered for publication.
Editors select manuscripts that are appealingly compatible
with previously published books. In scholarly and monograph
publishing, the lists of houses are, in effect, statements to
academics about what particular domains the publishers are
involved in. Marketing capability is also a concern. One
editor at Plum Press commented, and his editor-in-chief nodded vigorously in agreement,

> We couldn't publish a book in philosophy, even if it was the
> greatest book of the century on its topic. We've never pub-
> lished in philosophy; we lack the knowledge of the field, the
> mailing lists, and other related books to advertise along with it.
> We just wouldn't have the ability to do that kind of book.

The president of Apple Press voiced these related sentiments:

> You simply cannot sign just one book in an area. How in the
> world would you promote it? If you are going to move into a
> field, you have to sign three or four books; otherwise you
> don't stand a chance of breaking in and becoming noticed.

That is one reason why publishers like to do the kinds of books that they have done before. It's safer to work in an area that you are familiar with.

A good number of Plum Press publications were part of a series, and editors were always on the lookout for manuscripts that would complement earlier books in a series. It is much easier to market serial publications, since there is a ready-made audience consisting of those who have purchased previous books in the series. There were certain fields in which the house was well-established and for which it therefore showed a predilection. Editors at both houses were constrained by the types of books their firms had previously published. They would not suggest projects that would be considered out of bounds. Apple Press would not publish a resounding critique of the established authors whom they had published. Nor did they go in for "polemics or very speculative works."[15] Editors were able to bend the house's tradition, but they did so covertly. For example, when an editor wanted to publish a leading Marxist, the editor did not mention the author's politics but instead touted his academic credentials.

At Plum Press, the publishing program in the social sciences was less than a decade old. Plum had delayed moving into the social sciences because the firm's executives had doubts about the scientific respectability of these disciplines. Such concerns still loom large at Plum Press. The editor-in-chief continues to refuse to publish in the field of history because he maintains that "history is not a science." Hence, when the social sciences editor wanted to do a social-history book, he "advertised" it to the editor-in-chief as a work of comparative political economy.

The traditions of the two houses also put boundaries around the decision-making process in other ways. It was hard for editors to judge the significance of new subfields in which their house lacked good connections, so if they decided to publish a book in a new subject area and the book fared poorly, their interest in the subject waned sharply. They did not consider that what was responsible for the book's lack of success may have been not its subject matter but simply the fact that it was a very poor book. In addition, authors directly influence the future of a publisher's list. Authors who are satisfied with the publication of their books frequently act as informal scouts, referring others to the house. It stands to reason that authors are most likely to refer manuscripts by those who share their intellectual interests; hence they ultimately contribute to the maintenance of the house's tradition. Satisfied authors also continue to submit their own writings to the house. The editor-in-chief at Apple Press demonstrated his satisfaction with this arrangement by remarking, "One thing that can make your work a lot easier is to get a person's books throughout their life. That's quite an accomplishment, and, if you can do it, you can even count on them to have a new book for you every three years or so." The recurrence of a transaction reduces uncertainty and the need for search. Recurrent exchanges lead to familiarity between actors, the development of personalized exchange relationships, and a dependence of each actor on the other, resulting in a need to continue the exchange (Cook 1977).

Another way in which the premises of a house influence its decision-making is in the selection of outside reviewers. The most common source of reviewers at both Apple and Plum was their own authors and series editors. As a result, authors were called on to uphold the standards that they themselves had helped to establish. As one reader's report at Plum Press put it: "This manuscript is well written and probably publishable. But it is not as good as previous books in our series . . . I do not think it advisable that it be included . . . You might consider publishing it anyway, but not as a part of our series." And at Apple a reader's report said: "An intelligent and engaging study . . . from what I gather, however, this highly speculative, meta-theoretical treatment is not the sort of thing Apple usually does."

In their study of submissions to the British house of Macmillan between 1866 and 1887, Tuchman and Fortin (1980; also see Tuchman 1982 and 1984) found that the readers' reports strove to protect "the sanctity of their image of Macmillan and Company." Readers would comment that certain nonfiction books would bring no profit but would "be a credit to your list," and they commonly disparaged popular novels as "not suitable" for Macmillan. John Morley, one of the firm's primary readers, commented that a mysterious novel, "with blood and madness and dead men's bones . . . ought to be published and would sell—but [it is] certainly not of your style of publications."

Premise-setting is enhanced by standard operating procedures (March and Simon 1958). At both Plum and Apple, the print runs and prices of books were relatively fixed. The same forms, requiring the same information for each book, had to be filled out each time an editor wanted to propose signing a book. The process of obtaining approval was the same for every book. In cases where an editor wanted a larger advance for an author or a larger print run, he or she had to wage a special campaign to obtain approval. As the psychology editor at Apple Press told me after he had landed two very prestigious, popular authors within one week, "Publishing these guys is a real coup for us, but they do require a much bigger than normal investment. I had to anticipate the questions that the editor-in-chief would pose." This reflects a more general organization process, noted previously by Becker (1974): one can do things differently if one is prepared to pay the price in increased effort.

An organization's control over its operating premises is never perfect or total. Premises are not terribly useful during periods of rapid change or when organizations are faced with a string of unpredictable events. Premises are more likely to be resistant to change than supportive of it. Premises may be superstitious and contain the seeds of organizational obsolescence. They can even be viewed as part of the liability of aging (Aldrich and Fish 1982). Along with outdated premises, we commonly find a hardening of vested interests, an encrusting of tradition, and a homogeneity of perceptions. Continued poor performance by an organization may lead its members to question the value and nature of premises. Nevertheless, when successfully used, as they were at both

Apple and Plum, premises effectively guide behavior by providing reasonable and coherent boundaries. As long as the behavior of editors remained within these boundaries, they were free to carry out their duties in their own manner. Premises serve cognitive, ideological, and social-control functions, and they help management reduce uncertainty about employee performance.

Summary

In contrast to perspectives that emphasize the autonomy of craftsmen or the strategic power of the individuals who resolve critical uncertainties, I prefer a view that attends to the constraints faced by both an organization and the occupants of particular roles within it. In this chapter I have emphasized how patterns of exchange, the force of tradition, and an emphasis on complementarity serve as unobtrusive premises that guide editorial behavior. These situational, structural, and historical elements dispose editors to act in a particular manner. However, not only are editors socialized in an unobtrusive manner; publishing houses also are subject to both formal and informal pressures to adopt particular courses of action. Goal congruence is seldom individually tailored. There is ample borrowing of practices from other organizations that are viewed as legitimate role models. And, in turn, many less prestigious publishers tried to copy the successful policies of Apple and Plum. Moreover, as I shall maintain in chapter 6, publishers and highly productive members of the scholarly community at times engage in both subtle and not so subtle coercive efforts at furthering their own goals.

Editorial discretion is a negotiated order, a continual process of interaction and redefinition between an editor's preferences and the house's tradition and operating premises. Executives feel that, with proper socialization, editors acquire built-in regulatory mechanisms that shape their selection of manuscripts. Effective socialization and informal controls obviate the necessity of expensive and onerous surveillance. Editors, however, learn to use the premises and traditions for their own purposes. They know that unique situations become routine if repeated over time. Editors also have personal likes and dislikes, and these prejudices influence their work. Younger editors at both houses were more conformist. They did things by the book and were unlikely to intentionally take on books outside the house's tradition. Older, more experienced editors at Apple and Plum were more familiar with informal expectations; they knew, in addition to what were the "musts" of their role, what the "mays" were (Thornton and Nardi 1975). They had the ability to impose on their role their own personal style, modified in certain ways by their particular house. If they were successful, and their performance was accepted by others, they were in a position to create and expand the house's tradition in the course of their daily tasks.[16] Through them, the house published in new fields and, in a short time, incorporated these into the house's area of competence. More experienced editors also had their own "stable" of contacts and did not need to be wholly reliant on house authors as outside readers.

The individual initiative of editors is thus curbed and shaped but not stifled. Editors are never completely integrated into a fully cohesive order. Crozier (1981), in an analysis of a hospital, describes the balancing and managing of complex internal tensions within an organizational system as a game. The game must have rules so that collective association can continue, but, within the rules for playing it, different strategies are possible. In publishing, the rules can, on occasion, be broken. This is because decisions about which books to publish are significant events in an editor's professional career. Editorial performance of a high caliber must be rewarded in some fashion, because an editor-in-chief has to consider not only an author's career but the editor's as well—in particular, his or her recent track record. One senior editor at Apple felt that "one of the main criteria of a good house to work for is the extent to which an editor can debate an executive decision." If an editor had frequently been correct about books that others in the house were dubious about or had done several very successful books, then the editor-in-chief might decide it was "wise" to approve a manuscript proposed by this editor, even though his own judgment told him otherwise. An editor at Plum felt that an important consideration for him was how much "rope" he was given by his editor-in-chief. He recalled one instance where he received very poor reviewers' reports on a book for which he had recently proposed a contract. The editor-in-chief was disturbed and considered terminating the contract. The editor asked for patience and gambled on past experience with the author that he could turn the book around. He did, and the book did well.

An editor-in-chief must consider the morale of his editors when evaluating their proposals. An executive wants editors to be committed to the books they publish; therefore an editor-in-chief must think long and hard about the internal consequences of rejecting an editor's proposal. If a proposed book is very expensive, or if the author or manuscript will take up too much of an editor's time for what will be a modest return, the editor-in-chief may turn these projects down. It required careful combing of the editors' correspondence for me to find an occasional case where a proposal had been vetoed. This contrasted with the editors' frequent comments that their propsals were never turned down. The discrepancy comes from a selective memory: a project that an editor is passionate about is very rarely turned down; when an editor's commitment is weak, the possibility of rejection is higher. There are also a few proposals that editors are willing to use as tradeoffs or hostages to the future; when such projects are axed, the editors discount it, because these are not "real" proposals.

One of the most important influences on editorial behavior is work load. The decision process is very sensitive to decision load, hence editors must develop informal rules of thumb for managing their daily work load. In the next chapter I analyze the factors involved in the evaluation of manuscripts and discuss the consequences that information overload has on the process of making choices.

5

DECISION-MAKING AS A MEANS FOR ORGANIZING OBLIGATIONS

Making decisions, as everyone knows from personal experience, can be burdensome. In publishing, the burden is greatly increased by the fact that editors are inundated with "raw materials." At both Apple and Plum, editors received or acquired many more proposals, prospectuses, and manuscripts to evaluate than they could ever publish. Over the course of a two-year period (1975 and 1976), Apple Press received approximately 4,680 projects to consider. Fewer than 140 of them were accepted for publication. Such figures are by no means unusual. Editors at other houses also report that they receive a large number of "raw materials." In the fall of 1976, Columbia University Press noted in their brochure "The Pleasures of Publishing" that in 1975 they received 1,321 manuscripts and rejected all but 71 of them.[1] In 1981, Princeton University Press received 1,129 manuscripts and accepted 118. The Princeton data reflect steady growth over the previous decade, although submissions, which had risen by 52 percent since 1972, outpaced acceptances, which had increased by 42 percent (Darnton, 1983:533). Such low rates of acceptance are not unique to scholarly publishing (see Coser, Kadushin, and Powell 1982 for comparable data on other sectors of the book industry). Nor are high rejection rates merely a contemporary phenomenon. In the April, 1913, issue of the *Atlantic Monthly*, George Brett, who was then the president of Macmillan, asserted that "the number of books that appear in print is usually only about two percent of the total number of manuscripts submitted to the publishers for examination." Simon Michael Bessie, a distinguished editor, stated in 1958 that less than 3 percent of the novels written in America are published.[2]

For each of the editors at Apple and Plum, time was a scarce resource. The demand for editorial time far exceeded the available supply. Scarcity, whether of time, energy, or money, makes allocation decisions necessary. Editors cannot give each potential "product" an equal amount of attention. Only a small percentage of submitted manuscripts receives serious attention. This act of gatekeeping is an organizational necessity. In chapter 4, I emphasized how, at each house, both the backlist and the editors' network ties shaped editorial opinions. In this chapter I analyze how editors allocate their attention. What methods do they use to achieve an economy of effort, and how do they determine what are the most rewarding and morally demanding tasks? Editors manage these concerns through the use of a queue discipline. These rules for allocating attention are crucial, as the data on the numbers of manuscript submissions will vividly demonstrate. Yet location in queues is not the sole determinant of editorial attention; other factors—finances, an author's academic status, and the overall work load at the house—also influence the expenditure of an editor's time and ultimately determine the fate of manuscripts under review.

In a few cases, acquiring a manuscript and accepting it are one and the same. In the majority of cases, however, acquisition and evaluation are two separate and distinct processes. As we know from chapter 3, editors must keep track of many different streams of activity. There is a steady flow of unsolicited materials and referrals from people known by the editor, while other manuscripts are obtained as a result of editorial initiative or luck. At the same time that manuscripts arrive at the house, additional manuscripts are under review. Each manuscript is evaluated, and, if necessary, the editor will locate an appropriate reviewer to assess it. Once convinced of a manuscript's merit and marketability, the editor will "sell" the project to his or her superiors. Faced with so many demands and responsibilities, editors must develop strategies to cope with information overload. I found that most editors had personal rules of thumb. They conserved their energy by taking on projects that were either politically or financially expedient; or projects that were simple, meaning that the book did not require a great investment of time or energy; or projects that were enjoyable to work on—that is, the book dealt with a topic they were interested in. Therefore, one key to learning how decisions are made is to understand how an editor's attention is allocated. It seems logical to argue that the greater the amount of time that goes into evaluating a project, the more likely it is that the project will be published.[3] Even if we discount theories of cognitive consistency, we are left with the simple fact that spending time on some projects precludes giving attention to others.

I tried to map the various ways in which manuscripts are acquired by asking the editors at Apple Press to keep a record of all the materials they received.[4] This was a difficult request to comply with, because Apple did not keep records of submitted projects that were not published. Only rejection letters were kept on file. The editors were divided as to the utility of keeping these records for me. One editor said that now, for the first time, he felt organized. Another grumbled, saying, "Most of this stuff will never be published, so what's the use?" I abandoned this procedure after several months because it required too much of the editors' time. I decided that a more workable method would be to trace the manner in which all the books published during 1975 and 1976 had been acquired and to gather comparable information for all the books that were contracted for during 1975. In addition, I contacted the authors of the books that were published in 1975 and 1976 and obtained their version of how their manuscripts had come to be accepted. For projects that were signed while I was present, I was able to observe the evaluation process and ask questions as the acquisition took place. This research strategy was later partly replicated at Plum Press.[5]

Access and Waiting: Differential Chances of Being Published

The decision to perform one act before another implies an assignment of priorities. This does not mean that choices are necessarily purposive or based on stable preferences and expectations. Research suggests that preferences develop over time while decisions are being made, through a combination of education, socialization, and experience (March and Olsen 1976). My analysis of unobtrusive controls in chapter 4 suggests that decision-making most commonly represents the fulfillment of obligations and the maintenance of loyalties. Editors employ a variety of tactics to bring the supply of manuscripts and the demands on their time into a workable equilibrium. As Barry Schwartz (1975:80) contends, every organization that processes people or the "things" created by people must in some way make use of a queue discipline, a set of rules that govern the order in which service in rendered. In many organizations the standard policy is first come, first served; however, this is not the case everywhere. Queues can serve as a means of organizing obligations.

In some organizations there is a recognition of special circumstances or privileges that entitle a person to faster service. These preemptive priorities allow some clients to displace earlier arrivals. Schwartz (1975:78) also maintains that, in institutions as varied as hospitals and scientific journals, the longer the queue is, the less attention it gets. Effort expended on small queues produces a more visible impact than an identical amount of effort expended on longer ones. Moreover, as Schwartz (1975) and Schwartz and Dubin (1978) have shown in the case of academic journals, the reward that a journal editor experiences in finding papers to accept, and arranging to get the final drafts of each in hand in order to get the issue out on time, is very different from the reward he gets for rejecting papers on time. Thus, correspondence about rejections not only waits in a longer queue and takes more time than correspondence about acceptances; it is accorded a much lower priority.

A queue discipline is not the only way an organization can accommodate conflicting and competing claims. Excess demand may be responded to by omission or by cutting categories of discrimination, that is, by responding to tasks with less precision than would be the case at lower rates of input. One example would be for editors to rely on the institutional affiliation of an author as a way of reducing processing time. As Schwartz (1975, 1978a) points out, a client whose status is low cannot offer much to reward the service-provider for prompt service; this client will therefore wait. A high-status author of course has more to offer an editor in a reciprocal relationship. I was particularly attentive to the advantages in terms of access that were afforded to academics from prestigious institutions; however, as I discuss below, although academic status has a significant effect on network location, status alone is not a primary determinant in editorial decision-making.

Staffan Linder (1970) points out that under conditions of work overload or time scarcity, low-quality decision-making is the most sensible way to achieve organizational efficiency. A more effective decision-making process would be too time-consuming. For instance, a rational choice about a manuscript's value would require considerable information about both its intellectual contribution and its market potential. But to obtain that kind of information, an editor would have to read each and every manuscript, solicit reviews, investigate sales potential, and so on. To do so would mean that the editor was functioning very unintelligently, because such behavior would be an uneconomic way to allocate one's time. All editors recognize that decisions must be made in the absence of complete information. Nor is this a cause for great worry, as the comments of one editor vividly illustrate: "There are a lot of fish out there to be fried; if one gets away, you can't lose sleep over it. Everybody in publishing can tell you stories about great books that got away or were turned down." Linder's analysis helps account for this seemingly arbitrary aspect of the publication process.

In general, waiting time is reduced when there is financial competition between service-providers. But, as mentioned earlier, frenetic competition for authors, which is commonplace in trade publishing and to a lesser degree characterizes the college textbook field, is largely absent from the world of scholarly publishing. Competition for an author among scholarly houses usually involves high-quality service, the prestige of a house, and the author's affinity for the editor. The norms of peer review and first-rate scholarship are not typically associated with financial reward; therefore, waiting time is seldom reduced because of competition among scholarly presses.[6]

In an organizational society, delays in getting administrative decisions are a problem in a wide variety of settings (see Stinchcombe 1980). A pure case of red tape occurs when bureaucratic rewards are incongruent with bureaucratic purpose. In some cases there is neither a reward for prompt service nor any penalty for delay. Many service-rendering organizations do not lose clients by requiring them to wait a long time, because clients seldom have alternative services to which they may turn. The causes of delay at Apple Press, however, were not due to rule-bound behavior or to lack of reward for speed. Delays were caused by work overload; as a result, most manuscripts spent more time waiting in the queue than in being evaluated. The exceptions to this rule were those written by authors who had had some prior contact with Apple Press.

I argue that the time an editor spends on a project and hence its chances of being published are largely determined by the manner in which the project comes to the editor's attention. The data that I collected at Apple on manuscript acquisition yielded a list of approximately thirty means of obtaining manuscripts. These ranged from materials that arrived unsolicited to situations where the author was a personal friend of the editor. (The complete list is presented in an Appendix as the Manuscript Acquisition Code for Apple Press.) I collapsed these various methods of acquisition into three main categories:

1. The author initiates the contact with the publishing house. This category includes projects that come in over the transom or through an author's approaching a representative of the house at a convention or a meeting. In these cases the author has had no prior contact with the house.

2. The author has had some previous association with the house or with a person who has had such an association and is willing to act as a broker for the author or the house. This category includes both referrals from other publishers or from informal advisers to the house and also situations where the house has an informal arrangement with particular institutions to publish their materials.

3. The editor acquires a project as a result of his or her efforts or contacts. This category includes referrals from an editor's close personal friends and cases where the editor searches for projects.

The volume of materials received through these different channels varied considerably. The data I collected enabled me to place in one of these three categories all of the projects and manuscripts Apple received in the two-year period (1975 and 1976). Most fell into the first category; in fact, Apple Press was commonly swamped with over-the-transom materials. With some seasonal fluctuations, the house received an average of about thirty-five unsolicited projects a week. One editor noted that the sheer quantity of over-the-transom materials affected the quality of his work life; noting that most of his time was spent going over his mail, he lamented that "signing a book is actually something that happens rarely." The second category was less typical; approximately eight to ten projects a week arrived in this manner. The third category was the least frequently represented; during some weeks, no projects were obtained in this way, but at other times, especially if an editor was on the road, several projects could develop in a single week. I estimate that fewer than fifty projects a year were acquired in this fashion.[7]

After ascertaining the number of projects that were submitted to Apple, I spoke with both editors and authors to determine how the books that were published in 1975 and 1976 had been obtained. As the information presented in table 4 indicates, there clearly was a preemptive queuing system by which prospective authors' projects were processed in accordance with the extent of their previous association with the house or with a particular editor. Last to be processed were projects whose authors were unknown to the house and its editors, i.e., those who sent in unsolicited materials. The general result of this queuing system was that efficiency and short waiting times for one set of prospective authors resulted in ineffectiveness and long waiting times for unsolicited authors. This statement should be qualified somewhat by noting that, on occasion, an editor would scan an unsolicited project very quickly and then, if the manuscript was wholly inappropriate, reject it on the spot. A secretary would then return the author's materials. More commonly, unsolicited materials that had some appeal were added to the editor's pile of work and would, at some point, receive further scrutiny, although their chances of publication were quite slim.

The data presented in table 4 confirm the notion that the amount of attention an editor devotes to a manuscript depends on the manner in which it was acquired, and this attention subsequently affects its chances of being published. The more than 1,800 manuscripts submitted each year by authors who had had no prior contact with Apple Press had very small odds of getting published; in fact, their chances were considerably less than one in a hundred. Authors with some previous contact had chances of getting published of slightly less than one in ten. Projects that were obtained as a result of an Apple Press editor's efforts or connections—projects which averaged about fifty a year in number—had publication odds of about one in three.

Manuscripts that arrived as the result of a preexisting relationship with the house (category 2) illustrate how the house's previous history may influence editorial behavior. There are occasions when the relationship between the author and the house preceded a particular editor's tenure with the firm. The most common example was the "stepchild" manuscript, the

Table 4

Acceptance Rate for Books Published by Apple Press in 1975 and 1976

Acquisition Category	Estimated Number of Submissions	Books Published	Percentage of Submissions Published
1. Author had no prior contact with house	3,640	21	0.57
2. Author had previous contact with house	940	79*	8.4
3. Editor acquired materials personally	100	35	35.0
Insufficient information	—	2	—
Total	4,680	137	2.9

*Category 2 includes 32 titles that were revised editions, paperback editions of books that originally appeared in cloth, and old contracts, signed by the previous administration.

book that had been contracted for by a predecessor. There are also other relationships—with an author, an informal adviser, or an institution—that were established prior to an editor's employment with the house. In effect, a new editor inherits a complex network of contacts when he or she fills a position previously held by another editor. If the editor values these relationships or is strongly encouraged by management to cultivate them, he or she will pay attention to the material that is received as a result of these previous ties. This by no means ensures publication; but if the editor wants to continue the relationship, these materials must at the very least be attended to with care and some dispatch. Manuscripts that were directly acquired by an editor (category 3) obviously received the most immediate attention.[8]

It is important to note that authors in the high-priority queues (categories 2 and 3) would quite possibly transfer their allegiance to another house if they did not receive the prompt treatment and attention that their position in the queue merited. It is this priority service that creates the bonds of moral obligation and reciprocity that link authors to Apple Press. Editors gave their highest priority to what were morally their most demanding tasks—the tasks that gnaw at an editor's conscience when left undone. As Barry Schwartz (1978b:9) points out, "What this means is that the constraining elements in work are not altogether intrinsic to the task at hand but must be derived in part from its location in a queue."

I collected additional data from both Apple Press editors and authors for books that were signed, but not published, in 1975. This information appears in table 5. Both the means of acquisition and an author's chances for publication are quite comparable to the data presented in table 4.

Young unpublished academics will perhaps find some solace in the fact that their chances of publication are actually better than the odds facing unpublished authors of trade books (see Coser, Kadushin, and Powell 1982:128–35).[9] Some major trade houses will not even accept unsolicited materials. Menaker (1981) estimates the odds against pub-

Table 5
Acceptance Rate for Books Signed by Apple Press in 1975

Acquisition Category	Estimated Number of Submissions	Number of Books Signed	Percentage Published
1. Author had no prior contact with house	1,820	7	0.38
2. Author had previous contact with house	470	34*	7.2
3. Editor acquired materials personally	50	17	34.0
Insufficient information	—	2	—
Total	2,340	60	2.56

*Includes three revised editions

lication of unsolicited novels are approximately 15,000 to 1. The general prospects for unpublished writers who send in their materials over the transom are so poor that we advised:

> If the reader who is unfamiliar with publishing takes but one message away from this book, it should be that formal channels of manuscript submission are the very last resort of would-be authors. To get a book published, recommendation through an informal circle or network is close to being an absolute necessity. [Coser, Kadushin, and Powell 1982:73]

At Plum Press I was unable to collect data that were directly comparable to the data I had collected at Apple. I therefore solicited rough estimates from each of the editors and then fine-tuned their estimates by going through their correspondence files. I then asked the editors to go through their various methods of manuscript acquisition and tell me which manuscripts would receive the most serious attention. The Plum editors all accorded their highest priority to manuscripts that were directly referred to them by a series editor. They estimated that between 70 and 80 percent of these manuscripts were eventually published, although in a few cases a book did not appear in a specific series.

As I have noted, Plum Press was a relative newcomer to the social and behavioral sciences. Few Plum authors in these fields had done more than one book with the press. This is illustrated by the results of a questionnaire I sent to 58 randomly selected authors who had recently published a book in these fields with Plum. Of the 45 respondents, only 8 had had more than one book published by Plum. In the case of 22 authors, the book in question was the first one they had written. In contrast, Apple Press had many authors who had published four or five books with them and a few who had done eight or even more. Apple had a much larger circle of "friends and supporters" than Plum, and, as a result, far more manuscripts were referred to it by house authors than was the case at Plum. This was one reason why the behavioral and social science editors at Plum felt it was incumbent on them to travel and actively search for manuscripts, but, despite this additional effort, their traveling was slightly less productive than the search efforts of Apple editors. The Plum editors estimated that they eventually published one out of every three or four projects they acquired as a result of their travels—a somewhat lower percentage than at Apple. Because of Plum's late entry on the scene, its editors in the social and behavioral sciences devoted a good portion of their travels to spreading the word about Plum and their new publishing programs and were therefore less selective about the manuscripts they acquired. The editors wanted exposure for Plum, not just potential "products."

Plum also had other sources of manuscripts. They purchased several books each year from foreign publishers. They also had the option of publishing in the United States books that were originally published by their London branch office. In addition, Plum established ongoing relations with several research institutes, and they published most of the materials that were referred to them through these institutions.

At Plum, as at Apple, over-the-transom materials were not very likely to be published. A slight but important difference is that Plum was somewhat more hospitable toward over-the-transom materials because it received fewer of them. The editors at Plum estimated that "one out of every twenty-five or thirty" over-the-transom manuscripts was eventually published. Plum's late entry into the field and its resulting lower visibility among members of the social science community explain why it received fewer unsolicited submissions. The fact that its editors were not overwhelmed by over-the-transom projects meant that they could give more attention to them, and this increased these projects' chances of publication. In addition, the editors were buffered by the series editors, who handled many unsolicited manuscripts on their own. Often the series editors would reject unacceptable projects without contacting an editor at Plum.

I asked both the social sciences editor and the behavioral sciences editor at Plum Press to go over the list of their books that had been published during the two years 1975 and 1976 and describe how each had been acquired. The behavioral

sciences editor begged off, claiming a very faulty memory.
The social sciences editor was able to recall the way most of
his books had been acquired, and, when he could not, his
correspondence file was well-enough organized to enable me
to track down the needed information. I then double-checked
this information by contacting the authors and obtaining their
accounts of how their books had been acquired. The summary results are shown in table 6. In effect, this is a shorter
version of the manuscript acquisition code that I used at
Apple Press.

In order to compare Plum Press data with Apple Press
data, I assigned each of the methods of acquisition shown in
table 6 to one of the three categories I had used for analyzing
the Apple Press data. The results, shown in table 7, do not

Table 6
Methods of Acquisition of Social Science Books
Published by Plum Press in 1975 and 1976

Method of Acquisition	Number of Books Published	Percentage of Total Books Published
Editor's initiative	9	14.3
Recommended by a series editor	19	30.2
Originally published by Plum's London office	9	14.3
Arrangement with a research institute	4	6.3
Serial publication or proceedings of a symposium or conference	4	6.3
Signed by West Coast office	4	6.3
Import from a foreign publisher	3	4.8
Reprinted from a Plum Press journal or referred by journal editor	2	3.2
Author had previously published with Plum	2	3.2
Referred by well-known scholar because of Plum's backlist	1	1.6
Over the transom	4	6.3
Information not available	2	3.2
Total	63	100

Table 7
Social Science Books Published by Plum Press,
by Category of Acquisition, 1975 and 1976

Category of Acquisition	Number of Books Published	Percentage of Total Books Published
1. Author had no prior contact with house	4	6.4
2. Author had previous contact with house or one of its representatives	32	50.7
3. Editor acquired materials personally	21	33.3
Insufficient information*	6	9.5
Total	63	99.9

*Four titles were acquired by the West Coast office of Plum Press and could not be classified.

differ greatly from the Apple Press results. The overwhelming majority of Plum Press social science titles were acquired either through the direct efforts of a house editor or a series editor or through a preexisting relationship between the author and Plum Press. The data on the social science books, and the estimates provided by other editors, indicate that there is a preemptive queuing system in operation at Plum that influences how editors' attention is allocated and, ultimately, an author's chances of being published.

Manuscript queues operate as filtering systems. Not everyone in the high-priority queues gets published, nor is everyone in the lowly regarded queue rejected. As I observed above, a house's tradition and an editor's interests are important mediating influences. If a manuscript in the low-priority queue complemented books already published by the house and the editor found it to be interesting, its chances were naturally improved. On the other hand, if a manuscript in the highly regarded queue had these characteristics, its chances of publication were very high. There are other considerations editors must take into account in their decision-making, and in the next section I discuss these; but it must be kept in mind that location in the work queue differentially affects chances of publication.

Other Factors in the Decision to Publish: Inventory Considerations

From an author's point of view, timing must be viewed as pure chance. It is impossible for an author to know when a publishing house is short on "product" and is thus more likely to be receptive to new materials, and few authors will know whether or not an editor is looking for a manuscript on a particular subject. One reason why both Apple and Plum kept a backlog of materials was to ensure that there was ample "product." Editors are engaged in a delicate and continual balancing act in terms of scheduling; they must coordinate the signing of books with the release of new books, always checking to avoid periods of either inactivity or overproduction. At Plum Press it seemed that some books were signed so that a continual flow of product would keep their large work force busy. This opinion was routinely stated by production and manufacturing personnel. The following comments by a production editor touch on the issue of work flow:

> They often sign books just to keep us working . . . Oh, sure, the books fulfill other functions too—like they will sign up a guy's book even if they know it's not that good because he just got a big grant and they want to publish the results of the research . . . It's a big company . . . they want all these people to earn their money. [*How can you be sure of this? The editors don't tell you this, do they?*] Not in so many words, but they clue you in at transmittal meetings—where an editor turns a book over for production—by saying things like "This book is pretty dull, so don't bust your tail on it," or "There's not much you can do to improve this one; it's very dry, and we'll have to publish it as it is." The editor sort of lets you know when the book doesn't require the standard treatment.

At Apple Press, the twenty-odd employees were always busy, so there was no need to sign books just to keep the labor force working. However, maintaining a constant flow of materials is crucial to all organizations in order to avoid cash-flow problems. Thompson (1967:20) has suggested that "buffering on the input side" is essential and that organizations must stockpile materials acquired in an irregular market to maintain constancy in their service processes. This also explains why editors "sit" on manuscripts. I observed cases where manuscripts had been evaluated but editors held off on making a final decision, preferring to wait and see what the quality of forthcoming manuscripts would be. Such delays can be explained as protection against future contingencies. The concern with keeping up a constant flow of products is also a factor in relations between editors and management. The following entry in my fieldwork notes illustrates this:

> On the next-to-last day of the month, the editor-in-chief walked into a senior editor's office; he quite clearly looked worried. When asked what was wrong, he replied, "I'm wondering how the hell I can explain to the president why we didn't sign a single manuscript in the month of October." The senior editor responded that he had reached agreements with authors on at least seven projects during October but that the formality of the contract-signing probably wouldn't clear the parent company's bureaucracy until December. "It helps to know that," the editor-in-chief said, "but not that much. I'll just have to convince [the president] that this absence of projects won't create any scheduling problems for us sometime in the future. I just wish I had a book signed this month!"

Editors at several university presses reported that their presses have developed multitiered lists. This is a system for categorizing books based on their commercial potential. Each list has three types of books: C books are monographs on which the press expects to lose money; B books are expected to pay their own way; A books should earn money and pay for the Cs. These different categories of books receive dissimilar marketing attention. Obviously, in each season a university press will have to balance its mix of books. If a list needs to be cut back, a press may postpone some of the Cs. Another way of dealing with this problem, and of avoiding postponements, is for editors to defer making final decisions on C manuscripts. The rationale behind such a move is certainly reasonable; but, as I have argued elsewhere (Powell 1982a), it is incumbent on university presses to explain to their C authors—who are typically young and inexperienced—why a postponement or deferral is necessary. A key difference between university presses and Apple or Plum is that the latter will rarely knowingly publish a book on which they expect to lose money.

The Status of Authors

What effect does an author's location in the academic stratification system have on his or her chances of getting published? Hargens and Hagstrom (1967) demonstrated that having obtained one's Ph.D. at a major institution is a significant advantage to a scientist. Many of us are familiar with Merton's (1968) Matthew Effect, which echoes the gospel that unto him who hath shall be given, as when scientific recognition accrues to those who already have it. Merton argues that there is a continuing interplay between the status system, based on honor and esteem, and the academic class system, based on differential life-chances, which locates scientists in differing positions within the opportunity structure of science. Without deliberate intent, the Matthew Effect operates to penalize the young and the unknown, and, in the process, it reinforces the already unequal distribution of awards.

In deciding which books to publish, are editors reproducing the academic class system? If so, should this be cause for concern? Fulton and Trow (1974) suggest that only a limited number of academics are involved in research and that many American academics do little scholarly writing, opting instead for a teaching role. The Coles (1973) argue that the most talented scientists are located at the best schools and that science is a highly universalistic system that rewards merit. Clearly, scholars employed at elite colleges and universities have better facilities, greater research support, more release time, and lighter teaching loads. Such a system of accumulated advantages (Zuckerman 1970) would result in the rich getting richer at a rate that makes the poor become comparatively poorer.

Yet the amount of influence that accrues to an academic as a consequence of his or her affiliation with a prestigious department or university is not a simple thing to determine. It was certainly the case that authors from less prestigious universities were less likely to have contacts at Apple or Plum. My colleagues and I also found that writers affiliated with high-prestige schools were more frequently asked to review manuscripts (Coser, Kadushin, and Powell 1982).[11] In cases of multiple submissions of a manuscript by an author, we found that more than half of our sample of authors from top schools were offered a contract by more than one publisher, while only a third of the authors from nonelite schools enjoyed the opportunity to choose among several interested publishing houses. Authors from elite schools were also somewhat more likely to be offered larger advances. From a publisher's point of view, it is quite sensible to agree to publish the latest work of a widely known scholar. But to accept the work of a young Ph.D. candidate or an unpublished junior faculty member primarily on the basis of his or her university affiliation is a different matter. In his research on scientific reward systems, Stephen Cole (1978:176) found low correlations between measures of scientific output and the prestige rank of departments. He argues that this indicates that scientific talent is not concentrated in a handful of elite institutions.

Comments made by several editors revealed the importance they attached to academic reputation. For example, the psychology editor at Apple said, "Sure, if I get a project that has a Harvard letterhead, I'll handle it with dispatch . . . I might even take it home to read that night. There's no question but that someone from Harvard has an inherent advantage over others. Why shouldn't they?" The editor-in-chief at a competing scholarly house quipped, "People at good

schools write good books, and people at poor schools write
bad books or no books at all. It's that simple. You can't go
wrong publishing the books of people at the elite schools."

The majority of editors at Apple and Plum nevertheless
asserted that few decisions are made solely on the basis of
where an author is currently employed. Most editors felt that
academic credentials are increasingly difficult to evaluate.
One editor noted that the majority of graduates who remain
in academia received their Ph.D.s from elite schools. He
commented, "It used to be the case that the best ones stayed
at home or went to other top schools, but that's no longer the
case. The academy is unable to properly reward young people
these days. Heck, I know prize-winning authors teaching at
unknown schools." The contraction of university faculties
and the simultaneous increase in the number of new Ph.D.s
have greatly affected the academic job market. As a consequence, some editors have adjusted their thinking about
academic prestige. The following comments by the editor-in-
chief of a major university press illustrate this:

> As a matter of fact, our director was asking me about that just
> yesterday, whether I paid attention to what college the letter
> came from. It used to be that that was a fairly good criterion of
> what you could expect, because obviously so many of these
> places . . . well, it isn't that they may not be good colleges, but
> many of these colleges are teaching institutions almost exclu-
> sively; and they may be fine teaching institutions, but they
> don't allow much time for, or do anything to encourage,
> research and writing, and so they don't support this kind of
> thing. But the way things are now, people are getting jobs
> where they can find them. So I am reading a lot more carefully
> something recommended to me that comes from some college
> I've never heard of.

Academic staus is important because both graduates and
holders of positions in elite schools have much greater access
to effective socialization; that is, they are more confident,
they will probably write better letters of introduction, and
they will have better contacts, all because they have learned
the ropes from people who already know "what matters."

Caplovitz (1963) has made use of the concept "effective scope" in illustrating that the poor have a more restricted life-space; as consumers, for example, they are psychologically less mobile and more inhibited than well-to-do consumers; the latter, who can shop in a wider radius of stores, are not subjects of a captive market, to which sellers offer inferior goods at inflated prices. More generally, we know that, in the world at large, class position influences the degree of knowledge about, and the use people make of, labor- and money-saving opportunities. It is no accident that scholars in elite schools have a more "effective scope" than their counterparts at less prestigious schools, and they also develop a greater number of "weak ties" than do authors from the less elite schools. As Rose Coser (1984) argues, one's position in the social structure influences both the number and quality of opportunities one is afforded. Individuals with many weak ties (e.g., acquaintances as opposed to close friends) are far more likely to be involved in networks that enable them to contact an editor directly. Such individuals will have better access to information, and, as a result of their opportunities and enhanced awareness, they will gain experience and become more cosmopolitan (Granovetter 1974; Knoke and Burt 1982).[12]

Literary agents are little used in scholarly publishing. The stakes are small and unappealing, and agents lack the specialized knowledge needed to perform a bridging function between academic authors and scholarly editors. This function is served by a different group of intermediaries: an editor's friends; formal advisers to a house, who are paid an annual retainer; series editors; and senior academics, who play the roles of patron and broker. Just as authors located at the more prestigious universities are more likely to be called on to review manuscripts and to serve as formal advisers or series editors, so are brokers and patrons more likely to be located at top schools. Stephen Cole (1978) argues that academic sponsorship is primarily important in obtaining one's first job; from then on it has little effect. My observations at Apple and Plum made it clear that sponsorship can work in other ways as

well. It enhances the contacts and access enjoyed by the
graduate students and junior faculty who are members of the
same department as a senior broker or patron. This, in turn,
can raise the junior person's visibility and enhance the perceived quality of his or her work. This is critical for two
reasons. First, the greater the collegial recognition of a scientist's early work, the greater is the probability that he or she
will continue to be productive. Second, "successful scientists
are more likely to have their work perceived favorably independent of the content of the work" (S. Cole 1978:174–81).
Of course, sponsorship can be handled adroitly or poorly.
Some high-placed academics try to use their connections with
publishers as a way of paying off debts to students and colleagues. Others indiscriminately praise everything they refer.
A good editor learns which academics are reliable and which
ones' recommendations must be discounted.

The editors at Apple and Plum, who received unsolicited
material from scholars at prestigious universities almost every
day, were very selective; only a few of these projects were
accepted for publication. This suggests that young academics
at elite schools who, lacking contacts or connections, submit
unsolicited materials are treated much the same as anyone
else. A Chicago or Harvard letterhead alone does not guarantee publication. The social sciences editor at Plum, responding to a question I asked about a manuscript from a Harvard
junior faculty member, said, "Something must be wrong with
the guy. Doesn't he have any colleagues who think highly
enough of his work to recommend it to me?" The psychology
editor at Apple voices a similar concern in response to my
query about a manuscript from a young scholar at a top
school: "I know plenty of people there, and no one mentioned him to me; so I have to wonder."

Several things may limit an author's access to a high-quality
publisher such as Apple or Plum. For the most part, the
degree of access that authors enjoy depends on their location
in social networks. Academic status is important because it
enhances an author's ability to make personal contact with an
editor. Interestingly, academics at nonelite schools in the

New York metropolitan area are also more likely to be personally acquainted with someone in book publishing. Although I did not collect data directly on this, it is my impression that authors who teach in schools in the New York area have better chances of getting published than do authors from top schools located in America's heartland. Academic status can be important, but first-name familiarity with an editor is even more advantageous. Yet it is not surprising that people from elite schools are more likely to be found in the "right" queues.

Commercial Concerns

Financial and marketing considerations are involved in all publishing decisions. However much authors may regret it, the fact is that publishing is not an eleemosynary institution. Nevertheless, pecuniary concerns were not paramount at Apple or Plum, for two reasons. First, a financial evaluation was frequently colored by an author's location in the queuing system. If an expensive project came in via the lowly regarded queue, its chances were nil; but if an expensive project came from the high-priority queues, it would not be rejected out of hand. Editors would look for various ways of reducing the costs. Second, in scholarly and monograph publishing, most of the books are relatively inexpensive to produce; thus, in contrast to other branches of publishing, a different set of considerations—academic merit, originality, the quality of the reviews—may ultimately determine a book's success in the marketplace. For scholarly publishers, a book that sells well is almost always a success. This is not typically the case in trade or text publishing, where the various costs of doing a book—author's advance, size or print run, and promotion budget—may be so large as to render even a book with healthy sales unprofitable.

In comparison with trade and text houses, members of the sales or marketing staff at scholarly presses have little voice in the decision to accept a manuscript. One university press editor, who was delighted with this state of affairs, said:

> I'd like to stress the fact that most university presses really
> care a lot more about the quality of a book than its sales. I
> think most people in university presses are really enjoying
> themselves . . . because our jobs aren't dependent in such a
> hard fashion on sales . . . we don't have that much pressure,
> and that makes me much more comfortable.[13]

The attitude that the staff of trade and text houses must
take is quite different. Some editors question whether it is
responsible of them to push for books that marketing or sales
personnel are opposed to publishing on commercial grounds.
Roger Straus III, once a director of marketing but now an
editorial director, states the problem as follows:

> To publish a book that a number of us are infatuated with
> without making any marketing commitment to it is a real
> problem. I think in the long run you aren't doing yourself or
> the author any favor. If you are going to publish a book, you
> have to put a certain amount of money behind it or it's going to
> be a problem. So very often what I will say is, "Hey, we love
> the book, but can we envision making the kind of effort that
> will be necessary to secure the audience, and, if we don't, are
> we just going to lose the author, who'll be angry that we didn't
> do an aggressive enough job on his or her work?"[14]

In the course of our general study of book publishing, my
colleagues and I asked a sample of some 130 editors how
important a criterion, in deciding to publish a book, was the
profit anticipated from its sales in its first year of publication.
Almost 60 percent of the college text editors said that this was
a critical factor in the decision to publish; approximately a
third of the trade editors noted that first-year sales were
critical, but less than 20 percent of the scholarly editors listed
this factor as important. Trade editors were most concerned
about a book's subsidiary-rights potential. In general, we
found university-press editors least concerned about commercial prospects and scholarly editors at for-profit presses
somewhat more concerned but not as markedly so as trade
and text editors. This does not mean that money is unimportant to scholarly editors but that, in defining commercial
success, they take a much more long-term view than their

counterparts in other sectors of the book trade. Given the steady backlist sales of houses like Apple, this view seems appropriate.

At both Apple and Plum, most financial determinations, such as royalty rate, print run, and advertising budget, are made according to a standard format. Advances were rarely larger than $2,000 at Apple; at Plum they were less than $500 when they were given at all.[15] As a result, books are not often rejected because they are too expensive to do. As one Apple editor stated, when I asked him how he handled financial negotiations with a prospective author:

> My experience is that it's harder to convince the house than the author. Almost every author is *delighted* to be published by Apple. I therefore do the best I think that I can for the author when I make the proposal. If the author objects when the contract arrives, I'll see what I can do. It's often easier for me to get a change through then than it would have been to propose higher terms initially. Some editors may work the other way—they find out what the author will take, then make the proposal accordingly. I'm interested in getting the books I want and minimizing in-house hassles.

Apple and Plum authors can—very occasionally—through their affiliation with private foundations or research institutes, offer subventions that will help defray the costs of publication.[16] Obviously, editors find these helpful. Editors also keep their eyes open for books that are inexpensive to produce. Sometimes, for example, British publishing houses will sell the foreign rights to books originally done in England, and the economies realized on these projects are often very inviting. A less common example involves books that are short and by authors who are without previous publishing experience. Generally these are young people, and the book in question is often their dissertation. They are happy to be published and not overly concerned if various economizing steps are taken. Such ways of cutting costs include a lower royalty rate; omitting a jacket for the book; and requiring the author to submit the manuscript on computer tape, coded for typesetting.

Summary

In many respects, Apple and Plum compete for the same audience; but the competition is not of the zero-sum kind. I know of no evidence that suggests that a consumer of scholarly books buys only x dollars' worth of them and so must compare the latest releases of Apple, Plum, and other scholarly presses in order to decide which books to purchase. I do not imagine that a potential consumer considers whether a new book from Apple at $16.00 is a better buy than a new title by Plum at $20.00. I assume that most scholarly readers are motivated to purchase a new book because they read a prominent review, receive a recommendation from a reliable friend, or peruse a publisher's catalogue or exhibit and find a book that interests them. Apple and Plum can pursue a similar audience (although, as noted in chapter 2, the houses point in different directions along a continuum of audience size: Apple aims more broadly; Plum has a more specialized focus), but there are important differences in how they choose to market their books and—what is more germane to the topic at hand—how they decide which books to publish.

So far I have drawn a comparison of the two houses: Apple is smaller and more informally organized, and its editorial search methods resemble a garbage-can process, although the "stuff" that enters the garbage can is strongly shaped by tradition, external ties, and network relations; Plum is much larger, more formal, and more routinized, and it uses a strategy of clientelization, or reliance on a few series editors, to reduce uncertainty and make key choices. In the operation of the queuing systems we see that similar differences crop up: the authors who receive the most attention at Apple have either a close personal relation with an editor or an ongoing contact with the house. At Plum, contact with an editor helps improve one's chances, but the highest priority is accorded to the recommendations of series editors. Most of Plum's publications result from the efforts of their series editors, who serve boundary-spanning roles by virtue of their positions of prominence in academia. Plum Press also frequently publishes the proceedings of conferences and symposia; it also makes use of its journals to help with the acquisition of manuscripts. Furthermore, no projects are ever published without at least one review by a scientist in the manuscript's field. In short, Plum has successfully worked out a publishing strategy in which a few academics are coopted and utilized to perform a great many tasks for the press. In return, these academics enhance their own status and influence, in addition to receiving a modest financial compensation.

At Apple Press, editors more frequently rely on their own contacts, and they consult with academics, who then evaluate how good a choice the editor has made. Reviewers play a less significant role in the decision to publish than they do at Plum Press. Nevertheless, Apple Press often calls on its own authors for advice and assistance in promoting its books. The publishing philosophy at Apple is to create strong and lasting associations with eminent scholars, who then "spread the gospel," in the editor-in-chief's words, by directing potential authors to the press and speaking favorably about the press's publications.

At each house the particular queuing process acted both as a sorting system and as a means for organizing obligations. The odds in favor of publication for those in the lowly regarded queue were very slim, although, as a result of the efforts of the series editors, Plum paid more attention to young unpublished authors. But even authors in the highly regarded queues had no guarantee of publication. It is at this point that timing, finances, and academic status come into play, along with the concerns, discussed in chapter 4, about how well a manuscript fits with the backlist and with the house's image. The queuing system allows certain manuscripts to receive more attention than others; but once they have been scrutinized, the fate of these manuscripts depends on a considerable range of historical, network, and financial factors.

We can see that many aspects of the editorial process—in particular, editorial search behavior, the employment of series and journals editors, the use of outside readers, and the operation of the queuing systems—are integrally tied to the structure of the American academy. The motives and career-related needs of academic authors form a fragile alliance with the organizational demands of scholarly publishers. In the final chapter, I will discuss some of the effects that the specific publishing practices of Apple and Plum have on developments in social science research. More generally, I will discuss the interrelations between scholarly publishers and academics and the reciprocal influences they have on each other. I will also draw several theoretical implications from this comparative case study and discuss their relevance in light of recent debates in organization theory.

6

IMPLICATIONS

This comparative case study has illustrated the many ways in which organizations interact with their environments. In this concluding chapter, I will suggest that much of contemporary organization theory is not very helpful in accounting for the kinds of behaviors I observed at Apple and Plum. All theories are, of course, abstractions from reality, and it might be argued that networks of cooperation and affiliation are too informal and complex to model. Theories typically simplify complex social realities in the interest of parsimony. But such simplification runs the risk of ignoring precisely the aspects of reality that are the most crucial. For example, the "balance of payments" between Apple or Plum and its environment is not an easily quantifiable one-way exchange. Transactions at both of these publishing houses are highly interdependent, embedded in a history of previous associations, and guided by norms of reciprocity. Prestige is frequently the currency of exchange, and at times it even seems that editors and authors form their own quasi-organization, which is linked to the market as well as to the production and business side of the house.

I will also argue that the case studies I have presented here have a broader relevance, beyond simply helping us to understand the operation of two scholarly publishing houses; for other kinds of industries exhibit similar patterns of embedded relationships with their environments. But we know very

little about how the environments of organizations are organized. I will briefly compare scholarly publishing with public
television in order to show how variation in the collective
organization of environments influences the internal workings of firms. I will then conclude by discussing the ways in
which the organization of scholarly publishing creates an
opportunity structure for scholars and, in doing so, restricts
access to some and opens doors for others.

The Shortcomings of Orthodoxy

To a certain extent, the editorial departments of publishing
houses interpret and shape the environment in which they
operate. They try to define the reality of the external world
(this they do by searching for manuscripts in particular places,
not universally), and they socially affirm its salient features
(by publishing and promoting certain authors and by using
them as reviewers, they reinforce the external world they
have defined). Yet, from another perspective, these editorial
departments represent exogenous social forces contained
within the formal organization of the publishing house. This
dialectical process, between editors as agents of the publishing house and editors as friends and supporters of authors,
reflects the manner in which organizations incorporate certain aspects of their environment—certain techniques,
knowledge, and skills. These aspects are not invented inside
the organization but instead are brought within its purview,
sometimes by someone occupying a formal role, such as a
series editor or paid adviser, but, more commonly, by someone occupying an informal role, such as a talent scout or
friend and supporter.

Ongoing affiliations of this kind reflect more than a web of
resource dependencies. They are institutionally embedded,
often dating back to the earliest days of a company's history.
A good illustration of this historical linkage can be seen in the
genesis of Apple Press. It was established in the 1950s when a
noted academic contacted a friend who had an interest in
book publishing and suggested that translations of classic

works of European social science had a significant potential
for college-course adoption. Less than a year later, Apple
Press published its first list. Thus the recurring associations
between publishing houses and their friends and supporters
make it difficult to specify who is dictating what to whom. If it
is the publishers who are doing the controlling, they—the
controllers—routinely find themselves also being controlled.

I argue that close ties between a firm and its environment
are commonplace, even though a good deal of contemporary
organization theory downplays such ties.[1] The patterns of
behavior at Apple and Plum have meanings that exceed the
local circumstances that provide their occasion. Yet one
would not necessarily expect this if one used current organization theory as a guide.[2] Much of the current research in
organizational analysis is based on some or all of the following
simplifying assumptions: (1) the typical firm is organized as if
it were a single uncommonly intelligent individual; this implies a neat hierarchy, which can be modeled as a unitary
actor; (2) organizational boundaries are clear and distinct,
even though the actual line of demarcation between a firm
and its environment may be problematic, and boundaries
around task activities are drawn one way rather than another
in order to maximize efficiency; and (3) rational actors make,
in Simon's terminology, "intendedly rational," deliberate
decisions (Simon 1957). These assumptions, however useful
they have proved to be, may in fact not just simplify reality;
they may distort it and lead researchers in the wrong direction.

Two major organizational processes—the organization
and control of editorial activities and the making of editorial
decisions—have been analyzed in this book. Neither process
conforms to the neat assumptions of orthodox theory. With
respect to the organization of work, we have long known that
there is an informal organization that exists alongside the
formal hierarchy. Akerlof (1984:80) succinctly summarizes
decades of research on the sociology of work by noting that
these studies suggest "a complex equilibrium in which official
work rules are partially enforced, existing side by side with a

set of customs in the workplace which are at partial variance with the work rules, and some individual deviance from both the official work rules and the informal work norms." The data I have presented in chapter 4 go further and show that the customs found in the workplace are part of a complex game, some of whose rules stem from obligations owed to external constituencies. Much of the time, editors behave as if they are optimizing not their organization's welfare but their own or the welfare of the social networks to which they belong. Publishing executives are naturally aware of this, and they try to shape editorial behavior with a variety of unobtrusive controls. This is an ancient problem: formal controls get in the way of the motivation and flexibility that are needed in pursuing specific strategies; yet unobtrusive controls are never a complete proxy for authority (see White 1983). The premises that underlie informal controls are tied to the relational contexts in which the houses operate. Premises not only reflect patterns of exchange but also the history of a firm's previous associations. Premises may even be superstitious; fallacious rules of inference can persist for long periods of time. As a consequence, unobtrusive controls are nearly always incomplete, and many decisions are the result of complicated negotiations.

The discussion in chapter 5, of editorial decision-making as a means for organizing obligations, illustrates that the main point of a decision process may not always be a final choice. The central purpose may be the process itself. Orthodox decision theory assumes that no interdependencies affect decisions. Yet, clearly, people are resources for one another, and editors value certain persons more than others. Moreover, the limited information-processing abilities of editors force them to restrict their search for authors. The number of potential authors, reviewers, and advisers is finite, and the choice of one particular network of authors and sponsors not only may preclude the choice of other aspirants; it may serve to restrict access—either intentionally or unintentionally—to other potential authors. Information and opportunity, far from being open, are systematically distorted, depending on one's location in the social structure. Both houses adopted mechanisms to reduce the costs of search and to cope with uncertainty. Editors at Apple Press relied on extensive personal networks and on the loyalty of Apple authors. At Plum, external networks were brought inside the house and formalized in the person of series editors. These different arrangements are, in a sense, functional equivalents: not only do they allow editors to economize on search efforts; they are also means for introducing continuity and trust into business relations.

Organizations were never the simple entities that our theories suggest, and they are decreasingly so. The boundaries between firms and their environments have become increasingly blurry. Internally, firms have become more complex by introducing into their formal structure such market processes as profit centers and transfer pricing (see Eccles and White 1984). Current theory is also poorly designed to deal with the interconnectedness that characterizes the reality of organizational life. More broadly, the institutional foundations of organizational life remain largely unexamined. There is a great variety of such institutional supports, including trust, personal networks, norms of reciprocity, reputational effects, and tacit collusion, to name but a few. More recently, however, researchers have found that dense patterns of association between organizations and their environments are common in high-technology industries (Rogers and Larsen 1984), defense contracting (Stinchcombe 1983), cultural industries (Coser, Kadushin, and Powell 1982; Faulkner 1983), small businesses (Macaulay 1963), and family firms (Ben-Porath 1980).

What is striking about scholarly publishing is the degree of intimacy between the academic community and scholarly publishers. Personal friendships and extended networks among authors and publishers generate strongly defined standards of behavior. Bonds of allegiance shape the processes of access and discovery. Networks of personal relations are also vital to economic success. And, while competition among firms does influence the success or failure of particular publishing houses, these selection pressures are dampened by the dense associational ties and personal relations that support almost all publishing transactions.

The Organization of Environments

To illustrate the nature and the strength of the association between the social science community and Apple and Plum, it is useful to compare scholarly publishing with a somewhat similar institution: public television. Scholarly publishing is much less commercial than trade publishing, and competition among scholarly houses is frequently prestige-driven. Similarly, public television is widely seen as a less commercial alternative to network television. The stated mission of public television is to offer the viewing public higher-quality and more diverse programming. Indeed, John Ryden, director of Yale University Press, has remarked that "university press publishing is rather analogous to public television. We have somewhat the same mission."[3]

Nevertheless, a comparison of the relationships between scholarly publishers and their external constituents with the connections between the employees of a public television station and their external stakeholders reveals a sharp contrast. Exchanges between a scholarly publishing house and its clients are characterized by continuity and a commonality of interests. In public television, the demands of external constituents are typically in conflict not only with one another but with the interests of the television station. Transactions lack continuity—so much so that one public TV executive lamented "the sad fact that nothing that is successful on public TV endures" (Powell and Friedkin 1983:434).

The similarities in the mission and goals of public television and scholarly publishing mask significant differences in the nature of organization-environment relations. These differences require some description and elaboration. It is critical that we recognize that, although organization-environment relations may be a crucial factor in shaping the internal workings of a firm, environments differ greatly in the way they are organized. The consequences, as we shall see, can be significant.

A scholarly publishing house such as Apple or Plum receives its potential "products" from academic authors in search of a publisher. Authors' outputs are publishers' inputs. We know that these "suppliers" have varying rates of success, depending on the strength of their previous affiliation with Apple or Plum. The raw materials go through an editorial winnowing process, and a small percentage are selected for further review. For assistance in evaluating these manuscripts, editors call on academics, particularly those who have been published by the firm. If a manuscript is approved, it is put into production, and, upon publication, Apple and Plum again call on key members of the scholarly community for help in promoting the product. Academics provide blurbs and quotes for use in advertising copy and on the book's jacket. In fact, most authors actually begin the marketing of their book while they are in the process of writing it. Typically, academics ask their colleagues, members of their invisible colleges, to comment on their work in progress, thus helping to promote the book even before it is finished.

A great majority of the books published by scholarly houses are purchased either by members of the academic community or by university libraries. The latter are generally overwhelmed by the flood of new titles released every month. They are guided in their purchasing decisions by the advice of professors at their own universities and by book reviews in scholarly and library journals, the majority of which are written by academics. In sum, it is a community of shared interests: the suppliers, the consumers, and the gatekeepers of scholarly publishing are all members of the academic community. Moreover, inside the publishing houses, the decisions about what to accept are made by a very small number of people, each of whom is closely allied with certain key members of the academic community.

Economic exchange between members of the academy and scholarly publishers takes place within a normative context in which reciprocity, prestige, and career advancement are crucial considerations. Transactions are seldom isolated or atomistic; they commonly fit into ongoing patterns of obligation. The mutuality of interests between authors and publishers can be seen in both the sale of individual titles and in academic promotion decisions. The opinions that academics have with regard to particular books are important to university librarians, as well as to local booksellers. Both service the university community by distributing the products of scholarly publishers. Similarly, reputation and opinion also matter a great deal in academic promotion decisions; such evaluations are based on a candidate's publication record, and if the candidate's publishers are prestigious, that fact can figure prominently in any review.

Public television is also interpenetrated by external constituents, and, as in scholarly publishing, the activities and products of a public television station are a vehicle for the expression of the interests of key outsiders.[4] But we do not find shared understandings or a congruence between the interests of outside stakeholders and the goals of the organization. Instead, we find plural sovereignty, a situation rife with conflict, in which interests diverge and multiple incompatible demands go unresolved. In public television we observe little that is comparable to the close fit between the organizational goals of scholarly publishers and the professional goals of the academy. To demonstrate this point, I treat public television programs as the outputs of a large public television station and discuss the various inputs that are needed to produce a program and the way these resources are transformed by the station into a prime-time show that is disseminated to a national viewing audience.[5]

Public television is a peculiar hybrid, operating under both economic constraints and political control. A large public television station, such as WNET-TV in New York City, is a public agency, because nearly one-third of its operating budget comes from federal, state, and municipal governments, but it also receives as much as 25 percent of its financial support from its members. As in many voluntary nonprofit organizations, there is an ongoing tension between the need for promotional events, such as membership drives and auctions, and the possibility of so irritating supporters that they become disaffected. The remainder of a station's operating expenses, and the *majority* of the funding for nationally distributed programming, comes from corporate underwriters, private foundations, other public TV stations (who purchase the shows produced by the large stations), and the National Endowment for the Arts and the Humanities.

Programs come from a variety of sources, both within and outside the boundaries of a television station. The programming department generates ideas for programs. At the same time, it actively searches for suitable projects created by independent filmmakers, foreign broadcasters, and other public television stations. These outside sources also frequently contact public TV stations, seeking either to sell broadcast rights to their work or to negotiate a joint venture or cooperative financing for a project they are working on or have in mind.

The sources of program ideas may be diverse, but none will ever reach the television screen without financial backing. Public television stations have very limited capital of their own, and even a successful long-term show, such as *Great Performances*, requires new funding each year. Not only is money scarce, but external funding relationships can be unpredictable. A great deal of time and energy is spent by station executives in developing, maintaining, and smoothing relationships with key funding sources. The process of obtaining program-specific financing is labor-intensive and lengthy, sometimes taking several years. Proposals for federal grants usually require review by a panel of experts, and a consensus must be arrived at before final approval is received.

The interests of various funding sources are often at odds with one another. Although the federal government has been the most important continuous source of revenue for public TV, the history of federal support has been marked by political interference and budgetary uncertainty. State governments, through both overt and implied means, place strong constraints on local public-affairs programming.[6] Private foundations were once the largest source of funding for public television, but that support has declined sharply over the past decade. Today, foundation money goes to specific programs; this support has played a crucial role in bringing innovative, "risky" programming to public TV. As foundation support waned and federal money became entangled in political debates and budgetary battles, public broadcasting turned to large corporations for program-underwriting. Although a mere handful of large firms provides most of the corporate donations, which together constitute less than 15 percent of the total budget for public television, corporate underwriting is vital: approximately half of the nationally distributed programs are underwritten in part or in full by corporate sponsors. Corporations naturally prefer highly visible, splendidly produced, noncontroversial shows that reflect favorably on the sponsor.

In sum, both the sources of programming ideas and the financial support needed to translate ideas into viable projects are highly dispersed. The process by which ideas and financial backing are linked is ambiguous and politicized. A former president of the Public Broadcasting System has stated, "Every source of money is tainted. With federal funds we worry about becoming a governmental broadcasting arm. Corporate money makes you steer away from controversy. Membership money means you cater to upper-middle-class viewers. The saving grace is that we have diversified sources."[7]

Once funding for a program has been obtained, the station staff builds a temporary "organization" to produce it. This production team includes actors and actresses, the writing and filming crew, and the supporting staff. Because funding is always meager, considerable opportunity exists for differences of opinion to emerge among the members of this heterogeneous group. Program distribution is a further complication. The 300-odd PBS stations bid on programs offered by large public TV stations and independent producers. The selection process is slow and conservative, and new shows face formidable barriers. Eventually a program is ready for national broadcast. For a major series, this entire sequence of events can take a number of years. Just prior to the scheduled broadcast, the program is made available to television critics, whose reviews then appear in a large number of newspapers around the country. The reviewers seldom concern themselves with the problems of financing, production, and distribution. Like the national viewing audience, the critics are concerned with the merits of the final product. This cycle of production is constant. While not every program involves so complicated a process, the great majority of programs that are aired nationally between 8:00 and 11:00 P.M. do.

A public television station represents an assortment of mini-organizations, each made up of staff members who have their own priorities and varying amounts of allegiance to public TV. Each internal group has a different set of tasks and develops links to different parts of the environment. The environment of a public television station includes a number of large and powerful actors—major corporations, federal and state governments—as well as smaller but also influential constituents—private foundations, the station's members, the viewing audience, critics, and filmmakers. Collectively, these external groups are very loosely coupled and have few interests in common. The process of creating a television program is administratively complex and requires great skill at maneuvering through a minefield of obstacles.

Scholarly publishing and public television thus illustrate the varying ways in which the relational context of organizational environments may be organized. The environments of organizations differ in both the extent of their formal organization and the amount of consensus that is shared among external constituencies. This argument builds on the primary insight of industrial organization economics: the behavior of a firm can depend crucially on the organization of the industry of which it is a party. A key task for organization theory is, first, to extend the observation that many, if not most, organizations are embedded in a larger system of relations and then to begin comparative analyses of the collective properties of environments. We need to move beyond general characterizations of environments as either scarce or munificent and, instead, develop ways of specifying how environments are organized.[8]

A focus on variation in the collective organization of environments may enable us to better explain differences in internal organizational structures, processes, and performance. For example, editors at Apple and Plum had very high rates of success in getting projects approved, while the staff at WNET had low rates of internal approval. Obviously, the difference is explained in part by factors of risk and cost. That is, a scholarly book is neither expensive nor risky, while a public TV program is costly and may be controversial as well. Differential rates of approval also reflect the availability of resources. Less obvious, however, is the importance of patterns of exchange. The acquisition of resources at Apple and Plum takes place in the context of ongoing social relationships marked by loyalty and reciprocity. Both parties gain from the transaction. In public television, the acquisition of some key resources is mandated by federal budgetary allocations. Other resource exchanges are seldom reciprocal. One party (usually the public television station, except in the case of relations with independent filmmakers) is in a strongly dependent position. Transactions are politicized and often coercive; there is little loyalty or continuity. Hence, decision-makers have few commonly held premises to guide their decisions. Every decision seems unique, and it hinges on a particular and idiosyncratic mix of participants, resources, and constraints.

A comparison of Plum Press and WNET in terms of their formal organization is also illuminating. Both employ between 400 and 500 persons. Plum's annual sales in 1982 exceeded $60 million, and WNET's 1982–83 operating budget was of comparable size. Yet Plum has but three departments and one policy-making committee. In contrast, WNET has four divisions, each with six to eight departments, and it has several major policy-making committees. One might try to explain this difference by pointing to the more varied tasks that WNET must perform. But that explanation would not be sufficient. Organizations are constantly in search of external support and legitimacy. When financial support and much-needed credibility are provided by a dispersed and frag-mented environment, organizations respond with a varied mix of procedures and policies. Each response may in itself be formally rational, but collectively the responses will exhibit little internal coherence. Organizations located in environ-ments in which conflicting demands are made upon them will be especially likely to generate complex organizational struc-tures with disproportionately large administrative compo-nents and multiple boundary-spanning units (see Scott and Meyer 1983, especially pp. 140–49).

Organizations respond to the inconsistent claims gener-ated by pluralistic environments by incorporating structures and policies designed to please and report to a variety of organized constituencies. As a result, structural complexity increases, and the criteria for determining success become less clear. Thus it is not surprising that WNET is structurally more complex than Plum Press and that its control sytems are more cumbersome. Nevertheless, we should not ignore the tradeoffs inherent in these arrangements. The centers of au-thority and power in WNET's environment are fragmented. Control is primarily financial as opposed to control over the content of programs (although, clearly, the two are somewhat related [see Powell and Friedkin 1983]; in general, when the funding source is highly centralized, a greater degree of con-trol can be exercised over programs). Not surprisingly, indi-vidual corporations speak with a more unified voice than federal agencies do. Yet we find nothing comparable to the readers' reports, discussed in chapter 4, in which Apple and Plum authors suggested that manuscripts under review did not correspond to the style of previously published books. This is direct substantive control.

There is yet another and even more consequential tradeoff. Incongruent demands may generate complex re-porting and accounting systems, but they also encourage strategic behavior. Elsewhere I have documented how a pub-lic TV station is able to satisfy funding sources on a partial, ad

hoc basis by playing one funding source off against another
(see Powell and Friedkin 1983:431–34). In scholarly publishing such opportunism is very difficult. Social ties among
houses and authors are clustered and relatively exclusive, as
opposed to the dispersed and politicized relationships common in public television. As a result, scholarly editors know
that substitution is not easy; not only is it both difficult and
unethical to play one group off against another, but news of
any malfeasance travels quickly through academic networks.
This is even more important when one considers the quasi-
moral character of editor-author relationships, many of
which are close and enduring. The distinction between work
and social life is hard for many editors to draw. This makes it
all the more difficult to act strategically and treat authors as
impersonal providers of supplies that vary with respect to
both quality and marketability.

Access and Networks

What are the consequences of the close alignment between
scholarly publishers and certain influential academics? What
effect do these relationships have on the long-term health of
scholarly publishing houses?

It is my impression, based on hundreds of conversations,
that most academic authors regard the publishing process as
an open market. Academics submit their manuscripts and
assume that publishers will evaluate the merits of their work
as capably and equitably as possible. The process departs
somewhat from the submission of an article to a professional
journal—the author is not anonymous, nor are the initial
reviews done by an author's peers—but the evaluation is not
thought to be fundamentally dissimilar. In contrast, editors
conceive of the process in a completely different light. The
editorial task is like combing a beach that is covered with
rocks and shells of different shapes and colors in search of a
small quota of gems that nicely complement one's existing
collection. It is impossible to search widely or thoroughly;
instead, the skilled collector will learn, over time, to look

along the high-tide line near a certain jetty after a heavy storm.

There are a number of good organizational reasons for editors to restrict access to potential exchange partners. Searching for all the alternatives is a costly process. A system of priorities, such as a work queue, is an efficient means for dealing with overload. There are lower risks involved in dealing with known partners because the transaction is grounded in personal relationships. Recurrent exchanges reaffirm friendships. Trust and reliability are marvelously efficient lubricants to economic transactions. There are, however, drawbacks associated with this course of action. While the major burden is borne by the authors who lack access, the publishing house may suffer as well. Strong, established social networks can create a kind of social inertia, a rigidity that is analogous to a type of brand loyalty that precludes consideration of other, perhaps better, products. This social inertia has two related costs, and these accrue over time. Exclusive, repeat trading can result in parochialism, that is, an intellectual or ideological homogenization of a publisher's list. Authors with different theoretical viewpoints may either lack access to the house or choose not to contact it because its list has become so strongly identified with a particular type of scholarship. An editor's networks can also age or ossify. As an editor grows older, so does his or her network of authors and advisers. If this network has been tightly bounded and entry to it has been severely restricted, the editor may find it very difficult to learn about, or to acquire, work that is new and on disciplinary frontiers. Research in industrial organization has shown that it usually takes some kind of exogenous shock to jolt organizations out of a pattern of repeat purchasing (see Granovetter 1983a:34–37); change is seldom sought by the organization itself. Moreover, given the important resources provided by trading networks, changes that might create disaffection or withdrawal of legitimacy may be very difficult for the organization to pursue (see Hannan and Freeman 1984).

A variety of mechanisms limit an author's opportunity for

first- or even secondhand contact with an editor at a publishing house. There is also considerable variation within the academic community with regard to the willingness of prominent scholars to serve as brokers or patrons for their younger colleagues and thereby provide them with contact with a major publisher. Different degress of access also result from the differential location of individuals within a network of relations. Other things being equal, academics at geographically peripheral universities will have less access, as will scholars located at less prestigious universities. An important exception to this rule is that academics at less prestigious universities in the New York metropolitan area will profit from their geographic proximity to Apple and Plum. Another exception is that even at the most well-connected or prestigious universities the formal structure of academic organization may provide some individuals with more opportunities for access than it provides to others.

What are the implications of restricted access in scholarly publishing? Peter Marsden (1983:704) argues that, when the range of choice for some actors is restricted, they can be forced to exchange resources at a price less than market value because of their lack of alternatives. He then goes on to note that networks distort market value and give a higher exchange value to resources controlled by well-connected actors than these actors would receive under conditions of unrestricted access. Such a process could lead to the creation of a binary opportunity structure, with the rich getting richer and the poor getting poorer. In contrast to Apple and Plum, the leading journals in the social sciences are more pluralistic; they publish articles by authors from a wider variety of academic institutions.[9] This suggests that well-connected academics can easily publish their books, including books that may fall below the normal standards upheld by Apple or Plum, but that academics who unfortunately lack access may be forced to stake their careers and promotion prospects on the publication of journal articles.

Is the pattern of restricted access to Apple and Plum a less than optimal situation for many social scientists? Or, as Morton (1982:863) has argued, am I conflating concern over how manuscripts are evaluated at two publishing houses with concern over the control of the flow of ideas in the social sciences? Many editors contend that, since they determine only what their own house will publish, they are not the arbiters of a manuscript's ultimate fate. In part, this is correct. The number of publication outlets in the social sciences is not shrinking; indeed, the number of specialized scholarly publishers has burgeoned.[10] And the growth in the number of journals and of annual reviews, which bridge journal articles and monograph-length studies, has even outpaced the growth in the number of books published each year. These new publications seem to spawn like mushrooms after a good rain. Such developments in scholarly publishing are in part isomorphic with trends in the social sciences. Research is increasingly sophisticated. Written work now includes charts, tables, graphs, and mathematical notations. There has been a rapid expansion of subfields in the social sciences, and the rise of applied social research has grown apace. The primary danger is certainly not shrinkage of publication outlets. Instead, overproduction appears to be a greater cause for concern. Indeed, it often seems that the many new social science publications are not so much being read as received.

Despite the proliferation of scholarly publishing houses, it is my strong impression that the reputation and influence of the most prestigious ones have grown. This process operates as a contrast effect: in the midst of a large number of houses that are somewhat difficult to distinguish from one another, firms such as Apple and Plum stand out. The power of reputation depends in part on whether a good reputation is hard to obtain and in part on whether many people seek to acquire it (see Kreps and Wilson 1982). My evidence for this argument is fragmentary but strongly suggestive. For example, despite the number of new entrants, annual sales at Apple and Plum have outpaced both inflation and the overall growth rate for scientific and professional books. Interviews with a number of university librarians and booksellers have provided ample illustration of the power of reputational effects. One librarian responsible for her library's acquisitions said, "There are too many new publications to keep track of . . . basically I order the great majority of new titles from five or six of the best houses and wait for reviews or requests from the faculty before ordering other books." (Apple was included in her list of the "best" houses.) As a result, more options can actually lead to less-informed choices. Conversations with the book-review editors at a number of academic journals and journals of opinion also suggest that prestige is a valuable currency. A publisher's logo is particularly important to the fortunes of books by little-known authors. The books of highly visible scholars are typically sent out for review regardless of who their publisher is. But when the book-review editor does not know an author's work, the prestige of the publisher can be a major factor in whether or not the book receives a review. Thus, although acquisition editors do not actually determine a manuscript's ultimate fate, the fact that a prestigious house has selected a manuscript for publication can make an important difference. A book is more likely to be reviewed and to be purchased when it is published by an Apple or Plum press.

Journal articles are, to a certain extent, a barometer of an author's skill in a competition for scarce space. Books are different from journal articles: they are different in part because, while what one has to say is obviously important, whom one knows may determine one's success in getting into print. Books are also different in that we expect a good deal more of a book than of a journal article. A book should have a clear purpose—a detailed, systematic, coherent argument. A journal article need only report on a piece of research or a new idea. For most authors it is much harder to get a book published by Apple or Plum than it is to have an article accepted by a leading disciplinary journal. The publication system is a type of control system. A number of factors—prestige, tradition, and networks of affiliation—limit access and restrict diversity. Both Apple and Plum must, of course, maintain reputations that are reasonable proxies for reality. Otherwise the prestige system collapses.

The principal threat to such houses as Apple and Plum is

the possibility that their networks may either ossify or become too specialized. Many scientific fields are constantly fragmenting and splintering. Sometimes subgroups link up with subgroups in other disciplines; more commonly, subgroups become more and more specialized. This makes it all the more difficult to find books that appeal to broad audiences. The other danger is that, as the networks of authors and advisers age, the house finds that it increasingly lags behind new developments in research and theory. The house may experience a kind of downward mobility as its list becomes associated with the received wisdom of an old guard. The tighter and more homogeneous the circle of authors and advisers becomes, the more likely it is that this will happen. As Edward Shils (1981:213) has observed, "The existence of tradition is at least as much a consequence of limited power to escape from it as it is a consequence of a desire to continue and to maintain it."

I will not attempt to try to forecast the future direction of either Apple or Plum. It is my strong conviction, however, that both houses should be able to ride out periods of austerity. After all, both have prospered in the 1970s and early 1980s—hardly a prosperous era for higher education or for scientific research. Both have pursued strategies designed to lessen their dependence on external resources. Plum has healthy international sales and uses its serial publications as a means of convincing librarians to spend their shrinking budgets by filling out their many serial collections of Plum volumes. Apple continues to enjoy a strong identity, and its diverse list of scholarly, trade, and textbook titles allows it to keep a foot in several camps. The key issues for long-term viability are really perennial ones: how much autonomy will editors be afforded in the course of their duties, and how widely will the houses cast their nets in search of new authors? The answers to these questions will determine the future trajectory of both houses. Whatever that may be, the internal processes of decision-making and control are not likely to change in the immediate future.

APPENDIX

MANUSCRIPT ACQUISITION CODE
DEVELOPED FOR APPLE PRESS

Category 1.   Author initiated contact with the publishing house
  a. Over the transom—cold
  b. Over the transom with supporting materials (letters of reference, use of someone's name, etc.)
  c. Author approached editor/house at a convention, meeting, etc.
  d. Author contacted house cold—makes specific reference to backlist
  e. Author contacted house, but several houses are bidding for manuscript
  f. Other

Category 2.   Author had previous ties to the house or was referred by someone who had a connection with the house
  a. Referral from parent company
  b. Ongoing relationship between the house and an institution (e.g., a research institute or a private foundation)
  c. Serial arrangement (e.g., an annual publication or a referral by a series editor)
  d. Old contract—signed by a previous editor
  e. Paperback or new edition
  f. Referred by another publisher who recommends material

g. Referred by informal adviser or previous house author
h. Submitted by an agent known by the editor
i. Institution/foundation contacted house about manuscript by author affiliated with them, and they suggested a subvention to defray costs of publication
j. Author had previously been published by the house
k. Author had previously reviewed manuscripts for the house
l. Other

Category 3. Manuscript was acquired due to editor's initiative or contacts

a. Author is a personal friend of editor
b. The editor solicited the material either on the telephone, on a trip, or at a convention
c. The editor commissioned the book
d. An import purchased by the editor-in-chief or an editor on a trip abroad, or paperback rights to a book purchased from another American publisher
e. Editor signed the book at a previous house and brought it along to his or her new house
f. Author and editor had discussed manuscript, and the author sent material to the editor when it was completed
g. A friend told the editor about someone's work in progress, and the editor contacted the author
h. Serendipity—editor "stumbled upon" author
i. Other

Category 4. Insufficient information to categorize

NOTES

Notes to Introduction

1. In contrast to the dearth of research on book publishing, there are many studies of the policies and decision-making procedures used by the editors of scientific journals (see Crane 1967 and 1972; Zuckerman and Merton 1971; Schwartz 1975:63–87; Schwartz and Dubin 1978; and Lindsey 1978). The intellectual press is also a frequent target of scrutiny (see Lekachman 1965; Wrong 1970; Kadushin 1974; and Nobile 1974). The key difference between scholarly journals and scholarly books is that books are usually published with the aim of earning a profit. The decision to publish a book is never "pure"; it always rests on a guess about the market for a book as well as on an appraisal of the book's merits. Decisions about journal articles are more formalized and are subject to standards of scholarship, not market potential; as a result, the decision process is easier to study.

2. The weaknesses that characterize most company histories plague the majority of publishing-house histories as well. Many of them are commemorative works, produced to mark a festive occasion. Not surprisingly, the picture they present is rather bland and colorless. At worst, they are exercises in public relations. The best examples of this genre that I have encountered are Exman's (1967) account of Harper and Row, Ballou's (1970) history of the early years of Houghton Mifflin, and Sutcliffe's (1978) history of Oxford University Press.

3. The major histories of the publishing industry include Tebbel's (1972, 1975, 1978, 1981) extremely detailed volumes, Sheehan's (1952) account of publishing in the "Gilded Age," and Lehmann-Haupt's (1951) history of the making and selling of books in the United States from 1630 to 1950. Also valuable are Hart 1950, Madison 1966 and 1974, and Mott 1947.

4. It is not surprising that many of the people associated with the book trade tend to be self-conscious and self-reflexive. As a consequence, few of the memoirs and biographies of editors and publishers provide us with naive accounts. They are designed and intended as partisan documents. For sociologists, the real drawback of this kind of book, and of the company

history as well, is the scarcity of hard data; at best these books give figures on the extreme cases—the highest advance, the largest first printing, and so on. To my mind, Haydn's (1974) autobiography is in a class by itself. Also of interest are Canfield 1971, Cerf 1977, Commins 1978, and Gilmer 1970.

5. I have found Ross 1977, Braudy 1978, and Whiteside 1981 to be particularly useful.

6. Among the various books that deal with the business and financial aspects of book publishing, the following are among the most helpful: Miller 1949, Grannis 1967, Bailey 1970, Dessauer 1974, Balkin 1977, and Shatzkin 1982.

7. For a detailed discussion of the growth of various reading publics, see, in particular, Altick's (1957) entertaining study of reading habits in Victorian England and Watt's (1957) lovely account of the emergence of the novel in eighteenth-century England. Also see Bramstead 1964, James 1963, Q. D. Leavis 1965, and Ward 1974. On the social context in which literature is produced, see Bradbury 1971, Darnton 1971, Gedin 1977, Graña 1964, Sutherland 1976, and Williams 1961.

8. Among the few are Caplette 1981, Coser, Kadushin, and Powell 1982, Lane 1970 and 1975, Powell 1978b and 1982b, and Machlup and Leeson 1978.

9. Kurt Lewin (1951) coined the term "gatekeepers." He noted that information travels through particular communication channels and that specific areas within these channels function as gates, governed either by impartial rules or by individuals empowered to make the decision whether information should be let "in" or remain "out." Lewin's interest in the concept of gatekeeper did not spawn a great deal of subsequent research; however, one important line of inquiry has focused on newspaper editors. White (1950) discussed how a newspaper editor selects what news to print. His analysis of the reasons given for rejecting various types of news stories indicated how highly subjective and reliant on value judgments, based on the gatekeeper's own set of experiences, attitudes, and expectations, the selection of "news" actually is. Geiber (1964), in a review of his research on gatekeepers and civil-liberties news, on telegraph editors, and on editors of small Wisconsin dailies, argued that news is what newspapermen make it to be. Warren Breed's (1955) well-known contribution illustrated the ways in which newspapermen's reporting of the news is guided by the opinions and attitudes of their cohort of superiors and colleagues rather than by anticipation of their audience's reaction. Robert Darnton's beautiful article "Writing News and Telling Stories" (1975) is one of the best recent treatments of the subject. Also see Tuchman 1972, 1973, and 1978 and Roshco 1975.

10. Some attention is also given to the historical trends and large-scale changes that have marked both the past and more recent development of the book industry, but that is not the principal concern of this book. For a more thorough coverage of these issues, see Powell 1978a and Coser, Kadushin, and Powell 1982.

11. Unfortunately, we lack the data necessary to assess the accuracy of Sifton's claim. One of my more frustrating experiences was as a participant in the planning group for an issue of *Daedalus* (Winter, 1983) on the American reading public. While there was no shortage of opinions among

the planning group, there was an almost total absence of hard information on which to ground opinion. The small amount of empirical research that is available suggests that readership is not so much declining as shifting. Caplow et al. (1982:24–25), in their follow-up study of Middletown (Muncie, Indiana), find that the number of library cardholders declined from 48 percent of the population in 1925 to 31 percent in 1975. Yet the average number of books drawn annually by each cardholder increased from fifteen to twenty-two. In 1925, the public library was the principal supplier of books; in the 1970s, numerous bookstores and paperback racks offered the community additional access to books. Most important, library reading habits had shifted markedly: only one out of every six books checked out in the 1930s was nonfiction, but in the 1970s half of the books that circulated were nonfiction.

The Middletown data confirm my own opinion that fiction-reading has declined but that overall reading levels may possibly have increased as specialized reading tastes have burgeoned and popular nonfiction has become the major kind of recreational reading. Data that report the growth in the number of titles by subject area back up this view. For example, in the period 1955–75, there was a 212.7 percent increase in the number of books released annually. Yet, in this same period, the number of fiction titles increased by only 83.6 percent, while books on sports and recreation increased by 512.5 percent and titles in sociology and economics jumped by 1,167.3 percent. The subject categories are based on the Dewey system and are rather broad; still, there is a clear increase in nonfiction as compared to fiction. The information comes from *Social Indicators, 1976*, U.S. Dept. of Commerce, p. 516.

12. See Coser, Kadushin, and Powell 1982:chapter 4.

13. See ibid.: 112–17, 194–97.

Notes to Chapter One

1. Quoted from page 1 of the conference report, edited by Jean V. Naggar, *The Money Side of Publishing: Fundamentals for Non-Financial People* (New York: Association of American Publishers, 1976).

2. William Jovanovich, "The Structure of Publishing," a speech given in 1956 at the Center for Graphic Arts and Publishing of New York University; quoted in Tebbel 1981:722.

3. Quoted in Tony Schwartz, "A Publisher Who Sells Books," *New York Times Book Review*, December 9, 1979.

4. The 1959 and 1966 figures are from *Publishers Weekly*; the 1981 data are from the *U.S. Industrial Outlook*, (Washington, D.C.: U.S. Department of Commerce, 1983), pp. 7–6.

5. The data are from the final 1981 figures published in the Commerce Department's quarterly industry report, *Printing and Publishing*, vol. 22, no. 4, p. 7, edited by William S. Lofquist. The *U.S. Census of Manufactures* defines "company" as "a business organization consisting of one or more establishments under common ownership or control"; a "book-publishing establishment" is defined as "a place where books are published." There were 815 establishments in 1954; in 1977 there were 1,750.

6. The Authors Guild (1977a and b), a trade union representing American writers, has been a vociferous critic of these changes in the industry. It contends that:

> We have seen mergers in every imaginable permutation—hardcover houses merging with each other; hardcover houses merging with paperback houses; the combination thus formed being taken over, in turn, by huge entertainment complexes, involving radio-television networks and motion picture companies. And in some cases, perhaps most distressing of all, we have seen the business of choosing and purveying books, traditionally the province of more or less dedicated book men with one eye on profit and the other on literary and social values, falling under the control of businessmen with no prior interest in books—men, it has sometimes seemed to us, cursed like the Cyclops with having only a single eye, and that eye not trained on literary or social value but steadfastly on the bottom line of a company's financial statement. [Authors Guild 1977a]

In contrast, the industry's trade association, the Association of American Publishers (AAP), has argued that mergers and consolidations have made available the resources without which the remarkable growth of recent years could not have been sustained.

7. Quoted from a speech by Heather Kirkwood to the Pubmart Workshop on Concentration of Ownership in Book Publishing, New York, April 11, 1979.

8. Reported in *BP Report on the Business of Book Publishing*, September 14, 1981 (Knowledge Industry Publications, Inc.). One leading mass-market paperback line, Fawcett, was incorporated into the Ballantine line in 1982. Two smaller lines, Playboy and Ace, were sold to Putnam. And most of Popular Library's titles were sold to Warner. These acquisitions sharply increased concentration, but it should be noted that the rapidly declining number of firms reflects the severe illness of this industry sector; it does not indicate the market power of dominant firms.

9. Reported in *BP Report*, August 13, 1981.

10. U.S. Bureau of the Census report, quoted in *Publisher Weekly*, April 30, 1982, p. 22.

11. Recent developments in book retailing parallel the shifts in marketing strategy inside publishing houses. Some critics go further and charge that the rationalization of book selling is responsible for recent changes in book publishing. It is obviously hard to establish a causal priority, and, at any rate, the developments are mutually reinforcing. That there has been an effort to rationalize book selling is not surprising. Book distribution has always been a vexing problem because of the large number of books issued each year and the policy of publishers to allow booksellers to return unsold copies. ("Gone today, here tomorrow," was Alfred Knopf's sarcastic comentary on the returns policy.) Yet few in the industry anticipated the phenomenal rise of chain bookstores. The chains have spread throughout the country, attracting new buyers to their stores, which are stocked with such high-turnover items as bestsellers and books on the latest fads. For a good reading on how book selling has been transformed, compare Bliven's 1975 account of a traditional book traveler with Powell's 1983 analysis of the chain bookstores and specialty shops.

12. It is possible that this bifurcation of the market may even affect the manner in which authors convey their ideas. The literary critic Leslie Fiedler suggests that novels presently fall into the categories "art or show biz," and not just after they are written and have been sorted out by self-conscious critics and/or the blind mechanism of the marketplace, but in their very conception. Writers tend to write for the academy or for Hollywood, "which is to say as if to be taught, analyzed, and explicated—or to be packaged, hyped, and sold at the box office" (Fiedler 1981:143–44).

13. Richard Snyder, president of Simon and Schuster, did not exaggerate very much when he said, "In a certain sense, we are the software of the television and movie media" (quoted in Whiteside 1981:70).

14. For example, Dessauer (1983:107) reports that adult trade hardcover publishers are particularly dependent on subsidiary-rights income. This category of publishers had a net income of only 5.6 percent in 1980 but had earned-rights income of 15.5 percent, making their loss on their regular operations nearly 10 percent.

15. See Edwin McDowell, "The Loyalty of Authors to Publishers Has New Name: It's Spelled M–O–N–E–Y," *New York Times*, January 22, 1981, p. C12.

16. For data on salaries in publishing, see Stella Dong, "Publishing's Revolving Door," *Publishers Weekly*, December 19, 1980, pp. 20–23; see also Coser, Kadushin, and Powell 1982: chap. 4.

17. As industry analyst John Dessauer notes (1983:95–96), data on the book industry are notoriously scarce and incomplete. The most inclusive and widely used surveys, conducted by the U.S. Bureau of the Census, fall considerably short of capturing the full population of publishing houses. The 1977 *Census of Manufactures for Book Publishing* (SIC 2731) reports on 1,750 publishing establishments, but the R. R. Bowker Company's records suggest that "at least 8,000 bona fide book publishers were actually operating at the time." Late in 1982 Bowker listed 13,000 publishers who had contributed to *The Publishers' Trade List Annual* and *Books in Print*. In addition to excluding very small firms, the *Census* figures are most likely to fail to include publishing subsidiaries of educational, professional, and religious organizations.

18. John Brooks, speaking for the Authors Guild, in his remarks made at the Federal Trade Commission Symposium on Media Concentration, session on Cencentration and Conglomeration in Book Publishing, Washington, D.C., December 14 and 15, 1978.

19. Carroll (1984) notes strong similarities among specialist firms across industries. For example, specialist newspapers are less likely to have their own production facilities or distribution networks, and specialized music-recording labels are less likely than the large record companies to own production studios, to distribute their records, to manufacture them, or to promote their artists as widely.

20. As Freeman and Hannan (1983:1119) put it, "specialist organizations will appear to be leaner than generalists, to have less organizational fat."

21. Similarly, Peterson and Berger (1975) show that, unlike earlier periods in the record industry, when industry concentration was associated

with a narrowing of musical tastes, the renewed market concentration of the 1970s did not lesson musical diversity. A wide range of musical tastes was satisfied because of the institutionalization of the multidivisional form and the aggressive interdivisional competition within record companies.

22. Noble (1982:112) provides figures on book sales by distribution channel. The shares of the market in 1979 were as follows:

General retail stores	23.0%
College stores	14.3
Libraries/institutions	8.2
Schools	18.4
Direct to consumer	27.4
Other	0.9
Export	7.6

23. On the term "invisible colleges," see chapter 2, note 12.

24. In 1979, the eleven leading text houses accounted for 67 percent of college text sales (Noble, 1982:134).

25. For more details on the life-styles of editors, see chapter 4 of Coser, Kadushin, and Powell 1982.

26. Commercial houses tend to avoid these areas because few scholars who are active in them have research grants with which to purchase expensive monographs. Nor do many libraries allocate a large portion of their budgets for the humanities. University presses do, however, publish a considerable number of works in this area. Because trade publishers concentrate on the mass market and monograph publishers focus on the sciences, works of poetry, short stories, and translations are more frequently published by university presses. There is a clear parallel with television, where serious programming is also relegated to subsidized public television stations.

27. For a comparative analysis of the social circles in which scholarly, text, and trade editors are enmeshed, see chapter 3 of Coser, Kadushin, and Powell 1982.

28. Trade paperbacks, the "aristocrats" of paperback publishing, have a somewhat different life-span. Although the distinction between trade and mass-market paperbacks is sometimes blurry, the former are generally produced with better-quality materials and are sold chiefly in bookstores. Mass-market paperbacks are lower in price and smaller in size; intended for popular consumption, they are sold in newsstands, drugstores, supermarkets, bookstores, and anywhere else a paperback display rack can be located. Some trade paperbacks are serious works, of fiction or nonfiction, intended for a well-educated audience. A number of quality trade-paperback lines have been started in the past few years, and books of great merit are now available for the first time in paperback. To my mind, the success of these books has been one of the most exciting developments in recent publishing history. Nevertheless, not all trade paperbacks are books of distinction; much popular and trivial entertainment, such as *The Preppy Handbook*, is also published in trade-paperback format.

29. Harold T. Miller, president of Houghton Mifflin, quoted in *Business Week*, July 4, 1977, p. 50.

Notes to Chapter Two

1. One of the most pronounced changes in recent publishing history has been the shift from individual or family control to corporate ownership. Until the late 1950s most publishing houses were identified with one family or a single individual. In some cases the family's role could be traced back to the nineteenth century. Although there are a few exceptions, such as Harcourt Brace Jovanovich and McGraw-Hill, most large publishing companies today are run by group management. This change is directly tied to the period of expansion, diversification, and mergers in the 1960s and 1970s. With new product lines and specialization, the pursuit of worldwide markets, and the trend toward multimedia ownership, most large previously independent publishing houses became one of many companies operating under the same roof or the same corporate umbrella.

2. The advantages of a series may also extend to the editorial review process. Robert Darnton (1983), in a humorous reflection on the many hurdles that authors must surmount—a situation he observed at first hand during a stint on the editorial board of Princeton University Press—half-facetiously suggests that authors "submit a series." He notes that "we at Princeton turn down books by the hundreds, but as far as I know we have never turned down a series, and we took on half a dozen during my four years on the board."

3. J. David Sapir, an anthropologist who edits a series for a university press, suggests that the term "power" hardly captures his motivation for serving as a series editor. He notes, "If it is power, it is a rinky-dink sort of power." He correctly points out that the task of editing a series is arduous. It is not pleasant to turn people down, nor is it easy to help transform a dissertation into a book in which "several simultaneous levels—the facts of the matter, commentary on the facts, and the theoretical implications of the commentary—are operating together and are constantly at play" (Sapir 1983, personal communication). There is no question but that a well-edited series is difficult work. And certainly the hard work and the infrequent rewards, when a book gets some attention, may outweigh, in an editor's mind, his or her perceived influence. But if one compares the structural position of a series editor to that of an author looking for a publisher, the editor is seen to be in a powerful intermediary position, since his or her sponsorship dramatically increases the author's chances of getting published.

4. Perrow (1985), writing from the perspective of an "established author," argues that annual reviews, conference proceedings, and the like are ideal publication outlets for well-known scholars. These nonrefereed publishing options afford "the opportunity to work one's ideas out in print." They are more willing to accept new lines of inquiry and unconventional and reflective work. Of course, such volumes contain a certain amount of dross, but that is the price to be paid for escaping the orthodoxy of the mainstream journals.

5. For a more extensive discussion of the role of patrons and brokers in scholarly publishing, see Coser, Kadushin and Powell 1982:302–7.

6. We must be careful not to confuse either trust or a norm of reciproc-

ity with some notion of a generalized social morality. Trust is closely tied to self-interest; one trusts best the information generated in the course of one's own experiences. Granovetter (1983b:30) warns that "the widespread preference to transact with partners of known reputation implies that few of us are content to rely on general moral dispositions or on institutional arrangements if more specific information is available." It is evident that in cases of repeated reciprocal exchange, malfeasance is inhibited by the potential for damage to one's reputation.

7. For a discussion of how this myriad of individual transactions can overwhelm publishing houses, see Powell 1983.

8. Such small printings are still common and have changed little since the time of my fieldwork. In a 1983 study of 165 academic authors in economics departments and business schools, Shubik, Heim, and Baumol (1983:369) found that "most scholarly books are destined to have relatively modest sales in the range not exceeding 2,000."

9. Publishers commonly complain that because they produce hundreds of unique, individual products, consumers do not develop "brand-name loyalty." While this may be true for the general reading public, it is not true for librarians and booksellers. Our interviews revealed many instances of such loyalty; librarians and booksellers often base their decisions about which new books to order on a publisher's editorial and marketing reputation.

10. More recent data suggest that advances have not kept pace with inflation. Indeed, advances for scholarly or professional books appear to be the exception rather than the rule. In the study conducted by Shubik, Heim, and Baumol (1983:378), three out of four authors received no advance at all for their books, and the sample included authors of textbooks and trade books as well as professional books. This is unfortunate, though not necessarily because it means less money in authors' pockets. An advance reflects a commitment on the part of the publisher; it shifts part of the risk of publication from the author to the publisher. For example, if royalties never add up to the amount of the advance, the difference is usually borne by the publisher. In addition, it is not altogether uncommon for a house to be acquired by, or merged with, another firm while an author's book is in process. If an author has received an advance, the new owners have a stake in seeing that the book is published.

11. While I was involved in fieldwork at Apple Press, each of the senior editors received several job offers from other houses. The psychology editor left shortly after my observations ended. A year and a half later, unhappy at the house he had joined, he returned to Apple Press. At the time of his departure, the editor-in-chief noted that this editor "was irreplaceable." It was over six months before a suitable replacement was found. At the outset of my fieldwork, two editors had recently left Apple Press for better positions in other companies. Midway through my fieldwork, the marketing director resigned. The editors handled the promotion of their own books for a while, then a free-lance person assisted with the marketing for several months. Eventually a new marketing director was hired.

Only one editor left Plum Press during the course of my fieldwork there, but since then at least three editors have left for positions at other houses. The top administration of Plum Press has also changed significantly: the president has retired, and several top executives have been promoted to positions within the parent company.

12. For a detailed review of the concept of invisible colleges, see Crane 1972.

13. Since the primary focus of this study is on the way that editors select and acquire manuscripts, I have not provided a thorough discussion of the operations of the production, manufacturing, and marketing departments at either house. For an excellent discussion of these functions, see the accounts in the relevant sections of Bailey 1970 and Balkin 1977.

14. For details on interdepartmental conflicts in trade and textbook publishing, see Coser, Kadushin, and Powell 1982:185–99. The reactions of authors to the services provided by the different departments in commercial scholarly houses and university presses are summarized in Powell 1982a.

15. Epstein (1977:435) provides several humorous and incisive comments on this aspect of publishing. He recalls that, when he was an editor, he was visited by an editor from a distinguished English publishing firm:

> In a crisp Oxbridge accent he announced that he was here on a selling trip, attempting to sell the American rights to a number of his firm's titles. From his briefcase he extracted page after page, each one listing a title for sale, a brief description of its contents, a biographical note on the author, and a suggested price. I needed to concentrate, at various points, to recall that we were talking about books and not something else: costume jewelry, say, or cutlery. By the time he had arrived at my office, his better items had already been sold off, and the remaining ones—treatises on land reform in Wales, social scientific studies even more dismally specialized than those produced in the United States—were of no possible interest. We chatted pleasantly until, undefeated and indefatigable, he departed to make his next call. After he left, I thought of the old joke about the man in the circus whose job is to clean up after the elephants. When asked by a friend why he doesn't quit so undignified a job, the man replies, "What! And leave show business!"

16. Goodenough (1963:94) has discussed the social value of "established routines," pointing out that:

> Schedules provide for gratification of otherwise mutually incompatible wants. They acquire value also . . . by making it possible to have fairly reliable expectations . . . Finally, schedules help to space activities in such a way as to give the practice of each a fairly high net efficacy . . . Because they resolve so many different problems, schedules often represent a delicate balance that allows for little alteration without serious dislocation effects.

The disruption of one item in a tight publishing schedule frequently disrupts the entire schedule and throws the whole timetable off.

17. Openness is, of course, a two-way street. I believe, for example, that multiple submissions are reasonable, given the inevitable delays that authors face when they send their manuscripts to one publisher at a time. But it is incumbent upon an author to disclose to the publisher that he has submitted his manuscript to several houses simultaneously. On the other hand, as a book nears its publication date, its author is sometimes kept in

the dark about a number of key decisions. Publishers should provide authors with information about price, how royalties are calculated, the size of the print run, promotion plans, and where review copies have been sent. Such openness helps cement the relationship, and authors may even provide helpful suggestions when they are kept apprised of publication plans.

Notes to Chapter Three

1. A recent profile of editors working in the areas of science, medicine, technology, and the social and behavioral sciences is reported in Summers 1982. The survey presents salary data for editors in the United States, the United Kingdom, the Netherlands, and West Germany. Summers (1982:2109) begins his report by stating:

> Editors are . . . the most expensive and valuable human assets we employ . . . they are the most difficult staff to appoint. Good editors are also among the hardest of all staff to replace—every departure causes a loss of editorial momentum, a faltering of publishing rhythm which no house . . . can afford.

2. This chapter is based for the most part on my field observations at Apple Press and Plum Press. At Apple Press there were two senior editors who each signed approximately thirty books a year. The president of the company and an assistant editor annually signed about ten books between them. The editor-in-chief's "quota" varied, depending on how active his editors were. One year, when the press was without a sociology editor, he signed thirty-five books; the following year, after an editor had been hired, he signed sixteen titles. At Plum Press, my observations were concentrated on two senior editors, each of whom signed between thirty-five and forty books a year. I interviewed the editor-in-chief and an editorial vice-president of Plum, as well as editors who worked for the subsidiary company; however, I did not observe these people in the course of their daily affairs. I also spoke with Plum Press editors who worked in the physical and biological sciences.

In addition, I draw on interviews I had with the director of a leading university press and with his editor-in-chief, two senior editors, and one former editor. I also interviewed four editors at other commercial scholarly houses as well as three editors at three different university presses. I have also made use of interviews and field notes collected by Laurie Michael Roth in her participant-observation study of a large university press and by Annabelle Sreberny in her study of a small university press. Finally, I have utilized information from interviews with editors that were conducted by my research associates as part of a general study of book publishing (see the Appendix in Coser, Kadushin, and Powell 1982).

When I use the term "editor" without any other classification, I am referring to editors whose principal concern is acquisitions.

3. The reputation of a publishing house attracts many submissions. The younger authors whom I interviewed were aware that their chances for publication were somewhat better at Plum Press than at Apple Press. During the years 1975–78, Apple published, at most, three revised dissertations a year. Plum Press has a much larger list than Apple; even so,

dissertations constitute a higher percentage of their total output. From an editor's perspective, most dissertations devote inordinate attention to methodological issues and a review of the existing literature. Editors are more favorably disposed toward manuscripts that are intellectually more speculative and include policy recommendations. The prospects for young writers are not helped by the two- or three-year time lag between a book's publication and the appearance of a review in a professional journal. More prompt reviews could generate interest in what a young writer has to say. Thus it is more feasible for editors to publish established authors, for whom there are ready academic and library sales. Current cutbacks in library budgets, federal research grants, and operating subsidies for university presses now make it even more difficult for young scholars to publish their dissertations.

4. Economists have argued that transaction costs are lowered when there are "lubricants" to the exchange process. Such "lubricants" include personal relationships between actors, which facilitate understanding and reduce opportunism; precedents set by others; and reputational networks, which establish actors' credibility. In author-editor relations, however, the publishing house may suffer from too much familiarity between exchange participants. Not only are editors torn by twin loyalties, but authors may feel a greater allegiance to their editors than to the publishing house. For both authors and editors, the relationship to the publishing house is a formal, contractual quid pro quo, while the relationship between authors and editors may be intrinsically rewarding: the friendship itself is the source of value to the participants. Editors may, on occasion, find themselves in the unpleasant position of being accused by an author of betrayal and accused by their employer of cooptation.

5. Editors in university presses must go through a different and more formal decision-making process. In contrast to commercial scholarly houses, the review process at university presses typically requires two outside readings of a manuscript. If these reviews are contradictory, the editor may solicit a third opinion. In a few cases, particularly for very distinguished authors, outside reviews are not required. As a rule, outside readings are much more crucial in the decision-making process at university presses than at commercial houses. If the outside reviews are favorable, the editor recommends publication to the press's board of advisers, which consists of members of the senior faculty. Some boards are small, such as Princeton's four-member committee. Others are much larger; Chicago has a twelve-member board, California a seventeen-member board. The board's decision is usually based solely on considerations of merit; financial information is seldom provided. If the outside reviews are positive, board approval is typically granted.

The review process at university presses takes considerably more time than at commercial houses. Editorial boards commonly meet only once a month, ten months out of the year. To keep from losing manuscripts to commercial houses, where the pace is speedier and less deliberate, university presses have turned to offering letters of intent and advance contracts (see note 9). Nevertheless, the process at university presses is commonly quite time-consuming. Moreover, while commercial houses may sign a book on a promising topic even if the manuscript needs a good bit of revising, a university press would do so less frequently, because board approval would be hard to obtain.

There is currently much discussion of the need for faster publishing decisions by university presses. At the 1982 annual meetings of the Association of American University Presses, John Gallman, director of Indiana University Press, urged his colleagues to "cut down most in-house committees; they are too time-consuming. Get your faculty committees to allow you to accept a book without all that rigmarole" (Reuter el al. 1982).

6. The process of obtaining approval from the parent corporation of Apple Press has changed somewhat in recent years. A new top executive in the parent company now carefully reviews many of the proposals-to-publish from Apple Press. Proposals are sometimes returned with questions attached. This particular executive seems to enjoy a good argument. Final approval is still routinely granted, but the process now takes more time.

7. Would-be authors are strongly advised to speak with people who have had books published by the particular house to which they intend to send a manuscript. In addition, it is a good idea to examine any volumes that the publisher has released that are comparable to the manuscript that is being submitted. Nor does it hurt to review some of the publisher's relevant promotional materials or catalogues.

8. Twenty-five to thirty-five titles is a rough average of the annual work load for the senior editors at Apple and Plum. In general, scholarly editors handle more books each year than trade or college textbook editors do. Seventy percent of the scholarly editors my colleagues and I interviewed in our general study of book publishing signed more than twenty-five books a year (Coser, Kadushin, and Powell 1982:125). The "average" expectation of the sixty-three publishers from four Western countries, reported in Summers (1982:2111), was that editors would acquire at least twenty new books a year, although some houses expected as many as fifty. Given that a scholarly book earns less than a trade title or textbook, the heavier work load is to be expected.

9. Because of increased competition between university presses and commercial houses, more university presses are now willing to offer an advance contract, or a letter of intent to publish, for an incomplete manuscript. At university presses it is understood that the final manuscript will not be published without favorable outside reviews and board approval. Such quasi-official contracts may provide some security to the author; however, they are not legally binding on the publisher.

10. Editors in scholarly publishing maintain more extensive travel schedules than their counterparts in trade and textbook publishing; however, they are less likely than trade or text editors to initiate an idea and to commission an author to write a book on it.

Notes to Chapter Four

1. The study of the professions is the subject of much debate, as scholars are now questioning the attribute approach (Greenwood 1957; Goode 1960) and are suggesting that much of the research on professionals is

ahistorical and serves the ideological interests of powerful professions. Roth's (1974) vigorous critique of research on the professions points out that much of the literature does not focus on the process of professionalization but on its product, "and typically even this focus is contaminated with the ideology and hopes of professional groups rather than [being] an independent assessment of what they achieve." He claims that professional attributes are largely an ideology designed to protect professionals from threats to their power and demands that they become more accountable. Furthermore, most occupational cultures are composed of common values, folklore, symbols, and argot. What distinguishes the professions from other occupations is power, their ability to obtain a set of rights and privileges from society. Friedson (1970, 1976) has maintained that the constellation of characteristics that are accepted as denoting a profession should realistically be seen either as traits that are derived from the power that professions exercise or as a set of traits that the professions do not actually possess but have been able to convince significant others that they have.

2. Halpenny (1973) observes that students preparing for careers in library work must take advanced courses, become familiar with standard reference works, comprehend principles of classification, and acquire some experience with library research methods. There are even specializations that can be pursued: rare books, legal librarianship, business literature, audiovisuals, and data processing. She goes on to show the contrast between publishers and librarians:

> Librarians are major users of publishers' products, carefully trained to acquire, catalogue, and dispense them and to assist readers to gain access to and take fullest advantage of what has been set down in print or gathered onto film or in a data base. Yet the people in publishing who create these products receive virtually no training for their careers before they embark upon them, have to learn quickly what their responsibilities are and how to meet them, and must catch a general training from the remarks of their seniors, what they can read in a not extensive literature, and what they can acquire in this or that conference or work session to which they may be sent if funds and time permit. [Halpenny, 1973:166]

Johnstone and his colleagues argue that:

> There seems little doubt that, at least in the abstract formal sense, journalism can be considered a profession: it is clearly a full-time occupation; there are established training facilities for its practitioners; several professional associations for working news people are in existence; there is legal sanction, of a kind, for its work territory; and formal codes of ethics have been developed. [Johnstone et al. 1976:102]

On the other hand, neither journalism nor librarianship can be regarded as a powerful profession. Johnstone and his colleagues (1976:102) note that "the extent to which practicing newsmen identify as professionals is quite another question." Furthermore, what fledgling journalists should be taught is a controversy as old as journalism itself. Nevertheless, editors in book publishing have none of the formal professional characteristics of either journalists or librarians.

3. With but a few exceptions there is currently little in the way of formal educational training for careers in publishing. One goal of the AAP Committee for Education in Publishing was to identify existing educational

programs and to suggest how others could be started. Its report stated that publishing is

> A vocation "in which most people find themselves by accident, or at least by indirection, chance, family, or other quirky connections." It has long seemed (erroneously) a perfect refuge for those who "love to read" and/or wanted to write, or who didn't know what to do. Not more than a few publishers ever prepared themselves consciously for a life in publishing. [AAP 1977:11]

The Committee's report illustrates very well how occupational groups' attempts to expand their occupational license are inextricably tied to external forces over which they have limited control. The Committee stated that the industry should be concerned:

> (1) with education *for* publishing, which means the educating of those who might or who plan to enter publishing;
> (2) with the further educating *in* publishing, that is, the training and development of those already employed; and
> (3) with education *about* publishing, for those who do not work in publishing but whose good opinion and access to reliable information about publishing is of considerable importance.

With the latter point, the Committee recognized that there are special constituencies—among them, booksellers, librarians, authors, agents, the educational community, reviewers and critics, the financial community, printers, legislators, and the reading public—whose opinions affect the prestige and rewards of publishers.

4. For a detailed discussion of editorial careers, see chapter 4, "Climbing the Editorial Ladder," in Coser, Kadushin, and Powell 1982.

5. In the course of my fieldwork I saw many instances of manuscript referral. The editor-in-chief at a house that was one of Apple Press's prime competitors referred a manuscript to Apple because he felt that the manuscript was "a bit too academic for my tastes." The book subsequently became one of Apple Press's leading titles, selling well both in hardcover and in a later paperback edition. Both the editor-in-chief and the sociology editor at Apple Press frequently referred manuscripts they felt were "too specialized" to editors they knew in monograph houses. They remarked on several occasions that friends of theirs had started small publishing firms and that they were glad to send manuscripts their way. While I was at Apple Press, a manuscript came in from a monograph publisher (which in this case was Plum Press). It had been favorably reviewed by a Plum series editor; however, the acquisitions editor at Plum Press felt that it was too popular a treatment of the subject matter for Plum and suggested to the author that he send the manuscript to Apple Press.

6. The old cliché that variety is the spice of life obviously has some merit. Medoff and Abraham (1980:732) suggest that the "passage of time can come to have a negative effect on productivity, mediated by what might be called 'on-the-job sensory deprivation'" (also see Pfeffer 1983:320–26). For detailed reviews of the literature on turnover, see Price 1977 and Bluedorn 1982.

7. The comments the editor-in-chief at a competing scholarly house

made to me bear directly on the issue of editorial autonomy and the tolerance of mistakes:

> In general, every proposal is accepted as long as in a fundamental way it doesn't disgrace us or isn't a commercial disaster. I believe in a lot of discussion to bring the assumptions about a book out into the open. But it's very rare for a project which is proposed by an editor—one which he really wants—to be vetoed. It's very difficult to second-guess an editor. But if they make too many mistakes, I'll fire them. I believe in editorial freedom as long as they don't blow it.

8. The impact of several years of inflation may require these figures on editors to be adjusted upward. Summers' (1982) survey, drawing on 1981 data, reports a salary range of $23,000 to $43,000 for editors at monograph houses in the United States, with an average salary of $30,750. For salary information of the various branches of book publishing in the United States, see Coser, Kadushin, and Powell 1982:111–12. Our data were reported by editors in 1977 and 1978. Inflation does not, however, seem to have affected starting salaries. An August 15, 1982, *New York Times Book Review* column states that the average entry-level pay is about $9,000 a year.

9. The empirical support for contingency-theory or resource-dependence arguments has been modest. Critics of contingency theory argue that it exaggerates the constraints under which organizations operate (Child 1972). There have been weak empirical tests of contingency theory, in part because of inadequate conceptualization of technology, environment, and organizational effectiveness (Mohr 1971). Pfeffer and Salancik's (1978) resource-dependency theory avoids some of the problems that contingency theory has encountered in trying to explain the "fit" between an organization's structure and its environment. Their concern is to discover how the internal distribution of organizational power is determined by the differential ability of subgroups to solve problems related to critical environmental uncertainty. Critics such as Williamson (1981), however, contend that the power argument is both tautological and imprecise. Williamson's (1975, 1981) transaction cost approach would suggest that editorial discretion is the outcome of an efficient assignment of information and resources to the parts of the enterprise that are the most critical for competitive viability. The debate over whether aspects of organizational structure reflect power or efficiency maximization holds much promise as a research topic.

10. Perrow (1979:50–52) points out that this is an idea about which Max Weber was rather explicit, although few have properly recognized it. To Weber, a person has a set of skills, expertise, or experience and a sense of career with a firm. These skills, expertise, and experience can be developed, and he expects to utilize them; indeed, he wants to. It is therefore wise to allow him the freedom to exercise these skills and to use his discretion, for that is why experts are employed. He should, however, exercise his skills in the service of organizational goals that are set for him. He is not expected, or encouraged, to inquire into the legitimacy of those goals.

11. Warren Breed (1955:328) presents an excellent account of how reporters learn to please their editors. It is a process devoid of any formal instruction.

> When the new reporter starts work, he is not told what policy is. Nor is he ever told. This may appear strange, but interview after interview confirmed the condition. The standard remark was "Never in my —— years on this paper, have I ever been told how to slant a story." No paper in the survey had a "training" program for its new men; some issue a "style" book, but this deals with literary style, not policy. Further, newsmen are busy and have little time for recruit training. Yet all but the newest staffers know what policy is. On being asked, they say they learn it "by osmosis." Basically, the learning of policy is a process by which the recruit discovers and internalizes the rights and obligations of his status and its norms and values. He learns to anticipate what is expected of him so as to win rewards and avoid punishments. The staffer reads his own paper every day; some papers require this. It is simple to diagnose the paper's characteristics. Unless the staffer is naive or unusually independent, he tends to fashion his own stories after others he sees in the paper. This is particularly true of the newcomer. The news columns and editorials are a guide to the local norms. Thus a southern reporter notes that Republicans are treated in a "different" way in his paper's news columns than Democrats. The news about whites and Negroes is also a distinct sort. Should he then write about one of these groups, his story will tend to reflect what he has come to define as standard procedure. Certain editorial actions taken by editors and older staffers also serve as controlling guides. "If things are blue-pencilled consistently," one reporter said, "you learn he [editor] has a prejudice in that regard."

12. I was, at one point, offered a position as an associate editor by a leading scholarly publishing house. I met with their editorial director, and we discussed what my duties would be. I asked about my first assignment. He commented, "We have about four or five manuscripts in the house that desperately need an editor. You would inherit these. They need editing, and this would give you an idea of what we do around here. If you are interested, you can take one or two of them with you."

13. Perrow (1979) suggests that the consequences of effective premise-setting should lead organization theorists to reconsider traditional notions about the span of control. It has long been held that authority must be delegated if a manager has ten or fifteen people to supervise, because a manager cannot watch each employee; if a manager has four or five employees, then direct supervision and control are feasible. Perrow argues that a sensible alternative view is that a narrow span of control allows one to shape premises more effectively and thus avoid the costs of close supervision. A broad span of control is likely to be associated with little delegation, repetitive work, and little control over premises but much control over behavior. Perrow's hypothesis helps explain Blau's (1968) findings that a narrow span of control was associated with more decentralization of decisions than a broad span of control.

14. In houses where sales from the backlist are minimal, the influence of the house's tradition plays a minor part in the decision-making process. Generally this is the case in newly formed companies and in trade houses that do not publish "serious" fiction or nonfiction but produce, instead,

mass-market, trendy materials. At both houses I studied, the backlist accounted for more than 60 percent of total annual sales; hence the types of books previously done by the house were of major consequence in all publishing decisions.

15. One editor suggested that I overstated Apple's lack of interest in highly theoretical work. He said, "Sure, we have our own tastes, but we are also professionals." The difference lies in how various manuscripts are processed. The editor gave the following illustration:

> A book that is interesting and accessible in substance or style is likely to get signed faster, and perhaps without outside review. If we have reason to believe a very theoretical work is important, we certainly would do it. However, it is much more likely to be sent out for one or two reviews. And I'll have to have my facts together when I make a case for the manuscript.

16. Schudson (1978:16) makes a similar point with regard to print journalism, where there are important traditions that urge reporters to move beyond organizational routines. He suggests that "in journalism, as in medicine, one will get nowhere without mastery of the standard procedures, but one will not get somewhere unless one has also acquired and demonstrated the ability to exercise judgment in ways one's colleagues admire."

Notes to Chapter Five

1. As a member of a panel at the American Sociological Association meetings in Chicago, Illinois, in September, 1977, I presented the Columbia Press figures to illustrate the volume of materials with which publishers must cope. The editor-in-chief of Columbia University Press, also a member of the panel, was distressed by my presentation of this data, for he felt that I was implying that manuscripts do not receive sufficient attention. He responded, "Every manuscript gets looked at for at least ten minutes." I was tempted to interject, "I rest my case." Another panelist, Erwin Glikes, then president of Basic Books and an editorial director at Harper and Row, commented that if Basic "were to give every manuscript equal attention, they would each get a three-minute glance."

2. See Brett 1913 and Bessie 1958.

3. A notable exception to this rule occurs when a regular author submits an inferior manuscript; the editor is not impressed with it but does not personally want to say no. These are the "political" problems that can cause editors to lose sleep at night.

4. At Apple Press I initially used a network questionnaire, an instrument that my colleagues and I hoped to use at a number of publishing houses in order to keep track of manuscripts under review. We also anticipated that the responses to the questions would enable us to map both the informal organizational structure and the patterns of external ties—who works with whom, who consults with whom on what projects, and so on. The responses of the various editors to the questionnaire made us realize how extremely difficult such a mapping process would be. Regretfully, we abandoned our quest for network data. In particular, the senior

editors and the editor-in-chief replied that the question that asked for the names of the manuscripts or books on which they were currently working was not answerable. One senior editor wrote the following reply on the questionnaire:

> Not possible to answer. I'm always working on books and thinking about possibilities for new ones. I have twenty-three books scheduled for 1977; about half are in production, and the others are being worked on by me or by the authors. As of this writing, I have the same number scheduled for 1978, six of which are in and being worked on by me. About seven have been signed for 1979, but none is in the house. Also, of course, I have about forty books under active consideration, and consideration plus the red tape of doing a proposal equals "work." Zat what you mean?

The editor-in-chief could not interpret what "working on" was intended to mean. He responded, "Do you mean trying to sign, developing, on the spring list, the fall list, just out, or what? I am probably 'working on' over one hundred books at this time. I couldn't possibly recall the names of all the people I've spoken with in the course of my efforts."

5. The research strategy adopted at Plum differed from the approach I used at Apple for several reasons. My fieldwork could not be as detailed or intensive, because Plum had fifteen times the number of employees that Apple had. Second, at the outset we agreed that my fieldwork would last for a period of less than six months. And, third, individual editors operated much more on their own, working on their own lists and paying little attention to the overall Plum list. At Apple each editor felt that he or she was contributing to the overall list and was willing to talk about the character of the general Apple list. At Plum the editors were willing to talk only about their books, and, given the large number of books that each of them signed, it often happened that, unless they kept good records of correspondence, there were a number of books for which information on the method of acquisition was missing. In addition, the press had a west-coast office, staffed by several editors who also acquired books. The extensive use of series editors further confounded data collection; for Plum editors who received unsolicited manuscripts in a series editor's field of competence would often immediately forward the materials to the series editor, who would give the manuscript its initial scanning. Finally, many authors submitted their manuscripts to a series editor rather than directly to Plum.

6. This is not to say that speed is never a concern. Presented with an opportunity to publish a new book by Lester Thurow or Fernand Braudel (both of whom are published by trade publishers), scholarly publishers would surely move with dispatch. But this would be an exception to the general pattern. For an excellent case study of the "leisurely" decision-making process at scholarly presses, see Erwin and Sapir 1977 for a description of a project that involved six presses and more than three years of waiting time.

7. In category 3, editorial initiative, there are important differences between trade editors—who often hit on an idea for a book and then secure an author to execute it—and scholarly editors. The latter seldom initiate a project. After all, most scholars spend several years doing research before

they begin writing. More commonly, a scholarly editor learns about a research grant or a fellowship award or hears that someone is working on a project; the editor then visits the persons involved on their home campus or writes them and expresses interest. The key to category three for scholarly editors is to learn about a project in its early stages, actively follow up on this information, and eventually persuade an author to submit a manuscript for review.

8. Would-be authors should note that a five-minute conversation with an editor at a convention booth does not constitute "personal contact." In coding category 3 for personal contact, I asked each editor whether he or she expected the arrival of a manuscript. If the answer was yes, I asked several questions to assess the extent of the editor's personal knowledge of the author. A "no" to any of these questions meant that the manuscript was classified in category 1.

9. Authors with no prior contact with a publishing house should be aware that they face several disadvantages. Not only will the review process be perfunctory, but editors will also frown on the fact that an unsolicited manuscript has been simultaneously submitted to several other houses. In cases of extreme work overload, this fact alone may be grounds for rejection. For obvious reasons, publishers dislike multiple submissions. Granting a publisher the exclusive right to review a manuscript, however, puts an author at a considerable disadvantage (see Coser, Kadushin, and Powell 1982: chap. 9). I always recommend that authors be upfront and tell publishers about their intention to send a project to several houses, for to reveal this after a review has been completed can provoke considerable anger on an editor's part. It is, of course, reasonable for authors to stipulate that, if they have not heard from a publisher within a certain amount of time, they will submit their manuscripts elsewhere. But unpublished authors must recognize that, if they choose to send their manuscripts to many houses at once, they are probably hurting their chances of publication at each individual house.

10. There are occasional exceptions to this axiom. Some very prominent academics prefer not to be hounded by editors until they have completed their book. Once finished, they will contact the publisher of their choice. If an individual's reputation is widely known, he or she will receive more expeditious treatment than others who send in unsolicited manuscripts.

11. Barron's rating of the competitiveness of universities, measured on the basis of the SAT scores of the entering class, was used as a general rating of university prestige. Though not as accurate a measure as the various rankings of specific departments, the Barron's ratings are much easier to use.

12. The importance of networks is by no means unique to the contemporary publishing scene. In their study of the British house of Macmillan, Tuchman and Fortin (1980) found that previous contact with the house greatly enhanced an author's chances of publication. They argue that differential access to appropriate social networks and unequal educational opportunities account for the higher rate of rejection for women novelists at Macmillan during the period from the late 1860s to the late 1880s.

13. Although university-press publishing is probably still more "comfortable" than commercial publishing, the nature of this business has changed somewhat since this 1978 interview. Rising costs, the declining purchasing power of libraries, and, in some cases, cuts in support from parent universities have forced some belt-tightening on the part of university presses. The chief casualty of this economic regime appears to be the specialized monograph, particularly the revised dissertation. Nevertheless, university presses still receive support in a wide variety of ways, such as authors' waivers of royalties and submission of camera-ready copy, free rent, endowment income, and annual operating subsidies from parent universities.

14. Quoted in Wendroff 1980:25.

15. An advance is not, properly speaking, a production cost, for, if the book succeeds, the advance will be recovered by deductions from the author's royalties. However, it does represent an initial cost.

16. Subventions have become a controversial issue in scholarly publishing. At the 1982 annual meetings of the Association of American University Presses, a panel on subventions attracted the most controversy. John Gallman of Indiana University Press asserted that "books that require subsidy are not worth publishing." He went on to note that "subsidies mean loss of integrity; there is a subtle loss of control, since agencies giving money do expect special attention." He noted several exceptions, however, particularly in regard to translations and mammoth projects. Nor was Indiana averse to large block grants or endowments. Another panelist, Sheldon Meyer, of Oxford University Press, remarked that Oxford has several centuries-old subsidies, most notably various editions of the Bible and the *Oxford English Dictionary*. John Goellner, of Johns Hopkins University Press, argued that "the paramount reason for university publishing is to publish scholarly monographs, and such publishing is impossible without title subsidies." Moreover, he asserted that trade books (popular titles on health and diets, for example) could never support scholarly books and that, in fact, trade books are peripheral to a university press's purpose. Johns Hopkins has several operating rules for handling subsidies: "Never accept a subsidy from the author's own pocket; don't make publishing conditional on getting the subsidy; and don't ask the author to be solely responsible for obtaining the subsidy." (I was in the audience at this panel; however, the direct quotes are from Reuter et al. 1982). An article in the *New York Times* (September 30, 1983, p. C20) reports that, according to a study by the Association of American University Presses, 68.6 percent of the books published in 1982 by university presses were subsidized in some measure by endowments, foundations, or private organizations.

At both Apple and Plum, acquiring editors very rarely searched for title subsidies. On occasion, however, manuscripts arrived with support in hand. For example, a manuscript might report the results of a three-year research project, and the sponsoring foundation or agency would subsidize publication costs; or the manuscript might be a revised version of a United Nations or foundation-sponsored inquiry into a particular political or social problem, and the original sponsor wanted the report to reach a broader audience. Unlike some university presses, few commercial scholarly houses are engaging in widespread searches for title subventions.

Notes to Chapter Six

1. An important exception is Richardson 1972.

2. There are, of course, a variety of ways of carving up the terrain of organization theory. Astley and Van de Ven 1983, Barney and Ulrich 1982, and Pfeffer 1982 are among the more interesting recent efforts at synthesis. My reference in the text to the dominant perspectives in organization theory includes three schools of thought. (1) The *rational adaptation* perspective, of which there are numerous variants (the best known are structural contingency theory and resource dependence theory), argues that the key to organizational survival is adaptation to the threats and opportunities posed by the environment (see Thompson 1967; Pfeffer and Salancik 1978). (2) *Transaction cost analysis* argues that organizations are driven to engage in exchanges in a manner that minimizes overhead and enforcement costs. This effort is complicated by problems of uncertainty, asset specificity, and small numbers; thus various governance forms arise to mediate difficult kinds of transactions (see Williamson 1975 and 1981, and also Williamson 1985). (3) *Population ecology* focuses on the distribution of organizational forms across environmental conditions. It argues that organizational change is a consequence of an environmental selection process that operates via the replacement of organizations that are dominant at one period of time by a new set of dominant organizations (see Aldrich 1979; Hannan and Freeman 1977, 1984).

3. John Ryden, quoted in a news article by Edwin McDowell, "Publishing: What University Presses Are Doing," *New York Times*, April 20, 1984, p. C22.

4. For a more detailed comparative analysis of scholarly publishing and public television, see Powell 1984.

5. The discussion draws on interviews and fieldwork conducted between 1980 and 1982 at WNET-TV (New York, N.Y., and Newark, N.J.) and several smaller public TV stations. WNET is the largest public TV station in the United States and is commonly referred to as the public broadcasting system's "flagship" station. It produces a significant portion of the programs that are nationally broadcast by public TV stations.

6. As one former WNET executive noted, "Most stations simply can't do public affairs shows that look critically at their own state government . . . There is a terrible baggage that comes with state money" (Powell and Friedkin 1983:417–18).

7. Lawrence Grossman, quoted in *Newsweek*, November 20, 1978, p. 139.

8. For a promising approach of this type that deals with specific relations among the component parts of an organizational field, see DiMaggio 1984.

9. Compare the review process at Apple or Plum with a recent study by Cole, Cole, and Simon (1981) of the evaluation process used by the National Science Foundation for grant proposals in the fields of chemical dynamics, economics, and solid-state physics. They argue that the peer-review system at NSF is essentially free of systematic bias because grant proposals from eminent scientists do not have substantially higher probabilities of receiving favorable ratings than proposals from scientists who are

not eminent. Contrary to the view that science is characterized by general agreement about what constitutes good work, these researchers found real and legitimate differences of opinion among experts about what good science is or should be. They conclude (p. 885) that "the fate of a particular grant application is roughly half determined by the characteristics of the proposal and the principal investigator, and about half by apparently random elements which might be characterized as luck of the reviewer draw."

The disagreement found among reviewers of NSF grant proposals partially reflects the fact that the pool of reviewers is heterogeneous. The selection of reviewers is part of an effort to draw on a broad cross-section of scientists. In contrast, Apple and Plum, when they do call on academic reviewers (remember that this does not always occur), draw on a fairly small stable of authors they have published. The consensus is high. At NSF, unlike at Apple and Plum, there is no profit consideration that encourages prompt decision-making. NSF can afford to be pluralistic and to take its time; Apple and Plum cannot.

10. It is worth noting that the recent expansion of publication outlets has occurred in the context of a number of widely perceived and much ballyhooed threats to the health of scholarly publication. Library budgets have shrunk, federal support to higher education has failed to keep pace with inflation, soaring journal prices have cut into the already reduced acquisition budgets of libraries, and the demographics of higher education are not propitious. Scholarly books have become more expensive; hence there are fewer buyers, shorter print runs, and, as a result, higher price tags. So the vicious cycle goes. Nevertheless, the number of scholarly publishing houses has grown. The explanations are many and varied. In chapter 1 I noted that scholarly presses have moved into the niches vacated by large trade publishers, who have gone off in pursuit of "blockbuster" books. This newly opened terrain has afforded many houses important opportunities. Although widely available high-quality photocopying equipment enables some potential buyers to avoid purchasing new books, computer technology has greatly aided scholarly publishers in developing pinpoint mailing lists with which to target likely buyers. And, of course, the pressure to publish continues to increase within the academy. The demand for good books is fairly elastic, for scholars need to stay abreast of developments in their field in order to advance their own careers.

REFERENCES

Akerlof, George A.
   1984   "Gift Exchange and Efficiency-Wage Theory: Four Views."
          American Economic Review 74, no. 2 (May):79–83.
Aldrich, Howard E.
   1979   *Organizations and Environments.* Englewood Cliffs, N.J.:
          Prentice-Hall.
Aldrich, Howard E., and Donna Fish
   1982   "Origins of Organizational Forms." Paper presented at the
          American Sociological Association annual meetings, Septem-
          ber, San Francisco.
Altick, Richard D.
   1957   *The English Common Reader: A Social History of the Mass
          Reading Public, 1800–1900.* Chicago: University of Chicago
          Press.
Arrow, Kenneth
   1974   *The Limits of Organization.* New York: Norton.
Association of American Publishers
   1977   "The Accidental Profession: Education, Training, and the
          People of Publishing." Report of the AAP Education for
          Publishing Committee. New York: Association of American
          Publishers.
   1976   *The Money Side of Publishing: Fundamentals for Non-
          Financial People.* Report of a conference sponsored by the
          Association of American Publishers, General Publishing Divi-
          sion, prepared by Jean V. Naggar. New York: Association of
          American Publishers.
Astley, W. Graham, and Andrew Van de Ven
   1983   "Central Perspectives and Debates in Organization Theory."
          Administrative Science Quarterly 28:245–73.

234 References

Authors Guild
    1977a   Statement on the Continuing Trend to Concentration of Power in the Publishing Industry. Issued June 6, New York, N.Y.
    1977b   Supplemental Memorandum on Concentration in the Book Club Market and Mass Paperback Market. Issued August 2, New York, N.Y.

Bachrach, Peter, and Morton S. Baratz
    1963   "Decisions and Nondecisions: An Analytical Framework." *American Political Science Review* 57:632–42.
    1962   "Two Faces of Power." *American Political Science Review* 56:947–52.

Bailey, Herbert S.
    1970   *The Art and Science of Book Publishing.* New York: Harper & Row.

Balkin, Richard
    1977   *A Writer's Guide to Book Publishing.* New York: Hawthorn Books.

Ballou, Ellen B.
    1970   *The Building of the House: Houghton Mifflin's Formative Years.* Boston: Houghton Mifflin.

Bandura, Albert
    1977   *Social Learning Theory.* Englewood Cliffs, N.J.: Prentice-Hall.

Barnard, Chester
    1938   *The Functions of the Executive.* Cambridge, Mass.: Harvard University Press.

Barney, Jay, and Dave Ulrich
    1982   "Perspectives in Organization Theory: Resource Dependence, Efficiency, and Ecology." Unpublished manuscript, School of Management, University of California at Los Angeles.

Becker, Howard S.
    1978   "Arts and Crafts." *American Journal of Sociology* 83:862–89.
    1974   "Arts as Collective Action." *American Sociological Review* 39:767–76.

Ben-Porath, Yoram
    1980   "The F-Connection: Families, Friends, and Firms in the Organization of Exchange." *Population and Development Review* 6:1–30.

Bessie, Simon Michael
    1958   "American Writing Today." *Virginia Quarterly Review* 34: 253–63.

Blau, Peter M.
    1968   "The Hierarchy of Authority in Organizations." *American Journal of Sociology* 73:453–67.
    1964   *Exchange and Power in Social Life.* New York: Wiley.

Bliven, Bruce, Jr.
1975   *Book Traveller.* New York: Dodd, Mead.

Bluedorn, Allen
1982   "The Theories of Turnover: Causes, Effects and Meaning." In
        S. Bacharach, ed., *Research in the Sociology of Organizations*,
        vol. 1. Greenwich, Conn.: JAI Press.

Bourdieu, Pierre
1977   *Outline of a Theory of Practice.* Translated by Richard Nise.
        New York: Cambridge University Press.

Bradbury, Malcolm
1971   *The Social Context of Modern English Literature.* New York:
        Schocken Books.

Bramstead, Ernest K.
1964   *Aristocracy and the Middle Classes in Germany: Social Types
        in German Literature, 1830–1900.* Rev. ed. Chicago: Univer-
        sity of Chicago Press.

Braudy, Susan
1978   "Paperback Auction: What Price 'Hot' Book?" *New York
        Times Magazine*, May 21, pp. 18–19, 91–95, 106–9.

Breed, Warren
1955   "Social Control in the Newsroom: A Functional Analysis."
        Social Forces 33:326–35.

Brett, George P.
1913   "Book Publishing and Its Present Tendencies." *Atlantic
        Monthly* 111 (April): 454–62.

Burns, Tom, and G. M. Stalker
1961   *The Management of Innovation.* London: Tavistock.

Canfield, Cass
1971   *Up and Down and Around: A Publisher Recollects the Time of
        His Life.* New York: Harper & Row.

Caplette, Michele
1981   "Women in Publishing: A Study of Careers in Organizations."
        Ph. D. dissertation, Department of Sociology, SUNY at Stony
        Brook.

Caplovitz, David
1963   *The Poor Pay More.* New York: Free Press.

Caplow, Theodore
1964   *Principles of Organization.* New York: Harcourt, Brace &
        World.
1954   *The Sociology of Work.* Minneapolis: University of Minnesota
        Press.

Caplow, Theodore; Howard M. Bahr; Bruce Chadwick; Reuben Hill; and
Margaret Holmes Williamson
1982   *Middletown Families: Fifty Years of Change and Continuity.*
        Minneapolis: University of Minnesota Press.

Carroll, Glenn
  Forth-   "Concentration and Specialization: Dynamics of Niche Width
  coming.   in Populations of Organizations. *American Journal of Sociology,* in press.
  1984   "The Specialist Strategy." *California Management Review* 26, no. 3 (Spring): 126–37.
Cerf, Bennett
  1977   *At Random.* New York: Random House.
Chandler, Alfred D.
  1977   *The Visible Hand: The Managerial Revolution in American Business.* Cambridge, Mass.: Harvard University Press.
Child, John
  1972   "Organization of Structure, Environment and Performance: The Role of Strategic Choice." *Sociology* 6:1–22.
Child, John, and Janet Fulk
  1982   "Maintenance of Occupational Control: The Case of Professionals." *Work and Occupations* 9:155–92.
Cicourel, Aaron
  1970   "The Acquisition of Social Structure: Toward a Developmental Sociology of Language." Pp. 136–68 in Jack D. Douglas, ed., *Understanding Everyday Life.* Chicago: Aldine.
Cohen, Michael D., and James G. March
  1974   *Leadership and Ambiguity.* New York: McGraw-Hill.
Cohen, Michael D.; James G. March; and Johan P. Olsen
  1972   "A Garbage Can Model of Organizational Choice." *Administrative Science Quarterly* 17:1–25.
Cole, Jonathan, and Stephen Cole
  1973   *Social Stratification in Science.* Chicago: University of Chicago Press.
Cole, Stephen
  1978   "Scientific Reward Systems: A Comparative Analysis." *Research in Sociology of Knowledge, Sciences and Art* 1:167–90.
Cole, Stephen; Jonathan R. Cole; and Gary A. Simon
  1981   "Chance and Consensus in Peer Review." *Science* 214 (November 20): 881–86.
Collins, Randall
  1979   *The Credential Society.* New York: Academic Press.
Commins, Dorothy
  1978   *What Is An Editor? Saxe Commins at Work.* Chicago: University of Chicago Press.
Cook, Karen S.
  1977   "Exchange and Power in Networks of Interorganizational Relations." *Sociological Quarterly* 18:62–82.
Cooley, Charles Horton
  1929   "Case Study of Small Institutions as a Method of Research."

In Ernest W. Burgess, ed., *Personality and the Social Group.* Chicago: University of Chicago Press.

Coser, Lewis A.
1979 "Asymmetries in Author-Publisher Relations." *Society* 17: 34–37.

Coser, Lewis A.; Charles Kadushin; and Walter W. Powell
1982 *Books: The Culture and Commerce of Publishing.* New York: Basic Books.

Coser, Rose Laub
1984 "The Greedy Nature of *Gemeinschaft.*" Pp. 221–39 in Walter W. Powell and Richard Robbins, eds., *Conflict and Consensus: Essays in Honor of Lewis A. Coser.* New York: Free Press.
1961 "Insulation from Observability and Types of Conformity." *American Sociological Review* 26:28–39.

Crane, Diana
1972 *Invisible Colleges: Diffusion of Knowledge in Scientific Communities.* Chicago: University of Chicago Press.
1967 "The Gatekeepers of Science: Some Factors Affecting the Selection of Articles for Scientific Journals." *American Sociologist* 2:195–201.

Croce, Benedetto
1968 *Aesthetic.* Translated by Douglas Ainslie. New York: Noonday Press.

Crozier, Michel
1981 "Comparing Structures and Comparing Games." Pp. 97–110 in C. C. Lemert, ed., *French Sociology: Rupture and Renewal since 1968.* New York: Columbia University Press.
1964 *The Bureaucratic Phenomenon.* Chicago: University of Chicago Press.

Cyert, Richard M., and James G. March
1963 *A Behavioral Theory of the Firm.* Englewood Cliffs, N.J.: Prentice-Hall.

Darnton, Robert
1983 "A Survival Strategy for Academic Authors." *American Scholar* 52:533–37.
1975 "Writing News and Telling Stories." *Daedalus* 104:175–94.
1971 "Reading, Writing, and Publishing in Eighteenth-Century France: A Case Study in the Sociology of Literature." *Daedalus.* 100:214–56.

Dearborn, DeWitt C., and Herbert A. Simon
1958 "Selective Perception: A Note on the Departmental Identifications of Executives." *Sociometry* 21:140–44.

Dessauer, John P.
1983 "Book Industry Economics in 1982." Pp. 95–110 in *Publishers Weekly Yearbook, 1983.* New York: R. R. Bowker.

238 References

1974 *Book Publishing: What It Is, What It Does.* New York: R. R. Bowker.

DiMaggio, Paul J.
1984 "Structural Analysis of Organizational Fields." Unpublished manuscript, Department of Sociology, Yale University.

DiMaggio, Paul J., and Walter W. Powell
1983 "The Iron Cage Revisited: Institutional Isomorphism and Collective Rationality in Organizational Fields." *American Sociological Review* 48:147–60.

Doebler, Paul
1976 "Editors and Other Creative People Are Introduced to the Financial Side of Book Publishing." *Publishers Weekly*, March 15, pp. 33–35.

Driscoll, James
1980 "Myths about Work." Paper presented at the Academy of Management Meetings, August, Detroit.

Duncan, Robert B.
1972 "Characteristics of Organizational Environments and Perceived Environmental Uncertainty." *Administrative Science Quarterly* 17:313–27.

Eccles, Robert, and Harrison C. White
1984 "Firm and Market Interfaces of Profit Center Control." Working paper, Harvard Business School.

Edwards, Richard
1979 *The Contested Terrain: The Transformation of the Workplace in the Twentieth Century.* New York: Basic Books.

Emerson, Richard M.
1962 "Power-Dependence Relations." *American Sociological Review* 27:31–41.

Epstein, Joseph
1977 "Life and Letters: Marboro Country." *American Scholar* 46:432–40.

Erwin, Robert, and J. David Sapir
1977 "The Writer vs. the University Press." *Book Forum* 3:508–17.

Exman, Eugene
1967 *The House of Harper: One Hundred and Fifty Years of Publishing.* New York: Harper & Row.

Faulkner, Robert
1983 *Music on Demand: Composers and Careers in the Hollywood Film Industry.* New Brunswick, N.J.: Transaction.

Feldman, Martha S., and James G. March
1981 "Information in Organizations as Signal and Symbol." *Administrative Science Quarterly* 26:171–86.

Fiedler, Leslie
1981 "The Death and Rebirths of the Novel." *Salmagundi* 15:143–52.

Freeman, John, and Michael T. Hannan
    1983   "Niche Width and the Dynamics of Organizational Popula-
           tions." *American Journal of Sociology* 88:1116–45.
Friedson, Eliot
    1976   *Doctoring Together.* New York: Elsevier.
    1970   *The Profession of Medicine.* New York: Dodd, Mead.
Frugé, August
    1976   "The Ambiguous University Press." *Scholarly Publishing* 8:
           1–10.
Fulton, Oliver, and Martin Trow
    1974   "Research Activity in American Higher Education." *Sociol-
           ogy of Education* 47:29–73.

Gedin, Per
    1977   *Literature in the Marketplace.* Translated by George Bissett.
           Woodstock, N.Y.: Overlook Press.
Geertz, Clifford
    1978   "The Bazaar Economy: Information and Search in Peasant
           Marketing." *American Economic Review* 68, no. 2 (May):
           28–32.
Geiber, Walter
    1964   "News Is What Newspapermen Make It." Pp. 172–82 in
           L. Dexter and D. White, eds., *People, Society, and Mass
           Communications.* Glencoe, Ill.; Free Press.
Gilmer, Walker
    1970   *Horace Liveright: Publisher of the Twenties.* New York: David
           Lewis.
Gilroy, Angele A.
    1980   *An Economic Analysis of U.S. Domestic Book Publishing:
           1972–Present.* Congressional Research Service Report No.
           80-79E. Washington, D.C.: U.S. Government Printing Office.
Goode, William J.
    1960   "Encroachment, Charlatanism, and the Emerging Profession:
           Psychology, Sociology, and Medicine." *American Sociological
           Review* 25:902–14.
Goodenough, Ward H.
    1963   *Cooperation in Change.* New York: Russell Sage Foundation.
Graña, Caesar
    1964   *Bohemian versus Bourgeois.* New York: Basic Books.
Grannis, Chandler B.
    1967   *What Happens in Book Publishing.* 2d ed. New York: Co-
           lumbia University Press.
Granovetter, Mark
    1983a   "Economic Action and Social Structure: A Theory of Embed-
           dedness." Unpublished manuscript, Department of Sociolo-
           gy, SUNY at Stony Brook.

1983b   "Labor Mobility, Internal Markets and Job-Matching: A Comparison of the Sociological and Economic Approaches." Unpublished manuscript, Department of Sociology, SUNY at Stony Brook.

1974   *Getting a Job: A Study of Contacts and Careers.* Cambridge, Mass.: Harvard University Press.

Greenwood, Ernest
1957   "Attributes of a Profession." *Social Work* 2 (July): 45–55.

Hackman, J. Richard, and Greg R. Oldham
1980   *Work Redesign.* Reading, Mass.: Addison-Wesley.

Hage, Jerald, and Michael Aiken
1967   "Relationship of Centralization to Other Structural Properties." *Administrative Science Quarterly* 12:72–92.

Hagstrom, Warren
1976   "The Production of Culture in Science." *American Behavioral Scientist* 19:753–68.

Hall, Richard H.
1975   *Occupations and the Social Structure.* 2d ed. Englewood Cliffs, N.J.: Prentice-Hall.

Halpenny, Frances
1973   "Education and Training for Scholarly Publishing." *Scholarly Publishing* 4:165–74.

Hannan, Michael T., and John Freeman
1984   "Structural Inertia and Organizational Change." *American Sociological Review* 49:149–64.
1977   "The Population Ecology of Organizations." *American Journal of Sociology* 82:929–64.

Hargens, Lowell, and Warren Hagstrom
1967   "Sponsored and Contest Mobility of American Academic Scientists." *Sociology of Education* 40:24–30.

Harman, Eleanor, and R. M. Schoeffel
1975   "Our Readers Report . . ." *Scholarly Publishing* 6:333–40.

Hart, James D.
1950   *The Popular Book: A History of America's Literary Taste.* New York: Oxford University Press.

Haug, M. R.
1977   "Computer Technology and the Obsolescence of the Concept of Profession." In M. R. Haug and J. Dofny, eds., *Work and Technology.* Beverly Hills: Sage.

Haydn, Hiram
1974   *Words and Faces.* New York: Harcourt Brace Jovanovich.

Hickson, D. J.; C. R. Hinings; C. A. Lee; R. E. Schneck; and J. M. Pennings
1971   "A Strategic Contingencies' Theory of Intraorganizational Power." *Administrative Science Quarterly* 16:216–29.

Hirsch, Paul M., and Thomas Whisler
  1982   "The View from the Boardroom." Paper presented at the
          Academy of Management Meetings, August, New York, N.Y.
Inkeles, Alex
  1969   "Social Structure and Socialization." Pp. 615–32 in D. A.
          Goslin, ed., *Handbook of Socialization Theory and Research*.
          Chicago: Rand-McNally.
Jacobs, David
  1981   "Toward a Theory of Mobility and Behavior in Organizations:
          An Inquiry into the Consequences of Some Relationships
          between Individual Performance and Organizational Suc-
          cess." *American Journal of Sociology* 87:684–707.
James, Louis
  1963   *Fiction for the Working Man, 1830–1850*. London: Oxford
          University Press.
Jamous, H., and B. Peloille
  1970   "Work and Power." In G. Esland and G. Salomon eds., *The
          Politics of Work and Occupations*. Milton-Keynes, Eng.:
          Open University Press.
Johnstone, John W. C.; E. J. Slawski; and W. W. Bowman
  1976   *The News People: A Sociological Portrait of American Journal-
          ists and Their Work*. Urbana: University of Illinois Press.
Kadushin, Charles
  1974   *The American Intellectual Elite*. Boston: Little, Brown.
Kanter, Rosabeth Moss
  1983   *The Change Masters*. New York: Simon & Schuster.
  1977   *Men and Women of the Corporation*. New York: Basic Books.
  1968   "Commitment and Social Organization: A Study of Commit-
          ment Mechanisms in Utopian Communities." *American
          Sociological Review* 33:499–517.
Kelsell, R. K.
  1955   *Higher Civil Servants in Britain*. London: Routledge & Kegan
          Paul.
Kerr, Chester
  1974   "What to Publish at Yale." *Scholarly Publishing* 5:211–18.
Knight, Frank
  1921   *Risk, Uncertainty and Profit*. New York: Harper & Row.
Knoke, David, and Ron S. Burt
  1982   "Prominence." In R. S. Burt and M. J. Minor, eds., *Applied
          Network Analysis: Structural Methodology for Empirical So-
          cial Research*. Beverly Hills: Sage.
Kreps, David M., and Robert Wilson
  1982   "Reputation and Imperfect Information." *Journal of Eco-
          nomic Theory* 27:253–79.

Lane, Michael
    1980   *Books and Publishers*. Lexington, Mass.: D. C. Heath.
    1975   "Shapers of Culture: The Editor in Book Publishing." *Annals of the American Academy of Political and Social Science* 421:34–42.
    1970   "Publishing Managers, Publishing House Organization and Role Conflict." *Sociology* 4:367–83.
Larson, Magali Sarfatti
    1977   *The Rise of Professionalism*. Berkeley: University of California Press.
Lawrence, Paul R., and Jay W. Lorsch
    1967   *Organization and Environment*. Cambridge, Mass.: Harvard University Press.
Leavis, Q. D.
    1965   *Fiction and the Reading Public*. New York: Russell & Russell.
Lehmann-Haupt, Helmutt, in collaboration with L. C. Roth and R. G. Silver
    1951   *The Book in America: A History of the Making and Selling of Books in the United States*. 2d ed. New York: R. R. Bowker.
Lekachman, Robert
    1965   "The Literary Intellectuals of New York." *Social Research* 32:127–40.
Lewin, Kurt
    1951   "Psychological Ecology." In D. Cartwright, ed., *Field Theory in Social Science*. New York: Harper & Bros.
Lieberson, Stanley, and James F. O'Connor
    1972   "Leadership and Organizational Performance: A Study of Large Corporations." *American Sociological Review* 37:117–30.
Lin, Nan; Walter M. Ensel; and John C. Vaughn
    1981   "Social Resources and Strength of Ties." *American Sociological Review* 46:393–405.
Lindblom, Charles
    1959   "The Science of Muddling Through." *Public Administration Review* 19:79–99.
Linder, Staffan B.
    1970   *The Harried Leisure Class*. New York: Columbia University Press.
Lindsey, Duncan
    1978   *The Scientific Publication System*. San Francisco: Jossey-Bass.
Lorsch, J. W., and J. J. Morse
    1974   *Organizations and Their Members: A Contingency Approach*. New York: Harper & Row.
Luce, Robert Duncan, and Howard Raiffa
    1957   *Games and Decisions*. New York: John Wiley.

Macaulay, Stewart
  1963   "Non-Contractual Relations in Business: A Preliminary
          Study." *American Sociological Review* 28:55–67.
Machlup, Fritz, and Kenneth Leeson
  1978   *Information through the Printed Word.* Vol. 1: *Book Pub-
          lishing.* New York: Praeger.
Madison, Charles A.
  1974   *Irving to Irving: Author-Publisher Relations, 1800–1974.* New
          York: R. R. Bowker.
  1966   *Book Publishing in America.* New York: McGraw-Hill.
March, James C., and James G. March
  1977   "Almost Random Careers: The Wisconsin School Superin-
          tendency, 1940–1972." *Administrative Science Quarterly*
          22:377–409.
March, James G.
  1978   "Bounded Rationality, Ambiguity, and the Engineering of
          Choice." *Bell Journal of Economics* 9:587–608.
March, James G., and Johan P. Olsen
  1983   "Organizing Political Life: What Administrative Reorganiza-
          tion Tells Us about Government." *American Political Science
          Review* 77:281–96.
  1976   *Ambiguity and Choice in Organizations.* Bergen, Norway:
          Universitetsforlaget.
  1975   "The Uncertainty of the Past." *European Journal of Political
          Research* 3:147–71.
March, James G., and Herbert Simon
  1958   *Organizations.* New York: Wiley.
Marsden, Peter V.
  1983   "Restricted Access in Networks and Models of Power." *Amer-
          ican Journal of Sociology* 88:686–717.
Mechanic, David
  1962   "Sources of Power of Lower Participants in Complex Orga-
          nizations." *Administrative Science Quarterly* 7:349–64.
Medoff, James, and Katharine Abraham
  1980   "Experience, Performance, and Earnings." *Quarterly Journal
          of Economics* 95:703–36.
Menaker, Daniel
  1981   "Unsolicited, Unloved MSS." *New York Times Book Review,*
          March 1, pp. 3, 22.
Merton, Robert K.
  1968   "The Matthew Effect in Science." *Science* 159:56–63.
  1957   "Some Preliminaries to a Sociology of Medical Education."
          Pp. 3–79 in *The Student Physician,* edited by R. K. Merton et
          al. Cambridge, Mass.: Harvard University Press.

Meyer, John W., and Brian Rowan
  1977   "Institutionalized Organizations: Formal Structure as Myth and Ceremony." *American Journal of Sociology* 83:340–63.
Miller, William
  1949   *The Book Industry.* New York: Columbia University Press.
Mills, C. Wright
  1963   "Language, Logic, and Culture." In I. L. Horowitz, ed., *Power, Politics, and People: The Collected Essays of C. W. Mills.* New York: Oxford University Press.
Mintzberg, Henry
  1973   *The Nature of Managerial Work.* New York: Harper & Row.
Mischel, Walter
  1973   "Toward a Cognitive Reconceptualization of Personality." *Psychological Review* 80:252–83.
Mohr, Lawrence B.
  1971   "Organizational Technology and Organizational Structure." *Administrative Science Quarterly* 16:444–59.
Morton, Herbert C.
  1982   "The Book Industry: A Review of Books: The Culture and Commerce of Publishing." *Science* 216 (May 21): 862–63.
Most, Harry R.
  1977   "Today's Best Book Profits Are in Professional Publishing." *Publishers Weekly,* March 21, p. 39.
Mott, Frank Luther
  1947   *Golden Multitudes: The Story of Best Sellers in the United States.* New York: R. R. Bowker.
Nobile, Phillip
  1974   *Intellectual Skywriting: Literary Politics and the "New York Review of Books."* New York: Charterhouse.
Noble, J. Kendrick
  1982   "Book Publishing." Pp. 95–141 in B. M. Compaine, ed., *Who Owns the Media?* 2d ed. White Plains, N.Y.: Knowledge Industry Publications.
Oppenheimer, M.
  1973   "The Proletarianization of the Professional." Sociological Review Monographs no. 20, pp. 213–27.
Ouchi, William G.
  1980   "Markets, Bureaucracies, and Clans." *Administrative Science Quarterly* 25:129–44.
Perrow, Charles B.
  1985   "Journaling Careers." In L. L. Cummings and P. J. Frost, eds., *Publishing in the Organizational Sciences.* Homewood, Ill.: Irwin.
  1979   *Complex Organizations: A Critical Essay.* 2d ed. Glenview, Ill.: Scott, Foresman.

1977 "The Bureaucratic Paradox: The Efficient Organization Centralizes in Order to Decentralize." *Organizational Dynamics* 5 (Spring): 2–14.

1976 "Control in Organizations: The Centralized-Decentralized Bureaucracy." Paper presented at the Annual Meetings of the American Sociological Association, August, New York.

1974 "Is Business Really Changing?" *Organizational Dynamics* 2 (Spring): 31–44.

1967 "A Framework for the Comparative Analysis of Organizations." *American Sociological Review* 32:194–208.

1961 "The Analysis of Goals in Complex Organizations." *American Sociological Review* 26:854–66.

Peters, Thomas J.
1978 "Symbols, Patterns, and Settings: An Optimistic Case for Getting Things Done." *Organizational Dynamics* 6 (Autumn):3–23.

Peterson, Richard A., and David G. Berger
1975 "Cycles in Symbol Production: The Case of Popular Music." *American Sociological Review* 40:158–73.

1971 "Entrepreneurship in Organizations: Evidence from the Popular Music Industry." *Administrative Science Quarterly* 16:97–106.

Pfeffer, Jeffrey
1983 "Organizational Demography." Pp. 299–357 in L. L. Cummings and B. Staw, eds., *Research in Organizational Behavior*, vol. 5. Greenwich, Conn.: JAI Press.

1982 *Organizations and Organization Theory*. Marshfield, Mass.: Pitman.

1981 "Management as Symbolic Action: The Creation and Maintenance of Organizational Paradigms." Pp. 1–52 in L. L. Cummings and B. Staw, eds., *Research in Organizational Behavior*, vol. 3. Greenwich, Conn.: JAI Press.

1977 "Toward an Examination of Stratification in Organizations." *Administrative Science Quarterly* 22:553–67.

Pfeffer, Jeffrey, and Gerald Salancik
1978 *The External Control of Organizations*. New York: Harper & Row.

Porter, Michael
1980 *Competitive Strategy*. New York: Free Press.

Powell, Walter W.
1984 "Institutional Sources of Organizational Structure: A Comparative Analysis of Scholarly Publishing and Public Television." Paper presented at the American Sociological Association annual meetings, August, San Antonio, Texas.

1983 "Whither the Local Bookstore?" *Daedalus* 112:51–64.

1982a   "Adapting to Tight Money and New Opportunities." *Scholarly Publishing* 14:9–20.

1982b   "From Craft to Corporation: The Impact of Outside Ownership on Book Publishing." Pp. 33–52 in J. S. Ettema and D. C. Whitney, eds., *Individuals in Mass Media Organizations: Creativity and Constraint.* Beverly Hills: Sage.

1978a   "Getting into Print." Ph.D. dissertation, Department of Sociology, SUNY at Stony Brook.

1978b   "Publishers' Decision Making: What Criteria Do They Use in Deciding Which Books to Publish?" *Social Research* 45: 227–52.

Powell, Walter W., and Rebecca Friedkin
1983   "Political and Organizational Influences on Public Television Programming." Pp. 413–38 in E. Wartella and D. C. Whitney, eds., *Mass Communication Review Yearbook,* vol. 4. Beverly Hills: Sage.

Pressman, J. L., and Aaron B. Wildavsky
1973   *Implementation.* Berkeley: University of California Press.

Price, James
1977   *The Study of Turnover.* Ames: Iowa State University Press.

Pugh, D. S.; D. J. Hickson; C. R. Hinings; and C. Turner
1968   "Dimensions of Organization Structure." *Administrative Science Quarterly* 13:65–105.

Quant, Mary
1965   *Quant by Quant.* London: Cassell.

Quirk, Dantia
1977   *KIP Studies: The College Publishing Market, 1977–1982.* White Plains, N.Y.: Knowledge Industry Publications.

Reuter, Madalynne; John F. Baker; and Chandler B. Grannis
1982   "Scholarly Publishers Meet in a Can-Fix-It Mood." *Publishers Weekly,* July 30, pp. 30–42.

Richardson, G. B.
1972   "The Organisation of Industry." *Economic Journal* 82: 883–96.

Rogers, Everett M., and Judith K. Larsen
1984   *Silicon Valley Fever: Growth of High-Tech Culture.* New York: Basic Books.

Roshco, Bernard
1975   *Newsmaking.* Chicago: University of Chicago Press.

Ross, Irwin
1977   "The New Golconda in Book Publishing." *Fortune* 96 (December): 110–20.

Roth, Julius A.
1974   "Professionalism—The Sociologist's Decoy." *Sociology of Work and Occupations* 1:6–23.

Salancik, Gerald R., and Jeffrey Pfeffer
1977 "Constraints on Administrator Discretion: The Limited Influence of Mayors on City Budgets." *Urban Affairs Quarterly* 12:475–98.
1974 "The Bases and Use of Power in Organizational Decision Making: The Case of a University." *Administrative Science Quarterly* 19:453–73.

Schapiro, Meyer
1964 "On the Relation of Patron and Artist: Comments on a Proposed Model for the Scientist." *American Journal of Sociology* 70:363–69.

Schudson, Michael
1978 "A Critique of the 'Production of Culture' Perspective in the Study of Mass Media." Paper presented at the annual meeting of the American Sociological Association, September, San Francisco.

Schwartz, Barry
1978a "The Social Ecology of Time Barriers." *Social Forces* 56: 1203–20.
1978b "Queues, Priorities, and Social Process." *Social Psychology* 41:3–12.
1975 *Queuing and Waiting: Studies in the Social Organization of Access and Delay.* Chicago: University of Chicago Press.

Schwartz, Barry, and Steven C. Dubin
1978 "Manuscript Queues and Editorial Organization." *Scholarly Publishing* 9:253–59.

Scott, W. Richard
1965 "Reactions to Supervision in a Heteronomous Professional Organization." *Administrative Science Quarterly* 10:65–81.

Scott, W. Richard, and John W. Meyer
1983 "The Organization of Societal Sectors." Pp. 129–53 in J. Meyer and W. R. Scott, eds., *Organizational Environments: Ritual and Rationality.* Beverly Hills: Sage.

Shatzkin, Leonard
1982 *In Cold Type: Overcoming the Book Crisis.* Boston: Houghton Mifflin.

Sheehan, Donald
1952 *This Was Publishing: A Chronicle of the Book Trade in the Gilded Age.* Bloomington: Indiana University Press.

Shils, Edward
1981 *Tradition.* Chicago: University of Chicago Press.

Shubik, Martin; Peggy Heim; and William J. Baumol
1983 "On Contracting with Publishers: Author's Information Updated." *American Economic Review* 73, no. 2 (May): 365–81.

Sifton, Elisabeth
1982 "What Reading Public?" *Nation* 234:627–32.

Simmel, Georg
    1950   *The Sociology of Georg Simmel.* Translated and edited by Kurt
            H. Wolff. Glencoe, Ill.: Free Press.
Simon, Herbert
    1957   *Administrative Behavior.* New York: Free Press.
Stinchcombe, Arthur L.
    1984   "Contracts as Hierarchical Documents." Institute of Indus-
            trial Economics Reports, no. 65. Bergen, Norway.
    1980   "Three Origins of Red Tape." Unpublished manuscript, De-
            partment of Sociology, Northwestern University, Evanston,
            Ill.
    1959   "Bureaucratic and Craft Administration of Production: A
            Comparative Study." *Administrative Science Quarterly* 4:
            168–87.
Summers, David
    1982   "STM Editors in Profile." *Bookseller,* June 5:2109–11.
Sutcliffe, Peter
    1978   *The Oxford University Press: An Informal History.* London:
            Oxford University Press.
Sutherland, J. A.
    1976   *Victorian Novelists and Publishers.* Chicago: University of
            Chicago Press.
Tebbel, John
    1972,   *A History of Book Publishing in the United States.* 4 vols. Vol.
    1975,   1: *The Creation of an Industry, 1630–1865.* Vol. 2: *The Expan-*
    1978,   *sion of an Industry, 1865–1919.* Vol. 3: *The Golden Age be-*
    1981   *tween Two Wars, 1920–1940.* Vol. 4: *The Great Change, 1940–*
            1980. New York: R. R. Bowker.
    1974   *The Media in America.* New York: New American Library.
Thompson, James
    1967   *Organizations in Action.* New York: McGraw-Hill.
Thompson, James, and A. Tuden
    1959   "Strategies, Structures, and Process of Organizational Deci-
            sion." Reprinted in W. Rushing and M. Zald, eds., *Organiza-
            tions and Beyond.* Lexington, Mass.: D. C. Heath, 1976.
Thornton, Russell, and Peter M. Nardi
    1975   "The Dynamics of Role Acquisition." *American Journal of
            Sociology* 80:870–85.
Tuchman, Gaye
    1984   "When the Prevalent Don't Prevail: Male Hegemony and the
            Victorian Novel." Pp. 139–58 in Walter W. Powell and
            Richard Robbins, eds., *Conflict and Consensus: Essays in
            Honor of Lewis A. Coser.* New York: Free Press.
    1982   "Culture as Resource: Actions Defining the Victorian Novel."
            Media, Culture, and Society 4:3–18.

1978   *Making News.* New York: Free Press.

1973   "Making News by Doing Work: Routinizing the Unexpected." *American Journal of Sociology* 79:110–31.

1972   "Objectivity as Strategic Ritual: An Examination of Newsmen's Notions of Objectivity." *American Journal of Sociology* 77:660–79.

Tuchman, Gaye, and Nina Fortin

1980   "Edging Women Out: Some Suggestions about the Structure of Opportunities and the Victorian Novel." *Signs* 6:308–25.

Van Maanen, John

1978   "People Processing: Strategies of Organizational Socialization." *Organizational Dynamics* 7, no. 1:19–36.

Ward, Albert

1974   *Book Production: Fiction and the German Reading Public, 1740–1800.* London: Oxford University Press.

Watson, Tony J.

1980   *Sociology, Work and Industry.* London: Routledge & Kegan Paul.

Watt, Ian

1957   *The Rise of the Novel.* Berkeley: University of California Press.

Weick, Karl E.

1976   "Educational Organizations as Loosely Coupled Systems." *Administrative Science Quarterly* 21:1–19.

1969   *The Social Psychology of Organizing.* Reading, Mass.: Addison-Wesley.

Wendroff, Michael

1980   "Should We Do the Book? A Study of How Publishers Handle Acquisition Decisions." *Publishers Weekly* August 15, pp. 25–28.

Wheelock, John Hall

1950   *Editor to Author: The Letters of Maxwell Perkins.* New York: Scribner's.

White, David

1950   "The Gatekeeper: A Case Study in the Selection of the News." *Journalism Quarterly* 27:383–90.

White, Harrison

1983   "Agency as Control." Working paper, Harvard Business School.

1981   "Interfaces." Paper presented at the Social Science Research Council Conference on Organizational Indicators, December.

Whiteside, Thomas

1981   *The Blockbuster Complex.* Middletown, Conn.: Wesleyan University Press.

Williams, Raymond

1961   *Culture and Society, 1780–1950.* London: Penguin.

Williamson, Oliver E.
1985 *The Economic Institutions of Capitalism.* New York: Free Press.
1981 "The Economics of Organization: The Transaction Cost Approach." *American Journal of Sociology* 87:548–77.
1980 "The Organization of Work: A Comparative Institutional Assessment." *Journal of Economic Behavior and Organization* 1:5–38.
1975 *Markets and Hierarchies.* New York: Free Press.

Wrong, Dennis
1970 "The Case of the *New York Review.*" *Commentary* 50, no. 5 (November): 49–63.

Zerubavel, Eviatar
1979 *Patterns of Time in Hospital Life.* Chicago: University of Chicago Press.

Zucker, Lynne
1983 "Organizations as Institutions." Pp. 1–47 in S. Bacharach, ed., *Research in the Sociology of Organizations,* vol. 2. Greenwich, Conn.: JAI Press.

Zuckerman, Harriet
1970 "Stratification in American Science." *Sociological Inquiry* 40, no. 2 (Spring): 235–57.

Zuckerman, Harriet, and R. K. Merton
1971 "Patterns of Evaluation in Science." *Minerva* 9:66–100.

INDEX

Abraham, Katharine, 224
Academic Press, 31
Acceptance rates, 89, 161–62, 168–76
Acquisitions editor, use of term, 11
Ad Hoc Committee on What to Publish, 134
Advances, 54, 88, 117, 179, 185, 218
Agency accounts, 52, 54
Aiken, Michael, 135
Akerlof, George A., 191–92
Aldrich, Howard E., 157, 231
Altick, Richard D., 212
American Scholar, 29–30, 52–53
Apple Press, xxi, xxvii–xxix;
academic status of authors at, 179–82; acceptance rates at, 89, 161, 168–72; acquisition methods at, 163, 166–72, 209–10; author relations with, 40, 49–50, 65–67, 70, 74, 116–23; complementarity with backlist at, 154; conflicts at, 64–68; costing-out at, 103–4; description of, 36–37; domain of, 49–54; editorial autonomy at, 128–31, 133–34, 159–60; editor's tasks at, 73–75, 77; extraorganizational ties at, 142–43, 190–93; factors influencing accept-

ance at 81–87; financial considerations at, 178, 183–85; formal contracting process at, 78–81; future of, 207; hiring at, 103; history of, 38–42; informal controls at, 144–58; inventory considerations at, 176–77; occupational control by editors at, 137, 139–40; outside reviewers for, 78, 104–9, 133–34, 156, 187; and Plum Press, differences between, summarized 68–71, 186–87; and public television station, compared, 200; reference works published by, 116; rejections-handling at, 111–12; search behavior at, analyzed, 94–100; search process at, described, 88–92; structure of, 54–62, 68–69
Arrow, Kenneth, 51
Artist-dealer relationship, xxiv–xxv
Association of American Publishers, 1, 13, 49, 214; Education for Publishing Committee of, 139, 223–24; publishing categories of, 22–23
Association of American University Presses, 222, 230
Astley, W. Graham, 231
Atlantic Monthly, 29–30, 161–62

251

Invisible colleges, 24, 59–60, 195.
  See also Networks
ITT, 5

Jacobs, David, 126–27
JAI Press, 31
James, Louis, 212
Jamous, H., 138
Johns Hopkins University Press, 230
Johnstone, John W., 223
Jossey-Bass, 31
Journalism: as profession, 223; socialization in, 226
Journals, 164, 205; advertising in, 59–60, 63; of Plum Press, 43, 46, 114–16, 186–87; publishing of, and book publishing, compared, 202, 204, 206
Jovanovich, William, 2, 213

Kadushin, Charles, xxi, xxvi, xxviii, 28, 57, 63, 89, 161, 170, 172, 179, 193, 211–25, 229
Kanter, Rosabeth, xxii, 145, 151
Kelsell, R. K., 151
Kerr, Chester, 73, 134
Kirkwood, Heather, 6, 214
Knight, Frank, 135
Knoke, David, 181
Knopf, Alfred, 214
Korda, Michael, 2
Kreps, David M., 205

Lane, Michael, 22, 212
Larsen, Judith K., 193
Larson, Magali Sarfatti, 99
Launch meetings, 65
Law, occupational control in, 137–38
Lawrence, Paul R., 135, 136
Leavis, Q. D., 212
Leeson, Kenneth, 212
Lehmann-Haupt, Helmutt, 211
Lekachman, Robert, 211
Lewin, Kurt, 212
Lexicons, organizational, 151–52
Lexington Books, 31
Libraries, sales to, 53–54, 195–96

Library work, as profession, 223
Lieberson, Stanley, 61
Lin, Nan, 151
Lindblom, Charles, 93
Linder, Staffan, 165
Lindsey, Duncan, 211
Line editors, 11
Linkages with environment, establishment of, 101
Literary agents, 11, 34–35, 50–51, 74, 181
Lofquist, William S., 213
Loose coupling, 93–97
Lorsch, J. W., 135, 136
Luce, Robert Duncan, 135

Macaulay, Stewart, xviii, 193
McDowell, Edwin, 215, 231
McGraw-Hill, 3, 25, 31
Machlup, Fritz, 212
Macmillan, British house of, 156–57, 229
Macmillan Publishing Company, 3
Madison, Charles A., 3, 211
Manufacturing department, 58–59
Manuscripts: acceptance rates for, 89, 161–62, 168–76; conflicts over editing of, 119–22; costing-out of, 103–4; evaluation of, 103–10, 162–63; rejected, 110–14, 164; search process for, 88–93; unsolicited, 88–90, 162, 168–73, 182
March, James C., 151
March, James G., xxi–xxii, 63–64, 93–94, 96–100, 151, 157, 164
Marketing: by Apple Press, 59–60, 69; capability in, and decision to publish, 154; emphasis on, 10–11; by Plum Press, 47, 59–60, 69, 125; prior to publication, by authors, 195; and specialization, 19
Marketing department, 10, 59; and authors, 122–23; and editorial decisions, 64, 131, 183–84; and textbook publishing career, 28. *See also* Sales department

CONTENTS

NOËL COWARD

Present Indicative

With an introduction by

Sheridan Morley

Methuen Drama

Published by Methuen Drama 2012

Methuen Drama, an imprint of Bloomsbury Publishing Plc

3 5 7 9 10 8 6 4

Methuen Drama
Bloomsbury Publishing Plc
50 Bedford Square
London WC1B 3DP
www.methuendrama.com

Present Indicative first published by William Heinemann Limited 1937
Reissued 1986 in a volume with *Future Indefinite and Past Conditional*
by Methuen London Limited; reissued 1992, 1995 by Mandarin Paperbacks;
reissued 1999 by Methuen Publishing Limited.
This edition published in 2004 by
Methuen Publishing Ltd

ISBN 978 0 413 77413 2

A CIP catalogue record for this book is available from the British Library

Typeset by SX Composing DTP, Rayleigh, Essex
Printed and bound in Great Britain
By CPI Group (UK) Ltd, Croydon, CR0 4YY

ILLUSTRATIONS

[5]

INTRODUCTION

Present Indicative (first published in 1937) stands, in my admittedly unimpartial view, alongside Moss Hart's *Act One* and Emlyn Williams' *George* as one of the greatest autobiographies ever written about a life dedicated from an early age to the theatre. What all three books have in common, of course, is that they are largely pre-success stories: almost half of *Present Indicative* is over before we get to *The Vortex* in 1924, but it is in that half that Coward lays out the pattern of his life and explains the rules by which it was to be lived. The Teddington boyhood of genteel poverty, the failed father, the ambitious mother taking in lodgers to keep the family afloat, the child-actor meeting with Gertrude Lawrence, the desperate determination to succeed so that success could be a passport out of a suburban world he did not care for, the survival of failure and loneliness, the early passion for travel preferably by sea, the belief in work as a kind of religious discipline, the delighted discovery of New York's urgent pace and intensity, and then at 24 the success that was to change the face of London for him.

Though he was, as ever, totally discreet in print about his own sexuality, it is not hard to read, between the lines about early friendships and later bleak breakdowns, the truths about a private life that was often considerably less blithe than his own public facade would suggest. Noël himself was later to write one of the most perceptive of all the *Present Indicative* reviews: 'I read it through the other day and was pleased to find it was better written than I expected it to be. The style is sometimes convulsive, there are too many qualifying adjectives, it is technically insecure and there are several repetitive passages which slow up the narrative, but on the whole there is little in it that I regret having said: from it there emerges enough of my true character to make it valid within the limits of its intention, which was to record the factual truth about myself in relation to the world I lived in, the people I met and the rewards I worked for and often won'.

He also was in no doubt that this first autobiography had struck a chord in its readers, albeit probably the wrong one: 'For as long as it is in print or obtainable from secondhand bookshops there will be people, possibly in diminishing numbers, who will be fascinated or repelled, charmed or unimpressed by the story of an alert little boy who was talented and determined and grew up to attain many of his heart's desires and who, throughout his childhood, youth, adolescence and ten of his adult years, remained consistently fond of his mother. This fact inspired many hundreds of people to write to me in glowing terms. It apparently proved to doubting minds that in spite of success and adulation, and beneath a glittering veneer of wit and vintage playboyishness, I had managed, with extraordinary strength of character, to retain a few normal human instincts. I must admit that I resent the basic assumption that the first gesture of any young man who makes good is to kick his mother in the teeth, but alas it is one of the most annoying disenchantments of success to be praised for the wrong things'.

Present Indicative ends on a similarly rueful note about the general misunderstanding of *Cavalcade* as no more than a theatrical 'Land of Hope and Glory', and in the six years that separated the end of the book from its first publication Noël went on to *Design for Living* and *Conversation Piece*, before making the film of *The Scoundrel* and writing for himself and Gertrude Lawrence the series of one-act plays and musicals that made up *Tonight at 8.30*. So by the time his first autobiography reached the bookshops he was still two years away from his fortieth birthday, but already had behind him such theatrical hits as *The Vortex, Hay Fever, Fallen Angels, Private Lives* and *Bitter-Sweet*. 'This' wrote St John Ervine in an *Observer* review, 'is the book of a man who according to his capacity has taken the measure of life and does not shrink from coping with it'.

Other original reviews were similarly enthusiastic about Coward as a man and an autobiographer, with only one notable exception – a notice in the *New Statesman* from Cyril Connolly which is worth quoting here if only to establish that as early as 1937 the case against Coward was already being made more eloqouently, if in my view mistakenly, than in any of the subsequent 1950s rows about the angry young men of the Royal Court and Noël's temporary loss of theatrical favour.

After dismissing *Present Indicative* as 'almost always shallow and often dull', Connolly went on to wonder: 'What are we left with? The picture, carefully incomplete, of a success; probably of one of the most talented and prodigiously successful people the world has ever known – a person of infinite charm and adaptability whose very adaptability however makes him inferior to a more compact and worldly competitor in his own sphere, like Cole Porter; and an essentially unhappy man, a man who gives one the impression of having seldom really thought or really lived and who is intelligent enough to know it. But what can he do about it? He is not religious, politics bore him, art means facility or else brickbats, love wild excitement and the nervous breakdown. There is only success, more and more of it, till from his pinnacle he can look down to where Ivor Novello and Beverley Nichols gather samphire on a ledge and to where, a pinpoint on the sands below, Mr Godfrey Winn is counting pebbles. But success is all there is, and that even is temporary. For one can't read any of Noël Coward's plays now . . . they are written in the most topical and perishable way imaginable, the cream in them turns sour overnight – they are even dead before they are turned into talkies, however engaging they may seem at the time. This book reveals a terrible predicament, that of a young man with a Midas touch, with a gift that does not creep and branch and flower, but which turns everything it touches into immediate gold. And the gold melts, too'.

Thirty years after that review and *Present Indicative* were published, when in the later 1960s I was starting to write the first Coward biography, there were still a surprising number of critics around prepared to follow the Connolly line and assert that Coward was doomed to follow Lonsdale and Maughan into a theatrical mausoleum, rather than Wilde and Shaw into the ranks of the ever-revivable. Thirty years later still, at the time of this writing, it does not need a Coward apologist to point out to the unquiet grave of Mr Connolly that so far from being unreadable and unplayable, the comedies of Coward are revived more often around the country and the world than those of any other dramatist of his era.

Sheridan Morley

Present Indicative

PRESENT INDICATIVE: 1899–1931

WRITTEN: 1932–36
FIRST PUBLISHED: 1937

PART ONE

I was photographed naked on a cushion very early in life, an insane, toothless smile slitting my face and pleats of fat over-lapping me like an ill-fitting overcoat. Later, at the age of two, I was photographed again. This time in a lace dress, leaning against a garden roller and laughing hysterically. If these photographs can be found they will adorn this book.

In due course I was baptized into the Church of England and, I believe, behaved admirably at the font. No undignified gurglings and screamings. I was carried to the church, damped, and carried back home, preserving throughout an attitude of serene resignation.

Two years later, laced and beribboned, I was conveyed to church again, and was unimpressed by everything except the music to which I danced immediately in the aisle before anyone could stop me, and upon being hoisted back into the pew, fell into such an ungovernable rage that I had to be taken home.

There are many other small incidents of my infancy, some based on hearsay, and some that I actually recall, but I will try to employ a selective economy in setting them down, for it is a tricky business tracing the development of a character along the avenues of reminiscence. Too much detailed accuracy makes dull reading. I don't believe that my own childhood, until I went on the stage at the age of ten, was very different from that of any other little boy of the middle classes, except perhaps that certain embryonic talents may have made me more precocious than the average, and more difficult to manage. Several characteristics which have been commented upon in later years evinced themselves early. I was self-assured from the first, and intolerant of undue piety. I was also uncompromising in my attitude towards people I disliked, attempting to strike them in the face, or failing this, going off into screaming fits which frequently lasted long enough for the doctor to be sent for, but invariably gave place to chubby cluckings and smiles by the time he arrived.

I cherished a woolly monkey called 'Doris' for many years. She shared my bed until I was five, despite the fact that time and friction had denuded her of her fur, her tail, and one eye. I was also excessively fond of fish.

My mother came from what is known as 'Good Family,' which means that she had been brought up in the tradition of being a gentlewoman, a difficult tradition to uphold with very little money in a small suburb, and liable to degenerate into refined gentility unless carefully watched.

The family name was 'Veitch,' and there is a genealogical tree and a crest and engravings of the house in Scotland which my mother and her sisters never saw, as it passed into alien hands before they were born. My grandfather was a captain in the Navy, and the photographs we have of him show a handsome head with curly hair, wide eyes, and side-whiskers. He was, I believe, rather short, which doesn't show in the photographs, as in all of them he is sitting down. He painted a lot in his spare time, mostly water colours, some of them very large indeed. He was good at mountains and clouds and ships, and reflections in the sea, but consciously bad at figures, so he frequently cut these out from coloured prints, and stuck them, singly and in groups, on to his blue mountains, to give the landscapes 'life.'

He died in Madeira, comparatively young, and his wife and children came home to England, where my mother was born soon afterwards. There were, in addition to Mother, three girls and two boys, and an extra relation called Barbara, or 'Borby,' who had fallen out of a port-hole on her head at the age of two, and was consequently a little peculiar. In course of time both the brothers died, and two of the sisters married, one well, the other not so well, and in the year 1883 my grandmother, Aunt Borby, Aunt Vida and my mother, came to Teddington, still quite a small village on the banks of the Thames, where they lived gently and I think a trifle sadly, making over last year's dresses and keeping up appearances.

The social activities of Teddington swirled around St Alban's Church. It was an imposing building rearing high from the ground, secure in the possession of a copper roof which had turned bright green, and a militant vicar, the Reverend Mr Boyd, who was given to furious outbursts from the pulpit, in course of which his eyes flashed fire and his fingers pointed accusingly at old ladies in the congregation. He calmed down in after-years and became Vicar of St Paul's, Knightsbridge. Apart from him and the copper roof, the church's greatest asset was the Coward family, which was enormous, active, and fiercely musical. My Uncle Jim played the organ, while my father, together with my Uncles Randolph, Walter, Percy, and Gordon, and my Aunts Hilda, Myrrha, Ida, and Nellie, graced the choir. Aunt Hilda, indeed, achieved such distinction as a 'coloratura' that she ultimately became known as 'The Twickenham Nightingale.'

It was during choir practice that my mother (also musical) met my father. He courted her for a long time through many services. I like to think of him peeping through his fingers at her during the Litany, and winking fearfully at her under cover of Mr Boyd's vitriolic sermons. They appeared together also in various discreet theatricals, notably a performance of *The Gondoliers* at the Town Hall, in which all the Cowards played principal parts, and Mother demurely tra-la-la'd in the chorus.

When they were married they continued to live at Teddington. Father was very spruce. He always wore a blue cornflower in his buttonhole, and was justly proud of having a cold bath every morning, winter and summer. He went every day to London, where he worked for Metzler's, the music publishers. A boy was born and christened 'Russell,' but he died of meningitis at the age of six, a year and a half before I appeared on the morning of December 16th, 1899.

Teddington grew steadily. A new lock was built. There was a swifter train service to London, and electric trams began to screech along the High Street. There were lots more houses everywhere, with lots more people in them, and with this onset of urban progress the Coward glory began to fade. Nearly all the sisters married and dispersed, the brothers also; Uncle Percy, indeed, actually dispersed all the way to Toronto, where he married a professional pianist, and has never been heard of since, with the exception of a few vague rumours from Australia.

In 1905 we moved to a small villa in Sutton, Surrey. It had bow windows in the front, and a slim straight garden at the back. It also had coloured glass let into the front door. Father had left Metzler's and joined a piano firm which was just beginning. His position in the firm was at first not clearly defined, but on closer analysis proved to be that of a traveller. This necessitated his being away from home a good deal. Once he even went as far afield as Naples. I remember this distinctly, because post-cards of Vesuvius fluttered daily through the letter-box.

A little while after we arrived in Sutton, my brother Eric was born. Emma, our beloved 'general' who had been with us since before my birth, took me round to have tea with some friends, and when I got back I was led upstairs by Auntie Vida to see my 'new little brother.' He seemed to me to be bright red and singularly unattractive, but everybody else was delighted with him. Various things of minor importance happened to me in Sutton. I was run over by a bicycle and had concussion. The calf of my leg was practically torn off by a bull-terrier, and I was brave when it was cauterised.

When I was six I was sent to a day school which was kept by a Miss Willington, who wore blouses with puffed sleeves, plaid skirts and her hair done over a pad. I didn't care for her. On one occasion when she had been irritating me over some little question of English grammar I bit her arm right through to the bone, an action which I have never for an instant regretted.

I made my first public appearance at a prize-giving concert at the end of the term. I was dressed in a white sailor suit and sang 'Coo' from *The Country Girl,* followed by a piping little song about the spring for which I accompanied myself on the piano. This feat brought down the house, and I had to repeat it. I remember leaning over to Mother and Father in the front row and hissing exultantly: 'I've got to sing again.' The evening ended in tears, however, because I was not given a prize. Mother tried vainly to explain to me that the prizes were for hard work during the term and not for vocal prowess, but I refused to be comforted, and was led away weeping.

Mother had an old school friend who came to stay with us sometimes. Her name was Gwen Kelly, and she was a darling. She had large mournful Irish eyes, and a white tailor-made coat and skirt, and she sang and played exquisitely. Her voice was a husky contralto with a brogue in it, and it is to her that I owe the first real enthusiasm I ever had for music. She is dead now, after devoting her life to genteel poverty and an invalid mother, but she was the first artist I knew and I shall never forget her.

We went to the seaside every summer for a fortnight. Broadstairs or Brighton or Bognor. It was at Bognor that I met Uncle George's Concert Party. I shall always remember Uncle George and his 'Merrie Men' with tenderness. They held for me a romantic attraction in their straw hats, coloured blazers, and grubby white flannel trousers. They had a small wooden stage on the sands on which they performed every afternoon and evening. Uncle George himself was the comedian and Uncle Bob, I think, was the serious vocalist. I forget the names of the others excepting Uncle Jack, who was very jaunty and sang, 'Put a little bit away for a rainy day,' swaggering up and down the stage and jingling coins in his trouser pocket.

Uncle George gave a song-and-dance competition every week for the 'Kiddies,' for which I entered my name. I don't think Mother was keen on the idea, but she gave in when she saw how eager I was. On the evening of the competition I put on my sailor suit and waited in a sort of pen with several other aspirants, noting with satisfaction that those who appeared before me were inept and clumsy. When my turn came I sang, 'Come along with me to the Zoo, dear,' and 'Liza Ann' from *The Orchid.* I also danced violently. The applause was highly gratifying, and even Mother forgot her distaste of Uncle George's vulgarity somewhat and permitted herself to bridle. At the end of the performance Uncle George made a speech and presented me with the first prize, a large box of chocolates, which, when opened in our lodgings, proved to be three parts shavings.

From the age of five onwards Mother always took me to a theatre on my birthday. We went up to London in the morning and waited in the pit queue. I saw *The Dairymaids* and *The Blue Moon,* and a Spectacle at the London Hippodrome with a dam

9

bursting and tons of water pouring into the arena. We also went to the pantomime at Croydon which I enjoyed ecstatically from the first moment when the orchestra tuned up and the advertisement-covered safety-curtain rose, disclosing the faded old red tabs lit with an orange glow from the footlights, to the very end of the Harlequinade, when crackers were thrown by the clown and pantaloon to those fortunate enough to be in the expensive seats.

One Christmas I was given a toy theatre complete with two sets of scenery. One scene was a thick wood with a cottage in the distance, and the other was the interior of the cottage with a lot of painted beams. I used to augment this meagre *décor* with penny pantomime sheets which in those days were obtainable at any newspaper shop. There was *Cinderella, The Forty Thieves,* and a lurid melodrama called *Black-eyed Susan,* and many others as well. There were generally three scenes to each sheet, with all the characters brilliantly coloured and marked for each act. These had to be cut out with scissors and mounted on cardboard. I remember 'Fatima, Act III,' of the *Bluebird* sheet was one of my favourites. She was a bulbous girl with a turban. I was also very partial to 'Dandini, Act I,' in the *Cinderella* set. Later on I had a bigger theatre, and Father painted me some excellent scenery, and I used dolls on wires instead of the pasteboard figures, but in my heart I liked the pantomime sheets best.

When I was seven I spent the summer with my Aunt Laura in Cornwall. She was kind, pretty, and vain, and I was very fond of her. Her garden was lovely, and there was a large lake, very deep, with an island in the middle and jungle all round with small hidden waterfalls and secret paths. There was a swing, too, and a small blue punt which sank immediately if touched.

In 1908 we moved to Number 70, Prince of Wales Mansions, Battersea Park. It was a top flat with a little balcony looking out over the park to where the iron framework of Albert Bridge and Chelsea Bridge rose in the distance above the trees. I made a few friends in the adjacent flats and together we harassed the park-keepers, rang bells and ran away, and roller-skated up and down the pavements. Sometimes in the summer we skated all the way to St George's Baths in Buckingham Palace Road and back again, with our wet bathing dresses flapping round our necks.

At this period money worries were oppressing my parents considerably. Father's income from Payne's pianos was small, and Eric and I were both growing fast and had to be clothed and fed. Mother, realising that something had to be done in order to pay off the swiftly mounting debts, decided to take in paying guests. And so a Mr Baker and a Mr Denston came to live with us, and everybody dressed for dinner for the first time for years. This was really quite a jolly period. Emma was still with us and she was a good cook. Gwen Kelly often came to dinner and played the piano afterwards. Father was gay and sang all his old songs with Mother playing his accompaniments. She would take off her rings and place them on the side of the piano and then embark with a flourish upon the introductory chords of 'Mary Adeane,' or 'She and I Together,' while I sat in an Eton collar on the sofa watching for her little grimace when she struck a wrong note, and listening to Mr Baker whispering flirtatiously to Gwen Kelly in the corner.

Father had a light tenor voice of great sweetness, and he frequently shut his eyes tightly for the top notes, reliving, I am sure in those moments, not only the past glories of Teddington drawing-rooms, but the more austere occasions when he, together with Uncle Percy, Uncle Randolph, and Uncle Walter, had awakened the sophisticated echoes of the Caxton Hall, Westminster:

> 'So dainty fair, so gentle wise,
> Young love peeped forth from heaven-blue eyes,
> The lark poured rapture from the skies
> As we went through the heather.'

2

A short while after we had settled in Battersea Park a great agitation was started as to whether or not I was to join the Chapel Royal choir. Uncle Walter, then an eminent member of it, was approached, also Dr Alcock, the organist. It was agreed that I should go to the Chapel Royal school to begin with until I was old enough to have my voice tried for the choir itself. The school was in Clapham, and was run by a Mr Claude Selfe. It was small, consisting only of the twelve Chapel Royal boys, and seven or eight outside pupils of whom I was one. Mr Selfe was kind, sometimes jocular, and nearly always noisy. He had a slight paunch and the most tremendous calves which looked as though they were about to burst exuberantly through his trousers. Manliness was his strong suit, and he did everything in his power to foster this admirable quality in us. Boyishness was all right up to a certain age, but after that manliness was the thing. He wore a black gown and a mortar-board, and when he became in the least enthusiastic or excited over anything, bubbles of foam sprang from his lips like ping-pong balls.

I travelled to school daily by tram, or rather, two trams, as I had to change half-way. The second one landed me at the 'Plough,' Clapham, and from there I walked, in anguish in the mornings, and on wings of song in the afternoon when I was on my way home, loitering on autumn days to collect 'conkers,' and occasionally ringing a few bells just to celebrate the joyful hours of freedom separating me from the next morning. There was a second-hand book-shop on the way where I could buy 'back numbers' of the *Strand Magazine* for a penny each, and I hoarded my pocket money until I could buy a whole year's worth in order to read the E. Nesbit story right through without having to wait for the next instalment. I read 'The Phoenix and the Carpet,' and 'Five Children and It,' also 'The Magic City,' but there were a few numbers missing from that year, so I stole a coral necklace from a visiting friend of Mother's, pawned it for five shillings, and bought the complete book at the Army and Navy Stores. It cost four-and-six, so that including the fare (penny half-return, Battersea Park to Victoria) I was fivepence to the good. In later years I told E. Nesbit of this little incident and I regret to say that she was delighted.

Three days a week at the Chapel Royal school the choir-boys were absent, either in the mornings or afternoons, for choir practice. These days were blissfully quiet, the class-room seemed a pleasant place relaxed in a peaceful emptiness. When I arrived in the morning and saw that those horrible little mortar-boards were not on the pegs in the lobby I knew at once that lessons would be easier, that Mr Selfe would be in an amiable mood, and that the quarter of an hour interval in the middle of the morning would be an interlude of rest rather than a strained evasion of games I didn't want to play.

On the days when the choir-boys were all present the entire atmosphere seemed charged with gloom and foreboding. They were nasty little brutes as far as I can remember, and used to bully me mildly, putting ink pellets down my collar and forcing my head down the w.c. pan. Once during one of these boyish pranks I pretended to faint, having kicked one of them in the fork, an unmanly performance which frightened everyone very much indeed.

Eventually the day came when my voice was to be tried, a lot of assiduous practice having taken place beforehand with Mother at the piano and me hooting the praises of the Lord at her side.

I was dressed in my Eton suit with a slightly larger collar than usual in case of unforeseen throat expansion, and with my hair suitably plastered, I set off clutching a roll of music and Mother's hand.

Dr Alcock was distant and extremely superior. Perhaps his position as Chapel Royal organist, which automatically brought him into contact with the Royal Family as well as the Almighty, faintly upset his balance as a human being. However, undaunted by his forbidding expression, I sang Gounod's 'There is a Green Hill Far Away' at him from beginning to end. My voice was very good and I sang it well, although perhaps a shade too dramatically. I remember giving way to a certain abandon on the line 'There was no other goo-oo-oo-ood enough to pay the price of sin,' and later, lashing myself into a frenzy over the far too often repeated – 'Arnd terust in His redeeming blood.' I think, perhaps, it was this that settled my hash with Dr Alcock, for we were ushered out rapidly with the parting words that not only was I far too young, but that there was no vacancy anyhow. Mother was bitterly disappointed, and I felt miserable at having failed, also offended that my assured talent should not have been immediately recognised, but deep down inside me I was conscious of a secret relief, a certain lifting of the heart when I reflected that my near future was not after all to be spent singing sacred music in company with those unpleasant choir-boys. Mother simmered with rage against Dr Alcock and the whole Chapel Royal for weeks, ultimately arriving at the more comforting viewpoint that my not being accepted was a great stroke of good fortune, as Dr Alcock was silly and obviously didn't know a good voice when he heard one, and that the whole choir looked extremely common, including Uncle Walter.

3

Shortly after my failure for the Chapel Royal, our paying guests departed, and Mother made another of her sudden decisions. This time it was to let the flat for six months and take a small cottage in the country. I think that during all those years in London and the suburbs she had been secretly yearning for some quieter place in which to be poor. Small poverty is a greater strain in a town than in a village, and Mother was country-bred, and weary of whining cockney tradesmen and crowded buses and genteel makeshifts. She often talked wistfully of Chobham where she had lived as a girl; where there had been a garden to the house, a real garden, not a ruled-off passage sown with a few nasturtiums. An advertisement was put in the paper and we waited anxiously for results. Fate was kindly prompt, and in a very few days a Mrs Davis arrived without warning while we were having tea. She was gay and erratic and untidy, with a large green hat and a feather boa. She immediately joined us at tea, and intercepted Mother who was trying to nip into the kitchen in order to change the jam-jar for a more impressive dish.

After tea we went into the drawing-room which smelt rather frowsy as it hadn't been used for a long time, and Mrs Davis sang 'Mifanwy,' and 'My Dear Soul' in a piercing soprano, and then, encouraged, I think, by our obvious musical appreciation, said that she would like to take the flat on the dot providing that she could move in within three days. Mother assumed a dubious expression which wouldn't have deceived a kitten, and shook her head thoughtfully, trying hard to conceal the glint of excitement in her eyes and endeavouring not to appear too eager. I personally thought that she had gone raving mad. However, it was all fixed up satisfactorily, and we spent the next three days in a state of rapture, spring-cleaning, and having our meals off one end of the kitchen table.

We went first to stay with Grandmother, Auntie Borby, and Auntie Vida in rooms at Southsea, and Eric and I were left there while Mother and Father scoured Hampshire for a cottage. There were many enchanting things to do in Southsea. Trips backwards and forwards across Portsmouth Harbour in ferry-boats, sometimes expeditions as far as Ryde in bigger steamers, concerts on the Clarence Pier, and occasionally an actual play on the South Parade Pier. It was early April, and windy, and I frequently sat for hours watching the waves sliding up the slanting stone breakwaters just below the castle. I can remember, too, trudging home at dusk across the common after a long walk, with a flick of rain in the wind, and all the lights coming up along the parade. There is for me a certain romantic desolation about Southsea and I shall always be attached to it. Whenever I revisit it now it feels familiar and friendly. The South Parade Pier and the Clarence Pier may have shrunk a trifle, the Isle of Wight may seem a little less magical and not so far away, but the forts are still there patterned like chess-boards in the sea, and the castle, and Handleys, and the Cosham trams creaking round the corners; and there are still grey warships lying out at Spithead.

About this time I took a fancy for the most tremendously hearty schoolboy literature. I read avidly week by week *Chums, The Boy's Own Paper, The Magnet,* and *The Gem,* and loved particularly these last two. *The Gem* appeared on Thursday or Friday, and was devoted to the light-hearted adventures of Tom Merry and Co. *The Magnet* came out on Tuesdays, and dealt with the very similar adventures of Harry Wharton and Co. As far as I can remember the dialogue of the two papers was almost identical, consisting largely of the words 'Jape' and 'Wheeze,' and in moments of hilarity and pain respectively: 'Ha Ha Ha!' and 'Yow Yow Yow!' There was a fat boy in each. In *The Magnet* it was Billy

Bunter, who in addition to being very greedy and providing great opportunities for jam-tart fun ('Ha Ha Ha! – He He He! – Yow Yow Yow!'), was a ventriloquist of extraordinary ability, and could make sausages cry out when stabbed with a fork. They were awfully manly decent fellows, Harry Wharton and Co., and no suggestion of sex, even in its lighter forms, ever sullied their conversation. Considering their ages, their healthy-mindedness was almost frightening. I was delighted to find in a newspaper shop the other day that *The Magnet* was unchanged, excepting its cover, which used to be bright orange and is now white. I read a little of it with tender emotion. There they all were, Harry Wharton, Frank Nugent, and Billy Bunter, still 'Ha Ha Ha-ing' and 'He He He-ing' and still, after twenty-four years, hovering merrily on the verge of puberty.

Mother and Father finally discovered a minute cottage at a place called Meon in Hampshire, not far from the village of Tichfield. It had a thatch, and a lavatory at the end of the garden, the door of which always had to be kept shut because the goat liked to use it as well as the family. We lived there for six months completely happily. There was very little money, and at times I believe there wasn't enough food, but we were in the country, and so it didn't matter so much.

The sea, or rather the Solent, was only a mile away, and during Cowes Regatta Week we could see all the excitements going on just across the water. It was the year the German Emperor came and our Fleet saluted his yacht. For several nights all the warships were illuminated, and we had a moonlight picnic on the edge of the low sandy cliff, and let off some fireworks of our own that Father had bought in Fareham.

I learned a lot about the country during those six months. We went nutting and blackberrying and haymaking, and Mother and I were nearly caught stealing our landlord's plums after dark, and had to lie giggling in a ditch for half an hour.

Some little girls lived nearby, and I forced them to act a tragedy that I had written, but they were very silly and during the performance forgot their lines and sniggered, so I hit the eldest one on the head with a wooden spade, the whole affair thus ending in tears and a furious quarrel between the mothers involved.

Mrs Davis wished to keep our flat on in London for longer than she had originally intended, and at the end of our lease of the cottage we went back to Southsea for six weeks. A little while after Christmas Mother and Father became suddenly conscience-stricken over my lack of education, and so it was arranged for me to return to London a week before them in order to be in time for the first moment of the term. I was to stay with my Uncle Ran and Aunt Amy in St George's Square, and I travelled up to Victoria bleak in spirit at the prospect, not only of staying in a strange house, but of getting up early in the morning and going back to school. Mr Selfe loomed in my imagination like a black bat, the voluminous wings of his gown waiting to envelop me in the manly discipline from which I had been free for so long, and the day that I was to rejoin Mother in the flat seemed too far away in the future to be the least comfort.

That week more than came up to expectations; it was miserable beyond belief, although on looking back I am unable to discover exactly why I should have been so wretched. My aunt and uncle were kind, if somewhat remote in their attitude; perhaps if they had fussed over me a little at first and been less distantly correct in their manner towards me, or perhaps if I had not been so spoiled at home, I might have been happier there. As it was, I was conscious for the first time of being a very small boy indeed, forlorn, and badly mother-sick. There was a thick yellow fog throughout the whole week and school work was done with the gas on. The shadows of my snuffling classmates flickered over the walls, and the general smell of feet and linoleum smothered me. Mr Selfe was irascible and more frothy than ever, and one day caned me lightly on the hand which shocked and frightened me immeasurably. I remember crying all the way home in the tram to Victoria, and groping my way through the fog to St George's Square, where I managed to get to my bedroom at the top of the house without being seen by anyone but the housemaid who let me in. Once there I gave way to screaming hysterics. I was obsessed with the idea that Mother was going to have some sort of accident and die without my ever seeing her again. The dramatic scenes I visualised were terrifying: first the fatal telegram arriving at the house, and my aunt and uncle calling me into the drawing-room on the first floor to break the news, then a tear-sodden journey in the train and Auntie Vida meeting me at Fratton Junction, very small and morose, in black. Then, as a fitting climax I imagined the front bedroom enshrouded in funereal twilight with the blinds down and Mother lying still and dead under a sheet like a waxwork. My Aunt Amy appeared presently and admonished me kindly, she must have been startled, poor woman, at the sight of such abandoned despair. However, there was in her manner a certain dry efficiency that eventually suffocated my tears and reduced me to stillness, and a little later I dined downstairs in a state of splendid calm, and talked tremulously to the various nurses from the Westminster Hospital, several of whom were always present at meal-times. My aunt was then, and is still, a brisk dealer in nurses who, not being spoiled hysterical little boys, derive much comfort and warmth from that high clean house.

During the year 1909 my singing voice developed strongly. It was really a good voice, more full-blooded than the usual boyish treble. I occasionally sang anthems in churches but I hated doing this because the lack of applause depressed me. It irritated me when I had soared magnificently through 'God is a Spirit,' or 'Oh for the Wings of a Dove' to see the entire congregation scuffle on to their knees murmuring gloomy 'Amens' instead of clapping loudly and shouting 'Bravo.' Concerts were much more satisfactory, and I particularly enjoyed the annual church garden party at Teddington. It was a sort of fête and jumble sale, and there were stalls and amusements and a band. It was generally opened by someone suitably aristocratic, and my Aunt Myrrha ran the concerts, of which there were usually three or four in course of the afternoon. This was when I shone. I always sang a serious ballad to begin with, my principal successes being 'Through the Forest,' and 'Cherry Blossom Time.' The latter invariably was a great favourite, possibly owing to the redundance of its 'Hey Nonnys' and 'Ho Nonnys' and its winsomely pastoral sentiments. After this, I returned, smiling to the applause, and rendered a light musical comedy number with dance. It must have been surprising and, I should have thought, nauseating, to see a little boy of nine in a white sailor suit flitting about a small wooden stage, employing, with instinctive accuracy, the gestures and tricks of a professional soubrette, but they seemed to love it and encored me vociferously. Perhaps my lack of self-consciousness and my youth mitigated a little the horror of the situation, but I am certain that could my adult self have been present in that stuffy tent, he would have crept out, at the first coy gurgle, and been mercifully sick outside. I do not mean that I wasn't good. I was certainly good, far and away too good. My assurance was nothing short of petrifying, and although I look back upon myself in that saucy sailor suit with a shudder of embarrassment, there is envy in my heart as well.

The reader will probably gather from the above description that I was a brazen, odious little prodigy, over-pleased with myself and precocious to a degree; perhaps I was, but I was learning a lot, even from those kindly old ladies in their garden party finery; after all, I act to them still at matinées and I have a sad suspicion that I don't give them half as much pleasure now as I did then.

I was taken to *The King of Cadonia* on my ninth birthday, and fell in love with Gracie Leigh, and Mother bought me the *Play Pictorial*, and I cut out all the photographs and stuck them on my bedroom wall, where they remained until they turned yellow and curly at the edges and were replaced by new ones.

A little while after this, Mother, who was pleased but not surprised by my success in public, decided that my natural gift for dancing could be improved by a few lessons. So far I had tripped and flitted with much grace but little technique, often, owing to an inadequate knowledge of balance, losing control in my turns, and on one unfortunate occasion, actually finishing with my back to the audience on the final chord. The question of my going on the stage had been discussed several times. My talents and ambitions seemed obviously to lead towards it, but we were ignorant of the initial steps to take. Also I was only nine years old, and excepting a casual acquaintance with 'Mensa: A Table' in the first declension only, and a vivid mental picture of Flamborough Head, I was absolutely uneducated. The idea was therefore temporarily dismissed and lay fermenting in our minds waiting to jump out again the first moment a suitable opportunity offered itself. Meanwhile, the dancing lessons were a move in the right direction. It was no use concentrating on my voice, for that, alas, owing to certain processes in adolescence, would inevitably degenerate into humiliating croakings, and there was no physiological guarantee that when the raucous period passed, a silvery tenor would emerge in compensation for the lost soprano.

We interviewed a Miss Janet Thomas who ran a Dancing Academy in Hanover Square. Her manner was professionally brusque but sympathetic, and she seemed to take a fancy to me and agreed to give me a course of twelve lessons at a minimum fee. So, for the next six weeks I dispensed with school on Tuesday and Friday afternoons, and journeyed, first in the train from Battersea Park to Victoria, and then in a bus to the corner of Conduit Street.

It says a lot for Mother's self-control that she could sit at home, tortured by visions of street accidents, and allow me to gallivant about the town by myself at such a tender age; but she had fostered in me a spirit of independence, realising with remarkable foresight, considering how much she loved me, the valuable experience I should gain from learning to grapple early and alone with small adventures. This was brave wisdom and I profited by it. Long before I was twelve years old I was capable of buying tickets and counting change, ordering buns and glasses of milk in tea-shops, and battling in and out of trams and buses and trains. I could have found my way anywhere about London with ease, and above all, I acquired the inestimable habit of being completely happy alone. I also found that conversation with casual strangers was stimulating to the imagination. I shocked many kindly interfering old ladies with picturesque descriptions of my appalling life at home, making them cluck and shudder with horror at the drunken brutality of my father, and the squalid misery of our tenement room filled with ill-nourished brothers and sisters, many of them suffering from lingering diseases. One old body, I believe, actually went to the police about me. At any rate she said she was going, but as I had given her a false name and address, nothing ever came of it. It was also a pleasant game to be discovered sobbing wretchedly in the corners of railway carriages or buses in the hope that someone would take pity on me and perhaps give me tea at Fuller's. This was only rarely successful, the only two responses I can recall both being clergymen. One talked to me for a long time and told me to trust in God and everything would come right, and the other pinched my knee and gave me sixpence. Of the two, I preferred the latter.

I loved my dancing lessons with Miss Thomas. She started me off herself and then passed me on to her assistant, Miss Alice Hall, who put me through the whole routine of ballet dancing, including even point work for which I wore block-toed shoes. The room was long and large and smelt dimly of Ronuk. There were enormous mirrors all along one wall, and I had a fascinating view of my own front and Miss Hall's behind, which, while she was showing me the fleeter steps, jumped up and down merrily inside her black satin bloomers. There was another assistant, too, named Enid, who had slightly projecting teeth and was a dear. When Miss Thomas wasn't there Miss Hall and Enid used to ask me to stay to tea which was brewed on a spirit lamp in a little curtained-off recess in the corner of the studio. This treat was only possible when I was the last pupil, and I was often bitterly disappointed when, just towards the end of my time, some gangling débutante would appear for her deportment lesson.

Frequently on my homeward journey I walked all the way from Hanover Square to Victoria, through Green Park, thereby saving a penny to buy fudge at a little shop in the Buckingham Palace Road. It was a stern principle with me never to buy the fudge at any other shop before I reached Victoria, in case I broke my leg and hadn't the penny for the bus fare.

4

One day, just before I had come to the end of my dancing course, a little advertisement appeared in the *Daily Mirror*. Mother read it aloud to me while I was having breakfast. It stated that a talented boy of attractive appearance was required by a Miss Lila Field to appear in her production of an all-children fairy play: *The Goldfish*. This seemed to dispose of all argument. I was a talented boy, God knows, and when washed and smarmed down a bit, passably attractive. There appeared to be no earthly reason why Miss Lila Field shouldn't jump at me, and we both believed that she would be a fool indeed to miss such a magnificent opportunity.

I departed for school that morning late, leaving Mother to compose a not too effusive answer to the advertisement. In due course a letter arrived from Lila Field making an appointment for us to go and see her.

On the day specified we left the house in a flurry of grandeur, Mother very impressive in grey satin with a feather boa, and me burning bright in a new Norfolk suit with an Eton collar. Miss Field received us in a small bare room in George Street, Baker Street. She was smart and attractive with a charming voice, and her large brown eyes smiled kindly at us over highly-rouged cheeks and a beauty spot. My heart sank when I noticed that there was no piano, but after a little polite conversation we surmounted that difficulty and I sang 'Liza Ann' unaccompanied, and mother la-la'd for the dance. Miss Field was delighted and said that she would engage me for the part of 'Prince Mussel' and that the fee would be a guinea and a half a week, upon which Mother became sadly red and said that she was afraid we couldn't afford to pay that. Miss Field laughed and said that the guinea and a half a week was what I would receive, and that she'd let us know soon when rehearsals started. Mother and I floated down the narrow staircase and out into the street. The moment was supreme, and we could scarcely breathe for excitement. We went straight to Selfridge's and celebrated our triumph with ice-cream sodas over which we calculated how much a year I should be earning at a guinea and a half a week. Father was impressed with our news when we reached home and we sat up very late inaccurately visualising my future. A letter was sent to Mr Selfe announcing that my school attendance would be even more convulsive than it had been hitherto, as I was now a professional actor.

The rehearsals for *The Goldfish* took place about twice a week for many months; there seemed to be a hitch over the actual production and many mothers became impatient and snatched their children away, which naturally made holes in the cast and necessitated further rehearsals of the newcomers.

Ultimately a definite production date was announced and rehearsals became less spasmodic, the 'all children' cast sang and danced, and tried on elaborate costumes at Debenham and Freebody's in a state of wild excitement. Even the most hardened and cynical of the mothers were moved to enthusiasm.

The Goldfish was a fairy play in three acts, written by Miss Field herself. I believe it had originally been produced the previous year at The Playhouse for special matinées, but the production in which I appeared was entirely reorganised.

I can only vaguely remember the plot. The first act was a children's party with a spirited opening chorus 'School, School, Good-bye to School,' which I led in company with a pretty fair girl 'Little June Tripp' (later 'June' and later still, June Inverclyde). After this came some gay provocative dialogue, only one line of which I can recall: 'Crumbs! How exciting!'

In the second act for some reason or other all the children from the first act had turned into fish. June was 'Princess Sole,' Burford Hampden 'King Starfish,' and Alfred Willmore 'King Goldfish.' I, as 'Prince Mussel,' did not appear until the third act. There were many other fish characters, and a large girl with big knees and a rich contralto voice who played 'The Spirit of the Shells.' She sang a song at the beginning of the second act which always convulsed me, there was something about her strangely adult figure swathed in green tulle weaving up and down the stage, and that strong resonant voice bursting out of her, that was ridiculously at variance with the piping refinement of the rest of the cast. She also mouthed her words in a most peculiar manner.

> 'A so-unbeam fel-ler intew the sea
> Arnd waandered far and waide
> Oonteel eet found ar leetle shell
> Whoere eet coould safely haide.'

As 'Prince Mussel,' King Starfish's court jester, I had a good song in the last act. It was sure-fire sentiment as I was supposed to be torn between my duties as a jester and my unrequited love for the queen. I sang it with tremendous passion, and at the end tore off a top B flat with a Pagliacci sob in it. I was invariably encored, sometimes twice.

The play, having opened at the Little Theatre, ran a week of matinées, and during the following six months was revived twice, first at the Crystal Palace for two performances, and later at the Court Theatre for a week, matinées and evenings, when it was condensed into two acts and was part of a triple bill, the other two items of which were performed by adults.

During the over-long intervals between my public appearances I still attended school, but with even less enthusiasm than before. I developed the adventurous habit of playing truant which was made especially easy for me by the frequently genuine excuse of rehearsals. I used to leave the flat in the morning with a thrilling sensation of wickedness, and take quite a different tram and spend the whole day in Waterloo Station or Clapham Junction watching the trains. Once I bought a pennyworth of crêpe hair at a chemist's and walked up and down the embankment with a red beard.

5

After the Court Theatre engagement *The Goldfish* finally petered out, and as I had only received one week's salary I believe some acrimonious letters passed between Mother and Miss Field. My next appearance was in a less important role in a more professional atmosphere. I was sent for by Bellew and Stock, Theatrical Agents, and they (Mr Bellew) led me to E. M. Tarver, Charles Hawtrey's stage-manager at the Prince of Wales Theatre, who engaged me at two pounds a week (ten per cent commission to Bellew and Stock), to play a page-boy in the last act of a comedy called *The Great Name*. It was only three days before production, so my first rehearsal was a dress rehearsal, which should by rights have frightened me considerably although I only had one line, but I was buoyed up by some painstaking rehearsals at home with Mother. My line was to be addressed to Charles Hawtrey himself, playing the piano in the artists' room at Queen's Hall. I had to enter boldly in my buttoned suit and say: 'Stop that noise at once, please. In there they're playing *The Meistersingers.* Making such a horrible noise. We're used to good music here.' Mother and I did that scene over and over again in the dining-room of the flat with the table pushed against the wall, Mother, running the whole gamut of emotions, instructing me. 'STOP that noise at once, please,' was to be said with tremendous force, then with a barely perceptible note of awe creeping into the voice, 'in there [big gesture to the left] they're playing *The Meistersingers'* (pause for effect). Then (with biting contempt), 'Making such a horrible noise,' then (swelling with pride), 'we're used to good music here!' (rising inflection on the word 'good'). Having finally mastered this vocally to Mother's satisfaction we achieved an entrance and exit that would have been a lesson in deportment to a Ziegfeld show girl, and thus primed I bounced on to my first meeting with Charles Hawtrey. I have seldom seen a human being so astounded. He swung round on the piano stool with a glaze of horror in his eyes, while the members of the company seated in the stalls roared with laughter. After I had made my dramatic exit there was a slight pause, and I heard Mr Hawtrey say to the stage-manager in a weary voice: 'Tarver, never let me see that boy again.'

He relented later, and I was rehearsed by Mr Tarver, and ultimately gabbled the line hurriedly in Cockney, employing the minimum of gesture.

Charles Hawtrey smelt strongly of eau-de-Cologne, was infinitely kind to me, and I worshipped him. On the strength of my association with him I bought an autograph book with glacé sweetpeas on the cover which he signed continually. I followed him about like a sheep, seizing every opportunity that offered for polite conversation. Whenever there was a vacant chair near him at the side of the stage I grabbed it and chattered at him shrilly. Once I distracted him so that he missed an entrance in the first act, after which I was not allowed on the stage at all until there was a legitimate excuse for me to be there. If I shut my eyes now his image is clear to me. I can smell the eau-de-Cologne, see the twinkle in his eye and the stripes on his Paris shirt, and hear his quiet voice edged with exasperation saying: 'Go away, boy, for God's sake leave me alone.'

The bugbear of the child actor is the business of being licensed. The law insists that no child under fourteen may appear on the professional stage without the sanction of a Bow Street magistrate; consequently, before each production, a miserable morning is spent by the business manager, the Mother, and the child, standing about tortured with anxiety in draughty passages, oppressed by an atmosphere of criminality and surrounded by policemen. The magistrates vary. Some are easy-going and give the licence without any fuss, others are obtuse and disapproving, seemingly obsessed with the idea that the child is being forced against its will to act in order to support idle and dissolute parents.

We nearly failed to get a licence for me to appear in *The Great Name* because the magistrate, who had several feet in the grave and looked like a macaw, could not be persuaded that the whole thing was not a case of sweated child labour of the worst variety. After considerable pleading on the part of Mr Fitzgerald (Hawtrey's business manager), he squawked a refusal, whereupon I burst into loud sobs, and Mother, outraged beyond endurance, sprang to her feet and delivered a vehement protest to the effect that if the licence were not granted I should be so heartbroken that I should probably go into a decline and have to be sent to a sanatorium, and that far from using my meagre two pounds a week to support the home, she would willingly pay double that amount to ensure my happiness and peace of mind. After this she sat down, very red in the face and with her hat slightly on one side. The whole Court waited expectantly in dead silence for her to be led to prison; but the old magistrate seemed crushed and, without further argument, granted the licence and we left the court tearful with relief, after a dignified bow to everybody present.

The Great Name was not a success, and ran only two months, but before it finished I was already rehearsing for Hawtrey's production of *Where the Rainbow Ends* at the Savoy. Again I was playing a page-boy, but this time a much more important part, although only in the first act.

The whole company assembled on the stage for the reading of the play.

Parts were dealt out to everybody, and we sat following them while Mr Hawtrey read. He read beautifully and it was an afternoon of enchantment, only slightly clouded for me by the fact that I wasn't playing 'Crispian,' the leading part. For this, however, Master Philip Tonge had been engaged. I scrutinised him enviously along the front row of chairs (where I had placed myself with the principals). He was the great boy actor of London. His only serious rival was Master Bobbie Andrews, who had appeared with considerable success the year previously in *Where Children Rule* at the Garrick. Philip Tonge had a fresh red face; a large woolly overcoat, a 'Burglar Bill' cap with ear-flaps tied up on the top, and a formidable mother who regarded the other young juvenile males of the cast balefully, as though she expected them to rise up and fell Philip to the ground in a fury of jealousy. She proved on closer acquaintance to be kind, although domineering, and once during the run she had to be requested by the management not to monopolise our dressing-room basin for washing out her gloves, a proceeding which had become so tedious to the rest of us that we had complained.

Where the Rainbow Ends that first year was a glamorous entertainment. The leading lady was Miss Esmé Wynne, a podgy, brown-haired little girl with a bleating voice. Also in the cast was a strange fragile little thing named Mavis Yorke. She played Will-o'-the-Wisp and was exquisite; she flitted through the woods and glades of the production to Roger Quilter's gentle music, and there was in her a quality of magic. She was in no way a winsome prodigy, and utterly unlike all the other little actress children with their pert voices and black satin coats and ringlets. I often wonder what became of her, whether that tiny supple body ever became set in maturity, or whether she just snuffed out, to be remembered only as a Will-o'-the-Wisp in a children's play.

During that run several large parties were given for us, which generally took place at the Savoy. There were enormous silver trays with rows and rows of little chocolate éclairs, and crackers and paper caps and games, and our evening performances were frequently the worse for them.

The ballet mistress was Miss Italia Conti. She supplied then, as she does still, all sorts of children for all sorts of productions. They used to come shuffling into rehearsals in a great troupe, all those fairies and elves and frogs and caterpillars, gauntly escorted either by Miss Conti herself or her sister, Mrs Murray, a dragon in Astrakhan. It was a matter of constant amazement to me that she could so surely remember all their names, but she undoubtedly could and did. Mr Hawtrey winced many a time when suddenly in the middle of the ballet Miss Conti's commanding voice came shrilly out of the gloom of the dress-circle: 'Dorothy, do your coupé again,' or 'Grace, how many times have I told you never to push against Phyllis in your pirouette?'

Miss Conti insidiously suggested to me one day at the beginning of rehearsals that as my part was over after the first act, I might like to appear as a hyena and a frog in the later scenes as well. I was delighted with the idea, and rehearsed three times in a dingy basement room under the Bay Malton Hotel in Great Portland Street. Mother, having been dubious over the plan from the first, came with me to the third rehearsal and I never went any more. I was disappointed, but Mother soon convinced me that it was better to be content with my small part which was at least among the principals, than to lower my prestige by crawling about on all fours in a hot hyena skin.

6

After *Where the Rainbow Ends* finished I was out of work for a while, and I spent a good deal of time, now being an established actor, in writing in to the various theatres for free seats. I had had some professional cards printed with 'Master Noel Coward' in the middle, and 'Mr Charles Hawtrey's company, *Where the Rainbow Ends,* Savoy Theatre,' in the left-hand corner. These were sent to different managements with a stamped addressed envelope inside and a pompous little note in the third person, usually beginning, 'Master Noel Coward would be so very much obliged,' etc.

Usually, they were returned with callous regrets, but every now and then, as though to keep up my spirits, two pink dress-circle tickets would arrive with 'Complimentary' stamped across them. These were gala days. Mother used to frizz her hair and put on her evening dress. I put on my black suit and Eton collar, and off we'd go in the train and bus, always arriving far too early, long before the safety curtain had risen, but content with a box of chocolates and a programme. We used to have supper when we got home and discuss the play over it. Our greatest favourite of all was Gertie Millar. We had naturally never been able to get free seats for anything in which she was appearing, but we went in the gallery. My bedroom was plastered with photographs of her, for ever since the first time I had seen her in *The Quaker Girl,* I had adored her; and in my memory she is clearly the most graceful and charming artiste I have ever seen. Now that I know her well I can never look at her gay unchanged face without a little stab of the heart, to think that never again will she float down the stage, chuckling lightly and expressing with her hands a joy of living which was her own special charm. I often waited outside the Adelphi stage-door for hours to see her come out. She always smiled at me and said good night. Once she gave me a flower from a bouquet she was carrying which I pressed carefully in a bound volume of *Chums.*

A little while ago a party was given by Gladys and Leslie Henson – a good higgledy-piggledy theatrical party with a magnificent star cast of yesterday and today. Lily Elsie was there and Maurice Chevalier and Violet Loraine, and everybody balanced vol-au-vents on their knees and drank whatever they wanted, and gossiped and sang songs. Gertie Millar (the Countess of Dudley) sat on the stairs in chinchilla while I was at the piano strumming a few excerpts from bygone musical comedies in which everybody joined. Suddenly as I played 'Tony from America' the other sounds fell away, and from the semi-gloom of the stairs came 'He guessed I was all alone, so that's why he came along and found me,' in that funny, un-vocal little voice, bridging the years and for a strange instant filling our hearts with a pleasurable melancholy. Many of us cried because is was a most touching moment, and theatrical people are notoriously facile of emotion, and frequently victimised by their own foolish sentimentality.

7

During the spring of 1912 I spent a lot of time going the round of the agencies, a proceeding with which every struggling actor is bitterly well-acquainted. Blackmore's, Denton's, Bellew and Stock's, crowded waiting-rooms, with spangled principal boys on the walls, triumphant in their stardom, leering down at their seedy brothers and sisters in the profession; character actors, old lady parts, straight juveniles, singing soubrettes, standing about or sitting on the few shiny chairs, talking softly to each other in corners, not so much to impress as to bolster up their tremulous faith in themselves. Every now and then a man comes in and calls a name. There is a flutter of excitement and some wizened over-made-up little woman rises to her feet, gives a defiant tug to the frayed tulle round her neck and minces into the inner office in tight glacé shoes smelling of petrol. When she comes out again she nods brightly and goes down the stairs; if her nod is too bright everybody knows that she hasn't got the job, and hope flutters anew in those that are left.

I passed hours in those horrid waiting-rooms. Twice a week I devoted a whole day to doing the rounds. I had sixpence to spend on lunch which I took, not in an ordinary Lyons', but in the Corner House. Macaroni and tomato sauce fourpence, a roll a penny, and a penny for the waitress. Sometimes I was fortunate enough to find fourpence under the plate when I arrived at the table. This meant a chocolate éclair extra and twopence for the waitress.

One day I was actually sent for by Blackmore's Agency and engaged at two pounds ten a week to play in the Prologue of a big dramatic spectacle called *War in the Air* which was to be produced at the Palladium.

The writer and producer of the show was a little grey man, I think American. He was verbose and enthusiastic and seemed convinced that the production was going to revolutionise practically everything. I played the infant Aviator in the prologue and flew a small model aeroplane, which I was supposed to have made with my own chubby hands, backwards and forwards across the stage. Unfortunately it nearly always rushed into the stalls and had to be retrieved from under old ladies' seats while I waited politely for it to be returned to me by the musical director.

The end of my scene was deeply moving. I undressed and said a prayer at my mother's knee in a white spotlight. 'Please God, bless Mummy and Daddy and Violet [my slightly Cockney playmate] and make me a great big aviator one day,' whereupon the lights faded and all hell broke loose back-stage. I was whisked violently backwards into the property room, bed and all, and my gentle grey-haired mother skipped about like a two-year-old in order to avoid being knocked down by moving scenery. The rest of the entertainment was devoted to my adventures as a 'Great big Aviator' culminating in a tremendous aerial battle in which I (grown up) and Violet (also grown up and even more Cockney) swung out into the auditorium in an aeroplane amid a lot of banging and red fire. This hair-raising effect was spoiled at the third performance by the aeroplane becoming hitched on to the front of the upper-circle, where it remained for three hours. It was finally dislodged and slid back on to the stage, after the audience had gone home. Violet, I believe, disembarked in a fainting condition. After this the effect was resolutely cut by the management.

I always got to the theatre and made up before the performance started so that I could watch from the side the variety artistes who occupied the first part of the programme. Nellie Wallace was on the bill and Phil Ray, and Maidie Scott whom I loved; she always gave me tea and cake in her dressing-room at matinées.

8

It was some time during this year, 1912, that I was engaged by Miss Ruby Ginner for some special performances of a ballet she was producing at the Savoy Theatre. It was an artistic little morsel arranged to a selection of Chopin melodies and entitled *An*

Autumn Idyll, and was planned as a curtain-raiser to precede a two-act Operetta, *The Cicada.* Ruby Ginner herself was the Première Danseuse, and the *motif* of the ballet as far as I can remember was a day in the life of an Autumn Leaf (Miss Ginner) in conflict with the winter mists (members of Miss Ginner's Dancing School). As a mushroom I provided a few of the more light-hearted moments together with a little girl called Joan Carrol as a toadstool. I wore grey silk skin tights, a large grey silk hat like a gargantuan muffin, and a diaphanous frill round my middle to conceal any unaesthetic protuberances. My entrance consisted of a series of abandoned high kicks, slightly higher with the right leg than with the left, typifying the carefree *joie de vivre* of the average mushroom, until upon observing the toadstool (Joan Carrol in pink) my mood changed from gaiety to tenderness, and there ensued a refined *pas de deux* and exit to tepid applause. The really big moment of the ballet was undoubtedly Miss Gunner's valiant fight with the mists and ultimate death as the lights faded, although the effect of this was marred for me by the fact that she seemed so much larger and better developed than the mists that vanquished her.

My next engagement was with Charles Hawtrey again in a sketch *A Little Fowl Play* at the Coliseum. The magistrate refused to license me for the evening performances as the sketch didn't come on until just before eleven o'clock. I was heartbroken, and used to stand nightly in the prompt corner and listen to the assistant stage-manager playing my part (one line with a slight stutter to give character: 'I've brought the ch-ch-ch-chicken, sir'). It was typical of Hawtrey that he paid me my full salary for the whole four weeks' run when he could perfectly easily have dispensed with me altogether. I saw and learned a lot during that engagement. The entire bill was changed every Monday. The stage-manager, Mr Crocker, was kind, and allowed me to stand at the side except on Monday afternoons, when he was too harassed to bear me bobbing about under his feet. I had a close-up view of George Robey, Beattie and Babs, Madame Alicia Adelaide Needham and her choir, The Grotesques, and a Wild West show with property grass matting and cowboys and horses. During the last week Pauline Chase was on the bill with Holman Clarke in

Barrie's *Pantaloon*. In this also was a small girl called Moya Nugent who played the little clown. She was by then an experienced Barrie actress as she had played Liza in *Peter Pan,* I think for two consecutive seasons. We became great friends and have remained so ever since.

In between the matinée and evening performances the Coliseum stage had an even greater allure for me; with only a few working lights left on here and there, it appeared vaster and more mysterious, like an empty echoing cathedral smelling faintly of dust. Sometimes the safety curtain was not lowered, and I used to stand down on the edge of the footlights singing shrilly into the shadowy auditorium. I also danced in the silence. Occasionally a cleaner appeared with a broom and pail, or a stage hand walked across the stage, but they never paid any attention to me. An empty theatre is romantic, every actor knows the feeling of it: complete silence emphasised rather than broken by the dim traffic noises outside, apparently hundreds of miles away; the muffled sound of a motor-horn and the thin reedy wail of a penny whistle being played to the gallery queue. As a rule there are a few exit lights left burning, casting blue shadows across the rows of empty seats. It seems incredible that within an hour or two this stillness will awake to garish red-and-gilt splendour, and be shattered by the sibilance of hundreds of voices, and the exciting discords and trills of the orchestra tuning up.

9

After *A Little Fowl Play* I was re-engaged for my original part in *Where the Rainbow Ends.* This time it was produced at the Garrick, with more or less the same cast. The run was uneventful. There were the same parties given at the Savoy, and the same kindly clergyman eager to take the younger members of the cast to tea at Lyons' Corner House. As a step in my own development this engagement was negligible except for one all-important evening when I walked with Philip Tonge all the way to his home in Baker Street, and he told me the facts of life. I was tremendously excited, not only by the facts themselves, which were confined principally to the procreation of species, but also because it was a unique experience to be able to talk to Philip alone, without the didactic presence of his mother. I can't think what she could have been doing that night, but there we were on our own, trudging up Regent Street, along Oxford Street and down Orchard Street, Philip in his Sherlock Holmes' cap and overcoat, and me in a mackintosh, gloriously immersed in a sea of pornographic mis-information. We parted opposite the Baker Street tube station, and I climbed on to the top of the last bus to Victoria in an exalted frame of mind. Presently this heady intoxication of newly acquired knowledge began to wear off and give place to a fearful remorse. I felt smirched and unclean; I felt that God was angry with me and would probably visit me with some sharp punishment in the near future. By the time I arrived home I was in a state of hysteria. Mother was in bed, slightly anxious because I was so late, but reading a book in a sensible effort to calm her fears; her relief was obvious when I charged into her room, but her expression changed to alarm when she saw my face, as with perfect sense of the theatre I gripped the bedrail and cried in a tragic voice: 'Mother, I have lost my innocence!' She hoisted herself up on the pillows and after scrutinising me carefully for a moment did the very last thing in the world that I expected: she burst out laughing. Upon looking back I consider that gesture was a brilliant stroke of psychological intuition. Her laugh pricked my swollen hysterical ego like a pin, and I am certain that it cost her a good deal to do it. I dissolved into healthy tears, and the story of my fall from spiritual grace was gradually coaxed out of me. She was wise and gentle and said that there was nothing at all for me to be upset about, and that I was bound to find out all those things sooner or later, and that the fact that it happened to be sooner was really just as well, as in order to become a good actor it was necessary to know about life as early and as thoroughly as possible. I retired to bed serene and happy after a hot cup of cocoa made on her spirit lamp.

10

In the spring of 1913 Italia Conti wrote to Mother and offered me a three weeks' engagement in Liverpool and Manchester with the Liverpool Repertory Company. Several other children were to be in it and we were all to travel together and live together under Miss Conti's personal vigilance. I was very keen to go although Mother was not enthusiastic, never having quite forgiven Miss Conti for trying to transform me into a hyena in the *Rainbow.* However, we went to interview a young man with a rasping voice and dark glasses, Basil Dean, who was to produce the play *(Hannele,* by Hauptmann), and I was engaged at a salary of two pounds a week. In due course I was seen off by Mother at Euston, and in company of about ten other children and Miss Conti, travelled to Liverpool. It was a pleasant journey. We ate sandwiches and chocolate and played card games on a travelling rug stretched across our knees. Some of the children I already knew. Gracie Seppings and two sisters, Ivy and Dorothy Moody, had been in the *Rainbow* with me, and a very perky little boy in a yachting cap called Roy Royston I had met at one or two parties. The others were strangers, and still are, with the exception of Harold French and a vivacious child with ringlets to whom I took an instant fancy. She wore a black satin coat and a black velvet military hat with a peak, her face was far from pretty, but tremendously alive. She was very *mondaine,* carried a handbag with a powder-puff and frequently dabbed her generously turned-up nose. She confided to me that her name was Gertrude Lawrence, but that I was to call her Gert because everybody did, that she was fourteen, just over licensing age, that she had been in *The Miracle* at Olympia and *Fifinella* at the Gaiety, Manchester. She then gave me an orange and told me a few mildly dirty stories, and I loved her from then onwards.

We all lived in the same digs at Liverpool, and I was violently, wretchedly homesick. Miss Conti dosed me with Epsom Salts, doubtless in the belief that the root of all woe lay in the bowels. This failed to cheer me at all and merely succeeded in making

35

rehearsals extremely convulsive, to the great irritation of Basil Dean who was none too sweet-tempered at the best of times.

Roy Royston, Harold French and I were angels in the dream part of the play, then we did a quick change and became school-children in blue smocks and hard black hats, and then back again to angels for the end of the play. The whole production was definitely advanced, in the best and worst traditions of the repertory movement. There were steps leading from the stage to the stalls, odd and not always successful lighting effects, and a lot of curtains. Gracie Seppings played Hannele, and Baliol Holloway, Gottwald, the schoolmaster.

Roy and Harold and I had a little scene of our own in the early part of the play. We appeared through the inevitable curtains at the back and read verses from scrolls. We wore short tunics with green and red hieroglyphics stencilled on them, small and uncomfortable gold fillets on our heads and bare feet, which were usually pretty dirty because we nearly always forgot the slippers which we were supposed to wear down from the dressing-room.

My homesickness got a little better after the first few days, although it never entirely left me. When once the play had opened distractions were provided for us in the shape of trips to New Brighton on the Mersey steamers, personally conducted tours around the docks, and games of rounders in the park; in course of one of these, Gertie distinguished herself by striking Miss Conti's sister, Bianca Murray, a sharp blow on the head with a wooden bat, presumably by accident.

When we had played a week in Liverpool we went to Manchester. We arrived in the afternoon and settled into rooms in Ackers Street, and after a substantial high tea went off to the theatre in the tram for an evening rehearsal. That was my first view of the little Gaiety Theatre, and whenever I face it nowadays and see the garish movie posters outside, I shudder in my heart to think that it should have fallen so sadly from the grace and quality of its early years.

On Monday morning, those of us who were under fourteen were led to the police court, where a singularly disagreeable magistrate refused to grant us a licence unless we attended school every day during the week we were in Manchester. Then ensued a flustered consultation between Mrs Murray and the manager of the theatre, and we left the court dismal and anxious. In the course of the day a school was discovered which agreed to take us in. Saturday of course was a whole holiday and Monday had gone already, so it was only for four days that we were to be incarcerated. What high cultural grace the magistrate imagined we could acquire in that time I fail to see. Anyhow, the next morning we were taken to a large red board school in the Oxford Road. Harold and Roy and I were put in a class-room and questioned by a little master with pince-nez, and when it came to my turn to answer whatever it was he asked me I stood up and announced, quivering with rage, that I had not the faintest intention of answering that question or indeed any questions, and that I was not going to learn a lesson of any sort during the four days I was forced to come to the school, and that if I was caned or punished in any way I should go straight home to London. This tirade oddly enough was effective, and for the rest of the day I sat at the back of the class-room doing nothing at all but stare with distaste at the rest of my classmates. The next day, in spite of Mrs Murray's remonstrances (Miss Conti was in London), I took a book with me, nobody spoke to me in the school and I was allowed to keep it. Roy and Harold, more democratic-spirited, entered into everything with admirable zest and in the ten minutes' morning interval rushed out in the playground and fought and played football with the others. I think they were a trifle ashamed of me and felt self-consciously that perhaps a wholehearted participation in everything absolved them somehow from the stigma of association with me. On the Saturday night I went to bed deliriously happy. It was all over and I was going home. The journey the next day seemed interminable, but at last, as the train slid into St Pancras Station, I saw Mother standing on the platform and knew that the purgatory of those three weeks was ended.

II

While I had been away a long-discussed move had taken place, and the flat at Battersea Park had been left in favour of an upper maisonette on the south side of Clapham Common. It was a very tall house called 'Ben Lomond,' and was owned by a Mrs White and Miss Pitney, her sister, who inhabited the ground floor and basement while we had the rest of the house. The rooms were much bigger than those we had had in the flat, and looked straight out across the common in the front, and on to a large private garden at the back. I had a tiny bedroom at the very top, situated next door to the kitchen in which we usually had our meals, because we couldn't afford a servant. Mother, I think, was unhappy but she didn't show it, and for my benefit treated the cooking and washing and floor-scrubbing as a lark. Eric, my brother, then aged eight, and I, helped with the washing up, and enjoyed it, anyhow for the first few days.

Clapham Common was a nice place to live. There was a pond opposite the house on which Father used to indulge his passion for sailing a model yacht in the intervals of travelling for Payne's pianos. He never succeeded in infecting me with enough enthusiasm to last out longer than a quarter of an hour. Eric, however, was more docile, and used to squat on the opposite side of the pond from Father and turn the boat round with a walking-stick every time it crossed successfully. We used to take our tea out under the trees during the summer and play bat-and-ball afterwards.

There were pleasant walks in Clapham along tree-shaded roads, neatly spaced with refined suburban houses, secure in small prosperity with their conservatories and stained-glass windows and croquet lawns. From the 'Plough' onwards down the Clapham Road the atmosphere became palpably commoner, but it was very lively on Saturday nights, particularly at Christmas-time when the shop windows were gay with tinsel and crackers and paper-chains, and the poulterers' and butchers' and greengrocers' were glaring yellow caves of light, with the slow-moving crowds on the shining pavements silhouetted against them.

In order to get from Clapham Common to the West End you travelled either in a Number 88 bus, which took a long time, or in the City and South London Tube, changing at the Elephant and Castle into the Bakerloo, which was quicker.

The City and South London has now been transformed into a spacious network of efficiency, but then it was unique in uncomfortable charm. The trains were smaller than any of the other tubes and rattled alarmingly, and over it all there brooded a peculiar pungent stink which will live somewhere in the back of my nostrils for ever. I am dwelling upon this particularly because for several years it was an integral part of my life. I went through every sort of emotion in the City and South London Railway. Exaltation, having been sent for by some agent. Utter despair, returning home in the evening having failed to get the job. Or else hysterical delight with a typewritten part clutched in my hand and 'Rehearsal Monday morning at 11 o'clock' flashing before my eyes like an electric light-sign along the walls of the tunnel. I also managed to get through a lot of reading during those journeys back and forth from Trafalgar Square to the 'Plough': French Revolution stories whenever possible, and a welter of Guy Boothby, Phillips Oppenheim, William Le Queux, Stanley Weyman and the early novels of Edgar Wallace.

I can close my eyes and ears now and conjure up completely the picture of Mother and myself late at night on our way home from some theatre, Mother in a dust-coloured cloak over her evening dress, with a small diamanté butterfly in her hair, and me in a scrupulously pressed dinner-jacket suit (Lockwood and Bradley in the Clapham Road), rushing from the Bakerloo side at Elephant and Castle, down tiled passages with hot draughts flying up our legs until the well-known fœtid City and South London smell met our noses and a distant screeching and rumbling soothed us with the knowledge that we had not, after all, missed the last train.

12

In the summer of 1913 Auntie Vida and Auntie Borby took a small house at Lee-on-the-Solent, and we all went down to spend a month with them. It was lovely to be able to look across at the Isle of Wight again and watch the warships and liners steaming up and down the Solent. There was nothing to do at Lee but bathe and go for bicycle rides. My favourite occupation was to spend hours on the railway embankment waiting for the rare appearance of the fussy little train which connected Lee with Fort Brockhurst and put halfpennies on the line for it to flatten into pennies, after which I tried to coax them into the slot machine on the pier, with only occasional success.

A concert party called 'The Poppy Pierrots' played twice daily on the end of the pier. The stage was under cover, but the audience sat sparsely beneath the sky and scurried to the shelters at the side whenever it rained. Miss Maud Watson ran the company. She was dark-skinned and slightly *passée* and sang a number in the second part of the programme called 'Hush-a-bye, My Little Papoose,' during which she perpetually rocked an imaginary child in her arms until the dance, when she callously discarded it. There were two comedians, Teddy Baird and Fred Benton, and a soprano with the fanciful name of Betley Delacoste. I forget the names of the others, but I swiftly made friends with them all and was allowed to appear with them on benefit nights and sing a couple of songs.

One day in August a post-card arrived asking me to go and see Charles Hawtrey at his office at eleven-thirty. We looked at the postmark and discovered that Mrs White must have been negligent in forwarding it, because it was four days late. Nevertheless, Mother and I went pelting up to London in an excursion train and found that Hawtrey, having tried vainly to locate me, had engaged another boy for a good part in his new comedy, *Never Say Die,* which was already in rehearsal. He was sympathetic and charming as always, and when he saw my face fall told me that he would engage me as understudy. This was definitely better than nothing, because anyhow it meant that I should be in the theatre, and be earning two pounds ten a week; so we accepted gladly, and I started attending rehearsals right away. My natural hatred of Reggie Sheffield, the boy whom I was understudying, evaporated quite soon and we became great friends, although I never ceased to pray in my heart that he would be run over by a bus. Unfortunately he was a remarkably healthy little boy and remained uninjured, and in the pink of condition throughout the entire run. Doris Lytton was in the play and Winifred Emery, and there was a good dinner scene in the second act during which real asparagus was devoured nightly. Hawtrey always loved eating on the stage and I must say the food in his productions was invariably excellent. In *Never Say Die* I used to share the remains with Nelly Ayr, the wardrobe mistress.

13

In November I satisfied a long-cherished desire to be in *Peter Pan,* which was the Mecca of all child actors. I was engaged by Dion Boucicault at four pounds a week to play 'Slightly.' It was Mother who beat him up to such a high figure; flushed with nervousness and horribly conscious of my agonised expression, she argued and insisted and finally won, and we sailed out into St Martin's Lane dizzy with triumph. Playing in *Peter Pan* was all that I hoped it would be, and more, and after the London run the entire company went on tour.

Mother's travelling expenses were paid on condition that she undertook to look after a little boy called Donald Buckley, who played 'Michael,' and allow him to share digs with me. He was nice, really, but I was highly delighted when it was discovered that he had caught lice in his head at Newcastle. He had to be tooth-combed and disinfected while I remained aloof, clean and maddeningly superior.

We played at Glasgow, Edinburgh, Newcastle and Birmingham and all the suburban dates such as Wimbledon and Hammersmith and Kennington. When we were at Kennington Mother invited a lot of the company to tea between a matinée and evening performance and we were very excited when Pauline Chase consented to come. It's only a little way from Kennington Theatre to Clapham Common, most of us went by tram, but Pauline Chase and her friend Miss Berri (who played the mermaid) drove to our house in a shining and smart yellow two-seater which threw Miss Pitney, who was peering through the ground-floor lace curtains, into transports of excitement. The tea was elaborate, the white Worcester cups (wedding present) were brought out and Mother insisted proudly that I should sing, which I did, to my own and everybody else's acute embarrassment.

The tea-party, however, on the whole was considered a great success and the remains of the home-made coffee sponge with walnuts and the Fuller's almond cake brightened our lives for the rest of the week.

14

After the run of *Peter Pan* I was out of an engagement for a long while. These periods in my memory are difficult to recapture. They seem oddly jumbled and nebulous without the chain of the theatre to hold them together. I couldn't have been very happy really, because I was never completely happy when I wasn't working.

I met an artist named Philip Streatfield who had a studio in Glebe Place, Chelsea. He was painting a picture of Phyllis Monkman and I used to go to tea and watch it being finished. I don't really believe it could have been a very good picture, but I was most impressed by it. She was wearing the pink velvet dress in which she appeared in the 'Pom Pom' dance in the Alhambra revue; also, I think, a white feather head-dress. I met her once leaving the studio wrapped in fox fur and debated anxiously in my mind whether or not to ask her for her autograph, but by the time I had decided that I would she had hopped into a taxi and driven away. Philip also painted a model called Doris something-or-other, a pretty girl who posed casually in the nude and made tea afterwards. I soon became accustomed to the whole affair and spoke of it at home in a worldly manner.

It was about this time that an important friendship began, a friendship which for several years influenced me profoundly and is still clear to-day in spite of the fact that our two paths have diverged so definitely in opposite directions. Esmé Wynne was the little girl with the faintly bleating voice who had played the leading part in *Where the Rainbow Ends.* During the first two seasons of *The Rainbow,* I had no idea that she could ever mean anything to me in the future; in fact, I always found her pompous, podgy, and slightly superior, and although she sometimes betrayed a latent sense of humour by a misplaced giggle or so at rehearsals, these occasions were rare and her majestic deportment at parties filled me with awe and a certain indefinite dislike. In the spring of 1914 she suddenly appeared at 50, South Side, Clapham Common, wearing a white knitted jumper and skirt and hat and wheeling a brand-new bicycle of which she seemed extremely proud. She confessed that she didn't ride it very well and was terrified out of her life on any but the quietest thoroughfares. After tea I cycled back with her to Stansfield Road, Stockwell, where she lived with her family. It was a smug little road and the houses squatted back from contamination with the pavements, from which they were protected by grey strips of garden, barely enlivened here and there by dusty shrubs. The family consisted of Mother, Father, and Auntie Mona. Auntie Mona was seldom present as she was generally away on tour. But although corporeally absent, her successful aura pervaded every corner of the home and she was discussed with pride over the supper table. Esmé's mother herself was a handsome woman, who at one time had been in the original troupe of 'The Palace Girls.' I was certainly englamoured by the thought of this, but could never completely visualise her darting on and off the stage in line and waving her matronly legs with meticulous clockwork abandon, but of course my first view of her was when she was approaching fifty, and middle age had coaxed her figure into heavier shapes. I rode home that evening through the dim suburban roads, ecstatic in the thrill of new friendship, planning adventures for the future: bicycle excursions into the country, matinées at the Coliseum (early doors ninepence, with tea in the interval threepence extra). Long amicable evenings playing word games and listening to the gramophone (I had a new one that played flat disc records instead of the old-fashioned cylinders), and joyful shopping expeditions to the Woolworth's Threepenny and Sixpenny Bazaar in the Brixton Road, finishing up with the weekly melodrama at the Brixton Theatre. These romantic visions were realised quickly. Esmé and I became inseparable. Almost at the outset we gave each other nicknames, embarrassing now with the weight of years upon them, but at the time highly enjoyable. I was Poj and she was Stoj. We alternated between childishness and strange maturity. The theatre had led us far in precocity and we discussed life and death and sex and religion with sublime sophistication. We also dressed in each other's clothes and paraded the West End, rode for miles on the London and Brighton and South Coast Railway without tickets, evading station-masters, ticket-collectors and frequently even policemen. We stole chocolates from sweet-shops and cakes of soap from chemists; once Stoj got a large bottle of 'Phul-Nana' scent. We extracted, with the aid of bent hair-pins and latchkeys, packets of 'Snake Charmer' cigarettes from slot-machines and smoked them publicly with outward flamboyance and inward nausea. We explored the West End, the East End, the suburbs, and the near country with minute thoroughness. We even had baths together for the simple reason that we didn't wish to waste a moment's companionship and because it seemed affected to stop short in the middle of some vital discussion for such a paltry reason as conventional modesty. We quarrelled bitterly, usually over religion, Stoj at that time being given to spiritual ecstasies which fortunately seldom lasted long, but were remarkably alike for their violence and variety. Finally after many intensive arguments we evolved a list of rules for our 'Palship' which certainly saved us many unhappinesses and misunderstandings and was strictly adhered to for many years.

One of the most important aspects of this relationship was the fact that Stoj was determined to be a writer, an ambition that filled me with competitive fervour. She wrote poems. Reams and reams of them, love songs, sonnets, and villanelles: alive with elves, mermaids, leafy glades, and Pan (a good deal of Pan). Not to be outdone in artistic endeavour, I set many of the poems to music, sometimes, owing to the exigencies of my inspiration, changing her original scansion with disastrous results. One instance of this ruthlessness concerned a poem of which she was particularly proud, and an ugly battle ensued. The first lines were:

'Our little Love is dying,
On his head are lately crimson petals
Faded quite,
The breath of Passion withered them last night . . .'

I set these words to a merry lilt beginning: 'Our little Love is dying, on his head . . .'

Very soon I began to write short stories, beastly little whimsies, also about Pan, and Fauns and Cloven Hooves. We read a lot of Oscar Wilde and Omar Khayyám and Laurence Hope. Stoj even went so far as to sing 'The Indian Love Lyrics' for a short period until I put a stop to it, not so much from aesthetic principle, but because I knew with every instinct in me that her voice was quite horrid. Apart from these small skirmishings our mutual admiration was sincere and touching. Our Egos were battling for recognition and encouragement and we supplied one another generously with praise and mild, very mild criticism.

15

In the early part of May, Philip Streatfield, who had been discussing for a long time the possibility of taking a cottage somewhere suitably picturesque where he could paint landscapes, decided to make a motor tour through the west country and to my intense excitement invited me to go too. The car belonged to a friend of Philip's, Sidney Lomer, who was kind enough not to resent my inclusion in the party, and so, in due course, on a misty drizzling afternoon we set forth, slipping out of London over glassy roads, myself bouncing blissfully about at the back among the bags. The whole two weeks' trip was enchanting, doubly so for me as I had never been in a fast car in my life. We stopped in farms and inns along the coasts of Devon and Cornwall and lingered in small fishing villages while Philip made water-colour sketches, surrounded by admiring natives.

After a fortnight of the road I was dropped off at my aunt's house in Charlestown. Philip and Sidney Lomer stayed to lunch and I suffered tortures of apprehension in case my aunt should embarrass me with over-solicitude, but she behaved beautifully and was charming and social and, I hoped, impressive. When lunch was over I waved them away in the car and spent the rest of the day exploring the lake and the garden. Everything seemed to look smaller than when I was there as a little boy, but the spell of its beauty was as strong as ever and I was very happy. There was the old blue punt, still water-logged, the deep wide lake, coffee-coloured on account of the clay soil, and the mysterious damp-smelling jungle surrounding it. I walked down every path, crossed and recrossed all the little bridges, rowed myself out to the island in the dinghy, swung myself sick in the swing, and made up little verses, gay, winsome fragments redolent of Stoj's woodland influence and rife with whimsical pixie allusion. I fancied myself for a little as a half-wild creature and darted about among the trees, occasionally crouching in the bracken in faun-like attitudes. This peculiar behaviour was of course 'play-acting', although at the time I failed to recognise it. Intermixed with this self-conscious enjoyment of myself was a completely unself-conscious enjoyment of the country and, above all, of the sea. Perhaps a few drops of quarter-deck blood had seeped into my veins from my naval ancestors; at any rate I remember feeling a deep indefinable satisfaction, even when I was quite small, whenever I was taken on to a beach and could watch the waves sliding in over the shingle. The Cornish seas were much more exciting than the refined Sunny South Coast variety. Here were no neat breakwaters and trim stone esplanades, no rompered children patting at sand castles, while fat mothers lolled near-by in deck-chairs reading novels and knitting; there was no discreet band music here to interfere with the sound of the waves. The waves had it all their own way in Cornwall; grey and formidable, they hurled themselves endlessly against the rocks and swirled into the little sandy coves, leaving yellow suds of foam high up on the beach among the crushed shells and thick ridges of brown seaweed. There were sea-birds, too: cormorants and gulls in hundreds, wheeling and squawking round their nests on the cliffs, and diving for fish far out beyond where the waves curled and broke.

I was happy by myself in those days, a habit which I mislaid in later years, but have fortunately regained since. I spent many hours wandering along the cliffs, frequently returning drenched to the skin to eat large teas in my aunt's kitchen. Dripping-toast and splits and saffron cake, this last bright yellow and delicious.

On certain days I plastered my hair down, put on my best suit and went driving with my aunt in the dog-cart to pay calls. I was proud of her extreme prettiness and delighted that my extra years had made me more companionable to her. My uncle was seldom visible, as he was a determined invalid and preferred to stay in his room most of the time.

Later on in the same year I went again to Cornwall, this time to stay with Philip at Polperro, where he had found a pleasant little house perched up on the cliff overlooking the harbour. It was a lovely summer, hot and placid. There was nothing to do but bathe and lie on the rocks, or wander about the narrow streets of the village and talk to the fishermen. On the fourth of August we read in the paper that war had been declared, and later on in the day we saw three warships steaming slowly by, quite close in to the shore. They looked proud and invulnerable and almost smug as though they were secretly pleased.

The peace of the holiday broke at once, and I was sent back to London immediately where I was to spend one night at an hotel and then join the family and Auntie Vida at Lee-on-the-Solent. Philip saw me off at Looe and put me in the charge of Hugh Walpole, who treated me to lunch on the train and tipped me half a crown at parting.

16

The rest of that year, so eventful for the world, was quite uneventful for me. We stayed at Lee for a few weeks and I bicycled about the country and read books and went off by myself for whole day excursions into Portsmouth and Southsea. Presently we went back to Clapham and I set about looking for a Christmas engagement, a disheartening business because I was just reaching the awkward age midway between boy parts and young juveniles'. I was tall for my years and my voice was breaking, which made me croak unexpectedly in the middle of conversations, to my own mortification and Stoj's great amusement.

I was dreadfully disappointed when I heard that A. W. Baskcomb was going to play 'Slightly' in *Peter Pan* (his original part). This was my last hope gone and so I resigned myself miserably to the first Christmas I had spent without work for a long while. Mother did her best to cheer me up as much as possible and we went to one or two pantomimes, but I was really wretched until a sudden telegram arrived from Boucicault saying that Baskcomb was ill and that I could take his place immediately. It was heaven to be back in the theatre again, and I squeezed myself into my last year's furs (Act II, *Never Never Land*) and pink and black striped boots, and sniffed the grease-paint and the 'size' and that particular burnt-paper smell which always permeates every production of *Peter Pan* and is caused by the fire that the Indians make in the second act. I was immensely elated at the thought of actually appearing on the same stage with Madge Titheradge who was playing Peter; I had seen her in *Tiger Cub* at the Garrick and was deeply in love with her husky voice and swift, alert charm. That first matinée when I rejoined the company, I was going down the stairs on to the stage for the underground scene when I met her face to face; she shook hands warmly with me and said: 'My name's Madge, what's yours?' A never-to-be-forgotten, most characteristic gesture.

17

For the whole of the following year I did not work, as I developed a strange cough, which upon examination proved to be caused by a tubercular gland in my chest. Mother was very frightened, but Dr Etlinger, an old friend of the family's, assured her that it would be easily cured by a few months in the country away from theatres and smoky atmospheres. I spent a little time at the Pinewood Sanatorium at Wokingham. I was not an actual inmate of the sanatorium but stayed in Dr Etlinger's private house in the grounds. He was extremely kind to me and allowed me to accompany him on his rounds in the morning, play croquet with the patients and help him with small errands. He was a short weather-beaten man with twinkling blue eyes and a passion for Russian tea, which we used to brew at all hours of the day and night and drink out of long glasses. I learned a good deal about T.B. and its various symptoms and stages and became deeply interested. Most of the patients were officers and they were all extraordinarily cheerful, particularly the more hopeless ones. They played tennis and bowls and croquet on the lawn, dressed only in bathing trunks whenever the sun came out and in light sweaters when it didn't. It was strange to listen to these dying men talking so gaily of the future. They nearly all looked sunburned and well, and there was no trace of illness about them until they began to cough, and then in a moment their colour and vitality faded, and they seemed to shrink piteously. I remember sitting for hours in the doctor's library after dinner discussing their possible chances of recovery, and new cures and treatments and lung deflations, and the experiments of Professor Spahlinger. Then I would retire to bed rather bleakly comforting myself with the reflection that if I ever contracted T.B. seriously, I should at least know enough about it not to be fooled by false illusion when the time came for me to face the truth of dying.

My cough rapidly disappeared, and by the summer I was stronger and healthier than I had ever been in my life. The time passed slowly for me, but not really unhappily. Of course I had moments of irritable yearning for the theatre, but the sight of so much disease at close quarters had scared a lot of common sense into me, and I would have stayed away willingly for years rather than risk my cough recurring.

In June, entirely to please Mother, I consented to be confirmed and was duly prepared for this rite by Mr Tower, our Clapham vicar. I went to tea with him two or three times a week in his study and he was very affectionate and biblical.

Soon after my confirmation I received a letter written in a slanting illegible hand from Mrs Astley-Cooper, a friend of Philip Streatfield's. He had joined up and was training with the Sherwood Foresters in Essex and he had asked her to have me down to stay in the country. He seemed to think that she would like me and that I would not only derive much material benefit from her country air and excellent living, but also profit by the astringent wisdom of her friendship. He died the following year without ever realising to the full the great kindness he had done me.

I accepted her invitation to stay, and Mother came to see me off at St Pancras and left her bag in the tube, with all the money she had scraped together for my return ticket. It was a dreadful moment. Mother, however, rose above it as usual and depositing me in the waiting-room with my rather cheap suitcase, darted out of the station and asked a policeman the way to the nearest pawnshop. There happened to be one practically opposite and within five minutes she was back, without her only remaining diamond ring but with enough money for the ticket. She stood on the platform waving as the train slid away, triumphantly pink in the face but with the suspicion of tears in her eyes. The whole thing ended up well, because she regained her bag miraculously within two days and so the ring was with her for a little while longer.

Mrs Cooper lived at Hambleton in Rutland, about three miles from Oakham in the middle of the Cottesmore country. The village stands on a hill rising abruptly out of chequered fields, polite and green and neatly hedged. The whole county of Rutland is compact and tidy. In summer it sleeps gently and a little stuffily, but in winter it wakes for hunting.

Mrs Cooper was gay company. Her principal pleasure was to lie flat on her back upon a mattress in front of the fire and shoot off witticisms in a sort of petulant wail. She draped scarves over all mirrors because she said she could find no charm in her own appearance whatever. The principal characters in the house were Uncle Clem (Captain Astley-Cooper) and Fred. Uncle Clem was handsome, charming and vague. An aura of military distinction still clung to him as he passed to and fro through the village and read the lessons in church on Sunday mornings. The status of Fred when I first saw him was difficult to define. He was too young and unimposing to be a butler, but he undoubtedly ran the house thoroughly and efficiently, Mrs Cooper with it.

It was a pleasant experience staying in a well-run country house. The trappings of life there were new to me: a fire in my bedroom every night, dinner clothes laid out neatly on the bed, brass cans of hot water, and deep baths encased in shiny brown wood. People came over and lunched or dined occasionally. A flurry of wheels in the drive announced them and the murmur of different voices echoed up from the hall as I grandly descended the polished oak staircase, very careful not to slip in my new patent-leather shoes.

During my winter visits I used to go to meets in the dog-cart, driving myself and following the hunt for as long as the pony consented to gallop. It was never amenable for more than an hour or so and had a disconcerting habit of standing stock-still for no reason at all, completely obstructing the road, and quite impervious to my shoutings and belabourings. Later on in the war Mrs Cooper and Fred ran Hambleton as a convalescent hospital and I used to go down whenever I could, sometimes only for Sunday night when I was acting, and sing and play to the soldiers.

18

Just before Christmas 1915 *Where the Rainbow Ends* was produced again at the Garrick, its fourth consecutive season. Most of the original cast were re-engaged: Esmé Wynne (Stoj), Philip Tonge,

Sidney Sherwood, Mavis Yorke, and myself. This time I had grown too big for the Page-boy and was still apparently unacceptable for either 'Crispian' or 'Jim Blunders,' so I played a character part, 'The Slacker,' who was a cross between a man and a dragon. I wore a greeny-beige costume with a tail, and put on an elaborate make-up, masses of number five (yellow), cheeks carefully emaciated with blue pencil and glittering green sequins on my eyelids. The part was short but showy, and I gave a macabre performance, leading up to one of those hysterically laughing exits which never fail to get a round of applause.

After this Stoj and I were engaged to play Amy and Charlie in the spring tour of *Charley's Aunt* at salaries of two pounds and two pounds ten a week respectively. The men of the company were required to provide their own clothes, which from the point of view of elegance was an unwise decision of the management's. My undergraduate flannels in Act Two, which were remarkable both in cut and texture, shrank degradingly in the first week's wash and by the end of the tour were practically cycling knickers. The company was then, is now, and always will be run by Mr Cecil Barth, a kind man with an unbridled passion for respectability. He told us at the outset that Stoj and I were not to share rooms together because it would give the company a bad name, so I was paired off reluctantly with the leading juvenile, Arnold Raynor, who never cared for me much, while Stoj lived with a fair girl with long hair and a round face, called Norah Howard. In this Stoj was lucky, because Norah was the only other un-morose member of that exceedingly morose troupe. Kathleen Barbor (now Mrs Ernie Lotinga) was the Walking Understudy and was a little less under the pall of self-satisfied gloom that enveloped the rest, but it got her down eventually and she was only seen to smile about once a fortnight. Many of the cast of course had played the play month in, month out for years and years and years, notably James Page (Mr Spettigue), Sidney Compton (Brasset) and J. R. Crawford (Colonel whatever it was). Mr Crawford also directed rehearsals with all the airy deftness of a rheumatic deacon producing *Macbeth* for a church social. Sidney Compton had a deep rasping voice and unfolded his mouth like an Inverness cape. James Page was the gayest of these three veterans, a gossipy, slightly bibulous old thing.

In my opinion, of all the parts in that least funny of all plays 'Charley' is the worst. 'Jack' and 'Lord Fancourt Babberley' are the ones who get all the laughs and the wretched 'Charley' supplies the cues. I tried desperately at first to invest this high-spirited congenital idiot with some reality, but after a while I gave up the struggle and just bounded on to the stage nightly and said the lines with as much conviction as possible. We seemed to me to play interminably everywhere, frequently split weeks in smaller towns such as Rugby and Peterborough. These split weeks were very expensive owing to changing rooms so rapidly. Often I had only enough money for one meal a day and was forced to make do with buns and glasses of milk until after the show at night when I stuffed myself with fish and chips. The whole tour was alive with incident. In Peterborough we played during a blizzard to exactly six people. In Chester Stoj and Norah and I went rowing up the river for a picnic completely forgetting that there was a matinée. In Manchester I had a row with Arnold Raynor about the bath water and decided to share with Stoj and Norah henceforward and risk Mr Barth's disapproval.

The three of us started our alliance the following week in Hanley. The town was filthy, the rooms were filthy, and the other inmates of the house were four acrobats who used the bathroom at the same time for economy's sake and invariably left a rim of grey horror round the inside of the bath which we tried to rub off with wads of toilet paper.

Altogether that week was far from successful. No night passed without one or other of us retiring to bed in tears. I drove Stoj mad by strumming the piano and she lacerated my nerves by strumming the typewriter. I forget what poor Norah did to irritate us, but I expect she whistled, or didn't quite understand our jokes. At any rate we all quarrelled furiously to such an extent that Stoj and I (temporarily on the same side against Norah) defiantly determined to live alone together the next week and to give in our notices if there were any managerial objections.

We arrived in Chester late on Sunday afternoon in a downpour of rain. Norah, wearing a faintly superior smile, got herself and her luggage into a taxi and drove off to her combined room which she had had the forethought to reserve in advance. We left our bags at the station and set out in the rain. We trudged for miles, soaked to the skin. There was apparently only one street where theatrical rooms were available, and every room in every house seemed to be taken. We walked endlessly up and down it, averting our eyes as we passed Norah's window which was on the ground floor front. She had thoughtfully left the blind up so that we shouldn't miss the sight of her sitting by a crackling fire, cramming down hot cocoa and steak-and-kidney pudding and self-consciously reading a book propped up against the cruet. Finally we gave up the theatrical street entirely and found at the end of a lane a nice-looking house with an 'Apartments' board in the window. A flashily-dressed woman opened the door and greeted us with surprising enthusiasm. She showed us two well-furnished bed-rooms and said that we could use her dining-room and that dinner was just ready. Absolutely delighted, we rushed back to the station, retrieved our luggage and within half an hour were cosily installed in pyjamas and dressing-gowns eating roast mutton and red currant jelly. It was not until three different men had walked into Stoj's room in the middle of the night that we realised that we were in a brothel. Even then we were quite eager to stay because, as I truly remarked, Stoj's appearance at night with her hair scragged back in Hinde's curlers and layers of Icilma cream plastered all over her face was so repellent that she could pass unscathed through fifty brothels. Mr Barth, however, inevitably found out and back we went to Norah, Stoj sharing her 'combined,' and I sharing meals and inhabiting a lonely single attic down the road.

The tour pursued its dreary way through February, March, April and May. In Bristol I had a religious mania lasting exactly one day and based upon an inexplicable fear of death which descended upon me abruptly in the middle of a matinée. Homesickness started it, I think, a black nostalgia for Mother and the dear familiarity of my bedroom at Clapham Common. I felt definitely that I should never see my home again. I had been away too many weeks in frowsy lodging-houses and my nerves were raw with sudden loneliness. There was thunder in the air as well, and during that night a terrific storm broke convincing me that this was my destined finish. I wept thoroughly at the vivid picture of

Mother's face when she heard how the sharp lightning had struck her darling through the window of the second floor back. I murmured incoherent prayers, vowed many vows and promised many promises, if only I might live a little longer. These were apparently granted, for I woke up the next morning as bright as a button and rapidly forgot the entire episode, promises and all.

In Torquay we had charming rooms. It was May and the weather and sea were warm enough for bathing, so Stoj and I reverted to the 'Woodland' again and went for long picnics on non-matinée days. We frolicked in secluded coves and danced naked in little woods fringing the shore, shutting our aesthetic eyes to the fact that Stoj's hair always went straight as string when even slightly damped, and that owing to recent indulgences in sweets, my back was generously pimpled.

In Wolverhampton, Arnold Raynor finally lost his temper with me and knocked me down just before my entrance in the last act. I had no time to retaliate even if I had wished to, and I tottered on to the stage with my collar torn and my white tie under my left ear.

In the dressing-room afterwards he said in sinister tones: 'Now we'll have this out,' and hit me again, upon which I lost all control and threw my tin make-up box at him. He was shorter than I and much stronger. He then hit me again and I fell down and banged my head against the wall. As I did so I had the presence of mind to yell with what I hoped was enough volume and tone to indicate anger rather than stark terror; anyhow it was effective enough to bring Stoj flying into the room dressed in a brief camisole and a pair of knickers and waving a hairbrush with which she struck my aggressor so hard on the back of the head that he fell down too, whereupon everyone cried and apologised and we all went out affectionately to supper.

19

The tour came to an end in June and we said good-bye to the company with unqualified delight and rejoined our various families. The autumn tour started early in August gratefully shorn of our presence. Meanwhile I was busily preparing a single turn for the halls consisting of imitations of famous stars. This never amounted to anything as it was quite impossible for the acutest perception to distinguish one imitation from the other. I appeared at several auditions in evening clothes accompanied on the piano by Auntie Kitty (deserted in Toronto by Uncle Percy) in a black lace dress and a diamond slide in her hair. All we were ever offered was a trial week somewhere at our own expense, which I sadly and expediently refused.

A year or two before this I had met, I forget exactly where, a boy named John Ekins. He was a year older than I and had been at school at Walthamstow where I remember visiting him with Stoj and taking him a box of chocolates. We had procured this by the simple means of buying an empty box for threepence and going from sweet-shop to sweet-shop in the Clapham Road and stealing the chocolates off the counters while one of us distracted the shopkeeper's attention by asking for sweets which we knew he didn't stock. The chocolates suffered rather from joggling about in our pockets, so when we got home we rubbed them with margarine to restore their vanished shine. Anyhow, they looked alluring enough when arranged neatly with paper shavings, and John was becomingly enthusiastic about them and ate the lot. He was the son of the Rector of Rame in Cornwall and was more thoroughly stage-struck than I. He knew what every actor and actress had played in for the last thirty years, also what they had worn and whom they had married. We used to sit in the garden of the rectory overlooking the summer sea with our noses buried in back numbers of *The Play Pictorial,* staring avidly at Lily Elsie wearing a hat like a tea-cosy in *The Count of Luxembourg,* putting her hand through a screen and being married to Bertram Wallis in a velvet coat. Kate Cutler in *Bellamy the Magnificent,* clutching her neck with both hands and looking extremely agitated; Charles Wyndham and Miss Compton in *Eccentric Lord Comberdene,* very uneasy in yachting caps, and best of all our beloved Gertie Millar in *Our Miss Gibbs,* wearing a beehive and talking to Robert Nainby as a Duke. On Wednesdays or Saturdays we used to go into Plymouth to see the matinée at the Theatre Royal. This meant walking a mile or so into Cawsand Village and catching the morning bus, which sometimes missed the ferry, forcing us to wait on the wrong side of the harbour in a fever of impatience for fear we should miss the beginning of the first act. After the matinée we always had tea in the Palm Court of the Royal, very casual and grand in our carefully pressed navy blue suits and coloured silk socks. Coming home to Rame in the late evening was lovely except for the last drag up the hill which covered our shoes with dust and generally made us slightly irritable. The scenery all the way was beautiful, particularly in the dusk with the different coloured lights springing up behind us in the harbour, and, through the giant trees of Mount Edgecombe Park, the regular flash of the Eddystone fifteen miles out to sea.

The rectory itself was cosy and lamp-lit and rather faded; all the rooms felt lived-in except the drawing-room, which retained an aloof atmosphere and smelt of moth-balls. Mr Ekins, Mrs Ekins, Christine, Audrey and John comprised the family, and it was one of the nicest households I have ever known. Audrey was consumptive and we used to have tea parties in her room to cheer her up, although she seemed to me to be happier than most people in the best of health. John finally prevailed upon his parents to allow him to live with his uncle in Lewisham and try for a stage engagement, which he succeeded in getting remarkably quickly. He appeared with Hawtrey in *Anthony in Wonderland,* played my longed-for 'Crispian' in *Where the Rainbow Ends,* and was in a melodrama at Drury Lane called *The Best of Luck,* in which Madge Titheradge was the leading lady. I often used to walk on in the crowd scenes just to give myself the feeling of being in a job. We were inseparable friends until one morning in 1917 when a letter arrived from him from Farnborough where he was training as an Air Force cadet, explaining that he had a day's leave and asking me to go to a matinée with him. By the same post there was also a letter from his mother telling me that he had died suddenly of spinal meningitis. The violence of the shock robbed the day and myself of all reality, and I went to the matinée alone, remotely cheerful and feeling myself brave. It wasn't until the second entr'acte that I began to cry foolishly and had to go home. Memory is viciously insistent on such occasions. The City and South London Tube plunged through its tunnels interminably, while I bicycled down from Rame to Cawsand with John, picnicked with him below the fort on the rocks, slid wildly up and down the frozen pond on Clapham Common and made tea late at night in his uncle's kitchen at Lewisham. The finality of death is bewildering on first acquaintance and the words 'never again' too sad to believe entirely. It took a long while for my unhappiness to disperse and even now I feel a shadow of it when I think of him.

Tragedy certainly descended swiftly on that gentle, harmless rectory. Within a year or so Christine, the healthy elder daughter, had married and died in childbirth, and there was only Audrey left to linger on for a few months. Mr and Mrs Ekins live there still and Christine's daughter is with them, but even so the house must feel empty.

20

In the summer of 1916 Robert Courtneidge engaged me to play a small part in a new musical comedy, *The Light Blues,* which was to be tried out for three weeks in Cardiff, Newcastle and Glasgow, before coming to the Shaftesbury Theatre. The play was very clean-limbed and jaunty and good-fellowish and dealt with the excruciating adventures of a jolly actress called Topsy Devigne, who dressed up as an undergraduate at Cambridge during May week and got herself into a series of roguish scrapes. Cicely Debenham played 'Topsy' and Albert Chevalier was somebody's father, and Cicely Courtneidge and Jack Hulbert supplied a second-string love interest with a couple of dance duets. I can still recall fragments of the lyrics, as for example the finale of the first act when Topsy, having successfully squeezed herself into a navy blue suit, sang:

> 'I'm Cuthbert the Coconut,
> The smartest on the tree,
> Any girl who isn't shy
> Can try a shy at me—' etc.

And later on, Cynthia (Cicely Courtneidge), in a pink silk dress with panniers and a Dolly Varden hat, flitting backwards and forwards across the stage and singing with incredible archness:

> 'Don't you go a-counting of your chickens,
> Wait 'til they're all hatched out,
> For you never, never know
> What's going to happen next,
> And you may be vexed,
> And a little bit perplexed –' etc.

There was also a sentimental number sung by Albert Chevalier assisted by *bouche-ferme* refrains from the whole company during which he paraded up and down in an angry white wig and sang with intense feeling:

> 'I see Life through rose-coloured glashes,
> I see Lovers in ro-o-shy light
> Billing and coo-ooing,
> Tenderly woo-ooing,
> Oh, if you only would tesht your shight.'

This song was extremely long, and there was ample time for Chevalier himself and the company and the whole of Cambridge to change from amber to deep pink and back again to amber before the end of it.

I played what is technically described as a 'dude' part. Morning clothes, silk hat and false moustache (insecure). I was on for about five minutes in the first act and four in the second, and I was offended at not being included in any of the musical numbers, but I was given the understudy of Jack Hulbert and learnt all his dances quickly in the forlorn hope that he would be seized with some disease on the opening night, giving me the chance to rush on and become a star immediately.

I enjoyed the three weeks' tour and shared rooms with Stephanie Stephens and her mother, who were old friends of mine. I didn't have much opportunity to enjoy the London run, as it only lasted a little while, but on the whole I learned a good deal. Mr Courtneidge was violent at rehearsals and lost his temper gloriously. On one occasion when he was reviling me for being unable to peel a banana correctly, he actually flung his hat on the stage and jumped on it, which sent me into a flurry of nervous laughter. With all his rages he was really kind and just to everybody, but he happened to belong to that school of production which considers no later rehearsal complete without tears from someone.

In Glasgow I had a painful but salutary experience. There was a full rehearsal called and I went down to the theatre with Stephanie sublimely unaware of the trouble in store for me. I have never been able to look at the bare stage of the King's Theatre since without a shudder of remembrance. On that particular morning it seemed normal enough at first with pieces of scenery littered about and the company waiting expectantly for the arrival of Mr Courtneidge. I remember being gay and jocular myself and doing a saucy imitation of somebody or other to amuse some of the minor members of the cast. Presently the 'Guv'nor' arrived and the atmosphere changed somewhat, laughter dwindled into polite smiles and there was the usual silence while he stood by the prompt table talking to the stage-manager. I must explain here that during the course of the second act I played a little scene with Shaun Glenville, who used to gag a good deal and say anything that came into his head. I was never particularly amused by these 'impromptus' but I frequently allowed myself to be convulsed with ill-repressed laughter, because I felt that it was quite a good plan to be suitably responsive to the leading comedian. Before that miserable rehearsal started Mr Courtneidge called me out before the entire company and mortified me to the dust. He informed me that I was not only a very young actor but a very bad actor, and that in addition to this I was practically a criminal for accepting a salary of four pounds a week (I had told Stephanie I was getting five) when all I did to earn it was to fool about and giggle on the stage, and that if it wasn't for the fact that we were opening in London the following week he would sack me on the spot. He said a lot more which I forget now, but it was all in the same vein, and I slunk away more utterly humiliated than I had ever been in my life. Cicely Debenham, however, lent me her handkerchief, and

Cicely Courtneidge patted me on the back and said: 'You mustn't mind Father.'

The play opened in London with the mark of death emblazoned upon it, and although there were calls for author and several people made speeches, it actually ran only two weeks.

Just after this I became, briefly, a professional dancer. Not in the true 'gigolo' sense, for alas, my adolescence was too apparent, my figure too gangling and coltish to promote evil desire in even the most debauched night-club habitués. I partnered a girl named Eileen Dennis, and we were engaged by the Elysée Restaurant (now the Café de Paris) to appear during dinner and supper. A slow waltz, a tango, and a rather untidy one-step made up our programme. Later, owing to popular demand (from Eileen Dennis's mother), we introduced a pierrot fantasia for which we changed into cherry-coloured sateen and tulle ruffs. No South African millionaires threw diamond sunbursts at Eileen's feet. We were neither of us ever invited to appear naked out of pies at private supper parties, in fact the whole engagement from the point of view of worldly experience was decidedly disappointing.

Another brief engagement somewhere in those years was as a 'super' in a D. W. Griffith's film. I was paid, I think, a pound a day, for which I wheeled a wheelbarrow up and down a village street in Worcestershire with Lilian Gish. The name of the film was *Hearts of the World,* and it left little mark on me beyond a most unpleasant memory of getting up at five every morning and making my face bright yellow, and a most pleasant memory of Lilian, Dorothy and Mrs Gish who were remarkably friendly and kind to me.

21

In December 1916 I was engaged for a Christmas play by Cecil Aldin, *The Happy Family,* in which I played a Sandhurst cadet in a red-and-white-striped blazer and a pill-box hat. In the second act everybody turned into animals except Mimi Crawford and me, and I rendered a dashing military number: 'Sentry Go,' with a full chorus of ducks and pigs, which I drilled resonantly in the third refrain. In this play I was allowed to dance and sing for the first time since *The Goldfish,* so I was very happy. The steps I had learned from understudying Jack Hulbert came in useful, and a critic in one of the more obscure weeklies wrote that I combined the grace and movement of a Russian dancer with the looks and manner of an English schoolboy. This thrilled me, although I couldn't help regretting that *The Times* or the *Daily Mail* hadn't displayed the same acute perception.

The first act of *The Happy Family* was remarkable for a hilarious concerted number in which every member of the company took part and sang with enthusiasm:

> 'Isn't it awfully jolly
> Doing a little revue?
> Never could be a more happy idea,
> It's nobby and nutty and new.
> Laughter and frolic and folly
> Won't we be going ahead?
> None of us stopping
> Until we are dropping
> And then we'll have breakfast in bed.'

Ten years later I quoted this to C. B. Cochran after a twenty-seven-hour dress rehearsal of *On With the Dance* in Manchester and he smiled dimly.

The following summer I went to the Gaiety, Manchester, to play in *Wild Heather,* a play by Dorothy Brandon. I lived alone in a bed-sitting-room in Lloyd Street, and was mothered by Mrs Wood, my landlady. She waited up every night for me and brought me my supper on a tray. It was usually Heinz baked beans, or welsh rarebit or something equally delicious, and she used to sit on the edge of a large feather bed and gossip with me while I ate it. It was a bright room with a permanently crooked Venetian blind veiled demurely by white lace curtains. There was an incandescent gas bracket with the mantle broken at the end, which shed an acid yellow glare over everything and almost succeeded in taking the colour out of the eiderdown. There was a 'fire-screen ornament' in the grate made of crinkled paper, and on the mantelpiece several photographs of Mrs Wood's sister as Sinbad the Sailor in tights leaning against a log of wood. The bathroom was down one flight of stairs and contained a fierce geyser which blew up occasionally, and once completely destroyed the 'fringe' of a well-known character actress.

Edyth Goodall was the leading lady in *Wild Heather,* and Helen Haye and Lyn Harding were also in it. It was a strong social drama in which everyone seemed miscast. I played Helen Haye's son, and drifted in and out until the end of the second act, when I drifted out for good, which left me free to go and watch the variety bills at the Palace and Hippodrome. During the second week of the run I went to the Palace every night to see Clara Evelyn and Ivy St Helier playing and singing at two grand pianos placed back to back. I tackled them both one day in the Midland Hotel, and was invited to tea in their sitting-room where I immediately played them some songs I had written. Miss St Helier gave me a wise little lecture on the value of 'authority' in a piano entertainer; she also showed me some good striking chords to play as introduction to almost any song. I profited a lot from that afternoon.

During the last of our three weeks' run two important events occurred. The first was the appearance at the stage door one evening of a dark enthusiastic American who said his name was Gilbert Miller, and that he had come especially from London to see my performance, as Charles Hawtrey had suggested me for a part in the new Haddon Chambers comedy *The Saving Grace,* which they were producing jointly at the Garrick. He asked me to supper at the Midland, and I was flattered and amazed that anyone so important should be so human and unmanagerial. He told me that he had feared that I should look too young for the part, and that as there was only a cast of seven including Hawtrey himself, it was necessary for everyone to be absolutely first-rate, if not actually a star. I aged visibly in manner and deportment and became almost off-hand in my efforts not to appear too youthful, but he assured me that he thought me good and that I would certainly be engaged, whereupon I was too dazed to be more than mildly astonished when he suddenly asked me quite seriously whether I would care for Marie Lohr to play opposite me. By that time I should only have given a languid nod if he had told me that Ellen Terry was going to play my baby sister.

We chatted on, and he told me several plots of plays that his father, Henry Miller, had produced in New York. He told them in detail and with tremendous vivacity, occasionally rearranging the knives and forks and plates to illustrate the more dramatic passages; at one moment he actually sprang up from his chair and shouted: 'Never, never, never!' loudly, much to the dismay of the head waiter. Finally he left me in order to catch the midnight train back to London and as I was far too inflated to contemplate the squalor of the last tram, I grandly renounced it and took a taxi all the way to Lloyd Street.

The second important event of that week was the beginning of a friendship which has lasted hilariously until now, and shows every indication of enduring through any worlds which may lie beyond us, always providing that those worlds be as redundant of theatrical jokes and humours as this one is. I stepped off a tram outside the Midland Hotel on my way to play a matinée and met Bobbie Andrews and Ivor Novello. I had not seen Bobbie since we were boy actors in the dear old romantic days of Savoy parties and teas in Lyons' Corner House. He was now definitely grown-up, as well he might be, having advanced reluctantly into his early twenties, although I must admit that his years sat but lightly upon him. He introduced me to Ivor, and we stood there chatting while I tried to adjust my mind to the shock. My illusion of this romantic handsome youth who had composed 'Keep the Home Fires Burning' drooped and died and lay in the gutter between the tram-lines and the kerb. The reason for this was that I had caught him in a completely 'off' moment. He was not sitting at a grand piano. He was not in naval uniform. The eager Galahad expression which distinguished every photograph of him was lacking. His face was yellow, and he had omitted to shave owing to a morning rehearsal. He was wearing an odd overcoat with an Astrakhan collar and a degraded brown hat, and if he had suddenly produced a violin from somewhere and played the 'Barcarole' from *The Tales of Hoffmann,* I should have given him threepence from sheer pity.

They walked along to the stage door of the Gaiety with me, and Ivor asked me to come over to the Prince's Theatre when I had finished my performance to see the last act of his musical comedy *Arlette,* which was playing there before opening in London. I remember very little about *Arlette* except the score, which was charming. Winifred Barnes was in it and Joseph Coyne and the plot was Ruritanian.

Afterwards we had tea in Ivor's rooms at the Midland, and he shaved and changed into a dinner-jacket for a company supper party. I envied thoroughly everything about him. His looks, his personality, his assured position, his dinner clothes, his bedroom and bath, and above all, the supper party. I pictured him sipping champagne and laughing gaily, warm in the conviction that he was adored by everybody at the table. I envied the easy intimacy with which he referred to Winifred Barnes as 'Betty' and Joseph Coyne (my hero of *The Quaker Girl*) as 'Joe.' I don't think honestly that there was any meanness in my envy. I didn't begrudge him his glamorous life, nobody who knew Ivor for five minutes could ever begrudge him anything. I just felt suddenly conscious of the long way I had to go before I could break into the magic atmosphere in which he moved and breathed with such nonchalance. In bed that night in my combined room I devoured minced haddock on toast with a certain distaste. A sense of frustration oppressed me. Here was I, seventeen years old, bursting with remarkable talent, a witty and delightful companion, with an interesting if not actually good-looking face and an excellent figure, just wasting time, treading water, not getting anywhere. My forthcoming engagement in *The Saving Grace* was of course comforting, but an unknown young actor in an all-star cast would not stand much chance of sending the critics into hyperboles of praise. I admit that for a little while I did toy with the vision of an unforeseen ovation on the first night at the Garrick with Hawtrey and Marie Lohr and Ellis Jeffries pushing me in front of them and imploring me to make a speech, but common sense robbed this dream of any conviction, and I looked at the photograph Ivor had given me, propped up against Sinbad on the mantelpiece, with a lowering admiration not far removed from hatred.

To know theatrical stars by their Christian names seemed to me then to be the apex of achievement. So far I had very few to my credit. Madge (Titheradge), Debbi (Cicely Debenham), Cicely and Jack (Courtneidge and Hulbert), Peggy (Edyth Goodall), and Mary (Mary Glynne). With Pauline Chase I had never got further than Miss Chase, let alone 'Polly.' This appeared to be rather a meagre list, and I resolved to embellish it as soon as possible. I dropped off to sleep in the midst of an ecstatic dream-supper-party in which Gladys (Cooper), Elsie (Janis) and Irene (Vanbrugh) were all saying: 'We must get Noel to sing us something.'

22

The Saving Grace was a gentle, witty and delightful comedy, and it is a source of great pride to me that I had the good fortune to play in it. The cast were: Charles Hawtrey, Ellis Jeffries, Emily Brooke (not Marie Lohr), May Blayney, A. E. George, Mary Jerrold and myself. We opened at the Gaiety, Manchester, which I had left only a fortnight before, and on the opening night Hawtrey made a speech mentioning each member of the company and finishing up with a brief biographical sketch of me. He told how I had played for him on and off since I was a little boy of eleven, and that the public had better watch me carefully in the future as I was undoubtedly going to be a good actor. The audience applauded and he led me forward and shook hands with me, and I fear that I cried a little, but imperceptibly.

My part was reasonably large, and I was really quite good in it, owing to the kindness and care of Hawtrey's direction. He took endless trouble with me. I was nervous and scared at rehearsals and painfully aware that I was actually too young for the part. All this I endeavoured to conceal under a manner of uppish assurance which couldn't have deceived him because he was never impatient, and taught me during those two short weeks many technical points of comedy-acting which I use to this day. The play opened at the Garrick after Manchester and was an immediate success, despite the fact that the times were unhappy, and all optimism appeared to be fading into a dreary suspicion that the war was permanent and eternal. For several weeks we had a series of air-raids. Hawtrey used to stop the first act by advancing to the footlights to tell the audience that the warning had been given, and that if those present who wished to take shelter would kindly leave as quietly as possible, the play would proceed. Whereupon, a few usually shuffled out and we continued, with forced brightness, to prove that even actors could be brave in the face of danger. The full fury of the raids invariably occurred during my love scene with Emily Brooke; this irritated us considerably. The banging of the anti-aircraft guns and the reverberations from bombs falling, not only robbed us of the attention of the audience, but destroyed any subtle *nuances* we might attempt in the scene, for in order that any of the words might be heard at all we had to bellow like bulls. On several occasions small pieces of shrapnel fell through the roof over the stage and tinkled on the thin canvas ceiling immediately above our heads.

Meanwhile, drastic changes had taken place in my family life. Mother, growing weary of the purposeless, poverty-stricken gentility of existence in a maisonette at Clapham Common, suddenly revolted and determined to do something about it. She had a series of consultations with my Aunt Ida who had been successfully running a lodging-house in Ebury Street for several years, and decided that she would do the same thing. The tenants of III, Ebury Street, which was almost opposite to my aunt's house, wished to sell the remainder of their lease with all the furniture and what was ironically termed 'the goodwill of the business' thrown in. After a lot of discussion about inventories and instalments, and a series of scenes were enacted in the home in alternate moods of gloomy foreboding and the rosiest enthusiasm, Mother finally took the plunge, signed several incomprehensible legal documents, and we moved in *en bloc,* Auntie Vida included. There was quite a lot of additional argument over this as Auntie Vida had been nourishing a secret desire to live by herself in some sad building for deceased naval officers' daughters in Wimbledon.

Poor old Auntie Borby had died the previous year, the house at Lee-on-the-Solent had long been given up and she was completely alone except for us. We jumped on the Wimbledon idea firmly, suspecting misplaced martyrdom, so she came with us and was allotted a minute bedroom under the roof next to mine.

Number III was a tall house with an austere personality and passably good furniture. There was a wooden room built out at the back known as 'The Bungalow' which we inhabited together with our dining-room table and chairs, the walnut davenport, the Organo piano (which imitated an organ when anyone pressed its extra pedal), an old and much beloved sofa with its intestines coming out, and a lot of family photographs; also many of Grandfather's pictures, and his sword and dirk hung horizontally on the wall with a faded photograph of Uncle Ran, as a boy, on one side of them, and me as a mushroom on the other.

We had two servants to begin with, and nearly our full complement of lodgers, most of whom had stayed on after the house had changed hands. Mother worked like a slave, cooking meals, rushing up and down the high steep stairs, organising, dealing with tradesmen, income-tax collectors, rate collectors, and in later years occasionally brokers' men. Payne's Pianos had evaporated into an inconclusive mist of failure and Father had no work to do, so he contented himself with making model yachts for his own amusement. They were beautiful yachts and, I believe, structurally accurate in every detail, and he sailed them backwards and forwards across the Clapham Common pond, and the Battersea Park pond, and the Round pond and the Serpentine, while Mother discharged servants, engaged window-cleaners, found out how to make aspic jelly from *Mrs Beeton* and anxiously added up Eric's Manor House school expenses.

We soon discovered that two servants were too expensive and so we had to make do with one, which meant a lot of housework for Mother in addition to the cooking. The lodgers were amiable and frequently serenely inconsiderate. They left every once in a while, and grave apprehension reigned in the bungalow, until the empty rooms were occupied again. Mother became more or less inured to the drudgery, but her spirit drooped a little and she looked unbearably tired.

The Saving Grace ran for several months, and I began to be recognised a little bit for the first time in my life. Occasionally I noticed people nudging one another when I passed in the street, and once a strange woman spoke to me in a bus and said that she thought I gave ever such a good performance. In addition to being in a distinguished success with a distinguished cast, I had a dressing-room to myself for the first time, which, I think, pleased me more than anything.

I had a dresser called Terry, whom I shared with A. E. George, and I gave tea-parties on matinée days. Stoj generally came and Aishie Pharall, a big girl with a fox-terrier, who had been on tour with her. After we had been running a little while Mr Camplin Smith, the stage manager, took it upon himself to use my precious dressing-room in which to interview stray applicants for small parts and understudies. He did this while I was on the stage without saying anything about it to me. One day I came up after the second act and discovered Stoj and Aishie waiting on the stairs, having been refused admittance, whereupon, swollen with the importance of my position, I lost my temper and behaved very badly. I went straight to Mr Hawtrey's room and refused to go on in the last act. Hawtrey listened patiently to my incoherent tirade, sent for Camplin Smith, and told him he was never to use my room again without my permission, and then told me gently and firmly that if I gave myself airs and talked such nonsense I should not be given the chance of going on in the last act, nor indeed in any act, as I should be immediately sacked and never be allowed to appear in a company of his again. After that he hit me quite hard on the behind and sent me up to my tea-party.

I suppose if I had been with any other management, this appalling impertinence would have done for me completely, but Hawtrey knew a whole lot of things that other managers never even suspected. He knew how to bring out young talent without storming and bullying. He knew how to conduct the most irritating rehearsals without sacrificing one atom of his dignity or authority. He also knew that very youthful actors were frequently victimised by their own frustrated conceits, and that to deal harshly with them might crush down their small confidence and suffocate any genuine talent they might have. He had humour and kindliness, and a sure expert knowledge of the theatre, and he managed, without apparent effort, to be much beloved. It is one of my lasting regrets that he died before I had time to justify a little his faith in me.

PART TWO

My career in the British Army was brief and inglorious. In 1914 and 1915, when the first patriotic call to arms had sounded, I had been too young even to wish to respond. I was too concentrated on my own struggles and ambitions to be able to view the war as anything but an inevitable background. Air raids, darkened streets, familiar names in the casualty lists, concerts for the wounded, food rations, coupons, and the universal smear of khaki over everything were so much part of everyday life that any other conditions seemed impossible to visualise.

In January, 1918, I was examined by a medical board and informed that my slight T.B. tendency of three years ago would prevent me from being passed fit for active service and would also debar me from entering any of the Officers' Training Corps, but that I would be called up for some kind of service in due course, and was to hold myself in readiness. This was almost as great a relief to me as it was to Mother. The spirit of sacrifice, the conviction of speedy victory, and even the sense of national pride had faded in the minds of most people into a cheerless resignation. Four futile years had robbed even bravery of its glamour, and the far greater gallantry of courage in the face of anti-climax was too remote for dejected civilians to grasp. It was certainly too abstract an ideal to inspire a self-centred young actor. I remained in a state of relief tinged with uneasiness until the end of the run of *The Saving Grace,* and was rehearsing a meaty dramatic part in a play by Miss Hazel May, when a horrible little grey card fluttered through the letter-box of 111, Ebury Street, summoning me immediately to a medical board at the Camberwell Swimming Baths. I sent a telegram to Mr Ayliff who was producing the play, and set off in the tram for Camberwell. At the end of several hours of beastliness during which I stood about naked on cold floors and was pinched and prodded by brusque doctors, I was told to dress myself, given an identification card, and ordered to line up with a group of about fifty men in various stages of physical and mental decay. Presently a sergeant took charge of us and marched us untidily to Whitehall, where we were shut up in a stuffy hut overlooking the Park for about two hours while lots of papers were signed. This over, the sergeant again took us in charge and we marched up Whitehall, along the Strand and over Waterloo Bridge to Waterloo Station. I kept my head averted in case any of my friends should see me on their way out from their matinées at the Adelphi and the Vaudeville. We entrained at Waterloo and finally arrived at Hounslow where we marched to the barracks and were put into one hut, all fifty of us, and dealt out slices of bread and margarine, cups of greasy cocoa, and three blankets each for the night. There was a slight scene while we were undressing because the man next to me was found to be covered with sores. After a good deal of argument he was led away protesting, and I was generously offered one of his blankets extra, which, although shivering with cold, I thought it wiser to refuse.

The next morning we were given uniforms and boots and porridge and paraded in front of an irritable officer with a wart over one eye. We were also made to swill our mouths out with some bright pink disinfectant and wash our teeth over a long trough. By this time my despair had given place to a still, determined rage. I contemplated, alternatively, fainting suddenly in the middle of the barrack square, or making a wild dash for the gates, but my common sense told me that neither of these dramatic gestures would do me any good at all, and that the only thing was to keep my head and think out some more subtle means of escape. I had made up my mind definitely that in no circumstances whatever would I spend another night in that hut. At eleven o'clock, after we had done some perfunctory drill and been shown how to put on our puttees properly, we were given half an hour's rest. I waited until all the others were sitting around in the hut and smoking and cursing, and then I went boldly up to the sergeant and asked if I could speak to him privately for a moment. He led me outside, whereupon I pressed a ten-shilling note into his hand and asked him to lead me to the commanding officer. He told me to wait for ten minutes and disappeared. Presently he came back and took me across the square and passed me on to another sergeant, who in turn took me into an office where two clerks were sitting at typewriters. Here I waited until the commanding officer arrived. He looked me up and down searchingly and asked me what was the matter. I told him that I had been called up the day before without any preliminary warning, and without any time to settle up my private affairs, and that it was essential for me to have a day's leave in order to straighten things out. Finally, after a certain amount of questioning, he said I could have the rest of the day off providing I reported back at nine o'clock p.m. A railway pass was made out for me and within an hour I was sitting in the train wearing a uniform that was far too small, and a hat that was far too big.

I went straight home, and after an hysterical reunion with Mother, who greeted me with as much fervour as if I had spent four years in the front line, I changed into my own clothes and set off in a taxi. I had a hastily composed list in my pocket of everyone I knew who might conceivably be influential enough to help me. The list numbered two generals, two colonels, and a captain; with grim persistence I saw them all, and not one of them could offer me the faintest hope. If I had come to them before, they said, it would have been quite easy, but as things were, it was too late and the only thing for me to do was to resign myself to the inevitable. The last on my list was a captain in the Air Force whom I had met casually at one or two parties. He was as affable and kindly as the others and equally hopeless, except that he gave me a note to a friend of his, Lieut. Boughey at the War Office. I arrived at the War Office just as everybody was leaving. Someone told me that Lieut Boughey had gone five minutes before, then a small corporal interfered and said that he had not gone and was still in his office. I was led into his room, and I must have looked pretty exhausted for he offered me a drink at once and told me to sit down and take it easy. I explained my troubles to him as briefly and calmly as I could, and within ten minutes he had telephoned the commanding officer at Hounslow and informed him in a sharp official voice that there had been a disgraceful muddle over N. Coward, who was perfectly fit and had no earthly right to be in a Labour corps, and that his civilian clothes were to be sent home immediately, together with any papers there were concerning him. After this we had another drink and discussed Lord Kitchener, the war, the theatre, and my immediate future in the army. Lieut Boughey said that he could get me into the Artists' Rifles O.T.C., and that he would arrange for me to have a couple of weeks' leave before joining up. I thanked him as coherently as I could and went home, marvelling that a busy man at the end of a long day's work should take such trouble to help an insignificant stranger. I never saw him again, and a few months later I heard a rumour that he had been killed.

2

In due course my papers arrived from the Artists' Rifles, and I was sent down with a batch of about twenty recruits to the training camp at Gidea Park in Essex. It was only a little way from London, and we were allowed leave every other week-end. A sergeant-major lectured us all briskly at the outset and explained that as we were now soldiers of the King, our only thoughts henceforward must be of our country and our regiment. He commanded us to turn our minds from all trivial sentimentalities such as homes and sweet-hearts, and wives and brothers, and concentrate upon becoming fearless, hard-bitten fighters. This little homily depressed me, and I noted with a certain wan satisfaction that it also appeared to sadden my companions. When it was over, a group of us walked dismally into the town of Romford, our duties being finished for the day. We all tried hard to march along in an upright soldiery manner but the military spirit was as yet young in us. My puttees kept on coming undone, and I dropped my cane seventeen times.

The other men in my company (Company C) were pleasant. The food wasn't good, but on the other hand it wasn't bad. The routine was hard but not callous, and those weeks should by rights have done me a lot of good. Unfortunately, however, I couldn't adapt myself to these new circumstances. It wasn't that I didn't try. I did. I made tremendous efforts, but it was no use. My stage life had ill-prepared me for any discipline other than that of the theatre, and that discipline is peculiar to itself. In almost any branch of the theatre it is individuality that counts. In the army it is exactly the opposite. You are drilled and trained and lectured as a unit, one of thousands. I did my best and learnt a lot of things. I learnt how to fold blankets into a sort of bag and how to sleep inside it. I learnt how to polish buttons, how to roll and unroll puttees, how to carry a short cane, how to salute, and also how to stab sacks of straw accurately with a bayonet under the sharp eye of a bloodthirsty corporal with a highly developed sense of drama, who lashed our imaginations to the requisite pitch of fury by shouting: 'They're bellies, they're bellies, they're all German bellies!' The one thing I never learnt was to accept it all tranquilly. The sergeant-major's words had not sunk deep enough. I couldn't wipe my mind clean of Mother and home. I twisted about miserably inside my blankets at night wondering whether Miss Daubeney was inhabiting the third floor, and whether the drawing-room suite was still vacant, and how Mother was managing to pay Eric's school expenses without the help of my weekly salary. I was tortured with the thought that I was wasting time. The needs of my King and Country seemed unimportant compared with the vital necessity of forging ahead with my own career. It was a matter of pressing urgency to me that I should become rich and successful as soon as possible – soon enough, in fact, to be able to get Mother out of that damned kitchen for ever. All this, I fully realise, was reprehensible. There were millions of young men with far graver responsibilities than mine who were sacrificing their lives daily, and there were millions of mothers in far more tragic circumstances; but these reflections were powerless to jerk my spirit free of myself and my own personal problems, and as it is my object in this book to be as truthful as I can, I must confess that I was resentful and rebellious and profoundly wretched. Oddly enough, the thought of going to the front didn't worry me particularly. To begin with, the prospect was far away in the future, after months of training as a cadet and as an officer.

In addition to this, the fact that I had been graded B 2 instead of A 1 by the various medical boards, made the chance of any actual fighting even more remote. My unhappiness was concerned with the immediate present and cowardice had honestly no part in it. Soon the unfamiliarly hard routine coupled with my inward miseries began to affect me physically. I developed cracking headaches and was unable to sleep. I bought a bottle of aspirin in Romford, but it was only effective for a little while. It was ridiculous to hope for quiet in a hut with thirty men in it, and the noise every night before 'lights out' seemed to cut through my head like a saw. I used to twist string round my finger until it cut me, to prevent myself from giving way to nerves and yelling the place down.

One morning, a few weeks after I had been in the camp, we were all doubling back from musketry drill along the ribbed wooden paths that ran between the different huts. I caught my foot in one of the slats and fell heavily, striking my head against one of the stakes by the side of the path. I gather that I had concussion, because my memory of the next three days is almost completely blank, although I dimly remember Ivor's *Arlette* score running incessantly through my mind. This was accounted for a long while afterwards when someone told me that while I was lying on the corporal's bed in Hut 10 waiting for the arrival of the doctor, the regimental band was practising next door. I can only fix accurately upon two moments of consciousness. One, in the camp hospital, when I woke to the surprising vision of the company commander sitting on my bed, with his face, which was long and amiable with a moustache on it, seeming to weave up and down close to mine. I believe he asked me a lot of questions, but I forget what they were or whether or not I answered any of them satisfactorily. The only other clear moment in those strange hours was the sudden realisation that I was being conveyed rapidly backwards in bed, and that there was an orderly in khaki reading a book against a background of swiftly moving hedges. I awoke finally in the emergency ward of the First London General Hospital, with Mother bending over me and explaining tearfully that I had been unconscious for three days and nights.

3

I remained in the First London General Hospital for six weeks, in a large ward with about twenty other inmates, most of whom were shell-shock cases. I was examined by several different doctors, thoroughly, casually, suspiciously, and kindly. None of them seemed to know what was the matter with me. Some of them fired searching questions at me; abrupt and irrelevant questions obviously calculated to catch me out in the event of the whole thing being a hoax. Their suspicions were pretty adequately disproved by my temperature chart which resembled an outline of the Rocky Mountains drawn by a drunken child. They traced back my medical history and cross-examined Mother, who finally gratified them by remembering that I had been knocked down by a bicycle at the age of five. This apparently accounted for everything, and we all settled ourselves to wait until the brain tumour showed further signs of life. It didn't, and I convalesced gradually. My headaches became less frequent and less violent. My temperature returned to normal, and after a couple of weeks I was able to sleep at night without the aid of either aspirin or bromide. Mother visited me every day and brought me books and fruit, although where she found the money to pay for them I shall never know. I conceived a passion for the works of two authors, Sheila Kaye-Smith and G. B. Stern, and I wrote them both long letters of admiration to which they replied promptly. A considerable correspondence ensued, and when we ultimately met we discovered that we were already old friends.

During my really convalescent, out-of-bed period, when I wore hospital blue and helped to carry meals to the bedridden and sweep out the ward, I met in the Y.M.C.A. hut which was attached to the hospital, a young New Zealander named Geoffrey Holdsworth. He endeared himself to me by sitting wide-eyed by the rickety upright piano and imploring me to play him the 'Lilac Domino' waltz. This paved the way to mutual confidences, and he took me down to the kitchens to introduce me to a friend of his who was one of the cooks; thereafter, by means of various sly devices, Geoffrey and I were always given the slightly better quality food reserved for the officers. He also showed me a broken place in the wall at the end of the grounds by which it was possible to escape after the morning duties were finished, which was generally about eleven, and not return until roll-call at six. This was a dangerous proceeding but exciting. We were only actually allowed out for one afternoon a week from two until five, but with the aid of a broken wall and a convenient tree we enjoyed many hours of extra freedom. The initial steps were the most perilous – a casual walk along the path, then a swift glance all round, and a sudden dart into the shrubbery. Once over the wall there was only the brief agony of a nonchalant stroll to the tram stop, which was the worst of all really, because the desire to run whenever a sergeant or an officer appeared had to be sternly crushed down. There was always the dread of being accosted and asked to show a 'Pass.' However, I weathered all the dangers and was never caught.

Upon arrival at Ebury Street I bathed and changed, and set out for the West End, an actor once more, wearing coloured shirts and ties and silk socks, with shoes that felt strangely light after the heavy army boots, and a heart that felt lighter still. I saw a lot of Ivor and Bobbie and Gladys Gunn (now Gladys Henson), and one day Ivor gave me a dress-circle seat for the opening matinée of his new revue at the Vaudeville, in which Beatrice Lillie was the leading lady, and Gertrude Lawrence was understudying her. In his flat there was a delicious atmosphere of slight quarrels and gossiping. Everyone drank a lot of tea and discussed what Charlot had said and what Fay (Compton) had said and how Eddie (Marsh) thought it was marvellous anyway. This would have to be changed and that would certainly have to be changed. The whole conversation swirled around all the topics I loved best, occasionally enhanced, but never interrupted by peculiar noises from the next room in which Madame Novello Davies gave interminable singing lessons to small Welsh women in grey clothes.

4

I repaid Geoffrey Holdsworth's good offices by changing the course of his life. I lent him G. B. Stern's books and also showed him some of her letters, whereupon he immediately wrote to her himself and a few months later married her. As they are now divorced, I will deny myself the pleasure of romantic digression and dissociate myself firmly from the whole affair.

On my discharge from the hospital I was given a week's leave before returning to camp. This I spent in Devonshire with Stoj and her fiancé, Lyndon Tyson. He was tall and docile, and much in love with her; otherwise I am sure he would have objected to my presence during what was undoubtedly a sort of pre-nuptial honeymoon. It was a peaceful and pleasant week enlivened by only one serious row; caused by Lyndon meeting Stoj and me face to face on the hotel landing as we issued forth blandly from the bathroom together. It took several hours of threefold hysteria and many tears and recriminations to erase the unworthy suspicions from his mind, but by tea-time everything was rosy again, and we all sat on the bench and talked about life intellectually and without resentment.

When I arrived back at the camp I was put on 'Light Duties,' which consisted of polishing practically everything, and helping to clean out the latrines. This was far from enjoyable; but I had more leisure than before, and spent most of it sitting in the canteen drinking cups of tea and eating odd messes of bright pink jelly with whipped cream on top, which the local lady workers behind the bar arranged daintily in glass dishes.

I persevered wearily with my 'Light Duties' and tried, without much success, to keep my mind from dwelling too much upon the utter futility of the situation. I felt physically well enough for about three-quarters of every day, and then suddenly, unreason-ably, and without warning, a cloud of black melancholia would envelop me, draining all colour and vitality from everything and changing the friendly noises of the canteen into a nerve-racking din from which I fled to the Church hut. This, although gloomy, was at least empty and still. I lashed myself with accusations of hysteria and self-pity, aware that I was a poor weakling, a spineless creature of no integrity, unable to cope with anything more formidable than a row of footlights and a Saturday-night audience. These emotional orgies usually passed after an hour or so and I crept back, ashamed, to Hut 10, and scuffled into my blankets as unobtrusively as possible, in the hope that no one would comment upon my red-rimmed eyes.

After a few weeks my headaches began to recur, but not very badly; at least not badly enough to prevent me from applying for an afternoon's leave to attend the Theatrical Garden Party. Up to now I had helped Vane Featherstone every year with her 'Jarley's Wax-works,' and it had always been a day of ecstasy for me, hobnobbing with the stars on the more or less equal terms dictated by Charity. The company commander, with a slightly ironical smile, granted my request and I endured the next few days in a fever of anxiety in case anything should occur to prevent me from going. My anxiety was well-founded. The morning before the day of the garden party I woke with such a violent headache that I was incapable of standing up. The doctor came into the hut to examine me and I was carted off to the camp hospital. Later on in the day I was examined by two other doctors, and the next morning at eleven o'clock I was put in an ambulance and driven to the General Military Hospital at Colchester. It was a beautiful sunny day, fashioned by God for morning suits and silk hats and white gloves and flowered chiffons. I pictured the gay crowds at the Botanical Gardens, old ladies from the suburbs in black taffeta, character actresses of small standing in large feather boas, eminent male stars with button-hole cravats, and Gladys Cooper smiling immaculately, wearing shell pink and wheeling a barrow. I smelt the little 'Jarley's Wax-works' tent, hot canvas and trampled grass and tea, and knew wretchedly that I should never see any of it again, that the doctors at the first London General Hospital had been right about there being a tumour on my brain, and that I was lost for ever in frustration, misery and pain.

5

My first night in the Colchester Hospital was spent in a general ward. My head was bad and I couldn't sleep. The night nurse refused to give me aspirin because she said that I had not yet been diagnosed, so I twisted and turned and stared at the shadows the night lamp made upon the ceiling, wondering whether they would operate on my brain in the morning, and if so, whether they would use a hammer and a chisel as I heard they did in mastoid operations. I also wondered whether there would be time for Mother to get to Colchester for my death and whether I should be conscious or unconscious when she arrived.

They didn't operate on me in the morning. They thought of something far better, which was to move me straightway into an epileptic ward in the annexe. They also omitted to tell me that it was an epileptic ward, probably not wishing to deprive me of the full flavour of surprise, when the patient opposite to me proceeded to have several fits one after another before I had been in the place half an hour.

An epileptic fit is not a pleasant sight at the best of times, and as there were twelve epileptics in the ward and the moment one started they all started, my condition of acute neurasthenia showed no noticeable signs of improvement for the first week or so. As I remained there for two months I naturally became inured, and later on, even managed to be quite helpful to the nurses. I acquired the technique of squeezing the patients' tongues back into place by a deft pressure on the throat. I learnt how to hold their arms in a certain position to prevent their springing off the bed and out of the window, and I also learnt not to mind being flecked with their foam and saliva. I had a few bad moments at first, when I realised that not a single one of them suspected that he was epileptic. The minute anyone finished having a fit he generally went to sleep and woke up with no memory of it whatever. Most of them seemed rather bewildered at being there at all. The thought that I might be having fits myself all the time without knowing it was horrible, and when I questioned the nurses I wasn't quite able to believe their kindly denials, so I kept myself wide awake for twenty-four hours and checked off every ten minutes in an exercise book. I did this twice a week for the first three weeks. The strain of keeping awake all night long was awful, but the relief of finding every ten minutes safely marked was well worth it.

The rounds were made every morning by a lady doctor of bird-like appearance. She was brusque, efficient and quite idiotic. Once a week she was accompanied by the medical officer in charge of the whole annexe, and on these occasions her brusquerie became almost frantic. She yapped and poked and prodded and flounced from bed to bed, giving shrill orders to the nurses and snapping her teeth together like castanets.

Nobody seemed to consider it worthwhile to attempt to diagnose my case with any degree of thoroughness, and so there I remained through July and August, passing the time in bed by writing a bad novel, and reading a little and walking a little on the common whenever I could get a 'pass' for the afternoon. Sidney Lomer had a house in Colchester and I used to have tea with him sometimes. One day General (Splash) Ashmore, whom I had known when I was in *The Saving Grace,* made an official visit to the hospital. We all stood to attention when he clanked into the ward with some doctors and A.D.C.s in attendance, and he sent my stock up considerably by chatting to me for about ten minutes. Fortunately the dignity of the occasion was unimpaired by anybody having a fit, although a short while after he had left, a boy called Barnet, in the next bed to mine, had seven straight off, doubtless from sheer excitement.

Eventually the head medical officer called me into his office and told me that I was to go before the next medical board which occurred in a week's time, and that he had recommended me for complete discharge from the army. He said, reasonably, that my value as a soldier of the King amounted to a total loss, and that the sooner I got out of it the better for all concerned. I was stupefied with surprise and relief, but I retained enough sense not to give way to it too much. I believe I even managed to look a little wistful, which either deceived or amused him, for he patted me on the back and dismissed me amiably.

I went before the medical board after six days of feverish anticipation of freedom, during which I had written hysterical letters home and received correspondingly ecstatic ones back. My own medical officer was not present at the board and the doctors who were, after a cursory glance at me and my papers, marked me back for full duty with the Artists' Rifles and dismissed me curtly without argument.

I went back to the ward slowly, quite stunned, and trying to adjust my mind to the full bitterness of disappointment. To have been so near release, to have known so definitely that the futile wasteful months were at last over, and now, by the order of a few strange doctors who had glanced casually through my papers and knew nothing of my circumstances, to be sent back to the beginning again seemed too crushing a blow to realise.

I sat on my bed and opened a book, trying, while I was staring at the pages, to phrase in my mind a telegram to Mother, a telegram that would explain the truth adequately without upsetting her too much. While I was occupied with this, the head sister came in and, noting from my expression that something was wrong, called me outside and asked me what had happened. Under her sympathetic eye I managed to explain my doom more or less coherently. She thought for a moment or two and then, with surprising professional brusqueness, told me that I looked seedy and that I was to go to bed immediately for a week until the head doctor came back from his holiday; she also added stonily that it might be necessary to put me on a diet. With this she left me and I went to bed and wrote out a telegram to Mother saying that there had been a slight delay, but that she wasn't to worry as everything would be all right.

The head doctor returned from his holiday a day earlier than he was expected, and was astonished and angry to find me still littering up the ward. He interviewed me briefly in his office, and said that the medical board had behaved like bloody fools, and that not only would I be discharged within a week, but that he would see to it that I got a year's pension. Three days after this I was passed rapidly through another medical board and was signed finally out of the British Army. I still had to wait for a few days while the papers went through, but this I didn't mind in the least, as I was nominally free and could wander about the town and go to the pictures, providing I was back every night by nine o'clock.

The day before my actual discharge I was escorted up to London by a sergeant, who took me to the Pensions Office where I submitted to a good deal of questioning and was finally conceded a pension of seven shillings and sixpence a week for a term of six months. When all this was over we had a couple of hours to spare before catching the train back to Colchester, so I took the sergeant to Ebury Street and we had tea in the bungalow. Mother sent Auntie Vida round the corner to get a coffee cake at Barret and Pomeroy's and the whole occasion passed off delightfully. The sergeant, under Father's tutelage, experimented with the Organo piano and expressed great enthusiasm for Grandfather's pictures. Mother suggested that he might like a peep at my press-cutting book but I squashed this hurriedly, fearing that the early photographs of me in tights as 'Prince Mussel' might sully a hitherto successful afternoon.

The next morning, wearing a navy blue suit and carrying a kit-bag, I said good-bye to the epileptics and the nurses and my beloved head sister, and settled myself in a third-class carriage of the London train in a state of indescribable happiness. The fact that the train passed through Gidea Park and Romford gave an extra fillip to my joy. Somewhere between these two grim stations I observed a long line of Artists' Rifles tramping along the dusty road, but the train was travelling too quickly for me to be able to distinguish any familiar faces. At Liverpool Street I took a taxi and drove through the City streets. It was twelve noon, in the full tide of traffic and the hot August sun beat down upon taxis and trucks and drays and red friendly buses. It also beat down with kindly impartiality upon the Gaiety, the Vaudeville, the Savoy, and the Adelphi theatres and I pictured as I passed them the cool pre-matinée gloom of their interiors: cleaners swishing dust-sheets from the boxes and dress circles, understudies meandering about their stages under a working light, clutching scripts and mumbling inaudibly with an occasional sharp interruption from the stage manager at the prompt table, a genial hum of vacuum-cleaners from the front of the house, and strong shafts of alien sunlight striking down from open doors, and from the flies on to forlorn detached pieces of scenery; backings and flats against white-washed walls, unfinished staircases and shorn fragments of balustrade waiting about untidily to be set in Act One symmetry by the staff at two o'clock.

I almost wept with sentimental love for it all; it seemed that æons had passed since I had been part of it. I reflected then, without a shadow of embarrassment, upon my unworthy performance as a soldier. There was no room in my heart for anything but thankfulness that I was free again to shape my life as I wanted.

PART THREE

My first step after my discharge from the army was to look for an engagement. I sauntered into all the agents' offices and announced that I was free. I informed every management, verbally and by letter, that I was theirs for the asking, and discovered that although I had played a leading part in *The Saving Grace,* not one of them seemed to care. I appeared at crowded auditions wearing an immaculate suit and an air of amused condescension which deceived nobody and merely succeeded in irritating the other aspirants. I had written a number of light songs during the past years, and I sang them repeatedly, accompanying myself on the piano. There was a sentimental ballad: 'Tamarisk Town,' and a bright 'Point' number: 'Forbidden Fruit,' which I think is worthy of record as it was the first complete lyric I ever wrote. The perceptive reader will, I am sure, detect, even in this very youthful effort, that unfortunate taint of worldly cynicism which I am so frequently told, degrades much of my later work.

'Every Peach, out of reach, is attractive
'Cos it's just a little bit too high,
And you'll find that every man
Will try to pluck it if he can
As he passes by.

For the brute loves the fruit that's forbidden
And I'll bet you half a crown
He'll appreciate the flavour of it much, much more
If he has to climb a bit to shake it down.'

I can only suppose that this cold-blooded realism was too much for the managers, because they neither made any offers for me nor for the song. I remember on one occasion Beatrice Lillie incurred the grave displeasure of André Charlot by bringing me in to sing for him before an afternoon rehearsal. He informed her afterwards that he would not have his valuable time wasted by trivial young composers who played the piano badly and sang worse, and that never, in any circumstances, was she to do such a thing again.

In all theatrical experience I know of nothing more dispiriting than an average audition: a bleak denuded stage only illuminated by one or two glaring working lights; a weary accompanist at a rickety upright piano; in the second or third row of the stalls, with the dim auditorium stretching behind them, sit a small group of people upon whom your livelihood depends, who mutter constantly to each other and whose faces, on the rare occasions that they are turned towards the stage, register such forbidding boredom that gay words stick in the gullet, and voice-tones, so resonant and musical in the bathroom, issue forth in strangulated squeaks. An additional horror is the awareness that the sides of the stage are packed with implacable ambition. Every watching eye is steely with determination, marking with satisfaction each nervous shudder and each false note. The inexperienced of course suffer the most. They usually embark upon some lengthy song or aria and are stricken into bewildered silence half-way through by a sharp 'Thank you' from the stalls, and an abrupt cessation of all sound from the piano, after which, tremblingly, they give their names and addresses to the stage manager and go away, tortured by the knowledge that their top B flat, for which they had been conserving all their vocal energy, has not been heard at all. The wise ones sing only one refrain, sometimes only the last part of it if it happens to be overlong. Dancers have a very bad time as a rule, unless they bring their own accompanists, for in the hands of the lady provided by the management their carefully rehearsed tempos change inexorably from fast to slow and from slow to fast, heedless of their scurryings and gaspings and muttered supplications.

For most auditions ordinary day clothes are worn, embellished usually with borrowed finery. I believe that a white fox fur belonging to Beryl Norman was actually identified in the course of one month on nineteen different people. There are always a few, however, who put on fancy costumes and make up elaborately. Panniers, crinolines, insecure home-made bustles, and the inevitable pierrot suits with depressed tulle ruffles. Dancing girls used to wear imaginative 'practice dress,' but this in later years has gradually discarded its bows and frills and shrunk to nothing more or less than a plain one-piece swimming suit.

My own audition apparel was usually a navy blue suit with a coloured shirt, tie, socks, and handkerchief to match. I had not learned then that an exact duplication of colours ill becomes the well-dressed man. My bearing was a blend of assurance and professional vivacity; the fact that my bowels were as water I hope was not apparent to anybody. I used to walk on to the stage, bow politely in the direction of the stalls and say 'good morning,' sometimes, owing to nerves, a trifle more loudly than I had intended. Then, having banished the accompanist with a lordly gesture, I sat down at the piano on a stool that was invariably either too low or too high, and rattled off a few authoritative introductory chords, inwardly appalled by the tone and quality of the piano, but preserving an air of insouciance. I then swivelled round sharply, announced my song and started it before anyone had time to stop me. My voice was small but my diction clear, assisted by a violent interplay of facial expressions. My rendition of a song in those days was a model of exhaustive technique. Sustained pauses, gay laughs, knowing looks. All the paraphernalia of Harry Fragson and Margaret Cooper and Tom Clare. Frequently, if the dreaded 'Thank you' came in the middle of a verse, I pretended not to hear it and continued with only a faint quickening of tempo until either a second and louder 'Thank you' stopped me, or I was allowed to finish.

One day Grossmith and Laurillard held a big audition at the Shaftesbury Theatre. They were planning the production of an American musical comedy called *Oh, Boy,* with music by Jerome Kern. I received one of the usual audition cards, and arrived at the theatre in good time to force my way in front of those who had got there before me. When I had finally achieved the stage and the piano, and was half-way through my song, I noticed that

Grossmith and Laurillard and all their myrmidons in the stalls were so immersed in conversation that not one of them was looking at me. I stopped dead and waited until their voices had died into silence. Then, with what I hoped was icy dignity, I said that I saw no point in wasting my time singing to them if they continued to waste their time not listening to me. There was a horrified gasp from those waiting at the side of the stage, and the stage manager nervously rustled a lot of papers. Then, George Grossmith, whose manners have always been a long way above reproach, walked down to the orchestra rail and invited me gently to start my song again from the beginning. When I had finished, they asked me to come down into the stalls, where, after a few preliminary courtesies had been exchanged, I was engaged at a salary of twelve pounds a week. The actual part I was to play would be decided upon later, but in the meantime I could rest assured that my remarkable talents should have full scope.

2

Rehearsals for *Oh, Boy,* were not scheduled to begin for a few weeks, so I wrote to G. B. Stern, who was staying at St Merryn, in Cornwall, with the Dawson-Scott family, and suggested that now was the moment for our long-deferred meeting. She replied immediately that Mrs Dawson-Scott would be delighted to lodge me for a fortnight, which, I discovered later, was a slight over-statement, and that it would be a friendly gesture on my part to offer two pounds a week for my bed and board. This seemed a perfectly satisfactory arrangement and so I set forth for Cornwall, having sent a telegram on my way to the station, a blithe, cheerful and apparently quite fatal telegram: 'Arriving Padstow five-thirty. Tall and divinely handsome in grey.' I was met at Padstow by a strange man with a cart, and as we drove along the sandy roads, I listened to the surf thundering on the beach a mile or so away, and noted, with familiar pleasure, the Cornish shapes and sounds and smells. It was a glorious summer evening, and I was extremely happy. My future was assured. A good twelve-pound-a-week job in a musical comedy, which would certainly run a year. A chance to captivate London audiences for all time with my irresistible singing and dancing. Two weeks of sunshine and bathing and picnics and brilliant literary conversation. G. B. Stern and the kindly devil-may-care Dawson-Scotts entranced with my company and responding joyously to my witty sallies. All the gods were smiling at me without a trace of irony, and there seemed to be nothing to cloud my contentment.

These anticipations were, as usual, too good to be true. That holiday, although far from dull, was an established failure from the outset. G. B. Stern herself justified and surpassed my mental picture of her, and we were friends immediately, but the Dawson-Scotts, the kindly devil-may-care Dawson-Scotts, were a bad let-down, for not only did they dislike me on sight, but they had worked up a definite distaste for me long before I arrived. I was theatrical to begin with, and it was inevitable that I would be luxury-loving, unable to swim or climb rocks, unappreciative of the country, and very affected in my speech. On to this elaborate pyramid of prejudice my telegram fluttered, my odious, conceited telegram: 'Arriving Padstow five-thirty. Tall and divinely handsome in grey.'

Mrs Dawson-Scott, a writer of 'strong' books which reeked of earth, and sea-wrack, and primitive childbirth, and hot, sweet breasts, had had, I suspected, little time to cultivate social grace. She wore a red tea-gown and no shoes or stockings, and, as far as I was concerned, a remarkably forbidding expression. Her family dutifully followed her example and my first evening with them was far from cosy. I remember, during supper, when I suggested that they should call me 'Noel,' being painfully rebuffed by the reply, 'I think, Mr Coward, we would rather wait a little.'

Marjorie, the daughter, softened a little towards me later on in the week and we had an abortive heart-to-heart talk during a 'spratting' expedition in the moonlight. This melting might be explained by the fact that I was quite adept at plunging the curved knife into the wet sand as the waves receded and, in spite of my theatrical decadence, managed to catch more sprats than any of them. She informed me with compelling frankness, as we walked along the shore, that the whole family hated me, to which I replied, with equal candour, that the hatred was entirely mutual, and that I wouldn't have stayed a day with them had it not been for Peter (G. B. Stern), and that I had paid my two pounds a week in advance.

The elder son, Christopher, was less actively unpleasant to me, his only efforts to discomfit me consisting of sharp cries of 'Bet you can't do this,' followed by a flying leap on to a slippery rock, or something equally valorous. These manly exhibitions ceased when, in addition to cutting his knee quite badly, he discovered that I was unimpressed.

The younger son, Toby, was the nicest of the lot, and actually showed traces of a sense of humour.

Peter and I managed to get away by ourselves as much as possible, and these hours were peaceful and happy. We discussed plots for plays and novels. We dwelt untiringly upon the peculiarities of the Dawson-Scotts. We watched German submarines torpedoing cargo boats far out to sea, and wandered along the beach looking for pieces of wreckage, and wondering, fearfully, whether or not we should find any dead bodies.

Peter listened and nodded, and giggled appropriately, as we sat on the beach with our backs against a rock, and I enlarged, at great length, upon my ambitions as a playwright, composer, lyric writer, and novelist. Never once did she suggest that I seemed to be taking rather too much upon myself. Never once did she trot out the 'Jack-of-all-trades-master-of-none' bugbear, from which, even at that age, I had suffered a good deal. She recognised easily in me the familiar creative urge, and permitted my Ego to strut bravely before her.

My actual achievements up to date amounted to very little. I had written quite a lot, in spare moments, during the last few years: plays, singly, and in collaboration with Stoj; short stories, verses, and one meretricious full-length novel. I had also composed a good many songs, and written lyrics for some tunes of Max Darewski's and Doris Joel's.

I stayed for my full fortnight at St Merryn, having no intention of denying myself Peter's company just because that imperceptive family failed to respond to my charms. As a matter of fact, after the first few days they became much more agreeable and even, on one or two occasions, seemed disposed to be amused at my conversation, but these moments were too rare and ephemeral to form the basis of a lasting friendship. We met a few times during the following years, generally at the 'To-morrow' Club. I also dined with them once in Hampstead.

The introduction of celebrated names into autobiographies is a rule that I am too timorous to ignore, therefore I will put on record that, between the years 1917 and 1919, I knew G. B. Stern, Sheila Kaye-Smith, Charles Scott-Moncrieff, Fay Compton, Charles Hawtrey, Ivor Novello, Gertrude Lawrence and Beatrice Lillie. I was on pleasant, but not intimate terms with Rebecca West, Hugh Walpole, W. Somerset Maugham, Yvonne Arnaud, H. G. Wells, Rose Macaulay, Olive Wadsley, Billie Carleton, Viola Tree, Ronald Colman, Madge Titheradge, Lady Carisbrooke, Lady Londesborough and Nellie Wallace. I could also nod and be nodded to by Compton Mackenzie, Irene Vanbrugh, Violet Vanbrugh, Gladys Cooper, John Galsworthy, Gerald du Maurier, Nigel Playfair, E. F. Benson, John Lane, Elsie Janis, Maurice Chevalier and Lynn Fontanne. This last name was insignificant then and belonged to a scraggy, friendly girl with intelligent brown eyes and a raucous laugh. The above list must make it obvious to the meanest intelligence that I was progressing like wild-fire. The plans nurtured in my bed-sitting-room in Manchester were blooming and I could now use a considerable number of effective Christian names without fear of swift and crushing humiliation.

3

The day before the first rehearsal of *Oh, Joy* (it had been renamed, doubtless because the arrogant Americanism of *Oh, Boy,* might stir the English public's stomach to revolt), I was stricken with a bad attack of influenza. This was a bitter blow to me, and for several days I lay feverishly visualising the thrills and excitements taking place without me. At last, very weak, but determined, I was allowed to get up and take a taxi to the theatre. My head felt light and my legs wobbly, but I walked on to the stage as firmly as possible. The morning rehearsal was just about to begin and the play was being directed by an American producer named Austin Hurgon, who, when I approached him, regarded me from a tremendously high altitude. I asked him if he had received my telegram explaining why I had not been able to attend before, and he said: 'What telegram?' I then told him my name and he said: 'Noel what?' Discouraged but persevering, I went on to explain that I had been engaged by Mr Grossmith and Mr Laurillard to play one of the principal parts. He said, with sarcasm, that he was very sorry to contradict me, but that the principal as well as the small parts had been filled ages ago, in addition to which he was regrettably forced to admit that he had never heard of me in his life. All this took place before the amused gaze of the entire company. I replied, with as much dignity as I could muster, that there was obviously some mistake, and that if he would kindly telephone the office, the muddle would be rectified. He retorted that he had no time to waste telephoning while he was rehearsing, and that I had probably been engaged for the chorus, which was rehearsing elsewhere. Trying hard to keep emotion out of my voice, I said that I had certainly not been engaged for the chorus. Whereupon he snatched up the chorus list from the prompt table, glanced through it, and triumphantly read out my name. This called forth a titter from the company, and I walked off the stage and out into the street without another word. I went into a public-house in Shaftesbury Avenue, had a glass of neat brandy to pull me together, and took a taxi to the Grossmith and Laurillard offices in Golden Square, where I demanded to see Mr Laurillard. After about twenty minutes, I was ushered into his room where my pent-up emotions broke into a full-blooded fury. I think I must have roared very loudly indeed, for he looked startled, and kept on waving his hand in the air, apparently in an effort to dam the spate of words pouring on to his head. After a while I calmed down, and he expressed great sympathy and regret, admitting that there had indeed been a mistake, as there was no part suitable for me in *Oh, Joy!* I opened my mouth to launch a fresh tirade, but he silenced me with more soothing words, explaining that my performance in *The Saving Grace* had convinced him that I was far too good a straight actor to waste my time in anything so trivial as musical comedy, and that there was a good part for me in *Scandal,* the new Cosmo Hamilton play, which was to be produced at the Strand Theatre in December with a superb cast headed by Arthur Bourchier and Kyrle Bellew. This, although better than nothing, was still not enough to compensate me for the miseries of that morning, and I went unhappily home to bed, not particularly cheered by the reflection that I had ample time to recover from my influenza, as the rehearsals for *Scandal* were not due to begin for two months.

I occupied myself during those two months by starting another novel. It was a lush work called *Cherry Pan,* dealing in a whimsical vein with the adventures of a daughter of Pan, who, born into a modern world, contrived to be arch, and elfin, and altogether nauseating, for nearly thirty thousand words. She finally petered out, owing to lack of enthusiasm on my part, and lack of stamina on hers.

4

The house in Ebury Street was, at this time, running comparatively smoothly. Our faithful standby, Miss Daubeney, was still with us on the third floor. She was a niece of Lord Brassey, and had been known to sail on his yacht, a photograph of which adorned the mantelpiece in a silver frame. She was friendly and kind, and one of our temporary housemaids, in a transport of Irish enthusiasm, described her as being 'downright aristocratic.' On the ground-floor 'dining-room suite' we had a Mr and Mrs Farina, the most charming of all our lodgers. I dined with them frequently, repressing a sense of guilt in eating the excellently cooked food that I knew Mother had been labouring over in the kitchen. Mrs Farina evinced a kindly passion for being read to, and consequently had to listen, poor woman, to everything I had ever written. She was appreciative and only occasionally critical, and did me a power of good.

I managed to sell a few magazine stories here and there, and was once led by Stoj into the presence of a Miss Ethel Mannin, who was the editor or sub-editor of the *Blue Magazine.* I met her again many years afterwards at a literary dinner party given by Mr George Doran, and was flattered to discover, upon reading her book, *Confessions and Impressions,* recently, that these two brief encounters had obviously constituted, in her mind, a delightful intimacy.

Through the influence of Max Darewski, I signed a three years' contract with his brother Herman, who at that time was the head of a music publishing firm in Charing Cross Road. The contract was for lyrics only, and I was to be paid fifty pounds the first year, seventy-five pounds the second year, and one hundred pounds the third year. I appeared dutifully every week or so, for the first few months, armed with verses, and ideas for songs. I waited many hours in the outer office, and sometimes even penetrated into the next-to-the-outer office, but seldom, if ever, clapped eyes on Herman Darewski, and nobody seemed at all interested in my lyrics. At the end of the first year I began to get a little anxious about the second instalment of seventy-five pounds. But I needn't have worried because it was paid to me without rancour, on the day specified. During the third year of my contract I was too busy with other affairs to go near the office until the last day, when I called to receive my cheque for a hundred pounds. Herman Darewski's third or fourth secretary handed it to me with a charming smile, and, after a brief exchange of social amenities, I had a cup of tea in the outer office and went home. Some while after this, the Herman Darewski publishing firm went bust, a fact that has never altogether astonished me.

On Armistice Day I wandered about the streets during the morning and afternoon, and in the evening dined with Tony and Juanita Ganderillas, whom I had met originally at one of General Ashmore's musical parties. They were Chileans, wealthy, gay and kind. After dinner we drove in a dark red Rolls-Royce through the Park and into Trafalgar Square, where we stuck, while hordes of screaming people climbed on to the roof of the car, the footboards and the radiator. We screamed with them, and shook hands with as many as we could, and I felt ignobly delighted, in this moment of national rejoicing, to be in a tail coat, a Rolls-Royce, and obviously aristocratic company. After a couple of hours in Trafalgar Square, we managed to get to the Savoy, where everybody wore paper caps, and threw streamers, and drank champagne, and Delysia, in a glittering pink dress, stood on a table and sang the 'Marseillaise' over and over again to wild applause. It was a thrilling night, and I regret to say that the tragic significance of it was almost entirely lost upon me. I had not consciously suffered much from the war, apart from those unhappy months in training camps and hospitals. I had been a small boy of fourteen when it started, too young to realise what it was all about, and now that it was over, I could only perceive that life would probably be a good deal more enjoyable without it. I have noticed, just lately, a certain tendency among contemporary journalistic writers to class me with the generation that was 'ineradicably scarred by the war.' They have found, upon analysing my plays, a sense of profound disillusionment, a dreadful nerve-racked cynicism, obviously the heritage of those four black years, and I have searched myself carefully to discover any grounds for believing this dramatic implication to be true. I have found none. I was not in the least scarred by the war. It was little more to me at the time than a dully oppressive background, and although I certainly acquired a few nasty scratches from the years immediately following it, the reasons for my warped disenchantment with life must be sought elsewhere.

5

My part in *Scandal* was small, and as a character, nebulous. I made a brief appearance at the beginning of Act Two in a grey suit, and a still briefer appearance at the beginning of Act Three, dressed, I forget why, as Sir Walter Raleigh. The play was what's known as 'strong.' The 'big scene' took place in a bedroom, after all the smaller parts had gone home. Beatrice Hinchliffe (Kyrle Bellew), having tricked the strong and silent family friend (Arthur Bourchier) into a *mariage blanc,* suddenly discovered, on the wedding night, that she was deeply in love with him. This had the unfortunate effect of sending her into transports of coquetry. She bounced about on the nuptial bed, employing archness, defiance, tenderness, temper and tears, until Arthur Bourchier, goaded to a frenzy of suppressed passion, lashed her, cringing, on to her silken pillows, with a virile and dramatic speech concluding with the terrifying words: 'If you and I were alone on a desert island I wouldn't –' etc., etc., with which he turned definitely on his heel and left her as the curtain fell. In the last act, which took place on a yacht, after a comic seasick cameo contributed by Gladys Ffolliot, everything was smoothed out satisfactorily, and everybody forgave everybody else. I never considered it a good play, but perhaps I was prejudiced by the fact that my part in it was so unimportant.

Arthur Bourchier and Kyrle Bellew were charming to me, and arranged for me to have a little dressing-room to myself. Nora Swinburne was sweet and friendly, and I loved Mary Robson dearly, from the first rehearsal onwards. Apart from these pleasant contacts, my stock was low in the company. I behaved badly, and was accused, justifiably, by Millie Hylton of making hen noises whenever she came on to the stage. I was also heartily detested by Gladys Ffolliot, who had overheard me say to someone that her dog Daphne smelt like a drain. The truth of this statement in no way mitigated her rage, and she complained about me to the management whenever possible. Clare Greet lodged a few complaints too, from time to time, but I think this was only out of loyalty to the others. The theatre was frequently divided into camps, for and against me. Mary Robson's dressing-room was my refuge, where the various skirmishes were discussed with considerable hilarity. Our laughter was sometimes over-loud, and went echoing down the passage to torment the ears of my enemies. Arthur Bourchier and Kyrle occasionally admonished me with some attempt at severity, but they were seldom able to keep going for long without a twinkle appearing in their eyes, and when their door had closed upon my unconvincingly downcast figure, I used to hear them snorting with laughter. Finally Arthur Bourchier called me very seriously into his room, and informed me that the management were going to give me my notice at the end of the week. He suggested, kindly, that it would be a good idea for me to anticipate this, by writing them a letter of resignation, thereby saving myself the humiliation of being actually sacked. He said that he, personally, would be very sorry to lose me, as he considered me an excellent actor, but that in the future, I must behave much better, and be particularly careful never to offend women in the theatre, especially the slightly older ones, as their dislike, once incurred, was implacable and very, very dangerous.

When I got home that night I spent a happy hour composing a letter to Grossmith and Laurillard. I explained with dignity that owing to the peculiar behaviour of the old ladies in the cast, I felt myself compelled to tender my resignation, and that I should be exceedingly obliged if they could see their way to accepting my fortnight's notice. I remained, theirs very sincerely. They saw their way to accepting my fortnight's notice with unflattering clearness, and when I arrived at the theatre the next night, an envelope containing the salary due to me was handed to me by the stage-door-keeper, and I was allowed only half an hour to collect my things from my dressing-room. This was a shock, but not a bad one. I was already steeled to losing my job, and two weeks one way or another didn't make much difference. I detected in this waspish gesture from the powers, a certain lack of dignity, and although I should, by rights, have left the Strand Theatre for ever, burning with shame, and with my tail between my legs, my exit was actually a jaunty affair, untinged with sadness. I packed my things, said my good-byes to the Bourchiers and Mary and Nora, rattled blithely on all the old ladies' doors, and drove off in a taxi, feeling pleasantly free and in the best of spirits.

During that engagement I formed a fixed resolution to go to America. Mary, who had played in New York several times, thrilled me by her descriptions of it. We had dinner in the grill room of the Waldorf on matinée days, and she enumerated, at great length, the delights of American theatre life. The theatres themselves were the acme of luxury. The acting was far and away superior to anything that would be seen in London. There were apparently two very attractive brothers called Shubert, who produced masses of plays every season with a lavish disregard for expense, and welcomed any English actor, however small, with enthusiasm. There was also a kindly old body named Al Woods, who produced the best melodramas in the world, outside of David Belasco, who was of course a species of divinity. In addition to these brilliant philanthropists, there was the Flat Iron Building, the Woolworth Building, which I visualised as a pyramid of scarlet and gold, rising to the clouds in tier upon tier of ten-cent magnificence, the Pennsylvania Station, Times Square, Central Park (on a grander scale than Hyde Park), the Hippodrome stage, which could support and display at least fifty elephants abreast, the Metropolitan Opera House, glittering with Astors and Belmonts and Vanderbilts, Wall Street, the Bronx Zoo, Coney Island, and, most exciting of all, Broadway by night. Broadway by night seemed to be my cup of tea entirely. Its splendours and its noise and its crowds haunted my imagination. Its gigantic sky-signs dazzled my dreams, flashing in a myriad of lights, with unfailing regularity, the two words 'Noel Coward.'

Apart from the great American idea, I conceived a passably good plot for a play, and as, in those days, conception was only removed from achievement by the actual time required for putting the words on paper, it was completed inside a week. It was entitled *The Last Trick* and was a melodrama in four acts. The first and second acts were quite amusing, the third act good, and the last act weak and amateurish. The plot hinged on the 'revenge' motif and wasn't particularly original, but the dialogue was effective, and showed a marked improvement on my other work. I took the play to Gilbert Miller, and he seemed to be impressed with it. He said that he was leaving for New York in a few weeks' time and would like to take it with him, and that he might possibly be able to arrange for it to be produced. I lunched with him a few days later, and he told me the plots of several plays that he had seen in Vienna, Berlin, Paris and Budapest. He also gave me some useful pieces of advice on the art of play-writing. He said, among other things, that although my dialogue was nearly always good, my construction was 'lousy.' He said that someone had told his father, who in turn had told him, that the construction of a play was as important as the foundations of a house, whereas dialogue, however good, could only, at best, be considered as interior decoration. This I recognised immediately as being authentic wisdom. He said, on parting, that he was quite convinced that before long I would write a first-rate play, and that when I did, he would be only too delighted to produce it. He detained me for a few moments at the door by giving me an example of a really well-constructed scene. It was from the third act of a thrilling play he had recently attended in Stockholm.

Buoyed up by Gilbert Miller's encouragement, I wrote two bad plays and one better one. The first two are not worthy of discussion, but the third, *The Rat Trap,* was my first really serious attempt at psychological conflict. Even in the light of later experience, I can still see in it two well-written scenes. As a whole, of course, it was immature, but it was much steadier than anything I had done hitherto. The last act, as usual, went to pieces, but when I had finished it, I felt, for the first time with genuine conviction, that I could really write plays.

6

In the early spring of 1919, I went again to stay with Mrs Cooper at Hambleton. I drove a car for the first time. I rode a horse for the first time, with no fear but with little grace. I sang at village concerts, sometimes alone, sometimes with Mrs Cooper's daughter, Phyllis. With her soprano I harmonised breathily, making up for my lack of volume with the maximum of expression. We sang 'Trot here, trot there' from *Véronique,* also 'The Swing Song' from the same score. The villagers applauded us lustily, their hands and hearts warmed by the knowledge that, although my voice might seem to be a trifle reedy, I was actually, in manner and fact, a *bona fide* professional, accustomed to charming vaster multitudes from the vaster stages of the best London theatres.

Small memories are the most insistent, and I like to catch again, for a moment, the feel of the sharp spring air as we drove home at night after a concert, the smell of the wood fire in the library where we discussed, over hot soup and sandwiches, the triumphs of the evening. All the warm, comfortable ingredients of country-house life were there, the very unfamiliarity of the atmosphere enhancing its charm for me, and I felt happily aloof from the squabblings of angry old character actresses. This, I reflected, quite wrongly, was my rightful sphere, and I would go upstairs to bed, undress, and brush my teeth, still, until sleep closed down upon me, accurate in my performance of a country gentleman.

It must not be imagined that Mrs Cooper was my only contact with the shires. She was the first, but by no means the last. She, it is true, St Peter'd me into that bleak, horse-infested paradise, but once inside, I fended for myself. Other country houses opened welcoming doors to me. Some were larger and grander than Hambleton. Some were smaller and more exclusively concerned with the chase. None, however, was so individually agreeable, and I returned to the mattresses in front of the fire, the faded peach-coloured brocade curtains, and the brass hot-water-cans, with a sense of relief, a familiar home-sweet-home contentment.

Witham-on-the-Hill was one of my pleasanter excursions. It was a lovely old house, richly ordered, and belonging to the Keld Fenwicks. I was invited there, oddly enough, for a 'shoot,' I forget now what exactly was being shot, but it was probably duck. At least twenty people were staying in the house and some of them wore velvet smoking jackets in the evening, and there were two very large greyhounds, which fortunately took a fancy to me. The food was delicious, and I found several volumes of Marie Antoinette's secret memoirs in the library, which I read luxuriously during the day, while the 'shoot' was at its height. The evenings might have been a trifle dull for me if I had not been so enchanted with the authenticity of the atmosphere. The setting and the dialogue were perfect, the character performances superb, and there seemed to be, only every now and then, a suspicion of over-acting among the smaller parts.

The London managers during that year continued to disregard me, and I continued to write plays and magazine stories, occasionally selling some of the latter, and making enough money here and there to keep myself in clothes and help out with the house.

Now that I considered myself definitely 'set' as a writer, the horror of being out of an engagement was less dreadful. I could be my own master, and work alone, beholden to nobody. My plays were steadily achieving more 'body' and consistence. I flung aside all bastard whimsies and concentrated on realism. No pert elf or faun dared even to peep round a tree at me in 1919. Pan and pierrot retired, disgruntled, into oblivion as far as I was concerned and, I am glad to say, have remained there until this day. My mind, not unnaturally, jumped over-far in the opposite direction. I dealt, almost exclusively, with the most lurid types; tarts, pimps, sinister courtesans, and cynical adulterers whirled across my pages in great profusion. This phase finally passed owing to a withering lack of response from magazine editors, but it was all useful and I don't regret any of it.

Some new friends appeared. One of these was Betty Chester. Her real name was Grundtvig, and she lived with her mother and father in Chester Square.

Lorn Macnaughtan was a constant visitor at their house. She was tall and fair, with good hands and a nice speaking voice. She had been to school with Betty, and accepted a certain amount of Grundtvig patronage with slyly humorous grace. As she has been my personal secretary and close friend for nearly fifteen years, I find it difficult to describe her as I saw her then, for the first time. She seemed unremarkable in manner and personality, but there was authority in her quietness which was probably the heritage of many ancient, kilted Macnaughtans, who, in the long past, had stumped dourly over their Scottish estates. It was puzzling to try to reconcile her obvious distinction with the fact that she was, at the moment, in the chorus at the Empire, as she appeared to have no attributes whatever for that particular sphere. Her feet were large and her figure unvoluptuous; she could neither dance nor sing, and her movements were never especially graceful. She was slightly self-conscious, and her pale, clear complexion seldom conceded to wantonness more than an occasional dab of powder. When I knew her better, I discovered that her stage career was as surprising to herself as to everybody else. She had managed to get chorus and understudy jobs, sometimes through influence, some-times through grim determination, because the Macnaughtan splendour having faded into a small house in Wellington Square, it was essential for her to make enough money to live on.

All this accounted for the strange flashes of chorus-girl jargon which sprang from Lorn's lips bawdily, at the most unexpected moments, and frequently shattered the small, tightly encased propriety of Mr Grundtvig.

By this time I had moved down from my tiny top attic in III, Ebury Street to a more nobly proportioned room on the floor next to the top. In this, I was able to give occasional tea parties, with the social elements tastefully mixed. Gertie Lawrence used to come, bringing with her various haughty young Guards officers who sat about, puzzled by the theatrical conversation, but securely wrapped in regimental poise. Mrs Cooper came too and wailed agreeably at Stoj and Lyndon, and Peter and Sheila and Betty and Lorn. Every now and then I thoughtlessly chose the day of our housemaid's afternoon out, and was embarrassed to see Father waltzing into the room with the tea-tray. Everyone immediately rose to say 'How do you do?' and shake hands, to which he couldn't possibly respond until somebody relieved him of the tea-things. I glossed over those slight contretemps with, what I hoped, was easy Bohemian geniality, and tried not to intercept the ironic glances that any strangers present exchanged with each other.

One day a young man called Stewart Forster appeared. He was a lieutenant in the Coldstream Guards, with a deceptively guile-less personality, and a timid, butter-coloured moustache, which, with the passing of time, I regret to say, has become large and quite red. Then, however, it was innocuous and faintly apologetic, as though it knew perfectly well that it had no right to be there at all, and wouldn't be, but for the exigencies of military etiquette.

Stewart asked me, on leaving, if I would care to dine with him on guard at St James's Palace the following week. I accepted with alacrity and regretted that I had no decorations other than my army discharge medal with which to adorn the occasion. I hadn't even a tail coat. I didn't mention this, but hired one from Moss Bros the day before I was due to appear at the Palace.

I arrived on the stroke of eight o'clock, and was conducted to the mess by an austere corporal. The traditional pomp of the atmosphere felt chilly at first, but there was an underlying glamour in it which thawed me presently, and, with the aid of a glass of extremely dry sherry, I expanded sufficiently to make a joke about my tail coat, which no eye, however well schooled in good manners, could possibly regard in anything but a comic light. Moss Bros had certainly let me down badly. The sleeves had a Pagliacci fullness, and the tails rebounded from my calves as I walked.

At about eleven o'clock, Stewart imposed upon himself a gigantic bearskin, which looked as though it might slip down and extinguish him entirely at the slightest sharp movement. He also buckled on his sword, and clanked out into the courtyard, where I heard his voice barking shrilly to the accompaniment of shuffling feet. When he came back I had one more glass of port, said my goodbyes, and left, no longer oppressed by military tradition, but quite definitely part of it.

I walked home, down the Mall and past Buckingham Palace, much elated by my evening, and reflecting that uniform was undoubtedly very becoming to Englishmen, and that white-gloved orderlies, tawny port, a polished, shiny table decorated with silver regimental trophies, warm red-shaded lights, and large oil paintings of Their Majesties, all combined to impart to the most ordinary conversation an indescribable and imperishable charm.

7

In August 1919 I played 'Ralph' in *The Knight of the Burning Pestle* at the Birmingham Repertory Theatre.

For me, there was a quality of fantasy about the whole engagement. Nigel Playfair directed the production with a touching fidelity to Elizabethan atmosphere. No curtain. No footlights. A circular stage, fringed with uneasy gallants, who sat on stools, and smoked clay pipes. There was a musician's gallery high up on a rostrum at the back, containing a few local fiddlers, their upper parts correctly be-ruffed and be-wigged, and their lower parts more comfortably encased in their ordinary Birmingham trousers. Sometimes they forgot to leave off their pince-nez, and were flurried into doing so by urgent hisses from the conscientious gallants. I was not very good as 'Ralph,' owing to a total lack of understanding of the play. It was my first and only experience of Elizabethan comedy and, being unable to detect any great humour on it, I played that poor apprentice with a stubborn Mayfair distinction which threw the whole thing out of key. This was largely Nigel Playfair's fault. He directed with more elfishness than authority, and cheered the rehearsals with many little jokes, which, although vastly appreciated by Betty Chester and me, were not actually helpful to our performances. Betty played 'The Citizen's Wife' with youth, charm and great vivacity, which, considering that she was supposed to be a bawdy matron of about forty-five, was hardly appropriate.

The Knight of the Burning Pestle could not be considered a really progressive step in my career as an actor. I had mouthed and postured my way through it with little conviction and no sense of period. I was unaware of this, however, and, even if I had realised it, I doubt whether I should have cared very much, because, in course of those three short weeks, Fortune favoured me with such a violent and unexpected slap on the back, that not only Birmingham, but the whole world, seemed to be transformed. The people in the streets, hitherto rather dingy-looking, with grim, manufacturing faces, suddenly changed into happy smiling creatures, stepping lightly over pavements, no longer grey, and wearing gay colours. Not so much as one drop of rain fell for at least three days. And even my landlady, Mrs Hunter, a woman of sad regrets if ever there was one, seemed to forget for a spell her Bright's disease, and melt into cheerfulness. All this on account of one brief cablegram from Gilbert Miller in New York informing me, in lilting, business-like terms, that Al Woods wished to pay five hundred dollars for a year's option on my play *The Last Trick*.

Five hundred dollars, after calculations in Betty's dressing-room, resolved itself into the still fantastic but more understandable sum of one hundred pounds.

I remember rushing to the Queen's Hotel in full make-up, between the first and second acts of the matinée, sending an enthusiastic reply from the hall porter's desk, and, on my way back to the theatre, buying a very large bottle of toilet water at Boots Cash Chemists.

When I returned to London, the five hundred dollars was duly paid me, in pounds, by Gilbert Miller's secretary, and within a few days another cable arrived, this time saying that Al Woods would like to buy the play outright for a further fifteen hundred dollars, as it was necessary for it to be rewritten by a more technically expert playwright than myself.

Never having received more than a few guineas for anything I had ever written, this windfall was a shock which even my self-confidence was unable to meet calmly. I couldn't believe that there wasn't some mistake, some sinister catch in it, until Mother and I had been to a bank in the City and actually watched, with glistening eyes, the money sliding over the counter to us. Even the fact that at the moment I happened to be suffering from a degrading boil on the end of my nose, failed to depress the occasion.

I burst forth rapidly into several new suits, paid a large part of our overdue quarterly instalment on the Ebury Street house and bought a second-hand grand piano at Harrods, which contributed richness and joy to my room, and considerable pain to the lodgers immediately above and below it.

I glanced back happily upon recent penury, over which the haze of distance already seemed to be shimmering (a fancy which later proved to be distinctly premature), and walked on winged feet along Bedford Street, St Martin's Lane, Garrick Street, Charing Cross Road, Wardour Street, Green Street, Coventry Street, and Shaftesbury Avenue, crossing myself devoutly outside theatrical agents' offices, and finishing up daily with an expensive lunch at the 'Ivy.'

The 'Ivy' had been a generous friend to me in the past, allowing me many meals, when it knew perfectly well that the chances of their being paid for were slender. And so now, sheathed in sudden prosperity, it seemed only fitting that I should eat there until I burst.

I went to many parties in my new tail suit, savouring to the full the sensation of being well-dressed for the first time. The days of twirling anxiously before Moss Bros' looking-glasses were over. No more hitching of the arm-pits to prevent sleeves from enveloping the hands altogether. No more bracing of out-grown trousers to their lowest, with the consciousness that the slightest movement of the arms would display a mortifying expanse of shirt between waistcoat and flies. All that belonged to the past. Now I could dance and dine securely, feeling smart and *soigné,* and very, very smooth.

When relying upon my own funds, I chose a suitably under-standing partner such as Gertie Lawrence, or Meggie Albanesi, and we would dine frugally, and go to Murray's, or Rector's, or the Savoy, where it was possible to slip in by the Embankment entrance without a ticket.

When invited, I patronised the Grafton Galleries, the Ritz, Ciro's, and, on one occasion, even Claridge's.

Michael Arlen was also just beginning to blossom about this time. We used to wave languidly to each other across dance floors, shedding our worldliness later, in obscure corners. He was very dapper, and his Hawes and Curtis backless waistcoats aroused envy in me, which I soon placated, by ordering some for myself, but his exquisite pearl and platinum watch-chain was beyond competition, and all I could do was to admire it bravely, and hope, in my heart, that perhaps it was just a little bit ostentatious.

8

When Gilbert Miller returned to London, he asked me to go to see him in his office, where he continued his lecture on play construction where he had left off several months before.

He described to me the plots of *La Tosca, Fedora, The Easiest Way,* and *Within the Law,* which, incidentally, I had seen three times. He then went on to say that he himself had a good idea for a light comedy, but that he would like me to write it, preferably with Charles Hawtrey in mind, and that if I did it well enough, he would produce it in London during the following spring.

I was then, as I am now, extremely chary of the thought of writing anything based upon somebody else's idea, but I persevered, and within the next few weeks manufactured an amiable little play entitled (by Gilbert Miller) *I'll Leave It to You.*

The dialogue, on the whole, was amusing, and unpretentious, and the construction was not bad, but it was too mild and unassuming to be able to awake any really resounding echoes in the hearts of the great public, and although I was naturally entranced with it, Gilbert was not quite as enthusiastic as I had hoped he would be.

He suggested several alterations, some of which I agreed to, and all of which I made, and after a series of discussions, he departed for America again, having promised me that on his return he would arrange for a try-out production at the Gaiety Theatre, Manchester, in April. I had to content myself with this, and the reflection, that although six months was a long time to wait, I had at least had the sense to write a part in the play for myself, in which I should undoubtedly, when the moment came, score an overwhelming personal triumph.

9

In January, I went to Paris with Stewart Forster, according to a plan formulated during the summer at Rumwood, Stewart's home in Kent. We stayed at the Ritz for the first night, and at a small hotel in the Rue Caumartin for the rest of the week.

As it was the first time that we had, either of us, been out of England, our behaviour was entirely true to form.

We sipped *apéritifs* outside the Café de la Paix, visited the Louvre, Napoleon's Tomb, Notre-Dame, Versailles, the Moulin Rouge, and the Folies-Bergère.

We dined at Prunier's, and the Café de Paris, and danced endlessly round the cabarets of Montmartre with metallic tarts, who persisted in mistaking us for Americans.

We even quarrelled mildly over a young lady from Cincinnati, who drove us about in her car, accepted floral offerings, and flirted with us magnificently, never for one instant deviating from that fine line of conduct which separates racy conversation from staunch moral integrity. This we recognised as a racial peculiarity, and were duly impressed by it, if a trifle irritated.

We met a Russian Prince, *soi-disant,* who owned a racing car which looked like a red pepper, and a French mistress who looked like all the pictures of flaming adventuresses in the world rolled into one, but who, on closer acquaintance, turned out to be dull and deeply sentimental.

It was an enjoyable week, and we absorbed the sights and sounds and smells of Paris thoroughly and satisfactorily, and when we left, sadly, to return to England, we possessed a certain 'manner' which had not been apparent before. Our vocabularies also were the richer by several French phrases, and three complete sentences, two of which were unrepeatable.

In February, Mrs Cooper invited me to go to Alassio with her for a fortnight, and so for the first time I slept in a *wagon-lit,* experienced the thrilling, damp coldness of a frontier station at two o'clock in the morning, and whirled through Switzerland and down on to the Lombardy plains with my nose buttoned against the railway carriage window. In Alassio we stayed at the Grand Hotel, and breakfasted daily on a balcony overlooking dusty palm trees and glittering blue sea. Behind the hotel there were plaster houses in pale colours, olive groves, cypresses, lush curtains of wistaria and bougainvillaea, and serried ranks of snow-capped mountains.

I have returned there since, more experienced in travel, having seen higher mountains, richer foliage, and bluer seas, and realised that Alassio is really nothing out of the ordinary, that there are hundreds of other little towns nestling in the shadow of the Alpes Maritimes, with just the same coloured houses and twisted streets, and just the same palm trees, and fishing boats, and pungent smells. But that was the first time, the first thrill of discovery, the first proof I had ever had, that hot sunshine was anywhere possible in February.

Upon arriving back in London, I discovered that Gilbert Miller was not returning after all, and had put the producing of *I'll Leave It to You* in the hands of Robert Oswald, the general manager of the Gaiety, Manchester. Stanley Bell was to direct the play, and the cast chosen included Kate Cutler, Farren Soutar, Muriel Pope, Stella Jesse, Douglas Jeffries, Lois Stuart, Moya Nugent, Esmé Wynne (Stoj) and myself.

The first night in Manchester was tremendously exciting. The play went well all through and, at the end, the audience cheered, and Kate pushed me forward to make a speech. I was feeling far too emotional to be able to relinquish her hand, and so I stood there, clutching it, and experiencing the curious sensation of success. There was I, and there was an audience applauding and cheering, and as I advanced a step, the applause and the cheers swelled louder and then died away into complete silence. I made quite a nice little speech. It was boyish and modest, and had been carefully rehearsed alone in my digs beforehand. I had seen too many authors hauled on to the stage on first nights, trembling and confused, with goggling eyes, to make the mistake of being caught unprepared.

When it was all over and I went out of the stage door, there was a large crowd of gallery girls waiting on the pavement, and I signed their autograph books with a flourish and enjoyed myself deeply.

Towards the end of our first week in Manchester, Mrs Charles Hawtrey and Mrs Gilbert Miller came down from London to see the play. I was very nervous, and Kate and Stanley and I prayed ardently that there would be a good audience, and no hitches in the performance. Contrary to what generally happens on those occasions, there was a good audience, and the performance was smoother and better than it had ever been, and when, at the end, I had to make my speech in response to the cheers, I was visualising clearly an immediate production at the St James's Theatre, with Hawtrey playing Uncle Daniel. The faces of Mrs Hawtrey and Mrs Miller when Stanley Bell ushered them into my dressing-room afterwards were sadly disillusioning. They both stood there, shaking their heads slowly and tenderly, like china mandarins. They were both filled and brimming over with sympathy, as though they had just been present at the greatest theatrical catastrophe of modern times. They both kissed me, said that they would have to cable to Gilbert immediately to say what they honestly and truly thought. Upon this, I lost my temper inwardly, but fortunately not outwardly, and said that I was sorry that they were so disappointed in the play, but that luckily the audiences we had played to didn't seem to be quite so hard to please. I then added with firmness and a touch of hysterical bravado, that whether Gilbert Miller and Charles Hawtrey were interested, or whether they weren't, the play would definitely be produced in London within the next few months! Upon which, they both wobbled their heads again, and went out.

When they had gone Stanley took me to supper at the Midland and did his best to cheer me up, but without much success. With both Hawtrey and Gilbert Miller ruled out, our chances of a London production were small. However, I drove back to Lloyd Street, grimly determined that *I'll Leave It to You* was not going to peter out of existence with only three weeks in Manchester to its credit.

10

I'll Leave It to You opened in London at the New Theatre on July 21st, 1920, two and a half months after its try-out in Manchester. It was presented by Mary Moore (Lady Wyndham) with the same cast, excepting Farren Soutar, who had been replaced by Holman Clarke. The first night was a roaring success, and I made another boyish speech. Lots of my friends were there, including Bobbie and Ivor, neither of whom came round to see me afterwards, which hurt me bitterly. When I eventually tackled them about this, Ivor replied that the play, in the intervals of irritating him excessively, had bored him stiff. So that was that.

The critics were mostly very enthusiastic, and said a lot about it having been a great night, and that a new playwright had been discovered, etc., but unfortunately their praise was not potent enough to lure audiences to the New Theatre for more than five weeks, so the run ended rather miserably, the last week being rendered still gloomier by Lady Wyndham, who, with adamant economy, insisted that our lighting should be cut down to half.

However, I sold the amateur rights to Samuel French for a comfortable sum, and feeling much the better for my brief encouragement, both financially and spiritually, set to work with renewed vigour on a play called *Barriers Down,* which was awful.

In November, Nigel Playfair decided to produce *The Knight of the Burning Pestle* at the Kingsway Theatre, so we rehearsed it all over again, and finally opened, to tepid enthusiasm.

Mrs Patrick Campbell came one night in a box, and great excitement reigned behind the scenes. This excitement waned towards the end of the play, when it was discovered that she had been sound asleep since the beginning of the first act. I sent her an outraged message through a mutual friend, and the next night there she was again, in the same box, but far from sleepy. She wore long white gloves, and applauded wildly every time I stepped on to the stage. Elsie Janis and Mrs Janis brought a party to a matinée one day, prompted by sheer courtesy and kindness to me, and they sat, from the beginning to the end, bored and bewildered beyond relief, but infinitely polite. Many years later Elsie told me what they had really thought of the show, all of which goes to prove that Americans have very beautiful manners.

Just before Christmas, I developed suddenly a temperature of a hundred and two. The doctor forbade me to play, but, imbued with that misguided 'old trouper' bravery, I insisted, with the result that I gave sixteen members of the company 'mumps.' Nigel himself played my part for a little, but even his fine performance couldn't contend against the bad business and the 'mumps,' so the play closed, and I signed a contract to appear in Gilbert Miller's production of an American comedy, *Polly with a Past,* at the St James's Theatre. Rehearsals were not to start until February, so I had a few weeks free for a holiday.

I bought myself a second-class ticket to Rapallo, and stayed there for two days at the Casino Hotel. Then, as I knew no one at all, and couldn't speak a word of Italian, my independent spirit wilted a trifle, and I beat a hasty retreat to Alassio, where I knew Mrs Cooper was staying. She was delighted to see me, and once more I settled myself into the Grand Hotel.

After I had been there a few days, I was asked to sing at a concert at the English Club. The concert was bad, and the piano dreadful, but I sang several songs with lofty professional arrogance, only slightly deflated by a smartly dressed young woman in the front row, who appeared to be fighting an attack of convulsive giggles with singular lack of success. I remember frowning at her coldly several times, but this only seemed to send her into fresh paroxysms. When I met her afterwards with Mrs Cooper, she had regained control and was very poised indeed. Her name was Gladys Calthrop. I asked her what there was about my singing that had made her laugh so much, and, after a few evasions, she explained that it wasn't my singing exactly, but that I had looked funny.

It is strange how many really important moments in life slip by in the procession, unnoted, and devoid of prescience. No guardian angel whacks a sharp triangle in the brain, and the heavens remain commonplace. It is not my intention in this book to delve deeply into personal relationships, but as Gladys Calthrop has been so intimately concerned with all my best work, and so intrinsically part of my failures and successes, I feel that a small, retrospective fanfare is not entirely out of place. In appearance she was less attractive then than she is now. Her eyes and figure were good. Her brain was alert, and her sense of humour keen, though somewhat impaired by a slight bias towards highbrow Bohemianism.

The remaining few days of my stay in Alassio we passed almost entirely together. We went for walks. We went for drives. We sat on the beach, in olive groves, and on terraces overhanging the sea. We discussed vehemently Life, Love, Art, Marriage, Suicide and Religion. We went to a *festa* at the Combattente Club, and left politely with the English contingent, returning later when foreign constraint had fled, to enjoy ourselves. It was this *festa* that supplied the basis for my ill-fated play *Sirocco*. There was much tawdry glamour to it, contributed by sweet champagne, an electric piano, paper streamers, and the usual paraphernalia of Latin carnival.

II

Polly with a Past opened at the St James's Theatre on March 2nd. It was an American farce which had had a big success in New York, where the name part had been created by Ina Claire. In London, Polly was played by Edna Best, who was good, but appeared too adolescent in the latter part of the play when she was supposed to be a dashing French adventuress. Donald Calthrop was the leading man, and the rest of the cast consisted of Aubrey Smith, Helen Haye, Alice Moffat, Claude Rains, Arthur Hatherton, Edith Evans, Henry Kendall, and me. Donald Calthrop and Harry Kendall had the two best men parts, and, as in *Charley's Aunt,* I was the 'feed.' By the end of the run, however, I was embroidering and overacting to such an extent that they had to fight like steers to get their lines over at all.

During this run another lifelong friend made his appearance: Jeffery Amherst, or rather Jeffery Holmesdale as he was then. His father was the Earl Amherst, and he, Jeffery, held the rank of captain in the Coldstream Guards. He was small, and fair, and his gallant military record seemed slightly incongruous, until you had known him a little. He was gay and a trifle strained, and there was a certain quality of secrecy in him, entirely unfurtive, but stronger than mere reserve. It was as though he knew many things too closely, and was consequently over-wary. I dined with him several times, 'on guard' and at home with his family. I watched him twinkling and giggling through several noisy theatrical parties, but it took a long while for even me to begin to know him.

Polly with a Past bored me early in its run, but I was working hard outside the theatre. Songs, sketches, and plays were bursting out of me far too quickly, but without nearly enough critical discrimination. My best effort during that period was a comedy in three acts, *The Young Idea,* which was primarily inspired by Shaw's *You Never Can Tell.* Dolly and Phillip being my original prototypes for Sholto and Gerda, I felt rather guilty of plagiarism, however inept, and when the play was finished, J. E. Vedrenne kindly sent it to Shaw, to find out whether or not he had any objections. A short while afterwards, I received my script back from Shaw, scribbled all over with alterations and suggestions, and accompanied by a long letter, which, to my lasting regret, I was idiotic enough to lose. However, the gist of it was that I showed every indication of becoming a good playwright, providing that I never again in my life read another word that he, Shaw, had ever written. It was, as might be expected, a brilliant letter, and I took its advice only half-heartedly. But there was more than brilliance in the trouble that that great man had taken in going minutely over the work of a comparatively unknown young writer.

12

The rebirth of my determination to go to America occurred at one of Ivor's supper parties, and was caused, I think, by the presence of Jeanne Eagels, who had just made a big success in New York, in a play called *Daddies*. She talked vividly of the American theatre and I felt instinctively that she was a fine actress, and was thrilled to think that there were many others like her just on the other side of the ocean. In this I was wrong. Of all the actresses I have ever seen, there has never been one quite like Jeanne Eagels.

Ivor's parties, in those days, were great fun. In later years they seem to have become a trifle staid and less spontaneous, but perhaps the fault lies with me, perhaps I have grown blasé, and the thrill of star-gazing has turned sour and curdled. At any rate, at that time a party at 'The Flat' was a signal for general rejoicing. 'The Flat' sat, and still sits, on the very top of the Strand Theatre, and in order to reach it, a perilous ascent was made in a small, self-worked lift. Ivor's guests crushed themselves timorously together in this frightening little box, someone pulled a rope, there was a sharp grinding noise, a scream from some less hardy member of the party; then, swaying and rattling, the box ascended. Upon reaching the top, it would hit the roof with a crash and, more often than not, creak all the way down again.

Many people preferred to toil up seven long flights of stairs rather than face the lift, but I was one of the braver spirits, on one occasion actually making six complete journeys before I could induce it to stop.

The big room of the flat had a raised dais running across one end. Upon this, there were sometimes two, at other times no grand pianos, sometimes a gramophone, and nearly always Viola Tree. The high spots of the parties were reached in this room. Charades were performed, people did stunts. Olga Lynn sang, and Fay Compton immediately did an imitation of Olga Lynn singing. Visiting musicians were subtly lured to the piano. Native musicians rushed to it. Rival leading ladies had verbal scuffles. Divorced couples hobnobbed with each other, and with each other's co-respondents. Bitter enemies met face to face, and either swept majestically from the room or stayed to ruffle Ivor's hair.

Jeffery Holmesdale added an extra fillip to my American dream by telling me that he was sailing for New York at the end of May, to represent his father at some sort of centenary festival at Amherst College in Massachusetts. It seemed improbable at the moment that there could be the least chance of my going with him. *Polly with a Past* was still playing to good business, I had a run-of-the-play contract, and in addition there was the ever-present money difficulty. True, things were going better in Ebury Street, I had been earning a good salary for quite a long while, and had a certain amount in the bank, but not nearly enough to pay my return fare to America. I could, I suppose, have taken a passage on some little freight boat, but I was determined to make my first arrival as stylish as possible. I had heard a good deal about the American reverence for success, and on the strength of having had one play produced in London and having played several important parts, I felt that it would be bad policy to creep in, unannounced, by the tradesmen's entrance.

I brooded over all this for several weeks, and finally, by borrowing here and there and selling two songs to Ned Lathom, who didn't want them in the least and only bought them out of charity, I scraped together a hundred pounds, which was enough for my fare one way, on the *Aquitania*, with a little over for expenses.

The next step was to obtain permission from Gilbert Miller to leave the cast of *Polly,* which I did, a few weeks before it closed, and at the end of May, 1912, Jeffery and I set sail on the first of our many journeys together.

PART FOUR

I

To have embarked for America with a bundle of manuscripts, a one-way ticket, and only seventeen pounds to spare, was, I suppose, rather foolhardy, and when the *Aquitania* had left Cherbourg a few miles astern, fears twittered in my stomach like birds in a paper bag, and I reflected that from almost every point of view I was a fool. Admittedly, my faith in my own talents remained unwavering, but it did seem unduly optimistic to suppose that the Americans would be perceptive enough to see me immediately in the same light in which I saw myself. In this, I was perfectly right. They didn't.

However, the weather was warm, the sea calm, and I should have Jeffery to lean on for three weeks at least, so I snapped out of my despondency and sent a cheerful radio to Mother.

I appeared at the ship's concert, supporting the chief steward who sang 'Mandalay,' a wizened 'buck-and-wing' dancer from the second class, and a big woman in black satin, who played the fiddle, the piano, the xylophone, and, for an encore, the cornet.

New York rose out of the sea to greet us. It was a breathless June morning, and wads of cotton-wool smoke lay motionless among the high towers. The Statue of Liberty seemed insignificant but the harbour was glorious. There will always be a stinging enchantment for me in this arrival. Even now, when I know it so well in every aspect, my heart jumps a little. Then it was entirely new to me. We slid gently past Battery Park, still green with early summer, the skyscrapers moved gracefully aside to show still further vistas, and, a long way below us, platoons of straw hats passed by on ferry-boats. As we drew near the dock, several fussy little tugs came out to meet us and finally, after tremendous efforts, succeeded in coaxing and nuzzling us alongside.

We were met by Naps Alington, Gabrielle Enthoven, Cecile Sartoris and Teddie Gerrard. I knew Teddie and Naps, but had never met the other two, and was naturally unaware at the moment that I was destined to live with them for several months. Jeffery and I went, first of all, to the Algonquin, which I had heard was a comfortable, theatrical, and reasonable hotel. It was all that and more, and in later years I have grown to love it dearly. But then, in a violent heatwave, it seemed airless and stuffy, and so, after the first night there, we moved: Jeffery to share Naps' flat in Eighth Street, and I to the Brevoort, at the lower end of Fifth Avenue.

That first evening in New York is clear in my memory. I refused to dine with Teddie and Naps and Jeffery, because I wanted to go to a theatre. And so I promised to rejoin them all afterwards, and went off by myself. I sauntered down Broadway alone, gazing up at the sky-signs, being bumped into, pushed, and shoved by the endless, slow-moving crowds on the sidewalks. The sky was not yet quite dark and the million lights flamed against it, changing it from rich blue to deep purple. It was grander than Mary Robson had described, and more sharply beautiful than I could ever have imagined – a slightly tawdry beauty, detached, impersonal, and a little scarifying.

I walked up and down several side streets, looking at the pictures outside the theatres, and finally deciding upon one, went into the Klaw Theatre. The play was *Nice People* by Rachel Crothers, starring Francine Larrimore, and including among the smaller parts Tallulah Bankhead and Katherine Cornell. I thought the production and acting good, and the play poor, but what interested me most was the *tempo*. Bred in the tradition of gentle English comedy with its inevitable maids, butlers, flower vases, and tea-tables, it took me a good ten minutes of the first act to understand what anyone was saying. They all seemed to be talking at once. Presently I began to disentangle the threads, and learnt my first lesson in American acting, which was the technique of realising, first, which lines in the script are superfluous, and second, knowing when, and how, to throw them away.

After the play, I took a taxi down to Teddie's house in Washington Square, where I found the party in exceedingly full swing. From out of the haze of chatter, piano-playing, and cigarette smoke, I managed to extricate a dark, attractive woman, whose eyes slanted upwards at the corners, and who seemed unable to carry on a connected conversation in one language for more than three minutes. This was Poldowski, or to give her her non-professional name, Lady Dean-Paul. She had left her husband and children in England, and had come to America for much the same reason that I had: an urgent determination to make money.

Apart from her, the party bewildered me, and after a little while I crept away from it, and went back to the Algonquin, overtired and deflated after all the excitements of the day.

The first week in New York was great fun until the novelty had evaporated slightly and my spare cash had evaporated entirely. We did everything we should have done. We went up the Woolworth Building. We gaped appropriately at the majesty of the Pennsylvania and Grand Central stations. We battled our way along Wall Street during the rush hour. We went to Coney Island on a Sunday night, and were jolted and rattled and bumped at a terrific speed through pitch-black tunnels, over canvas mountains, disembarking, green in the face, to consume 'hot dogs' and non-alcoholic beer. We learnt to distinguish between 'expresses' and 'locals' in the Subway. We went to Harlem, and drifted from cabaret to cabaret, jigging to the alien rhythms, and listening to strange wailings and screechings, until our feet ached, our ears buzzed, and our eyes blinked, in the cool dawn.

We went to the New Amsterdam Theatre to see Marilyn Miller in *Sally,* and came away cheerfully enchanted. We went to the Globe Theatre to see the Ziegfeld Follies, and watched the famous, much-advertised beauties languidly boring themselves and the audience with their too perfect figures, their total lack of expression. In the same show there was, fortunately, Fanny Brice, to revive our interest in the theatre. She sang 'Second-hand Rose' with that particular brand of sentimentality sacred to Jewish-American comediennes. We even went, as the guests of Averill Harriman, to watch the scions of the rich play polo.

Apart from these excursions, I delivered the three letters of introduction that I had secured before leaving England. They were addressed to Al Woods, David Belasco and Charles Dillingham respectively. Al Woods was friendly, and told me that *The Last Trick* had been rewritten several times, by several different people, but that he feared nothing could ever be done with it. He also said he was going to Europe in a month or so, and that when he returned he would be delighted to read anything that I had to show him.

Charles Dillingham was away (I think in Colorado), but his manager, Fred Latham, was very amiable and let me go and talk to him in his office on many different occasions. He gave me a lot of kind advice about writing plays, and said that he was going away for a month or so, as he badly needed a holiday.

David Belasco was impressive, and wore a purple silk dressing-gown. He also told me a great deal about play-writing, emphasising his words with striking gestures and seeming, every now and then, to digress a little from the subject in hand. I tentatively suggested that he might be interested in reading one of my scripts, and he agreed that nothing would delight him more except for the unfortunate fact that, owing to doctor's orders, he was compelled to go away for a month or so.

These three stimulating contacts emboldened me to move from the small room that I was occupying at the Brevoort, to a much smaller one, practically in the eaves.

2

A little while before leaving England I had written, in collaboration with Lorn Macnaughtan, a short book of burlesque historical memoirs entitled *A Withered Nosegay*. Lorn did the illustrations and the book was published by Christophers. Some of it was funny, and the basic idea was good, but it was written with too much zest and personal enjoyment, and, consequently, fell a long way short of success. Burlesque at any time is dangerous ground and for young and inexperienced writers usually disastrous. In this particular book there was a lot that was crude and careless, and I have often regretted that the idea didn't come to me a little later, when I should have been more aware of its pitfalls and better equipped to grapple with it.

However, I took it with me to America and sold several of the separate parts of it to *Vanity Fair*. This happened only a few weeks after my arrival, and although the payment was small, it was encouraging.

After Jeffery had gone back to England, Gabrielle Enthoven and Cecile Sartoris offered me a room in their studio in Washington Square. They said that when I sold a play, or made some money somehow, I could pay rent, but until then I was to be their guest. They were neither of them in the least well-off and this was a blessed gesture of sheer charity. I accepted and moved in immediately, grateful not only for their kindness but for their company.

The studio was small, with white-washed walls and dark, polished furniture. Occasionally, in the evenings, we went out to the pictures, but usually we stayed at home and dined quietly in pyjamas. Candles flickered in sconces on the walls whenever there was enough breeze, and we drank red wine from the little Italian grocer's round the corner.

Irene Dean-Paul and Cecile sometimes made a little money by giving 'Verlaine' recitals in the homes of the wealthy. Irene had set, exquisitely, many of the poems to music, and sang them in her husky, attractive 'musician's voice.'

Cecile recited in a rhythmic monotone, her mouth twisted a little at one corner, and her eyes, apparently far away, gazing on enchanted woods and white moons.

There were frequently quarrels, smoothed over ultimately by Gabrielle's tact. Irene flew into rages easily, and delivered vitriolic tirades against American houses, American culture, and American hostesses in particular. On one occasion, after she and Cecile had trailed all the way to Boston to give a recital, she took exception to something that had been said about *l'heure exquise,* and tearing the hard-earned cheque into little pieces, flung them dramatically in the hostess's face. Repercussions of this scene occurred at intervals for many weeks afterwards.

Irene lived in a flat in West 70th Street. It was several flights up, and panelled in sickly pitch-pine. She had a grim but tender-hearted maid, from whom she was perpetually borrowing and who lived, silently, in the back somewhere and never seemed to go out farther than the delicatessen at the corner of the street.

Sometimes, when things looked especially black, we dolled ourselves up to the nines, she in an elaborate evening dress and I in a dinner-jacket, and went to the Ritz roof or Delmonico's to dine and dance. The dining, according to a prearranged plan, consisted of my ordering some light dish, and Irene feeling suddenly ill and being unable to eat a morsel. Later, when the waiter had left us, she would plunge a fork on to my plate, and we would eat hungrily to the last scrap. Occasionally, if we were in luck, some more or less rich acquaintance appeared and took us on to a night-club. When this occurred we at once demanded vast ham sandwiches, and considered the evening definitely a success.

One day when, as usual, we were at low ebb, Irene received an invitation to go and stay the week-end with a Mrs Magee in Mount Kisco, and asked me to go with her. It was a beautiful house and a nice house-party, and we refused to allow the fact that we hadn't enough money to tip the servants to detract one whit from our enjoyment, which was wise of us because, as it turned out, I happened to play 'rummy' on the Sunday night, and made six dollars fifty.

We returned, smoothed out by luxury, and feeling much better.

With all her lightness, humour and infectious high spirits, Irene was a tragic figure. Her integrity as an artiste was fine and uncompromising, too uncompromising to be satisfied with small success, and somehow not quite steel enough, not sufficiently swaddled in egotism to shield her from the irritation of failure. Not that her work was ever a failure, far from it. Her music has a strength and sincerity beyond the reach, I think, of contemporary criticism. Her failure lay within herself, in her abrupt pride, and sudden sharp intolerance, and her inability, when in certain moods, to accept the small change of friendship, even from those whom she knew loved her deeply. All this, I believe, she realised clearly at times, but she happened to be a genuine victim of that much overworked phrase 'artistic temperament,' and suffered accordingly. Her friends also suffered accordingly, but, in my opinion, were well repaid by the privilege of knowing her.

3

At the beginning of August Cecile and Gabrielle both went away, leaving me in charge of the studio and in command of a strange negress called Gertrude, who appeared for an hour or so every morning and ambled lethargically about with a broom. Her clothes were garish, oddly shaped, and a detached stay-busk reared itself up from the small of her back like a cane.

This, actually was a bad period for me. I was penniless and very lonely. The few people that I knew in New York were away, it being midsummer. Even Irene forsook me for a while. I saw Teddie Gerrard occasionally, and Naps, but they were both, although friendly, occupied with their own affairs.

Every theatrical manager in America seemed to have vanished completely, nearly all the theatres were closed, and several of the manuscripts I had brought with me had been consigned to some secret vault by the Theatre Guild, from which it was impossible to extricate them, or even hear news of how they were faring.

I acquired many of the stock habits of the forlorn and poverty-stricken, such as tramping the streets, contemplating daring robberies, and sitting on park benches. Unfortunately, owing to my carefully conserved wardrobe, I was invariably asked for money by my brother paupers, and was once addressed as 'sir' by an obviously prosperous Chinaman. Battery Park was really the nicest place in which to sit, but it was a long walk from Washington Square. Here, however, I found the company more varied and picturesque than in Central Park, also there was the sea to look at, and it was cooler. Sentimentally, of course, it had its drawbacks, because there were nearly always ships sailing away to England, and I had to avert my eyes and do a little honest, manly fist-clenching and shoulder-squaring.

I used to get packets of bacon, on credit, from the Italian grocer just near the studio, and cook it sparingly in the kitchenette. Luckily the weather was far too hot for me to want to eat very much. The kitchenette became suffocating quickly, and so I found it more comfortable, when actually frying, to be stark naked. This aroused the moral indignation of a 'cop,' who had been observing me from the other side of the street, and he came and banged loudly on the door. I put on a dressing-gown, and ran downstairs with the bacon fork still in my hand and upon opening the door received the full force of his rage, which evaporated quickly when I asked him if he would care for a little red wine. He came up into the studio and polished off three glasses. I offered him some bacon, which he refused, but at parting he kindly lent me his revolver because, he said, it was a dangerous neighbourhood, and living there as I was, completely alone, *anything* might happen. When he had gone, I lay awake for most of the night restraining the impulse to shoot at every shadow cast by the street lamp on to the white studio wall.

Later on in the month things began to look up a bit. I sold *A Withered Nosegay* to Boni and Liveright, and got a small advance for it. I made some new friends: Horace Liveright himself, Beatrice and George Kaufman, Blythe Daly, and Tallulah Bankhead. I also spent a pleasant evening in a cafeteria with an old friend, Ronald Colman, who had just opened in a play that was a flop, and was discouraged and unhappy. We cheered each other by formulating brave ambitions. He was determined to get to the coast to try his luck in pictures, and I was equally determined not to leave America until I had had a play accepted.

On the strength of this mutual stimulus, I started immediately to write *Sirocco* with Eva Le Gallienne and Joseph Schildkraut in mind for the leading parts. They were at that moment playing in Molnar's *Liliom*. I finished it quickly, and had no particular cause to regret it until several years later.

Florence Magee invited me to Mount Kisco a number of times, and I went, gratefully, whenever I had enough for the fare. Laurette Taylor and Hartley Manners returned to town from the country with Dwight and Marguerite, Laurette's children by her first marriage, and settled themselves into an odd demi-Gothic edifice on Riverside Drive. This house possessed one enormous room below-stairs, with an open fireplace, much tortured wood-work, and stained-glass windows, and, upstairs, many small rooms on different levels, varying in décor from Laurette's gilt and belaced bedroom and a formal mahoganied dining-room, to the correct and rather heavy-handed virility of Hartley's study, with its sports trophies, pipe-racks, and sturdy writing-table.

Hartley was a charming man, but his spirit seemed to be shut up permanently inside a sort of 'iron virgin' of moral principles. This, as far as I was concerned, made any lengthy conversations difficult. I had to tread lightly, and in the few literary discussions that we had, I soon learned not to allow enthusiasm to carry me too far, and to hop aside, nimbly, from any anti-social, anti-religious, or remotely sexual allusion. Laurette, on the other hand, was frequently blunt to the point of embarrassment. She was naïve, intolerant, lovable and entirely devoid of tact. Her humour was quick as lightning, and she could pounce from a great height with all the swift accuracy of a pelican diving into the sea, seldom failing to spear some poor, wriggling fish, and disquieting considerably the other fish present. Her taste in dress was poor, and her loveliness triumphed over many inopportune bows and ostrich feathers, but her taste as an actress was unassailable.

On Sunday evenings up on Riverside Drive we had cold supper and played games, often rather acrimonious games, owing to Laurette's abrupt disapproval of any guest (whether invited by Hartley, Marguerite, Dwight or herself) who turned out to be self-conscious, nervous, or unable to act an adverb or an historical personage with proper abandon. There were also, very often, shrill arguments concerning rules. These were waged entirely among the family, and frequently ended in all four of them leaving the room and retiring upstairs, where, later on, they might be discovered by any guest bold enough to go in search of them, amicably drinking tea in the kitchen.

It was inevitable that someone should eventually utilise portions of this eccentricity in a play, and I am only grateful to Fate that no guest of the Hartley Manners thought of writing *Hay Fever* before I did.

Lynn Fontanne returned from Chicago, where she had been

playing a trial run of *Dulcy,* her first star part, written especially for her by George Kaufman and Marc Connelly. Her career in America had hitherto been devoted almost entirely to supporting Laurette in various plays of Hartley's. On the strength of her comedy performance in one of these, *Dulcy* was created, and proved to be a decisive triumph for her. As yet, however, there were still two months to endure before New York production, and she was a prey to the usual nervous forebodings, her moods alternating between hysterical gaiety and the most intense melancholy.

She and Alfred Lunt were, to put it mildly, 'courting' at the moment, and lived in a theatrical lodging-house somewhere in the West Seventies, known as 'Doctor Rounds'.' Any actor, however vagrant, was welcome at Doctor Rounds'. The food was good, and the house comfortably untidy and Doctor Rounds herself quite remarkable. She had greyish hair and shrewd, wary eyes, which sized you up accurately on sight, and she would occasionally relate gruesomely medical stories from out of the mysterious limbo of her early years. There was also in the house, in addition to Barry Baxter and the other lodgers, a maid-of-all-work, *café au lait* in colour and correctly true to type in action, who crooned incessantly in and out of all the rooms, and bashed dust-pans and tin pails joyously against the banisters.

From these shabby, congenial rooms, we projected ourselves into future eminence. We discussed, the three of us, over delicatessen potato salad and dill pickles, our most secret dreams of success. Lynn and Alfred were to be married. That was the first plan. Then they were to become definitely idols of the public. That was the second plan. Then, all this being successfully accomplished, they were to act exclusively together. This was the third plan. It remained for me to supply the fourth, which was that when all three of us had become stars of sufficient magnitude to be able to count upon an individual following of each other, then, poised serenely upon that enviable plane of achievement, we would meet and act triumphantly together.

After these prophetic orgies, we often found it necessary to bring ourselves down to earth by taking brisk walks to the corner of the street and back, or going to the pictures. Once Lynn and I even sank so low as to make a charabanc trip to Chinatown.

In the meanwhile, we all had a long way to go and there was the immediate terror of the first night of *Dulcy* looming nearer and nearer. When the actual moment arrived, Alfred and I left Lynn in her dressing-room (to employ the hour and a half before the curtain rose by making-up, and dressing, and being methodically sick), and paced miserably up and down the street. We drifted in and out of soda-fountains, consuming endless Coca-Colas and frosted chocolates, and behaving generally like anxious fathers expecting twins. Presently we watched, in panic, cars and taxis beginning to arrive at the theatre, and so we went in, and clamping ourselves to our seats in the back row of the stalls, steeled ourselves to talk casually and wave and nod to acquaintances.

From the moment that Lynn flounced on in the first act, wearing a smart black velvet gown and appearing to be completely in command of herself and the play, we knew that everything was going to be all right, as indeed it was, and by the time the applause had died away after the second act we discovered that not only were we no longer pinching each other black and blue, but that we were quite relaxed and actually enjoying ourselves.

Soon after this I struck a bad patch again and, when I could really bear it no longer, I summoned up courage to go and borrow twenty dollars from Lynn. This courage was entirely my own concern and nothing whatever to do with Lynn. I knew that she would willingly give me anything that I asked for. But of all the many borrowings I have had to do in my time, I think I loathed that one the most. It wasn't humiliated pride that oppressed me, nor yet any false shame of my bad circumstances – all these things were too clearly understood among us – but somehow, in spite of my grey suit, blue shirt and tie and brightly shined shoes, I felt vaguely bedraggled, as though my spirit hadn't been pressed properly and was shabby and creased.

I arrived at the theatre too soon, a long while before the end of the matinée, and walked up and down the alley until I could tell, by the sound of applause, that the curtain had fallen. Of course, a troop of people came round to see Lynn, and I had to wait for several more years until they left. I finally had to interrupt Lynn in the middle of a detailed description of a new bit of business she had inserted in the second act, and pop the question, almost crossly, at her. She said: 'Darling, of course, don't be so silly,' delved in her bag, and handed me the money without deviating at all from what she was saying. The next morning I received a letter from Jim Whigham, the editor of the *Metropolitan Magazine,* asking me to lunch with him at the Brook Club. He had been staying at Mount Kisco with the Magees, and had read while there a copy of *I'll Leave It to You,* which I had sent to Florence, as a sort of bread-and-butter gesture, after my first visit. He said, in course of lunch, that if I would consider turning it into a short story he would pay me five hundred dollars for it. I nearly choked, but managed to say, casually enough, that I would try, and the rest of the meal passed in a sort of haze, which was rather a pity really, as I had not had the chance of eating such good food for a long time.

I reflected gleefully, on the way home, that for five hundred dollars I would gladly consider turning *War and Peace* into a music-hall sketch.

The result of all this was that, within three days, Lynn was paid back, swooning with surprise. The Italian grocer was paid back for two months of long-since consumed eggs and bacon. Gertrude received, with her usual lethargy, six weeks' arrears of wages. And I was able to send forty pounds home to Mother, to compensate for the loss of Mrs Herriot, who had inconsiderately abandoned our drawing-room suite early in June in favour of the grave.

4

With the beginning of the autumn season New York became cooler in temperature and much hotter in theatrical activity. Broadway awoke from its summer sleep, and the first batch of 'Fall productions' opened and closed in all directions. Homburgs took the place of straw hats, and coinciding with the return of all the managers to town, came the return of all my manuscripts. I was delighted to see them again, and read them through with keen pleasure, particularly *The Young Idea,* which, like *I'll Leave It to*

You, I turned into a short story and sold to the *Metropolitan* for a further five hundred dollars.

I felt now much more secure financially, which was just as well, as I had a letter from Cecile in Bar Harbour saying that she and Gabrielle were not coming back to the studio at all and were, in fact, going to give it up for good. Upon receipt of this I moved out immediately, and went back to the Brevoort.

I was rather glad to be in an hotel again, especially as I had the satisfaction of knowing that I should be able to pay my bill quite regularly every week for some time to come. The studio had, of course, been a godsend to me, but I had passed too many miserable days in it, and been too lonely there, to feel any deep regret at leaving it. Also, during the last few weeks, several unfortunate things had occurred. To begin with, my laundryman, a fat, jolly little Chinaman, had been murdered in a street fight on the next block, which depressed me, as his Monday morning vists were benign and friendly. Then, I arrived home late one night to discover that the downstairs passage window and the Yale lock on the door had both been broken, and although nothing inside had been touched, I felt, even with my carefully unloaded revolver, a little insecure. Finally, and worst of all, I had a plague of bed bugs. Having played in the pottery towns, these were not entirely strangers to me, but as, in America, the orange, apples, bananas and buildings are far bigger than anywhere else in the world, so it is with their bed bugs. I awoke one night to find the walls, the bed and myself covered with flat, slow-moving trouser buttons, which bit savagely, and, when squashed, smelt overpoweringly of almonds. I spent the hours until dawn shuddering in the kitchen, with all the lights on.

The next day, apart from a few corpses, there wasn't a sign of them, and the fumigators, when they arrived, expressed rather scornful scepticism, saying that I must have exaggerated, as the walls and ceiling and the floor showed no indications, and that there wasn't anywhere else they could possibly have come from. Nevertheless, upon my insisting, they fumigated the whole place and, in course of their labours, discovered several hundred hale and hearty bugs living cosily inside a tapestry picture of the Virgin Mary.

The various managers, although unenthusiastic about my plays, were most hospitable, asking me to lunch at the Astor, urging me to adapt sure-fire successes from the Hungarian, and sending me tickets for first nights. Even the remote Mr Belasco crashed through with a balcony seat for his revival of *The Easiest Way* with Francis Starr. This was interesting, as she gave a fine performance, and even though the play did appear to be a trifle dated, it was first-rate melodrama beautifully lit and directed. In the interval between the second and third acts, I contrived, by a casual word, to creep into the heart of Alexander Woollcott. The word was 'vexing.' I said, without any particularly witty intent, that I had found the performance of one of the actors in the play very vexing, whereupon the warm September night was instantly shattered by strange cluckings and gurglings and sharp, shrill wails of pleasure. I was unused to abandoned displays from eminent critics; as a matter of fact I was unused to eminent critics, and I regarded this capering figure on the sidewalk with astonishment. Later on I became accustomed to such outbursts, finding, to my occasional dismay, that they worked both ways. Alexander Woollcott, in a rage, has all the tenderness and restraint of a newly caged cobra, and, when striking, much the same admirable precision. He has written, during the last ten years, a good deal about me in various newspapers and magazines. He has, in criticism, brought me to the dust and raised me on to high pedestals, usually giving a sly, rococo twist to the pedestals. He has, in biographical sketches, sacrificed, without pang of conscience, many of my nobler characteristics to pertinent witticisms. He has coaxed, relentlessly, many hundreds of dollars out of me at backgammon and Russian banker, and been loudly and urgently clamorous for payment.

In 1928, when I was playing with Beatrice Lillie in *This Year of Grace,* he objected bitterly to my performance of a song, 'A Room with a View.' And as a final inducement to me to relinquish it to my understudy, he appeared one night in a stage box with a party, each member of which buried his and her face in a newspaper the moment I began to sing. All these gestures and many others of a like devilishness have, oddly enough, merely served to cement even more strongly my fondness for him, and there he sits, and will probably continue to sit for ever, firmly ensconced in my affections, wearing a dreadful old green dressing-gown, playing to me all the Gilbert and Sullivan records that he knows I hate, and ordering me shrilly from the house whenever I win one point from him at any game of chance.

For the moment, however, we must leave him in September 1921, whooping outside the Lyceum Theatre, and turn to more austere encounters – such, for instance, as my meeting with another critic at another first night, Mr George Jean Nathan. Him I found deeply impressive, if somewhat studied in manner, and even if I had known then how much time and ink he was going to waste in the future in roasting the pants off me, I should still have been unable to help liking the little man.

A little later on came the first really important opening of the season. This was an allstar production of *The Circle* by Somerset Maugham. Estelle Winwood, John Drew, and Mrs Leslie Carter played the parts originally created in London by Fay Compton, Allan Aynesworth and Lottie Venne. The night was particularly englamoured by the fact that it was the return of Mrs Carter to the stage after many years' absence.

I realised, after she had been on the stage for a little while, how superb she must have been in her flamboyant 'Zazas' and 'Dubarrys' of earlier years. I could visualise her clearly, through the brilliant web of Maugham's dialogue, posturing dramatically through bravura scenes, with scarlet hair piled high and her voluptuous figure dripping with Belasco jewels, but here, with sharp modern wit to express, she seemed strained and ill at ease. The most tawny lionesses wilt in captivity, and I couldn't help feeling that Mrs Carter was wilting considerably behind the polite bars of social comedy.

Lester Donahue appeared suddenly out of the gloom at the back of the stalls and reminded me that we had met in London, and that he had given me seats of his piano recital at the Æolian Hall. I remembered it with enthusiasm, not only because he had played beautifully that afternoon, but because I was delighted to see his pink, cherubic little face again.

A few days later he moved over from wherever he was and came to the Brevoort. This was nice for me because he had a piano in his room which I used frequently.

We went to a lot of parties together, at one of which we found a childhood friend of his, Peggy Wood. Unfortunately she was not playing in anything at the moment, and so I was unable to judge for myself whether or not Lester's ecstatic descriptions of her work were justified until nearly ten years later, when she walked with such exquisite distinction through the shiny double doors in the first act of *Bitter Sweet.*

With Lester also I saw Fred and Adele Astaire for the first time, in a musical comedy called *The Love Letter.* I hadn't realised before then that such rhythm and taste in dancing were possible.

Every Thursday and Saturday there were midnight performances of *Shuffle Along,* which was playing somewhere up in the West Sixties. This was, I believe, one of the first entirely coloured revues.

Throughout the whole jumble of songs and sketches and dances there darted the swift, vivid genius of Florence Mills, at one moment moving like a streak of quicksilver, the next still against some gaudily painted back-drop, nothing animated about her at all, except her wide smile and the little pulse in her throat, throbbing like a bird while she sang:

> 'Love will find a way
> Tho' skies now are grey,
> Love like ours can never be ruled,
> Cupid's not fooled that way –'

When she died a few years ago, many thousands of people followed her to the cemetery. Most of Broadway, and all of Harlem. And when the service was over and the hymns had been sung, there was no music until, just as the small coffin was being lowered into the grave, a sudden burst of singing rose to the skies, saluting her passing with the song that she had made so famous: 'Bye-bye, Blackbird.'

5

On the last day of October I sailed for home on the S.S. *Cedric,* one of the smaller White Star ships.

I stood on deck until the skyline had disappeared into the rain, and retired to my cabin in which I remained, prostrate with sea-sickness, for three days. When I ultimately emerged, still faintly green, the sea was calmer and the sun was shining, and I was able to sit wanly in a deck-chair nibbling, every now and then, a little cold beef and baked potato and allowing the events of the past five months to pass in stately review before my mind's eye, over the more unpleasant of which glamour was already beginning to settle.

I relived, with slight dramatic overtones, many hours of despair. I saw a brave, tragic youth trudging through the hot streets to his accustomed bench in Battery Park, friendless and alone, gazing out over the sea to where Green England lay, and sharing, perhaps, a crust with some kindly negro.

I saw the same gallant figure attired in deep evening dress attending the smartest first nights, with not even a nickel in his trouser pocket to pay his subway fare home. I also saw him, cowering naked in the kitchen, beset on all sides by voracious bed bugs.

I sorted my new friends with genuine pleasure. Lynn and Alfred, Alec Woollcott, Lester, Cecile and Gabrielle, Florence Magee, Irene, Laurette, Beatrice and George Kaufman, the Astaires, the countless others, all of whom had been charming to me, and all of whom I knew I should be enchanted to see again at any time, anywhere.

In addition to these there were some, who for some reason or other, possibly from sheer modesty, failed to appear in my memory while I was writing the preceding pages. Perhaps they felt that by shuffling late into their places they might interfere with the flow of my narrative. However, two at least were important to me, and if the others persist in lurking in the shadows that's their look-out. The two to be specified are Hoytie Wiborg and Gladys Barbour.

I stayed with Hoytie at Easthampton, where we ate good food, played bad tennis, argued on intellectual subjects, rode the surf on a large rubber mattress, and, on one occasion, nearly drowned.

Hoytie dabbled passionately in the Arts. She talked of Picasso, Van Gogh, Scriabin and Stravinsky. She lectured me austerely upon my own talents, intimating with great firmness that if I continued along my present lines, writing lyrics, sketches, plays and music, etc., that no good could ever possibly result from it. Facile versatility, she prophesied, would lead me surely to a dilettante's grave, and that if I must go on writing so much, and so quickly, at least I must give up imagining for one moment that I had the least talent for music. This, she said, she really knew about, and that as I could neither read it nor write it, and as my execution on the piano was only erratic in the right hand and non-existent in the left, the sooner I eliminated the whole idea from my bag of tricks the better.

Years later, on the first night of *Bitter Sweet,* remembering this conversation, I smiled at her from my box with a slight gleam of triumph in my eye, but she only shook her head gloomily, as though her worst forebodings had been incontrovertibly proven.

Gladys Barbour was chalk to Hoytie's cheese. She was small and fair, whereas Hoytie was tall and dark. She preferred dancing to Picasso, and Gershwin to Stravinsky. She shared in common with Hoytie a generous heart and an infinite capacity for taking trouble to help people she liked and, incidentally, was responsible, through the kind offices of her husband, for the comfortable free cabin on the *Cedric* which I was now occupying. One night in New York, during a party at some night club, she suddenly presented me with a mascot which was nothing more or less than a twenty-dollar gold piece. I am certain to this day that she gave it to me entirely because she knew I was broke, but sentimental to the last, I refrained for two whole weeks from changing it, and when finally I could resist the temptation no longer, I found that it had been stolen by one of the bellboys at the Brevoort. Altogether, I looked back tenderly across the sea to Gladys Barbour.

The S.S. *Cedric* was a small boat, compared with its enormous sisters, the *Majestic* and the *Olympic,* but it was comfortable enough. It was also old, and slow, and wallowed through the sea like a fat swimmer, past her prime, doing a perpetual breast stroke.

There were not many people on board. But among the few was one of definite interest, Doctor Marie Stopes. She had, appropriately, the eyes of a fanatic, but the rest of her was dim, excepting her conversation. This was surprisingly vivid, and almost exclusively concerned with the theatre. Naturally this was a comfort to me, and we discussed plays for hours in a small rustic tea-room aft of the promenade deck.

We docked at Liverpool in snow and sleet, and I went ashore hugging to myself the excitement of a surprise arrival. I couldn't resist sending Mother a telegram from Lime Street Station, and I spent the interminable five-hour journey in the train, imagining her face when she opened it and noted where it had been handed in.

The home-coming was entirely successful, and unspoiled by anti-climax. The bungalow was *en fête*. There were one or two new lodgers peering out of the windows, and a new and very young housemaid, who stood first on one leg and then on the other, and giggled loudly throughout the first flurry of reunion. Mother was flushed and hilarious, but I noticed a certain strain under her joy, and my heart sank a little, but rebounded again almost immediately with the realisation that whatever might be happening behind the scenes in that beastly house, we were at least all together again.

In so far as the complete success of my New York adventure was concerned, I felt a trifle dubious. Financially speaking, it had obviously been a failure, as I had returned with only seven pounds more than when I had landed five months before. However I had seen a lot, experienced a lot, and learned a lot. I knew New York thoroughly, better actually than I have ever known it since. The subway, the elevated, cheap cafeterias, park benches and loneliness have been no part of my later visits. But I felt, even then, certain small regrets.

To be poor in your own country is bad enough, but to be poor among strangers should, by rights, be very much worse. But, somewhat to my surprise, I realised that in my case it had not been worse at all. I remembered the Chinese laundryman, Gertrude, the Italian grocer and the Irish 'cop.' I remembered conversations in buses, and cinemas, and soda-fountains. I remembered the beauty of New York at night, viewed, not from a smart penthouse on Park Avenue, but from a crowded seat in Washington Square. And it seemed, in spite of its hardness and irritating, noisy efficiency, a great and exciting place.

PART FIVE

I

In reviewing the past, it is difficult to check off accurately, which, among the millions of small incidents, adventures, pleasures and pains, have been essential to the development of character, or at any rate interesting enough in themselves to be worth describing.

When this book is finished, corrected, revised and lying snugly bound in the publisher's office, I feel sure that many unrecorded events will arise to mock and torment me. Many people also. Already, I find that there are several that I have left out. Among these, oddly enough, some of considerable importance. Grace Forster, for instance, Stewart's mother. She should have made her entrance a long way back, swishing across shady lawns and night clubs, wrapped in gallant vanity, and smelling slyly of amber.

Farther back still, a hunt ball at Oakham seems to have been mislaid somehow. To this I was taken by Lady Londesborough, and was deeply, although not too rapturously impressed by it. I remember a lot of pink coats, and much deafening gaiety. I also remember a bad band and a worse floor and, more pleasantly, Burghersh, now Lord Westmorland, whose face, doubtless out of deference to the Cottesmore, seemed pinker than the pinkest coat present, and whose charm, even through the loudest din, remained inviolate.

Among other unrelated things floating in my memory, I can see clearly a man being run over by a bus just opposite the National Gallery. A Mercédès car, belonging to a gentleman called Harry Hart, which seldom got farther than Maidenhead, and a home-made turban of Joyce Barbour's fashioned saucily in 1916 from a bandana handkerchief.

The year of 1922 began for me in a welter of financial

embarrassment. The hows, whys, and wherefores would make dull reading, enough that there were borrowings, mortgages on my beloved piano, pawnshops, black moments of distress, brokers' men, and worst of all, days when even Mother's invincible spirit came near to being broken.

Nobody seemed to be interested in my plays. Nobody seemed anxious to offer me parts at even reasonable salaries. Every now and then I managed to sell a short story or a song, and once I got a hundred pounds for grinding out an adaptation of a French play for Denis Eadie. Altogether it was a gloomy and depressing period.

In former days, of course, I could probably have gone out on tour or procured a small job in London, but now, having played two or three leading parts, and actually appeared in my own play in the West End, I was in the awkward situation of being too well known to be able to accept little jobs, and not well known enough to be able to command big ones.

Every morning Mother used to come and sit on my bed while I had my breakfast. This was the one hour in the day that she allowed herself to relax, and I could always tell by her face, the moment it appeared round the door, if anything awful had happened. There was a certain artificial chirpiness about her on bad days, manufactured out of a determination not to let me see that she was worried, which generally broke down before I had finished my first cup of coffee.

We were getting more and more deeply into debt, and even with the house full, which it wasn't, the income from it was not sufficient to meet the quarterly instalments, the rent, the taxes, the electric light bills, and the living expenses of Father, Mother, Auntie Vida, Eric, and me.

What worried me most was the dread that Mother would suddenly break completely and become seriously ill. Her heart was not strong, and the strain of the last few years had been appalling. This I was determined to avert at all costs, even if the brokers took possession of the house and we were all flung into the street.

I went to see Ned Lathom, knowing how kind and generous he was, and also knowing how many hundreds of people had already sponged upon him, and asked him flatly, without preliminaries, to lend me two hundred pounds. He refused almost sharply, and he added that he would willingly give me two hundred pounds, but that never, in any circumstances, would he lend money to anybody ever again, it was too dangerous a commodity, he said, to pass between friends.

I have a lot of gratitude in my heart, towards many people, but it is too special and private an emotion to spill into print. There are hundreds of ways of describing unkindness and meanness and little cruelties. A sly dig at the right moment can work wonders. But just try to write of generosity. Try to frame in words an unrelated, motiveless gesture of sheer kindness and you are lost. The warmth behind the phrases dissipates before they reach the paper, and there they lie, under your hand, sneering up at you, coldly effusive and dead as mutton.

At any rate, with Ned's cheque in my pocket, the sun shone, temporarily, with all its might. About a hundred and fifty of the two hundred went immediately to various creditors. The remaining fifty I held on to, because I had a plan in mind which, after a discussion with Gladys Calthrop, I sprang on Mother, suddenly, and clinched before she had time to argue.

The plan was that Father was to take charge of the house, and that I was to find a little cottage in the country somewhere, where she could rest completely, for several months, and where I could come for week-ends, and write. She at once made a pyramid of small difficulties which I swept grandly away. There wasn't much conviction behind them anyhow, and a few days later Gladys and I went to Dymchurch, where Athene Seyler had lent me her cottage for a fortnight, and from this we set forth daily in search of a small, inexpensive house for Mother.

Dymchurch in March was bleak, windy, cold and full of charm.

We bicycled and walked for days over the marshes, with Fred, Gladys's brown spaniel, padding along behind us, and plunging in and out of the dykes. We zigzagged backwards and forwards between Ham Street and Ivychurch, Appledore and New Romney. We climbed up on to Aldington Knoll and looked at the cliffs of France glinting in the sun across the steely grey channel. We found some early primroses and a lame sea-gull, which bit us fiercely, and messed, with the utmost abandon, all over the cottage. We went systematically through every available habitation within a radius of twenty-five miles, and finally found a small and tender one, nestling up against a public-house in the village of St Mary in the Marsh. It had four rooms, outside sanitation, a rental of ten shillings a week, and a superb view from the upper windows of unlimited sheep.

Mother seemed to be quite pleased with it, and so we moved in, and very soon the sea and the sky and the marshes began to work a little homely Kentish magic. There was nothing to do but read and write, and make expeditions into Dymchurch or New Romney to get provisions, and a lot of the tiredness was smoothed away from Mother's face within the first few weeks.

I bought a black mongrel at the Battersea Dogs' Home, and conveyed him, radiant in a new collar, to New Romney Station, where Mother met us and fell in love with him at once. He was very young and spindly in the legs, and he promptly had a violent attack of distemper, which kept him hovering between life and death for seven weeks. However, nursing him provided an occupation for Mother during the days I had to spend in London.

There were a few neighbours for her to talk to: Mrs Hinds, the owner of the inn next door, Mr and Mrs Cook, the Vicar and his wife, Miss Hammond, the local school teacher. There were also the Bodys, who owned much of the property round about, and, not very far off, at Jesson, none other than E. Nesbit, who lived with her husband, and a gentle friend, in a series of spacious huts.

I called on her very soon, and found her as firm, as nice, and as humorous as her books had led me to expect. The skipper, her husband, was a grand old man, who loved her and guarded her devotedly through her last, rather sad years.

The friend, Miss Hill, was a wispy creature, with an air of vague detachment, which inspired Athene Seyler to christen her irreverently, 'The Green Hill Far Away.'

During that spring I spent most of my time at St Mary's. The churchyard just across the road was a peaceful place in which to work, and it was there, propped up against a family tombstone, that I wrote *The Queen was in the Parlour.* Nothing could be further removed from that play than the surroundings in which I wrote it. Its passionate love-scenes and Ruritanian splendours emerged from my mind to the gentle cawing of rooks and the bleating of new-born lambs. When I raised my eyes from a Palace courtyard, lit by the flare of torches and brimming with revolutionaries, I saw the marshes stretching to the dark line of the sea wall, broken every now and then by dumpy little Martello towers, and slightly inland on the right, a cluster of trees and houses and a square church tower – the village of New Romney.

On long summer evenings, Mother and I used to ride up to Aldington Knoll on our bicycles, and wait there in the growing dusk until the thin line of sea, four miles away, faded and disappeared in the white mist rising from the dykes, and then looking down over the darkening country spreading all the way from Folkestone to Hastings, we would see lamps twinkling in cottage windows, bats swooping down from the high trees, and the lighthouses flashing all along the coast.

It would have been cheering had we known, then, that the land just below us would belong to us one day. That the farm-house, the five poplars, the thick woods and lush fields stretching down to the Military Canal, would all be ours to do with as we liked. But even as it was, without clairvoyance and future certainties, those evenings were lovely enough, and we pedalled home happily through the dark, our bicycle lamps making wobbling shadows across the roads, feeling that, after all, money troubles, rate collectors, and brokers' men didn't matter so very much as long as we had a water-tight ten-shilling-a-week roof over our heads.

2

In June, Robert Courtneidge took up an option on *The Young Idea,* to produce it in the early autumn for a six weeks' trial run in the provinces. This was an obvious change of fortune, and we set about casting it right away. I firmly, and very much against Courtneidge's will, insisted upon playing 'Sholto' myself. I explained patiently, and at length, that as I had taken the trouble to write the part specially for myself, it would be both illogical and foolish to allow anyone else to get so much as a smell of it. Courtneidge's argument was that I was too old for it, that my personality was too sophisticated, and that in his opinion it would be much more effective played by someone with a more cherubic cast of countenance and a more naïve charm. What he really meant, of course, was that I was not a good enough actor for it. However, he finally gave in with as good grace as possible, and we went to work on the other parts.

I had written 'Gerda' for Edna Best, but owing to some other contract she was unobtainable, and so Ann Trevor was engaged. Kate Cutler, of course, was to be Jennifer. This also had been especially written for her, and of my other old *I'll Leave it to You* friends, Muriel Pope was cast for Cicely. The rest were Herbert Marshall, Clive Currie, Naomi Jacob, Phyllis Black, Molly Maitland (then Mrs Herbert Marshall), Ambrose Manning, and Martin Lewis, who was later replaced by Leslie Banks.

Rehearsals were to begin in August, and so I had nearly two months in which to enjoy myself, relieved, for the first time for a long while, of the horrible foreboding that I was never, never going to get work again as long as I lived.

Father, much to his own and everyone else's surprise, was not only running the house successfully, but deriving, on the whole, a great deal of personal gratification from it. Always naturally gregarious, he had a grand time talking to the lodgers and hopping in and out of their rooms with breakfast trays. Apparently, he was more sociable than Mother, and not only achieved extreme popularity inside the house, but outside as well. All the tradesmen in the vicinity welcomed his morning appearance with the dog (an obsequious Pomeranian), and even the window-cleaner was accorded fortnightly a brief but intimate chat. May Weaver, the now not so new housemaid who had been present on my return from the States, relaxed into delirious gaiety with Mother's restraining influence removed. She scampered madly up and down stairs singing shrilly, and never, except very, very late in the afternoon, dreamt of wearing a cap, a small gesture to refinement upon which Mother had obdurately insisted.

3

A short while after the contract for *The Young Idea* had been signed, I was invited by Lady Colefax to Oxford, where she had taken a house for a week, to entertain a party of young people for the Bullingdon dance. I knew her then only slightly, but we have been friends ever since.

Those few days were smooth and affable, and bathed in a gentle summer peace alien to me, and yet somehow vaguely familiar, which puzzled me at first, until I realised that my sense of having seen it all before was entirely due to the books I had read.

It was all there. All the paraphernalia of the eager young novelists, and touchingly accurate in detail.

There were the shady cloisters with the sun tracing Gothic patterns across the worn paving-stones. There were the rooks cawing in the high elms, the rich, over-laden rose gardens, the green velvet lawns, and the whacks and thuds of cricket bats and tennis rackets sounding gently from the other side of yew hedges.

There, beneath aged sycamores, were spread tea-tables, cushions, wicker chairs, 'Curate's Comforts,' and large bowls of strawberries and cream, the latter to be devoured by the returning game-players who were so much, much more suitably attired for the country than I. Their shirts and flannels were yellow and well used, against which mine seemed too newly white, too immaculately moulded from musical comedy. Their socks, thick and carelessly wrinkled round their ankles, so unlike mine of too thin silk, caught up by intricate suspenders.

Their conversation, too, struck a traditional note in my ears. I seemed to know what they were going to say long before they said it. I sensed in their fledgeling jokes and light unsubtle badinage a certain quality of youthfulness that I had never known. And although I was the same age, if not younger than many of them, I felt suddenly old, over-experienced and quite definitely out of the picture.

This was not exactly an unhappy sensation. I had then, as always, no wish to change places with anyone in the world. But I felt a slight strain, as though I were playing in a scene for which I had not been sufficiently rehearsed. This evaporated soon after the first day and after I had grown to know them all a little, but I noted carefully many points, without envy or disdain or wistfulness, but merely with a keen eye on future performances.

On the night of the Bullingdon dance itself, the whole atmosphere suddenly shivered and jangled into awareness of a very unfamiliar personality indeed. The elms shuddered a little when a large car drew up at the door and disgorged, amid raucous laughter, the bouncing, Michelin figure of Elsa Maxwell. She was accompanied, sedately, by Mrs Toulmin, fair and brittle and impressively *mondaine,* with her Chanel clothes and sleek contented dressing-case. Elsa beside her looked as incongruous as a large brindle bull-dog out walking with a white Russian cat. She at once proceeded to whistle through that house like a cyclone, strumming the piano, laughing, talking and striking the rose-white youth present into a coma of dumb bewilderment.

I loved her at once. I loved her round friendly face, with its little shrewd eyes darting about like animated currants in a Bath bun. I loved her high spirits and her loud infectious laugh. It was before the days when she became the Queen of Paris, and curdled her own personality with too much *crème de la crème.* In 1922 she was still a roystering buccaneer, and with all her boastfulness and noise and shrill assertiveness, intelligent and immensely lovable.

Why she suddenly appeared at Oxford that evening I shall never know. If I felt a little out of it in so fresh and young an atmosphere, Elsa must have felt like a visitor from another planet.

To write the true story of Elsa's life would be worth doing, but unfortunately quite impossible, for the simple reason that the details of it, the real mysteries and struggles and adventures are untraceable. The only authority for data would be Elsa herself, but to appeal to her would be worse than useless. Not that she wouldn't be willing and happy to supply information, not that she wouldn't be perfectly delighted to pour treasure-troves of anecdotes and incidents and startling experiences, glittering jingling heaps of them, into a lap of anyone sympathetically disposed to listen. She is nothing if not generous in everything, a magnificent egotist into the bargain, and loves few things better than talking about herself.

But unhappily for the author engaged in these tantalising researches, one of the principal gifts that the wise Californian fairies brought to Elsa's christening was an untrammelled and peculiarly vivid imagination. This provides a complete world for her, colouring to excess, not only the things she has done, and does, but creating for her with equal reality the things she never has done and never will do.

At the height of her Paris fame, Cole Porter inscribed the following little song for her, which she pounded joyously out of most of the pianos on the Continent:

'I met a friend of mine a week or two ago
And he was all togged out.
I said, "Excuse me, but I'd really like to know
What this is all about.
You're over-dressed, you're absurd!"
He answered, "Haven't you heard?

"I'm dining with Elsa, with Elsa, supreme.
I'm going to meet Princesses
Wearing 'Coco Chanel' dresses,
Going wild over strawberries and cream,
I've got Bromo Seltzer
To take when dinner ends,
For I'm dining with Elsa
And her ninety-nine most intimate friends!"'

After the Bullingdon dance she departed for London, but not before she had invited me to a party the following Tuesday.

The Oxford house-party seemed a trifle flattened after she had left, a hazy indecisiveness hung about it, as though it were just coming to after an anaesthetic. But by the next day it had regained its normal composure, and proceeded pleasantly, with various diversions, to the end of the week.

4

Elsa's party was great fun, with social and Bohemian graces tactfully mixed.

Dorothy Fellows-Gordon – 'Dickie,' a lifelong friend of Elsa's – was there, tall, nice-looking, with jet-black hair and a lovely singing voice. Later on in the evening, when I was sitting talking to her in a corner, Elsa came over and joined us, and after they had both exchanged significant raised-eyebrow looks, Elsa said that they had a little proposition to make to me and that on no account was I to be offended. I couldn't imagine what on earth she was driving at, and so I laughed nervously and said that I was never offended at anything. Then she explained that she and Dickie were going for two weeks to Venice, and wanted me to go with them as their guest. She added, as a palliative to my wounded honour, that they would feel far more comfortable with a man to look after them and that I would really be doing them a great favour if I would consent.

I saw through this in a minute. I knew perfectly well that they didn't in the least need anyone to look after them, but were only trying to gloss over for me the unmentionable horror of having my expenses paid by two defenceless women. But it was sweet and sympathetic of them, and they did it beautifully. Obviously I accepted with enthusiasm and a few days later travelled over to Paris to join them.

None of us had ever been to Venice before, and the first sight of it as we walked down the station steps into a gondola, sent us all off into a clamour of excitement. Elsa led, of course. Propped up against a cushion in the back seat, she let forth a stream of enthusiasm into the gathering dusk. Superlatives flew through the air, ricochetting off mouldering Palazzos and plopping into the water, as we swept under dark little bridges, swirled round sharp corners, and finally debouched on to the Grand Canal.

We were lucky that first evening. The air was clear and pure. A 'Serenata' passed close by us on its way to the lagoon, already lit with coloured lanterns and crammed to the gunwales with stout little tenors wearing white shirts and coloured sashes. One of them was tuning a guitar, another strummed absently on a small portable piano. Our gondoliers gave sharp atmospheric cries, and the sun set considerately as we arrived at the hotel, plunging the whole scene into a misty Turneresque beauty that robbed even Elsa of further adjectives.

That was certainly a glamorous fortnight. The loveliness of Venice alone would have been enough. The strange decayed magic of old palaces rising out of green canals, the dim archways, the remote misty lagoons stretching away behind the town towards Mestre. The brilliance and warm colour of the piazza in the evenings, a military band playing chirrupy selections from Verdi, gay crowds of people passing endlessly up and down through the arcades.

All this would have enraptured a far less impressionable mind than mine, and I could have returned home happily with such memories. More happily, perhaps, without the very different memories of the Lido and the myriads of feuds and scandals and small social rumpuses which took place there daily.

I found a few new friends – Muriel Draper, with plastered straw-coloured hair and full scarlet lips; Blanche Barrymore, with farouche Byronic locks flowing in the breeze and long billowing cloaks; and Mrs Spears, a small attractive woman with deep sleepy eyes and a rather nervous smile, who said that she had completed a novel which was to be published soon, and was to be called *Jane – Our Stranger.* She omitted to tell me that her pen name was Mary Borden and so I visualised a light, slightly 'jejune' little book written to pass the time, and dealing, probably amateurishly, with the adventures of some winsome housemaid.

When I finally left Venice in order to get back to London for rehearsals of *The Young Idea,* Dickie and Elsa stayed behind for an extra week. They insisted, however, upon giving me my ticket and seeing me off at the station. I hung out of the window for a long while watching Elsa's little bobbing figure growing smaller and smaller until it seemed to dissolve into the grey platform, and reflecting that the life of a gigolo, unimpaired by amatory obligations, could undoubtedly be very delightful indeed.

5

We rehearsed *The Young Idea* in hot, smelly rehearsal rooms, and later in cool empty theatres. I felt as nervous at first as if I had never acted before. Robert Courtneidge, although milder than in the old days, could still be scarifying, and I had the uncomfortable conviction all the time that he still disapproved of my playing the part. It was typical of his generosity, however, to take me aside a few days before we opened and tell me that he had been entirely wrong and that I was giving an excellent performance. Actually I believe that his kindness overstepped the truth. Perhaps I may have been better than he thought I was going to be, but I was a long way from giving a really good performance.

There was certainly an improvement in my acting since *I'll Leave it to You,* but I was still forcing points too much and giving knowing grimaces when delivering comedy lines. I had not learned then not to superimpose upon witty dialogue the top-heavy burden of personal mannerisms. In this instance, of course, I was both author and actor, and the former suffered considerably from the antics and overemphasis of the latter.

The play opened at Bristol. The notices and business were both good, and we settled down complacently for a pleasant little tour.

On returning to London I had a long talk with Courtneidge, who said that although there was no immediate chance of getting a theatre, it might be possible to find a suitable one after Christmas when the pantomime and fairy-play rush was over. And so, faced with November fogs and at least two months of idleness, I decided on another little excursion to foreign parts.

Ned Lathom, I knew, was in Davos recovering from his first bout of T.B. I also knew that he had only his sister Barbara with him, and that they both would be probably pleased to see me, so I sent him a telegram and waited hopefully for the reply. It was comfortingly enthusiastic, so after buying a few sweaters, thick socks and breeches, off I went; second-class on the trains, but first-class on the boat, arriving the next day, my eyes dazzled by leagues of white snow in strong sunlight and my ears pleasantly humming in the high altitude to the jingling of sleigh bells.

Ned looked better, but he still had coughing-fits from time to time. He managed, as usual, to be amazingly luxurious and had surrounded himself with books, cushions and large rich sweets which, I am sure, were bad for him.

I stayed there for three weeks with Barbara and him alone before anyone else arrived. The Christmas season had not yet begun, and the only other occupants of the hotel were T.B. patients, all in various stages of the disease. It was a strange life, gay in the evenings, when everyone made an effort to dress, dine in the restaurant and dance afterwards in the bar. During the days, of course, everybody had cures and treatments to undergo, and the whole hotel seemed dead and empty. At night, however, it regularly awoke. The gambling machine in the bar tinkled merrily, the band played, and there was the sound of corks popping and noisy conversation in many languages. Only very occasionally would someone slip away from the fun to flit upstairs, coughing, almost furtively, into a stained handkerchief.

Those evenings, with their noise and music and gaiety, were slightly macabre, but somehow not depressing. It was as though they were unrelated to ordinary existence – a few detached hours of pleasure, floating between life and death, untouchable by the sadness of either. The knowledge that practically everybody present, themselves included, would probably be dead within a year or so was, I suppose, tucked away behind the laughter of most of the people there, but it was in no way apparent. There seemed to be no strain in the air, no eager snatching at flying moments. Perhaps the disease itself carried with it a compensating illusion that ultimate cure was certain, that all the slow tedious intricate process of dying was nothing more than an interlude of small discomfort.

Ned, who had always been badly stage-struck, had financed Charlot's last revue *A to Z,* and still appeared to be avid for punishment. He made me play to him all the songs I had written, and when he realised that there were enough comparatively good ones to make up a score, he wired to Charlot commanding him to come out immediately. I was thrilled at the thought of doing a whole revue, but scared that Charlot, when he arrived, might not be quite as eager and appreciative as Ned. However, when he did arrive in due course he was expansive and benign, and a series of cigar-laden conferences ensued, during which *London Calling* was born.

I worked on sketches in the mornings, waking early when the clouds were still veiling the mountains, submitted them to Ned and Charlot in the afternoons, and within the space of a few days the whole plan of the show was roughly laid out. It was to be produced the following autumn, with Gertrude Lawrence, Maisie Gay, a comedienne as yet undecided, and myself.

Charlot took me aside and told me that he would be unable to pay me more than fifteen pounds a week, as I was inexperienced in revue work, but that as I was bound to make a great deal of money out of royalties I was not to worry about it. I didn't worry about it at the time as I was too occupied with the show as a whole, but later I gave it a certain amount of thought. Charlot went back to England, seemingly pleased with everything, and left Ned and Barbara and me in a ferment of excitement.

Christmas pounced on Davos and everything lit up. Trainloads of strange people arrived daily. A whole extra wing of the hotel was thrown open. The Kurhaus, down in the village, surprisingly produced a highly decorated bar and a jazz band. The whole place became, with abrupt thoroughness, a resort. Ned's Christmas guests, it is unnecessary to remark, were far and away the star turn of the hotel.

In order of appearance, rather than precedence, they consisted of: Clifton Webb, Mrs Fred (Teddie) Thompson, Gladys Cooper, Dick Wyndham, Edward Molyneux, Bobbie Howard, Dickie Gordon, Elsa Maxwell and Maxine Elliott. From their advent onwards life was less peaceful but certainly more stimulating. We went on tailing parties, stringing out in a long line of sleds behind a large sleigh in which Elsa sat screaming like a banshee. We went on skating parties, Swedish Punch parties and lugeing parties. In course of one of these, quite unintentionally, I got caught up in a time test race, and to my amazement on reaching the bottom was presented with a small silver cup. Apparently I came down the two and a quarter miles in just under four minutes, not, let it be understood, because I had the least desire to do so, but because, owing to the whole run having been rebanked and iced since Barbara and I had been on it, I was completely unable to stop myself.

Gladys Cooper took a marked dislike to me, and we had several acrid tussles, notably at a lunch party at the Kurhaus, where she remarked in a tone of maddening superiority that it was ridiculous of me to go on writing plays that were never produced, and that why on earth I didn't collaborate with someone who really knew the job, she couldn't understand.

I replied that as Shaw, Barrie and Maugham didn't collaborate I saw no reason why I should. Whereupon she laughed, not without reason, and said that she had never heard of such conceit in her life and that she might just as well compare herself to Duse or Bernhardt. I jumped in here quickly on cue and retorted that the difference was not quite as fantastic as that. After which the lunch continued amid slightly nervous hilarity.

Oddly enough, after this preliminary blood-letting, Gladys and I parted glowing with mutual affection, and the glow has strengthened through the years, with never so much as a breath of disharmony.

6

The Young Idea opened at the Savoy Theatre in February to even more enthusiasm than had greeted *I'll Leave it to You.*

The play proceeded smoothly and at the end I made my usual self-deprecatory speech with a modesty which was rapidly becoming metallic, but which had the desired effect of lashing the audience to further ecstasies, and when the curtain had fallen we all rejoiced appropriately, although my personal satisfaction was edged with wariness. I remembered the effusions of the first night of *I'll Leave it to You* – the kindly intentioned but over-optimistic voices which had dinned into my ears that it was 'marvellous' and 'divine' and would undoubtedly 'run a year,' and decided, before giving way completely to triumph, to bide my time until I saw the returns on Saturday night. In this I turned out to be wise, for in spite of excellent press notices and a deluge of superlatives from my acquaintances, the play folded up at the end of eight weeks.

But although brief, where the company was concerned it was a happy run. There were, of course, a number of the usual rumours that business was steadily going up or that we were to be transferred to a smaller and more intimate theatre, or that a friend of Muriel Pope's had heard from a friend of hers in Keith Prowse that the libraries were about to take up a big deal stretching right into May. But being on a royalty basis, I saw the returns every night and was able to watch without illusion, the sinister little figures growing weekly smaller and smaller until ultimately, after a sad but sympathetic conversation with Courtneidge, the fatal fortnight's notice was pinned up on the board.

Nevertheless, *The Young Idea* was one more step achieved and several perquisites accrued from it, among them the sale of the publication and amateur rights to Samuel French, and a letter of the most generous praise from Mr Charles Blake Cochran.

A few days later I lunched with him at the Berkeley, flushed with perfectly chosen wine and still more perfectly chosen words of encouragement. I don't remember any premonition sitting behind my chair and nudging me into realisation that this was the first of an endless procession of similar lunches that dotted through future years, that hundreds of restaurant tables, bottles of hock and *entrecôtes minutes* were waiting for us. It only seemed an extremely pleasant hour, significant because I hoped that he might be persuaded to produce a play of mine one day.

Meanwhile things were not going so badly. Mother had returned to Ebury Street from St Mary's, happier and in better health than she had been for a long time. She occasionally snatched the reins of management from Father and after a salutary crack or two with the whip, handed them back again so that the house jogged along amicably enough, like a dreary old family coach with Auntie Vida as a diminutive postilion hopping down every now and then to open the door for the lodgers.

When *The Young Idea* closed I went off to join Gladys Calthrop and Mrs Cooper at Cap Ferrat, where the latter had rented a villa.

It was a nice villa and the view from it was charming, but its peace and plenty were somewhat soured for Gladys and me by the presence of a Dominican Prior to whom Mrs Cooper was devoted, but who took a bleak dislike to us on sight. We bore his disapproval for as long as we could, and then, realising that our being there was not only making things uncomfortable for Mrs Cooper and for him but for ourselves as well, we departed in a deluge of Riviera rain for Italy.

We had very little money but it was a gay excursion and in due course we returned to Mrs Cooper and found to our horror that the Prior was still there. But this time we outstayed him and the rest of the holiday was peaceful and without incident.

7

In May a one-act comedy that I had written a year before was produced by the London Grand Guignol at the Little Theatre. It was called *The Better Half,* and was wittily played by Auriol Lee. In spite of this it was received with apathy; I think, possibly, because it was a satire and too flippant in atmosphere after the full-blooded horrors that had gone before it. Nevertheless it was quite well written and served the purpose, if only for a little, of keeping my name before the public. Meanwhile Ned was back from Davos, much improved in health and already beginning to dissipate the effects of his cure by giving the rich lunches, dinners and supper parties that he loved so much. With his return the preparations for the revue were resumed. The date was set, the title *London Calling* was set, and the cast was set, that is, with the notable exception of the leading juvenile. This state of affairs was brought about by my stubborn and unaccountable refusal to play it. At any rate it seemed unaccountable to those who had not been present during my brief fifteen-pound-a-week discussion with Charlot at Davos.

It had been arranged at the conference that I was to share the writing of the book with Ronald Jeans and the composing of the music with Philip Braham. This, although disappointing to me at first, I finally accepted as being a wise decision, as to do a whole show might have proved too heavy a burden on my inexperience. Also, during the conferences I had been unable to avoid noticing the fat and satisfying salaries that were to be received by Gertie Lawrence, Tubby Edlin and Maisie Gay, and the vision of myself, as the fourth of the quartette, earning five pounds a week less than I had received in both *I'll Leave it to You* and *The Young Idea* seemed unattractive. In consequence I announced (for which may God forgive me) that to appear in a musical show would injure irreparably my prestige as a straight actor.

After little argument my decision was accepted, but having in my contract as author a clause to the effect that I was to be consulted as to cast, I was able to raise the adequate objections to the name of every juvenile suggested, until ultimately, after many weeks' wear and tear, I allowed myself to be persuaded to change my mind.

This time my business conversation with Charlot was even briefer, but much more to the point, resulting in a salary of forty pounds a week and an additional clause permitting me to leave the cast at the end of six months if I wished.

Now I had ample time for misgivings. My dancing was rusty, but of course that could be remedied by hard practice. (My singing was rustier, and I feared could not be remedied by all the practice in the world.) However, I persuaded Fred Astaire, who was playing in *Stop Flirting*, to coach me privately, which he did with unending patience and not too frightful results.

Amid the hurly-burly of countless Charlot productions there had lived and breathed and strummed, for many years, a small sharp-eyed woman named Elsie April, whose mastery of musical technique was miraculous. She could transfer melody and harmony on to paper with the swiftness of an expert shorthand stenographer. Her physical endurance, too, was staggering. She could sit at the piano through the longest rehearsals, the most tedious auditions, seldom, if ever, playing a wrong note and only demanding for sustenance an occasional cup of tea.

When I had been working with her for some time I asked her why it was that she continued to lavish her musical talent and experience on the work of others and never composed anything herself. Her reply was evasive, 'Well, dear, I never seem to have any time.'

London Calling for me was certainly a gold mine of future alliances, for in addition to Elsie there was Dan O'Neil, the assistant stage-manager. Early on in rehearsals we all found ourselves relying upon him for everything. If any props were missing, it was Danny who restored them. If there was an untraceable draught, it was Danny who discovered a window open high up in the flies and closed it. If there was a noise at the side during a quiet scene, it was Danny who silenced it. And, above all, when we were tired after rehearsing all day and most of the night, feeling discouraged and certain to the depths of our souls that the whole thing was going to be a failure, it was Danny who invariably cheered us.

The dress rehearsals of *London Calling* were hectic, and the general frenzy was in no way mitigated by the frequent appearances of Ned in the stalls, accompanied by a few gay but critical friends. True he thoughtfully brought champagne and chocolates as a rule, but our insides were too twisted with nerves to be able to respond suitably to luxuries.

Gertie and I clutched each other in corners and listened morosely to 'Pa' Braham shouting staccato instructions to the orchestra, to Carrie Graham, the ballet mistress, haranguing the chorus girls, to Maisie Gay moaning that her material was the least funny that she had yet encountered in a long and varied career, to Edward Molyneux's quiet but deadly disapproval of the way the show girls were wearing his dresses, and to the show girls' equally deadly but less quiet disapproval of the dresses themselves. The only person who seemed to be completely peaceful and at ease was Charlot, who sat with Ned and his friends in the stalls and seldom raised his voice.

At last, however, we actually opened, oddly enough, with a matinée, according to an eccentric whim of Charlot's which, nevertheless, had a certain amount of common sense to it. He figured that as we were all tired, a matinée, which didn't matter very much, would tire us just so much more and ensure us playing the first night entirely on our nerves. In this he was perfectly right.

We did. We flagellated ourselves into giving a remarkably slick and good performance.

The hits of the show were primarily Maisie's singing of 'What Love Means to Girls Like Me,' and her performance of Hernia Whittlebot, my little burlesque on the Sitwells. Next in order of applause came Gertie singing 'Carrie,' and the duet, 'You Were Meant for Me,' which she and I did together, with a dance arranged by Fred Astaire.

Gertie sang 'Parisian Pierrot' exquisitely, and Edward had made it one of the loveliest stage pictures I have ever seen. Then there was Maisie as a tired soubrette singing 'Life in the Old Girl Yet.'

The only complete and glorious failure of the whole show was my performance of a single number. 'Sentiment,' which had gone so well at the dress-rehearsal and been so enthusiastically applauded by the friendly company in the stalls, that I bounded on at the opening performance fully confident that I was going to bring the house down. It certainly wasn't from want of trying that I didn't. I was immaculately dressed in tails, with a silk hat and a cane. I sang every witty couplet with perfect diction and a wealth of implication which sent them winging out into the dark auditorium, where they fell wetly, like pennies into mud. After this, discouraged but not quite despairing, I executed an intricate dance, painstakingly sweated over by Fred Astaire, tapping, after-beating, whacking my cane on the stage, and finally exiting to a spatter of applause led, I suspected, by Mother and Gladys.

Unfortunately the number could not be taken out, owing to the running order of the revue, and so nightly the audience and I were forced to endure it.

The revue was a tremendous success, and the Press notices, although a bit pernickety and fault-finding, were excellent from the point of view of box office. They were almost unanimous over one thing, however, and that was that I should never have been allowed to appear in it.

During the first two weeks of the run, I received, to my intense surprise, a cross letter from Osbert Sitwell; in fact, so angry was it, that I first of all imagined it to be a joke. However, it was far from being a joke, and shortly afterwards another letter arrived, even crosser than the first. To this day I am still a little puzzled as to why that light-hearted burlesque should have aroused him, his brother and his sister to such paroxysms of fury. But the fact remains that it did, and I believe still does.

Soon after *London Calling* was launched, Charlot became immersed in preparations for a revue which was to be produced in partnership with Archie Selwyn in New York. This was to be a conglomeration of all the best numbers and sketches from the Charlot shows of the last few years, and in it were to be starred Beatrice Lillie, Jack Buchanan and, much to my horror, Gertrude Lawrence. This obviously meant that she would be only able to stay in *London Calling* for, at most, three months, as the new company was to sail almost immediately after Christmas.

In addition to this serious loss, we soon learned that we were also to be deprived of Danny, Carrie Graham, and several of our best chorus and small-part girls. I could only hope that it was a comfort to Ned and the other wretched backers to feel that they still had Maisie Gay, Tubby Edlin, me and the scenery.

On account of this strange managerial juggling with success, the show began to deteriorate after the first three months, and although it ran for almost a year, it continued to deteriorate by leaps and bounds under the burden of successive new editions.

When Gertie left, Joyce Barbour took her place, and Charlot sailed away to America with his troupe, leaving us completely to our own devices. We continued, however, playing to more or less adequate business until his return in February, when he decided to plan still another new edition.

This time the revue was almost entirely reconstructed. Tubby Edlin left, and A. W. Baskcomb was engaged. Teddie Gerrard came in with a vague manner, and several diamond bracelets. I decided to leave the cast too. My six months were up, in fact I had played almost seven, and I had a longing to go to America again.

It was considered by some people to be very foolish of me to chuck up a forty-pound-a-week job, merely to satisfy my mania for travel and change, but to me it wasn't foolish at all. It was the result of careful thought.

To remain hopping about in a revue for which all my spontaneous enthusiasm had died ages ago, only for the sake of the salary, seemed to be a static, overcautious policy. I felt, sincerely enough, that my creative impulse was suffering from the monotony of eight performances a week, and although during the run I had managed to write two full-length plays, *Fallen Angels* and *The Vortex,* I was far from satisfied.

I was convinced that new experiences and inspirations and ideas were waiting for me, far away from the Duke of York's Theatre, Ebury Street, and the Ivy, and I felt that there was no time to waste, as the future was drawing near and I was already twenty-four.

8

I sailed for New York on the *Olympic* in Februray, enjoying to the full the contrast in circumstances between this and my first voyage on the *Aquitania* three years before. I had a comfortable cabin; took my meals in the Ritz restaurant; accepted small extra attentions from the ship's personnel as tributes to my fame which, although far from assured, had at least been enough to procure me a dignified pose for the White Star Line photographer at Waterloo, and an enquiry as to my American plans by the Press reporter at Southampton.

I had no premonition of what the year would bring. No seer had whispered that by the end of it I would be catapulted into real notoriety. I was pleased with the way things were going, and I had two hundred and fifty pounds to spend. Mother was well and happy; before leaving I had rented for her a cottage at Dockenfield, near Farnham in Surrey. True, we had taken it rather impulsively in a thick January fog which, when the lease was signed, lifted to disclose several villas in the too immediate vicinity. But still, it was country and cost only forty pounds a year.

I could look back cheerfully on the last six months and reflect with a certain irony how odd it was that my first two plays *I'll Leave it to You* and *The Young Idea,* having been praised almost unanimously by the critics, had failed, whereas *London Calling,* which had received only scant appreciation from them, had been a big success. The houses had been packed at every performance for the first three months. Society, with jewels and sables and white shirt-fronts, had come and come again, occasionally overflowing in driblets through the Pass door and trickling in and out of the dressing-rooms. I had observed the curious attitude of the *soi-distant* smart set towards a successful musical show, an attitude which is special and apart, and has nothing in common with that of ordinary straight playgoers. It is patronising, of course, to a certain degree, but not consciously nor disagreeably so; unaware of anything but the gay aspects of the performance and anxious to participate a little, at any rate to the extent of using Christian names and referring to 'Numbers' rather than 'Songs.' They have, these back-stage explorers, naturally no suspicion that it is a privilege for them to be there at all. They have paid for their seats, and, like children at a circus, they find it enjoyable to feed the animals afterwards. As a new animal I received many surprising visitors in my cage and learned quickly to do the little tricks that were expected of me.

London Calling had done a lot for me. For the first time I had experienced the thrill of hearing my own music played in restaurants. Also for the first time I had had the pleasure of seeing my name in electric lights outside a theatre. True, Maisie's and Gertie's names were on the best side of the sign facing down St Martin's Lane towards Trafalgar Square, while Tubby Edlin's and mine were visible only to pedestrians approaching from the direction of Seven Dials, but still there it was, 'Noel Coward' in gleaming pink bulbs, and never failed to please me every time I looked up at it, which was often.

Nineteen-twenty-four appears so far away now, much farther than earlier years. My vision of myself at eight and twelve and sixteen is clear, but at twenty-four I seem shadowy. I know how I looked, of course. The stage photographs show me in neat over-waisted suits, in pyjamas and dressing-gowns, and one in fanciful Russian dress with boots and a fur hat. My face was plumper and less lined than it is now, and my figure was good but a little weedy. Of what was going on inside me, however, there was no indication. There seems an emptiness somewhere, a blandness of expression in the eyes. There is little aggressiveness in the arranged smiles and no impatience apparent at all, and in this the cameras must have lied, for I have always been impatient. Nowadays there is more truth in my photographs. I hope there is more truth in me, too.

9

New York was still decorated with the remains of a blizzard as the *Olympic* steamed up the river. Everything was black and dirty grey; the New Jersey cliffs looked sinister, and white smoke from the ships lay heavily like clouds over the harbour. Nobody met me, which didn't matter, as I had had a wire from Jeffery at quarantine saying that he was busy on a job (*New York World*), had seats for *Rain* and would call for me at the Ritz. There was no disappointment anywhere that evening. Jeffery arrived, we dined and went to *Rain*. Jeanne Eagels had got us the management's seats in the second row. From the moment that she made her first entrance in those bedraggled trashy clothes and spoke her first lines, I knew from the timbre of her tough voice and the sullen slouch of her body that we were going to see great acting, and I was right. After we had been back-stage to see Jeanne we went to the Algonquin, for old time's sake, and had supper. Jeffery was now a full-fledged reporter on the *World* and had 'covered' a great deal of Life and Death in the raw. After his first spate was exhausted I managed tactfully to erase some of the bloodstains from his conversation and supper became more appetising.

I went home to the Ritz pleasantly tired and accepted the soft pink carpets, gold elevator doors and the general sense of rich comfort, almost as though it were all my usual background. Almost, but not quite. My small two-dollar-fifty room at the Brevoort was only two years away, still in sight and mind. I planned to revisit it soon, probably the next day. I meant to go to Washington Square, too, and sit on my old bench, jumping back for a little into loneliness and poverty, but this time with no sting of reality in it. The well-sprung mattress received me graciously, and I remember thinking just before I dropped off to sleep how sad it would be to have had Ritzes always and been denied the keen pleasure of earning them.

When I saw the bill at the end of the first week, however, I discovered that my grandeur had been both incautious and premature, and I moved hastily into Lester Donahue's flat in East 32nd Street and slept on a couch in the sitting-room. We had great fun in that little flat and gave several select cocktail parties, but I kept the Ritz as my address, feeling that as the gesture had been made it would be foolish to allow it to appear too short-lived.

The month passed swiftly with no miseries and anxieties to keep me awake at nights. It was a real holiday. I went to plays in the best seats. I experienced the mixed pain and pleasure of seeing Jack Buchanan bring the house down in the Charlot revue singing 'Sentiment,' watching to see why he should succeed so triumphantly where I had failed, and finding at first no adequate reason, except perhaps that it was because he apparently made no effort at all. It wasn't until later that I acknowledged to myself in secret that the truth of the matter was that his whole technique was superior to mine.

It was thrilling to see the three of them, Gertie Lawrence, Beatrice Lillie and Jack Buchanan hailed as great stars by the whole of New York. It invested them, for me, with a new glamour, as though I were discovering them too, and had never seen them before in my life. The appreciation of American audiences certainly gave an extra fillip to their performances. There was a shine on all of them, a happy gratification bursting through. I could swear that they had none of them ever been so good before.

I spent a lot of time with Lynn and Alfred, who were now married and living in a comfortable greenish apartment on Lexington Avenue. Lynn was just finishing a successful run of a comedy called *In Love with Love*. She was gay and attractive in it, utterly different from 'Dulcy' which had been a bleating, essentially comic characterisation. In *In Love with Love* she also began to be beautiful. There was a new fullness in her figure and her movements were smoother. She wore a pale pink dress in one scene which gave a warm glow to her skin, and when I noticed how she used her eyes and hands I suspected Alfred of rehearsing her in sex appeal. I think happiness and security had a lot to do with it, too. I have never known two people so happy together as the Lunts. If their whole-hearted engrossment in each other occasionally makes them a trifle remote from other people, so much the better. They could never be remote from real friendship.

Alfred was playing in *Outward Bound.* It was the first time I had ever seen him on the stage, and when I visited him in his dressing-room afterwards he went through all his hoops. I know those hoops so well now, that I can hear the paper crackling in anticipation before he dives through the first one; but then it was a surprise to me, rather a painful surprise. I had been deeply moved by his performance and was still feeling wrought up. I explained this to him from my heart, but no gleam of pleasure came into his rolling tragic eyes. He mowed down my praise with bitter self-recrimination. I had, he said, been privileged to see him give far and away the worst performance of his career. He had over-played, over-emotionalised, and used every ham trick that had ever been invented. Nothing I said could convince him to the contrary. At supper afterwards I observed that Lynn was unmoved by his despair. She said: 'Never mind, darling, you gave a lovely performance last Thursday matinée,' and went on with her scrambled eggs.

It must not be imagined that Alfred's dressing-room miseries are unreal or affected. His wretchedness, for the moment, is completely genuine, a nervous reaction from having tried too hard for perfection: an actor's disease from which we all suffer from time to time, although few can plumb the depths so whole-heartedly as he does.

In *Design for Living* we all three gave the worst performances of our career every night together for months, and managed to be very good indeed.

I found the personality of New York completely changed by winter. The sun, although brilliant enough, was detached and without warmth. Freezing winds whipped round the corners, and the buildings took on a knife-edged sharpness, casting shadows that looked as though they had been cut out of black paper. Park Avenue and Fifth Avenue were of course immaculate, but in many of the streets snow was still piled up in dirty mounds on the sidewalks. The hotels, the houses, the theatres and even the taxis were over-heated. The sensation of undressing in luxurious warmth, opening the window the last second before getting into bed, and feeling the icy fresh air swirling into the room was delicious. I could recall without regret the airless nights in Washington Square, and the dead oppressive days when the whole city shimmered in heat haze and the sun drained all colour from everything, softening the asphalt pavements into squelching rubber sponges, and cooking up the well-known champagne air until it felt like hot soup in the lungs.

I found several new friends, and together with them and some of my older ones I whirled through parties and trips to Harlem, and week-ends in the country. There were the Janis's, Eva Le Gallienne, Ethel Barrymore, the Kaufmans, Woollcott and many others. Among the new ones was Neysa McMein; beautiful, untidy, casual, and too difficult to know in a short month. I had actually met her during my first visit, and I think I found her rather tiresome. I was even more hasty in my judgments in those days than I am now, and as frequently inaccurate. I remembered having been taken to her studio a couple of times, where I had met a miscellaneous selection of models, journalists, actors and Vanderbilts, swimming round and in and out like rather puzzled fish in a dusty aquarium. Neysa paid little or no attention to anyone except when they arrived or left, when, with a sudden spurt of social conscience, she would ram a paint-brush into her mouth and shake hands with a kind of dishevelled politeness.

I was too inexperienced and edgy then to appreciate properly her unique talent for living, but I can salute it now.

It was at the Hartley Manners' house that I met Douglas Fairbanks and Mary Pickford. This was a big thrill, particularly as they were both charming to me. I discovered that we were sailing together on the *Olympic,* and my mind busied itself with secret plans to get to know them well. I was at that period a bad celebrity snob. Whether it was sheer undiluted snobbishness, or just part of my devouring ambition to become a celebrity myself I don't know, at any rate it was a strong passion and at least the memory of it has induced in me a quite admirable tolerance in my own dealings with lion-hunters. There is, I think, a real pleasure in reflected glory. I enjoyed it then tremendously and I enjoy it still. There is a technique to it, too. My method was always a careless indifference, so studied and practised that it could leave no doubt whatever in anybody's mind as to my easy intimacy with the object of the crowd's admiration. Other methods also can be equally successful, such as boorish irritation which I have seen used by stronger types with excellent effect – a let's-get-away-from-these-damn-fools-as-quickly-as-possible expression, apparent only when the chances of getting away are slight. With Douglas and Mary in 1924 any acquaintance of theirs could be surfeited with reflected mass-worship very swiftly. They were unable to go in or out of restaurants or theatres or hotels without dense hordes of people clamouring round them. Indeed, on the day that the *Olympic* was due to sail, the White Star Line had the forethought to send special warnings to all the passengers advising them to be on board at least two hours early. We sailed at midnight and I remember standing on deck (with Mary and Douglas, of course) as the ship moved slowly out into the river, and watching that vast sea of faces staring up from the lighted dock; hundreds of rows of pallid discs with black smudges on them where mouths were hanging open. It was an exhilarating sight, and I felt myself proudly to be the focusing point of a myriad sharp envies.

Much the same sort of thing occurred when we arrived at Southampton. The dock was black with people; so was the customs house and the station platform. Some hardy spirits actually sprinted along by the side of the train when it left, until at last the quickening pace caused them to fall back breathless, but still waving their arms like clockwork puppets that are beginning to run down a little.

Richard and Jean Norton had also been on the ship, and had planned a party for the Fairbanks to meet the Prince of Wales a few nights after their arrival in London. When they invited me too, my acceptance was so exquisitely casual that I am quite sure that it betrayed to them my obvious delight. However, I went and enjoyed it, although I must admit I suffered a little from strain afterwards. I remember that Douglas did a lot of conjuring tricks, a habit to which he was then, and still is, a keen addict, and that the Prince of Wales threw me into a frenzy by asking me to play a tune that I couldn't remember. Apart from these minor disadvantages the evening went with a swing.

10

London seemed dim to me on my return. I had not been away long enough to have missed it. Apart from seeing the family, Gladys and a few others, there was no thrill in my arrival. The weather was damp and the whole town looked sullen, as though it were cross about something. New York was hard and clear in my mind like a diamond, unsmudged as a memory by any sentimental glamour, but sharp with efficiency, strenuous ambition and achievement, in fact all the qualities that I felt were necessary to me at that time. I felt I knew London too well and had toiled in it too long, with no prospect of unexpected adventures or sudden surprises lurking round its gentle corners. It gave me a sense of frustration and a bad cold. I went to a few theatres and was irritated by both the actors and the audiences, the former lackadaisical and the latter apathetic. *London Calling* was still running, and there was an even worse air of dreariness over that. The company ambled through the show, the fade-outs and black-outs were untidy, and the smart Molyneux dresses looked as though they had been used to wrap up hot-water-bottles. I talked to Charlot about pepping it up a bit, but he wasn't interested, his mind being obviously occupied with more important plans, and so I went down to our cottage in Dockenfield and gave myself up to my cold. When this passed, my depression passed with it, and I wrote *Hay Fever*. The idea came to me suddenly in the garden, and I finished it in about three days, a fact which later on, when I had become news value, seemed to excite gossip-writers inordinately, although why the public should care whether a play takes three days or three years to write I shall never understand. Perhaps they don't. However, when I had finished it and had it neatly typed and bound up, I read it through and was rather unimpressed with it. This was an odd sensation for me, as in those days I was almost always enchanted with everything I wrote. I knew certain scenes were good, especially the breakfast scene in the last act, and the dialogue between the giggling flapper and the diplomat in the first act, but apart from these it seemed to me a little tedious. I think that the reason for this was that I was passing through a transition stage as a writer; my dialogue was becoming more natural and less elaborate, and I was beginning to concentrate more on the comedy values of situation rather than the comedy values of actual lines. I expect that when I read through *Hay Fever* that first time, I was subconsciously bemoaning its lack of snappy epigrams. At any rate I thought well enough of it to consider it a good vehicle for Marie Tempest, and so I took it up to London to read it to her. Both she and Willie Graham-Browne were kind and courteous as usual, and listened with careful attention, but when I had finished they both agreed with me that it was too light and plotless and generally lacking in action, and so back I went to the country again and wrote *Easy Virtue*. On this I worked hard and thought it excellent. I fully realised its similarity of theme to *The Second Mrs Tanqueray*, but the construction and characterisation on the whole seemed to me to be more mature and balanced than anything I had written up to date. The critics, later on, didn't agree with me, but by the time it came to their attention I was in too good a position to care. Meanwhile *The Vortex* and *Fallen Angels* were voyaging disconsolately in and out of most of the London managers' offices. H. M. Harwood at least displayed enough interest to say that he might consider producing *The Vortex* at the Ambassador's, providing that I did not play the part of 'Nicky' myself, but as one of my principal objects in writing the play had been to give myself a first-rate opportunity for dramatic acting, I refused his offer.

I had a much more hopeful nibble from Gladys Cooper, who wanted to play *Fallen Angels* with Madge Titheradge. They were both enthusiastic, and I, of course, was delighted. However, it all fell through during the next few months, more or less painlessly. Gladys had contracts to fulfil, so had Madge. When Gladys was going to be free, Madge was tied up, and vice versa, until everybody's interest and excitement died wearily, and *Fallen Angels* joined *Hay Fever* in oblivion.

Life in the Dockenfield cottage was pleasant but cramped. There was Mother and Auntie Vida, occasionally Father or Eric, and Gladys and me. I forget now where we all slept, but I do remember that no nocturnal cough nor sneeze nor digestive rumble went up unnoticed by any of us. We had a gentle wistful girl to help with the housework. Her name was Iris, and she meandered through the days in a sort of anaemic dream, from which she occasionally awoke to catch the afternoon bus for Farnham. Gladys and I drove about the countryside in a fast red tin bath which I had bought at the motor show. We visited, every now and then, acquaintances in the neighbourhood, among them one rather pompous family. Their name escapes me at the moment, but they were over-grand, and their house was large and ugly. It was filled with silver teapots, family paintings, tennis racquets, young people in flannels, sporting and hunting prints, mackintoshes, golf clubs, tweed coats, pipe-racks, and huge truculent cakes. I still retain a certain bitterness towards them, knowing that they were of the type that would fawn upon me now, and remembering how distantly, insufferably polite they were to me then. Mrs Whatever-her-name-was was quite palpably convinced to the depths of her Christian soul that Gladys and I were conducting a furtive, illicit honeymoon just a few miles away across the fields. No amount of references to Mother or Auntie Vida could budge her suspicions; I saw them in her eyes, eager and lascivious as they flickered at us over the tea-table. We left, thankfully, as soon as we could, feeling thoroughly uncomfortable and almost expecting Mother to greet us blind drunk in a dirty kimono.

II

In July I had a letter from Ruby Melville inviting me to stay with her in Deauville. Money was getting low again, but as I had enough to pay my fare, with a little over for expenses, I decided to go. So many of my earlier days seem to have been spent in a state of extreme penury among the very rich; Deauville couldn't have been smarter or wealthier or more fashionable than it was that year, at the height of its damp summer season. Nor could I have chosen a more thoroughly unsuitable place for a holiday, considering that I had about thirty pounds in the bank and no definite contracts to look forward to. However, I enjoyed myself watching people lose thousands at baccarat, and inventing thrilling dreams in which I suddenly found a mille-franc plaque under somebody's chair, sat down immediately at the big table, and in the course of a few hours won a vast fortune amid an envious crowd of onlookers. The dreams varied in superficial detail, but the climax was always the same.

A polo-playing friend of Ruby's lent us ponies and we rode them daily up and down the sands, borrowed riding-breeches spoiling for me a little the dashing picture I made. 'Noel Coward enjoying a brisk morning canter on the beach at Deauville,' seemed a nice caption for my mind's eye, but I suffered, when we dismounted for the morning *apéritif* from the consciousness that my seat was sagging behind me like the elephant's child.

Sir James Dunn arrived one day on a yacht with Lady Queensberry (now Lady Dunn), his daughter Mona, Diana and Duff Cooper, and several others. Large dinners were given nightly in the Casino, and certain private social dramas among the party enlivened the hours until dawn. I felt that I was seeing a side of life which should by rights be glamorous to eyes unfamiliar with it; all the correct adjuncts were there: champagne, beautifully-gowned women, high-powered gambling, obsequious *maitres d'hotel,* moonlit terraces – a perfectly arranged production with all the parts well cast according to type. I think, perhaps, that there must have been something wrong with the dialogue. The author must have had a common mind, because soon I became irritated and bored and wanted to go home. The leading lady, as far as I was concerned, was Ruby. She was good all through. Her wit saved the more tedious scenes and her performance was gallant to the last.

Jimmy Dunn took a sudden interest in me at about four o'clock one morning and informed me, to my immense surprise, that I was a genius! My astonishment was natural, owing to the fact that up till that moment he had paid no attention to me whatever. However, I concluded rightly that Ruby had been trying to do me a good turn on the side and that it was up to me to take advantage of it; so I interrupted him with no more than a routine smile of self-deprecation, while he went on to say that I obviously had a great career ahead of me, and that as he had been given to understand that I was oppressed by money worries, it would give him great pleasure to finance me for the next five years. I should like to say here that no one could have more personal charm than Jimmy Dunn, when he likes to turn it on. He can be gentle, kind, humorous and sympathetic all at the same moment, and before that little interview was over I believed that all my troubles were ended, and that all I had to do was to go back to England and write what I wanted to write in comfort, with the certain knowledge that on the first day of every month, for the next five years, a cheque for a hundred pounds was going to drop into the letter-box.

The next day I felt a trifle damped when he practically cut me dead at lunch, but in the evening his enthusiasm was reborn and he asked me, charmingly, to sing to him and Irene Queensberry in the deserted dining-room of the Royal Hotel, which was where the only available piano happened to be. It was a strange setting: piled-up tables, shuttered windows, a dust-sheet pushed half off the piano and a few palms in pots looking, under the sharp electric light, as though they were going to be sick. I felt somehow that I was singing for my life. Jimmy Dunn's personality was strong, and I expect the atmosphere of the whole place had nurtured in me a reverence for riches which, even in my most poverty-stricken moments, I had not been aware of before. They talked animatedly during my songs, but appeared to be quite carried away with appreciation at the finish and, when I went with them to the Casino and actually won forty-eight francs at *boule,* I felt that my star had definitely risen for good.

On my return to England, Gladys was the first person, and I think the last, to whom I broke my glorious news. It wasn't so much that she poured cold water on the idea; she submerged it in a sea of icy disapproval. She pointed out that having got so far in my career unaided, it was idiotic to lose faith in myself at a critical moment which, when analysed, was critical only because I happened to have a slight overdraft and no immediate prospects. I had been in far worse straits before and managed to come out unscathed, and that to contemplate tying myself up for five years to a strange financier was sheer lunacy. Worse than lunacy, it was craven cowardice, a mean clutching at expedience, an abysmal admission of defeat! Faced with this unexpected vehemence I was forced to take stock of the situation all over again from a different angle. The contract between Jimmy Dunn and me was to be drawn up on his return to London on the following lines: that he guaranteed to pay me twelve hundred pounds a year for five years, on the understanding that he was to take twenty per cent of anything I happened to earn during that period. This arrangement had seemed fair enough to me in Deauville, but in the cold light of Gladys's reasoning the glow of philanthropy faded from it. It seemed less munificent and more like a business deal than I had hitherto imagined it, and after discussion I decided, with a deep secret sense of relief, that she was unquestionably right. Having made this decision I nourished for quite a while a resentful anger against Jimmy Dunn. I can only suppose that my conscience was uneasy. I was ashamed somewhere inside because I had so nearly allowed myself to be made a fool of, not by him, but by myself through him. His charm, personality, perception and generosity changed, in my mind, into sinister sheep's clothing, and it wasn't until much later that I was able to see him as he really was: a man of blustering tempers, kind impulses and excellent business acumen.

12

In looking back now on those months, August, September and October, 1924, I can detect a glow of nostalgia upon them. They mark in my life such a definite end to a chapter. The weather was fine and clear, and nothing seemed to be happening. Whether or not I felt frustrated I cannot remember, but for that little while I was undoubtedly suspended – irritably, I expect – in a sort of vacuum. Several plays were written and ready for production, but nobody was interested enough to wish to produce them. My position was equivocal. As far as the theatre world was concerned I was well known and moderately popular. I was not yet 'unspoiled by my great success,' but in danger of being distinctly spoiled by the lack of it. The Press regarded me as 'promising' and were waiting, without any undue signs of impatience, for the day when they could tie on me a less ambiguous label. The general public, on the whole, were ignorant of my existence. Meanwhile the leaves fluttered down from the trees in Dockenfield, mist lay along the meadows in the evening, and London managers announced lists of interesting plays for the autumn, not one of them by me. Yes, the nostalgia is there all right, I can feel it strongly. It is like a sensation that every traveller knows when his ship steams away from a place to which he is sure he will never return. Not perhaps that he wants to. Not perhaps that he has been particularly happy there, but he feels a pang as the land slips down below the horizon. The little café where he used to have coffee. That boring walk along by the sea and back. The view from the balcony. The conversations with the barman. The hotel wallpaper. All part of living Time, never to be known again, the closing of a phase.

PART SIX

The Everyman Theatre, Hampstead, was, in its infancy, a Drill Hall, but by the time I knew it all military flavour had departed, and it was firmly and almost defiantly a theatre. Under the management of Norman Macdermott it had achieved an excellent reputation, and several plays had been successfully launched there, later to slide down the hill into the West End.

The theatre itself was small, intimate and draughty. Its auditorium, foyer and corridors were carpeted austerely with coconut matting, and there was a subtle but determined aroma of artistic endeavour pervading the whole place.

Norman Macdermott was a short, affable man with nice eyes and a faintly unreliable expression. He invited me to go to see him after he had read *Hay Fever* and *The Vortex,* and announced, to my joy, that he would produce one of them, but that he had not quite decided which would stand the greater chance of success. He had a slight bias towards *Hay Fever,* but as there was no good part for me in that, I managed to sheer him over to *The Vortex.*

Casting was even more difficult than usual owing to the rule of the Everyman Theatre that all actors appearing there must agree to do so, regardless of their position, at a fixed salary of five pounds a week. Naturally if the play was successful enough to be transferred to a West-End Theatre, they reverted to their normal London salaries. This was actually an admirable arrangement, but it limited our choice to actors who were sporting enough to take a chance. We finally collected a cast headed by Kate Cutler and myself, which included Helen Spencer, Mary Robson, Millie Sim, Bromley Davenport, Kinsey Peile, George Merrit, and Alan Hollis.

Macdermott, after a little argument, agreed that Gladys

Calthrop should design the scenery and dresses, and it wasn't until all the contracts were signed and we were about to start rehearsals that he called me to his office and told me that he was sorry to say that he couldn't do the play at all, as he hadn't enough money, and that unless two hundred pounds were procured immediately the whole thing would have to be abandoned.

This was the first of many horrible setbacks attending that production. I was in despair, and spent a black twenty-four hours racking my brains to think of someone whom I could ask for the money. Ned Lathom was out of the question, as I felt that I had already sponged on him enough. I scurried miserably through my address-book, marking with crosses the names of my richer acquaintances and later discarding them all on the fairly accurate assumption that, being rich, they wouldn't be good for more than a fiver, if that. Suddenly, on turning back at the beginning of the book again, I lighted on the name Michael Arlen. I had not seen him for a year or so, and during that time *The Green Hat* had been published and was a triumphant Best Seller. I remembered our casual meetings during the last few years. I remembered our occasional heart-to-heart talks sometimes in corners at parties, sometimes in his little flat in Shepherd Market. He knew all about being poor. He knew all the makeshifts of a struggling author. He also must have known, many times, the predicament I was in at the moment, that dismal resentment of being forced by circumstances into the position of being under obligation to people. He was the one to approach all right. Success was still new to him, and the odour of recent shabbiness must still be lingering in his nostrils. I telephoned to him straight away and he asked me to dine with him that night at the Embassy.

It was a smart evening at the beginning of the winter season. We had cocktails in the newly-decorated bar and smiled with affable contempt upon the newly-decorated clientele. Half-way through dinner I blurted out my troubles, and without even questioning me about the play or making any cautious stipulations about repayment, he called for a cheque form and wrote out a cheque for two hundred pounds immediately. After that the evening seemed even more charming than it had been in the beginning.

Rehearsals started and all went well for a few days. Then Helen Spencer developed diphtheria, and despair set in again. This was a bitter disappointment. However, Mollie Kerr was engaged to take over the part and played it excellently.

Our next obstacle appeared to be insurmountable and reared itself up in the most unexpected quarter. Kate Cutler, for whom I had written the part of 'Florence,' suddenly refused flatly to go on rehearsing. I have never quite known to this day what strange devil got into her. We were close friends and she had been my strongest and wisest ally through all the vicissitudes of *I'll Leave it to You* and *The Young Idea.* At all events she became surprisingly angry because, upon realising that the last act was too short, I had rewritten it, enlarging my own part considerably in the process. It was a painful and, I still think, unreasonable quarrel. Norman Macdermott was away for the week-end, and there was no one to whom we could appeal for arbitration. After a violent scene in which Kate and I both held our ground sturdily and refused to give way an inch, Kate left the theatre, and there I was, a week away from production, faced with two alternatives. I could either stick to my guns, in which case I should have to find a new leading lady immediately and rehearse her from the beginning, even supposing that I could persuade any first-rate actress to undertake such a task at such short notice. Or I could surrender to Kate by reverting to the original last act which I knew to be too short and lacking the correct emotional balance in the conflict between the mother and son. The fact that Kate seemed to imagine that I had rewritten it only in order to give myself better material as an actor made me extremely angry. I remember roaring out several grandiloquent phrases about my 'literary integrity,' etc., which, although pompous, were certainly justifiable in the circumstances.

Gladys and I drove back to Ebury Street in my red car, much too fast and sizzling with indignation. When all rage was spent and blood had resumed its normal circulation, I decided, quite firmly and without passion, that neither then nor at any time in my life would I allow myself to be dictated to in the old-age battle between actor and author: a resolution, I am proud to say, that I have kept more or less shining and unsullied to this day.

In the meantime a new mother had to be found, and all

through that night a grotesque ballet of middle-aged actresses whirled through my dreams. The next morning, having been forced to discard, for various reasons, all those who were even remotely suitable to the part, I decided to work from another angle and make a list of actresses as far removed from the type of 'Florence' as possible. This list was headed by Lilian Braithwaite. She was tall and dark. Florence should be small and fair. She was well-bred and serene. Florence should be flamboyant and neurotic. Lilian Braithwaite had been associated in the public mind for some years with silver teapots in Haymarket comedies. She was almost inextricably wedged in a groove of gentle, understanding motherhood. Her moral position was clearly defined, and her virtue unassailable. Even in *Mr Wu* a few years back, when by a hair's breadth she had, nightly for over a year, escaped dishonour at the hands of a Chinaman, she had still managed to maintain an air of well-bred integrity, all of which went to prove the foolish incongruity of casting her for Florence. On the other hand, there was the finally important fact that she happened to be a first-rate actress. And so, waiving aside all obvious objections, I telephoned to her and about twenty minutes later was sitting in her drawing-room in Pelham Crescent reading the play to her.

Before starting, I had explained the Kate Cutler situation and told her that before anything definite could be decided, Kate must be given one more chance to say either yes or no. Lilian also told me that she was about to start rehearsals for a new play, *Orange Blossoms,* in which her part was bad but her salary extremely good. She added, however, with a slight glint of her eye, that she had not yet signed the contract.

That being such a portentous interview, I am sorry that I cannot remember more details of it. I recall that the room was dimly green, and that there were well-arranged flowers and several silver photograph frames; I remember Gladys's hat, which was brown and perky; also her rather screwed-up position in an armchair. Lilian wore a far-away expression during the reading; she was looking out of the window beyond the trees of the Crescent, at herself in a blond wig, rather *outré* clothes, with perhaps a long cigarette-holder. I knew by the occasional nods she gave that she was liking the play and recognising the value of the part. At the end, without any quibbling, she said that if Kate refused finally, she would play it. I explained about the regulation salary being only five pounds a week at the Everyman, and that unless the play were successful enough to be transferred to the West End the engagement would only be for a fortnight; to which she replied that she was willing to take the chance providing that we let her know definitely within a few hours. It was a nice clean morning's work. There were no blandishments and no superlatives, no time wasted on inessentials. Gladys and I gulped down some sherry, dashed out of the house and drove straight off to see Kate. It was only a short way, but to our strung-up minds it seemed miles. By that time we had bolstered ourselves into the belief that Lilian was absolutely ideal casting for the part and must play it at all costs. This was actually unfair to Kate, but it provided us with a certain necessary impetus. We burst in on Kate and found her still angry and still adamant. This was, of course, a relief superficially, but I felt horrid and sad inside as though I were playing her a dirty trick by allowing her, and at this moment definitely encouraging her, to throw away one of the best opportunities of her life. But there it was. It had to be done. I told her that, after careful reflection, I had decided to keep the play exactly as I had rewritten it, and that I wished her to say finally whether or not she would play it. She said 'No, no, no,' with rising inflections, and that was that. Gladys and I left the house, thankful that the scene was over, and went back to Lilian for another glass of sherry.

Before the Monday morning rehearsal I had a stormy interview with Norman Macdermott, who, furious that an important decision had been made while his back was turned, struck the desk firmly with his clenched fist and said that Lilian Braithwaite was utterly wrong for the part, and would ruin the play, and that if she played it he would wash his hands of the entire production.

I tried to reason with him and was at length forced to remind him that as I had scraped up a good deal of the backing, the production was no longer his, anyway, and leaving him to his hand-washing, I went down on to the stage to rehearse Lilian.

That week was almost entirely beastly, and I should hate to live through it again. The weather was icy, damp and foggy. The roads were so slippery that driving to and from Hampstead was a nightmare. Gladys worked like a slave over the scenery and dresses, assisted by Mrs Doddington, 'Doddie,' the housekeeper at the Everyman. Doddie was a darling; fat and warm and dressed in untidy black. It was she who kept the fire going downstairs in the subterranean cavern where we all dressed. The dressing-rooms were little more than cubicles with a passage running between them which opened out into a small draughty space in front of the fireplace on either side of which were two frowsy, comfortable settees. Here, at any time of the day or night, Doddie brought us cups of strong tea.

Lilian learned her part in two days and devoted the rest of the time to developing and polishing her performance, with a dry, down-to-earth efficiency which was fascinating to watch. It was the only brightness in those cold, hurrying days. I knew, after her second rehearsal, that she was going to be superb, but in addition to all the extraneous details I had to attend to I was dreadfully worried about my own performance. The play as a whole I had, of course, never seen, as I was on the stage myself most of the time. I had no way of telling whether I was overplaying or underplaying, or whether my emotion was real or forced. Gladys emerged seldom from the basement, and as Macdermott remained up in his office, there was nobody out front to give me the faintest indication as to whether I was going to be good, bad or indifferent. Lilian remained a rock and allowed me to dash my miseries and hopes and fears and exaltations against her. Over and over that last act we went when everyone else had gone and the lights were reduced to one working lamp on the stage. That memory is vivid enough, anyway. Those blank rows of empty seats in the foggy auditorium; Lilian and I wrapped up in coats and tearing ourselves to pieces. 'That speech was bad – let's go back' – 'I must start crying later, if I start too soon the scene's gone' – back again – then suddenly an uninterrupted flow for a while – 'it's coming this time' – triumph! – then back again just once more, to set it – no life – no flow – despair! So on and so forth until gradually there began to grow into the scene the shape and reality we had been working for. Gladys came up one night towards the end of the week and saw it through. She was clearly excited by it, and we all went downstairs exhausted and drank tea by the fire.

The dress rehearsal staunchly upheld theatrical tradition by being gloomy and depressing to the point of suicide. The acting was nervous and unbalanced. The dresses looked awful, and the lighting was sharply unbecoming. The theatre cat made a mess in the middle of the stage, which everybody said was lucky, but which, to me, seemed to be nothing so much as a sound criticism of the entire performance.

An incident occurred which was remarkable only because it marked the first and last time that I have ever seen Gladys shed a tear over a production. At the end of the second act she appeared suddenly in my dressing-room trembling with rage and clutching a proof of the programme. The cause of her rage was a little paragraph which announced that the scenery of Act One and Act Three had been designed by G. E. Calthrop, and that of Act Two by Norman Macdermott. Considering that the whole essence of Gladys's scheme of *décor* lay in the contrast she had made between the highly-coloured modernism of the first and last acts and the oak-and-plaster simplicity of the country house in Act Two, her anger was understandable. True, Macdermott had contributed an idea for the construction of the fireplace, but apart from this the whole structure, colour and conception of the set had been Gladys's. We immediately went up into the stalls and tackled him about it, whereupon he said blandly that the complete set had been designed by him and that the programme must remain as is was. We then left him and went straight upstairs to his office, where we ransacked his desk and finally unearthed Gladys's original sketch with Macdermott's 'O.K.' scribbled across it in his own handwriting. We took it down to him triumphantly and he was very cross, and became crosser still when I said that I would not rehearse any further until the programme was changed. He ultimately gave in, however, and ordered his personal fireplace to be hacked out of the scene. This was done, and we were left with no fireplace at all for the opening night.

The next day Gladys was at the theatre early in the morning with the carpenter and George Carr, our stage-manager, and by about seven in the evening, an hour before the play was due to begin, the set was fixed satisfactorily.

Meanwhile I was having a spirited duel with the Lord Chamberlain (Lord Cromer) in his office in St James's. He had at first refused point-blank to grant a licence for the play because of the unpleasantness of its theme, and it was only after a long-drawn-out argument, during which, I must say, he was charming and sympathetic, that I persuaded him that the play was little more than a moral tract. With a whimsical and rather weary smile he finally granted the licence, and with this last and most agitating of all obstacles safely surmounted, I jumped into my car and drove up to Hampstead to help Gladys with the set.

We spent a couple of hours with hammer and nails hanging pictures and tacking bits of material on to the last act furniture, and at seven o'clock allowed ourselves a quarter of an hour to rush over the road and have some tomato soup, which, for the first time in the history of that particular café, happened so be so scorching hot that we were almost unable so drink it. Then back to the theatre again. Gladys changed into evening dress in my dressing-room while I made up. The call-boy called 'Half an Hour,' then 'Quarter of an Hour,' then 'Beginners.'

The stage was reached by a spiral iron staircase; I can feel the ring of it now under my feet as I went up, my heart pounding, to see that everything was in order and to listen, with a sort of dead resignation, so the scufflings and murmurings of the audience at the other side of the curtain. Gladys, with a tightened expression about her mouth, moved about the set arranging flower-vases and cigarette-boxes on small tables. George Carr made a few little jokes and animal noises in order to make us giggle and forget for a moment the lifts going up and down in our insides. Lilian appeared resplendent in pillar-box-red and a blond wig, wearing her 'emu' face, a particular and individual expression of outward calm masking inward turmoil. She was apparently placid – as cool as a cucumber. First nights were nothing so her, she had known too many of them! But yet there was a little twitch that occurred ever so often at the side of her jaw, as though she were biting very hard on something to prevent herself from screaming. Presently Kinsey Peile, Mary Robson, Millie Sim and Alan Hollis came on to the stage in various stages of alert misery. George Carr glanced at his watch and said 'Clear, please,' very softly, as if he were scared that we might all rush madly out into the street. Gladys gave one last hopeless look at the set. We all cleared to the side of the stage and, amid a sickening silence, the curtain rose on the first act.

That evening was altogether an extraordinary experience. There was a certain feeling of expectancy in the air, an acceptance almost that the play would be a success. The audience looked distressingly near owing to there being no orchestra pit and no footlights. Familiar faces suddenly jumped out of the darkness and accosted us in the middle of a scene. Lilian was cool and steady and played beautifully. I was all over the place but gave, on the whole, one of those effective, nerve-strung *tour-de-force* performances, technically unstable, but vital enough to sweep people into enthusiasm.

At the end of the play the applause was terrific. I happened to cut a vein in my wrist when, towards the end of the last act, I had to sweep all the cosmetics and bottles off the dressing-table. I bound it up with my handkerchief during the curtain calls, but it bled effectively through my author's speech.

The first person so clutch my hand afterwards was Michael Arlen. His face was white with excitement and he said: 'I'd be so proud, so *very* proud if I had written it.'

After him came the deluge. And a very gratifying deluge it was too. There was little or no empty politeness about it. People had obviously been genuinely moved and Lilian and I held court for a long time until finally the last visitor went away and we could relax.

There is was real and complete, my first big moment. I don't remember exactly how I felt. I do know that I was tired. We were all tired. I know also that I recognised a solidity underlying all the excitement; this time I really had done it. The cheering and applause had been no louder than it had been for *I'll Leave it to You* and *The Young Idea*. If anything it had been a trifle less, owing so the smallness of the Everyman Theatre. The back-stage enthusiasts had used the same phrases; their superlatives were still in my ears; the same superlatives as before; the same 'divines,' 'darlings,' 'brilliants,' and 'marvellouses.' The same fervent embraces and handshakes; the same glistening eyes. But this time there was a subtle difference. Lilian said wearily: 'Do you think we are all right?' And I knew, and she knew that I knew, that the question was merely rhetorical, a routine gesture of diffidence. We were all right, more than all right. We were a smash hit.

2

The Press notices the next day were, on the whole, enthusiastic, although most of the critics deplored the fact that the characters of the play were 'unwholesome,' which, of course, was perfectly true. Their insistence, however, on the cocktail-drinking, decadence and general smart-settishness of the play was good for the box office, and we played to packed houses.

Those two weeks at the Everyman were exciting. Bit by bit I improved my performance technically; controlling my emotion, holding tears in reserve until the right moment. Different scenes took shape and became more complete. Never in my life had I looked forward so much to getting down to the theatre at night. Lilian and I discussed, sharpened and polished our last act until it became almost as good as people said it was.

Meanwhile there was the anxiety of wondering which management would take us over in the West End. Finally Alban Limpus and Charles Kenyon offered us the best terms and the Royalty Theatre was decided upon.

Our last night at the Everyman was almost as exciting as our first. There was more cheering and speech-making and we felt sentimental and sad to be leaving that draughty, uncomfortable and loving little theatre. Doddie cried copiously and deluged us with tea and Gladys and I drove away down the hill for the last time, waving valedictions so our various landmarks: the pillar-box that we had run into after the dress rehearsal, the private gateway where we had had to leave the car all night in a pea-soup fog, the corner just by Lord's Cricket Ground where we had once missed a lorry by inches. Those drives from Ebury Street to Hampstead and from Hampstead so Ebury Street, so fraught with agitations and emotions, were now just part of the past, along with all the early rehearsals, the snatched meals at the café opposite the stage door, the arguments, she agonies, the crises. It was again the nostalgia of leaving a familiar shore. Several weeks of fever-pitch, strung-up heavens and hells, hours of desperate concentration, slipping away behind us as the road was slipping away behind us into the mist. I remember saying dolefully to Gladys: 'And now what?' But, oddly enough, I cannot recall her reply.

3

Success altered the face of London for me. Just for a little the atmosphere felt lighter. I'm not sure whether or not the people who passed me in the street appeared to be more smiling and gay than they had been hitherto, but I expect they did. I do know that very soon life began to feel overcrowded. Every minute of the day was occupied and I relaxed, rather indiscriminately, into a welter of publicity. No Press interviewer, photographer, or gossip-writer had to fight in order to see me, I was wide open to them all; smiling and burbling bright witticisms, giving my views on this and that, discussing such problems as whether or not the modern girl would make a good mother, or what would be my ideal in a wife, etc. My opinion was asked for, and given, on current books and plays. I made a few adequately witty jokes which were immediately misquoted or twisted round the wrong way, thereby denuding them of any humour they might originally have had. I was photographed in every conceivable position. Not only was *I* photographed, but my dressing-room was photographed, my car was photographed, my rooms in Ebury Street were photographed. It was only by an oversight, I am sure, that our lodgers escaped the camera.

I took to wearing coloured turtle-necked jerseys, actually more for comfort than for effect, and soon I was informed by my evening paper that I had started a fashion. I believe that to a certain extent this was really true; at any rate, during the ensuing months I noticed more and more of our seedier West-End chorus boys parading about London in them.

I found people difficult to cope with in my new circumstances. Their attitude to me altered so swiftly and so completely. Naturally my intimates and the few friends I happened to know well remained the same, but ordinary acquaintances to whom I had nodded and spoken casually for years, gummed strong affection to me like fly-paper and assumed tacit proprietary rights. Apparently they had always known that I was clever, talented, brilliant and destined for great things. 'How does is feel,' they cried, 'to be a genius?' To reply to this sort of remark without either complacency or offensive modesty was impossible, and so I chose the latter as being the less troublesome course and wore a permanent blush of self-deprecation for quite a long while. I can indeed still call it into use if necessary. Sometimes I became so carried away by my performance that I alluded to my success as luck! This monumental insincerity was received with acclaim. People were actually willing and eager to believe that I could throw out of my mind all memories of heartbreaks, struggles, disillusionments, bitter disappointments, and work, and dismiss my hard-earned victory as luck. Just glorious chance; an encouraging pat on the back from kindly Fate. I can only imagine that this easy belief in a fundamental schism in my scale of values must have been a comfort to them, an implication that such a thing might happen to anybody.

The legend of my modesty grew and grew. I became extraordinarily unspoiled by my great success. As a matter of fact, I still am. I have frequently been known to help old friends in distress and, odd as it may seem, I have actually so far forgotten my glory as to give occasional jobs to first-rate actors whom I knew in my poorer days. Gestures such as these cause widespread astonishment. The general illusion that success automatically transforms ordinary human beings into monsters of egotism has, in my case, been shattered. I am neither conceited, overbearing, rude, nor insulting to waiters. People often refer to me as being 'simple' and 'surprisingly human.' All of which is superficially gratifying but, on closer analysis, quite idiotic. Conceit is more often than not an outward manifestation of an inward sense of inferiority. Stupid people are frequently conceited because they are subconsciously frightened of being found out; scared that some perceptive eye will pierce through their façade and discover the timid confusion behind it. As a general rule the most uppish people I have met have been those who have never achieved anything whatsoever.

I am neither stupid nor scared, and my sense of my own importance to the world is relatively small. On the other hand, my sense of my own importance to myself is tremendous. I am all I have, to work with, to play with, to suffer and to enjoy. It is not the eyes of others that I am wary of, but my own. I do not intend to let myself down more than I can possibly help, and I find that the fewer illusions that I have about me or the world around me, the better company I am for myself.

Naturally in 1925 my reasoning on myself was not as clear as it is now, but the nucleus was fortunately there. I opened my arms a little too wide to everything that came, and enjoyed it. Later on, just a little while later – three years, to be exact – circumstances showed me that my acceptance has been a thought too credulous. The 'darling' of the London Theatre received what can only be described as a sharp kick in the pants. And while my over-trusting behind was still smarting, I took the opportunity to do a little hard thinking.

Perhaps, after all, in the above paragraphs I have been a little stingy with my gratitude. I hereby render deep thanks to those booing hysterical galleryites and those exultant, unkind critics and journalists for doing me more constructive good than any of their cheers or their praises have ever done.

As all this, however, belongs to a later part of the book, I will stop digressing and return to the Royalty Theatre in December, 1924.

4

The Vortex opened at the Royalty Theatre on December 16th, 1924. The first performance felt to all of us a little dull after the intimate excitement of the Everyman. The audience, although much larger, was further away, separated from us by an orchestra pit and footlights; also the nervous strain was lacking. We knew from our Press notices and from the advance sale that we were already an established success. The audience seemed to be conscious of this too, and so we just played the play as well as we could, and they appreciated it as well as they could, and despite the fact that many of them were obviously suffering from bronchial catarrh during the first two acts, they overcame their wheezings and coughings and cheered quite lustily at the end.

My dressing-room was large and comfortable, and there I sat nightly at the end of the play receiving people and giving them drinks and cigarettes and listening to praise. So much praise. So many various ways of expressing it. It was fascinating. Some would come in sodden with emotion and break down and have to be soothed. Others would appear to be rendered speechless for a few minutes and just sit nodding at me. The majority were voluble. There had apparently never been such acting or such a play in the history of the theatre. Many of them had friends who were the exact prototypes of Florence and Nicky. It was extraordinary, they said, how I had managed to hit off so-and-so with such cruel accuracy. No amount of protesting on my part that my characters were imaginary and that I barely knew the person in question convinced them in the least.

I arranged a series of code signals with Waugh, my dresser, by which means we contrived to get rid of visitors when the delight of their presence was wearing thin. He would vanish and reappear again with urgent telephone messages, and on one occasion became so carried away by his own virtuosity that he announced in ringing tones that Lady Biddle's car was waiting for me. I must have appeared rather over-excited at this news because in order to control my laughter I was forced to embark upon a sea of explanations relating to my lifelong connection with the Biddle family. However, it all passed off quite successfully, and from then onwards Lady Biddle and her car were used *ad nauseam.*

It must not be imagined that I was blasé and lacking in proper gratitude towards all those kind people who said so many charming things to me. I loved it all, but I had learned from experience that dressing-room opinions, unless based on sound theatrical knowledge, are actually worth little beyond the amiable impulse that prompts them. When fellow-actors or authors came backstage to see me it was quite different. It is deeply gratifying to be praised by one's peers, to know that that little bit of business by the window in Act One and that crushing out of the cigarette in Act Two was not only noticed, but appreciated and remembered. Laymen cannot be expected to note these small subtleties; indeed, it would be disconcerting if they did, but never let it be said that their appreciation, however untechnical, is unwelcome; far from it. It is warming and delightful and most comforting. It is only occasionally, after the performance of a strenuous part, that an actor may feel a little tired, a little hungry and a little anxious to get his make-up off and get out of the theatre to have supper.

The supper routine during the run of *The Vortex* is one of my pleasantest memories. There were two clubs flourishing at that time, clubs where it was not necessary to dress and where one could eat the kind of food one wanted to eat in comparative peace and quiet. The Gargoyle was practically next door to the Royalty Theatre and specialised in sausages and bacon and a small dance band consisting of a pianist and a trap-drummer who caressed, tenderly, the latest tunes, without imposing the slightest strain either upon the ears or the digestive tract.

The Fifty-Fifty was rather more flamboyant but equally theatrical in atmosphere. It was run by Constance Collier and Ivor Novello and catered exclusively to 'Us.' I put 'Us' in inverted commas advisedly, for although 'Us' were happy and contented with it at the beginning because we really could come in after the show in sweaters and old clothes without being stared at, this congenial state of affairs lasted only a little while. All too soon the news got around and various social liaison officers began to appear with representative groups, and the small-part actors, who were the basic reason for the club's existence, were seen to be shrinking away into the shadowy corners of the room until finally they no longer came at all. Personally I mourn to this day the loss of the Fifty-Fifty Club. I spent so many happy hours there. Constance, of course, was the spirit of it. Her table was enchantingly insular; the island of theatre, washed only occasionally, by wavelets from the outer sea. Conversation was amusing and gay and bound together by old understanding. Memories of early days suddenly took life again for a little. No one can talk theatre like Constance. There is a percentage of her tinsel quality in her book of memoirs, but inevitably only a small percentage. Anecdotes, particularly theatrical anecdotes, lose charm in print. Stage reminiscence needs a close intimate audience of stage people; people for whom it is not necessary to translate jargon; people from whom the mention of Crewe Station or Ackers Street, Manchester, will bring forth appropriate chuckles of recognition. Constance's principal asset as a raconteuse was self-laughter. Her humour rippled as lightly over tragic years as over gay ones. She was, I often suspected, an outrageous liar, and yet I found more truth in her than in many people. She has always epitomised for me the theatre world that I love and honour, and she will always have for me, like the glow of footlights on a red plush curtain, a deep and lasting glamour.

5

The house in Ebury Street blossomed perceptibly with the success of *The Vortex*. The feet of the lodgers on the high steep stairs trod more lightly. The water became more swiftly hot in the taps, and even the depressing little lobby separating the bungalow from the hall acquired a sheen of complacency.

I ordered new chintz covers for my sitting-room and had my bedroom done over in pillar-box scarlet, a decision which I afterwards regretted. Gladys set her seal on this by painting, out of the goodness of her heart and the deeps of her erotic imagination, a few murals to brighten up the room in case the scarlet paint became too monotonous. There were two pink nudes over the fireplace, and a third doing its languid best to disguise what was quite obviously a po cupboard. It was in the midst of this misguided splendour that I was unwise enough to be photo-graphed in bed wearing a Chinese dressing-gown and an expression of advanced degeneracy. This last was accidental and was caused by blinking at the flashlight, but it emblazoned my unquestionable decadence firmly on to the minds of all who saw it. It even brought forth a letter of indignant protest from a retired Brigadier-General in Gloucestershire.

Lorn, who had been my secretary intermittently for two years since the death of our much-loved Meggie Albanesi, for whom she had officiated before, was now established permanently. Every morning she arrived with my breakfast tray and sat on the side of the bed while we smoked, drank coffee and transacted what we were pleased to call the business of the day.

Later on, another room in the house was taken over and transformed into an office. We had two letter files, known as 'Poppy' and 'Queen Anne' respectively, and a sinister cardboard-box labelled 'Shortly,' into which we put all the letters we felt incapable of answering at the moment. About once in every month or so it overflowed and we had to concentrate, finding, to our delight, that lapse of time had made unnecessary to answer at all at least three-quarters of its contents. This admirable system, founded far back in 1924, we still employ with success. Of course there is occasionally a slip up, and I am attacked by some irate acquaintance whose urgent invitation to do something or other has been completely ignored, but, on the whole, our percentage of failure is small.

I indulged immediately a long-suppressed desire for silk shirts, pyjamas and underclothes. I opened up accounts at various shops, happy to be able to order things without that inward fear that I might never be able to pay for them. I wasted a lot of money this way, but it was worth it. My clothes certainly began to improve, but I was still inclined to ruin a correct ensemble by some flashy error of taste.

I went to a lot of lunch parties in the most charming houses which, in retrospect, appear all to be exactly the same. This may be a trick that Time has played upon me, but I have a uniform memory of pickled oak, modern paintings, green walls, a strong aroma of recently burned 'Tantivy' from 'Floris,' and eggs, mushrooms, cutlets, sausages and bacon sizzling in casserole dishes. The conversation, I am sure, was distinguished, but that too has become lost in transit. I only remember that I felt happy and confident and very pleased to be eating such nice food with such nice people. I loved answering the questions put to me by eminent politicians. I loved noting that fleeting look of pleased surprise in people's eyes when it was suddenly brought to their attention that, in spite of theatrical success and excessive publicity, I was really quite pleasant and unaffected. This, of course, was all nonsense, but I was at least no more affected than anyone else. A social intermingling of comparative strangers automatically imposes a certain strain, an extra politeness which is not entirely real. This, I think, may be described simply as good manners. I had been brought up by Mother in the tradition of good manners, and so had they, therefore everybody was extremely agreeable to everybody else. I think possibly what surprised them was that I could play the game as well as they could, but then, after all I had learned many different parts by heart long before I had ever met them.

6

Soon after the opening of *The Vortex* I started work on a revue for Cochran. This had been tentatively discussed before. There had been an interview with C. B. in his office in Old Bond Street in course of which we bickered for about two hours because he wanted me only to write the book of the revue, and I wished to compose the entire score as well. Finally his armour of evasive politeness cracked, and he was forced to say that he was very sorry, but he frankly did not consider my music good enough to carry a whole show, and that he intended to engage Philip Braham as composer. That settled it for the time being, and I retired, vanquished, to concentrate on ideas for sketches and burlesques.

The ideas came swiftly and, oddly enough, nearly every idea carried with it its accompanying song. In my planning of the show almost every scene led up to a number, and so when the revue was complete it was discovered, to the embarrassment of everyone but me, that with the exception of three numbers by Philip Braham for which I had written the lyrics, a few odd pieces of classical music for use in ballets, etc., and one interpolated song for Delysia, the whole score, book and lyrics were mine. A few days before we were due to open in Manchester I tackled Cochran and asked him to raise my percentage, which was for the book and lyrics alone. He explained painstakingly, with great charm but implacable obstinacy, that he could not in any circumstances ask his backers for any more money, but that I was to leave it to his discretion to decide upon some additional reward for me if the show happened to be a success.

In the face of his confidential gentleness and impressed by his financial dilemma which he outlined so clearly to me, I felt that there was nothing for it but to give in. It was altogether an exasperating interview and took place in a rehearsal room in the Helvetia Club. For the benefit of the untheatrical public I would like to describe here, briefly, the general horror of rehearsal rooms. There are several crops of them all over London, and they are a necessary evil, particularly in big musical productions. Stages are not always available, and even when they are it is usually only during the last week of rehearsals that they are occupied by the entire company. Until then a show is rehearsed in bits, dialogue scenes in one place, dance numbers in another and vocal numbers in another. This frequently necessitates members of a company scudding miserably from one side of the West End to the other. Touring companies are rehearsed almost exclusively in rehearsal rooms, seldom achieving the dignity of a stage at all until a hurried run through on the day of the opening night.

Cochran productions alternate monotonously between the Poland Rooms and the Helvetia Club. There is little to distinguish between the two except that the Poland Rooms are slightly larger. Both places are equally dusty and dreary. Each room in each place contains a tinny piano, too many chairs, a few mottled looking-glasses, sometimes a practice bar and always a pervasive smell of last week's cooking. Here rows of chorus girls in practice dress beat out laboriously the rhythms dictated by the dance producer. The chairs all round the room are festooned with handbags, hats, coats, sandwiches, apples, oranges, shoes, stockings and bits of fur. It is all very depressing, especially at night in the harsh glare of unshaded electric bulbs.

My interview with Cochran occurred during a morning rehearsal to the accompaniment of 'Cosmopolitan Lady,' which Delysia was rather irritably running through with the chorus. The general din was no aid to coherent thought, and I remember my attention being constantly distracted by wrong notes and sharp cries from the dance producer. I tried hard to remain adamant and business-like, but Cochran and the atmosphere and a certain bored weariness got the better of me, and the whole question was shelved.

We all travelled to Manchester on the following Sunday for the orchestra rehearsal, dress rehearsal and opening night. I had arranged to stay off for the Monday and Tuesday performances of *The Vortex* and allow my understudy to play for me. I would never behave so casually to the public nowadays, but then I was new to stardom and unencumbered by any particular sense of responsibility. Incidentally, my understudy happened to be a keen young actor named John Gielgud, so in the light of later events the public were not really being cheated at all.

On With the Dance, which was the title finally selected for the revue, was lavish to a degree and very good in spots. There were two ballets created and danced by Leonide Massine and an excellent cast including Douglas Byng, Nigel Bruce, Hermione Baddeley, Ernest Thesiger and several others. The star of course was Delysia. Everything she did she did well, with a satisfying authority and assurance. She was occasionally temperamental and flew into a few continental rages, but to me she was always easy to work with and extremely agreeable.

Those three days in Manchester were on the whole unpleasant, although fraught with incident. In the first place I discovered soon after my arrival that my name was not on the bills at all. The show was labelled 'Charles B. Cochran's Revue,' which, considering that I had done three-quarters of the score, all the lyrics, all of the book, and directed all the dialogue scenes, and several of the numbers, seemed to be a slight overstatement. I went roaring back from the theatre to the Midland Hotel and attacked Cockie in his bathroom. I'm not at all sure that I didn't deprive him of his towel while I shrieked at him over the noise of the water gurgling down the plug-hole. I will say, however, that he retained his dignity magnificently, far more than I, and in due course calmed me down and gave me some sherry. It is odd that in all the years I have since worked with Cockie, that show was the only one over which we have ever quarrelled. I think the psychological explanation must be that then, in those early days of our association, we had neither of us estimated accurately enough our respective egos. And a couple of tougher ones it would be difficult to find.

The dress rehearsal started at ten o'clock on Monday morning and continued without a break until lunch-time on Tuesday. I can never quite put out of my mind the picture of that large auditorium in the early hours of the morning. The limp exhausted bodies of chorus girls and boys strewn all over the stalls, some lying in the aisles, small miserable groups of people huddled in corners drinking coffee out of thick cups and trying to digest even thicker sandwiches. Meanwhile Frank Collins, Cochran's most admirable of Admirable Crichtons, dealt calmly with lighting men, property men, carpenters, and stage hands, never raising his voice and preserving to the end an expression of unrelieved gloom and an unquenchable sense of humour. Cockie himself sat in the front row of the dress circle supervising operations, with a grey felt hat at a rakish angle on the back of his head and a large cigar jutting truculently out of his mouth.

Cockie and I had still one more battle, this time over 'Poor Little Rich Girl,' which he considered too dreary and wished to take out of the show. I fought like a steer, backed up by Delysia, and fortunately for all concerned we won, as it turned out to be the big song hit of the revue.

Sibyl Cholmondeley travelled from London for the first night, and she and Mother and Gladys and I sat tremulously in a stage box. The dress rehearsal had ended only a few hours before, and we were taut with nerves and weariness. Cockie in his box was suave and calm. I know his first-night face now so well, but then it was new to me, and I must say that all my small angers and resentments were immediately swamped by admiration of his courage. There he sat with a beaming smile, occasionally waving a welcome to some acquaintance in the stalls, as though everything were smooth and in the best of order. Nobody could possibly have guessed from his bland expression that hardly one scene had gone through without a hitch at the dress rehearsal, that it was probable that every quick change in the show would last twenty minutes instead of thirty seconds, that the lighting men knew little or nothing about the running order of the scenes, that the stage hands and the company were dropping from exhaustion, and that Delysia was liable to lose her voice completely on the least provocation. Cockie continued to smile as he always does in a crisis, and also, as usually happens with a Cochran production, his smile was justified. The show went through without any noticeable accidents. There were spontaneous bursts of applause and cheering at frequent intervals during the evening, and a great deal of enthusiastic hullabaloo at the end. Cockie made a speech and led Delysia forward and me forward, and we all bowed and grinned over baskets of flowers. There was a festive party at the Midland afterwards, where all rancours and harsh thoughts were submerged in champagne, and a great many photographs were taken of everybody for the *Daily Mail*. Not only was all anger forgotten, but I may add, the possibility of my getting a larger percentage of the gross was also completely forgotten.

7

Almost simultaneously with the production of *On With the Dance* in Manchester came the rehearsals of *Fallen Angels* in London. This play had at last been bought by Anthony Prinsep as a vehicle for Margaret Bannerman. Edna Best was engaged to play opposite her, and the producer was my old friend Stanley Bell. Bunny Bannerman, one of the kindest-hearted and least troublesome leading ladies I know, was dead tired and heading for a nervous breakdown, having played a series of long parts at the Globe, none of which, with the exception of *Our Betters,* had been successful enough to enable her to relax. She tried bravely to remember her words, but every day they receded further and further away from her. This, not unnaturally, made her more and more hysterical and nervous until finally, four days before production, she had a brainstorm and said that she couldn't play it at all. We had advanced too far to be able to call the whole thing off, which might have happened if her breakdown had occurred earlier. Edna, as usual, was word-perfect and calm, and we were faced with the necessity of finding someone at once with a name of more or less equal drawing power. Once more that endless weighing of names in the balance. So-and-so was too old, So-and-so too young, So-and-so far too common, and So-and-so just about to have a baby. Finally, after a brief telephone conversation with Tony Prinsep and a slightly longer one with me, Tallulah Bankhead came flying into the theatre. Her vitality has always been remarkable, but on that occasion it was little short of fantastic. She took that exceedingly long part at a run. She tore off her hat, flipped her furs into a corner, kissed Edna, Stanley, me and anyone else who happened to be within reach and talking incessantly about *Rain,* which Maugham had just refused to allow her to play, she embarked on the first act. In two days she knew the whole part perfectly, and on the first night gave a brilliant and completely assured performance. It was a *tour de force* of vitality, magnetism and spontaneous combustion.

Edna pursued an orderly course of accurate timing and almost contemptuous restraint and skated knowledgeably over the holes in the script.

There was no sense of struggle between the two leading ladies. Their team work was excellent. They also remained entirely friendly towards each other all through the run which, considering that their parts were about equal and that they had to play the whole second act alone together, was definitely a strategic triumph.

The Press notices for *Fallen Angels* were vituperative to the point of incoherence. No epithet was spared. It was described as vulgar, disgusting, shocking, nauseating, vile, obscene, degenerate, etc., etc. The idea of two gently nurtured young women playing a drinking scene together was apparently too degrading a spectacle for even the most hardened and worldly critics. The *Daily Express* even went so far as to allude to these two wayward creatures as 'suburban sluts.'

All this was capital for the box-office and the play ran for several months. It had one disagreeable effect, however, which was to unleash upon me a mass of insulting letters from all parts of the country. This was the first time I had ever experienced such a strange pathological avalanche, and I was quite startled. In the years that followed, of course, I became completely accustomed to anonymous letters dropping into the letter-box. They have come in their hundreds, crammed with abuse and frequently embellished with pornographic drawings. Then I was still ingenuous enough to be amazed to think that there were so many people in the world with so much time to waste.

With *Fallen Angels, On With the Dance,* and *The Vortex* all running at once, I was in an enviable position. Everyone but Somerset Maugham said that I was a second Somerset Maugham, with the exception of a few who preferred to describe me as a second Sacha Guitry.

On With the Dance had opened at the London Pavilion and was a big success. 'Poor Little Rich Girl' was being played in all the restaurants and night clubs. I went to too many parties and met too many people. I made a great many new and intimate friends, several of whom have actually lasted. My old ones were still nearly all with me, with the exception of Stoj whom I saw only every now and then. She had married, had a baby, published two or three novels and embraced Christian Science with tremendous ardour. This depressed me but apparently gave her a great deal of pleasure, a pleasure, I may add, that was not entirely free from super-ciliousness. To this day we still meet occasionally and have a good time, but the paths back into the past are long and tortuous, and new faiths, like new policemen, are over-zealous in obstructing traffic.

The Vortex, having moved from the Royalty to the Comedy, was transferred once more, this time to the Little Theatre where I had made my first appearance in *The Goldfish* in 1910. This was the fourth theatre in which we had played it; a quiet intimate house peopled for me with ghostly hordes of small children dressed as fish. It was a far cry from 'Prince Mussel' in *The Goldfish* to 'Nicky Lancaster' in *The Vortex.* I sometimes imagined how the fond matrons of 1910, blissfully regarding the antics of their progeny, would have shuddered could they have visualised the podgy little boy with the throbbing treble voice, posturing on that same stage fifteen years later as a twisted, neurotic drug addict.

The theatre was so small that we were able to jog along for ages to adequate business. Our routine was set and, although the last act was a slight strain when we were tired after a matinée, we managed to uphold a pretty good standard of performance. On one occasion Seymour Hicks, that most generous of actors, came to a matinée, and stood up on his seat at the end, cheering wildly. This was thrilling to us because we had been long resigned to rather dim audiences and no 'bravos' had rung in our ears for many months. On another occasion Madge Titheradge came and fainted afterwards in Lilian's dressing-room which was equally gratifying.

One night in May a young man in the front row of the stalls caught our attention early in the first act. His rapt absorption in the play inspired Lilian and me to renewed efforts, and at the final curtain we both conceded him a gracious bow all for himself. This situation frequently occurs when actors have been playing a play for a long run. The routine has become dull, the repetition of the same words night after night has become so monotonous as to be almost automatic, when suddenly, out of the gloom of the auditorium, a single face emerges. Just for a fleeting second you note the attitude of intense interest, the gleam of enthusiasm in the eye, and if you are a conscientious actor, you refrain from looking again except only occasionally, and even then obliquely as though you are not looking at all. But the difference it can make to your performance is extraordinary. You play exclusively in your mind to that one stranger, and by the end you find that your most boring scenes have passed in a flash, and that you have probably played better than you have played for weeks. There are many unknown people in the world to whom I shall always be grateful because on some night in some play in some theatre somewhere or other, their little extra interest caught my eye and set a spur to my imagination, causing me to give a fresh and vital performance of a part which I had played and played until my nerves were sick and tired of it.

On that particular night in the Little Theatre the young man responded nobly to our bow, by applauding even more loudly. I remember remarking to Lilian that he must be an American because he was wearing a turn-down collar with his dinner-jacket. A few days later, a mutual friend told me that he knew a young American who was very anxious to meet me, and could he bring him round to my dressing-room one night, and the next evening Jack Wilson walked nervously, and with slightly overdone truculence, into my life.

Gladys was in my dressing-room and we both considered him amiable enough but rather uppish. He left after a drink and a little commonplace conversation, having asked me to lunch with him in New York when I came over with the play. We promptly forgot all about him, no clairvoyant being present to tell us that my trio of closest, most intimate friends, Gladys, Jeffery and Lorn, were fated, in those few minutes, to become a quartette. We should, I think, have laughed at the idea that that almost defiantly American stockbroker would become so much part of our lives that scarcely any decision could be made without him. That, however, is what ultimately happened.

8

My final efforts of that full season were concentrated upon *Hay Fever,* which, having mouldered sadly in a drawer for months, was suddenly taken out, dusted off and put into rehearsal at the Ambassadors Theatre.

This all came about because Alban Limpus and Charles Kenyon wanted a play for Marie Tempest, who was no longer under her own management but under theirs. I told them that I didn't think she would do it as she had already turned it down once. They insisted, however, that it would be a good idea for her to read it again. This she did, and, much to my surprise, said that she was delighted with it and that I must produce it. This scared me somewhat because, although my opinion of my own talents was reasonably high, I hardly, even in my most bumptious moments, visualised myself showing Marie Tempest how to act. Nevertheless I agreed and arrived at the first rehearsal probably more nervous than I have ever been in my life.

Actually I needn't have worried; moreover, I should have known that an artist as fine and experienced as Marie Tempest automatically takes direction with more graciousness and docility than a dozen small-part actresses rolled into one. She stamped her foot at me early in rehearsals and said sharply with the utmost decision: 'Come up here, Noel, and play this scene for me. You wrote it and you know it, I didn't write it and don't!' I clambered obediently on to the stage and played the scene as well as I could, whereupon she kissed me and said: 'Excellent, my dear, you've shown me exactly where I was wrong. Let's go back.'

She touched me, thrilled me, and enchanted me all through those rehearsals, and she has touched, thrilled and enchanted me ever since. I have seen her on occasion snappy and bad-tempered, particularly with actors whose lack of talent or casualness in the theatre exasperated her. She has a personal imperiousness that demands good behaviour in others, but if you give in to her too much she'll bully the life out of you. She is lovable as a person and unique as an artist, and her charm is ageless. And if it were not that my intention in this book is to write about me, I should probably continue indefinitely to write about her. In any event she is bound to appear again, for even the most impersonal book dealing with the theatre could not avoid frequent reference to the first lady of it.

We gave an invitation dress rehearsal of *Hay Fever* to which all the actors in London came. They greeted it with hilarious enthusiasm although the general consensus of opinion was that the play was fundamentally too theatrical in flavour and too thin in plot ever to be a success with the public. On the first night I remember dear Eddie Marsh, that Dean of first-nighters, wobbling his head sorrowfully at me and saying: 'Not this time, Noel. Not this time.' He was fortunately wrong. And I went on at the end in response to the calls for 'Author' with a slightly less modest demeanour than usual. I was still smarting from the insults I had received over *Fallen Angels,* and I announced, with some tartness, after I had correctly thanked Marie Tempest and the company, that although the audience and the critics may have found the play a trifle dull, they would at least have to admit that it was as clean as a whistle. This called forth delighted laughter and was later alluded to in the Press as being amusing and witty, thereby proving that my stock that winter was still obstinately high.

The bulk of the notices referred to the play variously as being dull, amusing, thin, slight, tedious, witty and brittle. It ran to excellent business for over a year.

Since *The Vortex* had opened in November I had received several offers from different American managements who wished to present it in New York. For a long while I was undecided which to accept and also, which way to do the play. Either with an all American cast and an American star to play 'Florence,' or else with Lilian and the principals from the English cast. I had a shrewd suspicion that, all personal feelings aside, it would have to be a very fine actress indeed, star or no star, to give a better, or even as good a performance as Lilian. Also the thought of rehearsing from the beginning and playing that heavy last act with somebody else depressed me, and so finally I arranged with Basil Dean that he should take over the play and produce it in New York under the auspices of Charles B. Dillingham and Erlanger. This seemed really to be the most satisfactory arrangement. I knew Basil well and admired his work, and I didn't want to carry the burden of producing the play myself as well as acting in it.

It was ultimately agreed between Basil and me, after a lot of dogged haggling over percentages in course of which Basil became more and more business-like, and I became more and more vaguely artistic, until I finally won from sheer dreamy stubbornness, that we would take with us, in addition to *The Vortex, Easy Virtue* and *Nadya.* (This was later re-titled *The Queen was in the Parlour.)* *The Vortex* was to open first with Lilian, Mollie Kerr, Alan Hollis and me and new people for the other parts, and the other two plays were to come later. September the 7th was set for our try-out week in Washington, and as it was now only June I set about making plans for a holiday. I was certainly in need of one, and I persuaded Alban Limpus to let me leave the cast of *The Vortex* and go away. John Gielgud took over my part and played it beautifully, and the play continued for a considerable while after

I left. Lilian, I need hardly add, stood staunchly to her post and never missed one performance.

9

I sailed for New York on the *Majestic* in the middle of August. It was a gay, nervous voyage and far from peaceful. In addition to Lilian, Alan Hollis, Basil Dean, Mercy (his wife), Mother, Gladys and me, there were on board, Leslie Howard, Ruth Chatterton, Laura Hope-Crews, Mercédès de Acosta and Eva Le Gallienne. Laura was delightful, and we seemed to know each other well at once. Ruth Chatterton was still and reticent, and it wasn't until long afterwards that I grew to know her as a devoted friend. Eva I had known before. She and Mercédès had been in Paris presenting, rather disastrously, Mercédès' play on Joan of Arc. I think they were sad about it, at any rate they alternated between intellectual gloom and feverish gaiety and wore black, indiscriminately, for both moods. Leslie was vague and amiable and spread his own particular brand of elusive charm over every gathering. The whole trip consisted of gatherings. We had bathing parties, cocktail parties, dinner parties and poker parties. We discussed the theatre exhaustively and from every angle. We were all anxiously looking forward to the autumn season. Leslie was going to play *The Green Hat* with Katherine Cornell. Laura was to do *Hay Fever,* Eva had plans for a few Ibsen revivals. Ruth was going to do *The Man With a Load of Mischief,* Basil and Gladys and I were twittering with our own projects. The sea was calm and the weather fine, but the air on that ship felt definitely electric.

New York looked more beautiful than ever in the early hours of the morning, but by the time we docked most of the colour had been drained away by the full glare of noon. We went to the Plaza for the first few days, and then moved to a singularly inappropriate apartment in East 54th Street, which seemed to have been designed exclusively for the blonde plaything of a tired business man. It was dainty to the point of nausea; however, we saw very little of it, as rehearsals started almost immediately, and there were lots of things to be done. Gladys and I left Mother to deal with the intricacies of American housekeeping, and she shopped, mastered the Frigidaire and engaged coloured maids without turning a hair.

Those first few days were overcrowded and breathlessly hot. I was received with genial kindliness by Charlie Dillingham, who lent me his car and sent us masses of flowers. Everyone we met welcomed us with the utmost enthusiasm and seemed cheerfully convinced that *The Vortex,* although most of them had never seen it, could be nothing but a tumultuous success. Nevertheless, in spite of all this encouragement, an unpleasantness happened very soon. Charles Dillingham and Abe Erlanger were to present the play in conjunction with Basil Dean, and in due course, a conference was called in the Erlanger offices. This was my first meeting with Mr Erlanger, and I had not been in the room five minutes before he informed me that the play could not open in New York until I had rewritten the last act. Although he never removed his feet from his desk throughout the entire interview, he was patient and fatherly with me, explaining that mother-love in America was a real and universally recognised ideal, and that the public would assuredly rise as one man and leave the theatre at the spectacle of a son so vilely abusing the woman who gave him birth. He added, gently, that the little question of reconstruction would not be difficult as he could come to rehearsals and tell me what to do.

He talked for a considerable time. I regarded the over-furnished office, his perspiring form leaning back in shirt-sleeves with a cigar stub in one hand and a lily cup of ice water in the other; the dusty beams of sunlight slanting through the open windows catching refractory gleams from a gargantuan spittoon in the middle of the floor; the 'We must be tactful at all costs' expression on the faces of Basil Dean and Charlie Dillingham; and my spirit revolted.

I remembered that *The Vortex* had been turned down cold by many managers in London and New York, and that I had had finally to borrow money from Michael Arlen to get it produced at all. I remembered the obstacles we had had to overcome during rehearsals. The difficulties, the disappointments, the battles and the despairs. I remembered also the impact of that last act upon the first-night audience. And here was this theatrical magnate, soggy with commercial enterprise, prattling smugly to me about the ideal of mother-love, and imagining that I would agree to rewrite my play at his dictation. I knew, in that moment, that I would far rather go back to England the next day and not do the play in America at all, than submit to such insolence.

I must say, to my credit, that I controlled any outward display of temper and waited, politely, until he had finished. Then, ignoring Dillingham's frantic grimaces, I said quite calmly that I intended to play the play exactly as it was, and that, far from listening to any of his suggestions for the altering of the script, I would not even allow him inside the theatre while I was rehearsing. With which I made a swift exit. Not too swift, however, to miss a gratifying roseate suffusion of Mr Erlanger's face and neck. I was overtaken by Basil and Charlie Dillingham in the passage, where they assured me that I had been over-hasty, and that they would guarantee that Erlanger wouldn't worry me at all during rehearsals, and that, with a little tact, he was perfectly easy to manage.

I replied that I had not travelled three thousand miles to manage Mr Erlanger, but for him to manage me, and left them to go back to the office and be as tactful as they liked. The upshot of the whole thing was that Sam Harris and Irving Berlin took over the play, and Erlanger and Dillingham absolved themselves, misguidedly, from any connection with it.

The important additions to our New York cast were Leo Carril as 'Pawnie' and Auriol Lee as 'Helen.' Auriol was an old friend. She had a witty mind and gave a fine performance.

We had been fortunate in getting the Henry Miller Theatre. It was one of the nicest theatres in New York and perfect, both in size and atmosphere, for the play.

Henry Miller himself was extremely hospitable, and on the first day turned over his private office to me. It was well furnished and comfortable, and had its own shower-bath and dressing-room, and I looked forward to cooling myself luxuriously in it after tiring rehearsals. A few days later, however, Henry Miller went away, and from then onwards the office was inexorably locked, and all my protestations to the house manager were unavailing. He said that there was only one key, and *that* Mr Miller had taken away with him. This seemed to be rather eccentric of Mr Miller, but I remained deeply appreciative of his initial gesture.

Gladys had only two weeks in which to collect all the furniture and get the scenery built, and so we seldom met until evening. She disappeared early each morning into the maw of New York in search of scene-painters and standard lamps and sofas and chairs. It will always be a mystery to me how she managed to get everything done in time, but she did, and with apparent ease.

During the first week of rehearsals I had a letter from Jack Wilson asking me to lunch. Flushed with pride at having even remembered his name, I dictated a letter of acceptance and waited, in a mounting rage, for three-quarters of an hour on the day specified, and finally was forced to lunch alone in a cafeteria. It later transpired that my secretary had never posted the letter.

10

In later years I have travelled extensively. I have sweated through the Red Sea with a following wind and a sky like burnished steel. I have sweated through steamy tropical forests and across arid burning deserts, but never yet, in any Equatorial hell, have I sweated as I sweated in Washington in September 1925. The city felt as though it were dying. There was no breeze, no air, not even much sun. Just a dull haze of breathless discomfort through which the noble buildings could be discerned, gasping, like nude old gentlemen in a steam room. The pavements felt like grey nougat and the least exertion soaked one to the skin.

We floundered through a dress rehearsal on the Sunday night with the make-up streaking down our faces, every extra dab of powder creating gloomy little rice puddings round the corners of our nostrils, and every word we uttered crackling in our throats like brown paper. We prayed ardently for a thunderstorm, prayers to which the Almighty responded with unparalleled thoroughness, granting us not just one thunderstorm during the day to cool the air, but one every night of the week without cooling the air. The first one was timed, with perfect accuracy, to burst in the middle of the second act on the opening night, and from then onwards, in spite of our frantic shrieks, not one word of the play was heard. On the second night the storm broke at the beginning of the last act, and so on throughout the week with monotonous regularity, until we were forced to conclude that God shared Mr Erlanger's views on the sanctity of mother-love and that by offending one I had obviously offended the other.

The only coolness in that unpleasant week was supplied by the Press. The notices referred to the play as unwholesome, dull and mediocre. One critic even went so far as to say that if, as he had heard on good authority, I was considered to be the white hope of the English theatre, God help the English theatre.

We played on the week to a little over six thousand dollars and returned to New York on the Sunday miserably prepared for certain failure. Lilian, I believe, actually had the forethought to make tentative steamship reservations.

We were due to open on the Wednesday night, and Mother and Gladys and I occupied those agonising days by going to plays and moving into a new apartment.

The apartment we had taken was in the Hôtel des Artistes on West 67th Street, and belonged to Miss Mae Murray. Its assets were that it was spacious and high up, and commanded a grand view over Central Park. Its defects were that it was exceedingly expensive and rather trying to the eye. The main studio was Italian Gothic in intent but papier-mâché in reality. There were two elaborately wrought-iron gates which flew away lightly at a touch, and a set of really wrought-iron chairs which were quite immovable. There was a stained-glass window depicting a ship at sea, which lit up at night unless we were careful. Also a tall Renaissance chair with a red velvet cushion under which lived an electric victrola.

In the dining-room there was a wooden trellis over which clambered festoons of tin ivy. I remember looking at it abstractedly as I tried to eat a light meal at six o'clock on the evening of September the sixteenth, 1925.

II

I remember driving from West 67th Street through Central Park and down Sixth Avenue trying, with all the will-power I could exert, to coax myself into a more detached frame of mind. The play was going to be a failure, of that I was convinced. It would be a horrible evening, tense and depressing; certain people I knew would come backstage afterwards and be as sympathetic and comforting as they could, saying, with almost defiant enthusiasm, that I had given a wonderful performance and that they had liked the play anyhow. I knew that behind their kindness I should be able to detect the truth, and have to steel myself to the additional strain of putting up a good show for them; not letting them know that I knew; accepting their politeness with as good a grace as possible; betraying, neither by bitterness nor over-jocularity, that my heart was sick inside me.

I strove vainly to project my mind a few weeks ahead when I should be able to view this dreadful night in perspective, set in its right proportions. After all, it didn't matter as much as all that. My whole career was not going to be blasted by one failure in New York. I had written other plays and intended to write still more. The fact of failure would not, in this instance, necessarily mean that the play was bad; it had been a proven success in London and dealing, as it did, with an extremely small and typically English social group, there was no earthly reason why a New York audience should recognise its values at all; the dialogue, to them, would be nothing but an alien jargon; Washington, by all accounts the most cosmopolitan of cities, had regarded it with blank distaste; the New York reaction would be just so much blanker and, after some bad notices and a week or two of bad business, the show would close, and that would be that.

In this mood of dreary resignation I arrived at the theatre and went in to talk to Lilian for a little while. She was making up lethargically with a white cloth tied round her head, looking remarkably like an early photograph I had seen of her as the Madonna in *The Miracle,* but wearing an expression that was less tranquil and a good deal more pessimistic. 'We can only do our best,' she said, slapping her face viciously with a powder puff, 'and if they don't like it they can do the other thing!'

Both our dressing-rooms were crowded with boxes of flowers and there was a pile of about a hundred and fifty telegrams on my table; many of them from total strangers. All the managers, all the stars, everyone, it seemed, connected with the American theatre, wanted me and the play to be a success. It was my first professional experience of the tremendous warmth and kindness that New York people extend to strangers, and I was touched by it almost beyond endurance. There was a lot of time, far too much time, and I made up slowly and methodically, opening fresh batches of telegrams as they came, and occasionally wandering round the room looking gloomily at the cards on the flowers. Mother and Gladys arrived in due course, dressed up and scented and looking as though they might break if anyone touched them. Basil appeared too, in an opera hat that was a little too small for him. His manner was pathetically breezy, and he slapped me on the back rather harder than he meant to and made me choke. Eventually the 'Five Minutes' was called, and they all went round to the front of the house.

My dressing-room was on the stage level, and I heard the curtain rise. A few minutes later I heard, to my astonishment, a laugh from the audience; then, almost immediately, a bigger one. I could only conclude that either Leo Carril or Auriol Lee had fallen flat on their faces. A little while later there was a prolonged round of applause. That was Lilian's entrance. I got up then and after a final dab at my face and the usual nervous gesture to discover if my fly-buttons were properly done up, I went on to the stage. Lilian was playing her scene at the telephone; I noted a certain strain in her voice, but she was timing beautifully and getting laugh after laugh. Remembering the damp unresponsiveness of Washington I could hardly believe it. I paced up and down gingerly on the strip of coconut matting at the side of the stage and was told by the theatre fireman to put out my cigarette. At last it was near my time to go on, and I stood holding the door knob with a clammy hand, frowning in an effort to keep my face from twitching. My cue came and I made my entrance. There was a second's silence, and then a terrific burst of applause which seemed to me to last for ever. Fortunately the first thing I had to do was to embrace Lilian, which I did with such fervour that her bones cracked. The applause continued, and there we stood locked in each other's arms until I felt her give me a little reassuring pat on the back, and I broke out of the clinch and managed, in a strangulated voice, to speak my first line.

Never before or since in all my experience have I received such a direct personal stimulus from an audience. First nights are always over-strung and nerve-racking. There is always a certain tension and, for leading actors, always a reception on their first entrance. This comes to be regarded less as a tribute than as an inevitable part of a first performance. Some actors like it and say so, some like it and pretend they don't, some really hate it. I belong to the first contingent. To me a round of applause, even though it may interfere for a moment with the action of the play, even though it be conventional rather than spontaneous, almost always sets my performance off on the right foot. On that particular night, however, it did more than that, it saved me. I had expected a little clapping – after all even Washington had accorded me that – but this sound was of such a different quality, and the genuine ring of it uprooted my deep-set conviction of failure and substituted for it a much stronger conviction of success.

There was no false modesty in my astonishment at such an ovation. I had never appeared in New York before. They had no reason to make the smallest demonstration until the end of the evening when they could decide whether or not I merited it. As it was, they made me feel as though I were one of their most beloved and established stars, and I tried with everything I had in me to deserve it. I do know, to my lasting satisfaction, that I gave the best performance that night that I have ever given in my life.

In *The Vortex* we had made it a rule not to take any curtain calls until the end of the play. This was not a new idea in America, although in London, where the public were inured to watching a row of actors bowing and smiling after every act, it was considered to be quite an innovation. It is now, I am thankful to say, usual in both countries. On that first night in New York the play ran more smoothly than it had ever run. Everyone in the cast seemed to be inspired, and when the curtain fell after the piano-playing scene at the end of the second act, there was prolonged cheering, so prolonged, indeed, that we could still hear it while we were changing in our dressing-rooms.

We had now only the last act to be got through, but it was technically the most difficult of all, and we enjoined each other urgently to keep clear and cool, and to hold everything in reserve until the last few minutes.

We played it with the utmost wariness, feeling the audience completely with us. There wasn't a fidget or a sneeze or a noseblow, or even a cough. The whole act was received in absorbed silence. The curtain fell and rose again on the final picture of me kneeling with my head buried in Lilian's lap while she mechanically stroked my hair, still in dead silence, until, just as it fell for the second time, the cheering broke over us, and we struggled trembling to our feet.

I had rehearsed a polite little speech in my mind in case it should be called for, but when the time came for me to say it, my throat was so constricted that I was able only to mumble a few incoherent words of thanks and clench my hands tightly to prevent myself from breaking down.

We stood in our dressing-rooms afterwards for over an hour receiving. A few faces in that procession stand out in my mind: Mother's, very pink and powdered over tear-stains; Gladys's aloof and almost expressionless except for a triumphant glint in the eye; Jeanne Eagels's, with little rivulets of mascara trickling down her cheeks. I was hugged and kissed and crowned with glory, and that night is set apart in my memory, supreme and unspoilt, gratefully and for ever.

12

The Press notices the next day were enthusiastic and the advance sale tremendous. Ticket speculators bought up seats and sold them, sometimes on the side-walk outside the theatre, for as much as twenty and twenty-five dollars a pair. It was obviously a violent and glittering success, and I became, extremely happily, the talk of the town. I was photographed and caricatured and interviewed and publicised with even more thoroughness than in London. I was the guest of honour in all directions and made brief speeches at immense ladies' luncheons. I was invited to restful week-ends in large houses on Long Island, but these I had to give up very soon, as they were far too strenuous, and I was too tired after such clamorous relaxation to be able to give a good performance on Monday evenings.

Jack Wilson appeared at the stage door of the Henry Miller after the first matinée. He had been to a cocktail party where he had drunk enough to give him enough courage to come and attack me for not having answered his invitation to lunch. Fortunately I remembered his face and after a moment's scurried thinking, his name, which mollified him somewhat and after a few high words in the alley, I took him back to dine at the studio where Gladys, with royal thoroughness, also remembered him at once, so that his outraged feelings were soon smoothed out.

From then onwards we became close friends, and a few months later he gave up being a stockbroker in order to be my personal manager, in which capacity he has bullied me firmly ever since.

The Vortex being safely launched I had to start work immediately on *Hay Fever*. There had been a considerable muddle over the casting owing to the eccentric behaviour of the Shuberts, who were given to engaging people recklessly without even a cursory knowledge of the types required by the script.

On the morning of the first rehearsal I walked on to the stage of the Broadhurst Theatre and was startled to find a company of over thirty which, for a comedy of nine characters, seemed excessive. I weeded them out gradually, but one lady gave me a great deal of trouble. She was a brassy blonde in a *décolleté* afternoon dress of black lace, and was lying on her back on a wooden bench chewing gum with an expression of studied languor. At first she replied to my questioning laconically, but even in her monosyllables it was not difficult to detect a strong Brooklyn accent. I asked her what part Mr Shubert had promised her and, shifting the gum from one side of her mouth to the other, she replied, 'Myra,' and turned her head away wearily as though the whole interview were distasteful to her. Out of the corner of my eye I observed Laura Hope-Crews at the prompt table convulsed with laughter. I persevered, with as much tact as I could manage, and said that I was extremely sorry, but that Myra was such a typically English character she could obviously not be played with such a thorough-going American accent; whereupon the blonde rose in a sudden fury, spat her gum neatly into a chiffon handkerchief, said: 'Accent Hell! I've got a contract,' and flounced off the stage.

The fact that she had indeed got a contract cost me many wasteful hours in the Shubert office later.

Eventually after days of argument the cast was set – never, I must say, to my satisfaction – but I was at a loss in New York, and had, more or less, to accept actors on other people's recommendation.

Hay Fever played a trial week in Brooklyn, and opened in New York at the Maxine Elliot Theatre to a specially invited audience on a Sunday night.

I had decided, with careless optimism, to give a large party at my studio after the show, to celebrate its success, and I sat, during the performance, wishing with all my heart that I hadn't. It was, without exception, one of the most acutely uncomfortable evenings I have ever spent in the theatre. Everyone of artistic importance in New York was there. All the stars, all the writers, and all the critics. Not only were they there in the theatre, but most of them were coming to the party afterwards, and I, being in a box with Mother and Gladys and Jack, had an uninterrupted view of their faces as the play proceeded majestically, and with measured tread towards complete failure. The cast, never inspired at best, seemed utterly crushed by the splendour of the audience, all of them, that is, excepting Laura, who, in a praiseworthy but misguided effort to lift the play and her fellow-actors out of the lethargy in which they were rapidly congealing, gave a performance of such unparalleled vivacity that it completely overbalanced everything.

The critics tore her to pieces the next day for over-acting, which indeed she did, but what they didn't realise, and what I realised fully, was that in the circumstances it was certainly excusable. She lost her head a bit and hit too hard, but she was surrounded by a cast who were lying down and not hitting at all.

The applause at the end was polite, and the atmosphere in Laura's dressing-room strained. She knew, and I knew, and everybody knew, that the play was a flop; however, there was the party to be got through, and Laura gallantly agreed to come to it in spite of everything.

Many of the guests had already arrived by the time I got back to the studio, having left the theatre as quickly as they could in order to evade backstage condolences. Apprehensive social smiles seemed to be glued on to the face of everyone, and the preliminary gaiety was forced, to say the least of it. Looking back at it, that party was hilarious; at the time, however, it was pretty dreadful, especially for the first hour or so before the dampness of the play had been dispelled by liquor. Laura's social performance was superb; this time she didn't overact a fraction; she was gay and gracious and accepted guarded compliments with the most genuine of smiles.

The Press notices the next day were extremely depressing and the advance sale non-existent, and the play, having played to rapidly diminishing business for about six weeks, gently expired.

13

Christmas came and went with its attendant festivities, and owing to a throat infection, my voice went with it, and I was forced to stay out of the cast for a whole week. My understudy was a boy called Allen Vincent, who played the piano excellently.

Basil Dean was busy producing John Van Druten's first play, *Young Woodley,* and when that had been successfully launched we devoted ourselves to Jane Cowl and *Easy Virtue.*

Although Jane Cowl has been described with amusing malice by Mr Joseph Reed in his book *The Curtain Falls,* I should like to have a slap at her too; my slap, however, will be more in the nature of a loving pat, as I found her, both in spite of and because of her temperament and capriciousness, a most enchanting personality. To begin with, she is everything a famous theatrical star is expected to be; beautiful, effective, gracious, large-hearted, shrewd in everything but business, foolishly generous, infinitely kind to lesser people of the theatre, extremely annoying on many small points, and over and above everything else, a fine actress. She and Basil inaccurately measured each other's quality early on, and proceeded firmly to misunderstand each other on every possible occasion.

The production of *Easy Virtue* was tricky, especially the dance scene in the last act which Basil, with his usual passion for detail, polished within an inch of its life. The cast, on the whole, was excellent, and the play opened, after a trial week in Newark, at the Empire Theatre where it was received with only moderate acclaim. Jane's performance was smooth and touching, but she always played the big scene at the end of the second act too dramatically, thereby jerking the play too far back into the Pineroism from which it had originally sprung. My object in writing it had been primarily to adapt a story, intrinsically Pinero in theme and structure, to present-day behaviour; to compare the *déclassée* woman of to-day with the more flamboyant *demi-mondaine* of the nineties. The line that was intended to establish the play on a basis of comedy rather than tragedy, comes at the end of the second act when Larita, the heroine, irritated beyond endurance by the smug attitude of her 'in-laws,' argues them out of the room and collapses on to the sofa where, suddenly catching sight of a statuette of the Venus de Milo on a pedestal, she shies a book at it and says: 'I always hated that damned thing!'

Jane invariably delivered this line in a voice strangled with sobs and brought the curtain down to tremendous applause. If, however, she had said it and played the scene leading up to it with less emotion and more exasperation, I don't think that the play would have received quite so much criticism on the score of being old-fashioned. On the other hand there would probably not have been so much applause, and so I expect that Jane, from her point of view, if not from the play's, was quite right.

At all events she made an enormous personal success, and if I had to bear the gleeful laughter of Alexander Woollcott and a few stinging comments from the other critics, I had, at least, the satisfaction of knowing that Jane was filling the theatre to virtual capacity, and that the play would certainly run for months.

14

I remember drinking-in the year 1926 alone with Mother. We had a bottle of champagne all to ourselves, and stood at the window looking out over Central Park. There had been a heavy fall of snow, but the night was clear and starry; the traffic far below us looked like a procession of toys illuminated for some gigantic children's party, and when we opened the window the noise of it sounded muffled and unreal.

All along upper Fifth Avenue and West 59th Street the buildings glittered with lights; it was a beautiful sight, but so alien to us that it made us homesick. We both sighed for the gentle familiarity of London. Mother kept on saying: 'I wonder what Eric and Arthur and Vida are doing,' and refraining from the obvious surmise that they were probably bickering like mad, I allowed the sentimentality of the moment to have its fling, and pictured the Ebury Street house *en fête*, left-over Christmas decorations looped from the ceiling of the bungalow and festooned over Grandfather's sword; Father sipping inferior port and cracking nuts, and Eric and Auntie Vida wearing firemen's hats and laughing immoderately.

We stood with our glasses correctly poised while the ice-cold air blew over us through the open window; syrens were blowing and bells were ringing, and a wave of depression engulfed us. I knew, from the trembling of Mother's lip, that she was remembering too much, but my own thoughts were occupied more with the future than with the past. I think I realised in that moment how warily I should have to go; how infinitely more dangerous the achievement of ambition was than the struggle to achieve it. Here we were, Mother and I, having survived many despairs, at last safe, financially safe at any rate, for quite a while, providing we weren't too foolishly extravagant and providing that my grip on my talents didn't become loosened with too much success. How dreadful it would be, having got so far, to sink slowly back; not perhaps this year, nor even the next year, but later, when praise and publicity and 'stage centre' had insidiously become necessary to me, too necessary to be discarded without heartbreak. The picture of a one-time white-headed boy advancing bitterly into middle age with yesterday's Press headlines yellowing in a scrap-book, and only an occasional Sunday night performance by the Stage Society to remind him of past glories, seemed far from improbable and almost too depressing to be borne. Perhaps I was over-tired. Perhaps I was wiser than I knew, but instead of welcoming that new year with a grin of triumph, which in the circumstances I had every right to do, I greeted it suspiciously, with guarded politeness, like a newly-crowned King receiving the leader of the Socialist Party at his first levée.

However, natural resilience and another glass of champagne dissipated the mood, and we both began to giggle at the spectacle of ourselves, hovering on the verge of sentimental tears in a Metro-Goldwyn-Mayer mausoleum. We retired to bed early in a gale of hiccups, and the next morning 1926 seemed happily indistinguishable from 1925.

15

By this time I had whittled down my large circle of New York acquaintances to the small group of people I really liked. I had for some weeks been gradually eliminating big parties, finding them tiring and almost always disappointing. Before, I had accepted every invitation with a little thrill of anticipation; So-and-so was going to be there, and also Such-and-such, and it would sure to be gay, and I should probably meet someone new and exciting. It didn't take me long to realise that there was little or no novelty in any large party; people looked the same and talked the same and sang the same songs and made the same jokes. Only very occasionally, for a brief hour or two, generally round about three in the morning when most of the guests had gone, a certain magic occurred, and the few who were left really relaxed and enjoyed themselves; but these moments were rare, and you could never be sure that the various elements were really going to fuse successfully. Even if they did, awareness that there was a rehearsal the next morning, or a matinée to be played the next afternoon, made the dreary hours of waiting hardly worth while.

Frances Wellman, whom I had known since my first visit to New York, administered, like Elsa Maxwell in Paris and Sibyl Colefax in London, the best social mixtures. At the crack of her whip Park Avenue clapped Broadway on the back, and Broadway generously went through its hoops for Park Avenue. I soon discovered, however, that Park Avenue, like Mayfair, had not yet acquired the estimable habit of keeping quiet when someone was entertaining them. It appeared that life was too swift for them, too crowded with excitement and endeavour, to permit them to sit still and listen to some fine musician such as George Gershwin or Vincent Youmans or Richard Rodgers, without breaking the spell by whispering shrilly, or demanding, over-loudly, the few songs they happened to know. It was on account of this odd restlessness that one had to wait so long for most parties to become good. However, Frances organised well as a rule, and professionals were allowed to show off to their hearts' content, without too much competition from amateurs.

My own entertaining was usually confined to small suppers after the show, when nobody was expected to dress, and music and conversation were possible without strain.

16

After a run of just over five months *The Vortex* closed in New York, and we went off on a short road tour. Mollie Kerr returned home to England and an excellent actress, Rose Hobart, took over the part of 'Bunty.' With this exception, the cast remained the same.

I cannot say that I look back on that tour with any pleasure. The business was good for the first few weeks, but I was too tired of playing that heavy part night after night to care much. It was then that I made a vow that never again in any circumstances would I play a play for longer than six months, preferably three months in London and three months in New York. For an actor alone, this decision would seem to be rather high-handed, but I was a writer too, and the routine of eight performances a week, with all the attendant obligations, precluded any chance of concentration on new ideas. Nobody but an actor knows the vitality that has to be expended during a single performance; even after months of playing, when you move through the play automatically and without nerves, you still have to be strung up to a certain extent in order to get yourself on to the stage at all. In *The Vortex* there was always the last act hanging over me; the interminable physical strain of lashing myself, on cue, into the requisite frenzy. There were bad nights when the tears wouldn't come at the right moment, or when they came too soon and dried up completely just before they were really wanted. There were scarifying moments when suddenly my mind went blank, and I had no idea what came next or what had gone before. This happens to many actors when they play long runs. The displacement of a chair; the ticking of a clock; a sudden unexpected sound, either backstage or in the front of the house, or a new intonation on one of the other actor's lines is quite enough to dry them up dead. It is a horrible sickening sensation and leaves you shaken and insecure, not only for the rest of the evening, but for several performances afterwards.

Audiences, too, after the first month or so, begin to deteriorate in quality, and whereas during the first part of a run you can count on at least five good audiences a week, later, the percentage gets lower and lower until every performance seems drearier than the last, and it is only very rarely that you feel, on your first entrance, that blessed electric tension in the front of the house which means that for once you won't have to pump the words over the footlights, and nurse and coddle every line until your nerves ache with boredom.

The Mecca of our tour was Chicago. The company reminded each other at frequent intervals of the delights of that city. 'Wait,' they said, ignoring the kindly enthusiasm of Newark, Brooklyn and Cincinnati, 'wait until we get to Chicago. There, they'll really appreciate the play. There they'll eat it up!'

We arrived in Chicago having been advertised to play a six-weeks' season, but reserving smugly to ourselves the right to prolong this indefinitely. Mother was with me and Jack; Gladys wasn't, as she was on tour with Eva Le Gallienne working with her on plans for the formation of the famous Civic Repertory Company for which she, Gladys, was to be art director. On the advice of Mary Garden we had reserved an expensive suite at the Lake Shore Drive Hotel, in addition to which I had ordered my car to come from New York and be there to greet us when we arrived. The car had been, at the outset, a wild extravagance. It was a vintage Rolls-Royce with a shining new Brewster body which successfully concealed from the casual eye the aged dilapidation of its engines. Ravished by its appearance, I had bought it against all unprejudiced advice. After all it was a Rolls-Royce, and Rolls-Royces were well known to last for ever, also the drive was on the right-hand side, which would be very useful in England. The fact that I had often stepped in to it outside the stage door and been forced to step out on the other side into a taxi, I merely ascribed to the inadequacy of the chauffeur. At all events, it looked marvellous, and although in the long run it cost me as much as three new Bentleys, I am still grateful to it for the many plutocratic thrills it gave me.

It managed to reach Chicago all right, and met us at the station, and we drove out to the Lake Shore Drive, none too impressed with the atmosphere of the town, but determined to enjoy our stay there as much as we could.

Mary Garden had lovingly and generously written a squib for the papers – 'My divine breezy city, you have with you four words that spell "Genius": Noel Coward, *The Vortex*!' – and we opened to a packed house at the Selwyn Theatre on the night of George Washington's birthday.

They seemed unappreciative of the comedy in the first act, but we struggled manfully across the damp patches where the laughs should have been, deciding in our minds that they were a dramatic audience rather than a comedy one. In this we were wrong. They were essentially out for comedy, and they got their first big belly-laugh at the curtain of the second act. This struck me like a blow on the head. With every audience I had ever played it to, I had always been able to rely on complete absorption at the particular moment; it was really the most tragic scene of the play, when the son plays jazz more and more feverishly in order to drown the sound and sight of his mother abasing herself before her young lover. Chicago, however, saw it only as supremely comic, and Lilian and I retired to our dressing-rooms with prolonged laughter instead of prolonged cheers ringing in our ears. I was trembling with rage; I wanted to go out before the curtain and inform that gay holiday-spirited audience that this was the first and last time that I would ever appear in their divine, breezy city, and that to save themselves and me further trouble they could go back to their dance-halls and speak-easies immediately as there was not going to be any last act at all. Lilian restrained me by gripping me by the shoulders and hissing in my face: 'Remember you are English! Remember you are English!'

The last act was worse than I could ever have imagined it to be. The sight of me in pyjamas and dressing-gown started them off happily, and from then onwards they laughed without ceasing. Never, since *Charley's Aunt* on a Saturday night in Blackpool, have I heard such uproarious mirth in a theatre. The curtain fell to considerable applause, and I even had to make a speech, which, remembering that I was English, was a model of grateful restraint.

I have regretted ever since that I didn't tell them what I thought of them; it wouldn't have made any difference, as the play was a dead failure, and it would, at least, have given me a little satisfaction.

The two principal critics of the town wrote two such diverse notices that they nullified each other. Ashton Stevens said that the play was great and fine and subtle and tragic, while his confrère, whose name I forget, said it was cheap and comic and stupid and dull. Unfortunately we couldn't close at once because there was no other attraction ready to come into the theatre. Pauline Lord was playing next door in *They Knew What They Wanted,* and came popping in as often as she could to cheer us up, but apart from her my theatrical career in Chicago was miserable.

Socially, however, everyone was extremely kind. I was made a member of the Riding Club, and rode every morning with Diana Cooper and Iris Tree, who were playing *The Miracle* at the Auditorium. There were gay supper parties given almost every night, and when they weren't, we gave impromptu ones in our hotel and ran up and downstairs between each other's kitchenettes bearing bacon and cheese and ginger-ale.

Diana and Iris and Rudolph Kommer were at the Lake Shore Drive; Pauline Lord, Helen Hayes and Judith Anderson were not far away, and apart from the horrible hours I had to spend in the theatre, I had quite a good time.

Before leaving the Selwyn Theatre, Chicago, I wrote on the wall of my dressing-room in indelible pencil, 'Noel Coward died here,' and when I visited Clifton Webb in the same room years later, I was delighted to see that the inscription was still there.

Cleveland received us kindly, and we finished our tour to good business. I don't ever remember feeling so relieved and happy as I did on that last night. I had played the part over four hundred and fifty times, and although during the tour I had forced myself to write a play, it had been a tremendous strain, and I felt that many months of creative impulse had been frustrated. The play I wrote was called *Semi-Monde,* and the whole action of it took place in the public rooms of the Ritz Hotel in Paris over a period of three years. It was well constructed and, on the whole, well written; its production in London or New York seemed unlikely as some of the characters, owing to lightly suggested abnormalities, would certainly be deleted by the censor; Max Reinhardt, however, was enthusiastic about it, and it was translated into German by Rudolph Kommer and taken in due course to Berlin, where for years it escaped production by a hair's breadth until eventually Vicky Baum wrote *Grand Hotel,* and *Semi-Monde,* being too closely similar in theme, faded gently into oblivion.

Mother and I had reservations on the *Olympic* which didn't sail for two weeks, and so I left her in New York and went to Palm Beach to stay with my old friends, Florence and John Magee. It was an uneventful but lovely holiday. The air was soft and the sea blue, and I bathed and lay in the sun. There were dinner parties, lunch parties and picnic parties. Perhaps they were dull, perhaps they weren't; I only know that I enjoyed every minute of them. I was out of prison; free! Not for as long as I liked would I again have to be in any theatre every night at a certain time. I could have a nice strong cocktail before dinner with a clear conscience, and no fears that it might spoil my performance. Of course it was conceivable that too strong a cocktail might spoil my performance at dinner, but I don't think it ever did, and I returned to New York decently tanned and feeling a great deal better.

17

Jack, having already wisely invested a lot of my money in American securities, and having convinced his family that a career as my business manager would ultimately prove more lucrative than that of a stockbroker, was sailing to England with Mother and me. We had drawn up an elaborate contract in a lawyer's office, bristling with legal technicalities, options and percentages, so that in the event of sudden unforeseen mutual hatred, we could still continue to work together, however dourly, on a business basis.

Happily that situation has not, to date, occurred and as during the last ten years we have weathered more storm and stress than the average business association has to combat in a lifetime, I think it can safely be said that our original summing up of each other's characters was fairly shrewd. During that voyage home I remember feeling a little apprehensive over Lorn. I wondered how she would welcome the introduction into our slap-dash business lives of a hard-headed and extremely uncompromising American. Fortunately, however, my fears were groundless, as they took to each other on sight; in fact, the only scenes that have ever taken place since have been the result of both of them, for some reason or other, basely combining against me.

18

The Rolls-Royce was brought over to London at great expense, and on the rare occasions when it was not being overhauled at Derby, I drove about in it with considerable satisfaction and found that the streets of London, although retaining their well-worn familiarity, took on a new sheen viewed through Rolls-Royce windows. Bouncing along on gracious, buff-coloured upholstery, I noted with a thrill of conscious pleasure various landmarks of my still very recent past. Garrick Street, Bedford Street, Leicester Square, Shaftesbury Avenue, St Martin's Lane, looking in the warm May sunlight so exactly the same, still, in the mornings, thronged with actors hurrying in and out of agents' offices, stage doors, and rehearsal rooms. Even the chocolates and cakes in the windows of the Corner House seemed unchanged except for the difference that now I no longer yearned for them. It felt strange after months in America to be back again as an established star. True, I had been that when I left, but now Time had allowed the sediment of novelty to settle a bit, and I could accept the situation more tranquilly. The success in New York seemed to have added assurance to my position. This was all right, concrete. The sense of unreality had faded, and I no longer felt as though I were flying faster and faster through a nervous dream.

Easy Virtue was playing its last weeks in New York, and Basil had arranged to present it in London with Jane and practically the same cast in June. Meanwhile there was nothing much to do, and so I went off for a trip to the South of France, Sicily and Tunis. While in Palermo I wrote a new comedy called *This Was a Man*. It was primarily satirical and on the whole rather dull; the bulk of its dullness lay in the second act which was an attenuated duologue between two excessively irritating characters. The fact that the characters were intended to be irritating in no way mitigated the general boredom, and this vital error in construction ultimately cost the play its life.

On my return to London I showed it to Basil, who thought it excellent, and so we sent it to Lord Cromer for a licence with the intention of producing it immediately after *Easy Virtue*. The licence, however, was refused, principally, I think, because of a scene in the last act when the husband, on being told that his annoying wife had committed adultery with his still more annoying best friend, bursts out laughing. The fact that the circumstances of the story made this behaviour more than permissible weighed not a jot with the board of censors, who like the commandments broken solemnly or not at all; and so, after a little gleeful publicity in the Press, the play was shelved for later production in America.

Jane arrived three days before we were due to open *Easy Virtue*, and we travelled up to Manchester. The Manchester Watch Committee, for some strange reason known only to itself, refused to allow us to use the title *Easy Virtue*, and so it was announced merely as *A New Play in Three Acts*. At the cinema next door to the theatre a film entitled *Flames of Passion* was complacently advertised for the whole week: perhaps, however, the vigilance of the Watch Committee did not extend to mere celluloid. *A New Play in Three Acts* was a big success, and Jane made a gracious first-night speech, explaining that she was a stranger and rather scared, but that she already felt absolutely at home in dear Manchester. She was appropriately mobbed by the gallery girls at the stage door and conveyed in triumph to the Midland.

London fell into Jane's lap like a ripe plum. She made a tumultuous success and was immediately adored. She still played the end of the second act too emotionally, and the dramatic impact she gave to it still brought forth terrific cheering. The bulk of the critics sniffed superciliously at the play, but I was prepared for this and didn't mind much. The business was excellent, and everybody rightly felt that the London Theatre was the richer by the presence of a new and glamorous star.

19

Almost immediately after the production of *Easy Virtue*, *The Queen was in the Parlour* went into rehearsal at the St Martin's

Theatre. The cast, headed by Madge Titheradge, included Herbert Marshall, Francis Lister, C. M. Hallard, Ada King and Lady Tree. The rehearsals were remarkable for the fact that Madge and Basil worked together in complete peace and harmony. By this time, having worked with Basil a good deal, I had grown to know him very well, not only as a producer but as a person. The two were in no way synonymous. As a man he was pleasant, occasionally gay with an almost childish abandon, and in his more relaxed moments exceedingly good company. As a producer he could be and frequently was a fiend. It was not that he means to be in the least, but his genuine passion for perfection of detail, his technical thoroughness, and his tireless energy as a rule completely shut him off from any personal contact with his companies. He often blinked at me in amazement when I told him how bitterly he had offended So-and-so, or how unnecessarily cruel he had been when poor Miss Such-and-such had been unable to get the right intonation. I don't think it ever occurred to him that actors' feelings are notoriously nearer to the surface than average people's; if they weren't they wouldn't be good actors. Every good surgeon knows that no operation, however swift and brilliant, can ultimately be considered a complete success if sensitive membranes and organs and viscera have been handled carelessly in the process. A first-rate theatrical producer should learn early on in his career that most actors wear their intestines on their sleeves. Basil's only real failing in the theatre was lack of psychological perceptiveness. His actors on the whole were terrified of him; frequently even stars of big reputation quailed before him. True, their fear took various forms, but it was there all right, under their blusterings and ragings and tearful refusals to do this or that. His knowledge and efficiency were undeniable and his personality was strong, but generally, rehearsals under Basil were nerve-racking. Jane, who had fought him stubbornly step by step, finally won hands down, slightly at the expense of the play. Madge never fought him at all. She took his direction with enthusiasm automatically changing anything she didn't approve of, but with such expert technique that I don't believe he ever noticed. She agreed wtih everything he said and emerged triumphantly at the end of it unruffled by anything but her own temperament. Her performance of *The*

Queen was in the Parlour was flawless both in its comedy values and its moments of tragedy. She gave to the play more reality and pathos than it actually deserved, and although as an experiment in Ruritanian romanticism it wasn't so bad, it was Madge, I am sure, aided by a brilliant cast and production, who made it the success it was.

20

We gave up the little house in Dockenfield and set to work to find somewhere less cramped and villa-ish and in deeper country than Surrey. There were many kindly memories attached to it: the first day when it had risen out of a thick fog to welcome us; long spring evenings when we had made toffee on its inadequate stove and listened to the rain dripping through the bathroom ceiling into a tin basin; lovely summer nights when we had driven down late from London, tearing much too fast over the long straight stretch of the Hog's Back, whirling through Farnham with only a few lights winking at us from the sleeping houses, finally arriving at that kind, silly little villa squatting on its haunches in a field.

I wanted, if possible, to be near the sea, and I naturally turned towards Kent where we had been so happy before. We stared at advertisements of houses to let in the *Kentish Times* until our eyes ached. None of them were any good. They were either too old and falling to pieces, or so new that they were horrible. Finally we were on the verge of fixing upon a more or less passable-looking red-brick house at Stone near Rye, when we had a letter from Mr Body, our one-time neighbour at St Mary's. He wanted to let his farmhouse at Aldington and move into one that he had just built on the Marsh. Mother went down and saw it first and said it was all right, but rather poky; I went down a little later on and agreed with her, but as the rent was only fifty pounds a year and it had six acres of ground, electric light and a garage, it seemed a good idea to take it for a year or so, still keeping a lookout for something better. It was called, floridly enough, 'Goldenhurst Farm.' There was the house proper which was lop-sided and had a Victorian air; jammed up against this was the 'new wing,' a square edifice wearing perkily a pink corrugated tin roof and looking as though it had just dropped in on the way to the races. There was a muddy yard enclosed by thatched barns which were falling to pieces, there were two small ponds, five poplars, a ramshackle garden consisting almost entirely of hedges, and an ancient, deeply green orchard with thick grass and low-growing apple-trees. At the end of the garden the land sloped away to the Military Canal and one could see across miles of marshes to Dymchurch and the sea-wall. Beyond this the sea looked high as though it were painted on the sky; on clear nights the lights on the French coast glimmered along the horizon.

The house itself was indeed poky and quite hideous, made up into dark little rooms and passages, but there was a certain atmosphere about the place that felt soothing and somehow right, and so we decided to move in the moment the Bodys moved out in October.

21

Easy Virtue and *The Queen was in the Parlour* ran along together for a little, and when *Easy Virtue* closed because Jane had to go back to America, *The Queen was in the Parlour* was transferred from the St Martin's to the Duke of York's. In the meantime Basil was planning *The Constant Nymph* and suggested that I should play Lewis Dodd for the first month of the run. I wasn't at all keen, as it was a heavy part and I was feeling exceedingly tired, also it meant postponing until November our production of *This was a Man* in New York. However, Edna Best was to play Tessa, and after a good deal of argument both she and Basil prevailed upon me and we started rehearsals.

It was a crowded play and Basil tore himself and us to shreds over the production of it. As an actor it was excellent experience for me, being utterly unlike anything I had ever played before.

Basil adamantly refused to allow me to use any of myself in it at all. I wasn't even permitted to smoke cigarettes, but had, with bitter distaste; to manoeuvre a pipe. I had grown my hair long and put no grease on it for a month, consequently it was dry and fluffy and sparks from the pipe frequently blew up and set fire to it. In addition to the pipe, I wore purposely ill-fitting suits, and spectacles through which I peered short-sightedly; altogether I don't remember ever having been so thoroughly uncomfortable on the stage in my life. I hated Lewis Dodd whole-heartedly from the first rehearsal onwards. In the book his character was clearly defined and understandable; in the play he seemed to me to be a clumsy insensitive oaf with little to recommend him over and above the fact that he was supposed to be a musical genius. I say 'supposed to be', because, beyond a few modern piano chords and a burlesque opera in the first act and a little Scarlatti and a doggerel rhyme in the second, he betrayed no marked talent whatsoever. I was told, even by my most uncompromising critics, that I gave a fine and convincing performance, which still comforts me, as I was under the impression then, and am still, that I was awful.

Edna gave a tender, exquisite portrayal of Tessa and was so gallant and moving in the death-scene at the end that she almost made me forget my own dreariness.

The whole production, with its multitude of small parts, ensemble scenes and minute details, was magnificently done; the doing of it, however, was gruelling work. The party scene was Basil's pet, and we went over and over it endlessly until, whatever spontaneity there might have been at the beginning, set like cement in our joints, and we were unable even to remember our words. There was also a supper scene in the first act to which he was extremely attached. It had more props in it than *Ben Hur*: plates, mugs, knives, forks, spoons, bread, jam, cheese, biscuits, ham, all of which had to be manipulated on cue. Wooden benches and tables and chairs had to be moved on to their correct marks for the opera scene immediately following it. Owing to there being so many of us, there were no consecutive sentences lasting for more than a few lines, and so we had to listen like hawks and spear our cues out of the general chaos like fish from a boiling cauldron. The effect from the front was, of course, masterly, but the strain on the stage was unbelievable.

In the second act alone I had three two-minute changes: lounge suit to tails, back to lounge suit, and back to tails again; these changes were achieved frenziedly at the side of the stage, usually in the pitch dark. Before the death scene I had only one minute in a black-out in which to change completely from evening clothes to flannel trousers, shirt, tie, thick socks, shoes, hat and coat, with the result that I generally shot on to the stage like a rabbit with no breath at all. It was worse than revue because once on, the scenes were long and difficult, whereas in revue nothing lasts longer than a few minutes.

That rehearsal period was a bad time for my unfortunate intimates. Lorn and Jack bore most of the brunt of it. I gave up the part publicly on Mondays, Wednesdays, and Saturdays, and privately every night of the week. Basil, impervious to my wailings, kept my nose firmly to the grindstone, and I know whatever good there was in my performance was entirely due to him. Margaret Kennedy, the authoress, twittered in and out endeavouring, with sudden bursts of the most obvious tact, to persuade me how good I was going to be, although I am certain that she had an unshakable conviction that I was as much like her beloved Lewis Dodd as the Queen of Sheba.

Mrs Patrick Campbell rang me up on the day of the last dress rehearsal and implored me to allow her to come, explaining at length that she was a poor unwanted old woman and couldn't afford seats for the first night. She arrived rather late, bearing in her arms a Pekinese which yapped insistently through the quieter scenes. The next morning, the actual day of production, she rang me up again. Her voice sounded sympathetic over the telephone; she said that she had enjoyed the play very much and that the little fair girl (Edna) was quite good, but that, why, oh why, had I ever consented to play the part? 'You're the wrong *type*!' she moaned. 'You have no glamour and you should wear a beard!'

The play opened and was an immediate smashing success. I moved through the opening performance in a dull coma of depression. Jack appeared in my dressing-room after the second act and told me that everyone was saying how marvellous I was;

this I took to be a well-intentioned but transparent lie, and asked him gloomily to go away and leave me alone, which, to my considerable irritation, he did. I played Lewis Dodd for just over three weeks, and then my nerves, resenting at last the strain that had been imposed upon them for the past two years, finally snapped and I went through one whole performance weeping for no reason whatever, to the bewilderment, not only of the audience but of the cast as well. Edna guided and upheld me as well as she could, and at the end I subsided on the floor of my dressing-room, where I remained until my doctor arrived and gave me a strychnine injection and put me to bed.

I stayed in bed for a week without seeing anybody, and then, feeling slightly rested, insisted, against the doctor's advice, on sailing for New York.

I was certainly in no condition to enjoy the rehearsals of *This was a Man*; indeed, even if I had been as radiant with health as a Phosferine advertisement, I doubt if I could have derived much pleasure from that dreariest of dreary productions.

My withdrawal from the cast of *The Constant Nymph* made no more difference to the business than if an aunt of Margaret Kennedy's had died in Scotland. John Gielgud took over Lewis Dodd and played it successfully for a year, pipe and all.

22

My first serious play, *The Rat Trap,* was produced at the Everyman Theatre while I was on the *Olympic* bound for New York, and so I never saw it; however, from what I gathered later from eye-witnesses, I didn't miss much.

The leading parts were played by Robert Harris, Joyce Kennedy and Mary Robson, and the smaller ones by Adrianne Allen, Elizabeth Pollock and Raymond Massey. But in spite of the effulgence of the cast, the play fizzled out at the end of its regulation two weeks. I was not particularly depressed about this; *The Rat Trap* was a dead love. Seven years had passed since I wrote it with so much ardour, and during those years its glory had been eclipsed by more balanced and mature work. It had achieved publication at least, and I could read it in my first volume of *Three Plays* with indulgent cluckings of the tongue at its youthful gaucheries. The two big scenes were still good, but the first act with its strained epigrams and laboured exposition of character, and the last act in which the heroine bravely admits that she is going to have a baby, thereby tying up the plot with a bow on the top, made me shudder, nostalgically, but with definite embarrassment. It was neither good enough nor bad enough to merit a West-End run, and it was perhaps a mistake to have allowed it to be produced at all; however no harm was done, and I am sure that it was admirable exercise for the actors.

On arrival in New York we set to work to find an attractive star to play the extremely unattractive part of Carol in *This was a Man.* This was difficult, and it was only after considerable blandishments that we persuaded Francine Larrimore to do it. As a type she was miscast, but her name was a draw and she was a first-rate actress. The other principals were Auriol Lee, Nigel Bruce and A. E. Matthews.

The rehearsals were slow and uncomfortable and the tension increased by the fact that Basil's effect on Nigel Bruce was much the same as that of a python on a rabbit. Like so many large, bluff and hearty actors, Nigel was acutely sensitive and tremulous with nerves. He knew his lines perfectly until he stepped on to the stage, when, confronted by the menacing figure of Basil in the stalls, his moral legs became like spaghetti, his tongue clove to the roof of his mouth and all coherence was lost in a flurry of agonised stammering. Francine was calm and doggedly efficient, although occasionally tearful; A. E. Matthews ambled through the play like a charming retriever who has buried a bone somewhere and can't remember where, and Auriol Lee snapped in and out like a jack-knife.

The first night was fashionable to a degree. Everybody who was anybody was there, that is, they were there up till the end of the second act, after which they weren't there any more. Jack and Gladys and I sat with neatly arranged first-night faces in a box and watched the theatre slowly emptying until the stall floor was almost deserted except for a few huddled groups of the faithful. We had the feeling that even they were only staying because the theatre was warm.

I must say that Basil had not done his best with the play; if the writing of it was slow, the production was practically stationary. The second-act dinner scene between Francine Larrimore and Nigel Bruce made *Parsifal* in its entirety seem like a quick-fire vaudeville sketch. The scene between Nigel Bruce and A. E. Matthews in the last act might have livened things up a little if A. E. Matthews had not elected to say the majority of his lines backwards; however, it didn't really matter, for by then the play was down the drain, anyhow. Gladys and Jack and I, after a few jocular condolences with the company, went back to the Ritz where we lapped up neat brandy in order to prepare ourselves for the inevitable party which was being given by Schuyler Parsons ostensibly in my honour.

It turned out to be a highly successful party where fortunately the glaring failure of the play was quickly dimmed by the arrival of the Queen of Roumania.

We all had some more brandy, and recent agonies receded farther and farther away until suddenly George Jean Nathan appeared from behind somebody, shook me warmly by the hand and said that he thought the play was excellent and had enjoyed it thoroughly. This was so unmistakably the crack of doom that I gave up even pretending to be cheerful and went disconsolately home to bed.

That two months' sojourn in America was altogether unsatisfactory. I felt far from well and lacking in energy when I arrived, and soon my nerves began to get really bad again. For so many hours of each day I felt all right and then, suddenly without warning, melancholia enveloped me like a thick cloud, blotting out the pleasure and colour from everything. It was a difficult malady to explain; a bursting head that didn't exactly ache but felt as though it were packed tightly with hot cotton-wool; a vague, indefinable pain in my limbs when I lay down to rest, a metallic discomfort as though liquid tin had somehow got mixed up with my blood-stream, making sleep impossible and setting my teeth on edge.

I went off for two weeks to White Sulphur Springs with Jack in order to get fresh air and rest. I was unused to being in anything but the best of health, and was irritable and unhappy. We got up early every morning and rode peaceful horses up and down the mountain trails until lunch. There was nothing to do in the afternoons but lie about and read or write, and so I of course wrote.

I really should have rested completely, but I had promised Marie Tempest that I would write a comedy for her, and as an idea had been kicking about inside me for some time, I huffed and puffed and poured out nervous energy which I should have been conserving, and finally completed a pleasant little eighteenth-century joke called *The Marquise*. The last act was a bit weak, but I thought on the whole it would make a good evening's entertainment.

When it was finished I sent it to England and came back to New York in time to attend, with resigned lassitude, the last performance of *This was a Man*.

There was no reason for me to stay any longer in America, and I didn't feel equal to going back to the cold and damp of London and facing the casting and rehearsing of *The Marquise*. I felt suddenly sick of the theatre and everything to do with it, sick of cities and high buildings and people and screeching traffic. I decided that the time had come for me to go away, right away from everyone I knew and everything that was familiar, so I procured hurriedly, before my determination cooled, passport visas, typhoid inoculations, some new suitcases and a ticket for Hong Kong.

This sudden drastic decision jumped me for a little out of my nervous depression, and I set off across the continent with Jack, who, disapproving of the whole idea, insisted at least upon coming as far as San Francisco with me. He was right to disapprove because I was actually too tired and out of condition to make such a long trip all by myself, but I argued and insisted and finally convinced him that it was a case of kill or cure. If I didn't make a clean break and let a little new air into myself I should probably, within a few months, subside into some gloomy mental nursing-home in a state of complete nervous collapse. By going boldly out into the blue the very adventure of the thing would uphold me for a little while, and although I was fully prepared for days, perhaps weeks of acute loneliness, Time in the long run, together with new sights and sounds and climates, would be sure to cobble up the rapidly widening holes in my nervous fabric.

Finally, on Christmas Day, in the evening, I sailed for Hong Kong on the *President Pierce.* It was foggy and cold and, up to date, the wretchedest and most forlorn moment of my life. Syrens were blowing and a brassy band was playing. The air was filled with loud, sharp noises, and coloured-paper streamers fluttered and stretched between the ship and the dock.

I watched Jack, my last link with familiar life, disappearing down the gangway wearing my fur coat which he was taking back to New York. He turned and waved once, with a very forced, gay smile, then as I couldn't see any more I went below to my cabin.

PART SEVEN

I

The reconstruction of despair is difficult. I find that now it is only with the utmost concentration that I can catch for a moment or two a clear memory of the profound unhappiness I suffered during those seven days on the *President Pierce* between San Francisco and Honolulu. It is grey and nebulous in my mind like the cloudiness on an X-ray photograph that marks a diseased area.

I can remember a few hours when I emerged from my cabin and, with almost hysterical vehemence, endeavoured to fling my miseries over the rail and into the past. But I was too tired and weak to sustain the gesture and back came the hosts of darkness, crowding me down into my cabin again, twitching my nerves with sharp fears for my sanity and clouding the future with the most dismal forebodings.

Too much had happened to me in too short a time. I had written too much, acted too much and lived far too strenuously. This was the pay-off; possibly, I thought, the full stop to my creative ability which I had strained and overworked beyond its strength. My talent or flair for formulating ideas and dressing them up with words was squeezed dry and I felt convinced that I should never be able to write again. To add to my troubles, sleep evaded me and I spent many hours of every night trudging round the deserted decks until finally I persuaded the ship's doctor to give me some sort of sedative.

He was an amiable man but obtuse and offered me, in addition to the sedative, some kindly meant but irrelevant words of comfort. He seemed to be obsessed with the idea that lack of money was the only vital ill that the flesh was heir to, and regaled me with sad little stories about the engineer who only got so much a month and had three children, and the stoker who got even less and had five children and a wife with diabetes.

If my illness had been of the variety that profits from a counter-irritant, that foolish man would undoubtedly have effected a complete cure. As it was, his dullness and lack of understanding only served to emphasise my loneliness. I do not know if there were any amusing people on board, because I rarely came on deck except at night when everyone was asleep. I had a couple of radios from Gladys and Jack, whose intent to cheer made me almost suicidal, with a temperature of a hundred and three, and a black loathing for the *President Pierce,* the ship's doctor, my Chinese room steward, the entire Dollar Line and everything connected with it.

Florence Magee had telegraphed to her friends the Walter Dillinghams, who lived in Honolulu, asking them to entertain me, and I was met on the dock by a smart Japanese chauffeur, who placed a *lei* of sweet-smelling flowers round my neck and informed me that Mrs Dillingham was expecting me at the Peninsular. I of course had no idea where the Peninsular was, and he omitted to tell me that it was twenty miles away. We drove out through the town and into the country. I noted feverishly and without particular enthusiasm the luxuriant foliage and bright new colours. Bananas, palms, sugar canes, Flame-in-the-Forest, poinsettias and hibiscus flashed by, and the air was soft and cool, for it was still early. I wondered what Mrs Dillingham would be like and whether she would think I was drunk when I fell flat on my face at her feet. I had definitely decided not to continue my journey in the *President Pierce,* but I doubted whether I could hold out long enough to explain coherently that I was ill and wanted to go to bed.

We arrived at a Japanese house in a Japanese garden and Louise Dillingham came flying out, surrounded by dogs and children. She was a woman of abundant vitality, charming-looking and smartly dressed, and almost before I had finished my halting explanations she had bundled me back into the car together with herself, the dogs and the children, and back we went at a great rate to the town I had just left. She expressed a hope en route that I was not too ill to come to the lunch party she had arranged for me; she said that the people she had invited were all absolutely delightful, and that I couldn't possibly fail to adore every one of them. After lunch, she added, we would see about getting me a comfortable room in the hotel, unless of course I preferred to come and stay with her. I gave a hurried glance at the dogs and the children and said in a weak voice but with a firm intonation that I would rather go to the hotel.

We whirled through the town and along a coast road fringed with gigantic palms until we reached 'La Pietra,' the Dillingham home on Diamond Head. Even ill as I was I couldn't fail to notice the loveliness of that cool, pink house with its terraces and *patios* and tinkling fountains. The children and dogs disappeared miraculously the moment we arrived and I was left alone on the terrace with a strong whisky and soda, while Louise Dillingham changed her dress to receive the lunch guests. I lay in a swing chair under a 'Hau' tree looking out over a green valley to the deep blue sea; the town was in the middle distance and purple mountains lay along the horizon. The whisky went to my head at once, and I could hardly stand up to receive the first guest, who happened to be a doctor. His name was Withington and sensing sympathy in his manner, I explained quickly how dreadful I felt, and he promised to keep his eye on me. Then other people arrived and I have only a vague recollection of summer dresses, small talk and hot little sausages on sticks.

We went into lunch and sat down at a shiny table. I concentrated on my plate because, whenever I looked up, people's faces seemed to rush close to me and then recede again like a badly cut film. About half-way through the meal I happened to see through the window the car turn into the drive and, suddenly realising that I could bear it all no longer, I got up from the table with a mumbled apology to Louise Dillingham, rushed downstairs and, jumping into the car, directed the chauffeur to drive to the boat. There I dismissed him and staggered on board and down to my cabin. The boat was deserted, and there was nobody to help me, but I managed by degrees to pack everything, collect a couple of deck hands and get my luggage off and into the Customs House. I had to wait for about half an hour because another ship had just arrived, so I sat down on the ground with my back against a trunk until the officials were ready to deal with my bags. When they had passed them I had them piled on to a taxi and drove off to the Moana Hotel. By then I think my fever must have mounted still higher, because there were strange noises inside my head and I could hardly see. However, I contrived by a great effort of will to register my name at the desk and send a cable to Jack explaining my change of plans; after that I don't remember any more until I woke up in bed. Paul Withington, the doctor I had met at lunch, was in the room. He was calm, reasonable and wonderfully quiet; everything about him was quiet – face, movements and voice. He explained to me gently that I had a slight fever that was nothing to worry about and which would go down soon, and that he had given me a strong sleeping draught and something to make me sweat.

Of the two concoctions, the 'something to make me sweat' won easily. I woke up soaked every hour or so during the night and had to rub myself down and change beds.

The din outside on the beach and in the streets was terrific owing to it being New Year's Eve; it seemed as though the entire Chinese population of Honolulu had chosen the immediate vicinity of the Moana Hotel to blow their squeakers and let off their fire-crackers.

The next morning, and several times a day for a week, Paul Withington appeared bringing me books and more sedatives and bunches of vivid tropical flowers from Dillinghams' garden. My fever gradually subsided and towards the end of the week I was able to sit up for a few hours a day and watch from the window the beach boys riding the surf. They came flying in over the rollers like animated bronze statuettes; and marvelling at their grace and agility, I wondered miserably whether I should ever be able to lift a hand or a foot again without gasping with exhaustion.

Paul Withington gave me a meticulously thorough examination when I was strong enough to get to his surgery. Everything about me was tested in order to discover the cause of my fever, for which there seemed to be no apparent reason whatever. Finally, in the X-ray photographs, he pounced on the long-since-healed tubercular scar on my lung and announced with clinical triumph, but strange lack of psychological consideration, that I had T.B.

This I didn't really believe for a moment, but it was an unpleasant possibility to go to bed with. Fortunately my earlier T.B. experiences at Dr Etlinger's sanatorium and with Ned Lathom at Davos reassured me a good deal. As far as I could see I had none of the symptoms. I had lost only a little weight from the fever and now that it had gone I didn't sweat at night at all; my breathing was sound and I had no cough. All the same, my imagination worked overtime for a few days, visualising the future years as an attenuated procession from sanatorium to sanatorium surrounded by the well-known T.B. paraphernalia: doctors, nurses, lung inflations, sputum cups, and chill beds on snow-covered verandas. It was not a cheerful vision, but it gave me something definite to fight and, oddly enough, stimulated my nerves. I decided that however long it took I would lie in the sun and fresh air until all possibility of such horror should be completely eliminated.

The Dillinghams, with infinite kindness, told me that their ranch at Mokuleia on the other side of the island was at my disposal for as long as I liked. A French caretaker and his wife lived nearby and would cook meals for me; apart from them nobody would speak to me or worry me and I had nothing to do but sleep and relax and get well.

I accepted gratefully and a day or two later Paul Withington drove me there, with a suitcase and a few books packed into the back of his car.

There are some places in the world that charm the spirit on sight; Mokuleia was one of them. A soothing graciousness seemed to emanate from it.

The ranch itself lay at the foot of a high mountain and was built on three sides of a square. The middle part was one big room opening on to a veranda; the bedrooms were on either side. At the back, an avenue of enormous royal palms led to the foot of the mountain. In the front was a sweep of grass, a tall eucalyptus tree and then a banana and sugar plantation, through which a little road led to a small copse of pines and then the sea. Although it was over a mile away, you could hear from the veranda the noise of the surf pounding ceaselessly on the reef like muffled thunder. The beach itself was a semi-circle of gleaming white sand that shelled steeply into deep water and in which it was perfectly safe to bathe because the reef was a protection against barracudas and sharks.

We arrived in the evening, just after sundown. Madame Thevenin, the caretaker's wife, greeted us with an omelette and coffee and freshly baked bread. She was a round little woman with a kind, comfortable face.

The twilight changed swiftly to darkness and then the moon came up as suddenly as though someone were jerking it through the sky on a string. After supper we drove down to the sea; the pinewood was ghostly with shadows but the beach was almost as light as day and we took off our clothes and swam out through the warm surf into deep water.

Presently it was time for Paul Withington to go back to Honolulu, so he dropped me at the ranch and drove off. I watched the tail lights of his car disappearing down the road and when the noise of it had died away I stayed for a little, sitting on the veranda rail and listening to all the various unfamiliar sounds of the night. There were tree-frogs and cicadas and lizards and some strange hooting little bird in a tree not far off. The air was heavy with the sweet scent of night-blooming cereus, and presently, fearing that the spell might be broken by a sudden attack of scare or loneliness, I went to bed and slept deeply and dreamlessly for the first time in weeks.

2

I stayed at Mokuleia for several weeks. Occasionally Paul and Constance Withington, his wife, drove out to visit me, and we had picnics on the veranda or on the beach; apart from them I saw no one but the Thevenins. Their house was at the end of the garden, and I had all my meals with them; breakfast at six-thirty, lunch at one and dinner at seven. Although their English was reasonably good, we spoke mostly in French. Monsieur Thevenin had a fine face, white hair and piercing blue eyes which flashed cold fire whenever he was propounding his extremely violent political opinions; and as this was practically all the time, they flashed a good deal. My French was not fluent enough for me to be able to argue really satisfactorily, and so I filled in agreeably with enough '*ouis*' and '*c'est vrais*' to make him feel that his eloquence was not being entirely wasted.

There was a ferocious bull-terrier chained up in the yard who bared his teeth and snarled whenever anyone went near him. The Thevenins assured me that he was dangerous, but I had a feeling that he was bluffing and so one day I boldly offered him my hand to bite. This embarrassed him horribly, and he seemed at a loss to know what to do with it. Finally, he licked it apologetically and from then onwards he spent most of his time with me, accompanying me down to the beach every morning, sleeping on my chest during my afternoon siesta on the veranda, and walking with me through the plantations in the cool of the evening.

The big moment of every morning was eleven o'clock, when one train a day rattled across the little wooden bridge just behind the beach, and disappeared into the hills. 'Owgooste' always heard it before I did and started barking, whereupon I sprang up from the sand and raced to the top of a dune in time to wave my towel, forgetting in the excitement of the moment that I was stark naked. This, the Dillinghams told me later, shocked immeasurably many of the native passengers and also the engine-driver.

Frequently, during the early part of my time there, I had bad hours when the peaceful charm of the place turned suddenly sour and I felt neglected and far away. These black patches were usually caused by the arrival of a cable from Mother or Gladys or Jack asking how I was and when I planned to return. In the instant of reading them peace slipped away from me and a troubled restlessness took its place. My mind's eye blinked resentfully at the vivid colours all round me and ached for the gentle greens and greys of Kentish marshes, the familiar procession of red buses trundling down Piccadilly, or the garish lights of Broadway at night. A longing to be within reach of the things and people I knew tugged at my heart-strings, robbing me of my appetite and making me irritable and snappy with the Thevenins.

I could, of course, go back quite easily. There was nothing to hold me there except my own private vow not to budge until I felt, beyond doubt, that I was completely cured.

There were many things to be adjusted before I could consider myself really fit to plunge once more into the strenuous life that had so nearly wrecked me. Not only my physical health – that was coming along beautifully; I was already burnt black by the sun and sleeping and eating well – but my mind needed a great deal more solitude and a great deal more time before it could safely be guaranteed to function as I intended it to function. I meant to take no more chances. Never again would I allow myself to sink into that pit of unreasoning dreads and despairs. I had scrambled out by the skin of my teeth and intended to stay out for the rest of my life. In those long hours alone, lying on the hot sand with the noise of the sea in my ears, or on the veranda, rocking gently in the swing chair, or wandering along the dark roads in the evening, I had had time to round up an imposing array of past mistakes. It seemed that I had not only burnt the candle at both ends, but in the middle as well, and with too strong a flame. From now onwards there was going to be very little energy wasted, and very little vitality spilled unnecessarily.

People, I decided, were the danger. People were greedy and predatory, and if you gave them the chance, they would steal unscrupulously the heart and soul out of you without really wanting to or even meaning to. A little extra personality; a publicised name; a little entertainment value above the average; and there they were, snatching and grabbing, clamorous in their demands, draining your strength to add a little fuel to their social bonfires. Then when the time came when you were tired, no longer quite so resilient, you were pushed back into the shadows, consigned to the dust and left to moulder in the box-room like a once smart hat that is no longer fashionable.

I remembered the *chic,* crowded first night of *This was a Man* in New York. Three-quarters of the people present I knew personally. They had swamped me, in the past, with their superlatives and facile appreciations. I had played and sung to them at their parties, allowing them to use me with pride as a new lion who roared amenably. I remembered how hurriedly they left the theatre the moment they realised that the play wasn't quite coming up to their expectations; unable, even in the cause of good manners, to face only for an hour or so the possibility of being bored. True, there was no reason why they should stay. They had paid for their seats, most of them, and they were under no obligation to me or the management. I felt no bitterness towards them, no bitterness, that is, beyond a realisation of their quality, a forewarning of what to expect if I continued to fail.

I sorted them out, those names and the chinchilla wraps and piqué evening shirts, and stacked them neatly along the rail at the end of the veranda. On the other side, a few more dimensional individuals sat at ease. These were a little cleverer, more reliable, and could be counted on for certain hours of pleasant companionship providing one didn't ask too much or allow the burden of acquaintanceship to weigh too heavily on their shoulders. In the centre of the lawn, against the shadow of the eucalyptus tree, half a dozen figures moved into the light moonshine. These were my friends and I was glad that there were so many.

3

I firmly resisted the temptation to work during those weeks. This was difficult, as I had soon got through most of the books in the ranch that were readable, and there was nothing whatever to do in the evenings.

A tune certainly did slip through the barricade one day while I was on the beach and, between waking and dozing in the sun, I lazily fitted words to it. It lay forgotten at the back of my mind for many months until it emerged, nearly a year later, as 'A Room with a View.'

Apart from this, my vegetation was complete, until one day the urge to return home became too insistent to disregard any longer, and I went back to Honolulu to make plans for sailing.

At last, on a still, crystal-clear evening, I sailed on a stumpy little ship called the *Wilhelmina*. Few passengers were on board, but those were nice, particularly the Paepckes, a young American couple whom I had already met with the Dillinghams. Lots of people came down to see us off and we were loaded with *leis* of every flower imaginable.

The *Wilhelmina* sailed out of the harbour to the strains of 'Aloha,' played and sung by a band of Hawaiians on the dock; the coloured streamers snapped and broke, and the plaintive music followed us out over a sea that looked like grey oiled silk. There was so little breeze that the tall palms on Waikiki could only wave languidly as we passed.

I stayed on deck looking out through the gathering dusk until Diamond Head loomed over the port bow. I could see lights in the Dillingham' house and others springing up along the coast.

There is a superstition in Hawaii that travellers who are sailing away, and wish to return to the islands, must drop the flower *leis* that have been given them into the wake of the ship.

I remembered Mokuleia, the little road winding down through the plantations, 'Owgooste,' the light shining from the cosy sitting-room of the Thevenins' house and making shadows across the lawn, the pine wood and the thunder of the surf on the reef, and with a nostalgia that a few weeks ago I could not have believed possible, I dropped my *leis* one by one into the sea.

PART EIGHT

During the ensuing year the realisation that my nervous disorders, fevers and despairs, culminating in those rejuvenating weeks in Honolulu, had come at a very opportune moment, was brought, forcibly home to me. I discovered that I had need of every ounce of the moral and nervous stamina that the rest had stored up in me.

My various reunions went off satisfactorily. Jack and Gladys met me in New York, both looking much younger and nicer than when I had left them..The *Olympic,* in which Jack and I sailed to England, had been repainted. Lorn was gay and in the best of spirits, Mother was well and delighted with Goldenhurst, and *The Marquise* had opened at the Criterion Theatre and was a big success. I went to it on the night of my arrival. It was beautifully played by Marie Tempest, W. Graham Browne and Frank Cellier; and William Nicholson had designed an accurate and charming setting.

The spring and summer passed agreeably and without agitation. To begin with, Jack and I discovered during the first week-end we spent at Goldenhurst that, beneath its tiled fireplaces and hideous wallpapers, it was really a fine old seventeenth-century farm-house groaning with oak beams which a surveyor from Folkestone told us were free from dry-rot and in perfect condition. We immediately bought the house and grounds freehold at a ridiculously small price and set to work to make improvements.

We knocked walls down right and left and banished all family horrors of sentimental value into Mother's and Auntie Vida's bedrooms, substituting for them solid oak furniture from every antique shop within a radius of fifty miles.

Mother and Auntie Vida wailed a good deal at first, but we

overrode their protests; later on they admitted that they were very proud and pleased that we had.

In the late spring Jack and I went to Vienna to see the first performance of *The Marquise* at the Volkstheater. It was played by a celebrated German actor named Albert Bassermann, who, I believe, only consented to play it because the Marie Tempest part provided a fine opportunity for Frau Bassermann, his wife. She, I gathered from current gossip, was not quite such a public idol as he was.

The whole thing was rather bewildering. We arrived only an hour before curtain time, dressed hurriedly at the Bristol Hotel, and were escorted to a stage box by several directors and the translator, who, in the scramble, had omitted to explain to me that he had taken the liberty of transposing the period of the play from the eighteenth century to the present day.

My lack of knowledge of German prevented me from discovering this until about ten minutes after the beginning of the first act; up to then I had been under the impression that we were watching a curtain-raiser. When finally I caught the word 'Eloise,' which was the heroine's name, and observed Frau Bassermann enter in a red leather-motor coat, the truth dawned upon me and I laughed so much that I nearly fell out of the box.

I gathered from Albert Bassermann's performance that he was primarily a tragedian, as his idea of comedy consisted of little beyond sudden bull-like roarings and noisy slappings of his own face. Frau Bassermann, on the other hand, was going to be a comedienne or die. This, apparently, was her big opportunity to establish herself once and for all as a light soubrette, and it was clear that she intended to leave not a stone unturned. Unfortunately, her stage experience, like her husband's, had obviously been hitherto confined to heavier roles and her comic resources were limited to a repeated wrinkling of the nose as though she were going to sneeze, and an incessant giggle.

There was, however, an utterly delightful performance of the *ingénue* part by a comparatively unknown young actress named Paula Wessely, who, I am gratified to know, is now one of the greatest stars in her own country.

At the end of the play I was called on to the stage and, hand-in-hand with the Bassermanns, took endless curtain calls. Finally a group of students clambered over the footlights with a zeal that I could not but feel was out of proportion to the merits of either the play or the performance, and we all signed autographs, thereby setting the seal of success upon what had been, for me at any rate, a thoroughly hilarious evening.

2

During the summer I wrote a comedy called *Home Chat*. It had some excellent lines and a reasonably funny situation, but I was not entirely pleased with it. However, I read it to Madge Titheradge, for whom I had visualised the leading part, and she liked it, and as Basil also thought it good, we settled to do it in the early autumn.

Gladys came back from America with a hard black hat and mumps, having severed finally her connection with the Civic Repertory Company.

Lynn and Alfred appeared too, later on in the summer and came down to Goldenhurst. They had just finished playing S. N. Behrman's comedy *The Second Man* for the Guild, and were extremely enthusiastic about it as a play for me. A cast of only four characters made it comparatively simple for them to play the whole thing through for me in the drawing-room, which they did immediately. A certain amount of argument sprang up between them, and Alfred forgot one of the most important scenes and burst into tears, but I gathered enough inspiration from their performance to set about getting hold of the rights of the play at once.

I discovered that Macleod and Mayer held the English rights and were planning to do it in the late autumn, but I managed to persuade them to wait for me and do it in January instead.

Basil had for a long while been anxious to produce *Sirocco*, the play I had written in New York in 1921, and after we had had a series of discussion about it, I rewrote a great deal of it and we decided to put it into rehearsal directly after we had launched *Home Chat*.

Having thus light-heartedly sealed my doom, I spent a charming holiday with the Cole Porters in Venice and returned home fairly crackling with health and optimism to start work. The cast of *Home Chat* was good and rehearsals proceeded with sinister smoothness.

On the first night I suspected, early, with growing certainty, that we were in for a bad failure. The audience was restless, particularly in the cheaper parts, and I recognised danger in their whisperings and scufflings. Basil had not been insistent enough on *tempo* during rehearsals, with the result that the play moved with admirable realism, but too slowly. Poor Nina Boucicault, who was playing Madge's mother, and had not acted for some time, was horribly nervous and dried up on several of her lines, thereby causing long pauses which, in addition to those that Basil had put in purposely, brought the action frequently to a standstill. I writhed about on my chair in the box, sniffing disaster and seeing no way of averting it. Madge, with her unfailing ear, did her best to quicken things up, but it was of no avail, and at the final curtain there was booing from the gallery and the pit.

I dashed through the pass door and on to the stage as quickly as I could, feeling that it was unfair for the company to bear the brunt all by themselves. Basil was nowhere to be seen and the stage manager was in a panic.

The moment I appeared the booing became a good deal louder and then subsided as I advanced to the footlights. My intention was to ignore all hostility, thank the audience briefly but insincerely for their kind reception, and get the curtain down as quickly as possible, but just as I was about to speak, a voice yelled 'Rotten!' from the pit and another one shouted from the gallery: 'We expected a better play!' whereupon I snapped back that I expected better manners, and the curtain fell amid considerable tumult.

The notices the next day were all bad. Some contented themselves with supercilious patronage while the rest were frankly abusive and the business, needless to say, did not profit by them.

3

The two principal parts in *Sirocco* were played by Ivor Novello and Frances Doble, and the only theatre available was Daly's, which had housed nothing but musical comedies for many years.

Basil took infinite pains over the production, and although the *festa* scene in the second act was considered by some to be over-elaborate, I personally thought it a superb piece of ensemble work.

Ivor was a difficult proposition. Although his looks were marvellous for the part, and his name, owing to film successes, was a big draw, his acting experience in those days was negligible. I must say, however, that he worked like a slave and endeavoured, to the best of his ability, to do everything that Basil told him. Unlike Nigel Bruce, he was not in the least fussed or nerve-stricken and, although Basil at various times brought up all his artillery, gentle sarcasm, withering contempt, sharp irascibility, and occasionally full-throated roaring, Ivor remained unimpressed, behaving on the whole gaily, as though he were at a party.

Frances Doble was frankly terrified from beginning to end. She looked lovely, but, like Ivor, lacked technique. On the whole she gave a good performance, although it ultimately transpired that neither she nor Ivor had at that time strength or knowledge enough to carry those two very difficult parts. The play, I think, was fairly good. The characterisation was clear, and although the story was a trifle thin in texture, it seemed to me that it should be strong enough to hold.

On the evening of the first performance Mother, Gladys, Jack and I, elaborately dressed and twittering with nerves, dined at the Ivy. Abel, the proprietor, stood us champagne cocktails, and we drove to the theatre in good time to go backstage and wish everybody success.

When we went into the box I noticed, over the squeaking and scraping of the refined quintet in the orchestra pit, the familiar sound of restlessness in the upper parts of the house. The gallery was jammed – mostly, I suspected, with Ivor's film fans. The atmosphere in the theatre was certainly uneasy, and when the house lights went down, my heart went down with them.

4

Probably nobody not connected with the theatre could appreciate fully the tension and strain of that dreadful evening. The first night of any play is uncomfortable enough for those who are intimately concerned with it.

And in the case of *Sirocco* it was a losing battle from the word 'Go!'

The first act was received dully. Ivor got a big reception from the gallery when he came on; apart from that there was nothing but oppressive stillness, broken, only very occasionally, by two or three half-hearted titters on certain comedy lines.

The curtain fell to scattered applause, and in the orchestra pit a quintet, with almost shocking vivacity, struck up the Henry the VIII dances. G. B. Stern came to my box and said that she was sitting at the back of the stalls close to the pit, and that there was going to be trouble.

Jack's face assumed a slightly greenish tinge, Gladys's chin shot up so high that I was afraid she would rick her neck. Mother, unaware of impending disaster, waved to Madame Novello Davies at the opposite side of the theatre, and the second act started.

The storm broke during Ivor's love scene with Bunny Doble. The gallery shrieked with mirth and made sucking sounds when he kissed her, and from then onwards proceeded to punctuate every line with catcalls and various other animal noises.

The last act was chaos from beginning to end. The gallery, upper circle and pit hooted and yelled, while the stalls, boxes and dress circle whispered and shushed. Most of the lines weren't heard at all. Ivor and Bunny and the rest of the cast struggled on doggedly, trying to shut their ears to the noise and get the torture done with as quickly as possible.

The curtain finally fell amid a bedlam of sound, and even

Mother, who was slightly deaf, was forced to realise that all was not quite as it should be. I remember her turning to me in the darkness and saying wistfully: 'Is it a failure?'

I replied, without quibbling, that it was probably the bloodiest failure in the history of English theatre, and rushed through the pass door on to the stage.

During the first act I had felt utterly miserable. The sense of hostility was strong in the house and I knew it was directed against me. The second-act commotion jumped me from misery into angry, and by the last act I was in a white-hot fury. I don't ever remember being so profoundly enraged in my whole life. I could think of no way to account for this violent change of public feeling towards me. The failure of *Home Chat* had not been important enough to cause it, and *Sirocco* as a play, although far from perfect, was at least superior in quality and entertainment value to many plays running successfully in London at the moment.

Whether or not the demonstration was organised by personal enemies I neither knew nor cared; I was conscious only of an overwhelming desire to come to grips in some way or other with that vulgar, ill-mannered rabble. When I reached the side of the stage, Basil, who never attended first nights of his own productions, and had been quietly dining somewhere, was standing in the prompt corner smiling and ringing the curtain up and down. From where we stood, the tumult in the front of the house might conceivably be mistaken for cheering and he, having no idea of the horrors of the evening, was happily convinced that it was.

I quickly disillusioned him and walked on to the stage. Without once looking at the audience I went along the frightened line of the company to the centre, shook hands with Ivor, kissed Bunny Doble's hand, presenting my behind to the public as I did so, and walked off again.

This, as I expected, increased the booing ten thousandfold. I whispered hurriedly to Basil that I was going on again and that he was to take the curtain up and keep it up until I gave him the signal. If we were to have a failure I was determined that it should be a full-blooded one.

I went on again and stood in the centre, a little in front of Bunny and Ivor, bowing and smiling my grateful thanks to the angriest uproar I have ever heard in a theatre. They yelled abuse at me, booed, made what is known in theatrical terms as 'raspberries,' hissed and shrieked. People stood up in the stalls and shouted protests, and altogether the din was indescribable.

It was definitely one of the most interesting experiences of my life and, my anger and contempt having reduced me to a cold numbness, I was able almost to enjoy it.

I stood there actually for about seven minutes until their larynxes became raw and their breath failed and the row abated a little. Then someone started yelling 'Frances Doble'; it was taken up, and she stepped forward, the tears from her recent emotional scene still drying on her face and in the sudden silence following what had been the first friendly applause throughout the whole evening, said in a voice tremulous with nerves: 'Ladies and gentlemen, this is the happiest moment of my life.'

I heard Ivor give a gurgle behind me and I broke into laughter, which started a fresh outburst of booing and catcalls. Bunny stepped back, scarlet in the face, and I signalled to Basil to bring the curtain down.

Ivor's behaviour all through was remarkable. He had played a long and strenuous part in the face of dreadful odds without betraying for an instant that he was even conscious of them, and at the end, with full realisation that all his trouble and hard work had gone for less than nothing, his sense of humour was still clear and strong enough to enable him to make a joke of the whole thing. Nor was he apparently in the least ruffled by the inevitable Press blast the next day. He made no complaints, attached no blame or responsibilities to anyone, and accepted failure with the same grace with which he has always accepted success.

The evening for me, however, was not quite over. The fireman sent a message to me in Ivor's dressing-room where we were all drinking champagne in a state of dazed hysteria, to say that there was a hostile crowd outside the stage door and that it would be wiser for me to leave by the front of the house. This information refuelled my rage and I went immediately up to the stage door. The alley was thronged with people who yelled when I appeared. I surveyed them for a moment from the steps, wearing what I hoped was an expression of utter contempt, and then pushed my way through to the car. Several of them spat at me as I passed, and the next day I had to send my evening coat to the cleaners.

5

The next morning Lorn appeared early in my bedroom and peered at me sympathetically over an armful of newspapers. 'This time, my darling,' she said, 'we have undoubtedly bought it!'

I read carefully through every notice and was interested to discover that in not one of them was there so much as a kindly word. I noted also, however, that the notices themselves were much longer than those usually accorded to failures.

There was an unmistakable note of glee discernible in most of them. It seemed that all along, for the past three years, since *The Vortex,* the bulk of the critics had known that my success was ephemeral, merely a foolish whim of the public's and based upon little merit beyond a superficial facility for writing amusing lines. There was little or no surprise that a play of mine should be so appallingly bad, for, in their minds at least, I had never been anything but a flash in the pan, a playboy whose meteoric rise could only result in an equally meteoric fall into swift oblivion. In fact, so general was the conviction that I was done for, that several journalists announced it in so many words.

There were, however, two notable exceptions. One was St John Ervine, who wrote an impartial, careful criticism of the play with no malice, and even a certain amount of praise, and the other was Edgar Wallace who, although we had never met, took the trouble to write a long article in my defence, warning the gentlemen of the Press that their announcements, in his opinion at any rate, were not only unsporting but distinctly premature; this heartened me a great deal.

We certainly passed a gloomy enough morning; Lorn, Jack, Gladys and I, sitting round in my bedroom, drinking coffee and deciding what was best to be done. Even the comfort of knowing that the house was sold out for three days was denied us, for when we rang up the box office we were told that more than half the seats already booked had been returned.

My first instinct was to leave England immediately, but this seemed too craven a move and also too gratifying to my enemies, whose numbers by then had swollen in our minds to practically the entire population of the British Isles.

We finally came to the conclusion that the best plan was for me to brazen things out for a week, to be seen everywhere, and to try, as convincingly as possible, to make light of the whole fiasco. After that it seemed best to go away, preferably to America, writing first, of course, to Macleod and Mayer asking them to release me from my *Second Man* contract, and also to Cochran, for whom I had agreed to write a new revue.

It seemed absurd to embark on further theatrical enterprise in London with the Press and the public so obviously against me. An absence of a year or so would give them time to forget and enable me to make a come-back with a more reasonable chance of success.

Having decided upon this, we strapped on our armour, let down our visors and went to the Ivy for lunch.

The Ivy looked much the same as usual. Perhaps it was our overwrought nerves that sensed a sinister quality in the atmosphere. So often, after success, we had filed in triumphantly to our usual table in the corner, just to the right of the door; receiving congratulations modestly and trying not to allow too much cocksureness to colour our jokes. This time our task was more difficult. A line had to be drawn between what we felt and what we wanted people to think we felt. It wasn't unfriendliness exactly that we had to combat. Most of the Ivy's clientele were essentially well disposed towards us; indeed, on this occasion, kindly sympathy was all too apparent in every eye.

This had to be accepted with tempered gratitude. Condolences were harder to handle than congratulations, particularly as we felt them to be more wholeheartedly sincere.

Our table was in no way isolated. We were not ostracised for a moment, in fact the rush was quite flattering. Expressions of shocked horror, revilings of the shameful manners of first-nighters, scornful recriminations of the Press, rattled on to our plates and splashed into our dry Martinis. If I had expected even the most embittered character actresses to rise up and spit at me, I was doomed to disappointment. In fact the whole thing, after the first few difficult moments, went with a swing.

Realising that the eyes of Lorn and Gladys and Jack were set upon me with an almost clinical watchfulness, I was constantly wary that no undue bitterness should sully my replies, nor, on the other hand, any overdone jocularity either. A too casual attitude would be obviously false and recognised at once, whereas any indication of the real anger and humiliation I felt would not be in keeping with the gay, cynical, playboy-of-the-theatre tradition which had proved such a useful façade for so long. Also, I considered, without rancour, that my real feelings were nobody's business but my own.

Doubtless the reader will wonder why, in the circumstances, we went to the Ivy at all. Why, in addition to the strain and anxiety of the night before, and in the face of such thorough-going disaster, we elected to make ourselves the target for possibly still further slings and arrows. The reader will also probably say to himself or herself: 'How foolish, how unnecessary and, above all, how conceited to imagine that the mere failure of a play was of such importance. To believe, for an instant, that the Press and the public were really interested enough in so small an event as to feel exultant.'

In this the reader would be completely justified. Even at the time we realised in our hearts that the bulk of the public knew nothing about *Sirocco* and cared less. The theatre world, however, was different, and it was with the theatre world that we had to deal. We went to the Ivy that day as a gesture – not to our friends, nor our acquaintances, nor our enemies, but to ourselves. Nor was it entirely a gesture of defiance. To hang our heads in private and not be seen about anywhere would only make our ultimate emergence more embarrassing, and it seemed much more sensible to take the bull, however fetid its breath, by the horns at the outset.

Ivor, we were delighted to see, had decided upon the same course, and was sitting, surrounded by his coterie, at a large table just opposite to us. His gaiety seemed, even to me, to be genuine, and we all joined up for coffee and discussed the miseries of the night before with growing hilarity, and it wasn't until we had separated and gone our different ways that I realised that, on the whole, I had enjoyed myself.

6

After an unpleasant week in London, a week of lunches and dinners and suppers during which *Sirocco* was discussed interminably, by me with an air of semi-humourous resignation, nicely adjusted and not too semi-humorous, and by everyone else with various degrees of anger, conjecture, pleasure, wit, shocked astonishment and sympathy, I went to Paris, where Jack and I stayed with Edward Molyneux in Neuilly for a while before going on to St Moritz for Christmas.

Macleod and Mayer had gallantly refused to release me from my contract for *The Second Man* and Cochran had almost laughed at me for wishing to postpone doing his revue. He said, with a kindly wisdom born of many years of battling with success and failure, that in a few weeks' time any hubbub over *Sirocco* would be entirely forgotten and that he was quite sure that the revue would turn out to be a triumphant one in the eye for the lot of them.

I was grateful to him for this. His faith in me was so genuinely unimpaired, and although I wouldn't have blamed him if it hadn't been, I was extremely glad. It was altogether a sentimental interview, sentimental in the best sense of the word. He, more than most people, perceived beneath my business-like nonchalance, a certain vague scurry of apprehensions. I was scared inside, scared that perhaps, after all, the Press were right, that I was really nothing better than the flash-in-the-pan, the over-bright little star they had so caustically described. These fears were far from concrete, and received from me, even in my dimmest moments, no actual recognition. But, on looking back, I know they were there, swimming about in my subconscious, trying to clamber out and shake themselves like beetles striving to escape from a bath-tub. I rescued them later, quite a while later, and, after scrutinising them thoroughly, squashed them with murderous satisfaction.

Then, however, I needed outside manifestations of confidence in my ability, and Cockie bolstered me generously. No gleam in his eye indicated that he remembered my past shrill quarrel with him, no suggestion of veiled patronage. It was, as I said before, a thoroughly sentimental interview because, above all things, Cockie's sentiment rises supreme in failure. It is, I am sure, through his failures that he has made his friends. No other theatrical manager that I have ever known can rally adherents so swiftly in catastrophe. Temperamental stars demand to be allowed to pawn off their jewellery for him. Chorus girls, stage managers, members of his office staff eagerly offer him their services indefinitely for nothing. Even hard-boiled backers rush through the flames with their cheque-books over their mouths to aid him, regardless of the fact that the flames are probably consuming many of their own investments.

We discussed some of my already formulated ideas for the revue. This time there was no question raised as to the advisability of anyone else having anything to do with it. The whole show was to be mine: music, book, lyrics and supervision of production. The cast was to be headed by Maisie Gay, Jessie Matthews, Sonnie Hale and a Viennese dancer called Tilly Losch, whom Cockie had seen with Reinhardt and considered brilliant.

I remember leaving his office much cheered and with a new tune whirling round in my head, a tune to which the words 'Dance, Dance, Dance, Little Lady' had resolutely set themselves even before I got home to the piano.

I fear, however, that Jack and Edward had a bad time with me in Paris, as for many hours of the day I was what is known as 'a prey to melancholy.' My moods of depression were in no way mitigated by the English papers, which can be obtained far too easily in that gayest of gay cities.

In every one I chanced to look at, daily or weekly, I was confronted by either unpleasantly veiled or direct allusions to my recent débâcle. I should, of course, far from being upset, have congratulated myself on the stringy persistence of my news value;

no other dramatist that I could remember, with the exception of Bernard Shaw, having been the object of such a sustained attack for many years. However, I was upset, exceedingly upset. It seemed strange that the various editors should permit such redundant flogging of a dead donkey, unless perhaps they had a suspicion that after all the donkey might not be quite dead, and wished to make sure. At all events I formed a vicious little resolution then and there that in the future, however many triumphs I might achieve, I would never again, in any circumstances, give an interview to the London Press.

Never again should their readers be gratified by my opinion of 'The Modern Girl.' Henceforward my views on Birth Control, Television, Long Skirts, D. H. Lawrence, Free Love and Bicycling Waitresses should be locked in my own bosom and, strange as it may seem, good resolutions as a rule being so frequently trodden into the dust by the march of Time, I have adhered to that vow ever since.

With the passing of the years, of course, even the memory of my disgust has evaporated and my feelings towards the Press are friendly in the extreme and I hope will remain so. But the resolution still holds firmly and gratefully, for the simple reason that it saves me an incalculable amount of time.

Edward's quiet, lovely little house in Neuilly presently began to soothe me down a bit. It had been at one time a royal pavilion attached to the French Court, and there was enveloping it an atmosphere of departed glory. The high trees in the garden bowed sadly in the winter wind; they seemed tremendously dignified and long since resigned to the shock of a revolution which had swept away all familiar charm and elegance, a revolution, I could not help reflecting, whose impact on world history had on the whole been more serious than the screeching of a few gallery girls in a London theatre.

7

The Second Man was a witty comedy, with only four characters in it and my part, Clark Storey, a cynical, intelligent dilettante, was the pivot around which the play revolved. It was, in consequence, extremely long and, owing to the author's unrestrained passion for the *Oxford Dictionary*, very difficult to learn. There was, however, much wisdom and charm in the lines, and by devoting a few hours of every day to it in St Moritz, I managed to learn it by the time rehearsals started.

The other three parts in the play were played by Zena Dare, Ursula Jeans and Raymond Massey. Basil Dean produced with commendable gentleness which was only occasionally ruffled into irritability by the fact that Zena Dare was constantly bathed in tears.

This happened to be one of her peculiarities and really reflected very little on his directorial manner. She was the victim of a desperate inferiority complex, which was enhanced rather than minimised by a strong sense of humour directed principally against herself, with the result that every time she cried, she laughed at herself for crying, becoming in the process more and more hysterical until eventually rehearsals were brought to a standstill. Owing to early and arduous training in musical comedy, her first ingrained instinct was to smile, this smile often persisting even while the tears were cascading down her face. I think one of the most entrancing spectacles I know was Zena's expression when something untoward occurred on the stage, or when she lost a line and knew that she hadn't the remotest idea what to say next. On would flash the smile immediately, stretching into a mirthless grimace; meanwhile her eyes, in deathly panic, searched wildly the ceiling, the floor and the furniture for inspiration. Still smiling, she would hiss out of the corner of her mouth: 'For God's sake, dear, agony dear, what do I say, dear?'

At rehearsals, of course, such contretemps were the signal for tears; in actual performance, however, the trouper spirit was too strong in her to permit collapse, and she persevered gamely until, the danger over, her smile changed from macabre ferocity to relief and wafted her off the stage. She was a darling in the theatre and we all adored her.

Raymond Massey was another slight thorn in Basil's side, owing to his eccentric habit of behaving like a windmill whenever he dried up on a speech. Horrified at the outset by the fact that I was practically word-perfect, he lashed himself into a frenzy several times a day, tearing at one particular long-suffering lock of hair and rending the air with incoherent Canadian curses, not at me, which would have been understandable, but at himself. There is nothing so irritating as rehearsing scenes with someone who already knows them, and I was fully conscious that my unethical slickness was putting him off. I apologised profusely, explaining that the reason I had played such a dirty trick on him was that my part was long and I wanted to get the actual learning of it out of the way in order to give myself time to polish.

He moaned at me wretchedly, alluding to his obtuseness and slowness with a wealth of invective that was nothing less than masochistic; the fact that he was giving one of the most expert performances of his career never occurred to him, and he continued to wallow. However, long before the dress rehearsal he vanquished his troubles and became word-perfect, which was, in a way, disappointing, as the picture of that tall, gyrating figure with arms and legs waving had grown dear to me.

Ursula Jeans was the fourth member of the cast. She was ebullient, quick and only occasionally flustered. She rushed at her scenes as though she were about to vault over a high gate, but eventually, the first exuberance over, she simmered down into a charming performance.

Altogether, it was well acted. I was happy with my part and I think I was good in it; at all events, when Sam Behrman, the author, arrived from America, he said that he was delighted with all of us. I trembled at his arrival even more than the others did, realising that he had known the inestimable pleasure of seeing the play acted by Alfred and Lynn. I didn't want him to say that I was better than Alfred; if he had, I should not only have disliked him for saying so, but not believed him. However, I needn't have worried; Sam Behrman was tactful and kind to a degree. He insisted that there was no comparison between the two per-formances, that they were completely different both in approach and technique; and if in his secret heart he considered Alfred better than I in certain scenes and me better than Alfred in certain other scenes, I am convinced that no amount of cajoling would ever have got it out of him.

He was encouraging and charming to us all and instead of hating him coming to rehearsals, which we had all been doing in anticipation, our hearts sank whenever we looked out and noticed that his shining bald head and quizzically gleaming spectacles were missing.

8

The first night of *The Second Man* should by rights have been particularly nerve-racking for me, but somehow or other it wasn't.

To begin with, I had so often, during the past two months, visualised the horror of it, that when it arrived I was conscious of little beyond a steely hatred of the first-night audience even before they came into the theatre. I wondered dispassionately whether they would shriek anything offensive at me on my first entrance, or just sit in sullenness, daring me to be good. As a matter of fact they did neither. They applauded me politely when I came on and I judged, from an early laugh or two, that they were quite willing to be amused.

By the middle of the second act I knew the play was a success. There was a pleasant tension in the house and considerable laughter and applause. No hitches occurred. The champagne bottle opened with a good resounding pop (ginger-ale pro-fessionally bottled for us by Messrs Mumm), and Raymond's revolver in the last act went off without any of those abortive clickings which are often so mortifying to an actor. In fact everything was smooth and satisfactory and the cheering at the end would have been undoubtedly gratifying if, through it, I had not been listening ironically to crueller noises.

The notices were good and there were many sly suggestions to the effect that there was in reality no such person as S. N. Behrman, as the play had obviously been written by me under a pseudonym, apparently in the craven hope that it would thus be received more favourably.

Several writers even went so far as to assert that they had discerned definite examples of my wit in many of the lines. They were palpably delighted to have uncovered such a juicy secret, and it seemed almost unkind to have to undermine such proud assurance, but although Sam and I both acknowledged to each other how sincerely flattered we were, truth *was* truth and it had to be stated that there wasn't even one phrase or word of mine in the whole play.

9

Rehearsals for the revue started almost immediately after the opening of *The Second Man,* beginning as usual with a week or so of auditions for the chorus and small parts.

Daily, morning and afternoon, we sat in the dust-sheet enshrouded gloom of the London Pavilion, Lorn, Jack, Gladys, Frank Collins and me, while Elsie April, perched on the stage at an upright piano, pounded out accompaniments and drank endless cups of tea. With us also in the stalls was Cissie Sewell, the ballet mistress for all Cochran productions, her job being to remember accurately all dance movements originated by me or Max Rivers, the dance producer, and rehearse the girls apart at different hours of the day. Cissie was red-haired, smart, nice-looking, and efficient. Her memory was fantastic, and enabled her to catch the most fleeting movement of the leg or shoulder or hand and reproduce it later in the rehearsal room with precision. She possessed, in addition to her other virtues, an outspoken critical faculty allied to the kindest heart imaginable. This combination frequently set up a considerable conflict within her during the audition period. She knew, from years of experience, most of the aspirants who appeared before us. She knew whether they were kept or not kept, whether they needed the job or merely looked on the stage as a side-line, whether they were good workers or bad workers.

She and Elsie, who were bosom friends, had a series of code signals which they exchanged whenever one of their particular favourites or *bêtes noires* appeared. Elsie, with one swift twiddle round of the piano stool, would shoot a knowing look at Cissie in the stalls. If genuine talent was imminent she would give a satisfied little nod; if, on the other hand, some poor inexpert creature of old repute came on, she would shrug her shoulders and fling her eyes up to heaven with an expression of such untold resignation, that we knew, long before the poor thing started, what to expect.

They were usually pretty accurate in their judgments, although occasionally, owing to private knowledge of some girl's sad circumstances, they would argue tooth and nail to get her the job, even if her talents were not quite up to scratch. These kindly, sentimental efforts were generally frustrated by Frank Collins, who also knew a thing or two, but as a rule, it worked both ways, for he too had his special loves and hates, and auditions were often greatly enlivened thereby.

The atmosphere of those dim auditoriums; the dust-sheets, the large brass pot for cigarette ends, the bars of chocolate contributed by Lorn, are indelibly stained on to my memory. I will always remember the weariness at the end of a long day when Elsie finally clambered down from the piano to join us in the stalls, while we added up the odd hundred people we had seen and selected dispiritedly about three possible ones. So tired were we as a rule that the effort of getting up and going home seemed too much for us, and we sat around lethargically, gossiping a little, wondering whether Phyl would be strong enough for such and such a part or whether Vera – 'You remember, dear, the one that sang "Love, Here is my Heart," and did a buck and wing' – would be, although less pretty, more reliable.

Cockie himself seldom attended these general hurly-burly auditions, preferring to wait for the later ones at which, having weeded out most of the drearies, we recalled those whom we thought were really worthy of his consideration. Naturally nobody could be definitely engaged without his OK and we were often on tenterhooks lest our selected pets should appear less talented than we thought, and let down our faith in them.

The finding of a title for the revue caused us all many racked hours of the day and many sleepless nights. We sat round with pencils and papers flogging our brains and shooting forth anything we thought of, however inappropriate, in the hope that the very fatuity of our suggestion might inspire somebody else with an idea. All the ideal revue titles seemed to have been done: *Vanity Fair, Bric-à-Brac, London, Paris and New York, Odds and Ends,* etc., etc. Finally Lorn said *This Year of Grace,* and we instantly knew that we were all right. *This Year of Grace* it was, and I still think it one of the best revue titles I have ever heard.

The show opened, as usual, in Manchester. This time I did not stay off and allow my understudy to play for me, but I went up all the same for the Sunday dress rehearsal, which went on, as was expected, all through the night but was not, on the whole, nearly as depressing as *On With the Dance* had been.

Arnold Bennett was with us, I cannot at the moment remember why, and appeared to be enchanted with the whole thing, enjoying keenly with detached amusement every hitch and every hold-up. It was nice having him there, because he cheered up our blacker moments with a joke or two, and generally emanated good will from every pore.

This Year of Grace opened at the London Pavilion in March, and was an immediate success. I was still playing *The Second Man,* but as this didn't begin until just before nine, and the revue, on the first night, rang up at eight, I was able to watch, from the back of the dress circle, the first three-quarters of an hour of it.

Quite early in the first half came my series of short one-line parodies on current plays, the final one of the series being announced as 'Any Noel Coward Play,' and I was particularly anxious to see the effect of this on the first-night audience. The scene consisted merely of a row of people, with an author in the centre, bowing, until at a given moment the leading lady stepped forward and, with tears in her voice, said – 'Ladies and gentlemen, this is the happiest moment of my life!' whereupon she burst into sobs and the entire orchestra and any of us in the audience who happened to be in the know, booed and raspberried with the utmost fervour.

The response of the first-nighters to this was interesting. There was first of all dead silence, then a titter of shocked amazement and then a full-bellied roar of laughter.

That night the performance of *The Second Man* must have been exceedingly bewildering to the audience. The management had kindly agreed to cut the intervals down to half, and I had primed Ray and Zena and Ursula to play as quickly as they could, in order that I might get back to the Pavilion in time for the finale.

I don't suppose that a play has ever been performed with such speed without losing coherence. We all four rattled through it like express trains and it was not until nearly the end of the last act that I was suddenly conscious-smitten by the sight of a poor old gentleman in the front row of the stalls, leaning forward with a strained expression and his ear cupped in his hand.

I slowed down for the last few minutes, but we all managed to get to the Pavilion, still in make-up, for part of the second half of the revue.

Everything in the show went well. Tilly Losch made a huge success. Maisie Gay triumphed with 'The Bus Rush' and her Channel-swimmer song, 'Up, Girls, and At 'Em.' Sonnie Hale and Jessie Matthews were charming in 'A Room with a View' and 'Try to Learn to Love,' and Sonnie brought down the house with 'Dance, Little Lady,' which he did with Laurie Devine against a group of glittering, macabre figures wearing Oliver Messel masks.

A great sensation was caused by Jack Holland and Jean Barry, who danced 'The Blue Danube' in the finale of the first half and a Spanish dance in the second half. They were certainly magnificent, swift, graceful and handsome to look at. Everybody fared well, and the notices were ecstatic. It appeared, from reading them, that I was the most brilliant man of the theatre that England had ever known, and the delightful audacity of parodying my own recent failure shook journalistic admirers of the sporting instinct to the marrow. In fact, far from creeping back into favour I was shot into it with the drum accompaniment and velocity of a Star Trap Act.

10

The idea of *Bitter Sweet* was born in the early summer of that year, 1928. It appeared quite unexpectedly and with no other motivation beyond the fact that I had vaguely discussed with Gladys the possibilities of writing a romantic Operette. She and I were staying with Ronald Peake, her family solicitor, in Surrey, and an hour or so before we were due to leave, Mr Peake happened to play to us on the gramophone a new German orchestral record of 'Die Fledermaus.' Immediately a confused picture of uniforms, bustles, chandeliers and gas-lit cafés formed in my mind, and later, when we were driving over Wimbledon Common, we drew the car to a standstill by the roadside, and in the shade of a giant horse-chestnut tree mapped out roughly the story of Sari Linden.

The uniforms, bustles, chandeliers and gas-lit café all fell into place eagerly, as though they had been waiting in the limbo for just this cue to enter.

There had been little or no sentiment on the London musical stage for a long while. The Daly's operettas, with their crashing second-act finales in which the heroines dissolved in tears, or danced with the footman, had given place to an endless succession of slick American 'Vo do deo do' musical farces in which the speed was fast, the action complicated, and the sentimental value negligible.

It seemed high time for a little romantic renaissance, and very soon, a few of the preliminary melodies began to form in my head. However, the whole idea had to be shelved for a while owing to the urgency of other plans.

The Second Man had finished its run, and Cockie and Archie Selwyn were trying to persuade me to play in *This Year of Grace* in New York in the autumn. The idea was for me to rewrite certain of Sonnie Hale's material to suit my own talents and to co-star with Beatrice Lillie, who was to use the bulk of Maisie's numbers and sketches. There would, of course, have to be an entirely new cast, as Cockie wisely and resolutely refused to break up the London company, which was playing to capacity.

I was not particularly keen on the project at first, but presently the idea of dancing, singing again and playing a series of different rôles during an evening instead of only one, began to seem more attractive, and finally I decided to do it, and signed my contract.

In July Cockie and I travelled over to New York for a couple of weeks, a little outing that we both agreed should come under the heading of 'Managerial Expenses,' considering that the object of our visit was to discover fresh talent and discuss with Archie various arrangements for theatres, try-outs, etc.

As a matter of fact, we didn't find much talent beyond George Fontana and Marjorie Moss, whom we had both known for years, and one girl who could do side splits and walk on her hands with an air of social nonchalance that was exceedingly fetching. But we had a pleasant time.

We stayed at the Ritz and went out constantly to theatres and parties. Constance Collier was in New York, staying at the Algonquin in her usual slightly rusty splendour, surrounded by cats, dogs, monkeys, parrots and coffee percolators. She had become close friends with the new phenomenon of Broadway, Jed Harris, who had produced already, in rapid succession, several sure-fire successes.

He was an extraordinary creature, with an authentic flair for the theatre. He talked brilliantly, and turned on, whenever he considered it worth while, a personal charm that was impossible to resist. He had made a large fortune, but beyond a shining Packard car, the evidence of it lay only in his conversation, and then only occasionally. His was one of the most interesting self-devouring egos I had ever met, and I found him enchanting company. Now and then he suggested to my mind that strangely ruthless insect, the Praying Mantis. I couldn't help wondering how long it would be before Jed's ego, prompted by sheer passion, ate up every scrap of him. We went to his production of *Coquette* in which Helen Hayes gave an agonisingly perfect performance and tore our emotions to shreds. We saw *Funnyface,* in which Fred and Adele Astaire were more electric than ever, and also the Guild production of the negro play *Porgy,* which Cockie immediately bought for London.

In fact, theatrically speaking, that was one of the richest two weeks I have ever spent.

As all the ships were crowded, on the voyage home Cockie and I were forced to share a cabin on the *Berengaria*. Although we had both viewed this prospect with slight apprehension, it turned out to be extremely cosy. Neither of us snored, apparently, and conversation after lights out was stimulating.

During that voyage I wrote, roughly, the first act of *Bitter Sweet,* and when I read it to Cockie and explained to him the story of the rest of it, he became at once enthusiastic. One of his greatest qualities is his amazing flair for visualising a play completely from the barest outline, and he decided then and there that he would do it, providing that I could finish it in the time, in the spring of the following year, 1929.

II

Meanwhile at home the family fortunes continued to pursue an upward course. We had sold the lease of the Ebury Street house, although as I had recently had my rooms done up at great expense I decided to keep them on.

Father, at last free from the burden of lodgers, tax-collectors, window-cleaners, etc., was installed at Goldenhurst, where he gardened to his heart's content, dealing with the wider landscape problems, while Auntie Vida had charge of the bulbs, potting and flower beds. With this arrangement, of course, a certain amount of friction was inevitable, and high words frequently winged their way across the velvet lawns.

Mother drove recklessly about the countryside in a new car. She drove well, but with an unchristian spirit of truculence towards any other vehicles that happened to be on the road. Her mishaps, on the whole, were few. She once upset the Vicar of St Mary's and his wife into a ditch in a fog, and on another occasion, owing to mistimed acceleration, she advanced triumphantly through the plate-glass window of Pearks' grovers' shop in Ashford, remaining at the wheel in a state of splendid calm, while pots of blackcurrant jam, light plum, dark plum, strawberry and

Golden Shred marmalade ricochetted gaily off the wind-screen on to the radiator. Her rage over this incident simmered for days and was not soothed by the fact that the local Ashford paper grudgingly awarded her only a paragraph or two instead of the full column she had expected.

My brother Eric, then aged twenty-three, was rather at a loose end. He had had two or three jobs, in none of which he had been particularly happy. I felt, and I know that he felt too, that to be the brother of anyone as spectacular as myself was far from comfortable. True, there were certain perquisites accruing from it, but, on the whole, I fear that my shadow lay heavily upon him.

If he had possessed any outstanding marketable talent it would, of course, have been different, but alas, apart from a genuine passion for music and sufficient ability to play it quite well on the piano, his assets were little above the average.

We discussed his prospects at length, and eventually, as he had a keen desire to see something of the world, we arranged for him to go out to Ceylon in the autumn as a tea-planter.

It was about this time that the great Barn Battle took place. This campaign, started quite unintentionally by Jack and me, flared up violently and showed every indication of continuing with all the futile persistence of the Hundred Years' War.

The beginning of it was simple. There was an old barn near to the house which we had left intact, feeling that later on it might be useful to us.

In the early spring of 1928, realising that for all of us, Mother, Father, Eric, Auntie Vida and me, supplemented frequently by Lorn, Father, Jack or Jeffery, to live together in one small house was really asking too much of human forbearance, Jack had evolved a plan for rebuilding the interior of the barn and transforming the whole into a home for the family, while I took over the house. The view from the barn was much lovelier than from the house and, with bathroom, dining-room, bedrooms, living-room, etc., we considered that it ought to be the acme of comfort.

At this suggestion the family rose to a man, alternatively furious, outraged, martyred, hurt, and bitterly resigned. The basis of the trouble was apparently a deeply embedded conviction that I had grown to be ashamed of my loved ones and wished to banish them beyond sight and sound of my new-found 'grand' friends, for whom I obviously considered them not good enough.

As my new-found 'grand' friends that year had consisted solely of Bobbie Andrews, who had come down for a couple of weekends, this argument seemed unjust. Jack and I, terrified by the storm we had created, surrendered, but as it seemed a shame that all our elaborate schemes for the expansion of Goldenhurst should be grounded on the shoals of family pride, we set to work, and with the aid of builders and plumbers from Folkestone, made over the barn and cottage into an establishment for my exclusive use.

When ultimately finished, the family were enraptured with it, and, to this day, use it a great deal in my absence, for entertaining their new-found 'grand' friends.

12

My determination that in this narrative the reader shall take the rough with the smooth impels me to relate that, two days before rehearsals for the American production of *This Year of Grace* were due to begin, I was operated on for piles.

This meant postponing everything for two weeks, during which I lay, in bad pain and a worse temper, in a nursing home.

The newspapers described the affair with light-hearted reticence as 'a minor operation,' and I couldn't help reflecting that if that were a minor operation, I should have been far happier with a Caesarian.

The night before I was to go under the knife, having been respectfully shaved and offered some barley sugar, I was left dejectedly alone in a small bed in a minute white room. Realising that after the anaesthetic I should probably have all, if not more, sleep than I was usually accustomed to, I passed the long hours until dawn pleasantly enough by writing the second act of *Bitter*

Sweet, and in the morning conscious that I had accomplished a considerable job of work upheld me throughout the routine indignities that I had to endure.

The nursing home was conservative to a degree, and so nineteenth century in atmosphere that I fully expected the nurses to come in in crinolines.

There was one bathroom on the fourth floor which contained, in addition to the usual offices, a forbidding geyser. This snarled angrily at those patients who were strong enough to survive a long, frightening ascent in a lift which, I imagine, must assuredly have been the pride of the Arts and Crafts Exhibition at Earl's Court in 1842.

I had several visitors during my convalescence, all of whom were kind and sympathetic, and seldom referred, except obliquely, to the mortifying nature of my complaint.

Marie Tempest was the exception. She came a lot to see me, and we discussed every detail with enthusiasm, and I need hardly say that her visits were far and away the most welcome of all.

It was my first experience of nursing-home life, and once the acuter discomforts were over I settled down to enjoy it. There was, first and foremost, a pleasant sense of timelessness. The moment the early morning washing and prinking were done with I could sink back in clean pyjamas on to a freshly made bed with the heavenly sensation that there was no hurry and no necessity to do anything whatever.

There came a beaten-up egg in milk at eleven, and possibly a visit from the Surgeon at twelve; apart from these minor interruptions the hours stretched lazily ahead towards lunch, my afternoon snooze, one or two amiable visitors, an early supper and then the night.

The nights were the nicest of all. When the bed had been remade, the curtains drawn, the dark green shade put over the light, and the night nurse had whisked out of the room, a different kind of peace descended. There was no obligation to sleep. I had rested a lot during the day and could rest more on the following day. A gentle dimness enveloped me, a detachment from affairs. The life outside seemed incredibly remote.

Occasionally a taxi drew up on the other side of the road. I could hear the screech of the tyres, the sound of the door opening and shutting, a murmur of voices, a sharp little ting as the driver reset the fare meter, then the grinding of gears and a diminishing hum until there was silence again. I pictured, without envy, those strangers letting themselves into their houses, switching on the lights in the dining-room and finding the usual decanter, siphon, glasses and sandwiches curling slightly at the edges in spite of having been covered with a plate.

I imagined problems for them: jealousy perhaps, suspicions of infidelity, a business crisis to be dealt with the next day, a brief to be prepared, or a political speech. Sleep was essential to them; they must get to bed and sleep because Time was whirling them along too fast. Not for them the luxury of lying still and making faces out of the shadows on the ceiling. Not for them the delight of a sudden cup of tea at three in the morning with a couple of Marie biscuits and one chocolate one. They had to be active and energetic and get things done, as I should have to in a week or so, but in the meantime I could relax, comfortably aware that I was not imprisoned by a long illness and that I should be up and about again before this delicious enforced rest had had time to become tedious.

13

We rehearsed the American production of *This Year of Grace* on the Pavilion stage and in the Poland Rooms. I had, during the summer, taken the precaution of going for six weeks to a dancing school in order to get limbered up, a necessary but painful procedure, for although I was not called upon to dance much, I had to be reasonably agile.

The show was unchanged except for the interpolation of two single numbers for Beattie, 'World Weary' and 'I Can't Think' (an imitation of Gertrude Lawrence); two duets which we did together: 'Lilac Time,' an *opéra bouffe* burlesque, and 'Love, Life and Laughter,' a sketch and song of Paris night life in the eighties, which had originally been created by Maisie Gay in one of the Charlot revues.

The cast was surprisingly good considering how difficult it always is to duplicate an entire production, and we all sailed off to America to play a try-out week in Baltimore, before coming to the Selwyn Theatre in New York.

The Lunts, who happened to be playing in the next-door theatre to us in Baltimore, came to our Sunday rehearsal and assured me that I was going to be fine, but I was depressed and perfectly certain that I was going to be nothing of the sort. In 'Lilac Time,' 'Love, Life and Laughter' and 'Dance, Little Lady,' which latter I did with Florence Desmond, I was all right, but in 'A Room with a View' with Madeleine Gibson, and in the ballet announcement, I wasn't half as effective as Sonnie had been, and in most of the other things I had to do in the show I felt myself to be only adequate.

Beattie was good all through, but being, like all of us, in a bad state of nerves and fright, she contrived to be completely and utterly devilish throughout the whole week. Before I continue further, I should like to say that she was then, and is now, a much-loved friend. The fact that she was an uppish, temperamental, tiresome, disagreeable, inconsiderate, insufferable friend during that one week of her life in no way sullies my steadfast love for her. It may have temporarily dimmed it to the extent of my wishing ardently to wring her neck, but once we had opened in New York all rancour disappeared, as the mist on a glass disappears with the application of a damp rag, the damp rag in that instance being the re-emergence of Beattie's real character. Whether it was the stimulus of the triumphant success she made, or a letter from her son at home, or the General Election, I don't know. I do know, however, that the moment the first night was over she changed miraculously back to her old self, just as though some magician had whacked her sharply over the head with a wand, and became, what I had always expected her to be, one of the most generous and delightful partners it had ever been my privilege to work with.

There was even more than the usual first-night excitement going on when we opened in New York. Everyone was running in and out of everyone else's dressing-rooms, the passages were stacked high with boxes of flowers, Frank Collins and Dan O'Neil were conducting a gloomy little conference with the heads of departments on the bare stage.

I felt as though I were in a sort of coma. The outlook was so black, the past week had been so gruelling, and although I was sure that the scenery was bound to fall down, the lights go wrong all through and the audience walk out on us, I was really too exhausted to care.

We went through the first half in a trance, more and more astounded, as each scene concluded, that no hitches had occurred. The second half went, if possible, even more smoothly than the first. Not a light was wrong (Frank Collins had stationed himself in the limelight box in the front of the house), not a property was out of place, and the cast, stimulated by the responsiveness of the audience, played magnificently. Altogether it was a triumphant evening, and Beattie and I fell into each other's arms sobbing with relief at the end.

From then onwards Beattie and I co-starred not only theatrically but socially in all directions. We appeared together everywhere. At large Charity Balls where we sang 'Lilac Time,' at select Ladies' Clubs where we sang 'Lilac Time,' at fashionable night-clubs where our entrance was the signal for an immediate flood of requests for us to sing 'Lilac Time,' and at small convivial theatrical parties to which we were invited on the strict understanding that in no circumstances would we sing 'Lilac Time.'

A week or so after the opening of the revue we gave a midnight performance which theatrical New York attended *en masse,* and which completely unbalanced our performance for several days afterwards. However good the audience were following that midnight show, they inevitably seemed flat and uninspiring.

In order to chasten our spirits and bring us down from our high altitude with a bump, Archie Selwyn had arranged that the next night should be a 'Benefit.' This benefit business is a custom in America, and although from the point of view of the charity concerned it is unquestionably profitable, from the point of view of the actors concerned it is Hell.

One of the most remunerative and popular means of raising funds for a pet cause is the buying out of the house for a performance of a successful play. Once bought and paid for, the tickets are resold at fabulous prices to the supporters of the charity in question. This, of course, is not effective unless the show is new and the demand for seats high.

The managements obviously have no objection to the arrangement, as it ensures the house being sold out at box-office prices, which is as much, if not more than they can ordinarily expect. For the actors, however, it is miserable in the extreme. A 'Benefit' night means, as a rule, an audience of such soul-shattering dreariness that it is as much as one can do to give even the semblance of a good performance.

The reason of this is difficult to discover. Whether the fact that they have all paid far too much for their seats, and are consequently in a mood of sullen resentment to start with, accounts for their behaviour, I do not know. But I do know that whether I have been warned beforehand that it is a charity audience, or whether I haven't, I can tell the first moment I step on to the stage.

To begin with, the stalls are usually half empty during the first act, and one is continually distracted by the noisy arrival of late-comers, who churn down the aisles, generally in parties, and discuss loudly, with complete disregard for the performers or those already present, who is to sit next to whom. Once seated they scan the house anxiously with opera-glasses to discover whether or not their dearest enemies have better seats than they have. Their response to the play is apathetic, to say the least of it. Lines which, with an ordinary audience, always get big laughs, are unrewarded by so much as a twitter, and the play proceeds with almost as little reaction as if one were playing a dress rehearsal in an empty theatre.

Generally, in one of the intervals, a lady arrives back-stage covered with pearls, sables and orchids, to make a speech before the curtain, appealing for funds, which invariably enshrouds the house in still deeper gloom, so that the effort to re-establish the mood of the play afterwards is similar in sensation to remounting a horse immediately after you have fallen off it and broken three ribs.

During the last act there is a certain awakening of activity as people rise and leave in chattering groups in order to get to their cars before the rush begins. At the final curtain there is a general exodus, and the cast is lucky if it gets one curtain call.

14

This Year of Grace continued to play to packed houses. I had originally contracted to play it only for three months, but in the face of the business and Archie Selwyn's persuasions, I agreed to carry on for longer. During that winter Alec Woollcott inaugurated his Sunday morning breakfast parties. These peculiar functions, starting at nine a.m. and continuing until three or four in the afternoon, were adorned by a varied mixture of personalities ranging from Ethel Barrymore and Harpo Marx to lady novelists, osteopaths, *soi-disant* foreign princesses, cub-journalists, and grey university professors.

Alec, although lacking the essential grace and fragility of an eighteenth-century marquise, being as a rule unshaven and clad in insecure egg-stained pyjamas, managed in his own harum-scarum way to evoke a certain 'salon' spirit.

There was always a din of voices augmented by the crash of crockery and the rattle of dice and backgammon men, above which Alec could sometimes be heard crooning to himself in ghastly baby language – 'Evwy night my pwayers I say, I learn my lessons EVWY day' – until his opponent happened to throw double sixes, whereupon he would scream shrilly – 'Bitch delivered of a Drab' in tones of such, apparently, ungovernable fury that any strangers present who were unaccustomed to his particular brand of badinage would hastily brush the breakfast crumbs from their laps and edge, nervously, towards the door.

In addition to Dorothy Parker, Ben Hecht, Charlie MacArthur, Herbert Swope, George and Beatrice Kaufman, Alice Duer Miller, and Marc Connelly, you would be almost certain to find the Lunts, Margalo Gillmore, Thornton Wilder, twittering gently in a corner, Kathleen Norris, in majestic black satin and pearls with a rowdy look in her eye, and, if she and Alec happened to be on speaking terms, Edna Ferber.

It was at one of these strange galaxies that I met William Bolitho. His name I knew from his book *Murder for Profit* and his articles in the *New York World,* and the first thing that struck me about him was his intensity. It was not an obvious intensity, in fact his manner was on the whole singularly detached. He looked, if anything, a little irritated, as if the close proximity of so many people irked him and made him uneasy. He was tall and fair with blue eyes and a biggish nose, which he had a trick of whacking with his finger when he wished to emphasise some particular point. I liked him immediately, and when he invited me to dine the following evening before the show, I accepted with pleasure.

We dined at the Plaza: he, Sybil (his wife), and me. We talked incessantly, frequently all three of us at once. It was as though we were together again after a long absence; a reunion of close friends rather than an introductory meeting.

They lived near Avignon at Montfavet. Their house, they said, was surrounded by trees and there was a swimming-pool that William was very proud of, and several fruit trees and a vegetable garden of which he was still prouder. They spent six months of every year there and were returning quite soon.

I told them to expect me some time during the summer, and left them in a rush, having allowed myself only a bare ten minutes in which to get to the theatre.

15

During that winter, January and February, 1929, I finished *Bitter Sweet,* on which I had been working intermittently for the last few months. The book had been completed long since, but the score had been causing me trouble, until one day, when I was in a taxi on my way back to the apartment after a matinée, the 'I'll See You Again' waltz dropped into my mind, whole and complete, during a twenty minutes' traffic block. After that everything went smoothly, and I cabled to Cockie in London suggesting that he start making preliminary arrangements regarding theatre, opening date, etc.

My first choice for Sari had been Gertie Lawrence, but when the score was almost done, she and I both realised that her voice, although light and charming, was not strong enough to carry such a heavy singing rôle. She was naturally disappointed and I promised that the next play I wrote would be especially for her.

In the meantime a leading lady who could sing beautifully, look lovely and act well, had to be found. Evelyn Laye was the obvious choice in London, but she, unfortunately, owing to various previous contracts, was unobtainable.

One afternoon, in the lobby of the Algonquin Hotel, I ran into Peggy Wood. She had just come in from the country and was wearing a raincoat, an unbecoming rubbery hat on the back of her head, and horn-rimmed glasses, and she looked as far removed from my vision of Sari Linden as Mrs Wiggs of the Cabbage Patch.

I had known her on and off for several years, in fact ever since my first visit to New York in 1921, but oddly enough, in all that time I had never once seen her on the stage. I had, of course, heard on all sides enthusiastic accounts of her acting and her looks and the loveliness of her voice, but never having been able to judge for myself, and confronted by that rubber hat, that face devoid of make-up and those horn-rimmed glasses, it was with some trepidation that I heard myself asking her if she would care to come over to London and do an operetta.

She replied that she'd love to, but that hadn't I better hear her sing first? And so we rushed off immediately to my studio in the Hôtel des Artistes. On arrival, Peggy realised that she hadn't any music, and so she darted out and down the street where, fortunately, her music teacher happened to live, and returned in a few minutes with the score of *Manon*.

She sat down at once and started to sing, but had to stop owing to lack of breath.

After she had rested a little and had a glass of water she started again, and the first few bars she sang assured me that here was the ideal Sari.

I was impressed by her surprising lack of 'star' manner. With a long list of distinguished successes behind her she behaved as though she were being offered a good part for the first time. She was enthusiastic over the music I played to her. I knew from that moment that she would be a delight to work with, and I was right. In due course Cockie cabled a contract to Peggy, and with that primary difficulty settled, I continued to add finishing touches to the score and lyrics, until the whole show was complete.

16

Bitter Sweet went into rehearsal at the Scala Theatre at the end of May. We were ultimately bound for His Majesty's, but the Guitrys were at the moment in possession of it, and as the show was booked for a three weeks' try-out in Manchester, it was more convenient to rehearse in an empty theatre, where we could set up our scenery and work at nights as well as in the mornings and afternoons.

From the beginning *Bitter Sweet* went smoothly. Cockie and I, having taken an arduous trip to Berlin and Vienna in an effort to find a foreign tenor to play 'Carl,' had returned to London empty-handed and engaged George Metaxa, who had been available all the time. Ivy St Helier, for whom I had written the rôle of 'Manon La Crevette,' was already engaged, and the rest of the cast fell into our laps with hardly any trouble on our part at all.

We had had the usual auditions, and the chorus we had engaged sang well and looked pleasant. The scenery was well under way, the first and last acts having been designed by Gladys and the middle act by Ernst Stern. Peggy Wood arrived in good time from America and proceeded slowly but surely to build her distinguished performance. In fact, I reflected, with everything going so marvellously, the play, according to all theatrical tenets, couldn't escape being the gravest fiasco.

Cockie, who had tactfully left the production entirely to Gladys and me, came to the last rehearsal before the dress rehearsal. Before he arrived I made a little speech to the company through my microphone which I had had installed in the dress circle, imploring them to play up for all they were worth. The scenery was up but there was no orchestra, so Elsie officiated at the piano at the side of the stage. The company wore their ordinary day clothes and the lights consisted merely of a few battens and the footlights. In fact it was a thorough-going working rehearsal.

In due course Cockie arrived and he, Lorn, Jack, Frank, Cissie, Gladys and I took our places in the front row of the dress circle and waited apprehensively while Elsie scampered through the overture.

Of all the performances I ever saw of *Bitter Sweet* that rehearsal was far and away the most exciting. Each and every member of that always fine company, from Peggy down to the smallest walk-on in the café scene, was perfect. There were no dry-ups, no muddles in the dance routine and no undue waits between the scenes. Dan O'Neil, even with a skeleton staff, was, like everyone else backstage, inspired.

At the end Cockie thanked the company through the microphone in a voice husky with emotion and added that he wouldn't part with his rights in the play for a million pounds.

It was an unforgettable, glorious three hours and the dress parade the next day, according to the law of compensations, was correspondingly ghastly.

Many of the dresses had not been finished in time, and several of those that were, didn't fit. Half the shoes were missing. The stage was littered with squabbling dressmakers, shoemakers, wigmakers, fitters, and resentful chorus girls who hated their wigs and their bonnets, complained about their feet, and said they couldn't sing unless their collars were loosened. Several of them appeared with their bustles on back to front, and the smart uniforms of the Austrian officers looked as if they had only recently evacuated the front-line trenches.

Peggy sailed on and off in a series of lovely gowns, causing no trouble and minding her own business. Ivy, on the other hand, carried on like fifty prima donnas in one. She loathed her dresses, refused to wear her wigs, tried to insist on silk stockings which for the period would have been quite inappropriate, wept and wailed and entreated, until Gladys and I sprang at her like tigers and nearly murdered her.

At the dress rehearsal in Manchester she cheered up a bit, and after the opening night when she had given a splendid performance and had made a triumphant success, she changed back, like Beattie in New York, into her old gay, humorous self.

The Manchester first night was riotous. Peggy made a gracious speech and so did Cockie, in which he touchingly and generously handed me the credit for the whole production which, I may say, without his enthusiasm, his lavishness, and his unwavering trust in me, could never have been possible. The Press notices the next day were almost incoherent with praise, and the house was immediately sold out for the entire three weeks.

I think that of all the shows I have ever done *Bitter Sweet* gave me the greatest personal pleasure. My favourite moments were: the finale of the first act when Carl and Sari elope; the café scene when the curtain slowly falls on Carl's death, in a silence broken only by Manon's sobs; the entrance of Madame Sari Linden in her exquisite white dress of the nineties and, above all, the final moment of the play, when, to the last crashing chords of 'I'll See You Again,' Sari, as an old woman, straightens herself with a gesture of indomitable pride and gallantly walks off the stage. That gesture was entirely Peggy's idea, and the inspired dramatic simplicity of it set her for ever in my memory as a superb actress.

The London first night was definitely an anti-climax after Manchester. The audience were tremendously fashionable, and, for the first part of the play, almost as responsive as so many cornflour blancmanges.

Later on they warmed up a little, and at the end the upper parts of the house cheered. I sat with Gladys at the end in the dome of the auditorium where the spotlights were housed. It was pleasant to look down upon the audience unobserved. None of them seemed anxious to leave their seats and go home, from which I gathered that they were waiting for me to appear to make a speech. But my speech-making days were over, I did not appear, and when an hour or so later I was hailed at the stage door by a mob of vociferous gallery girls who demanded why I had not come out in response to their calls for me, I replied, with genuine irritation, that I only came on when they booed.

The Press notices the next day and on the Sunday following were remarkable for their tone of rather grudging patronage. It seemed as though the critics were ashamed of their recent outburst of enthusiasm over *This Year of Grace* and wished to retrench themselves behind a barricade of non-committal clichés. It would be too bad, after all, if I were encouraged to believe that there was anything remarkable in writing, composing and producing a complete operetta. I might become uppish again and this was an excellent opportunity of putting me gently but firmly in my place. Some praised the book, but dismissed the music as being reminiscent and of no consequence. Some liked the music, but were horrified by the commonplace sentimentality of the book. The lyrics were hardly mentioned, and although the acting and *décor* were favourably received, the general consensus of opinion was that the play would probably run for six weeks or, at the most, three months.

17

Cockie, already occupied with plans for an American production of *Bitter Sweet* in the autumn, had persuaded Evelyn Laye to play 'Sari.' This settled, he and Gladys and I went to France to start off again on the discouraging search for a tenor to play 'Carl.' This time, in addition to a tenor we had to find a soubrette to play 'Manon.'

Paris was hot and uncomfortable. We were surrounded by active theatrical agents who produced tenors and soubrettes by the score, until we were dizzy. None of them seemed anywhere near good enough.

Finally we engaged a little French comedienne called Mireille for 'Manon.' She was actually a bit young for the part, but her English was good and she sang well.

We were still without a 'Carl,' and were becoming more and

more disheartened, when a handsome young Roman appeared with a letter of introduction from Princess Jane San Faustino. He had a good voice, long eyelashes, short legs, no stage experience and a violin, and although at the moment he couldn't speak a word of English, he swore with fervour that he would learn it in two months if we would only give him the part. We all felt a little dubious, but he seemed the likeliest possibility so far and so, after a certain amount of weary discussion, we engaged him.

This achieved, Gladys went back to London to devote herself to scenic problems, and I went to Avignon to stay with the Bolithos.

There was nothing to do at Montfavet but swim in the pool, lie in the garden, and occasionally drive into Avignon. William was just completing his book *Twelve Against the Gods* and was seldom visible before lunch.

The house was indeed thickly surrounded by trees, and might have been gloomy had anyone but the Bolithos been occupying it. As it was, the atmosphere was gay enough and indescribably peaceful. The food was plain and good, and we drank a sourly delicious *vin du pays* with every meal. Also with every meal William talked, and Time being serenely unimportant in that house, we often sat on for hours arguing and discussing and shouting at one another. He talked with fire and grace and beauty, and with apparently a profound knowledge of every subject under the sun. His vocabulary was brilliant and varied. He was often violent but never didactic, and he never appeared to monopolise the conversation or to show off or to try for too long to hold the floor.

Of all the minds I have ever encountered, his, I think, was the richest and the most loving. Those all too brief ten days I spent in his company turned me inside out, stimulated the best of my ambitions, readjusted several of my uneasy values, and banished many meretricious ones, I hope, for ever; and I went back to London strongly elated and bursting with gratitude to him for the strange new pride I found in myself.

18

The rehearsals for the American production of *Bitter Sweet* also took place at the Scala, and whereas with the original company everything had been easy, with this one it was exactly the opposite. The stimulus of building something new, watching the play grow, fill out and develop day by day, was naturally lacking. Everything was set, the formula was laid down, and with no excitement and no sense of discovery, it was all dreary to a degree.

Evelyn was delightful to work with, and the one bright spot in the whole business.

Jack, Gladys, Frank, Danny, Evelyn and I travelled over on the *Mauretania,* while the company followed on a slower boat. Cockie, much to our dismay, was unable to come at all, which meant that I was nominally in charge, and had to deal with Selwyn and Ziegfeld. If I had realised at the time the exasperation that this entailed, I should have insisted on Cockie's coming, even if it had meant shanghai-ing him. The voyage was comparatively uneventful. Ina Claire and John Gilbert, who had been staying with me at Goldenhurst in the course of a rather strained honeymoon, were on board, and enlivened the trip to a certain extent by their conjugal infelicities, quarrelling and making up and quarrelling and making up again unceasingly, all the way from Southampton to the Statue of Liberty.

Eventually we arrived in Boston for our two weeks' try-out, and embarked on a full Sunday-night rehearsal with orchestra in the Colonial Theatre.

It was at that rehearsal that we realised once and for all that our Roman tenor could never open without doing incalculable harm to the play. We had been buoying ourselves up with the hope that his English, over which he had been slaving, would improve sufficiently for him to be understood, but it was no good; up against the orchestra he was not only unintelligible but inaudible as well, also his lack of acting experience was so apparent, that even if he could have been heard, his important scenes would have gone for nothing. I felt desperately sorry for him. He had worked hard and done his best, but Evelyn and the play had to be considered, and so I told him that he couldn't appear. It was a painful scene, as those scenes always are, but there was no time to waste, and I left Dan O'Neil to comfort him and devoted my attention to Gerald Nodin, whom I had decided to put in his place. Nodin had originally sung 'Tokay' in the London production, and although quite wrong in type for 'Carl,' he had the advantage of knowing the show thoroughly, and was ambitious enough to make the utmost of himself.

All that night and all the next day he worked. Evelyn played her scenes with him over and over again, encouraging him and helping him in every way she could think of. Watching her and knowing how tired and nervous she was, I found it easy to understand why she was so adored by every company she had ever worked with.

On the day of production Ziegfeld asked me to lunch and told me in course of it that, as I had so resolutely refused his offer of a smarter male chorus and twelve ravishing show-girls (an offer, incidentally, which had been made daily since our arrival in America), he was going to refrain from any undue display over the New York first night and, contrary to his usual custom, was not even going to raise the prices. I received this dispiriting announcement apathetically, being far too exhausted to care whether he gave the seats away with a packet of chewing-gum.

The show, however, was an enormous success in Boston, and by the time the New York first night arrived, it had been so publicised that a special cordon of police had to be called out to control the traffic in Sixth Avenue. Floodlighting was used to illuminate the gratified audience as they came into the theatre. Flashlight photographs were taken of every celebrity that entered the lobby, and seats on the orchestra floor were sold by speculators for as much as two hundred and fifty dollars a pair. Ziegfeld, whom I now addressed affectionately as 'Flo,' had placed his office and private box at the disposal of Gladys, Jack and me. He had generously stacked it with flowers, caviare and champagne, and whenever, during the performance, we found a certain scene too wearisome to be borne, we retired to it and had a drink, with the result that by the end of the evening we were merrily unconcerned as to whether the show was a success or not. As a matter of fact, it was. The company, although I never felt them to be up to their London equivalents, played, on the whole, remarkably well. But it was Evelyn who turned the scale. It was Evelyn's night from first to last. She played as though she were enchanted. Never before at any of the rehearsals or at any of the performances in Boston had she given a quarter of the grace and charm and assurance that she gave that night. Early on in the ballroom scene she conquered the audience completely by singing the quick waltz song, 'Tell Me, What is Love?' so brilliantly, and with such a quality of excitement, that the next few minutes of the play were entirely lost in one of the most prolonged outbursts of cheering I have ever heard in a theatre.

Her performance was magnificent all through, and she fully deserved every superlative that the Press lavished upon her the next day. It would, of course, have been impossible for her to play with such inspiration at every subsequent performance, and I don't suppose for a moment that she either could or did, but it was she, and she alone, who put the play over that night.

PART NINE

I sailed from San Francisco in one of the Dollar Line ships, the *President Garfield* at four p.m. on the 29th of November, 1929.

The day was grey and chilly, and an angry wind swept through the Golden Gate, whipping the harbour into waves and tearing the smoke out of the ship's funnel in a straight black line.

The important fact that this holiday was an escape that I had been planning for a long while dwindled under a general sense of futility. Jeffery, who had given up his job on the *New York World* in the spring and gone off in a freight boat to the South Seas and Australia, had arranged to meet me on the 23rd of December in the Imperial Hotel, Tokio. We had sat in the garden at Goldenhurst with a globe between us on the grass planning the places we were going to, picturing (inaccurately) the Temple of Heaven in Peking, the Ruins of Angkor, vivid tropical jungles and the road to Mandalay, flying-fish and all. Then, with soft Kentish greens all around us and grey Kentish sheep punctuating our imaginative flights with gentle bleats, the whole scheme seemed glamorous beyond words; now, however, in the grip of inevitable 'boat-departure' anti-climax, I was lonely and depressed, and felt that I should have been far wiser to have stayed at home and read a travel book.

I looked dismally at the packages of fruit and flowers and books which various friends had sent me, and even more dismally at a map hanging by the purser's office. Far over in the corner of it, among a welter of greens and browns, I could discern a minute reddish speck which was England and with the aid of the pin from my tie I fixed approximately the spot where, probably at this very moment, Auntie Vida was battling through the weather with a trowel to attack the weeds in the orchard.

After dinner – an interlude of polite conversation at the captain's table – I sat on deck for a while. It was getting dark, and far away astern a few lights were shimmering on the coast. The weather was clearing and the sea calm.

It was a good moment for retrospection, so I put my feet up on the rail and relaxed, aware suddenly that time was no longer exigent. I had nothing to do, hours stretched before me into the future, hundreds and thousands of hours. No more rehearsals, no more first nights, no more leading ladies to be cajoled, no more theatrical anxieties, arguments and irritations. My dramatic sense saw me picturesquely languid, wearier than I really was, and a self-conscious peace descended upon me as I lay there looking up at the stars.

I journeyed back into the past without any particular aim or direction, allowing events of the past few months to hobnob with more elderly memories. I saw myself in a sailor suit singing 'Come Along with Me to the Zoo, Dear'; in a tail-suit singing, 'Dance, Little Lady'; in a sweat-stained dressing-gown in New York pounding out short stories on my typewriter; in baggy riding-breeches riding along the sands at Deauville. I heard, dimly, the cheers for *The Vortex* and, less dimly, the catcalls for *Sirocco.* I heard orchestras tuning-up and fateful, shuffling sounds of curtains rising. People, too, popped up briefly out of the limbo and then sank back again like the little white letters in vermicelli soup when you churn it with your spoon. Gwen Kelly singing 'Every Morn I Bring Thee Violets'; Mary Garden singing 'Vissi D'Arte'; Mother in grey satin and a feather boa smiling exultantly over an ice-cream soda in Selfridge's – Mother again, hot and tired, cooking in the Ebury Street kitchen; Charles Hawtrey patting me on the back; Robert Courtneidge saying 'You're not only a very young actor but a very bad actor!'; Stoj in a white knitted coat and skirt riding along suburban roads on a bicycle; John Ekins buying vivid artificial silk socks with me for two shillings a pair in the Berwick Market. I suddenly remembered William Bolitho talking to me just before I left New York. I had told him of a novel I intended to write, rather a neurotic novel about a man who committed suicide because he was bored.

William whacked his nose with his finger and said, almost sharply: 'Be careful about Death, it's a serious business, big and important. You can't go sauntering towards Death with a cigarette hanging from your mouth!'

I didn't know then that those were the last words he would ever speak to me, and he effaced himself along with the others to make room for some clamorous new friends I had found in Hollywood.

Looking back over my ten days in Hollywood made me gasp a bit and wish for a little neat brandy. I felt as though I had been whirled through all the side-shows of some gigantic Pleasure Park at breakneck speed. My spiritual legs were wobbly and my impressions confused. Blue-ridged cardboard mountains, painted skies, elaborate grottoes peopled with familiar figures: animated figures that moved their arms and legs, got up and sat down and spoke with remembered voices.

The houses I had visited became indistinguishable in my mind from the built interiors I had seen in the studios. I couldn't remember clearly whether the walls of Jack Gilbert's dining room had actually risen to a conventional ceiling or whether they had been sawn off half-way up to make room for scaffolding and spluttering blue arc-lamps.

I remembered an evening with Charlie Chaplin when at one point he played an accordion and at another a pipe-organ, and then suddenly became almost pathologically morose and discussed Sadism, Masochism, Shakespeare and the Infinite.

I remembered a motor drive along flat, straight boulevards with Gloria Swanson, during which we discussed, almost exclusively, dentistry.

I remembered, chaotically, a series of dinner parties, lunch parties, cocktail parties and even breakfast parties. I remembered also playing a game of tennis with Charlie MacArthur somewhere at two in the morning, with wire racquets, in a blaze of artificial moonlight and watching him, immediately afterwards, plunge fully clothed into an illuminated swimming-pool.

I remembered Laura Hope-Crews appearing unexpectedly from behind a fountain and whispering gently: 'Don't be frightened, dear – this – THIS – is Hollywood!'

I had been received with the utmost kindness and hospitality, and I enjoyed every minute of it; it was only now, in quietness, that it seemed unreal and inconclusive, as though it hadn't happened at all.

It occurred to me that I had been living in a crowd for too long; not only a crowd of friends, enemies and acquaintances, but a crowd of events: events that had followed each other so swiftly that the value of them, their causes and effects, their significance, had escaped me. My nervous energy, always excessive, had carried me so far. My determination, ambition and almost hysterical industry had been rewarded generously, perhaps too generously. I remembered driving with Gladys down the long road from Hampstead after the first night of *The Vortex* – 'And now what?'

Then there had been no time to answer; success had to be dealt with, adjustments had to be made to my new circumstances, more money, more people, more noise, more diffusion of experience, new attitudes to be acquired, a thousand new tricks to be learned. And now, after only five years, here was that offensive little query bobbing up again. The acquired attitudes were no longer new, I could slip them on and off with ease to suit every occasion. The social tricks, then so fresh and shiny, were now creaking mechanically. There were the demands I had made, miraculously granted, looking a bit smug. Most of my gift horses seemed to have bad teeth – and now what?

I comforted myself with the thought that perhaps this uneasiness, this vague sense of dissatisfaction was a good sign. If I was as superficial as so many people apparently thought – a subtle whip this, always guaranteed to raise a weal – if my mind was so shallow, if the characters I had written were so meretricious and unreal, if my achievements fell so far short of the first-rate, surely this moment of all moments, this relaxed contemplation of recent triumphs should fairly swaddle me in complacency. I should be able to smile, a smooth, detached smile – 'People say – what do they say? – let them say!' I should be able to boast, not loudly but with a quiet satisfaction – 'at least I have done this and that in a remarkably short space of time.' I should be able to defy the envious, the jealous, and the unkind – come on, if you're so critical – come on and do better! I should be serene, content with my light-weight crown, without a headache and without doubts.

On the other hand, however, I felt no conviction that this reasoning was in the least accurate. It seemed arbitrary to assume that a superficial mind was necessarily invulnerable. Perhaps my uneasiness was the true indication of my worth, the inevitable shadow thrown by thin facility; a deeper mind might suffer more, win less spectacular laurels and in the long run stake a richer claim.

There seemed no criterion by which I could judge my quality, or rather so many criteria that they nullified each other.

How, from all the written and spoken praise, blame, admiration, envy, prejudice, malice, kindness and contempt that these last few years had brought me, could I abstract a little of what was really true? Which of all those critical minds had been the most unbiased – nearest to hitting the nail on the head? How much had the precipitate flamboyance of my success prejudiced not only those who criticised my work, but the work itself? In fact, where was I and what was I? Had I done what I thought I'd done or what others thought I had done? Was my talent real, deeply flowing, capable of steady growth and ultimate maturity? Or was it the evanescent sleight-of-hand that many believed it to be; an amusing, drawing-room flair, adroit enough to skim a certain immediate acclaim from the surface of life but with no roots in experience and no potentialities?

Among all the thousands of people I knew I searched vainly in my mind to find one who could give me an answer or, at any rate, a comment accurate and honest enough to restore my sense of direction. The simple single track of earlier years seemed far away. There had been no necessity to look either to the right or to the left then, success was the goal – 'Noel Coward' in electric lights. Now I found the electric lights so dazzling that I couldn't see beyond them. It was no use asking for help, jogging policemen's elbows and enquiring the way. The lights blinding me would probably be blinding the policeman too. Solutions and answers would fall into place in time. Nobody, however well-intentioned, could find my own truths for me, and only very few could even help me to look for them. In moments of private chaos it is better to be alone; loving advice merely increases the chaos. At all events I could congratulate myself whole-heartedly on one count: I had realised, I hoped not too late, the necessity for space, and had deliberately broken away. Perhaps the next few months would answer a few of my questions for me; perhaps new countries, sights, sounds and smells, the complete cessation of familiar routines, this strange sense of timelessness would release from the caverns of my mind the most gratifying profundities. It would be enjoyable to return to my startled friends with, in addition to the usual traveller's souvenirs, a Strindbergian soul. I remember leaving the sea and the sky and the stars in charge of my problems and going below to my cabin chuckling a little at my incorrigible superficiality.

2

We arrived at Honolulu at six a.m. on a calm opalescent sea. I looked out of my port-hole as we passed Diamond Head towering above the palm trees; perched half-way up it I could see the Dillinghams' house where I hoped, at that very moment, breakfast was being prepared for me.

It all looked so gay and different from that horrible morning three years before when I had arrived and collapsed in the Moana Hotel. Then, seen through a haze of fever and unhappiness, everything had seemed too bright and highly-coloured and somehow unfriendly. But now it was enchanting.

Walter Dillingham's secretary met me at the dock and we drove off past the outlying buildings of the town, along that lovely road with the palm-fringed surf on one side and the mountains rising, clear-cut, out of the plains on the other.

Louise was unfortunately away visiting her eldest son in the States, so Walter and I had breakfast by ourselves, sitting on the terrace and looking out over descending green lawns to the town in the distance. The wide sweep of the sea outside the reef was deep blue, but inside near the shore the water was streaked with jade green. I could hear distinctly in the stillness the cries of the beach boys riding the surf at Waikiki, although they were nearly two miles away. A freighter with a jaunty red-and-black funnel was trundling across the bay, rolling so lackadaisically in the slight swell that I almost expected it to yawn.

Walter gave a dinner party for me that night, and while we dined a small Hawaiian orchestra played and sang softly outside. After dinner we all went out on to the moon-flooded patio and lay in long chairs drinking coffee and liqueurs, listening to further music and gazing up at Diamond Head above us.

The four days in Honolulu passed swiftly. I motored over to Mokuleia and bathed from that beach where before I had spent so many homesick hours. I retrod the road from the ranch through bananas and sugar-canes where the white dust had formerly been furrowed by tears of self-pity. I walked through the pine trees, with the roar of the surf growing louder and louder in my ears until I came out on to the sand and saw the enormous waves advancing endlessly like rolls of blue velvet, unfrilled and unruffled until they broke in thunder on the reef, sending smaller editions of themselves to splay the beach with foam. I went out at night on a fish-spearing expedition and wandered about the reef waist-deep in water, making ineffectual dabs with my spear whenever I saw anything move in the light cast by the torches until finally, in triumph, I transfixed a wriggling pink octopus and handed it graciously to the natives to kill, which they did by biting its eyes out.

I visited the Thevenins who had left Mokuleia and were living in a small house just outside the town, and learned to my sorrow that poor 'Owgooste' had had to be destroyed owing to an outburst of indescribable savagery in which he had bitten the behind of a Filipino coolie.

Finally, a trifle exhausted but warmed by Hawaiian sunshine and hospitality, and conscious that I had laid for ever a number of personal ghosts, I sailed on the *Tenyo Maru,* a distinctly *passé* vessel of the N. Y. K. Line, for Yokohama.

3

The eight days on the *Tenyo* were more or less uneventful, except that we completely lost a whole Saturday, which worried me rather.

I worked hard on my novel *Julian Kane,* but became increasingly discouraged by its obvious dullness, until I finally decided that if it continued as it was going the future readers of it would commit suicide from boredom long before the hero ever reached that point of defeat, and so discarding it I proceeded to concentrate on finding an idea for a play.

Gertie Lawrence, the night before I had left New York, had given a farewell party for me and, as a going-away present, a little gold book from Cartiers's which when opened and placed on the writing-table in my cabin disclosed a clock, calendar and thermometer on one side, and an extremely pensive photograph of Gertie herself on the other. This rich gift, although I am sure prompted by the least ulterior of motives, certainly served as a delicate reminder that I had promised to write a play for us both, and I gazed daily, often with irritation, at that anxious *retroussé* face while my mind voyaged barrenly through eighteenth-century salons, Second Empire drawing-rooms and modern cocktail bars in search of some inspiring echo, some slight thread of plot that might suitably unite us in either comedy, tragedy or sentiment.

However, nothing happened. I was aware of a complete emptiness. The Pacific Ocean, bland and calm, swished by with the perpetual off-stage effect of rice in a sieve; flying-fish skittered away from the bows, skimming along the surface for a while and disappearing with little plops; my fellow-passengers paraded round and round the deck providing me with nothing beyond a few irrelevant and purposeless conjectures, until I finally gave up. This was a holiday after all, and I refused to allow my writer's conscience to agitate it any further. I also resolved never again to make any promises that implicated my creative ability. They were limiting and tiresome and imposed too great a strain. I would write whatever the spirit moved me to write, regardless of whether the subject matter was suitable to Gertie Lawrence, Mrs Patrick Campbell or Grock, and in the meantime, feeling no particular urge to write anything at all, I closed Gertie's clock with a snap and read a book.

4

At about five o'clock on a bitter December afternoon the *Tenyo Maru* came to a standstill in the bay of Yokohama. There was a blizzard raging and, through it, I could see from the smoking-room window the quarantine launch approaching like an asthmatical old lady fussing through bead curtains.

Shapes of land appeared at intervals through the driving sleet; strange nobbly mountains dotted here and there with white specks which I gathered were lighthouses.

The drive from Yokohama to Tokio takes as a rule about fifty minutes, but mine took longer as a wheel came off the taxi when we were half-way. I sat inside in a pool of water watching, in the downpour, several excited Japanese put it on again and feeling, on the whole, discouraged by my first view of the 'Glamorous Orient.'

The Imperial Hotel was grand and comfortable, and was renowned for having stood firm during the big earthquake. A wire was handed me from Jeffery saying that he had missed a boat in Shanghai and wouldn't be with me for three days which, although disappointing, was a relief, as I had begun to think I was never going to hear from him at all.

The night before he arrived I went to bed early as I wanted to greet him as brightly as possible at seven in the morning, but the moment I switched out the lights, Gertie appeared in a white Molyneux dress on a terrace in the South of France and refused to go again until four a.m., by which time *Private Lives*, title and all, had constructed itself.

In 1923 the play would have been written and typed within a

few days of my thinking of it, but in 1929 I had learned the wisdom of not welcoming a new idea too ardently, so I forced it into the back of my mind, trusting to its own integrity to emerge again later on, when it had become sufficiently set and matured.

We found Tokio flat and painfully ugly: a sad scrap-heap of a city, rather like Wembley in the process of demolition. The streets were all muddy and everything appeared to be in course of reconstruction owing, we supposed, to perpetual earthquakes and an excess of zeal in the way of Western improvements. Fortunately, however, Tokio is far from being representative of Japan. Nikko is only four hours away with its snow-capped mountains and gurgling streams, and its temples and shrines peacefully sheltered in groves of trees.

We spent a couple of days there in a neat, shiny little hotel with paper walls, a few back numbers of *Woman and Home* and excellent food.

After three weeks in Japan we crossed the Yellow Sea to Fusan, and travelled by train up through Korea to Mukden in Manchuria where we were met, at six in the morning, by a gentleman in furs who turned out to be not only the British Consul, but the brother of Frank Tours, the musical director of *Bitter Sweet* in New York.

He gave us a delicious, thoroughly English breakfast and a hot bath, after which we went out in rickshaws to see the town; but we soon came back with tears of agony running down our faces, as the wind happened to be blowing from Siberia that morning, and the temperature was thirty below zero.

That evening we spent a pleasant hour or two in the English Club. The English and American residents, of which there were few, had organised a fancy-dress dance to celebrate the passing of 1929. It was a strange party and, beneath its gaiety, exceedingly touching. Pierrots, Columbines, Clowns, red rep Cardinals and butter-muslin Juliets, all pulling crackers, drinking punch and crossing hands to sing together 'Should auld acquaintance be forgot,' while outside the wind blew like ice over the Manchurian wastes and the snow piled high on the window-sills. If they had not all been so kind and hospitable to us we might have had time to feel a little guilty. We were only passing through. We were free to go where we pleased, whereas the bulk of the people present were condemned to stay in that grim, remote place perhaps for years.

I will spare the reader a detailed description of a twenty-four-hour journey to Peking in an unheated train in which we sat, wrapped in fur coats, in a wooden compartment trying unsuccessfully to conquer intestinal chills by eating nothing at all and drinking a bottle of brandy each, while the frozen Chinese countryside struggled bleakly by the windows.

Lady Lampson, the wife of Sir Miles Lampson, the British Minister, was particularly charming to us in Peking. She showed us the incredible beauties of the city; organised our shopping expeditions, and took pains to prevent us from buying soapstone instead of jade, and plaster instead of Ming pottery.

We travelled as far as Shanghai with her and her little boy, who was going home to school in England. A few days later we heard that she had been taken seriously ill with spinal meningitis on her arrival in Hong Kong and, a little later still, that she was dead. This saddened us horribly. We had only known her for a few weeks, but during that time she had been so hospitable and kind that we felt we had lost a much older friend.

5

A bout of influenza laid me low in Shanghai, and I lay, sweating gloomily, in my bedroom in the Cathay Hotel for several days. The ensuing convalescence, however, was productive, for I utilised it by writing *Private Lives*. The idea by now seemed ripe enough to have a shot at, so I started it, propped up in bed with a writing-block and an Eversharp pencil, and completed it, roughly, in four days. It came easily, and with the exception of a few of the usual 'blood and tears' moments, I enjoyed writing it. I thought it a shrewd and witty comedy, well constructed on the whole, but psychologically unstable; however, its entertainment value seemed obvious enough, and its acting opportunities for Gertie and me admirable, so I cabled to her immediately in New York telling her to keep herself free for the autumn, and put the whole thing aside for a few weeks before typing and revising it.

With influenza and *Private Lives* both behind me I entered the social whirl of Shanghai with zest. There were lots of parties and Chinese dinners and general cosmopolitan junketings, which, while putting a slight strain on our lingual abilities, in no way dampened our spirits. We found some charming new friends, notably Madame Birt and her twin daughters who, apart from being extremely attractive, could quarrel with each other in six different languages without even realising that they were not sticking to one; and three English naval officers, Ascherson, Bushell and Guerrier, with whom we visited many of the lower and gayer haunts of the city and sailed as their guests on our first but, as far as I was concerned, not my last voyage in one of His Majesty's ships.

Ever since then I have become increasingly indebted to the Navy. To me, the life of a guest in a warship is deeply satisfactory. I have passed some of the happiest hours of my life in various ward-rooms. The secret of naval good manners is hard to define; perhaps discipline has a lot to do with it and prolonged contact with the sea; perhaps a permanent background of such dignity makes for simplicity of mind.

Perhaps all this is an illusion, perhaps it is merely the complete change of atmosphere that so englamours me; if so I shall certainly take good care never to outstay my welcome long enough to break it.

Ascherson, Bushell and Guerrier, having firmly inoculated me with the naval bug, obtained permission from their captain, Captain Arbuthnot, for us both to travel as far as Hong Kong with them, and we sailed down the river from Shanghai in the H.M.S. *Suffolk* on a cold sunny morning in February. The warships of other nations, American, French and Italian, saluted as we moved down-stream. Jeffery and I, well placed out of everyone's way on the gun deck, stood, uncertain whether to keep our hats on or off, knowing only that we mustn't smoke and must wait there, however cold, until fetched into the ward-room for a drink. We watched the busy water-front slide away. The air was sharp and clear, and the blue of the coolies' coats on the bund took from the sun such vivid brightness that, in the distance, it looked as though the river had climbed up into the streets and was swirling among the houses.

The voyage took five days, as we stopped every now and then on the way for various exercises. I think we behaved adequately well on the whole. We learnt, and remembered, various little lessons in naval etiquette and jargon as we went along. We had a comfortable cabin each, and the captain allowed us the use of his bathroom. There is a permanent humming noise in a warship which is soothing to the nerves, and a clean, efficient smell, impossible to describe, but quite unique. No one paid much attention to us and we were free to wander about and observe the life of the ship, and a very cheerful and energetic life it seemed to be. There was an incessant orgy of polishing and swabbing and scrubbing from the moment we left Shanghai to the moment we arrived in Hong Kong. There was also a great deal of bugle-blowing and fast running, crabwise, up and down narrow iron ladders. At night we dressed for dinner and sat round the shiny ward-room table while the marine band fought its way gallantly through the intricacies of *Bitter Sweet* and *This Year of Grace,* the parts of which the bandmaster had hurriedly bought in Shanghai when he heard that I was to be a passenger.

The ship changed for dinner, too. It changed its personality entirely, becoming silent, purposeful and almost sinister. There was no activity and hardly any noise except for the humming of the engines. We usually went up on the bridge for a little while before going to bed, and put the final seal upon the drinks we had drunk in the ward-room by swallowing a mug of ship's cocoa with the officer of the watch. Then, of all moments, we were most conscious of the good old layman's romantic 'thrill of the Navy.' The ship slid quietly through the darkness and we felt the pulse of her strength beneath our feet. The water cut away from the bows and swished and gurgled alongside, occasionally streaked with phosphorus, while overhead strange and larger stars appeared. There was a slight panic one night because Guerrier, who happened to have the middle watch, sent a frantic message down to the ward-room to say that he'd mislaid an island and did anyone know where it was! A good deal of agitation ensued, and it was finally located several miles off the port bow. This joke lasted everyone for quite a while.

Finally, on the fifth evening, Hong Kong sprang abruptly at us out of a fog. The sun was just setting, and the island against a suddenly clear sky was a fantastically beautiful sight, but at that moment sad and unwelcome for us both because it meant that we had to go ashore.

We loitered on board as long as we could. Long after the captain had left in his launch, long after night had fallen, we were still standing about in the ward-room accepting with gracious melancholy 'gimlet' after 'gimlet' until finally we clattered unsteadily down the ladder behind our luggage and went bouncing off across the harbour to the Peninsula Hotel at Kowloon, where we ate some caviare and drank still more gin. Jeffery indeed was so sunk in depression that he signed the hotel register 'Mackintosh' without my noticing, a slip of the pen which caused us considerable trouble later on.

We stayed a week in Hong Kong. I spent most of it sitting in my hotel bedroom typing and revising *Private Lives*. When it was completed I sent copies of it to Gertie and Jack in New York, and told them to cable me in Singapore what they thought about it.

The night before we left we gave a farewell dinner to all the officers of the *Suffolk*. They were going to sea early next morning and that evening, although tinged with regret, was, to say the least of it, a success.

We rose with cracking heads to watch from our windows the *Suffolk* sail away. We felt very proud to know her as she steamed with slow dignity out of the harbour, and also so low that we ordered a bottle of champagne then and there, a drink that we both detest, and drank it to the last drop sitting miserably in a hot bath.

We embarked that same afternoon on one of the filthiest little freight boats I have ever encountered. We were bound for Haiphong in Indo-China, and there were no other boats available. This one, whose name I will withhold owing to the laws of libel, was French-owned, and manned by a crew of murderous-looking Annamites and three French officers with singularly untidy personalities. Our cabin contained two cast-iron bunks and a tin basin, and we shared it with hordes of cockroaches, bed bugs and fleas, and a dead mouse which we buried at sea as soon as the tragedy was discovered.

We were immured in that God-forsaken tub, with a cargo of copra and salt fish, for five days and nights.

On arrival at Haiphong we hired a car and drove to Hanoi, which is the capital of Tonkin. Here we were not allowed out of the hotel as there was a revolution in progress; however, Monsieur Pasquier, the Governor-General, to whom we had a letter of introduction, sent his A.D.C. and car to fetch us, and we spent a strange evening in the Government Palace with Monsieur Pasquier, two Generals, an Admiral and the A.D.C. Outside the revolution was in full swing, and there was occasionally the sound of gun-fire. Inside all was peaceful and well-ordered. The dinner was delicious, the wine excellent, and Monsieur Pasquier the most delightful host.

We hired a car and a driver and set off the next day down the length of Indo-China to Saigon. The journey took the best part of a week, the scenery alternating violently between the steepest of steep mountains and the flattest of flat plains, with a little jungle thrown in every now and then, and a never-ending series of rivers across which we were ferried on creaking, insecure barges. We were deeply impressed by the admirable French colonisation which enabled us to procure excellent coffee and rolls in the remotest villages.

The night before we were due to arrive in Saigon we stopped at a small village called Nah Trang. The rest-house was clean but primitive, and we went to bed early as we were getting up at dawn to make the last lap of our journey. At about a quarter to five, before it was light, I was wakened by Jeffery demanding, in a shaky dry voice, a thermometer. I struggled out from under my mosquito net, lit a candle and took his temperature which, to my horror, was nearly a hundred and four. I disguised the truth from him and told him it was just on a hundred and, having roused our driver and dressed as quickly as we could, we set off, hell for leather, for Saigon. It was a hideous journey – our driver, none too good at any time, became demoniac when urged to drive fast. We slaughtered countless chickens and ducks, two dogs, a snake and a cat. Jeffery was delirious part of the time, and I watched him anxiously for symptoms of coma, because my mind all the while was haunted by the memory of Lady Lampson and spinal meningitis.

We arrived in Saigon in the full glare of midday. Every blind was down and there wasn't a creature moving. The streets were white with heat, and Jeffery by then was almost unconscious. I got him into a room in the hotel and set off in a rickshaw, the hotel porter having directed me to a clinic, where I managed to persuade a pompous little doctor to rouse himself from his siesta and come with me.

The result of all this was that Jeffery was moved into the clinic, with what the French doctor hilariously diagnosed as *'mal au foie – rien que mal au foie.'* He was given a few injections and some vegetable soup immediately, and why he didn't die I shall never know, because several weeks later when he was properly examined in Singapore he was found to be suffering from amoebic dysentery.

However, he lay in the clinic in Saigon for close on a month, and finally emerged looking more like a hat-pin than a human being, but pronounced fit enough to continue our journey up through Angkor and into Siam. In the meantime I spent those four weeks in isolated splendour in the Grand Hotel. Saigon is very small and is referred to proudly by the French as the Paris of the Orient. This, I need hardly say, is an over-statement. It is a well-arranged little town and it has several cafés and a municipal opera house, but it is *not* very like Paris.

I visited Jeffery twice a day and discovered a pleasant little café and brothel combined which catered mostly for the lower-class mercantile marines and a floating clientele of tarts of all nations; apart from these distractions I spent most of my time sitting on a cane chair outside the Grand Hotel watching the *beau monde* bouncing up and down the Rue Catinat in rickshaws. The hotel orchestra played selections from *Tosca, Madame Butterfly* and the tinkling French operettas of the nineties every evening, and for a little while the scene took on a certain forlorn charm. But even this faded after the first few days, because it took only a very short while to know every single person that passed by sight.

When Jeffery so strangely recovered from the ministrations of that doctor we set off to Angkor, where we stayed for ten days. We wandered through queer magnificent ruins; we watched the temple dancers in the vast courtyard of Angkor Vat, swaying and stamping to harsh music in the flickering light of torches and coloured flares; we drove through the jungle roads, coming upon villages still in the process of excavation, still in the grip of the jungle, houses with strong trees growing right up through them and grey monkeys chattering on the crumbling roofs.

From Angkor we motored to Aranya Pradesa, the Siamese frontier, over the most appalling road I have ever encountered; from there, after a night in a surprisingly German rest-house, we took a train to Bangkok, where we stayed for two weeks. The Phya Tai Palace, which had once belonged to the Royal Family, was now a hotel, cool, spacious and reasonably comfortable, although I must admit that I once woke up from my after-lunch siesta to find a majestic procession of red ants making a forced march from one side of the mattress to the other, by way of my stomach.

We saw all the sights the city had to offer, and they were many and varied, ranging from an emerald Buddha the size of a football to the Pasteur Institute, where they extracted the venom from snakes by the apparently casual method of seizing them by the neck and making them bite little parchment saucers.

6

During that holiday, I think my spirits reached their lowest ebb on the first evening I spent in Singapore. I sat on the veranda of the hotel, sipping a gin-sling and staring at the muddy sea. There was a thunderstorm brewing and the airless heat pressed down on my head. I felt as though I were inside a hot cardboard box which was growing rapidly smaller and smaller, until soon I should have to give up all hope of breathing and die of suffocation.

My state of mind was not solely due to the climate. Jeffery had been taken badly ill again in the little Danish freighter which had brought us from Siam, and I had just left him in the hospital, looking like death and waiting to be diagnosed. My imagination was busy wording, as gently as possible, the fatal telegram to his mother. I pictured her receiving it in the cool quietness of her Wilton Crescent drawing-room while I, in this God-forsaken hole, dealt sadly but efficiently with grisly funereal details; in fact, by the time my second gin-sling was brought to me Jeffery was dead and buried.

Presently the thunderstorm broke and raged violently for about an hour. It was the most thorough-going storm I had ever seen. The sky split in two; the sea lost its smooth, oily temper and rushed at the hotel as though it wanted to swallow it up, and then the rain came. I recognised it as rain only because I knew it couldn't possibly be anything else; it certainly bore no resemblance to any rain I had ever met before. It fell like a steel curtain, and its impact on the roof of the veranda was terrific. Then, abruptly, the whole performance stopped. The sea relaxed, the skies cleared, the stars came out, and in the cooler air my imagination became less fevered. I drove up to the hospital after dinner and found Jeffery enjoying a cigarette and an animated conversation with the night nurse.

The next day the doctors said that he had dysentery and would be able to leave the hospital in about a month if all went well. Once resigned to this enforced pause in our travels we both felt better, and while Jeffery concentrated on his discomforts and treatments, I set out to discover what Singapore had to offer in the way of distractions.

The first and principal distraction I found was an English theatrical touring company called 'The Quaints.' They were appearing at the Victoria Theatre and their repertory was almost shockingly varied. They played, with a certain light-hearted abandon, *Hamlet, Mr Cinders, Anthony and Cleopatra, The Girl Friend, When Knights Were Bold,* and *Journey's End.* I was taken to their opening performance of *Mr Cinders* by the manager of the theatre and from then onwards I never left them. My chief friends among them were Betty Hare and John Mills, both of whom have worked with me a great deal since, and the general major-domo of the whole enterprise, Jimmy Grant Anderson. Jimmy was rich in quality; he was 'of the dust the theatre bore, shaped, made aware,' his blood was the best grease-paint. I had met him before in a thousand people, but never so concentrated, never such triple distilled essence. His mind was a prop hamper crammed to the lid with theatre finery. To him the sea and the sky were only painted on canvas, and not any too well painted at that. Behind the immediate Singapore act drop there were other scenes being set, there always had been and there always would be. I had the feeling that even after his own death he would merely retire, to some celestial dressing-room and take off his make-up.

There were other Quaints, a dozen of them. *En masse* we went to supper parties and swimming parties after the show at night. Some of the more refined social lights of Singapore looked obliquely at us, as though we were not quite the thing, a little too rowdy perhaps, on the common side. I'm sure they were right. Actors always laugh more loudly than other people when they're enjoying themselves, and we laughed most of the time.

Intoxicated by so many heady draughts of familiar vintage theatre, I allowed myself to be persuaded by Jimmy to appear as 'Stanhope' in *Journey's End* for three performances. The Singapore Press displayed gratifying excitement and my name glittered proudly in blue bulbs across the front of the Victoria Theatre. I learnt the part in two days and had three rehearsals. The *élite* of Singapore assembled in white ducks and flowered chiffons and politely watched me take a fine part in a fine play and throw it into the alley. The only cause for pride I had over the whole business was that I didn't dry-up on any of the lines. True, I became slightly lost during the second performance in a maze of military instructions, and commanded a surprised sergeant-major to take number eight 'platoolian' into the back trenches; and I was never actually certain which scene I was playing, and how long it was going to last, but Bob Sherriff's lines remained, on the whole, intact, although I spoke the majority of them with such overemphasis that it might have been better if they hadn't. John Mills, as 'Raleigh,' gave the finest performance I have ever seen given to that part, and Jimmy Grant Anderson was excellent as 'Trotter.' The whole company was good and the production admirable. The outstanding failure was undoubtedly me. Of course there were many excuses: only two days to learn it, insufficient rehearsals, etc., etc.; all the same I should have been ashamed of myself for attempting anything as important as *Journey's End* in such circumstances. In discussing it beforehand it had seemed a lark, great fun, an amusing experiment; it wasn't until I got on to the stage in a temperature of about 115 in the shade, with the sweat rolling off me, that I began to be aware of my folly, and it wasn't, mercifully, until the three performances were over that I relaxed enough to realise my impertinence.

The third performance was a little better than the first two, and probably with a few weeks of hard work I might ultimately have played it properly. If it had been a bad play I should have accepted the lark at its surface value and been content that I had, at least, amused The Quaints; as it was, however, my retrospective embarrassment afterwards was mortifying and I have never quite forgiven myself.

Singapore's behaviour to me was beyond reproach, with the exception of one of the gentlemen of the Press, who was indelicate enough to hint that I was not quite as good as the man he had seen play it before. I saluted him, wanly, for his honesty.

7

I have often thought I should like to write a travel book. Not the *Through Tibet on a Bicycle* variety, nor yet the Richard Haliburton formula with pictures of myself swimming unswimmable rivers and straddling ancient statuary. Rather a casual travel book, in which the essence and charm of every strange place I visited would be captured in a few apt and telling phrases; in which I could devote pages and pages to gentle introspection; sketching lightly my opinions of Life, Love, Art and Letters on to incongruous backgrounds of mountains and deserts and shrill tropical vegetation.

My body has certainly wandered a good deal, but I have an uneasy suspicion that my mind has not wandered nearly enough.

It is a well-trained mind, disciplined to observe, record and store up impressions without any particular wear and tear or exhaustive effort. It is capable of functioning quickly, and making rapid and usually intelligent decisions. It is at its best when dealing with people, and at its worst when dealing with the inanimate. Its photographic propensities are good, but something goes wrong with the developing, because the pictures it takes of landscapes and seascapes fade too easily. Faces, events and tunes remain clear, fragments of past conversations also, and the sudden stinging memory of long-dead emotions. But visual experience, that glorious view when you reach the top of the hill, that moment in the Acropolis just before sunset, those pale dawns at sea, all these become smudged and half-rubbed out until, frequently, not even an outline remains.

My travel book would be difficult to write, for in addition to these defects, my mind resents certain kinds of information; it cannot or will not accept history for history's sake. Remote foreign churches, carved, sculpted and decorated by remote foreign monks centuries ago; ruins, museums and cathedrals, unless for some specific reason they happen to catch my imagination, leave no imprint whatsoever. In fact, many of the world's noblest antiquities have definitely irritated me. Perhaps the sheen on them of so many hundreds of years' intensive appreciation makes them smug. I feel that they bridle when I look at them. Once, in Ceylon, I saw an enormous sacred elephant sit up and beg for a banana; I don't believe it really wanted the banana, it merely knew what was expected of it. I have also seen the Pyramids give a little self-deprecatory simper at the sight of a Kodak. I have not, as yet, seen the Taj Mahal at all, but I feel that when I do it will probably lie down in a consciously alluring attitude and pretend to be asleep.

I freely admit that this blindness is perverse; perhaps it's a repressed complex, perhaps I was frightened by a Bellini Madonna when I was a tiny child, but there it is, complex or not, a permanent obstacle to a respectable travel book. On the other hand, although insensitive to history for history's sake, I am keenly responsive to travel for travel's sake. I love to go and I love to have been, but best of all I love the intervals between arrivals and departures, the days and nights of steady, incessant movement, when the horizon is empty and time completely changes its rhythm. Then I can sleep, wake, write, read and think in peace. It is in these hours I feel that, after all, there may be a chance for me, less likelihood of opportunities missed, less intolerable distraction. It is probably a temperamental defect in me that I can only catch this elusive quietness when moving, a maladjustment of my nervous system, but it is certainly the reason above all others that I go away, not to get anywhere, not even to return, just to go.

Jeffery emerged from the hospital in Singapore more emaciated than ever, but definitely on the way to recovery. We lingered on a little. The Quaints left for Hong Kong and we celebrated their going with a party, waving them hazily into a small P. and O. at two in the morning. We went to a few dinners, picnics and cocktail parties, and finally went on to Ceylon by way of Kuala Lumpur and Penang. From Penang to Colombo we travelled in a Prince Line freighter; an enchanting few days, most of which we spent lying in a canvas swimming tank rigged up on the fo'c'sle.

At Colombo we were met by my brother Eric, in shorts and a sola-topee. We stayed with him in his bungalow in the hills for a few days, and then came down again to the Galle Face Hotel, where there was a jazz orchestra, curry, Cingalese waiters with elaborate combs in their hair and, surprisingly enough, Cole and Linda Porter. They were on their way from Java and Bali, and looked splendidly immaculate. The climate did its best to flurry Linda's coolness, but without success; she remained serene and smooth, and bought a lot of emeralds. Meanwhile, a tremendous telegraphic bickering was taking place between me and Gertie Lawrence in New York. She had cabled me in Singapore, rather casually, I thought, saying that she had read *Private Lives* and that there was nothing wrong in it that couldn't be fixed. I had wired back curtly that the only thing that was going to be fixed was her performance. Now cables were arriving at all hours of the day and night, with a typical disregard of expense, saying that she had foolishly committed herself to Charlot for a new revue – could we open in January instead of September – could I appear in the revue with her, just to fill in – could I wire to Charlot to release her from her contract – that it wasn't a contract at all, merely a moral obligation – that it wasn't a moral obligation at all, but a cabled contract – that her lawyers were working day and night to get her out of it – that she would rather do *Private Lives* than anything in the world – that she couldn't do *Private Lives* at all? In her last telegram she remembered to give me her cable address which, had she done so sooner, would have saved me about forty pounds. I finally lost patience and cabled that I intended to do the play with someone else, and I heard nothing further until I arrived back in England.

8

Our journey from Ceylon to Marseilles was accomplished in one of the older P. and O. ships, in fact so old was she that we expected her to hoist enormous bellying sails when a light wind sprang up in the Red Sea. The voyage started badly for me; I was awakened from a deep sleep at eight o'clock on the first morning out by the games organiser, who walked peremptorily into my cabin and told me that I was to play shuffle-board with Mrs Harrison at eleven, and deck-quoits with Miss Phillips at ten-fifteen. I replied that I intended to pass most of the day in the lavatory and that if Mrs Harrison and Miss Phillips felt like a little Russian bank or backgammon, he could tell them where to find me.

Owing to this reasonable outburst of irritation, both Jeffery and I were considered snobbish and exclusive by our fellow-passengers and were, mercifully, excluded from most of the ship's social activities, with the exception of the fancy-dress ball at which I was invited to give the prizes. Here I disgraced myself again by giving the first prize to a woman who had been ignored by most of the ladies on board, apparently because they suspected her of coloured blood. Had I known this, I should have given her the first prize, even if she had been a Zulu.

During that voyage I wrote an angry little vilification of war called *Post-Mortem*; my mind was strongly affected by *Journey's End,* and I had read several current war novels one after the other.

I wrote *Post-Mortem* with the utmost sincerity; this, I think, must be fairly obvious to anyone who reads it. In fact I tore my emotions to shreds over it. The result was similar to my performance as 'Stanhope': confused, under-rehearsed and hysterical. Unlike my performance as 'Stanhope,' however, it had some very fine moments. There is, I believe, some of the best writing I have ever done in it, also some of the worst. I have no deep regrets over it, as I know my intentions to have been of the purest. I passionately believed in the truth of what I was writing; too passionately. The truths I snarled out in that hot, uncomfortable little cabin were all too true and mostly too shallow. Through lack of detachment and lack of real experience of my subject, I muddled the issues of the play. I might have done better had I given more time to it and less vehemence. However, it helped to purge my system of certain accumulated acids.

9

Back in London again, the Far East receded swiftly. Once the various presents had been doled out and the principal anecdotes related, all memories fused in a highly-coloured jumble.

I sat in the garden at Goldenhurst in the sunset, worrying about pneumonia rather than malaria; I no longer shook my bedroom slippers to see if there were any scorpions inside them, although I must admit I was badly frightened one night by a daddy-long-legs falling on to my face. Jungles, mountains and seas looked up at me from snapshots. Yes, I had been there and there and there – there was Saigon, that suffocating little Paris of the Orient – in the right-hand corner was the hotel terrace where I sat interminably night after night – the little orchestra – *Tosca, Bohème, Véronique* – the rickshaws passing back and forth – podgy French business men in creased, tropical suits, clambering in and out – Jeffery in the clinic, lying yellow and wretched under a mosquito-net. There was the Tartar Gate in Peking – I'd been through that – ice-cold winds blowing across from the Gobi Desert – clouds of stinging grey dust. Hong Kong harbour, unrecognisable in the photograph, just a view, no suggestion of its reality – that gigantic island rising out of the sea – the peak with white veils of cloud round it, as though it had been washing its head – at night the millions of lights – the little ferry-boats chugging to and fro across the harbour. There was the *Suffolk* looking glossy and prim and over-posed – there was the scuttle through which I stared at the China Sea – the cross marks my bedroom window. Indo-China – Siam – monks in faded yellow robes – temples and palaces with porcelain roofs – emerald Buddhas – silver mesh floors – cobras hooded and angry, snapping at bits of parchment – ships of all shapes and sizes – freighters, P. and O.s, Dollar Line, N.Y.K., sampans, junks – Singapore – a thunderstorm like the breaking of the sixth seal – straight, flat streets lined with coloured shops – palms, flame-in-the-forest, hibiscus, poinsettias – the Victoria Theatre, with large electric punkahs eternally scuffling round and round, while I sweated and ranted in a British warm and full trench equipment – Kuala Lumpur, Penang, Colombo, Kandy, Aden, Suez – names on a map no longer, but places that I had been to; I – me – sitting here in a familiar garden – I had walked along those streets, eaten and drunk, gone to sleep and wakened up in those strange hotel rooms; crossed those wide seas; bumped over those faraway roads, and here I was again; the world was round all right, one small circle had been completed, perhaps Time was round, too. I remember going indoors, twirling the globe and looking towards future journeys.

10

We played a short provincial tour of *Private Lives* before bringing it to London. Gertie had arrived back in England in gay spirits and, by hook, crook, love and money, managed to extricate herself from her moral, legal and financial obligations to Charlot. She seemed happily unaware that there had ever been any question of her not playing *Private Lives*. All the cables and muddles and complications hadn't existed. Here she was, eager, enthusiastic and looking lovely; the play was perfect, nothing had to be fixed at all. Gertie has an astounding sense of the complete reality of the moment, and her moments, dictated by the extreme variability of her moods, change so swiftly that it is frequently difficult to discover what, apart from eating, sleeping and acting, is true of her at all. I know her well, better, I believe, than most people. The early years of our friendship set her strongly in my mind. I knew her then to have quick humour, insane generosity and a loving heart, and those things seldom change. I see her now, ages away from her ringlets and black velvet military cap, sometimes a simple, wide-eyed child, sometimes a glamorous *femme du monde,* at some moments a rather boisterous 'good sort,' at others a weary, disillusioned woman battered by life but gallant to the last. There are many other grades also between these extremes. She appropriated beauty to herself quite early, along with all the tricks and mannerisms that go with it. In adolescence she was barely pretty. Now, without apparent effort, she gives the impression of sheer loveliness. Her grace in movement is exquisite, and her voice charming. To disentangle Gertie herself from this mutability is baffling, rather like delving for your grandmother's gold locket at the bottom of an overflowing jewel-case.

Her talent is equally kaleidoscopic. On the stage she is potentially capable of anything and everything. She can be gay, sad, witty, tragic, funny and touching. She can play a scene one night with perfect subtlety and restraint, and the next with such obviousness and over-emphasis that your senses reel. She has, in abundance, every theatrical essential but one: critical faculty. She can watch a great actor and be stirred to the depths, her emotional response is immediate and genuine. She can watch a bad actor and be stirred to the depths, the response is equally immediate and equally genuine. But for this tantalising lack of discrimination she could, I believe, be the greatest actress alive in the theatre to-day.

Adrianne Allen (Mrs Raymond Massey) played 'Sibyl' in *Private Lives,* and Laurence Olivier, 'Victor.' The whole tour was swathed in luxury. Adrianne travelled in a car, so did Gertie and so did I, the touring days of the past belonged to another world. Assurance of success seemed to be emblazoned on the play from the first, we had few qualms, played to capacity business and enjoyed ourselves thoroughly. We felt, I think rightly, that there was a shine on us.

In London we opened in a new theatre, the Phoenix. We were an immediate hit, and our three months' limited engagement was sold out during the first week. It was an interesting play to play, naturally more interesting for Gertie and me than it was for Larry and Adrianne. We had the parts, or rather, the part, as 'Elyot' and 'Amanda' are practically synonymous. The play's fabric was light and required light handling. Gertie was brilliant. Everything she had been in my mind when I originally conceived the idea in Tokio came to life on the stage: the witty, quick-silver delivery of lines; the romantic quality, tender and alluring; the swift, brittle rages; even the white Molyneux dress. Adrianne played 'Sibyl' with a subtle tiresomeness and a perfect sense of character, more character actually than the part really had. Larry managed, with determination and much personal charm, to invest the wooden 'Victor' with enough reality to make him plausible. I frequently felt conscience-stricken over them both, playing so gallantly on such palpably second-strings. Gertie and I certainly had most of the fun and, with it, most of the responsibility. Our duologue second act, when, for some reason or other, we were not feeling quite on the crest of the wave, was terribly exhausting. We both knew that if we let it sag for a moment it would die on us. On the other hand, when it flowed, when the audience was gay and appreciative, when our spirits were tuned to the right key, it was so exhilarating that we felt deflated when it was over.

We closed, at the end of our scheduled three months, with the gratifying knowledge that we could easily have run on for another six. This arbitrary three months' limit of mine brought me a certain amount of criticism. 'It was a sin,' people said, 'to close a play when it was doing so well.' Some even prophesied, darkly, future catastrophes: 'A day will come,' they said, 'when you will bitterly regret this.' I am told that even Sir Cedric Hardwicke sprang into print about it. However, I remained convinced that that policy, for me, was right. Perhaps a day will come, as the Cassandras foretold; perhaps in later years, when I'm looking for a job, I shall indeed regret those lost grosses, but I don't really think that I will. I consider myself a writer first and an actor second. I love acting, and it is only during the last few years that I have become good, although, as yet, limited in scope. If I play the same part over and over again for a long run, I become bored and frustrated and my performance deteriorates; in addition to this, I have no time to write. Ideas occur to me and then retreat again because, with eight performances a week to be got through, there is no time to develop them. For me, three months in London and three months in New York once in every two years is an ideal arrangement. It is, of course, more than possible that I might write and appear in a play that wouldn't run three weeks. In that bleak moment, age permitting, I shall turn gratefully to a revival of *Private Lives.*

I spent Christmas at Goldenhurst before sailing for America. Goldenhurst was growing; bedrooms and bathrooms were multiplying rapidly, so also was acreage. I could now walk proudly for quite a long way over my own land. Goldenhurst was a continual pleasure. Even then, in 1930, it was unrecognisable from what it had been a few years before. Now, of course, at the moment of writing, it has almost over-reached itself. It has completed its metamorphosis from a tumbledown farmhouse to a country estate. To do it justice, it hasn't got a self-made look. It has no vulgar '*nouveau-riche*' mannerisms, it doesn't eat peas with its knife, but I am beginning to feel a little awed by it, especially when I come across its photographs in the smarter illustrated weeklies.

I employed that Christmas week by writing some numbers for a revue that Cochran was preparing. Two of them, 'Any Little Fish' and 'Half-caste Woman,' were reasonably successful, although the revue – which I never saw – wasn't.

II

During the London run of *Private Lives,* I discussed with Cochran the idea of doing a big spectacular production at the Coliseum. I felt an urge to test my producing powers on a large scale. My mind's eye visualised a series of tremendous mob scenes – the storming of the Bastille – the massacre of the Huguenots – I believe even the Decline and Fall of the Roman Empire flirted with me for a little. Soon my imagination became overcrowded, and I began to simplify. These mass effects were all very well, but they couldn't sustain a whole evening; they should be, at best, a background for a strong story; at worst, padding for a weak one.

Cockie was enthusiastic and settled himself blandly to wait until I delivered him a more concrete proposition; meanwhile history continued to parade through my mind, usually at night, when I was tired and wanted to go to sleep. Events, grand and portentous, battles, sieges, earthquakes, revolutions and ship-wrecks, but no story, not the shadow of a theme. The Second Empire was the most tenacious of all; gaslight – chandeliers – richly apparelled courtesans driving in the Bois – Englishmen in deer-stalker caps climbing out of smoky trains at the Gare du Nord – the Empress herself, haughty, beautiful, crinolined; somehow a little synthetic – the whole scene a little synthetic – Winterhalter figures moving to Offenbach tunes. At the time perhaps a trifle shabby, but now, set in retrospect, charming. A sentimental, daguerreotype sort of charm, belonging to the past, but not too far away.

However, as an idea for the Coliseum it seemed too pale, too lacking in action; so away it went with the chariot-races and carmagnoles and blood-and-thunder, and I continued the search, until one day I happened to buy, at Foyle's in the Charing Cross Road, some ancient bound volumes of *Black and White* and the *Illustrated London News*. This was chance, and extremely happy chance. In the first volume I opened there was a full-page picture of a troop-ship leaving for the Boer War, and the moment I saw it I knew that I had found what I wanted. I can't explain why it rang the bell so sharply, I only know that it did. The tunes came into my mind first, tunes belonging to my very earliest childhood; 'Dolly Gray,' 'The Absent-minded Beggar,' 'Soldiers of the Queen,' 'Bluebell' (later this, but I neither knew nor cared). I played them on the piano immediately. G. B. Stern, who was coming to tea, found me in a state of high excitement; by then I had progressed, musically, quite a long way through the years; I'm not sure, but I think she entered to the tune of 'Tipperary.'

The emotional basis of *Cavalcade* was undoubtedly music. The whole story was threaded on to a string of popular melodies. This ultimately was a big contributing factor to its success. Popular tunes probe the memory more swiftly than anything else, and *Cavalcade,* whatever else it did, certainly awakened many echoes.

That afternoon in my studio, Peter (Stern) tottered a bit under the full impact of my enthusiasm, but she rallied after a while and, renouncing any personal problems she might have wished to discuss, obligingly retired with me to the beginning of the century. She remembered Mafeking Night, the Relief of Ladysmith, 'Dirty old Kruger,' One-armed Giffard, and newsboys – particularly newsboys – shrill Cockney voices shouting victories and defeats along London streets; cooks and housemaids running up foggy area steps to buy halfpenny papers; elderly gentlemen in evening capes stopping hansoms in order to read of 'Bob's' latest exploits. Then the illness of the Queen – newsboys again – the Queen's sinking – latest bulletin. She remembered vividly, graphically, and became as excited as I was. Later on I dedicated the published play to her in gratitude for those two hours.

My original story was different from what finally emerged, but the shape was the same, New Year's Eve 1899 to New Year's Eve 1930. Events took precedence first in my mind, and against them I moved a group of people – the bright young people of the nineties, the play was to finish with their children – the same eager emptiness, but a different jargon. After a while, I realised that the play should be bigger than that. I had flogged the bright young people enough, my vehemence against them had congealed, they were now no more than damp squibs, my Poor Little Rich Girls and Dance, Little Ladies. Thirty years of English life seen through their eyes would be uninspired, to say the least of it. Presently my real characters appeared in two classes: 'the Marryots,' and 'Ellen' and 'Bridges.' 'Jane Marryot' displayed a greater fecundity in my original conception, there were several more children than just 'Edward' and 'Joe;' however, these fell away, stillborn, into oblivion, discouraged by my firm determination to keep the whole thing as simple and uncomplicated as possible, and gradually the whole story completed itself in my mind.

I knew I couldn't attempt the actual writing of it until I had finished with *Private Lives* in New York. It would obviously require a lot of time, concentration and research, so I outlined it, in brief, to Cockie and promised it vaguely for the following year.

12

Private Lives was as gratifyingly successful in New York as it had been in London. Adrianne Allen was unable to come, and so Jill Esmond (Laurence Olivier's wife) played 'Sibyl' excellently, in a blond wig. The New York critics resented the thinness of the play less than the London critics, and enjoyed the lightness of it more; in fact, many of them came to see it several times. I think we retained, on the whole, the shine that we had started with; at all events, we strained every nerve to justify the almost overwhelming praise that was most generously lavished upon us.

I lived in a little penthouse on West 58th Street, with a lot of rather 'Ye Olde Teashoppe' furniture, a French cook and an uninterrupted view of the Empire State building. Here, with the extremely twentieth-century sounds of New York in my ears, I embarked on my researches for *Cavalcade*. I had brought stacks of books with me from London, even the faithful bound volumes of the *Illustrated London News*. I started at an earlier date than 1899, feeling that to work slowly through the seventies, eighties and nineties would give my people a more solid background than if I just let them appear, untouched by any past experience whatever, in leg-of-mutton sleeves. For some of the later scenes of the play I could, of course, draw on my own memory.

The 1910 seaside scene – Uncle George and his Merrie Men from Bognor would be useful there – the war scenes – 'We don't want to lose you, but we think you ought to go,' 'On Sunday I walk out with a soldier.' I could remember Gwennie Brogden singing that in *The Passing Show* at the Palace. The Victoria Station scene – hospital trains coming in, leave trains going out – I remember that clearly – walking home from the theatre at night after the show, a sinister air-raid consciousness in the air – hardly any lights anywhere, the Mall ghostly and almost deserted. I often walked through Victoria Station, it was practically on my way, and there was always activity going on. It seems, looking back on it, more dramatic than I expect it actually was. In those days everybody was quite used to that interminable anti-climax. Khaki everywhere. Tommies laden with trench equipment. Tired officers in thinner khaki and Sam Browne belts – movable canteens on wheels – movable Red Cross stations, too – nurses, V.A.D.s, chaplains, R.A.M.C. corporals, military police with red bands round their arms – groups of anxious civilians and always, always the tarts mincing about on high heels, with their white fox furs and neat navy blues and checks – permanent grimaces at our national morality – hoping to squeeze a little profit from a few last drunken moments of leave.

Armistice night – I could certainly remember that – thousands and thousands of human beings gone mad – very effective on a revolving stage – yelling, dancing, fighting, singing, blowing squeakers. Then – later on – a night club; a gigantic noisy brassy night club – Dance, Little Lady again – Twentieth-century Blues – a comment accurate enough and empty enough.

'Jane Marryot' took shape in my mind quite early. She seemed real to me and still does, a bit of my own mother and millions of others, too; ordinary, kind, and unobtrusively brave; capable of deep suffering and incapable of cheap complaint. I was proud of 'Jane Marryot' from the first.

In March I had a cable from Cockie saying that we couldn't have the Coliseum, but that we could have Drury Lane if I could guarantee him an opening date. This flurried me a bit, I have always loathed working to set time-limits; however, I made a few rapid mental adjustments, bade a sad adieu to the revolving stage and cabled back that I would have the play completed and ready to open at the end of September.

Gertie got ill towards the end of our three months' run, so we closed the theatre for two weeks. This naturally put a little additional time on to the end of the run, and I arrived back in England to start on *Cavalcade* at the beginning of May.

13

It was a long time before I could settle down to the actual writing of the play. Mother was taken ill with appendicitis, and an anxious time ensued, during which concentration was impossible. It was then discovered, after a series of scenic conferences at Drury Lane, that certain structural alterations would have to be made, and a lot of new lighting equipment installed. Frank Collins, Dan O'Neil, William Abingdon, the Lane stage manager, all the heads of departments, the Strand Electric Company, Gladys and I, spent hours on end trying to solve, on paper, a mass of complicated technical problems. We planned the production so that there should be never more than thirty seconds' wait between any of its twenty-three scenes. The stage was divided into six hydraulic lifts. These had to be timed to sink and rise on light cues from the prompt corner; at the same moment, other light cues would cause the hanging parts of the scenery to be whisked up into the flies and simultaneously replaced. We installed a row of automatic lights along the front of the second balcony. These had five changes of colour and could be regulated by the electricians from the stage. The footlights were reconstructed so that they could silently disappear altogether for the big scenes, and rise into place again for the small interiors when needed. When all the estimates were passed and the work under way, Gladys and I retired to Goldenhurst and set ourselves to a rigid daily routine, until every word of the play and every scene design were completed. We worked from eight in the morning until five in the afternoon, with an hour's break for lunch, Gladys downstairs in the library, I upstairs in my bedroom. We passed through every emotional phase: the height of exhilaration, the depths of despair and all the intermediate grades between. Fortunately, our moods were, as a rule, mutual. On gay, successful days, when everything had gone well, we drove into Folkestone in the evening, relaxed and happy, and went to the pictures. At other times, when everything had creaked and stuck, when there had been no flow, we sat miserably in the garden, hardly speaking, convinced that we had bitten off a great deal more than we could chew, and sick to death of chewing.

At last it was finished; the dialogue all written and typed, the sets designed and coloured, the changes approximately timed, the dresses and uniforms sketched, individually for the principals, in blocks for the crowd.

While the scenery was being built, we took a short breather in the South of France, but the holiday, although outwardly peaceful, lacked inner tranquillity. The sun was hot; the sea blue. We drank a lot of Pernod, and watched brightly-dressed crowds passing to and fro. They looked care-free and irresponsible, no recalcitrant hydraulic lifts haunted their sleep; no obstinate, unautomatic, automatic lights bedevilled them. The Alpes Maritimes, the smooth Mediterranean, the coloured houses, the harbours, the beaches, seemed to us to be only so many act drops, liable to rise at any moment and disclose a vast stage, dimly lit and crowded with odds and ends of furniture and mumbling actors. Most of the cast had been engaged before we left London, and on our return we dealt with the crowd auditions. This was a depressing business. We needed about four hundred, and over a thousand applied. Hour after hour we sat on the stage at a long table set against the lowered safety-curtain, while an endless stream of 'out-of-works' passed by us – all of them professional actors or actresses, every one of them so in need of a job that the chance of being engaged as a super for thirty shillings a week was worth queueing up for. Many of them, at some time or other, had been comparatively successful; in fact, we had several in our crowd who had actually played important parts on that very stage. The old ones were naturally more pathetic than the young; little thin old women, rather dressy, terrified of not being engaged, but quibbling a bit at the salary, asking time to think it over, then giving in suddenly – 'Very well, I'll take it.' Pride was all very well, but times were hard, almost too hard to be borne.

They were tragic, those auditions, and they lay heavily on my conscience for a long while. I felt sentimentally ashamed at having succeeded so quickly, faced with those old lives who had worked all their years and never succeeded at all. I knew that thirty shillings a week was hopelessly inadequate, but the production was budgeted down to the last penny, and couldn't be put on at all if the crowd were paid any more.

I discovered, to my horror, that Cockie, in past moments of expansiveness, had promised three stage-struck society girls walk-ons in the show. There they stood, rather nervously, wearing excellently-cut clothes, good furs and discreet jewellery. One of them whispered sweetly to me that she believed I knew her aunt. I told them, all three, that they were not the types I wanted, but Cockie intervened and insisted on engaging them. After a long argument, I finally gave in on condition that for each of them I engaged two extra for the ranks of those who really needed the work.

In September rehearsals started. The carpenters and electricians were still in possession of the stage, and so I worked with the principals in the bar for the first ten days, getting all the dialogue scenes learnt and polished before I dealt with the crowd. As with *Bitter Sweet,* I felt a direct enthusiastic response from the cast. Everyone seemed to know their lines almost immediately, nobody was obtuse, tiresome or temperamental. I had lots of old friends with me: Moya Nugent, always efficient, gentle and utterly reliable; Maidie Andrews, Phyllis Harding, Betty Hare, John Mills, and several others. The newcomers seemed imbued with the same spirit; in fact, the amount of work achieved in those first ten days was remarkable. Mary Clare played 'Jane' with simplicity, tenderness and complete reality. Irene Browne was stylish and effective as 'Margeret.' Una O'Connor and Fred Groves, as 'Ellen' and 'Bridges,' set themselves securely in the framework of the play from the first. Everybody was admirable, and the smaller parts were as expertly handled as the bigger ones. I woke up on the morning of my first crowd rehearsal frankly terrified. All night long a shouting mob of four hundred people had shared my bed, pushing and clamouring and asking me what I wanted them to do. I was in a bad panic, but the dreadful day had to be faced, so off we went, Lorn, Jack, Gladys and I, to the theatre.

I had decided to break the ice with the seaside scene, and it sat on the stage, complete in every detail, lowering forbiddingly at us as we filed into the front row of the dress circle. Below us, in the stalls, was the full strength of the company, chattering and whispering. There was an extra buzz of expectancy when we came in, and then silence. I had thought out, in advance, a plan for handling such large numbers of people which, as it saved us endless trouble and time, I will explain. I had divided, on paper, the entire cast into groups of twenty. For each group there had been made a set of large plaques in different colours and numbered from one to twenty. Number one in each group was the captain, and was virtually in charge of the other nineteen. Each captain was responsible for his group having their plaques tied on before rehearsal started, and was also empowered to collect them at the end of the day and deliver them to the property master. This scheme, after a little preliminary confusion, worked splendidly. I could direct, through my microphone in the dress circle, without the strain of trying to memorise people's names, entirely by numbers and colours: 'Would number seven red kindly go over and shake hands with number fifteen yellow-and-black stripe?' etc.

At that first rehearsal it naturally took a long time to get everybody correctly numbered and sorted. Finally, however, it was done, and there they stood, serried ranks of them, waiting for what was to appear next. That was the moment that I nearly broke. I had an insane desire to say, quite gently, into the microphone: 'Thank you very much, everybody, I shan't be wanting you any more at all' – and rush madly from the theatre. Fortunately, I conquered this impulse and gave them a brief explanation of the scene. I told them that it was a seaside resort in the year 1910, and that when I blew a whistle I wished them all to walk about and talk and behave as though they really were at the seaside. There was the parade (number two hydraulic lift), the beach, the steps leading down, the small stage for Uncle George's Concert Party, sand-castles for the children, bathing-machine and the bandstand. All they had to do was to use their imaginations and circulate until I told them to stop. I gave them full permission to use any by-play and bits of business that they could think of, with the proviso that any undue overacting would be discouraged. Then I arranged Uncle George's Concert Party round their small stage, commending my soul to Heaven, blew the whistle. The effect was fantastic – immediately the scene came to life, whole and complete. People laughed and talked, promenaded to and fro along the esplanade, children patted their property sand-castles, Uncle George besought the crowd to listen to his concert. It was a most thrilling and satisfying moment, and from then onwards I had no more fears.

We did the scene over again several times, until it was set. Little bits of excellent business crept in; a child burst its balloon and screamed, and its mother smacked it; an old lady collapsed in a deck-chair, and one young woman shut herself up in her parasol when she heard the noise of an aeroplane. The by-play was prodigious and hardly any of it overdone. I was considerably praised later on for my little touches of sheer genius in that scene, and few believed me when I replied that the only genius I had displayed was in blowing a whistle!

Scene after scene was accomplished in that way, and rehearsals progressed rapidly. There were several comic interludes and a few tragic ones. In time we grew to know the names of nearly everyone, numbered or not. One of our lighter diversions was the 'Shy Bride.' This was the locomotive in the Victoria Station scene. All it had to do was to advance, amid clouds of steam, for a few yards, on rollers, and stop at the buffers. This it resolutely refused to do. It went backwards, it went sideways, it tangled itself in the black velvets and the fog gauzes, but never, until almost the last dress rehearsal, did it come in on cue.

We had a full week of dress rehearsals which, although chaotic at first, gradually righted themselves. The whole thing was the most thrilling theatrical adventure I could ever have imagined. The play grew and lived just a little bit more each day. The first time the Queen Victoria funeral scene went without a hitch, we found ourselves crying. Suddenly, unexpectedly, the emotional content of the play caught us unawares; once set, of course, and rehearsed over and over again, the scenes became familiar and lost their sting, but there were always certain moments in *Cavalcade* that touched me however often I saw them.

Cockie came to rehearsals during the last weeks, and encouraged everybody, as he always did, with just the right amount of praise and criticism. Frank Collins and Dan O'Neil achieved miracles of stage management. Elsie April pounded the piano, sorted band parts and evolved brilliant ideas for the blending of the popular tunes; in fact, everybody concerned with the production worked with untiring diligence and enthusiasm.

Gladys remained calm throughout. She had designed and ordered the entire scenic part of the production; sketched, planned and chosen about three thousand seven hundred costumes; selected and hired every stick of furniture, and managed to be at my side through almost every rehearsal. Without undue modesty, I can truthfully and most gratefully say that *Cavalcade,* apart from its original moment of conception, was as much hers as mine.

14

The first night of *Cavalcade* will remain for ever in my memory as the most agonising three hours I have ever spent in a theatre. This, I am sure, will appear to be an over-statement to any reader who happened to be present at it. But nobody in that audience, excepting Cockie and a few who had been concerned with the production, had the remotest idea how near we came to bringing the curtain down after the third scene and sending the public home.

The evening started triumphantly. The atmosphere in the auditorium while the orchestra was tuning-up was tense with excitement. Many people had been waiting for the gallery and pit for three days and nights. Gradually the stalls and dress-circle filled; Reginald Burston, the musical director, took his place. I came into my box with Mother, Jack, Gladys and Jeffery, and received a big ovation. The overture started and we settled ourselves to wait, while the house-lights slowly faded. The first scene went smoothly. Mary was nervous, but played with experienced poise. The troop-ship, with our military band and real guardsmen, brought forth a burst of cheering. The third scene – inside the house again – went without a hitch. Half the strength of the orchestra crept out during this to take their place on the lower hydraulic lift, on which they played for the theatre scene.

It was a very complicated change. The second two lifts had to rise so many feet to make the stage. The first lift had to sink and rise again with the orchestra in place on it. The preceding interior had to be taken up into the flies, and the furniture taken off at the sides. Two enormous built side-wings, with two tiers of boxes filled with people, had to slide into place on rollers, when the first lift had risen to its mark. All this was timed to take place in just over thirty seconds, and had gone perfectly smoothly at the dress rehearsals.

We sat in the box on the first night with our eyes glued on to the conductor's desk, waiting for the little blue warning light to show us that the scene was set. We waited in vain. The conductor played the waltz through again – then again – people began to look up at us from the stalls; the gallery became restless and started to clap. Neither Gladys nor I dared to move, there were too many eyes on us, and we didn't want to betray, more than we could help, that anything was wrong. I hissed at Jack out of the corner of my mouth, and he slipped out of the box and went down on to the stage. In a few moments he returned and said, in a dead voice: 'The downstage lift has stuck, and they think it will take two hours to fix it.'

Gladys and I talked without looking at each other, our eyes still set on where the blue light should appear. She said, very quietly: 'I think you'll have to make an announcement,' and I said: 'I'll give it another two minutes.' Still the orchestra continued to grind out the 'Mirabelle' waltz, there seemed to be a note of frenzy creeping into it. I longed passionately for it to play something else – anything else in the world. The audience became more restless, until suddenly, just as I was about to leave the box and walk on to the stage, the blue light came on, the black curtain rose and the scene started.

From then onwards there wasn't a moment's peace for us. The effect of the hitch on Dan O'Neil and the stage staff had obviously been shattering. The company caught panic too, and the performance for the rest of the evening lost its grip. I don't think this was noticed by the audience, but we knew it all right. That unfortunate accident took the fine edge off the play, and although the applause at the end was tremendous, we were heart-broken. I appeared at the end against my will, but in response to frantic signals from Cockie in the box opposite. It was one of the few occasions of my life that I have ever walked on to a stage not knowing what I was going to say. However, standing there, blinded by my own automatic lights, and nerve-stricken by the torment I had endured in course of the evening, I managed to make a rather incoherent little speech which finished with the phrase: 'I hope that this play has made you feel that, in spite of the troublous times we are living in, it is still pretty exciting to be English.' This brought a violent outburst of cheering, and the orchestra, frantic with indecision as to whether to play my waltz or 'God Save the King,' effected an unhappy compromise by playing them both at once. The curtain fell, missing my head by a fraction, and that was that.

15

Lorn came in the next morning and plumped all the papers down on my bed. 'I think,' she said, 'that our little piece is a success!' We read the notices through carefully. Mounting paeans of praise – not a discordant note. Jack and Gladys appeared presently, and we had lunch at the Ivy, where our reception was most satisfactory. Abel gave us all cocktails and drank to us solemnly, trembling a little with kind, friendly emotion. Congratulations bombarded the table. Our little piece was a success. Such a success, indeed, that I knew the moment had come for me to disappear. It seemed to me that there was danger in the air – a private, personal danger. I was happy enough, more than happy, delighted, but somehow, somewhere, not quite comfortable. Everybody seemed to be more concerned with *Cavalcade* as a patriotic appeal than as a play. This attitude I realised had been enhanced by my first-night speech – 'A pretty exciting thing to be English' – quite true, quite sincere; I felt it strongly, but I rather wished I hadn't said it, hadn't popped it on to the top of *Cavalcade* like a paper-cap. I hadn't written the play as a dashing patriotic appeal at all. There was certainly love of

England in it, a certain natural pride in some of our very typical characteristics, but primarily it was the story of thirty years in the life of a family. I saw where my acute sense of the moment had very nearly cheapened it. The Union Jack stretched across the back of the stage – theatrically effective jingoism. 'It's pretty exciting to be English' – awareness of the moment, not quite first-rate, a nervous grab at success at any price. Fortunately the essence of the play was clear. A comment mostly, emotional at moments but, on the whole, detached enough. The irony of the war scenes had been missed by the critics – naturally, they couldn't be expected to see it in a time of national unrest with a General Election looming in the immediate future. The Queen Victoria funeral was good – dignified, reticent and touching – the *Titanic* scene excellent, too, in a different way – the 1914 outbreak of war was again touching, but there was irony here, the beginning of bitterness. 'My world isn't very big.' The Trafalgar Square scene, obvious, not quite psychologically accurate, but undeniably effective, all that noise and movement against 'Land of Hope and Glory.' Best of all the Toast speech – 'Let's couple the Future of England with the Past of England. The glories and victories and triumphs that are over, and the sorrows that are over, too. Let's drink to our sons who made part of the pattern and to our hearts that died with them. Let's drink to the spirit of gallantry and courage that made a strange Heaven out of unbelievable Hell, and let's drink to the hope that one day this country of ours, which we love so much, will find dignity and greatness and peace again.'

That was all right. That was deeply sincere and as true as I could make it. I do hope, profoundly hope, that this country will find dignity, greatness and peace again – no cheapness there, that came from the heart, or rather perhaps, from the roots – twisted sentimental roots, stretching a long way down and a long way back, too deep to be unearthed by intelligence or pacific reason or even contempt, there, embedded for life.

With reasoning I felt better; better for myself, but sadder for poor *Cavalcade*. It was already becoming distorted and would, in time, be more so. 'A message to the youth of the Nation.' 'A Call to Arms.' 'A shrill blare on a trumpet,' blowing my decent, simple characters into further chaos. I could stay in England and cash-in if I wanted to, cash-in on all the tin-pot glory, but I felt that it would be better for me, and much better for my future work, if I went away.

On the twenty-ninth of October, 1931, Jeffery and I left for South America. It was a casual departure, without the strained courtesy of long farewells; in fact, there weren't any farewells at all. England slipped away into the mist behind us without waving a single handkerchief. A slightly complacent England, basking in pale sunlight and the ambiguous security of a vast National Government majority. I compared her in my mind to a gallant, unimaginative old lady convalescing after an abdominal operation, unaware of the nature and danger of her disease, and happy in the belief that it could never possibly recur, because all the doctors had told her so.

Seagulls followed the boat for a little way, screeching with what may well have been national pride, and as we rounded the harbour jetty we could see the whole of Folkestone greyly spreading over the hills. Small figures promenaded along the Leas, invalids probably, sad, flat women and rheumaticky old gentlemen in Bath chairs. There were nursemaids sitting in the shelters, easily distinguishable by the perambulators drawn up before them; other figures, too, huddled on iron chairs, seeking protection from the sharp wind in the shadow of the empty bandstand.

Far and away to starboard, Dungeness point crept into the sea from the marshes, and nearer, dominating the picture, just before the cliff dipped towards Sandgate, rose proudly the Grand Hotel and the Metropole Hotel, sisters in impressiveness and flushed with gentility.

We were catching a small German-Spanish ship at Boulogne, for Rio de Janeiro – seventeen days of the Atlantic were ahead of us, not our well-known Atlantic of violence, wind and icebergs, but a gentle ocean growing hourly gentler, later becoming warm and phosphorescent under new stars.

We planned to be away about nine months. We had no itinerary. After Rio we intended to drift in whatever direction the spirit moved us; our anticipatory flights included jungles, orchids, lianas, turgid tropical rivers, squawking, coloured parakeets, vast mountains, Inca ruins, deserts and languorous Latin-American cities with white houses, green jalousies and dark-eyed, attractive people sipping cool drinks on palm-shaded patios. Most of these things, we knew, would drop into place, modified a little, perhaps, by actuality, but glamorous enough on the whole. England receded a little farther, and only a few gulls remained with us.

The whole world seemed remarkably empty to me, probably because the last weeks had been so full. From the first night of *Cavalcade,* until this moment, I had been unable to put myself down at all. The tempo of everything had increased alarmingly. If I had been working all these years merely for the outward trappings of success, I had certainly achieved my destiny, and there was nothing left for me to do but hop over the side of the ship and triumphantly drown.

I was almost surprised that my incorrigible sense of the right moment didn't force me to do it. I had had a lot of this 'right moment' business dinned into me just lately. There seemed to be a set conviction in many people's minds that I had dashed off *Cavalcade* in a few days, merely to help the General Election and snatch for myself a little timely national kudos. The rumour was fairly general that I had written it with my tongue in my cheek, in bed, probably, wearing a silk dressing-gown and shaking with cynical laughter. This I knew was partly my own fault – that good old Union Jack – 'Land of Hope and Glory' – my redundant theatre sense over-stepping the mark a bit. But still, there it was – a louder success than I had ever dreamed – vulgarised a bit, but real and satisfactory within its limits. The apex had been reached the night before I sailed, the night immediately following the election results, when Their Majesties, the King and Queen, and the entire Royal Family had come to the play. A thrilling, emotional event, everything in its place. Sitting in our box, exactly opposite the Royal Box, Gladys, Jack, Lorn and I had heard the roar outside the theatre as the Royal Party arrived. The house was crammed to the roof, the dress circle presented an unbroken line of diadems, tiaras, sunbursts and orders – people sat on the steps and stood in the aisles. When the Royal Family came into the box, the whole audience stood and the orchestra played 'God Save the King.' We stood rigidly to attention. I remember trying not to cry, trying not to let the emotional force of the moment prevent me from discovering what it was that was so deeply touching. I didn't succeed, the force was too strong.

The play started and went smoothly from the first; everybody played perfectly; none of the effects failed; even the 'Shy Bride' steamed in eagerly on time.

After the second act, Cockie and I were received in the ante-room behind the Royal Box. Six Royal bows, one after the other, were rather agitating, but we were kindly and graciously put at our ease. I repressed a nervous desire to describe to Their Majesties the extreme squalor of that very ante-room in the early hours of the morning during our first lighting rehearsal, when Gladys and I had used it as a sort of combined rest-room and snack-bar. My mind's eye could still see curling ham-sandwiches in greasy paper – crumbling Banbury cakes and bottles of gin and tonic littering that smooth, correct table. I think Their Majesties were pleased with the play, and the Prince of Wales asked me several searching questions. I was a little too nervous entirely to enjoy the conversation, but I hope I acquitted myself favourably; at all events, it was a proud moment for me, and I set it gratefully in my memory.

The end of the evening was even more exciting than the beginning. When Mary Clare spoke the Toast speech, there was such a terrific burst of cheering that I feared the chandeliers would fall into the stalls. At the final tableau the audience rose again, and sang 'God Save the King' with the Company. The curtain fell, and the Royal Family left the box, but the cheering persisted with increasing volume until, after a while, they came back.

Of all emotional moments in that very emotional evening, that, somehow, was the most moving; the Queen drew back a little, leaving His Majesty in the front of the box to take the ovation alone. He stood there bowing, looking a little tired, and epitomising that quality which English people have always deeply valued: unassailable dignity.

It had been a tremendous night for me; a gratifying theatrical flourish to my twenty-one years of theatre.

Twenty-one years since I had sung 'Liza Ann' unaccompanied to Lila Field, in a small bare room off Baker Street – a rich, full, and exciting twenty-one years – 'Jam yesterday; jam to-morrow, but never jam to-day!' wasn't quite true of me. I had enjoyed a lot of immediate jam, perhaps a little too much. I didn't want it to cloy, I didn't want to lose the taste for it, but I comforted myself with the assurance that there were lots of different varieties. This was another holiday, another escape, another change of rhythm. In the months before me, I should have a little breathing-space in which to weigh values, reassemble experience, analyse motives, and endeavour to balance the past and present against the future. I waved a loving *au revoir* to Mother, Gladys, Lorn and Jack, to my family and to my friends, and went below to have a drink with Jeffery. When we came up on deck, there was no England left. Nothing but sea and sky!

INDEX